To Brian Chenault

Congratulations
on Your MBA

May Your reading of
This book add to
Your knowledge
of who You are and
where You have come
from and... Well..."
leave it there"!

PROMISE
UNFULFILLED

PROMISE
UNFULFILLED

THE FAILED

STRATEGY

OF MODERN

EVANGELICALISM

ROLLAND MCCUNE

AMBASSADOR INTERNATIONAL
Greenville, South Carolina • Belfast, Northern Ireland

Promised Unfulfilled:
The Failed Strategy of Modern Evangelicalism

Cover design & page layout by A & E Media — Paula Shepherd

ISBN 1 932307 31 1

Published by the Ambassador Group

Ambassador Emerald International
427 Wade Hampton Blvd.
Greenville, SC 29609
USA
www. emeraldhouse.com

and

Ambassador Publications Ltd.
Providence House
Ardenlee Street
Belfast BT6 8QJ
Northern Ireland
www. ambassador-productions.com

The colophon is a trademark of Ambassador

TO MY WIFE, DAISY

TABLE OF CONTENTS

PART 5: THE BIBLE AND AUTHORITY

PART 6: APOLOGETICS

PART 7: SOCIAL INVOLVEMENT

PART 8: DOCTRINAL STORMS

PART 9: CONCLUSION

ACKNOWLEDGMENTS

Those who contributed directly or indirectly to this study are legion. I could not possibly remember who they all are. There are also those who molded my thought or supplied insight and bits of information who were oblivious of doing so. But first I am grateful to the living and true God who showed grace to me in eternity past (2 Tim 1:9) and so ordained that I would arrive on this planet in a fundamental, Bible-believing Christian home and church environment in which I came to a saving knowledge of His Son Jesus Christ at an early age.

I must mention several men who, as my pastors and teachers, had a significant influence on my thinking regarding the subject of this book and of the Christian ministry. The late Dr. Alva J. McClain, my mentor in systematic theology, was a very careful scholar and knowledgeable theologian. He was an unashamed fundamentalist who had a gracious spirit and firm convictions about the importance of truth. He along with another of my professors, the late Dr. Herman A. Hoyt, were in hand-to-hand combat with liberalism in the Ashland College and Theological Seminary.

The late Dr. Richard V. Clearwaters was my pastor at Fourth Baptist Church, Minneapolis, during my fourteen years on the faculty of Central Baptist Theological Seminary. Dr. Clearwaters gave me a clear understanding of the primacy and function of the local Baptist New Testament church. Having pastored Fourth Baptist for nearly forty-two years, he was a stalwart for Baptist fundamentalist separatism. His first-hand accounts of experiences during the fundamentalist-modernist controversy in the old Northern Baptist Convention and in the rise of the new evangelicalism among fundamentalists were not only interesting but gripping as well. Being able to observe his spirit, knowledge, and experience in the heat of battle for fundamentalism and the Word of God was an experience of incalculable worth. His keen understanding of various leaders, his recall of what was said and done by individuals over the decades, and his ability to cut to the heart of issues and proposals never ceased to amaze me.

Dr. John C. Whitcomb was my teacher in Old Testament and apologetics. His class on Biblical Fundamentalism formally introduced me to the literature on the subject of the new evangelicalism and the necessity of a strong biblical stand for fundamentalism and separatism. His biblically analytical approach to the new coalition, which was still taking shape as we were studying, not only provided a wealth of academic material but also insight as to why things were happening as they were.

Dr. William R. Rice was founder of Inter-City Baptist Church and Detroit Baptist Theological Seminary in Allen Park, MI. He was my pastor during my first eight years of teaching at the seminary. His long tenure as pastor of Inter-City (42 years) demonstrated to me the ability to preach expositionally and mold a church knowledgeable in the Bible and theology. He witnessed first hand the rise of the new evangelicalism and knew well some of its early participants. He spoke against the first encroachments of the new evangelicalism into Inter-City's fellowship of churches, and finally had to lead the church out of that circle because it was unwilling to resist those inroads and put its house in order. That association of churches cannot as a whole be put into the fundamentalist camp any longer. It apparently hears the sound of a different trumpet, one that is alien to the Scriptures and to its own separatist history and heritage.

I owe a word of thanks to my colleagues at Detroit Baptist Theological Seminary for their Christian and fraternal friendship and fellowship and for reading and interacting with portions of the manuscript. Their advice, suggestions, and corrections were valuable and appreciated. The labors of Dr. William W. Combs, editor of the *Detroit Baptist Seminary Journal*, deserve special appreciation. The Journal published some of the chapters in this work and they are included here with its permission.

A special thanks goes to Dr. David M. Doran, the successor to Dr. Rice as pastor of the Inter-City Baptist Church and president of the seminary. He and the deacons of Inter-City, who are the governing board of the seminary, have generously allowed me to be relieved of many of the rigors of teaching in order to devote time to research and writing. Dr. Doran has consistently maintained the historic fundamentalist position in his preaching and teaching and in the administration of the church and seminary. His fidelity to the Cause is an encouraging sign that there can be those of the younger generation of fundamentalists who have large and responsible ministries and are capable of exegetical preaching with an articulate correlated doctrinal base while maintaining a consistent separatist position.

I also acknowledge the many students who through the decades of teaching have contributed research papers, insightful ideas and comments, as well as probing questions, all of which have increased my fund of knowledge and understanding of the subjects in this book.

Gratitude is owed to Brenton Cook of Ambassador International for his courteous expertise in publishing this work. Also my liaison to Ambassador International, Dr. Claude Wiggins, assistant to the president of Detroit Baptist Theological Seminary, was an intrepid and tireless worker, and a constant encouragement, in the final completion of this task. Robert Vincent did a tremendous job editing the manuscript. Thanks are also due to Paula Shepherd for her work in graphic design and layout.

And finally, I owe deep personal thanks to my beloved wife Daisy who has been my life's companion for over fifty years. Her love and patience through the many decades of schooling and teaching, often on what Spurgeon called a "slender apparatus" since, as any professor knows, there are often the Spartan times, have been an encouragement to keep pressing on.

BDAG throughout refers to *A Greek-English Lexicon of the New Testament and other Early Christian Literature*, 3rd edition, F. W. Danker, ed. (Chicago: University of Chicago Press, 2000).

ABOUT THE AUTHOR

Dr. Rolland D. McCune has been Professor of Systematic Theology at Detroit Baptist Theological Seminary, Allen Park, Michigan, since 1981. During that time he was also President for ten years and Dean of the Faculty for six years. He was born and raised near Berne, Indiana, and was graduated from Hartford Township High School in 1952. He earned the Bachelor of Arts degree at Taylor University, Fort Wayne (Indiana) Campus, and the Bachelor of Divinity, Master of Theology, and Doctor of Theology degrees at Grace Theological Seminary, Winona Lake, Indiana. He has made five trips to the Middle East, visiting such countries of the Bible as Italy, Turkey, Greece, Jordan, Israel, and Egypt. Twice he participated in the Bible Geography Seminar at the Institute of Holy Land Studies in Jerusalem. He was ordained to the ministry by the First Baptist Church of Warsaw, Indiana.

Dr. McCune pastored churches in Missouri and Indiana, and has had numerous interim pastorates in Indiana, Minnesota, Iowa, and Michigan. For fourteen years he was on the faculty of Central Baptist Theological Seminary of Minneapolis, serving as Professor, Registrar, and Dean. He at one time was on the Board of Trustees of the Minnesota Baptist Association and on the faculty of Indiana Baptist College in Indianapolis. In 1977 he was chosen by his college alma mater for honorary membership in Delta Epsilon Chi, the honor society of the American Association of Bible Colleges. In 1986 he was conferred with the honorary Doctor of Divinity degree by Pillsbury Baptist Bible College, Owatonna, Minnesota.

Dr. McCune has written numerous articles and extensive course syllabuses in Systematic Theology, Apologetics, New Evangelicalism, History of Israel, Basic Bible Doctrine, and Dispensationalism, as well as a handbook on the Book of Daniel.

Dr. McCune is married to the former Daisy Heller of Berne, Indiana. The McCunes have three married children. He teaches during the fall semesters at Detroit Baptist Theological Seminary. The rest of the year he resides in Bonita Springs, Florida, where he is doing research and writing on subjects he has taught.

FOREWORD

I have had the privilege of observing Dr. Rolland McCune's life and ministry from several different perspectives. He was my theology professor while I was in seminary. I was Chairman of the Board while he served as the Seminary President. He is a member of the church where I serve as pastor. I have preached with him in pastors' conferences. We have shared rooms together on the road for the seminary, and family occasions together at home. I watched him face two bouts with cancer with confident trust in His God. I have seen him take difficult stands on biblical principles with gracious strength. In all of these varied life situations, Dr. McCune's commitment to the truth of God's Word and the God of that Word has been unwavering. His dedication to study, love for the local church, and desire to communicate biblical truth have had a profound effect on my life and ministry. Whenever he speaks or writes, I listen carefully because I know it reflects a life of study and devotion to the cause of Jesus Christ.

While in seminary, I had the privilege of taking Dr. McCune's course on the History and Theology of New Evangelicalism, and it turned out to be one of the most influential courses I have ever taken. Since I was not born until after Harold J. Ockenga announced the launch of the New Evangelicalism and did not begin to think seriously about such matters until almost two decades later, it was eye-opening to learn this history and see its implications for the world of ministry I was entering. Frankly, before taking the course I knew what the Fundamentalist position was, but I didn't fully understand why. The material contained in that course, and in this book, helped me understand the dangers of the compromises which had been made before I was born but were bearing very bad fruit by the time I was entering ministry. Now, almost another two decades later, the costs of these compromises continue to mount. I pray that the material in this book will have the same effect on others that it has had on me, and I hope that it will receive a wide audience among Fundamentalists and Evangelicals. It is a serious and solemn call to faithfulness that desperately needs to be heard.

—DR. DAVID M. DORAN
President, Detroit Baptist Theological Seminary
Senior Pastor, Inter-City Baptist Church, Allen Park, MI

INTRODUCTION

I first heard that there was such a movement called the "new evangelicalism" when I entered Grace Theological Seminary in the fall of 1957. The leadership and professors of the seminary at that time were very much aware of the new position within the fundamentalist ranks and were not sympathetic toward it. Some were in a position to write and speak out against what was happening and where the new coalition was going. I refer to some of my mentors such as Dr. Alva J. McClain, Dr. Herman A. Hoyt, and Dr. John C. Whitcomb. Since that time I have had a continued interest, and disappointment, in watching the leftward trend of this break-away group that chose to separate themselves from their fundamentalist brethren and comrades in arms during the great fundamentalist-modernist controversy of the 1920s and later.

The new evangelicals were annoyed with certain fundamentalist characteristics that to them were quite objectionable, such as a supposed mean spirit that lacked the love of Christ, an intellectual inferiority that could only produce second-rate scholarship in Bible and theology, a majoring on minors, and the like. But in the seminary I attended and its circle of friends and fellowship I did not observe these negatives; this observation raised more questions about the new evangelical complainants than anything else.

At this time in the 1950s a spate of books and articles were published that vividly framed the issues of the fundamentalist-new evangelical controversy. These publications were accompanied by actual events taking place in the public arena that furnished a running commentary on the dispute taking place in the literature. Meanwhile my files and book shelves expanded as the controversy continued animatedly until the later 1970s when the new evangelicalism suffered an internal upheaval over the inerrancy of the Scriptures. At that time its own founders had to admit that the pinnacle of the movement had been reached. They lamented that the second generation was going in a direction that they never envisioned in the beginning. The movement, which began in the 1940s with such self-assurance and optimism that it would change the face of evangelical thought and American culture, in thirty-five years was already in a virtual free fall toward irrelevancy. In 1967 I began teaching on the seminary level and annually lectured on the new evangelicalism. This book is a partial harvest of all my years of research, study, and teaching on the subject.

Defining the "new" evangelicalism is part of the greater problem of defining evangelicalism itself. Usually evangelicalism means a Protestant view of the "good news" (from the Greek word *euangelion)* of salvation by grace through faith in Jesus Christ. Timothy Weber said, "Defining evangelicalism has become one of the biggest problems in American religious historiography."[1] Mark Noll is undoubtedly correct when he says, "The term 'evangelical' is a plastic one."[2] George Marsden sees no fewer than fourteen evangelicalisms in the mix![3] For our purposes the term "new evangelicalism" applies to a strain of conservative, traditional, Protestant, religious thought that coalesced into a movement in the mid-twentieth century, purporting to avoid the fundamentalist right and the neo-orthodox/neo-liberal left.[4] Although David Wells claims that evangelicalism was never a "movement,"[5] it appears difficult to sustain that assertion. In the sense that Joel Carpenter describes fundamentalism as a movement,[6] the new evangelicalism can also meaningfully be classified as such.

Harold John Ockenga coined the term "new evangelicalism" in an address at the newly-formed Fuller Theological Seminary in 1947.[7] Like all theological groups or movements, the new evangelicalism has a general motif of belief and

---

[1]Timothy P. Weber, "Premillennialism and the Branches of Evangelicalism," in *The Variety of American Evangelicalism*, eds. Donald W. Dayton and Robert K. Johnston (Downers Grove, IL: InterVarsity, 1991), p. 12. He sees four kinds of evangelicals: classical, pietistic, fundamentalist, and progressive.

[2]Mark Noll, *Between Faith and Criticism* (Grand Rapids: Baker, 1986), p. 1. For further detail on the history of the term "evangelical" and the question of the antecedents of the movement in America, see, among others, Alister E. McGrath, *Evangelicalism and the Future of Christianity* (Downers Grove, IL: InterVarsity, 1995), pp. 17-51; Donald G. Bloesch, *The Future of Evangelical Christianity: A Call For Unity Amid Diversity* (Garden City, NY: Doubleday, 1983), pp. 11-22; John H. Gerstner, "The Theological Boundaries of Evangelical Faith," in *The Evangelicals: What They Believe, Who They Are, Where They Are Changing*, eds. David F. Wells and John D. Woodbridge (Nashville: Abingdon, 1973), pp. 21-37; *The Evangelical Dictionary of Theology*, s.v. "Evangelicalism," by R. V. Pierard; and Donald W. Dayton, *Discovering an Evangelical Heritage* (Peabody, MA: Hendrickson, 1976).

[3]George M. Marsden, *Understanding Fundamentalism and Evangelicalism* (Grand Rapids: Eerdmans, 1991), p. 110.

[4]R. Albert Mohler, Jr. characterized the new evangelicalism as a "middle way between the increasing heterodoxy accepted by the mainline denominations and the obscurantism, cultural isolation, and separatism of the fundamentalists" ("Evangelical: What's In a Name?" *The Coming Evangelical Crisis*, ed. John Armstrong [Chicago: Moody, 1996], p. 31). J. Elwin Wright, director of the New England Fellowship in the 1940s and perhaps the most energetic personality behind the formation of the National Association of Evangelicals (1942), wanted a new coalition that would form between the two polarities of modernism and fractious fundamentalism (Joel A. Carpenter, *Revive Us Again: The Reawakening of American Fundamentalism* [New York: Oxford, 1997], p. 149). Edward John Carnell, certainly a representative of the new evangelicalism if there ever was one, "personified the tensions that would emerge in this new movement that sought to distinguish itself from sectarian fundamentalism on the right, and liberal and neo-orthodox theology on the left" (L. Joseph Rosas III, "The Theology of Edward John Carnell," *Criswell Theological Journal* 4 [1990], p. 351).

[5]David F. Wells, *No Place For Truth* (Grand Rapids: Eerdmans, 1993), p. 8. Decades earlier Bruce Shelley had expressed similar thoughts. He said, "Evangelical Christianity is not a religious organization. It is not primarily a theological system. It is more of a mood, a perspective, and an experience" (*Evangelicalism in America* [Grand Rapids: Eerdmans, 1967], p. 7).

[6]He says that fundamentalism had "a whole panoply of aims and aspirations" (*Revive Us Again*, p. 15). Elsewhere he described fundamentalism as a movement that had "leaders, institutions, and a particular identity" with its own ideology and agenda ("Fundamentalist Institutions and the Rise of Evangelical Protestantism, 1929-1942," *Church History* 49 [1980], pp. 64, 74).

[7]News Release by Ockenga, December 8, 1957, and his chapter, "From Fundamentalism, Through New Evangelicalism, to Evangelicalism," in *Evangelical Roots*, ed. Kenneth Kantzer (Nashville: Thomas Nelson, 1978), p. 78.

practice, with varying shades attached corresponding to the backgrounds and beliefs of those involved. This motif expresses itself in many areas, many of which will be examined and analyzed in this book.

The procedure in this study will be to begin, Part 1, with a history of the major theological antecedents to the formation of the new evangelical coalition, namely the rise of liberalism and the great fundamentalist-modernist controversy it precipitated (Chapters 1 and 2). Part 2 will analyze the contributing factors to the actual formation of the new evangelical movement historically (Chapters 3 and 4). Part 3 deals with the pervasive effects of ecumenism on new evangelical thought and activity (Chapters 5 through 9). Part 4 explores the main issue that divided the new evangelicals and the fundamentalists practically—ecclesiastical separation (Chapters 10 and 11). Part 5 sets forth the most basic concern with the new evangelicalism, its deviations on biblical revelation, inspiration, inerrancy, and thus on ultimate religious authority (Chapters 12 through 15). Part 6 goes behind the thinking of the early new evangelical mentors and leaders in the area of apologetics and finds that intellectual autonomy appears to be the headwaters for the misfortunes of the doctrine of Scripture and the Bible's final authority in the minds of many (Chapters 15 and 16).

Part 7 looks closely at the perennial complaint of the new evangelicals against fundamentalism, namely its alleged lack of social sensitivity (Chapters 18 and 19). Part 8 deals with three major doctrinal storms that shook the new evangelical movement in the closing years of the 20th century, namely the status of the unevangelized (Chapter 20), the destiny of the finally impenitent (Chapter 21), and the radical open theism view of God (Chapter 22). Part 9 wraps up the study with a hindsight evaluation of the new evangelicalism as well as a forward projection of the movement, both in terms of its early goals and aspirations and its present relevancy in a post-modern, non-authoritarian culture (Chapter 23). Two addenda close off Part 9, namely a review article of the latest expression of the new evangelicals and the radical proposals they make for doing theology and church in the 21st century (Chapter 24), and a time line of the major events in the formation and ongoing of the new evangelical movement from 1942–2003 (Chapter 25). A selected annotated bibliography rounds out the study as an aid to some of the important literature on the topic of evangelicalism and fundamentalism.

PART 1: HISTORICAL ANTECEDENTS

The purpose of this section is to give a general account of the formation of the new evangelical movement in the 1940s and 1950s. It will note the historical, philosophical, and theological antecedents that formed modernist theology. It will describe the fundamentalist-modernist controversy that was the milieu out of which came the appearance and subsequent historical rise of the new evangelical coalition.

1

THE RISE OF THEOLOGICAL LIBERALISM

Liberalism (here used synonymously with modernism) arose out of European upheavals in the eighteenth and nineteenth centuries. These upheavals were political (the French Revolution, the Thirty Years War), technological (the industrial revolution, advances in science), and religious or philosophical (Protestant and Roman Catholic scholasticism, Pietism, and the Enlightenment, among others).[1] The "Wars of Religion" left people in Europe in a state of weariness, religious fatigue, and toleration.[2]

EARLY 18TH CENTURY EUROPEAN THOUGHT
The early 18th century has been called "from orthodoxy to enlightenment."[3] This period is an important antecedent to what later became American liberalism or "modernism." The theological/philosophical scene in 18th-century Europe consisted of the following aspects.

Protestant Scholasticism
The post-Reformation era witnessed intense theological conflicts between the Lutherans and the Calvinists, the rise of Arminianism, and the formulations of confessions and statements in dogmatics. Protestant scholasticism embraced a form of rationalism and often drew conclusions based upon logic rather than scriptural exegesis.

Roman Catholic Scholasticism
Roman Catholic scholasticism was a return to compromise between Aristotelian philosophy and Middle Ages theology, a conflation commonly known as Thomism, after Thomas Aquinas (1225-1274). Plato dominated pre-Aristotelian Greek thought from the fifth century BC, insisting on an absolute dichotomy between form/spirit and matter. Forms were inherently unknowable, and "God" was the form of the good. Aristotle, an empiricist, united form and

---

[1]William C. Fletcher, *The Moderns: Molders of Contemporary Theology* (Grand Rapids: Zondervan, 1962), pp. 15-20. Alister E. McGrath, *Historical Theology: An Introduction to the History of Christian Thought* (Malden, MA: Blackwell, 1998), pp. 214-20.

[2]Alister E. McGrath, *Historical Theology*, p. 214.

[3]John Dillenberger and Claude Welch, *Protestant Christianity Interpreted Through Its Development* (New York: Scribners, 1954), p. 151.

matter. He repudiated the independent existence of the Platonic form apart from the thing that embodied it, arguing that sense perception is the basis of all the knowledge we receive. Mixing Aristotle's philosophy with theology, Aquinas held that by natural reason converging on sense data one could pursue theology and philosophy independently of Scripture, special revelation, or even grace. He developed "theistic proofs" for the existence of the true God. On this first floor of natural theology, God added an upper story of special revelation concerning the things of grace. Scholastic Thomism is a nature-grace scheme. Ironically, Francis Schaeffer credits (correctly, it seems) Aquinas with being the fountainhead of the intellectually autonomous, humanist philosophy that led down the slippery slope to the dialecticism of G. W. F. Hegel (1770-1831) through which autonomous human thinking sank below "the line of despair"—a point where philosophy abandoned any hope for a unified field of knowledge.[4]

Pietism

Pietism represented a strong protest against Protestant scholasticism, especially German Lutheranism. Pietism emphasized Christian experience, inner feeling, the individual's personal relationship with God, and high religious idealism. It was a reaction to rigid, dead orthodoxy.

The Enlightenment

The roots of the Enlightenment reached into the seventeenth century. The Enlightenment, sometimes known as the Age of Reason, articulated a totally secular mindset and has been called the modern paganism because of its magnification of the here and now. Everything is to be understood in terms of temporality; nothing is transcendent. Life can be pursued without regard for an eternal God or religion. Some of the main characteristics of the secular spirit are contingency (the universe is the result of causes that are neither necessary, rational, or purposive), relativism (there are no absolutes), transience (constant change and the becomingness of all things), and intellectual autonomy (the total independence of human thinking).[5] The Enlightenment aimed to emancipate the human mind from its alleged philosophical and religious shackles, making the mind of man totally autonomous. Thinkers refused to be bound by special revelation, dogma, and tradition. Immanuel Kant likened the Enlightenment to the emergence of man from a self-inflicted state of minority. While some positive contributions to learning came out of the Enlightenment, the theoretical underpinnings were anti-Christian, pagan, and secular. The Enlightenment ended in a deadlock between the rationalists (Hobbes, Descartes, Spinoza, and Leibnitz) and the empiricists (Locke, Berkely, and Hume), preparing the way for the synthesis philosophy of Immanuel Kant. In theology, Enlightenment thought filtered into Protestantism through Christian Wolfe (a disciple of Leibnitz; d. 1754) who blended Protestant

---

[4]Francis A. Schaeffer, *Escape From Reason* (Downers Grove, IL: InterVarsity Press, 1968), pp. 9-13, 40-42. For Hegel, the field of knowledge was open-ended, always "becoming" through the dialectical process of thesis, antithesis, and synthesis.

[5]Gary Scott Smith, *The Seeds of Secularization: Calvinism, Culture, and Pluralism in America: 1870-1915* (Grand Rapids and St Paul: Consortium of Christian University Press and Eerdmans, 1985), p. 36.

scholasticism with philosophy, especially that of Leibnitz.[6] The Enlightenment eventually effected a transition "from a new scholasticism to a new religion" through a series of "transitional" theologians and "innovating" theologians.[7]

The Enlightenment affected Christianity by exalting the complete autonomy of human reason, making man totally free intellectually.[8] Man was not to be bound by church creeds, theological statements, revelation, or any particular world view or presuppositions of any kind. Man was intellectually independent in an open universe of chance, relativity, and inevitable change in *all areas*. This freedom was almost religious in nature and offered the brightest prospects for the future of both mankind and religion. Part of the fallout of this liberated intellectualism was the detachment of faith from knowledge; God could be "thought" but He could not be "known."[9] The Kantian synthesis developed this idea with its radical dichotomy between the phenomenal and noumenal realms.

The Enlightenment also destroyed the need for divine revelation. Revelation became dispensable since it largely duplicated knowledge man might glean naturally. Culture and religion were practically synonymous, both gained, not by divine revelation, but by the Enlightenment rubric of the "omnicompetence of human reason."[10] This rationalism destroyed the doctrines of inspiration, inerrancy, miracles, and the like. Hermeneutically, the Bible became a completely culture-bound book.

A third and equally devastating impact of the Enlightenment was the detachment of religion from history. Religion could now reach forward without being manacled to the past and historical events such as the resurrection of Jesus of Nazareth and events in His life and ministry. Gotthold Lessing, for example, separated the truth of Christianity from the truth of history and called this uncrossable chasm "an ugly, broad ditch."[11] Thankfully, however, the "ditch" did not need to be crossed. A religion's truthfulness, Lessing declared, is not dependent on its nexus with history's "facts" but on its ability to transform lives through its "teaching." Theology became more concerned with spiritual "life" or the practical interests in the field of religion.[12]

Theoretical thought ended in a philosophical stalemate between the Renaissance rationalists (knowledge is the product solely of the mind) and the Enlightenment empiricists (knowledge comes from sense experience). Meanwhile Protestant thought lost all uniqueness and distinctiveness. Immanuel Kant (1724-1804) forged a synthesis between the two factions and in so doing laid the

---

[6]Dillenberger and Welch, *Protestant Christianity*, p. 152.

[7]Ibid., pp. 153-56 give further explication and detail concerning these theologians.

[8]For a good overview, see Bruce Demarest, "The Bible in the Enlightenment Era," in *Challenges to Inerrancy*, eds. Gordon Lewis and Bruce Demarest (Chicago: Moody, 1984), pp. 11-47.

[9]John Jefferson Davis, "Kant and the Problem of Religious Knowledge," in *Perspectives on Evangelical Theology*, eds. Kenneth Kantzer and Stanley Gundry (Grand Rapids: Baker, 1979), p. 236.

[10]Alister E. McGrath, *Historical Theology*, p. 221.

[11]Bruce Demarest, "The Bible in the Enlightenment Era," p. 27.

[12]Dillenberger and Welch, *Protestant Theology,* p. 156.

groundwork for liberal theological opinion. Kant derived from Hume the idea that we have nothing beyond the data of our senses (his empiricism), and further held that the human mind is latent with certain "categories" by which it comes to the raw data of experience. These categories are innate aptitudes of, or a certain structure of, the mind. Kant also sharply distinguished between "reality" and "appearance." What we "know" is not a thing-in-itself but its appearance, or what our minds have told us about the realm of appearances via the categories. Thus the human mind makes a contribution to knowledge (his rationalism). This made man's mind totally autonomous and the ultimate referent. In effect, Kant put a "wall,"[13] consisting of the human mind, between a person and the "real" world. He limited knowledge to the experienced world—the phenomenal realm, the world of apparitions that comes to us via the categories. Metaphysics was excluded from this realm. Kant did not deny the existence of a higher realm of God, freedom, reality, immortality, and the like; instead he said that this realm—the "real" world, the noumenal realm—while not a source of knowledge can be a domain for faith. In this system God was not a proper object of knowledge because He is not of the phenomenal realm. God could be *postulated* as a matter of "practical" reason for religion, ethics, and morality, but He could not be cognitively known as a matter of "pure" reason.

THE RESULTANT THEOLOGICAL LIBERALISM

German rationalism was the well from which liberal theology sprang, for various reasons. A large number of full-staffed German state universities enabled scholars to research and write unencumbered by students. The German mind prided itself on exactness and analytical ability. Wide doctrinal latitude characterized the faculties of the universities. Scholars had the time, ability, and means to specialize in biblical themes.[14]

The Influence of Schleiermacher and Ritschl

In addition to the general contributions of Enlightenment thought to the formation of liberalism were the special views of Friederich Schleiermacher (1768-1834) and Albrecht Ritschl (1822-1889),[15] both of whom were influenced by Kant. Schleiermacher came out of Pietism (Moravian Brethren) and heavily imbibed Kantian ideas as well as philosophical Romanticism. Romanticism stressed the imagination, creativity, freedom, individuality, and the spontaneity of

---

[13]Ronald Nash, *The Word of God and the Mind of Man: The Crisis of Revealed Truth in Contemporary Theology* (Grand Rapids: Zondervan, 1982), p. 27. Kant's "wall" is philosophically akin to Lessing's "ditch" between faith and history and Hume's "gap" between faith and knowledge.

[14]Examples of German scholars and universities include G. W. F. Hegel (University of Berlin), F. C. Bauer (University of Tubingen), Friederich Schleiermacher (Universities of Halle and Berlin), Albrecht Ritschl (Universities of Bonn and Gottingen), Adolph von Harnack (University of Berlin), Ernst Troeltsch (Universities of Heidelberg and Berlin), and Johannes Weiss (Universities of Gottingen, Marburg, and Heidelberg).

[15]Ronald Nash, *The Word of God and the Mind of Man*, pp. 28-34. Dillenberger and Welch, *Protestant Christianity*, pp. 182-89, 198-200. On Ritschl specifically, see Alan P. F. Sell, *Theology in Turmoil: The Roots, Course and Significance of the Conservative-Liberal Debate in Modern Theology* (Grand Rapids: Baker, 1986), pp. 73-87.

life, especially in the realm of the human spirit, which was not being reached by the rationalism of the day.[16] Through the influences of Pietism and Romanticism, Schleiermacher identified the locus of religion in man's feelings, affections, and emotions. "God" was what one accepted with "absolute dependence"—a consciousness of the inner unity of all things. Thus he put God and religion in the realm of sense experience, not in the realms of doctrinal formulations or a system of beliefs. For him, God and faith were united, i.e., one cannot speak of God without knowing and trusting Him. As such God was not simply a postulate (answering Kant's denial of a true knowledge of God), and religion was not reduced to a system of intellectual beliefs (answering orthodoxy's claim to an infallible Bible).

Ritschl opposed Schleiermacher's subjectivism and sought to ground Christianity in history by seeking to restore the historical Jesus. His Kantianism prevented much progress in this endeavor because he accepted Kant's limitation on the knowledge of God; God was not an object of theoretical judgments. From Kant he also borrowed the notion that one cannot know the thing-in-itself but only the effect that it has on us, i.e., what our minds tell us about the empirical realm. Thus his quest for the "historical" Jesus in the apparitional world, apart from metaphysics and divine revelation, was extremely difficult; in fact it was doomed from the start. Furthermore, like Kant he also accepted the identification of religion and morality. Ritschl's theology thus became a matter of unanalyzable value judgments (derived from the unreachable noumenal realm), and Christianity became a system of ethics.[17]

Protestant liberalism therefore retained the essentials of Lessing's ditch, Hume's gap, and Kant's wall. These essentials added up to a God who was ultimately detached from the historical and cognitive processes, hence impersonal and ultimately unknown and unknowable, a nineteenth-century version of the ancient Athenians' Unknown God (Acts 17:23).

The Influence of Higher Criticism

Higher criticism significantly influenced the formation of liberal theology because it produced a hermeneutic or a method of interpretation that viewed the Bible as a culture-bound book. Higher criticism dealt with authorship, date of composition, purpose in writing, parallels to other forms of literature, and the like. In themselves these were legitimate areas of scholarship, but with the post-Enlightenment presuppositions the discipline drastically undermined the Bible through the development of the historical-critical methodology. Dillenberger and Welch note correctly:

> The decisive issue was not the specific interpretations of historical criticism, but lay at a deeper level—viz, at the level of the *significance* and *authority* of the

---

[16]Harold O. J. Brown, "Romanticism and the Bible," in *Challenges to Inerrancy*, pp. 49-65. McGrath, *Historical Theology*, pp. 227-29.

[17]Ronald Nash, *The Word of God and the Mind of Man*, p. 33. Alister E. McGrath, *Historical Theology*, p. 283.

Bible as a whole, i.e., precisely in the giving up of traditional conceptions of biblical revelation. The acceptance of biblical criticism meant the abandonment of the belief that the Bible is an infallible record of divine revelation.[18]

The Bible came to be regarded as a record of the religious experiences of men and not as the infallible, verbally inerrant revelation of God.

The Influence of Science and the Theory of Organic Evolution

The dichotomy which existed between science and religion brought about by Galileo and Kepler, who destroyed the universally-held geo-centric idea of the universe, was further sharpened by Charles Darwin's *The Origin of Species* (1859). Darwin proposed a scheme of amoeba-to-man organic evolution. This theory of organic evolution directly contradicted the Bible in at least two ways—the interpretation of Genesis (especially chapters one through three) and the need to believe in God in order to account for origins. Charles Hodge of Princeton Seminary said that Darwinism was atheism.[19] Conservatives almost universally condemned Darwinism. Others countered the Darwinian notion of natural selection as a contradiction between the moral law and natural law that blurred the biblical picture of God as loving, wise, beneficent, powerful, and just. Overproduction, the struggle for existence, and the survival of the fittest seemed incompatible with the biblical view of God.

Darwinism scorned the theistic proof for God's existence from "design" previously used by both faith (theology) and reason (science).[20] Darwinian evolution demoted man as a special creation of God with a special position of honor. Most importantly, Darwinism led the way for evolutionary ideas in other fields, especially religion.

Evolution had many effects on the formation of a new theology. One, it reinforced the growing emphasis on the immanence of God; God, man, and nature were actually on the same continuum. Evolution also brought a reinterpretation of the ideas of sin and redemption. Redemption became the extremely optimistic idea of the gradual education of man from a brute state to obedience to God. Harry Emerson Fosdick, a chastened and reconstructed Twentieth-century liberal (i.e., a neo-liberal), in his autobiography quotes Samuel Butler, an early (old) liberal, who predicted that through the simple process of evolution, man would one day become

---

[18]Dillenberger and Welch, *Protestant Christianity*, p. 195.

[19]Charles Hodge, *What is Darwinism? And Other Writings on Science and Religion*, eds. Mark A. Noll and David N. Livingston (Grand Rapids: Baker, 1994), p. 156.

[20]George M. Marsden, *Understanding Fundamentalism and Evangelicalism* (Grand Rapids: Eerdmans, 1991), p. 141. Gary Scott Smith, *The Seeds of Secularization*, p. 109. It was *Darwinism* to which Hodge objected. He and some of the other Princetonians were not totally opposed to evolution as such. Hodge's objection to Darwinism was aimed primarily at the denial of divine design on which the Darwinian scheme was actually predicated. See David B. Calhoun, *Princeton Seminary*, 2 vols. (Carlisle, PA: Banner of Truth, 1996), 2:10-21, 80-82, 256-59, and especially George M. Marsden, "The Collapse of American Evangelical Academia," in *Reckoning With the Past: Historical Essays on American Evangelicalism From the Institute for the Study of American Evangelicals*, ed. D. G. Hart (Grand Rapids: Baker, 1995), pp. 221-38. Charles Hodge himself held to a day-age theory concerning the opening chapters of Genesis (*Systematic Theology*, 3 vols. [London: James Clark, 1960 edition], 1: 570-74).

"not only an angel but an archangel."[21] That thought was too starry-eyed even for Fosdick. In the same vein, non-Christian religions were looked upon by some liberals as stages in the development of man's religious climb toward monotheism.

In summary, the basic ideas of liberalism were: (1) A spirit of free inquiry and open-mindedness. Nothing was off-limits to the inquiring mind. This spirit was the genius of liberalism.[22] (2) An optimism concerning the abilities, natural goodness, and future of man. Man was not thought to be perfect but was certainly perfectible. The dignity of man, even though demoted and diminished, was emphasized and his depravity deprecated or denied. Harry Emerson Fosdick quoted Newell Dwight Hillis, pastor of Plymouth Church, Brooklyn, New York, as saying,

> Laws are becoming more just, rulers more humane; music is becoming sweeter and books wiser; homes are happier, and the individual heart is become at once more just and more gentle....For today art, industry, invention, literature, learning and government—all these are captives marching in Christ's triumphant procession up the hill of time.[23]

Another said, "Over the crest of the hill the Promised Land stretches away to the far horizon smiling in eternal sunshine."[24] (3) The immanence of God; i.e., that God works within the world not just upon it. There is no fundamental disjunction between the natural and the supernatural, man and God. Both are on the same essential continuum. Other tenets included: (4) Sympathy and tolerance among Christians. (5) Confidence in science and the methods of modern science. (6) Skepticism about achieving absolute truth or a knowledge of ultimate reality. (7) Idealism about society and social progress.[25]

THE RISE OF LIBERALISM IN AMERICA

The Influence of the Social Gospel

Although the "social gospel" is primarily an American phenomenon arising during the last quarter of the nineteenth century, there were European precursors such as the Christian Socialist movement in Britain which began in 1848 (F. D. Maurice, Charles Kingsley, and J. M. Ludlow).[26] The value-judgment theology of Albrecht Ritschl strongly influenced a concern for social betterment on the Continent.

---

[21]Harry Emerson Fosdick, *The Living of These Days* (New York: Harper and Bros., 1956), p. 250.

[22]Daniel Day Williams well said concerning liberalism: "In its theological context it designates the spirit and attitude of those who sought to incorporate in Christian theology the values of freedom of thought, tolerance, and the humanitarian motives in modern western culture. Theological liberals have always asserted the claims of reason against a petrified orthodoxy, and have sought freedom for diversity of belief in the Church" ("Liberalism," in *A Handbook of Christian Theology*, eds. Marvin Halverson and Arthur A. Cohen [New York: World Publishing, 1958], p. 207).

[23]*The Living of These Days*, p. 237.

[24]Ibid., p. 239.

[25]Dillenberger and Welch, *Protestant Christianity*, pp. 211-17.

[26]Dillenberger and Welch, *Protestant Christianity*, p. 242. They also note that 1848 was "the year in which the *Communist Manifesto* appeared and popular insurrections swept over continental Europe, and [the Christian Socialist movement] was explicitly an effort to provide a Christian method of social reform as an alternative to the class struggle."

Among the precursors of the social gospel in America was Horace Bushnell (1802-1876), a Congregationalist who stressed the corporate, social involvement of man in sin. He taught that if sin can be social in dimension, so can virtue. He is most famous for his book, *Christian Nurture* (1847), in which he taught that conversion should come by a process of education or nurture and not in a sudden, instantaneous manner.[27] He also understood the atonement of Christ in terms of love rather than penal satisfaction. Josiah Strong, a Congregational minister who wrote *Our Country: Its Possible Future and Its Present Crisis* (1885), said that money, greed, immigration, Roman Catholicism, and Mormonism were corrupting America. Strong was the executive secretary of the American branch of the Evangelical Alliance (formed in England in 1846) from 1886 to 1898.[28] The American branch became the Federal Council of Churches in 1908. Other precursors of the social gospel were William D. P. Bliss, George Herron, and Graham Taylor.

Charles M. Sheldon (1857-1946) was a Congregationalist who did the most to popularize the social gospel. He wrote *In His Steps: What Would Jesus Do?*, a social gospel novel that sold over 100,000 copies within a few months, 23 million within a generation. Washington Gladden (1836-1918) has become known as "the father of the social gospel." He was also a Congregational minister and was influenced by Bushnell. He believed that a competitive basis of economics was unchristian. He stressed love and moral persuasion as the means of achieving a more ideal society.[29] His hymn, "O Master Let Me Walk With Thee," was a statement of the social gospel. His books included *Working People and Their Employers* (1876), *Applied Christianity* (1887), and *Social Salvation* (1902).

Walter Rauschenbusch (1861-1918) also led in the development and spread of the social gospel in America. He taught church history at the Rochester Theological Seminary after having been a pastor for eleven years among immigrant workers in a difficult section of New York City. His major publications were *Christianity and the Social Crisis* (1907), *Christianizing the Social Order* (1912), and *A Theology For the Social Gospel (1917)*. Rauschenbusch maintained that social sins were more devastating to morality than personal sins. He followed Bushnell's idea that personal existence is social in nature, i.e., that society was an organization and not just a collection of individuals. There existed a solidarity to society. Rauschenbusch's ideas for social betterment rose chiefly from his concept of the kingdom of God. The kingdom would emerge from the existing social order and redeem it without destroying it. This feat would be accomplished by God working immanently in society, not merely by the efforts of people. Through moral, economic, and social reform a new order, not based on competition, would emerge. Rauschenbusch understood that the realms of education and democratic

---

[27]Sydney E. Ahlstrom, "Horace Bushnell," in *A Handbook of Christian Theologians*, eds. Martin E. Marty and Dean G. Peerman (New York: World Publishing, 1965), pp. 39-40, 43-44.

[28]*Dictionary of Christianity in America*, s.v. "Strong, Josiah (1847-1916)," by R. T. Handy, pp. 1140-41.

[29]Dillenberger and Welch, *Protestant Christianity*, p. 246.

principles had already made great social advancement, but the kingdom of God needed advancement in the economic realm.[30] Although definitely a liberal, his theology was not characterized by the "sentimental optimism" that marked much of the social gospel; "many of his deepest convictions ran counter to the prevailing liberal theology."[31]

The social gospel in America achieved notable status when the Federal Council of Churches began in 1908, partly for the purpose of centralizing Protestant concern for social problems. The Council drew up a Social Creed of the Churches which called for equal rights for all, child labor laws, old age benefits, a shorter work week, and labor arbitration. The theoretical underpinnings (philosophical and theological) for the social gospel are patently Enlightenment-liberal in origin and content.

The Influence of a Secularized American Society

Several factors contributed to a trend toward the secularization of American society in the last quarter of the nineteenth and the first quarter of the twentieth centuries. One was the urbanization of the nation and the acceleration of the transition from an agrarian society to an urban one. In 1870 about one fifth of the population was urban; by 1890 the percentage increased to one third, and continued to increase until 1910 when suburbs began to form.[32] The motif and power structures of society by then were no longer agrarian. The metropolis influenced everything, even the surrounding rural communities. Compared to an agrarian society, in an urban-oriented culture the home began to lose its influence and the community church waned. Urban churches became affluent as millionaires (such as the Colgates and Rockefellers) gave heavily of their means. Church-related educational institutions expanded dramatically. Then, as now, "there was a tendency to treat the Gospel much as a corporation might treat the promotion of its product."[33] Urbanization had secularized the large Protestant denominations.

The development of the public school system had a secularizing influence on American culture.[34] Public education combined rationalism with statism. Two figures were especially prominent. Horace Mann (1796-1858), "the father of the American public school" was a Unitarian who believed in the natural goodness of man. He believed that man by universal, compulsory education, could ultimately develop a perfect society. John Dewey (1859-1956), a humanist and "the father of American progressive education," believed that man by cosmic evolution had finally reached a state whereby he could control all future evolution. He applied evolutionary concepts to the curriculum and the teaching methods of education.

---

[30]Dillenberger and Welch, *Protestant Christianity*, pp. 247-50; William C. Fletcher, *The Moderns*, pp. 52-59; R. T. Handy, "Walter Rauschenbusch," in *A Handbook of Christian Theologians*, pp. 192-211.

[31]Dillenberger and Welch, *Protestant Christianity*, p. 251.

[32]Clifton E. Olmstead, *Religion in America: Past and Present* (Englewood Cliffs, NJ: Prentice Hall, 1961), p. 123.

[33]Ibid., p. 125.

[34]See Henry M. Morris, *Education For the Real World* (San Diego: Creation-Life Publishers, 1977).

A. A. Hodge, a theologian at Princeton Seminary, prophesied the moral and social deterioration that the proposed method of public education would bring. He said,

> I am as sure as I am of Christ's reign that a comprehensive and centralized system of national education, separated from religion, as is now commonly proposed, will prove the most appalling enginery for the propagation of anti-Christian and atheistic unbelief, and of anti-social nihilistic ethics, individual, social and political, which this sin-rent world has ever seen.[35]

Immigration also contributed to the secularization of America. Between 1865 and 1900 some 13,500,000 aliens arrived in America, and even more after that in the decades of the twentieth century.[36] Consequently, denominations grew in size, and new ones were formed, particularly among the ethnic and language groups. A number of immigrants rejected evangelical values and further diluted the hope for an evangelical religious consensus in America. Many were absorbed by the secular spirit, swelling the ranks of secularism in America.

The Influence of Postmillennialism[37]

Postmillennialism prevailed among American evangelicals between the Revolution and the Civil War. Although secularization had been gaining ground in America, it did not appear, initially at least, to be anti-clerical or hostile to Christianity. Americans thought that materialism, capitalism, and nationalism were gifts from God and were therefore evidences of His blessings. Others thought that secularism was a "public" philosophy and that individual values could be found in private religion.[38] Postmillenialism granted theoretical support for the expansion of secularism and liberalism. Postmillennialists were optimistic about the spiritual progress of culture. Those who were more literal (albeit historicist) in interpreting the Bible believed that the (papal) antichrist was in decline and would fall in the 1860s. They believed the Mohammedans (the little horn in Daniel 8) had reached their apogee of power and were diminishing, and that the United States under God would lead the new world in cultural advance.[39]

Postbellum liberalism, however, began to abandon the supernatural aspects of historic postmillennialism. For example, a leading liberal Baptist, William Newton Clarke, viewed the formerly supernatural aspects of the Kingdom of God as natural and normal; i.e., the Kingdom was *now* (a prime ingredient of secularism) and not future.

The leading early American liberals/modernists included several important figures. Henry Ward Beecher (1813-1887), pastor of Plymouth Church, Brooklyn,

---

[35]A. A. Hodge, *Popular Lectures on Theological Themes* (Philadelphia: Presbyterian Board of Publications, 1887), p. 283. See also J. Gresham Machen, *Christianity and Liberalism* (Grand Rapids: Eerdmans, 1923), pp. 13-14.

[36]Clifton E. Olmstead, *Religion in America*, p. 106.

[37]See George M. Marsden, *Fundamentalism and American Culture: The Shaping of Twentieth Century Fundamentalism: 1870–1925* (New York: Oxford, 1980), pp. 48-55.

[38]Gary Scott Smith, *The Seeds of Secularization*, pp. 37-38.

[39]George M. Marsden, *Fundamentalism and American Culture*, p. 49. For the leading historicist ideas of the period, see Leroy E. Froom, *The Prophetic Faith of Our Fathers*, 4 vols. (Washington, DC: Review and Herald Publishing, 1946), 3:687-723.

NY, was a progressive who ended his ministry as a liberal. He was very popular as a pulpiteer, political activist, and social reformer. William Rainey Harper (1856-1906) taught Semitics and Biblical Literature at Yale, and in 1891 he became the first president of the University of Chicago, a Baptist school built with Rockefeller money which became the educational hotbed of the social gospel. Shailer Matthews (1863-1941) was Dean of the University of Chicago and taught New Testament and theology. He contributed heavily to the liberalism of the Northern Baptist Convention. A. C. McGiffert (1861-1933) was a Congregationalist and professor of church history at the liberal Union Theological Seminary of New York. C. A. Briggs (1841-1913) was professor of Hebrew and cognate languages at Union. Briggs repudiated the verbal inspiration of the Bible and was eventually condemned and put out of the Presbyterian ministry, only to be ordained by the Episcopal church and retained at Union. William Adams Brown (1865-1943) taught theology at Union Seminary in New York. He wrote *Christian Theology in Outline* (1906) in which he centered theology on experiencing the life and teachings of the historical Jesus and not on the objective authority of the Bible or an understanding of sin and atonement. William Newton Clarke (1841-1912) taught at Colgate University and wrote *An Outline of Christian Theology* (1906), the first liberal systematic theology in America. Harry Emerson Fosdick (1878-1969) was a Baptist liberal, trained under Clarke, who pastored the First Presbyterian church in New York City. In 1925 he became pastor of the Park Avenue Baptist Church in New York where John D. Rockefeller, Jr. was a member. In 1930 Riverside Church, constructed largely with Rockefeller money, was built as a place for Fosdick to preach. Fosdick called himself an "evangelical liberal." More technically, he would qualify as a neo-liberal—still a liberal but not of the extremely optimistic old liberal vintage. He said, "We do not believe in automatic, inevitable social progress, supposing that by some inherent necessity the world is growing better and better."[40]

---

[40]*The Living of These Days*, p. 237.

2

THE GREAT CONTROVERSY

New evangelicalism began formally in the 1940s as a break from the fundamentalist movement of which it had been a part. This chapter discusses the great theological and ecclesiastical controversy, principally of the 1920s, between the fundamentalist/evangelical coalition and the liberals/modernists. This controversy would eventually give rise to the great fundamentalist/new evangelical division. Part two discusses the events and issues surrounding the formal break from the fundamentalists by the new evangelicals.

FUNDAMENTALISM AND THE FUNDAMENTALIST-MODERNIST CONTROVERSY IN AMERICA

The term "fundamentalist" has its most primitive starting point with *The Fundamentals: A Testimony to the Truth,* a series of booklets published in 1910-1915 on crucial fundamental doctrines which were under attack by the liberals. More directly, the name seems to have originated with Curtis Lee Laws, editor of a Baptist publication, *The Watchman Examiner*, who stated in an article that "we suggest that those who still cling to the great fundamentals and who mean to do battle royal for the fundamentals shall be called 'Fundamentalists.'"[1]

Fundamentalism is a distinct movement not merely a mood or mentality. David Wells maintains that a movement needs a commonly owned direction, a common basis on which the direction is based, and an *esprit* that informs and motivates those united in the cause.[2] On those bases, he maintains evangelicalism was not a movement. Joel Carpenter argues for identifying fundamentalism as a movement because of its leaders, institutions, and clear identity.[3] He broadens his comments by saying that "fundamentalism bears all the marks of a popular religious movement which drew only part of its identity from opposition to liberal trends in the denominations. The movement had its own ideology and program to pursue."[4] Wells's point that evangelicalism was not a movement is debatable. Fundamentalism, on the other hand, is definitely an identifiable historic religious

---

[1]"Convention Side Lights," July 1, 1920, p. 834.

[2]*No Place For Truth* (Grand Rapids: Eerdmans, 1993), p. 8.

[3]"Fundamentalist Institutions and the Rise of Evangelical Protestantism, 1929-1942," *Church History* 49 (1980), 64.

[4]Ibid., p.74

movement. It has moved in a specific (conservative) direction well-chronicled by historians. Its common basis is a set of biblical doctrines and beliefs, and its *esprit* is principally its militant separatism. Fundamentalism is a movement, not an attitude of belligerence, ugliness, or a negative mentality as often depicted.

Fundamentalism has always been defined by its beliefs on biblical doctrine. Historically, fundamentalists have held core biblical truths, principally those concerning Christ and the Scriptures, as well as the doctrine of ecclesiastical separation. Together with the practical distinctive of militancy, these common biblical convictions have formed the essence of the fundamentalist movement.[5]

In this regard, exception must be taken to those who define fundamentalism as essentially a negative social, cultural, or religious reaction. Donald Bloesch describes fundamentalism as "a movement of reaction in the churches in this [present] period of history."[6] Alister McGrath likewise concentrates almost exclusively on social and cultural factors, seeing fundamentalism as a reaction within American culture to the emergence of a secular culture. He terms fundamentalism, "oppositionalism," a "countercultural movement," and a "separatist attitude toward culture."[7] These sobriquets would be partially correct if he had noted that it was *godless* culture that fundamentalists oppose. More appalling is the approach of Douglas Frank who contends in terms of fundamentally Marxist socioeconomic factors, that Bible-believers awkwardly blundered their way into the twentieth century. He impugns the testimony of those who claimed to be following biblical mandates and principles.[8]

Joel Carpenter, on the other hand, is far more historically perceptive at this point when he notes that fundamentalism drew only "part" of its identity from its opposition to liberalism.[9] He puts little weight on socioeconomic and cultural factors, noting that "fundamentalism's commitment to urban evangelism and foreign missions suggests that the movement was primarily concerned with preaching the evangelical gospel in the twentieth century, both at home and abroad."[10]

George Marsden's four stages of evangelicalism beginning with the 1870s serve, with slight modification, as suitably paradigmatic for a concise mapping of the fundamentalist movement and its battle with the rising liberal tide in America. His periods are: (1) The 1870s to the end of World War I, a period when evangelicalism was intact in America; (2) 1919-1926, the fundamentalist-

---

[5]See my "The Self-Identity of Fundamentalism," *Detroit Baptist Seminary Journal* 1 (Spring 1996), and "Doctrinal Non-Issues in Historic Fundamentalism" 1 (Fall 1996).

[6]*The Future of Evangelical Christianity: A Call For Unity Amid Diversity* (Garden City, NY: Doubleday, 1983), p. 22.

[7]*Evangelicalism and the Future of Christianity* (Downers Grove, IL: InterVarsity, 1995), pp. 28-29.

[8]Douglas W. Frank, *Less Than Conquerors: How Evangelicals Entered the Twentieth Century* (Grand Rapids: Eerdmans, 1986). See my review in *The Sentinel* (published by the Detroit Baptist Theological Seminary) 4 (1987).

[9]Joel A. Carpenter, "Fundamentalist Institutions and the Rise of Evangelical Protestantism, 1929-1942," p. 74.

[10]Ibid. See also Mark Sidwell, "Defining Fundamentalism: A Question of Theology or Sociology?" *Biblical Viewpoint* 30 (1996), p. 73.

modernist controversy; (3) 1926-1940s, a time of withdrawal and regrouping; and (4) 1940s-1970s, the emergence of the new evangelicals, whom he calls "self-conscious evangelicals."[11]

The Period of Conflict and Beginnings: 1876–1919

Many institutions, movements, and personalities converged during this period to form historic fundamentalism. Foremost was the Bible Conference movement. The annual summer Bible conferences were a powerful means of combatting liberalism and promoting biblicism. The main characteristics of the Bible Conference era were the teaching and preaching of premillennialism, the exposition of major doctrines of the Bible, and the defense of the Bible as the Word of God. The flavor of the movement was interdenominational, although the Baptists and Presbyterians were dominant. The conferences ignored denominational distinctives due to the transdenominational character of liberalism and the perceived need to unitedly confront unbelief. The Bible Conference era began with the Niagara Bible Conference in 1876[12] and died out by the early 1960s.

Another tributary of fundamentalism was the Training School/Bible Institute movement. Originally the Training School or Bible Institute had a two-year curriculum that emphasized Bible content and evangelism. In the 1920s the curriculum became a three-year program, and in the 1940s developed into a four or five-year program in a Bible college framework. Liberal arts courses were added to the Bible major. Some of the prominent schools begun in this period were Nyack, NY (1882); Moody, Chicago (1886); Gordon, Boston (1889); Trinity Bible Institute, Chicago (1894); Practical Bible Training School, Binghampton, NY (1900); Providence, RI (1900); Northwestern, Minneapolis (1902); Bible Institute of Los Angeles (1907); Northern Baptist Seminary, Chicago (1913); and the Philadelphia School of the Bible (1916).

Another impetus in the rise of the fundamentalist coalition of this period was the presence of popular and influential pastors and evangelists such as D. L. Moody, J. Wilbur Chapman, Billy Sunday, Sam Jones, Gypsy Smith, A. J. Gordon, W. E. Biederwolf, C. I. Scofield, James Brooks, A. T. Pierson, W. J. Eerdman, W. B. Riley, R. A. Torrey, A. C. Gaebelein, and Bob Jones, Sr. These men affirmed the cardinal doctrines, saw souls saved, and started schools and publications. Most were moderately Calvinistic and espoused varying degrees of dispensational premillennialism.

Another major contributor was the stream of literature that developed during this period. One of the most important works was the *Scofield Reference Bible* (1909), whose influence is incalculable.[13] *The Fundamentals: A Testimony to the Truth* (1910-15), was a series of twelve paperbacks containing essays on doctrines

---

[11]"From Fundamentalism to Evangelicalism," in *The Evangelicals: What They Believe, Who They Are, Where They Are Going*, eds. David F. Wells and John D. Woodbridge (Nashville: Abingdon, 1973), p. 122.

[12]See Larry D. Pettegrew, "The Historical and Theological Contributions of the Niagara Bible Conference to American Fundamentalism" (Th.D. dissertation, Dallas Theological Seminary, 1976).

[13]David O. Beale notes that the *Scofield Reference Bible* was "the single most influential publication in Fundamentalism's history" (*In Pursuit of Purity: American Fundamentalism Since 1850* [Greenville, SC: Unusual Publications, 1986], p. 37).

and themes crucial to Bible believers. Conceived of by Lyman and Milton Stewart, successful Christian businessmen of the Union Oil Company, some three million copies were distributed. The Moody Bible Institute, the Bible Institute of Los Angeles, and the Philadelphia School of the Bible each had publishing or colportage ventures.[14] Other noteworthy publications of the time were *The Pilot, Our Hope, Princeton Theological Review, The Watchman Examiner, The Watchward, The Truth, The King's Business, The Christian Workers Magazine,* and *The Sunday School Times.* These and other publications gave analytical expression to the issues facing conservatives, exposed the unbelief of liberalism, expounded the truths of Scripture, and gave publicity to men and causes standing for evangelism and the fundamentals of the faith.

The Period of Conflict and Battle: 1919–1929
   This period witnessed the great fundamentalist-modernist controversy, a gigantic theological and ecclesiastical clash between the old-line conservatives (fundamentalists) and the purveyors of post-Enlightenment religion (liberals/modernists).[15] The controversy concerned the truth-claims and belief-system of fundamental Christianity versus an essentially new religion. It was a fight over the retention and control of denominations, mission agencies, colleges, and seminaries. The clash raged between those who had founded and nurtured these organizations and those with alien intentions who were endeavoring to infiltrate and capture them for the spread of theological and philosophical novelties. No one understood the antithesis of the times better than the editor of the liberal *Christian Century.*

> The differences between fundamentalism and modernism are not mere surface differences, which can be amiably waved aside or discarded, but...they are foundational differences, structural differences, amounting in their radical dissimilarity almost to the differences between two distinct religions. Christianity according to fundamentalism is one religion. Christianity according to modernism is another religion. [The antithesis implies] that the differences which characterize fundamentalism and modernism are so broad and deep and significant that, if each group holds its respective views consistently and acts upon them with conscientious rigor, they find an alienating gulf between them....There exists in present-day Christianity two structurally distinct religions, irreconcilable not alone on the side of apologetics but of churchly function and ideal and of missionary propagation.

> Two worlds have crashed, the world of tradition and the world of modernism. The God of the fundamentalist is one God; the God of the modernist is another. The Christ of the fundamentalist is one Christ; the Christ of modernism is another. The Bible of the fundamentalist is one Bible; the Bible of modernism is another. The church, the kingdom, the salvation, the consummation of all things—these are one thing to the fundamentalists and another thing to modernists. But that the issue is clear and that the inherent incompatibility of the two worlds has passed the stage of mutual tolerance is a fact concerning which there hardly seems room for any one to doubt.[16]

---

[14]Joel A. Carpenter, "Fundamentalist Institutions and the Rise of Evangelical Protestantism, 1929-1942" pp. 66-67.

[15]I note again the dubious idea that fundamentalism and the controversy of the 1920s were simply cultural matters. This is a wholly reductionist notion that fails to capture and explain the genius and spirit of the time.

[16]Charles Clayton Morrison, "Fundamentalism and Modernism, Two Religions," *The Christian Century* (Jan 3, 1924), pp. 5-6.

J. Gresham Machen had seen the issues equally as clearly when in the previous year (1923) he published *Christianity and Liberalism*. He wrote,

> We shall be interested in showing that despite the liberal use of traditional phraseology modern liberalism not only is a different religion from Christianity but belongs in a totally different class of religions....Our principal concern just now is to show that the liberal attempt at reconciling Christianity with modern science has really relinquished everything distinctive of Christianity.[17]

The bulk of the controversy of this period affected the northern churches of the United States, principally the northern Presbyterians and the northern Baptists. In the main, new evangelicalism emerged from the northern tier of fundamentalism. While dissertations and books have been devoted to the period, only a few high points of the time can be noted here.

The World's Christian Fundamentals Association: 1919

The WCFA grew out of the Bible conferences, especially the 1918 Prophecy Conference in Philadelphia. The driving personality behind the WCFA was W. B. Riley, pastor of the large First Baptist Church of Minneapolis, a dynamic speaker who possessed exceptional organizational skills. Riley was a militant fundamentalist. The association consisted of churches, individuals, and other organizations. It published literature, held rallies, and had aspirations in the field of education.[18]

Large anti-evolution rallies were the chief accomplishment of the WCFA. Evolution became a prominent national issue, highlighted by the famous Scopes trial in Tennessee in 1925. W. B. Riley traversed the nation holding public rallies and debates.

The WCFA attracted many prominent names of the time. Riley noted in 1943 that of the original number of ministers who joined the WCFA those still living were himself, J. C. Massee, P. W. Philpot, Lewis Sperry Chafer, William Pettingill, and George McNealy. Those who had gone to be with the Lord were Charles Alexander, R. A. Torrey, James M. Gray, Paul Rader, C. I. Scofield, W. H. Griffith Thomas, John Roach Straton, L. W. Munhall, I. M. Haldeman, Joseph Kyle, George E. Guile, and A. B. Winchester.[19]

The WCFA began to wane in the late 1920s. The issues became less attractive, and other groups developed similar emphases or became more popular in their own right.[20] W. B. Riley served as president from 1919-1929, Sidney Smith from 1929-1931, and Paul Rood from 1931-1952, after which the WCFA merged with the Slavic Gospel Association.

---

[17]*Christianity and Liberalism* (Grand Rapids: Eerdmans, 1923), p. 7.

[18]Out of the WCFA the idea of a fundamentalist seminary was proposed, which eventually saw the establishment in 1924 of the Evangelical Theological College in Dallas, TX, now the Dallas Theological Seminary. W. H. Griffith Thomas and others were the founders.

[19]"World's Christian Fundamentals Association," *The Pilot* (June 1943), p. 259.

[20]The Research Science Bureau, begun by Harry Rimmer in 1920, the Anti-Evolution league, begun by Riley himself in 1923, the beginning of the American Council of Christian Churches by Carl McIntire in 1941, the formation of the National Association of Evangelicals in 1942, and the denominational concerns and struggles among fundamentalists beginning around 1930 all proved to be in competition with the WCFA and its goals and emphases.

The Fundamentalist Fellowship: 1920

The fundamentalist-modernist controversy in the Northern Baptist Convention had its principal locus around the upstart Fundamentalist Fellowship. The Fellowship formed in 1920 in opposition to the liberalism that had infected the Convention from its beginning in 1907 but which had now begun to dominate the convention infrastructure. The main impetus that triggered the controversy in the Convention and the subsequent establishment of the Fundamentalist Fellowship was the Interchurch World Movement. Begun after World War I, the movement was an interdenominational relief organization controlled by liberals that wanted $100 million from the Baptists. The 1919 Convention voted to participate, but the fundamentalists strongly objected. The Fundamentalist Fellowship grew out of the 1920 pre-Convention conference, June 21-22, in Buffalo, NY.

The Fundamentalist Fellowship was initially non-separatist. It did not intend to leave the Convention but to be a catalyst for fundamentalism within. It hoped to purge the modernists and recapture the Convention's political machinery—a "loyal opposition" mentality. Its principal mode of operation was to hold pre-convention meetings to plan strategies for combating the modernists. There were militant fundamentalists in the Fellowship (such as W. B. Riley, John Roach Straton, William Pettingill, and Robert T. Ketcham) and moderate fundamentalists (such as Russell Conwell, Curtis Lee Laws, J. C. Massee, James Whitcomb Brougher, John Marvin Dean, and Frank Goodchild). Of the original call for the pre-Convention conference, few ever actually left the Northern Baptist Convention. The first president of the Fellowship was J. C. Massee, pastor at the Baptist Temple, Brooklyn, NY, and later the Tremont Temple, Boston.[21]

Despite the Fellowship's strategies, fundamentalists were almost routinely defeated on the Convention floor. The 1922 gathering in Indianapolis was a telling defeat for the fundamentalists. The chief combatants were W. B. Riley and Cornelius Woelfkin, former professor of Rochester Seminary and pastor of the Fifth Avenue Baptist Church, New York City. Speaking for the fundamentalists, Riley recommended the adoption of the historic, conservative New Hampshire Confession of Faith as the confessional basis of the Convention, thereby hoping to gain the ecclesiastical leverage necessary to deal with the modernists. Woelfkin shrewdly substituted a motion that the New Testament itself serve as the basis. The modernists sided with Woelfkin and prevailed overwhelmingly. The Fundamentalist Fellowship finally withdrew from the Convention in the early 1940s and launched the Conservative Baptist movement.

The Baptist Bible Union: 1923[22]

Considerable agitation existed within Baptist fundamentalism for a much larger testimony that would transcend its Northern Baptist Convention denominational boundaries. There was also dissatisfaction in some quarters with the "loyal opposition," moderate approach of J. C. Massee and the Fundamentalist Fellowship.

---

[21]For a biographical study on Massee, consult C. Allyn Russell, *Voices of American Fundamentalism* (Philadelphia: Westminster, 1976), pp. 106-34.

[22]A definitive work on this subject is that by Robert G. Delnay, "A History of the Baptist Bible Union" (Th.D. dissertation, Dallas Theological Seminary, 1963).

In 1923 The Baptist Bible Union formed in Kansas City, MO, under the leadership of W. B. Riley, J. Frank Norris, pastor of the First Baptist Church of Fort Worth, TX, and T. T. Shields, pastor of the Jarvis Street Baptist Church of Toronto. Shields served as president. The Union represented a more organized, more separatistic, and more militant stance than the Fundamentalist Fellowship. It withheld financial support from non-sympathetic schools and mission agencies rather than supporting them while trying to purge them of bad elements. On a more aggressive front, the Union projected the organization of new schools,[23] publishing efforts,[24] and missionary endeavors.[25]

The Union men also met continual defeat within the Northern Baptist Convention. One of the leaders of the Union, J. Frank Norris, was involved in the fatal shooting of D. L. Chipps, a local adversary of Norris, in 1926.[26] This incident earned Norris a great deal of opprobrium even from men within the Union, causing a serious disruption of the fellowship. Another setback was the controversy, amid rumors of improprieties, and the subsequent student riot at the Des Moines University in 1929, causing the school's eventual dissolution.[27] The Baptist Bible Union declined and became the General Association of Regular Baptist Churches in 1932.

The Northern Presbyterian Conflict: 1920s

Presbyterian ministers had been prominent in the Bible conference and Bible college movements, such as James H. Brookes, W. J. Eerdman, L. W. Munhall, Billy Sunday, William E. Biederwolf, A. T. Pierson, Thomas C. Horton, William Evans, William Jennings Bryan, Charles G. Trumbull, and Lewis Sperry Chafer. Liberalism crept into the Presbyterian Church USA through lax presbyteries, especially the New York presbytery, that ordained men with liberal views. In the late 1890s, three prominent heresy trials occurred: Henry Preserved Smith (1892), C. A. Briggs (1893), and A. C. McGiffert (1899). There was also an attempt, agitated by Philip Schaff and C. A. Briggs, to revise the Westminster Confession and tone down its Calvinism to give space to new ideas of a liberal slant. While all of these ended in technical victories for the conservatives, the denomination eventually succumbed to the new thought.

Several issues precipitated the controversy of the 1920s: liberalism on mission fields, the case of Harry Emerson Fosdick, a liberal Baptist who had become the associate pastor of the First Presbyterian Church of New York City,[28] and the issue of the Auburn Affirmation.

---

[23]For example, it took over and ran Des Moines University as a separatist, fundamentalist institution from 1927-1929 (Ibid., pp. 180-226).

[24]The Union published a magazine, *The Baptist Bible Union Herald*, later named *The Fundamental Baptist*. Some of the pastors had their own publications. Riley, for example, published *The Baptist Beacon*, Norris had *The Searchlight*, and Shields put out *The Gospel Witness*, the latter becoming sort of the official organ of the Union when Shields was the leader. A wide and aggressive colporteur endeavor for the Union was planned early on (ibid., p. 71).

[25]Ibid., pp. 73-80.

[26]George W. Dollar, *The History of Fundamentalism in America* (Greenville, SC: Unusual Publications, 1973), p. 168.

[27]Ibid., p. 110. Delnay said, "The collapse of Des Moines University...ruined the Baptist Bible Union" ("A History of the Baptist Bible Union," p. 238).

[28]For a description of the Fosdick issue, see Beale, *In Pursuit of Purity*, pp. 153-55 and David B. Calhoun, *Princeton Seminary*, 2 vols. (Carlisle, PA: Banner of Truth Trust, 1996) 2:338-39, 347, 350.

In 1910 the General Assembly had adopted the famous "five fundamentals,"[29] and they were reaffirmed in 1916 and 1923. A committee of fifteen located in Auburn, NY drew up an affirmation denying that the fundamentals should be required beliefs for ordination, however the General Assembly of 1924 declared the "five fundamentals" to be unconstitutional, a bitter defeat for the Bible-believers.[30]

In the wake of the Auburn Affirmation controversy, the General Association established a Peace Commission of fifteen (liberals and conservatives) to deal with unrest in the church. In 1927 the commission recommended that the five-point doctrinal statement no longer be required for ordination, opting instead for a bland statement, passed by the General Assembly, that the standard is "the Word of God as the Spirit speaks through it."[31]

The final indignity for the fundamental conservatives proved to be the reorganization of Princeton Theological Seminary. Turmoil between the hard-line conservatives and those with less restrictive views had been brewing in the Seminary for a number of years.[32] A committee was appointed in 1926 to look into the turbulence. Princeton Seminary had been operating with two boards, one for education and the other for finances. The committee recommended a reorganized administration with one board. The new board tipped the balance of power towards the liberals. The reorganization brought a degree of religious syncretism to the Seminary and precipitated the exodus of several professors to form Westminster Theological Seminary in 1929.[33]

The Scopes Evolution Trial: 1925

One of the more celebrated events of the 1920s religious controversy was the Scopes evolution trial in Dayton, TN, in 1925. William Jennings Bryan served as prosecutor of John T. Scopes, a school teacher accused of violating the anti-evolution law of the state of Tennessee. The flamboyant Clarence Darrow, retained by the American Civil Liberties Union, was one of the defense attorneys. The trial attracted national attention. While the verdict announced a victory for the prosecution, the media fallout was almost wholly negative for the fundamentalists. Bryan, out of his league as a trial lawyer in a civil-religious-scientific suit, appeared to have been outmaneuvered by Darrow in the eyes of the public. The national media portrayed fundamentalism as archaic and ridiculous.

The Period of Consolidation and Building: 1929-1940s

Fundamentalist associations of churches, schools, and mission agencies coalesced around strong fundamentalist leaders. In most cases there had been

---

[29]They were the inerrancy of the original manuscripts of Scripture, the virgin birth of Christ, the vicarious atonement of Christ, the bodily resurrection of Christ, and the reality of biblical miracles.

[30]Calhoun, *Princeton Seminary*, 2:350.

[31]Beale, *In Pursuit of Purity*, p. 161.

[32]David B. Calhoun acknowledges the problem with designations for the two groups at Princeton Seminary at the time. While not strictly divided into liberal and fundamental, one group was militantly antagonistic toward liberalism and the other was tolerant; one stressed doctrine and the other peace and unity (*Princeton Seminary*, 2:512).

[33]Beale, *In Pursuit of Purity*, p. 169.

attempts to purge an organization of liberalism, and these attempts had failed. In the first stage fundamentalist "separatism" amounted to an attempt to separate liberals from their organizations. Having failed, fundamentalists resorted to a second stage and were forced to separate themselves from the liberals in a formal practice of ecclesiastical separation.[34]

Westminster Theological Seminary, 1929: J. Gresham Machen

The reorganization of Princeton Theological Seminary in 1929 represented a victory for the liberals. The conservatives' outspoken leader in the struggle was J. Gresham Machen, a Princeton graduate and faculty member since 1906.[35] Machen and three other Princeton faculty members resigned and formed Westminster Theological Seminary in Philadelphia on September 25, 1929.[36]

The Independent Fundamental Churches of America, 1930: William McCarrell

The IFCA grew out of the American Conference of Undenominational Churches, formed in 1923 in Iowa. The ACUC met for six annual conventions and grew from 24 members to 150 by 1929.[37] After the Illinois State Congregational Conference united with the Universalists, the fundamentalists eventually withdrew. William "Billy" McCarrell's church voted itself out of the Congregational Association in January 1930.[38] On January 22, McCarrell and other interested men met at the Cicero Bible Church to consider uniting with the ACUC. On February 6, thirty-nine men met at the same church under the leadership of McCarrell resulting in a motion to affiliate with the ACUC. In June 1930 the annual convention of the American Conference of Undenominational Churches met at the Cicero Bible Church at which time it enlarged and strengthened its doctrinal statement and became the Independent Fundamental Churches of America. Influential men in the IFCA movement were M. R. DeHaan, Wendell P. Loveless, W. L. Pettingill, M. H. Reynolds, Sr., J. Oliver Buswell, Jr., Louis Talbot, John Walvoord, and William E. Ashbrook.[39]

The General Association of Regular Baptist Churches, 1932: Robert T. Ketcham and Others

The GARBC succeeded the Baptist Bible Union that had been declining for several years. The last annual meeting of the Union occurred in May 1932, in the Belden Avenue Baptist Church, Chicago, with only thirty-four delegates

---

[34]Beale rightly describes these two stages as "nonconformist" fundamentalism and "separatist" fundamentalism (*In Pursuit of Purity,* pp. 5-6). Carpenter notes: "Fundamentalist efforts to cleanse the denominations of liberal trends had seemed to fail. Rather than persisting along the 1920s lines of conflict, fundamentalists during the 1930s were developing their own institutional base from which to carry on their major purpose: the proclamation of the evangelical gospel" ("Fundamentalist Institutions and the Rise of Evangelical Protestantism, 1929-1942," p. 73).

[35]Calhoun, *Princeton Seminary,* 2:233.

[36]Machen was accompanied by Robert Dick Wilson, Oswald T. Allis, and Cornelius Van Til from Princeton. These men were joined by four Princeton graduates: Allan MacRae, Paul Wooley, Ned Stonehouse, and R. B. Kuiper (ibid., 2:395-66).

[37]James O. Henry, *For Such A Time As This: A History of the Independent Fundamental Churches of America* (Westchester, IL: Independent Fundamental Churches of America, 1983), pp. 29-31.

[38]Ibid., p. 37.

[39]Dollar, *A History of Fundamentalism in America,* p. 223. *Dictionary of Christianity in America,* s.v. "Independent Fundamental Churches of America," by C. E. Hall, p. 573.

in attendance. Apparently no meeting had been held in 1931. Out of the Bible Union the GARBC was formed by Baptist fundamentalist leaders such as Robert T. Ketcham, Harry Hamilton (president), O. W. Van Osdel, and Earle Griffith (vice president), among others. Ketcham and Griffith pastored in Ohio and were instrumental in forming the Ohio Association of Independent Baptist Churches. Hamilton pastored First Baptist Church, Buffalo, NY. Van Osdel pastored Wealthy Street Baptist Church in Grand Rapids, MI, and started the Michigan Orthodox Baptist Association.

The GARBC initially had three general characteristics: it was composed of churches and not individuals, it was a fellowship not a convention, and it maintained the practice of "approving" existing agencies rather than starting them. It also required churches to sever all connections with modernism, direct or indirect, before membership in the GARBC could be obtained.

Ecclesiastical separation became a hallmark of the Association from the beginning. The Baptist Bible Union, as originally envisioned and implemented, was a separatist movement. However, some of the early leaders, notably W. B. Riley and T. T. Shields, came to disavow separatism. Riley steered the Bible Union away from separatism when it formally organized in May 1923.[40] The Baptist Bible Union became more of a separatistic protest group within the Northern Baptist Convention rather than a strictly separatist movement. The separatist mentality, however, was still a viable though subliminal stratum in the Bible Union. It became obvious to many after the defeats of the Union men in the 1926 and 1927 Conventions that separation was the final solution to the modernism issue.[41]

The Independent Board For Presbyterian Foreign Missions, 1933: J. Gresham Machen
Liberalism on the mission fields of the Presbyterian Board for Foreign Missions had been a problem for some time. In 1920 W. H. Griffith Thomas and Lewis Sperry Chafer visited China and reported the prevalence of modernism and higher criticism among Presbyterian ministers.[42] J. Gresham Machen spoke out against modernism in missions and presented evidence of liberalism on mission fields. He soon founded the organization of the Independent Board For Presbyterian Foreign Missions in 1933. The General Assembly declared the Board to be divisive and ordered the members who were Presbyterians to withdraw or stand ecclesiastical trial. Machen and others refused to withdraw and consequently were suspended from the Presbyterian ministry. In 1936 Machen led the formation of the Presbyterian Church of America, which was later named the Orthodox Presbyterian Church.[43]

Grace Theological Seminary, 1937: Alva J. McClain and Herman A. Hoyt
Liberalism had invaded the Ashland College and Theological Seminary, Brethren schools in Ashland, Ohio. Alva J. McClain, from the beginning of his

---

[40]Delnay, "A History of the Baptist Bible Union," pp. 52-54.

[41]Ibid., p. 238. J. Murray Murdoch, *Portrait of Obedience: The Biography of Robert T. Ketcham* (Schaumburg, IL: Regular Baptist Press, 1979), p. 128.

[42]Beale, *In Pursuit of Purity*, p. 317.

[43]Russell, *Voices of American Fundamentalism*, p. 156.

ministry, opposed the inroads of modernism in the Brethren Church. He was a professor in the college (1925-1927) and later (1930) the directing leader, dean, and, supported by Professor Herman A. Hoyt, the guiding light for fundamental conservatism against the incursion of worldliness and liberalism in the seminary. McClain and Hoyt were dismissed from the faculty of the seminary in 1937, precipitating the founding of Grace Theological Seminary in the fall of that year. In 1939 the National Fellowship of Brethren Churches formed after two stormy years of controversy between the Ashland and Grace groups within the Brethren Church.[44]

The American Council of Christian Churches, 1941: Carl McIntire

The ACCC began in New York City on September 17, 1941. The leader and first president was Carl McIntire, a militant fundamentalist who, along with J.Gresham Machen had been suspended by the Presbyterian Church a few years earlier. The initial impetus for the founding of the Council was to be a protest against the Federal (now National) Council of Churches, a liberal federation, and to be a witness for fundamentalist separatism. The Federal Council had become the representative for Protestantism with the federal government. McIntire challenged that right and gained recognition for fundamentalist chaplains in the military as well as securing free radio time.[45] The stated purpose of the ACCC was and still is

> to expose and oppose liberalism, socialism and...communism...to unify those Protestants who believe in an inerrant Bible, each denomination however, retaining its identity and full autonomy; to obtain advantages for the historic Christian Faith in America and all lands.[46]

The Conservative Baptist Movement, 1943: R. V. Clearwaters and Others

For over twenty years the Fundamentalist Fellowship within the Northern Baptist Convention continued to agitate against liberalism and endeavored to capture the machinery of the convention from the modernists. The "loyal opposition" and "separation from within" mindset prevented these fundamentalists from an open break with the convention as had been done earlier by the Baptist Bible Union/GARBC men.[47]

After decades of failure to accomplish a cleansing of the Northern Baptist Foreign Mission Society from liberal control,[48] the Fundamentalist Fellowship

---

[44]See Alva J. McClain, "The Background and Origin of Grace Theological Seminary," in *Charis: The History of Grace Theological Seminary 1931-1951*, ed. John C. Whitcomb (Winona Lake, IN: Grace Theological Seminary, 1951), pp. 9-38, and Homer A. Kent, Sr., *250 Years...Conquering Frontiers: A History of the Brethren Church* (Winona Lake, IN: Brethren Missionary Herald, 1958), pp. 125-68.

[45]*Dictionary of Christianity in America*, s.v. "American Council of Christian Churches," by The Editors, p. 45.

[46]Constant H. Jacquet, Jr., ed., *Yearbook of American and Canadian Churches 1984* (Nashville: Abingdon, 1984), p. 8, quoted in Beale, *In Pursuit of Purity*, p. 368.

[47]The framers of the (later) Conservative Baptist movement took criticism over the years for this delay and for allowing churches membership in the Northern Baptist Convention while joining the CB movement; i.e., a *complete* break with the apostasy was not required for membership in CB organizations. Justification of the criticism was tacitly admitted decades later (R. V. Clearwaters, "The GARB Guilt Complex of Dr. Merle R. Hull, Editor of The Baptist Bulletin," *Central Testimony* [published by Central Baptist Theological Seminary of Minneapolis] 10 [1968]).

[48]Chester E. Tulga, *The Foreign Missions Controversy in the Northern Baptist Convention: 30 Years of Struggle for a Pure Missionary Society* (Chicago: Conservative Baptist Fellowship, 1950). Bruce Shelley, *A History of Conservative Baptists* (Denver: Denver Conservative Baptist Seminary, 1960), pp. 26-47.

(renamed the Conservative Baptist Fellowship in 1946) launched several Conservative Baptist organizations by first establishing the Conservative Baptist Foreign Mission Society in 1943. Vincent Brushwyler served as the general director. The Conservative Baptist Association of America began in 1947 with I. Cedric Peterson as the general director, followed by B. Myron Cedarholm a short time later.[49] The Conservative Baptist Home Mission Society was formally organized in 1950, having operated with provisional organization since 1948. George Washburn was the first general director, followed by Rufus Jones in 1952.[50]

The Conservative Baptist movement began as a separatist fundamentalist movement. The statement of purpose of the Conservative Baptist Association of America said explicitly that the organization aimed to "provide a fellowship of churches and individuals upon a thoroughly Biblical and historically Baptistic basis, unmixed with liberals and liberalism and those who are content to walk in fellowship with unbelief and inclusivism."[51]

Other Formations

Bob Jones College was established by Evangelist Bob Jones, Sr. in 1927 at St. Andrews Bay, FL. John R. Rice commenced the *Sword of the Lord* on September 28, 1934. The Los Angeles Baptist Seminary began in 1927, Baptist Bible Seminary (Johnson City, NY) in 1932, Western Baptist Bible College in 1935, Baptist Bible Seminary (Ft. Worth, TX) in 1939, and Grand Rapids Baptist College in 1941.

Thus by the 1930s fundamentalism had gone through a major struggle with liberalism, had regrouped, and had made a fresh start with new organizations and institutions around strong leaders. At this point, the terms fundamentalism and evangelicalism were still used interchangeably as they would continue to be well into the 1940s and 1950s.[52]

---

[49]Bruce Shelley, *A History of Conservative Baptists*, pp. 48-62.

[50]Ibid., pp. 63-66.

[51]"CBA: Its Mission" (Chicago: Conservative Baptist Association of America, B. Myron Cedarholm, General Director, pamphlet, n.d.).

[52]Joel A. Carpenter, *Revive Us Again*, p. 152.

PART 2: THE FORMATION OF THE NEW EVANGELICALISM

In the late 1930s and early 1940s dissatisfaction with fundamentalism arose from among those within the general pale of the fundamentalist cause. Their historical and educational roots were in fundamentalism, and organizationally they were within the broader fundamentalist/evangelical coalition. Their feelings came to light in various publications and actions. Over the course of fifteen years they planned, and eventually launched a coalition self-styled the "new" evangelicalism.

3

FOUR CRUCIAL ISSUES

The rise of new evangelicalism is traceable through a series of intricately interwoven issues and events reflecting dissatisfaction with fundamentalism. These issues overlap in many cases, so that it must not be construed that separate and unrelated factors gave rise to the new ideas. Dispensationalism was frequently a debated issue. Ecclesiastical separation was another cause for dispute between moderate evangelicals and fundamentalists in the struggles of the 1940s and 50s.

THE UNITY/SEPARATION ISSUE: THE NATIONAL ASSOCIATION OF EVANGELICALS (1942)

The formation of the National Association of Evangelicals (NAE) marks the conception of new evangelicalism. A distinction between "fundamentalist" and "evangelical" began to take shape.[1] Ecclesiastical separation proved to be the "most explosive issue" and "dilemma"[2] for the dissatisfied element within fundamentalism. Agitators for change initially attempted to be loyal to the fundamentals of fundamentalism, but they also wanted to be loyal to their own denominations that were capitulating to liberalism. The agitators desired to reclaim their denominations for orthodoxy,[3] and to present themselves as a genuine positive alternative to fundamentalism, neo-liberalism, and neo-orthodoxy. Ellingsen well describes the unity/separation issue and its precipitated change:

> In many ways this desire to present the old fundamentals of the faith in a positive, not merely defensive, way was to set the agenda and rationale for the emergence of Evangelicalism out of its original Fundamentalist heritage.[4]

The vision for a cooperative, unified evangelical voice that did not have the stigma of fundamentalist negativism nor the doctrinal heresies of liberalism is ascribed to J. Elwin Wright, leader of a group of evangelicals called The New

[1]Joel A. Carpenter, *Revive Us Again: The Reawakening of American Fundamentalism* (New York: Oxford, 1997), p. 152. Elsewhere he noted that part of the significance of the call to form the NAE was that it represented "a ferment within Fundamentalism." "The Fundamentalist Leaven and the Rise of an Evangelical United Front," *The Evangelical Tradition in America*, ed. Leonard I. Sweet (Macon, GA: Mercer University Press, 1997), p. 260.

[2]George M. Marsden, *Reforming Fundamentalism: Fuller Seminary and the New Evangelicalism* (Grand Rapids: Eerdmans, 1987), pp. 6-7.

[3]Ibid.

[4]Mark Ellingsen, *The Evangelical Movement: Growth, Impact, Controversy, Dialog* (Minneapolis: Augsburg, 1988), p. 99.

England Fellowship, founded by Wright in 1929. Referring probably to the World's Christian Fundamentals Association (begun in 1919) and the American Council of Christian Churches (begun in 1941), if not obliquely to the Federal Council of Churches (begun in 1908), Wright declared at the organizational meeting of the NAE in April 1942:

> Although several movements having similar objectives are in the field, it is evident that none of these have succeeded in winning the confidence and support of that vast section of Protestantism still loyal to the historic doctrinal positions of the Church.[5]

Wright had been touring the country from 1939 to 1941 stirring up revival fires and pressing for a new coalition of evangelicals.

Another energetic and capable leader in the efforts to form a new united evangelical organization was Harold John Ockenga, pastor of Park Street [Congregational] Church, Boston (1936-1969). He was a graduate of Taylor University, attended Princeton Seminary, and graduated from Westminster Seminary in 1930. He received a Ph.D. from the University of Pittsburgh in 1939. In 1936, after serving for five years as an assistant to Dr. Clarence MacCartney at First Presbyterian Church, Pittsburgh, Ockenga became pastor of Park Street Church. In 1940 and 1941, he and J. Elwin Wright planned and promoted what became the NAE. Ockenga served for several years as its first president.[6]

At the Moody Bible Institute on October 27-28, 1941, several evangelical leaders met for prayer and discussion concerning the formation of the new endeavor. Another organizational meeting followed in St. Louis on April 7-8, 1942.[7] The three primary threats identified by these men were Roman Catholicism, liberalism/modernism, and secularism (generally in the form of Franklin D. Roosevelt's political liberalism, and international communism).[8] Even liberals at the time were concerned about the growing strength of Roman Catholicism.[9]

---

[5]"An Historical Statement," *Evangelical Action! A Report of the Organization of the National Association of Evangelicals for United Action*, compiled and edited by the Executive Committee (Boston: United Action Press, 1942), p. v.

[6]Data on Ockenga was gleaned from "Harold J. Ockenga: Chairman of the Board [an interview]," *Christianity Today* (Nov 6, 1981), pp. 26-30; Randy Frame, "Modern Evangelicalism Mourns the Loss of One of Its Founding Fathers," *Christianity Today* (Mar 15, 1985), pp. 34-36, and *Evangelical Dictionary of Theology*, s.v. "Ockenga, Harold John (1905-1985)," by J. A. Carpenter, p. 837.

[7]Joel A. Carpenter, "From Fundamentalism to the New Evangelical Coalition," in *Evangelicalism and Modern America*, ed. George M. Marsden (Grand Rapids: Eerdmans, 1984), p. 12.

[8]Harold John Ockenga, "The Unvoiced Multitudes," *Evangelical Action! A Report of the Organization of the NAE*, pp. 26-31. These three items were the main reasons given for considering the formation of a new body. See also his "The Last Word," *Christian Life and Times* (October 1947), p. 52. Ockenga saw in the increase of government at the expense of private interests and capitalism "the most tremendous danger of all" ("The Unvoiced Multitudes," p. 31). William Pettingill called Catholicism, Modernism, and Secularism the "Big Three" (*Christian Life and Times* [October 1947], p. 101). Carl F. H. Henry feared fundamentalism would become a despised and oppressed sect "in the event of Roman Catholic domination in the United States" (*The Uneasy Conscience of Modern Fundamentalism* [Grand Rapids: Eerdmans, 1947], preface).

William Ward Ayer deplored the advancing "statism" and the government's recognition of the Federal Council of Churches as representative of Protestantism. He declared, "evangelical Christianity has the America of our fathers to save. Evangelicals have the 'keys of the kingdom'" ("Evangelical Christianity Endangered By Its Fragmented Condition," in *A Report of the Organization of the NAE*, pp. 42, 46).

For the fear of communism, see Carpenter, "From Fundamentalism to the New Evangelical Coalition," pp. 6, 9.

Harold Ockenga's formula for meeting the spiritual enemies of the day began with seeking to unite evangelicalism against them. Fundamentalism's effectiveness had been stifled by its "failures, divisions, and controversies." Rugged individualism, the alleged catalyst to fundamentalism's weaknesses, must be repudiated. Second to ecclesiastical unity, Ockenga targeted doctrinal purity and "consecrated love."[10]

Many separatist fundamentalists were in sympathy with the early aims and goals of the NAE despite the recently-formed fundamentalist American Council of Christian Churches (1941). John R. Rice and Bob Jones Sr. and Jr., worked within the NAE to promote evangelistic campaigns throughout the country.[11] However, during the early 1950s Rice and the Joneses, who "led the fundamentalist faction,"[12] and other fundamentalist leaders left the NAE because of its weak position on separation. These departures consolidated the leadership of the NAE in the hands of those with less restrictive convictions who wanted a softer stand and a far less militant direction. NAE polemics against unorthodoxy accordingly died down.

The NAE received criticism from both the left and the right. Charles Clayton Morrison, editor of the liberal *Christian Century*, noted that "in the formation of the National Association of Evangelicals For United Action, the atomistic sectarianism which has long been a scandal of Protestant Christianity appears to be receiving a new lease on life."[13] Fundamentalist W. B. Riley decried the NAE as a "divisive organization."[14] He forcefully reproved the NAE leaders for not joining in with the World's Christian Fundamentals Association (in whose formation he had a principal role in 1919) because it did not fully represent them, and strongly suggested that pride of leadership among the NAE men fostered

---

Eerdmans, 1984), pp. 6, 9; George M. Marsden, *Reforming Fundamentalism,* pp. 154-55; and H. H. Savage, "United Evangelical Action" (presidential address at the 1955 NAE convention), *United Evangelical Action* (May 1, 1955), p. 3. An implicit polemic against communism can be seen in Carl F. H. Henry, "Christianity and Social Reform," *Bulletin of the Moravian Theological Seminary* (1960), pp. 22, 24, 27. For an outright polemic see Edward John Carnell, *A Philosophy of the Christian Religion* (Grand Rapids: Eerdmans, 1952), chapter 4, "Bread Alone?" pp. 83-128, as well as Henry, "Christianity and Economic Crisis," *United Evangelical Action* (May 1, 1955), pp. 7-9, and L. Nelson Bell, "Christianity and Communism," *Christianity Today* (Jan 19, 1959), p. 19. See also Wilbur M. Smith, *The Atomic Age and the Word of God* (Boston: W. A. Wilde, 1948) and his *World Crises and the Prophetic Scriptures* (Chicago: Moody, 1951).

[9]Harold Fey, "Can Catholicism Win America?" a series of eight articles, *The Christian Century* (Nov 29, 1944 through Jan 17, 1945). Even liberals were trying to "win America."

[10]"Unvoiced Multitudes," pp. 32, 34

[11]Farley P. Butler, "Billy Graham and the End of Evangelical Unity" (Ph.D. dissertation, University of Florida, 1976), p. 29. Mark Taylor Dalhouse, *An Island in the Lake of Fire: Bob Jones University, Fundamentalism, and the Separatist Movement* (Athens, GA: University of Georgia Press, 1996), p. 53.

[12]Farley P. Butler, "Billy Graham and the End of Evangelical Unity," p. 29. See also Dalhouse, *An Island in A Lake of Fire*, p. 73, and Marsden, *Reforming Fundamentalism*, p. 159. For a brief account by Bob Jones Jr. see *Cornbread and Caviar: Reminiscences and Reflections* (Greenville, SC: Bob Jones University Press, 1985), pp. 103-04.

[13]Charles Clayton Morrison, "Sectarianism Receives New Lease on Life," *The Christian Century* (May 19, 1943), p. 596.

[14]"The Fatal Weakness of Fundamentalism," *The Pilot* (May 1942), p. 227. The "weakness" was the failure to unite together strong leaders with sound doctrine in an established organization, doubtlessly meaning the World's Christian Fundamentals Association.

division.[15] One of his final comments on the NAE was that "it has effected some very positive divisions, and doubtless will itself become just another semi-fundamentalist movement, illustrating afresh the fact that Fundamentalists defeat themselves by divisions."[16]

Carl McIntire, instrumental in starting the American Council of Christian Churches in 1941, wanted the NAE men to join the ACCC. Various talks transpired between the two groups, but it became obvious that the NAE was less restrictive on ecclesiastical separation, and thus it refused to join the ACCC.[17] Clyde Taylor, past general director of the NAE, on the thirtieth anniversary of the NAE (1972), recalled the three issues separating the NAE and the ACCC: ecclesiastical separation, the question of creating a council of churches vis-a-vis a fellowship of evangelicals, and the difference between a "polemical" and a "constructive" approach in dealing with the theological and ecclesiastical issues of modernism.[18] In short, the ACCC fundamentalist separatism offended the NAE moderates such as Harold Ockenga, Donald Grey Barnhouse, John Bradbury, Will Houghton, and J. Elwin Wright, and union was impossible.[19] From then on McIntire constantly chided the NAE. J. Oliver Buswell, Jr., who was part of the original organization of the ACCC, reported the difference between the two groups.

> Our interests and purposes were similar in many ways. With others of the ACCC I attended the meeting [the NAE organizational meeting in St. Louis, 1942] and prayed for rapprochement and understanding. But our differences came clearly to light. The NAE view crystallized in opposition to the ACCC constitutional provision that constituent membership be limited to denominations not in the Federal Council. Thus the NAE was formed of brethren who sincerely desired to spread the Gospel but who did not see the doctrine of the purity of the visible Church as we believe the Bible sets it forth.[20]

While there was criticism from both the left and the right, most evangelical pastors and leaders were sympathetic to the new group. Typical were the encouraging words of Lewis Sperry Chafer, editor of the *Bibliotheca Sacra*:

> There is genuine ground for encouragement in the nationwide movement which has been styled the *National Association of Evangelicals for United Action,* which has as its objective the uniting of the vast evangelical forces in America for the fair and reasonable expression of their convictions. This movement was born by the Holy Spirit in the minds of certain prominent evangelicals in the East....This

---

[15]"National Association of Evangelicals For United Action," *The Pilot* (November 1942), pp. 53-54. He proposed a clearing house for fundamentalist activities composed of representatives from the various groups (WCFA, NAE, and ACCC).

[16]"National Association of Evangelicals," *The Pilot* (October 1943), p. 31.

[17]Farley P. Butler, "Billy Graham and the End of Evangelical Unity," p. 16. The issue was the ACCC position of separation from the Federal Council of Churches and from any denomination which was a member of the Federal Council. One compromise proposal that was finally rejected by the NAE leaders was that membership in the NAE could be predicated on the fact that there was at least a *willingness* formally to go on record as being opposed to and repudiating the Federal Council.

[18]Clyde W. Taylor, "NAE Celebrates 30 Years of Service," *United Evangelical Action* (Spring 1972), p. 9.

[19]Joel A. Carpenter, *Revive Us Again*, pp. 145-46.

[20]"The American and International Council of Christian Churches," *Christianity Today* (Jan 29, 1965), p. 9.

new undertaking for united action deserves the support by prayer and gifts of all those who have a heart for the vital things of God.[21]

The formation of the NAE ultimately proved to be a watershed event in the rise of the new evangelicalism and in the history of fundamentalism/ evangelicalism. It constituted a part of an agenda of certain leaders who were convinced that the fundamentalism of the 1920s and 30s did not suit the new generation of evangelicals and their vision for the future. That being the case, Clyde Taylor's observation is significant that most of the agitators for change, and the majority of those at the first meeting of the NAE, had not personally been involved in the fundamentalist-modernist controversy.[22] With the NAE the "refurbishing" of fundamentalism had begun.[23] Nevertheless, Carpenter correctly observes: "…fundamentalists provided the initial vision and leadership for 'united evangelical action.'" Like the Methodists in the early nineteenth century and the holiness people in the late nineteenth century, "the fundamentalists were the salient evangelical movement in the 1920s."[24]

One can only speculate what might have been if the separatist fundamentalists had prevailed in the progress and direction of the NAE. Farley Butler muses pensively:

> Had the NAE men, the Baptist fundamentalists led by [John R.] Rice, the independent fundamentalists represented by [Bob] Jones, and the men of the American Council been joined together in a strong organization with a clear platform, the history of evangelicalism in the next years might have been far different.[25]

Indeed, efforts to unite the sparring factions (separatists and moderates) marked the early years. Bob Jones and John R. Rice were heard to discuss the hope of bringing the two groups together.[26] In fact, in the *Sword of the Lord* Rice urged people to pray for such a reconciliation.[27] But it was not to be. The separatists were outnumbered. As Weber observed,

---

[21]"United Action of Evangelicals," *Bibliotheca Sacra* 39 (Oct-Dec 1942): 385-86. See also his testimonial in *Evangelical Action! A Report of the Organization of the NAE*, p. 144.

[22]Clyde W. Taylor, "NAE Celebrates 30 Years of Service," p. 9. Taylor was the general director of the NAE from 1963-1974, having served in various other capacities since 1944.

[23]George M. Marsden, *Reforming Fundamentalism*, p. 153.

[24]Joel A. Carpenter, *Revive Us Again*, p. 155. Elsewhere he said that the NAE was a "fundamentalist-initiated but genuinely inclusive fellowship that signaled the formation of a new coalition" and "the new evangelical coalition was made possible to a large extent because fundamentalism, as the era's most vocal and visible evangelical movement, had influenced many other evangelical groups" ("From Fundamentalism to the New Evangelical Coalition," pp. 12, 13).

[25]"Billy Graham and the End of Evangelical Unity," p. 30.

[26]Ibid., p. 19.

[27]May 14, 1944, p. 6. In 1947 Carl F. H. Henry was suggesting a meeting between the two groups "in a spirit of mutual love and compassion" to seek a united voice (*The Uneasy Conscience*, p. 81). And as late as 1968, in his own words, "I tried to close ranks...between evangelicals per se and radically independent fundamentalists." He was invited, and prepared to go, to address the Seventh World Congress of the International Council of Christian Churches (1968), intending to speak on "Demythologizing the Evangelicals." But, due to correspondence confusion between him and Carl McIntire, he never made it (Carl F. H. Henry, *Confessions of a Theologian: An Autobiography* [Waco, TX: Word, 1986], p. 300). Henry's would-be address to the ACCC was printed in *Christianity Today* (Sept 13, 1968), p. 13.

> By the 1940s...many more moderate fundamentalists were convinced that their movement had become needlessly marginalized. They longed for the days when evangelical religion really mattered in American culture and decided to rid fundamentalism of its excesses and negative image and create a "new evangelicalism."[28]

With the founding of the NAE the basic difference between the militant fundamentalists and the moderate evangelicals was clear,[29] although the terms evangelical and fundamentalist would be used somewhat interchangeably for another decade more.[30]

THE SOCIAL ISSUE: THE UNEASY CONSCIENCE OF MODERN FUNDAMENTALISM (1947)

Carl F. H. Henry published the above book describing and decrying the lack of social concern in the fundamentalist movement of which he considered himself a part. He felt it his duty to "perform surgery" on fundamentalism and call it back to the cultural consciousness squandered by fundamentalists during their reaction to the threat of modernism. The "uneasy conscience" was not about the verities of the faith, but about the "frequent failure to apply them effectively to crucial problems confronting the modern mind." Henry betrayed a keen sensitivity to what non-evangelicals of the time were thinking of fundamentalism. He said fundamentalists had "needlessly invited criticism and ridicule" from liberals and others for majoring on minors and replacing the primary aspects of the fundamentalist position with secondary and sometimes obscure aspects. To that extent, he believed fundamentalists failed to oppose the social gospel with the "full genius of the Hebrew Christian outlook." This lack of social concern was "almost wholly unintelligible to the naturalistic and idealistic groups." "From the standpoint of not a few religious modernists, ethical idealists and humanists," humanitarianism had evaporated from fundamentalism. Henry tuned in to the "suspicions on the part of non-evangelicals" of fundamentalist failures to mount campaigns against social evils. According to him, a philosophical world view that has no social world program will not get a hearing from "contemporary speculation" in the "struggle for a world mind." He was anxious that fundamentalism's theology of a future millennial kingdom (a "kingdom then" message) not "identify Christianity further

---

[28]Timothy P. Weber, "His Life and Ministry" [referring to former Fuller Theological Seminary president David Allan Hubbard], *Studies in Old Testament Theology: Historical and Contemporary Images of God and God's People*, ed. Robert L. Hubbard, Jr., et al. (Dallas: Word, 1992), p. 23.

[29]I would have to disagree in principle with George Marsden's conclusion: "Almost no one seems to have regarded the formation of the NAE as a sign that 'evangelicals' were now breaking from 'fundamentalists' over the principle of separatism" (*Reforming Fundamentalism*, p. 48). This may have been the understanding of the liberals. It is true that the terms "fundamentalist" and "evangelical" had not yet developed all of their peculiar connotations and innuendos; and it is also true that some separatist fundamentalists thought they could work inside and thus direct the new group. And to be sure W. B. Riley was about the only fundamentalist leader in outspoken, public opposition to the new body (some would say this was due to his vested interest in the WCFA). But given the backgrounds, statements, and actions of its organizers of the time, it should have seemed clear where the NAE's toes were pointed despite which way its face was turned.

[30]Joel A. Carpenter, *Revive Us Again*, p. 152. In fact, as late as 1978, Harold John Ockenga said, "Doctrinally, the fundamentalists are right, *and I wish to be always classified as one*" (italics added). "From Fundamentalism, Through New Evangelicalism, to Evangelicalism," *Evangelical Roots*, ed. Kenneth Kantzer (Nashville: Thomas Nelson, 1978), p. 40.

to the modern mind in terms of an escape mechanism" (italics added) [that is, as an evasion of present social responsibilities].[31]

Henry denied that he had been influenced in his social views in the post World War II era by his encounters with the social gospel as a graduate student at Boston University and by its leading light, Edgar S. Brightman, a liberal Methodist personalist theologian. However, one is nearly compelled to agree with Carpenter that "it is hard to believe that it was only a coincidence that Henry was putting the finishing touches on *The Uneasy Conscience* in the summer of 1946 when he was studying in Boston."[32] Furthermore, Carpenter also suggests that Henry maintained a strong dislike for the penurious background of fundamentalist Christian service that Henry and his evangelical graduate school colleagues experienced, in contrast to their respectable gentlemen teachers and scholars in liberal institutions. This fact plus their desire for more upward social mobility undoubtedly contributed to the new impetus to social betterment.[33]

Harold John Ockenga introduced *The Uneasy Conscience* by saying that "the church needs a progressive Fundamentalism with a social message," noting there was a "growing revolt in evangelical circles on ethical indifferentism." Henry's book, Okenga believed, articulated that "revolt," and reflected the tension in evangelicalism to "vacillate between Fundamentalist isolationism and cooperation with the World Council of Churches." He believed that a message addressing world questions, the needs of society, and education, as well as evangelism, should spring from the Great Commission in Matthew 28:18-20.[34]

Henry bemoaned the "evaporation of fundamentalist humanitarianism." He disliked the inveighing of fundamentalists almost exclusively against individual rather than social evil. He sensed a growing awareness in broader fundamentalism that "evangelical Christianity [had] become increasingly inarticulate about the social reference of the Gospel."[35] He said that "the rejection of non-evangelical solutions does not involve—at least not logically—a loss of the social relevance of the Gospel. A globe-changing passion certainly characterized the early church...."[36] In rejecting the social gospel, "fundamentalism," he said,

---

[31]Quotes taken from *The Uneasy Conscience*, preface, pp. 17, 20, 23, 52.

[32]Joel A. Carpenter, *Revive Us Again*, p. 193.

[33]Ibid., p. 203. Carpenter also notes that both Henry and E. J. Carnell were able to buy new houses and Buicks when they arrived in Pasadena as faculty of the newly-formed Fuller Theological Seminary in 1947 (pp. 203, 310). He concludes that this upward mobility was an "important dimension in the neo-evangelical impulse. Bound up with doctrinal revisions and the recovery of social concern was the determination to stake a fresh claim on middle-class respectability" (p. 203). This is also an implication of Mark Ellingsen's note concerning the contacts of certain evangelicals with the wider culture during and after World War II (*The Evangelical Movement*, pp. 94-95).

[34]*The Uneasy Conscience*, introduction.

[35]Ibid., pp. 16, 20, 26.

[36]Ibid., p. 28. Henry made sweeping, unsupported claims for a social consciousness of the early New Testament church, such as this quote. He spoke of apostolic Christianity "turning the world upside down," presumably socially (p. 28). He lamented that "no voice is speaking today *as Paul would* either at the United Nations sessions, or at labor-management disputes, or in strategic university classrooms whether in Japan or Germany or America" (p. 34, italics added).

seemed also to revolt against the Christian social imperative. It was the failure of Fundamentalism to work out a positive message within its own framework, and its tendency instead to take further refuge in a despairing view of world history, that cut off the pertinence of evangelicalism to the modern global crisis.[37]

Henry derived his cultural agenda from the social comments of the Old Testament prophets, John the Baptist, Jesus of Nazareth, and the Apostle Paul.[38] But more to the point theologically, Henry extracted his social imperative from the central message of Jesus Christ which concerned the kingdom of God. While admitting that he was "broadly premillennial," he had no interest in dispensationalism and its "postponement theory of the kingdom."[39] He held to what in modern parlance is the "already/not yet" kingdom view; the kingdom exists today in "incomplete realization" and will be further realized before Christ comes back, and will be fully realized in the millennium.[40] The "kingdom now" view has far-ranging social implications for the present-day church. But one legitimately wonders whether for Henry the kingdom came first and brought its social implications, or if a preconceived social agenda brought its kingdom implications. It may well have been the latter, for he says,

> Whatever in our kingdom views undercuts [the world relevance of the Gospel] destroys the essential character of Christianity as such. No study of the kingdom teaching of Jesus is adequate unless it recognizes His implication both that the kingdom is here, and that it is not here.[41]

It appears that the "world relevance of the Gospel," which is simply code language for societal concerns, is that to which kingdom theology must conform. Thus the view of dispensational futurism that prevailed in fundamentalism/ evangelicalism almost from the beginning had to be expunged as being totally inadequate to carry the social relevance of Christianity. In Henry's mind, this view had cut the nerve of social activism by placing the messianic kingdom *after* the second coming, leaving little or no basis for a world wide social mandate for the institutional church of the New Testament in the present age.

The new evangelical platform for the social implications of the gospel is predicated on a present form of the messianic kingdom of God with its wide social dimension. To that end, the already/not yet kingdom theology of George Eldon Ladd became the de facto view of the early new evangelicalism.[42] Ladd's

---

[37]Ibid., p. 32.

[38]Ibid., pp. 38-43.

[39]Ibid., p. 52. He said there were "remote affinities" between the liberal "consistent eschatology" [i.e., wholly future] of Johannes Weiss and Albert Schweitzer and the postponement theory of dispensationalism.

[40]Ibid., p. 53.

[41]Ibid.

[42]Ladd became a New Testament professor at Fuller Theological Seminary in 1950 and had a profound influence on his generation of students, especially concerning the doctrine of the kingdom of God. His first book-length contribution to kingdom thought was *Crucial Questions Concerning the Kingdom of God* (Grand Rapids: Eerdmans, 1952). With his powerful mental energy and abilities, Ladd almost single-handedly turned the tide within the new evangelicalism in favor of "historic" (covenant, posttribulational) premillennialism and against dispensational, pretribulational premillenialism. In the later 1960s, posttribulationalism was declared to be the official view of the new evangelical theology (Millard Erickson, *The New Evangelical Theology* [Westwood, NJ: Revell, 1968], p. 126). Some of the

view of the kingdom of God and end-times scheme was "more conversant with classic Christian beliefs and more able to sustain evangelical social engagement."[43] "Evangelicals had to recover a theology of the kingdom that would enable them to be its advance agents and effect significant social transformation before Christ's return to establish the kingdom in its fullness."[44]

Surely much of the anti-dispensational bias so evident in the development of the new evangelicalism stems from Henry's view.[45] Dispensationalism, with its doctrine of the professing church and society each growing more apostate toward the end-times, and its concept of a utopian kingdom of God that was being delayed until the *eschaton*, was simply too pessimistic to sustain any hopes of present global betterment through the church and its gospel. Harold Ockenga saw this clearly as he chronicled the formation of the new evangelicalism thirty years after *The Uneasy Conscience*. He said, "The social theory of the fundamentalists was governed by eschatology. It was believed that conditions would grow worse and worse so that until Christ came again, the only effective application of the gospel could be to the individual."[46] Dispensationalism as an inhibitor of the efforts and the success of early new evangelical endeavors has been duly noted (and usually deprecated) by different commentators on the fundamentalist and evangelical movements.[47]

THE SCHOLARSHIP/INTELLECTUALISM ISSUE:FULLER THEOLOGICAL SEMINARY (1947)

A common complaint in the 1940s during the developing new evangelicalism was fundamentalism's lack of scholarship and general intellectual ability. The leaders of fundamentalism were supposedly deficient in their educational backgrounds.

second generation new evangelicals, self-styled as "young evangelicals," virtually canonized Ladd, along with Clarence Bass of Bethel Theological Seminary, St. Paul, MN, as the theological mentors whose kingdom views emancipated them from dispensational pessimism and gave their societal activism biblical legitimacy. See Richard Quebedeaux, *The Young Evangelicals* (New York: Harper & Row, 1974), pp. 38, 74-81.

[43] Joel A. Carpenter, *Revive Us Again*, p. 195.

[44] Ibid., p. 203.

[45] Dispensationalism also impacted other areas of the developing new evangelicalism. Its rubric of "literal interpretation" was predicated on the verbal inspiration/inerrancy of Scripture, an issue which festered in the new evangelicalism for some twenty years before reaching a breaking point in the latter half of the 1970s. Dispensationalism's doctrine of an apostate church in the end-times and a need for the purity of the visible church in the present age had a direct bearing on the separatism controversy. The idea of a pure church also made dispensationalism one of the chief anti-modernist systems of biblical thought, which tended to retard the success of new evangelical dialogue and cooperation with non-evangelicals in various settings. Helpful in understanding these matters and the place of dispensationalism in early fundamentalism is the sketch by Mark Ellingsen, *The Evangelical Movement*, pp. 60-72.

[46] Harold John Ockenga, "From Fundamentalism, Through New Evangelicalism, to Evangelicalism," p. 43.

[47] For example, Carl F. H. Henry, "The Vigor of the New Evangelicalism," *Christian Life* (April 1948), p. 34; E. J. Carnell, *The Case For Orthodox Theology* (Philadelphia: Westminster, 1959), pp. 117-19; Leon McBeth, "Baptist Fundamentalism: A Cultural Interpretation," *Baptist History and Heritage*, 133 (1978), p. 32; Joel A. Carpenter, *Revive Us Again*, p. 310, fn. 54; Donald W. Dayton, "'The Search for the Historical Evangelicalism'; George M. Marsden's "History of Fuller Seminary as a Case Study," *Christian Scholar's Review* 33 (1993): 30-33; "Is Evangelical Theology Changing?" (Symposium of Evangelicals), *Christian Life* (March 1956), p. 18; George M. Marsden, *Reforming Fundamentalism*, index, p. 314; Thorwald W. Bender, "What Is New In Theology?" *Bulletin of the Evangelical Theological Society* 2 (1959): 17, 21-22; Millard J. Erickson, *The New Evangelical Theology*, pp. 122-26; Ronald Nash, *The New Evangelicalism* (Grand Rapids: Zondervan, 1963), p. 178 (philosopher

The universally acknowledged exception was J. Gresham Machen of Princeton Seminary. A more mature perspective, however, shows that much of this criticism was prejudicial and exaggerated. Many of fundamentalism's leaders were very well trained and had taken degrees from academically respectable institutions of the day.[48] Abrams is correct to note that "As a group, fundamentalist leaders were well-educated."[49] Nonetheless, the charge that fundamentalism was intellectually challenged seemed to stick.[50]

The original milieu for this complaint seems to have been the intellectual climate of secularism and liberalism at the non-evangelical institutions where many evangelical scholars were earning graduate and post-graduate degrees. In the 1940s over a dozen new evangelical scholars studied for Ph.D.s at Harvard alone.[51] In this atmosphere many of them concluded that their fundamentalist contemporaries simply were not up to par intellectually, could not interact with modern thought on an academic level, and consequently were not turning out cogent scholastic material that commanded the attention of non-evangelicals. Fundamentalism's intellectual dimension needed a drastic overhaul if it were to gain a hearing in the marketplace of ideas and the cultural centers of the USA and beyond. As Erickson noted, the early leaders of the new evangelicalism had undergraduate training in conservative schools, but "they then sought graduate experience at a leading liberal or secular institution. Somewhere in this development the men became aware of the shortcomings of fundamentalism, and the need for reconstruction."[52]

Nash calls dispensationalism, which is a biblical/theological formulation, a "dismal morass"); Alister E. McGrath, *Historical Theology: An Introduction to the History of Christian Thought* (Malden, MA: Blackwell, 1998), p. 251; and Mark A. Noll, *The Scandal of the Evangelical Mind* (Grand Rapids: Eerdmans, 1994), pp. 115-20, 132.

[48]For example, W. B. Riley (1861-1947) earned degrees from Hanover College and Southern Baptist Theological Seminary; R. A. Torrey (1856-1928) studied at Yale and in Germany; and J. Frank Norris (1877-1952) graduated from Baylor University and Southern Baptist Theological Seminary. More recent fundamentalist leaders likewise were not educationally deficient. William E. Ashbrook (1896-1977) was educated at Westminster College, Pittsburgh Theological Seminary, Cambridge University, and New College in Scotland; R. V. Clearwaters (1900-1996) took degrees from Moody Bible Institute, Northern Baptist Theological Seminary, Kalamazoo College, and the University of Chicago (M.A. and all but a dissertation for the Ph.D.); B. Myron Cedarholm (1915-1997) graduated from the University of Minnesota, Eastern Baptist Theological Seminary, and Princeton Theological Seminary (Th.M. and residence work completed for a doctorate); John R. Rice (1895-1980) earned degrees from Decatur Baptist College, Baylor University, and Southwestern Baptist Theological Seminary; and Carl McIntire (1906-2002) studied at Princeton Seminary and finished at the newly-formed Westminster Theological Seminary. What was said of James M. Gray, dean of the Moody Bible Institute, could be said of the leaders of fundamentalism in general: He "was never one to disparage scholarship" (Joel A. Carpenter, *Revive Us Again*, p. 40).

[49]Douglas Carl Abrams, *Selling the Old-Time Religion: American Fundamentalists and Mass Culture, 1920-1940* (Athens, GA: University of Georgia Press, 2001), p. 9.

[50]It is easily granted that in its basic motif fundamentalism was evangelistically/revivalistically and not scholastically oriented as to ministry, certainly not so in comparison with the aspirations of the new evangelical complainants in this regard. The issues, priorities, and bustle of the controversy with modernism did not give fundamentalists the leisure to pursue the life of the mind. But the frequent and usual broadside against the fundamentalist intellect of the time seems greatly overdrawn.

[51]Joel A.Carpenter, *Revive Us Again*, p. 191. Some of them were Harold B. Kuhn, Samuel J. Schultz, Kenneth Kantzer, John Gerstner, Burton Goddard, Roger Nicole, E. J. Carnell, Gleason Archer, George Ladd, and Paul King Jewett. Carl F. H. Henry was studying at Boston University at the time. Millard Erickson paints a somewhat idyllic picture of Henry, Edward John Carnell, and Harold Ockenga in this regard as they viewed the intellectual (and social) scene in 1946 (*The New Evangelicalism*, pp. 13-16).

[52]Millard J. Erickson, *The New Evangelical Theology*, p. 43.

The complaint against fundamentalism's intellectual deficiency took many different forms. As a matter of fact, some accused fundamentalism not only of lacking scholarship, but also of despising it.[53] Norman Furniss gave as characteristics of the fundamentalist movement anti-intellectualism, ignorance, and illiteracy.[54] "An increased emphasis on scholarship" was one of the changes taking place in new evangelical theology's beginnings.[55] Ronald Nash notes that "during the early years of the orthodox [i.e., fundamentalist] reaction [to liberalism], the controversy was generally waged on a high intellectual level," but gradually fundamentalists developed "a spirit of anti-intellectualism."[56] Even current evangelical critics of fundamentalism still echo the early complaint.[57]

The prodigious pen of Carl F. H. Henry in the 1940s and 50s did the most to raise the issue of fundamentalism's intellectual want and in turn tried to elevate the standard of evangelical/fundamentalist scholarship and intellectualism. Henry also did as much early on to set the scholastic tone and academic standards of the new evangelicalism's flagship center of learning—Fuller Theological Seminary.

In 1946 Henry undertook an extensive (and enlightening) critique of modern thought in *Remaking the Modern Mind*.[58] He organized his analysis around the then-current, modern (i.e., 1914-1945 era of world wars) philosophical revolt against the assumptions that had prevailed for the previous 350 years—those assumptions being (1) the inevitability of human progress, (2) the inherent goodness of man, (3) the absolute uniformity of nature, (4) the ultimate reality of nature, and (5) the ultimate animality of man. While the book is a polemic against the modern revolt and not a criticism as such of fundamentalism's lack of philosophical input, his goal is still clear and the warning is patent.

> It remains that the modern philosophical scaffolding has proved so unfruitful and so unempirical that contemporary thinkers must be schooled as thoroughly in its disillusioning denouement as they were in its utopian prophecies and, beyond this, they must be driven to a satisfactory metaphysics for the alternatives demanded by the sobered western mind. Such a metaphysics will surely be one which is radically different from that to which the modern mind is accustomed *and that evangelical is visionless indeed who does not see in such an hour a time ripe for proclaiming his convictions* (italics added).[59]

In a similar volume Henry reiterates compactly much of the same thought but with a more pointed criticism of fundamentalism.[60]

---

[53]E. M. Blaiklock, "Conservatism, Liberalism, and Neo-orthodoxy," *Eternity* (August 1960), p. 23.

[54]Norman F. Furniss, *The Fundamentalist Controversy, 1918-1931* (Hamden, CT: Archon Books, 1963 reprint), pp. 38-41.

[55]"Is Evangelical Theology Changing?" (Symposium of Evangelicals) *Christian Life* (March 1956), p. 18.

[56]*The New Evangelicalism*, pp. 22, 26.

[57]For example, Alister E. McGrath, *Historical Theology*, p. 251.

[58]Carl F. H. Henry, *Remaking the Modern Mind* (Grand Rapids: Eerdmans, 1946).

[59]Ibid., pp. 274-75.

[60]Carl F. H. Henry, *The Drift of Western Thought* (Grand Rapids: Eerdmans, 1951), pp. 151-52.

In 1948 Henry was quite explicit in inveighing against fundamentalism's intellectual and philosophical deficiency, and set forth the new evangelical agenda in this area. Fundamentalism had "permitted the philosophic implications of Christianity to become obscured."[61] To avoid fundamentalism's deficiencies, "the new evangelicalism aims to clarify the philosophic implications of Biblical theism."[62] "Because the fundamentalism of the past generation was not interested in a salvation emphasis formulated in philosophic as well as Biblical terms," evangelical students had gone to schools that taught non-Christian philosophy and had "gradually lost their faith."[63]

In his *Evangelical Responsibility in Contemporary Theology*, Henry forthrightly expressed his dissatisfaction with fundamentalism's failures in the intellectual field, especially in chapter two, "The Fundamentalist Reduction." He gave at least six criticisms of fundamentalism's intellectual deficiencies: (1) "Concentration on 'the fundamentals' often displaced doctrinal responsibilities of the Church in the wider dimensions of historic creeds and confessions of faith." (2) Fundamentalism's "theological emphasis and temperament" were primarily concerned to correct the social matrix and social philosophy shaped by liberalism" and thus neglected "to exhibit Christianity as a comprehensive world and life view." (3) Fundamentalism "lacked theological and historical perspective." (4) "Fundamentalism neglected the production of great exegetical and theological literature" relying instead on reprinting "the theological classics of the past." (5) Fundamentalism neglected "the doctrine of the Church, except in defining separation as a special area of concern," leading at times to anti-denominationalism instead of interdenominationalism. (6) Fundamentalists "identified Christianity rigidly with premillennial dispensationalism." He went on to say, "Fundamentalism paid scant attention to basic principles with which its theological positions were integrally connected. Had evangelical theology pursued the tasks of Christian philosophy, emphasis would not have been placed upon isolated doctrines." "A fresh exploration of the interrelations of revelation and reason...is one of [evangelicalism's] present imperatives." "Evangelical theology's best hope for a relevant and aggressive impact in our turbulent times lies in a bold, biblical, emphasis on the relation of revelation and reason."[64]

In many minds fundamentalism was anti-intellectual and anti-science because it was anti-evolution. The theory of organic evolution had captured secular philosophical thought and liberal religious opinion since the last quarter of the nineteenth century. Anti-evolutionism was a major plank in the fundamentalists' platform in their clash with modernism in the great 1920s controversy. W. B.

---

[61]Carl F. H. Henry, "The Vigor of the New Evangelicalism," *Christian Life* (March 1948), p. 35.

[62]Ibid. Harold B. Kuhn stated that fundamentalism [which he called orthodoxy] "had not developed a definitive philosophical grounding" ("Philosophy of Religion," in *Contemporary Evangelical Thought*, ed. Carl F. H. Henry [Great Neck, NY: Channel Press, 1957], p. 217).

[63]"The Vigor of the New Evangelicalism," p. 37.

[64]Carl F. H. Henry, *Evangelical Responsibility in Contemporary Society* (Grand Rapids: Eerdmans, 1957), pp. 32-36, 61, 63, 66.

Riley and the World's Christian Fundamentals Association (founded in 1919), for example, held large anti-evolution rallies around the country and entered into numerous debates with evolutionary scientists and educators.[65] The apogee of anti-evolutionism was the Scopes Evolution Trial in Dayton, TN, in 1925. John Scopes had violated the Tennessee law that prohibited the teaching of evolution in the public schools. Due to media coverage, the trial was sensationalized and followed nation wide. Press and radio reporting of the trial, especially on the aging William Jennings Bryan, the trial leader for the prosecution and thus in a direct sense for fundamentalism, was caustic and hostile. Both Bryan and fundamentalism were depicted as wallowing in intellectual backwaters totally out of their depth with reference to modern thought.[66] National pundits, such as H. L. Menchen, issued scathing denunciations of the fundamentalist presence and mentality. After Dayton, fundamentalism did not fare well at least in public opinion, especially since Bryan's testimony as a self-professed expert witness on creationism was somewhat deficient scientifically and biblically.[67]

New evangelical leaders of the 1940s and 50s were embarrassed by the mentality of some of their fundamentalist forebearers and peers. In a landmark article in *Christian Life*, the author postulated that "a friendly attitude toward science" was the first component in the changing evangelical thought.[68] Thorwald Bender preferred the term "Critical Conservatism" to describe the new evangelicalism, and went on to criticize intellectual aspects of some types of fundamentalism.

> By Critical Conservatism we mean to emphasize the *self-critical* open-mindedness of science at its best, as over against the spirit of some types of Fundamentalism in which criticism and suspicion of *others*, nursed by an attitude of self-righteousness, unteachable arrogance, spells the essence of being orthodox (italics his).[69]

Ronald Nash boldly declared, "Fundamentalism's attitude toward science was typical of its deprecation of scholarship in all fields."[70]

Bernard Ramm chastised fundamentalists more than any other new evangelical for their attitude toward modern science. He electrified the evangelical community with his synthesis of the Bible and science called "progressive creationism."[71] He

---

[65]It was principally the Darwinian amoeba-to-man evolutionism of the time that was opposed. Some fundamentalists were sympathetic to an old earth and the rubric of scientific uniformitarianism.

[66]Robert D. Lindner, "Fifty Years After Scopes: Lessons to Learn, A Heritage to Reclaim," *Christianity Today* (July 18, 1975), pp. 7-9.

[67]Fundamentalism's losses were more perceived than real after 1925. The movement flourished in the decades following Scopes. See Carpenter, *Revive Us Again*, pp. 13-32 and George M. Marsden, *Fundamentalism and American Culture: The Shaping of Twentieth Century Evangelicalism* (Oxford: Oxford University Press, 1980), pp. 193-95.

[68]"Is Evangelical Theology Changing?", p. 17.

[69]"What Is New in Theology?" *Bulletin of the Evangelical Theological Society* 2 (1959), p. 17.

[70]*The New Evangelical Theology*, p. 26.

[71]*The Christian View of Science and Scripture* (Grand Rapids: Eerdmans, 1954). While not original with him, Ramm's ideas made a tremendous impact on evangelical thinking. George M. Marsden noted, "By the next summer [i.e., 1955] Ramm's book had indeed caused the largest stir in fundamentalism since the RSV controversy"(*Reforming Fundamentalism*, p. 159). I was in Bible College at the time and observed and felt firsthand this impact. Ramm summarized the principles of progressive creationism

called the scientism of his fundamentalist forbearers an "ignoble tradition." They were the "hyperorthodox."[72] Ramm's book and the kind of thinking it represented were a great boost to the fortunes of new evangelical thinking vis-a-vis old fundamentalist mentality. Farley Butler noted, "Orthodoxy was to be rendered intellectually respectable by the appearance of concessions to the scientific viewpoint. This first surfaced in a book by Bernard Ramm published in the fall of 1954, *The Christian View of Science and Scripture*."[73]

The foregoing discussion gives a general backdrop to appreciate the attempts by the new coalition of evangelicals to gain academic and intellectual respectability in the founding of Fuller Theological Seminary. This new seminary represented a tangible effort to correct the perceived intellectual shortcomings of fundamentalism, and it was symbolic of the new evangelical mindset regarding academia itself.

As noted, the leaders of fundamentalism were not adverse to genuine scholarship. Nor did they consider education and training a waste of time. In fact, Bible institutes and colleges developed within fundamentalism as well.[74] Fundamentalists disparaged the godless, pagan, and critical post-Enlightenment presuppositions and philosophical underpinnings that imbued secular education. They perceived the need for a distinctively Christian, biblical education for their youth in order to have a trained ministry and perpetuate the faith of their fathers. And in so doing they were in the best of company and tradition; the early schools and colleges in America were just such learning centers. But in the minds of the new evangelical thinkers, such education was top-water, superficial, and inadequate to grapple with modern thought and leave a mark on the contemporary culture.

The original idea for what became Fuller Theological Seminary came to Charles E. Fuller in a night in November 1939. God awakened Fuller and burdened his heart "for a Christ-centered, Spirit-directed training school, where Christian men and women could be trained in the things of God, to become steeped in the Word, so as to go out bearing the blessed news to lost men and women."[75] Such a proposal, of course, sounded quite "Bible-Institutish," although Fuller wanted the school to be on a higher level than the typical Bible institute. Actually he wanted something on the college level but oriented to

---

on pp. 112-17, and his summary statement on p. 256 says, "we accept progressive creationism which teaches that over the millions of years of geologic history God has been fiatly creating higher and higher forms of life." A similar scheme, described briefly and non-technically, and termed "threshold evolution," had been put forth earlier by Edward John Carnell (*An Introduction to Christian Apologetics* [Grand Rapids: Eerdmans, 1948], pp. 238-39). Not all evangelicals accepted Ramm's synthesis and its presuppositions. See the quite negative assessments by Joseph T. Bayly, "*The Christian View of Science and Scripture*: A Critical Review of Bernard Ramm's Book," *Christian Life* (August 1955), p. 4 ff.

[72]*The Christian View of Science and Scripture*, preface, p. 47.

[73]"Billy Graham and the End of Evangelical Unity," p. 6.

[74]See the excellent summary by Joel Carpenter on "Training Leaders," *Revive Us Again*, pp. 16-22. His conclusion is well-taken: "Educational institutions did much to hold fundamentalism together, form its future leaders, and give expression to its beliefs and concerns" (p. 22).

[75]Daniel P. Fuller, *Give the Winds a Mighty Voice: The Story of Charles E. Fuller* (Waco, TX: Word, 1972), p. 189.

practical Christian service.[76] However, the capable and tireless leader and organizer of new evangelical projects, Harold John Ockenga, persuaded him of the need for a graduate level, scholarly institution where the nation's top-notch evangelical scholars could work.[77] Fuller Theological Seminary was in business by the fall of 1947 with Ockenga as the first president.[78] It was not long before the new seminary was being called "a Cal Tech of the evangelical world" and "a research center of evangelical scholarship" engaged in "rebuilding western civilization" and "redefining the fundamentalist mission."[79] At the school's opening convocation address in 1947, entitled "The Challenge to the Christian Culture of the West," Ockenga eloquently intoned,

> Now there is a task to be done. And that task is not going to be done by the ordinary Christian alone. It's going to be done by those who are prepared to do it. It must be done by the rethinking and restating of the fundamental thesis and principle of Western culture. There must be today men who have the time and energy and the inclination and the ability and the support to be able to redefine Christian thinking and to fling it forth into the faces of unbelievers everywhere....We need men who can once again in an intellectually respectable way present an apology for God, and for His creation of the world, and for the soul, and for eternal life, and these things must be brought so that our young men, and those who are going to take the places of leadership, will once again believe in the eternal law of an eternal God....I envisage a school that can become the center of missions and evangelism on the basis of a Gospel of which we need not be ashamed because we can give a reason for the hope that is within us.[80]

In keeping with the academic/intellectual philosophy of the new evangelicalism, the early faculty of Fuller consisted of men with earned doctorates from accredited and recognized universities: Everett F. Harrison (University of Pennsylvania), Carl F. H. Henry (Boston University), Harold Lindsell (New York University), George Eldon Ladd (Harvard), Edward John Carnell (Harvard, Boston University), Charles J. Woodbridge (Duke), and Gleason Archer (Harvard). The faculty in the first years of Fuller were mainly Presbyterians or those with a Presbyterian background; a few were Baptists. The opening class consisted of "graduates of accredited universities and colleges."[81] On the early faculty was also Wilbur M. Smith, an erudite evangelical who, in the early 1940s, called for a new center of scholarship and academics that could turn out men "for the powerful defense of the faith in the great citadels of unbelief in our country,"[82] by producing a stream of high caliber literature in defense of the faith.

---

[76]Joel A. Carpenter, *Revive Us Again*, p. 194.

[77]Ibid.

[78]Ockenga went on to serve for eleven years as president in absentia of Fuller Seminary.

[79]George M. Marsden, *Reforming Fundamentalism*, pp. 53, 56, 69.

[80]Daniel P. Fuller, *Give the Winds a Mighty Voice*, pp. 209-10. It was in this same address that Ockenga coined the term "new evangelicalism," a conscious self-designation of the new coalition of conservatives in distinction from fundamentalism.

[81]So stated in an early ad for the seminary in *United Evangelical Action* (Sept 1947), reproduced in George M. Marsden, *Reforming Fundamentalism*, p. 55.

[82]Wilbur M. Smith, *Therefore Stand: A Plea For a Vigorous Apologetic in the Present Crisis of Evangelical Christianity* (Boston: W. A. Wilde, 1945), p. 498. See pp. 498-507 for an expansion of his vision of an intellectual penetration of unbelief by evangelicals.

Fuller Theological Seminary emerged as the enfleshment of Smith's dream and a showcase of the new evangelical corrective to the philosophy and practice of old fundamentalism. In the eyes of the new evangelical coalition, it embodied what was right in Christian academia and stood against what was wrong with the old fundamentalist mentality. Theoretically, the seminary was the ideal evangelical school. Or so it seemed. But it was not long before tensions arose concerning the motif of the school. Charles E. Fuller desired a heavy emphasis on the practical. The faculty were generally predisposed to the philosophical and the academic.[83] Finding professors for the practical courses "proved to be the lowest priority."[84] The administration deferred to the practical leanings of Charles E. Fuller, but the ambivalence was felt by the faculty. The same pull accompanied the separation issue. General sympathy for the separatists' cause existed, but little or no sympathy for separatism.[85] The Baptist and Presbyterian connections of the school's founders made projecting a truly interdenominational outreach difficult.[86] A tension existed between the individualism and high expertise of the scholar-teachers and the development of a faculty team spirit.[87] In addition, the dispensational leanings of Charles E. Fuller, Everett F. Harrison, and Wilbur Smith encountered unsympathetic if not hostile attitudes toward dispensationalism by Carl Henry, George Ladd, and others in and around the seminary.[88] The greatest strain was the need to forge a new position between fundamentalism and non-evangelicalism (neo-liberalism and neo-orthodoxy). In this challenge "the seminary faced in two directions at once....In the early days, hopes were high that it could carve out a large middle ground where a healthy third force in Protestantism could operate between the separatist fundamentalists and the modernists."[89]

The scholarship/intellectualism issue of the early new evangelicals resolved into the Fuller experiment of the ideal. "The Fuller professors were renowned for their hard work. They were going to rise to the top of their professions, fill the Christian world with outstanding books and popular literature, be great teachers...."[90] They were to teach about eight academic hours a semester, have one month in the summer for vacation, and two months for research, writing, and outside travel and speaking. "Each scholar was endeavoring to make a contribution that the theological world would have to take seriously, that would signal the emergence of a new evangelicalism, that would contribute to Christian cultural renewal in the West."[91]

---

[83]Ockenga, for example, wanted evangelism backed by "apologetics based on impeccable scholarship" (George M. Marsden, *Reforming Fundamentalism*, p. 36). Marsden notes that "the tension between Fuller Seminary's two missions—being a center for apologetic scholarship and a training base for sending out spiritually empowered missionaries—dominated its quest for a self-image" (p. 83).

[84]Ibid., p. 122.

[85]Ibid., p. 46.

[86]Ibid., pp. 38, 76, 95-98, 103-07, 133.

[87]Ibid., pp. 28-30.

[88]Ibid., pp. 6, 71, 72, 76, 81, 189.

[89]Ibid., pp. 67-68.

[90]Ibid., pp. 128-29.

[91]Joel A. Carpenter, *Revive Us Again*, p. 195.

Whether the seminary ever reached those lofty goals is another question. As with most new endeavors, the goals were only partially realized at best. Carnell, for example, complained bitterly:

> After pouring the fruit of my philosophical labors into it [*A Philosophy of the Christian Religion*, released in 1952], it has received little or no acclaim; at least not in a measure of what I thought it was deserving in light of the effort expended....There is a parochialism in evangelicalism from which I must withdraw....I want to command the attention of Tillich and Bennet; then I shall be in a better place to be of service to the evangelicals. We need prestige desperately."[92]

Three decades after Fuller's founding, Carl Henry would still write: "Evangelical Christianity has not yet in fact very deeply penetrated the radically secular mentality evident in schoolroom and society today and reflected by the media."[93] In Henry's autobiography, the final chapter, "The Evangelical Prospect in America," consisting of nine points, is in the main quite pessimistic.[94]

With Fuller Theological Seminary and all it represented up and running, the distance widened between the new coalition of moderate evangelicals and the old fundamentalist/evangelical alliance.

THE EVANGELISM ISSUE: BILLY GRAHAM (1949–1957)

Both the fundamentalists and the new evangelicals remained committed to evangelism, revival, and missions.[95] It was a substantial and integral part of their common heritage. Both groups worked in tandem to further this mutual conviction until the 1950s. It was an issue that was often used to quell an outbreak of ecclesiastical hostilities in the fundamentalist-modernist controversy in various provincial settings,[96] and its legacy kept some fundamentalists within the more moderate National Association of Evangelicals for about ten years.[97] However, evangelism eventually made the growing cleavage between the moderate evangelicals and the militant fundamentalists permanent. The battle over the 1957 Billy Graham New York Crusade finally made the two camps irreconcilable.

---

[92]Letter to Carl F. H. Henry, reported by Henry in his *Confessions of a Theologian*, p. 137. Some five years after Carnell's lament, Henry put forth a more sophisticated complaint that *The Christian Century* and neo-liberals were retaining too much of the outdated old liberalism and had not taken evangelical criticism seriously, if it had noticed it at all ("Dare We Revive the Modernist-Fundamentalist Conflict?" *Christianity Today* [June 10, 1957], pp. 4, 6).

[93]Carl F. H. Henry, "Evangelical Summertime?" *Christianity Today* (April 1, 1977), p. 38.

[94]*Confessions of a Theologian*, pp. 381-401. More recently Mark A. Noll was similarly disappointed: "The general impact of Christian thinking on *Christians* of our country, much less the nation's academic culture, is slight" ("The Evangelical Mind," in *The Evangelical Landscape: Essays on the American Evangelical Tradition*, ed. Garth Rosell [Grand Rapids: Baker, 1996], p. 31).

[95]Carl F. H. Henry put it this way: "Both the American Council of Christian Churches and the National Association of Evangelicals cast their weight—in principle at least—behind mass evangelism" ("Theology, Evangelism, Ecumenism," *Christianity Today* [January 20, 1957], p. 21).

[96]For example, J. C. Massee, a moderate fundamentalist but a prominent leader in and first president of the Fundamentalist Fellowship in the old Northern Baptist Convention, grew weary of the denominational infighting over liberalism and ended up calling for the fundamentalists to lay down their swords and join the liberals in denominational evangelism and missions. See George W. Dollar, *A History of Fundamentalism in America* (Greenville, SC: Bob Jones University Press, 1973), p. 157.

[97]Mark Taylor Dalhouse, *An Island in the Lake of Fire*, pp. 53, 73; George Marsden, *Reforming Fundamentalism*, p. 159; Farley P. Butler, "Billy Graham and the End of Evangelical Unity," p. 29.

The United States (and other parts of the world as well) in the 1940s was in a chastened frame of mind because of the ravages of the Great Depression and the Second World War, the aggressiveness of international communism, and the beginning of the tensions of the Cold War. A general mood of God-consciousness among the populace and a hunger for inner peace and ultimate reality existed. Already in the 1930s mass evangelism in the United States had reached a low ebb, although a few evangelists saw good results in city-wide campaigns. Local church evangelism, on the other hand, proved quite successful and continued to be successful into World War II.[98] But, "by 1942 a vigorous evangelistically aggressive wing of Fundamentalism now believed that it stood on the threshold of revival,"[99] and in the mid 1940s mass evangelism began to ascend again. Hyman Appleman, Bob Jones, John R. Rice, Monroe Parker, Paul Rood, and others conducted successful city-wide campaigns. Other evangelists entered the field such as Merv Rosell, Torrey Johnson, Bob Cook, Jack Shuler, Phil Shuler, Chuck Templeton, Percy Crawford, Jack Wyrtzen, T. W. Wilson, Jimmie Johnson, J. Edwin Orr, Armin Gesswein, and others. Campus revivals occurred at Northern Baptist Seminary, North Park College, California Baptist Seminary, Wheaton College, Asbury College, Seattle-Pacific College, and Greenville College. Charles E. Fuller's Old Fashioned Revival Hour weekly radio program became extremely popular. The Christian Businessmen's Committee hosted well-attended prayer breakfasts around the country. These were certainly "extraordinary times" when "evangelical religion was carving out some new cultural space for itself."[100] Fundamentalist evangelism prospered again as local church and city-wide campaigns began seeing remarkable results. Evangelism and revival were "in the air." Virtually everyone with a heart for souls and a modicum of evangelistic abilities and techniques witnessed some success.

An important development in this religious awakening, and the stratum out of which came the most far-reaching evangelistic impact, was the youth rally movement, especially Youth for Christ, organized in 1945. Billy Graham, the acknowledged titular head of evangelism since 1949, was a product of the original Youth for Christ evangelistic thrust. He was the first YFC full-time, traveling evangelist and one of the early popular speakers of the youth rally movement.[101] Graham held large and successful Youth for Christ evangelistic rallies in the United States, Great Britain, and Europe in 1945-47.[102] Graham's evangelistic team eventually consisted of former Youth for Christ evangelists and workers such as George Wilson, Walter Smyth, Cliff Barrows, and Tedd Smith.

---

[98]Farley P. Butler, "Billy Graham and the End of Evangelical Unity," pp. 52-53.

[99]Joel A. Carpenter, "The Fundamentalist Leaven and the Rise of an Evangelical United Front," p. 266.

[100]Joel A. Carpenter, *Revive Us Again*, pp. 229, 231. See also his description of the post-WWII spiritual awakenings on pp. 213-17.

[101]A concise but helpful account of the beginnings of Youth for Christ, Young Life, and Inter-Varsity Christian Fellowship (in the USA) is Bruce Shelley, "The Rise of Evangelical Youth Movements," *Fides et Historia* 18 (986). See also Mel Larson, *Youth For Christ* (Grand Rapids: Zondervan, 1947).

[102]See Billy Graham's own account of his Youth for Christ years in *Just As I Am: The Autobiography of Billy Graham* (San Francisco: Harper Collins, 1997), pp. 92-111.

Mass evangelism and the eventual impasse that ended any remaining fundamentalist/evangelical unity was propelled by the 1949 Christ For Greater Los Angeles tent campaign of Billy Graham that lasted from September 25 to November 20, 1949. After traveling for Youth for Christ, Graham held city-wide meetings in 1947 at Grand Rapids, MI, and Charlotte, NC. In 1948 he was at Augusta, GA, and Modesto, CA. In 1949 he held meetings in Miami, FL, Baltimore, MD, Altoona, PA, and then in Los Angeles. The Los Angeles campaign drew unbelievably large crowds and an astonishing response, including the conversion of several well-known celebrities. This crusade was followed in the next several years by equally amazing campaigns in Boston, MA, Columbia, SC, Portland, OR, and many others. 1954, 1955, and part of 1956 were spent holding mammoth crusades abroad.[103] The crusade of greatest importance to new evangelicalism and fundamentalism was the 1957 New York Crusade that ran from May 15 to September 1. Two issues raised during the New York Crusade established precedent, setting decisions over which the moderate evangelicals and the militant fundamentalists became permanently polarized—sponsorship and convert referrals.

Billy Graham's roots were in fundamentalism. Modernism and neo-orthodoxy do not practice true evangelism, and consequently their churches and denominations typically wither into irrelevancy. However, Graham's crusade provided them an opportunity to ride the crest of the evangelical wave of evangelism and revivalism and thus fill their empty churches. Their strategy proved to be productive once evangelical evangelists, principally Billy Graham, acceded to their involvement.[104] Both evangelical and non-evangelical churchmen lived off each other's wealth to promote a common goal—reaching the masses.

Originally Graham operated on the policy of being sponsored in evangelistic endeavors exclusively by fundamentalists. That policy changed with the New York Crusade when new evangelical evangelism made a calculated effort to receive broad-based approval and support, including that of non-evangelicals. The Los Angeles campaign of 1949, while certainly interdenominational, was sponsored only by evangelicals/fundamentalists. (Graham now seems to demur slightly on this point.)[105] Graham had always solicited fundamentalist support, and his early years in crusade evangelism reflected this fact.

---

[103]See a complete itinerary of Graham crusades from 1947 to 1996 in *Just As I Am*, pp. 736-39.

[104]Nothing is more revealing of this liberal strategy than the report by Michael Boland on the Graham Harringay Crusade in England of 1954 ("Co-operative Evangelism at Harringay," *The Banner of Truth* 42 [May/June 1966]). He said "one constant feature [of the Harringay campaign] is the participation of leading ministers who could not be described as evangelical" (p. 7). He then documents the testimonies to liberal gains of the two Archbishops of Canterbury, Michael Ramsey and Geoffrey Fisher, the Anglican bishop of London, J. W. C. Wand, and the former pastor of City Temple, Leslie Weatherhead, all liberals. The latter's assessment is quite plain: "...any Minister who frequently preaches to small congregations might rejoice that Billy Graham is helping to fill our churches for us" (p. 10). Boland's conclusion is apt: "Billy Graham was to non-evangelical ministers at Harringay,...a recruiting sergeant filling their churches for them. He was providing them with congregations in whom they could inculcate their liberal and Anglo-Catholic teachings" (p. 10).

[105]In *Just As I Am*, Graham says that he insisted that the LA Campaign Committee broaden its church support to include as many denominations and churches as possible because the Committee "represented too limited an evangelical constituency to make an impact" (p. 144).

He had spoken against 'apostasy' as strongly as other fundamentalists, and there was little to indicate that he would become the struggle which would cause great bitterness among conservative Christians. Eventually Billy Graham came to be *the* issue in the division of conservative evangelicalism.[106]

A litany of statements made by Graham and others around him during his early crusade years disclaim anything but fundamental sponsorship for his early campaigns. Robert P. Shuler, militant fundamentalist pastor of the Trinity Methodist Church, Los Angeles, and editor of *The Methodist Challenge*, noted:

> None of the great evangelists had ever before accepted the sponsorship of modernists. Billy himself had not only refused to hold a campaign under their sponsorship but had openly declared that he never would. In his Los Angeles campaign, I personally saw and heard him turn down and politely decline the approval and cooperation of the Church Federation, which represented the Federal Council, now the National Council.[107]

As president of Northwestern Schools, Minneapolis, Graham apologized profusely that an ad for a book by liberal Harry Emerson Fosdick inadvertently appeared in *The Pilot*, the school's publication.[108] In a written reply (April 20, 1951), to Robert T. Ketchem, national representative of the General Association of Regular Baptist Churches, who in his travels had been asked scores of times about some of the statements and practices of Billy Graham, Jerry Beaven said simply, "It grieves me to the very depths of my heart to think that another fellow servant of Christ...could suggest any compromise in his [Graham's] message or ministry."[109] In a letter to John R. Rice (May 10, 1952), Graham said, "We have never had a modernist on our Executive Committee, and we have never been sponsored by the Council of Churches in any city, except Shreveport and Greensboro,...I do not think you will find any man who has sat under my ministry in any of these campaigns who would testify that I ever pulled a punch."[110] At the 1948 annual Conservative Baptist Association meeting in Milwaukee, when asked about the upcoming World Council of Churches meeting in Copenhagen, the evangelist replied, "I believe they are going to nominate the Anti-christ."[111] In a reply (May 29, 1951) to a fundamentalist committee who wanted to bring the evangelist to New York for a crusade, Graham said the committee did not represent the churches in the area, and he wanted an "ecumenical spirit," but further stated, "I have never been, nor will I ever be in favor of a modernist being on the committee or in any way having any working

---

[106]Farley P. Butler, "Billy Graham and the End of Evangelical Unity," pp. 9-10.

[107]Robert P. Shuler, *The Methodist Challenge* (Oct 1957), p. 3, quoted in Brad K. Gsell, *The Legacy of Billy Graham: The Accommodation of Truth to Error in the Evangelical Church*, revised and expanded edition (Charlotte, NC: Fundamental Presbyterian Publications, 1996), p. 15.

[108]He said, "We do not condone nor have fellowship with any form of modernism" (*The Pilot* [April 1951], p. 222). On assuming the presidency of Northwestern Schools and the editorship of *The Pilot*, Graham noted that the magazine had "indeed been militant in its stand against Modernism in every form," and he pledged that there would be no change under his leadership (*The Pilot* [March 1948], p. 113.)

[109]Robert T. Ketcham, "The Billy Graham Controversy," *The Baptist Bulletin* (December 1952), p. 25.

[110]Quoted by Robert Dunzweiler, *Billy Graham: A Critique* (Philadelphia: Faith Theological Seminary, n.d.. This booklet is an address by the author given March 4, 1961.), p. 11.

[111]G. Archer Weniger, "The Position of Dr. Graham Before He Embraced Ecumenical Evangelism," Fundamentalism Archives, Bob Jones University, Greenville, SC.

fellowship in this meeting."[112] Replying to Chester Tulga (December 27, 1951), Graham asserted, "My separation and my theology have not veered one iota from that of W. B. Riley."[113] In a letter to Bob Jones Sr. (June 3, 1952), Graham declared, "The modernists do not support us anywhere….We have never had a man on our committee that denied the virgin birth, the vicarious atonement, or the bodily resurrection."[114] John R. Rice, in a letter to Graham (May 2, 1957), recalled an earlier conversation they had: "You told me about the Atlanta campaign that modernists were put on the committee before you were there and when you had no control of the situation, and you said, 'I promised God I will never let that happen again.'"[115] After Rice visited Graham at the Scotland Crusade (1954), he reported in the *Sword of the Lord*: "Dr. Graham…told me frankly that he felt that he must not have any man speaking for him as an official of the campaign or taking part on the public program of the campaign who is not true on the great fundamentals of the Christian Faith."[116] After the fracture in fellowship between Rice and Graham, Rice would write:

> I talked with Dr. Graham again and again about the danger of yoking up with modernism. Again and again he assured me that he had vowed to God he would never have a man on his committee who was not right on the inspiration of the Bible, the deity of Christ, and such matters.[117]

In the same vein, Graham constantly disavowed the practice of sending crusade converts back to modernistic and even Roman Catholic churches, the second issue that permanently divided the evangelicals from the fundamentalists in 1957. By 1950, rumors already abounded about converts being referred to liberal and Catholic churches,[118] but these were routinely denied. Jerry Beaven, for example, secretary to Dr. Graham, wrote to Robert Ketcham: "That you should give any credence to the idea that Mr. Graham would ever turn over any decision cards to the Roman Catholic Church seems inconceivable."[119] In November 1957,

---

[112]Quoted by James E. Bennet, "The Billy Graham New York Crusade: Why I Cannot Support It," *A Ministry of Disobedience: Christian Leaders Analyze the Billy Graham New York Crusade*, ed. Carl McIntire (Collingswood, NJ: Christian Beacon Press, n.d.), p. 12. The article first appeared in the *Christian Beacon* (Nov 22, 1956).

[113]Excerpt from the letter to Tulga, a copy of which was sent to Bob Jones, Sr., Fundamentalism Archives, Bob Jones University, Greenville, SC.

[114]Fundamentalism Collection, Bob Jones University, Greenville, SC.

[115]John R. Rice, "Billy Graham and Editor Exchange Letters," *Sword of the Lord* (May 24, 1957), p. 2.

[116]John R. Rice, "Questions Answered About Billy Graham," *Sword of the Lord* (June 17, 1955), p. 9. On the same page Rice also said: "As I understand Billy, he has definitely pledged that he will not have any man in his campaigns to represent him officially who is not true to the inspiration of the Bible, the deity of Christ, His blood atonement and such fundamental truths."

[117]John R. Rice, "Cooperative Evangelism," *Sword of the Lord* (June 20, 1958), p. 12.

[118]Robert T. Ketcham documented numerous instances of these charges in *The Baptist Bulletin* (December 1952), pp. 8, 23-24. Carl McIntire also asserted the same: "His [Graham's] ministry is devoid of any recognition or any consciousness of the apostasy in the church, and the converts which are led to the Lord in the campaigns are left to go to 'the church of their choice' without any instruction or indoctrination. They go into the modernist, apostate churches, into the National Council of Churches, and some even, as any number have gone, according to reports, into the Roman Catholic Church itself" ("Graham, Sockman Meet on America's Town Meeting: Sockman Wins Round," *Christian Beacon* [Jan 18, 1951], p. 8).

[119]Letter from Jerry Beaven to Robert T. Ketcham, April 20, 1951,"Graham-Ketcham Correspondence" (distributed by R. T. Ketcham, 431 S. Dearborn, Suite 1205, Chicago, IL), p. 12.

Walter Smyth, from the Billy Graham headquarters, told a group of Conservative Baptist ministers in the San Francisco Bay Area in view of the upcoming Cow Palace crusade that "the New York crusade was not sponsored by the Protestant Council of New York" and that "Billy Graham has never at any time in history given any cards to the Catholics."[120]

Despite the clarity of all the foregoing disclaimers and assertions, there is evidence that they were at best disingenuous. When John R. Rice finally broke with Billy Graham, the evangelist wrote Rice, somewhat disbelievingly, that "the sponsorship that has disturbed a few was far more liberal in Glasgow than in New York, yet you sensed the presence of God and did not have adjectives enough to describe it."[121] Graham has implied that there had already been broad sponsorship (i.e., some of which was non-evangelical) for the 1949 Los Angeles campaign.[122] In addition, the Los Angeles practice with reference to convert referrals was to direct them to the church of choice, a fact that does not seem to have been known or at least comprehended by fundamentalists at the time. Nevertheless, J. Edwin Orr was quite forthright about the policy as he wrote shortly after the campaign:

> The Christ for Greater Los Angeles committee handled the distribution of the cards, sending cards to the pastor of any church specified, or to the nearest co-operating church of any denomination specified, or to the nearest co-operating evangelical church if no denomination were specified.[123]

The response of the Roman Catholic Church to the 1950 Boston Crusade was "heartening" to the Graham team, as the evangelist now recalls.[124] In the 1950 ecclesiastical atmosphere, fundamentalists and conservatives would have found Graham's comment upsetting. In 1950, Graham considered Jesse Bader, then the evangelism secretary of the Federal/National Council of Churches, and later the chairman of Visitation Evangelism that followed up the New York Crusade, a "wise older friend."[125] Willis Haymaker joined the Graham team for the 1950 Columbia, SC, Crusade. "He would also call on the local Catholic bishop or other clerics to acquaint them with Crusade plans and invite them to the meetings." Graham notes that this was pre-Vatican II, "but we were concerned to let the Catholic bishops see that my goal was not to get people to leave their church; rather I wanted them to commit their lives to Christ."[126] In an interview with Graham before the 1954 Paris campaign, the evangelist was asked:

---

[120]Letter of inquiry about these and other assertions by Pastor G. Archer Weniger to Walter Smyth, December 20, 1957, Fundamentalism Archives, Bob Jones University, Greenville, SC.

[121]This was "Dr. Graham's Kindly Letter" to Rice, April 27, 1957, reproduced in the *Sword of the Lord* (May 24, 1957), p. 2. Regarding Rice's effusiveness over the Scotland Crusade, which Rice attended and had private conversations with the evangelist, Graham is correct. But the admission of liberal involvement is telling.

[122]Billy Graham, *Just As I Am*, p. 144.

[123]J. Edwin Orr, "Preparing For Revival," *Revival In Our Time* (Wheaton: Van Kampen, 1950), p. 38.

[124]Billy Graham, *Just As I Am*, p. 161.

[125]Ibid., p. 186.

[126]Ibid., p. 163.

> If Catholics made decisions at your meetings will you encourage them to return to the faith they were born into? Answer: My objective is to get the people to accept Jesus Christ. The names of the converts will be turned over to the Evangelistic Alliance which invited us to France. Question: Are there any Catholic members of the Alliance? Answer: No. (A member of the Alliance interrupted to say that cards of people requesting reaffirmation in the Catholic faith would be turned over to the Catholic church).[127]

In an interview concerning Graham's 1954 European Crusade, the evangelist stated: "If a person in one of these campaigns makes a commitment to Christ, we don't drop him. He is followed up. The ministers all do that. His name and address and a lot of information about him is taken, and within 24 hours that is sent to a minister of the church of his choice, regardless of denomination."[128] Jerry Beaven attempted to summarize the referral policy:

> Billy has always adopted the view that he is merely the messenger boy. He delivers God's message and what happens to those who receive it is not his responsibility....
> Following each meeting when the invitation to make a commitment to Christ was given, [the] counselors met with those who responded. They conducted careful interviews and in turn referred those who responded to the church they indicated they preferred.[129]

So by the time of the preparations for the 1957 New York Crusade, when the new inclusive policy was officially acknowledged, announced, and implemented, it appears that there was a pattern regarding sponsorship and referrals already well in place. For whatever reason, it seems that this pattern was not generally known. However, the testimony of Pastor Bryce B. Augsburger concerning the Detroit Crusade (1953) is quite clear. Augsburger, then pastor of the Gratiot Avenue Baptist Church, Detroit, testified as a first-hand eyewitness of the participating presence of liberals in the Detroit Council of Churches, the Northern Baptist Convention, and others from whom his church had separated.[130] Carl McIntire as well was perceptive at this point, declaring that "Billy Graham has been building up to this position over a period of years. The New York campaign, under the modernist-inclusivist Protestant Council of New York City, the voice of the National Council of the Churches of Christ in the U.S.A., has brought all these matters into focus."[131]

Antecedents for the first New York Crusade can probably be dated to 1951 when a group of fundamentalist preachers invited the Graham team for an evangelistic campaign in 1952. They had heard and seen what had happened in Los Angeles (1949) and Boston (1950). A committee of eighty-seven was formed, sixty-six at a breakfast and twenty-one chosen later by the sixty-six, "largely at the selection

---

[127]George Burnham, *Billy Graham: A Mission Accomplished* (Westwood, NJ: Revell, 1955), p. 113.

[128]"Billy Graham's Story: New Crusade in Europe," *U. S. News and World Report* (August 27, 1954), p. 89.

[129]Jerry Beaven, "The Billy Graham I Know," *Christian Herald* (August 1966), p. 72.

[130]Bryce B. Augsburger, "Shall We Co-operate With Graham Campaign?" *Sword of the Lord* (June 15, 1962), p. 10.

[131]Carl McIntire, "The Graham Debate," *A Ministry of Disobedience*, p. 35.

of Billy Graham."[132] John Sutherland Bonnell, a liberal Presbyterian, among other liberals, was chosen for the committee. Jack Wyrtzen, a popular and influential youth evangelist in New York City, objected to the heterogeneous composition of the committee, and a group of about ten ministers drew up a statement of faith for the committee members to sign. Bonnell and others refused to sign. Graham then felt that the committee no longer represented the area churches. In a letter of May 29, 1951 he indicated he wanted the committee to endorse an "ecumenical spirit," but that he had never been in favor of having a modernist on the committee or of having a working relationship with modernists.[133] The group dropped its efforts to bring Graham to New York. In 1954 Wyrtzen proposed to his friends that Graham again be invited to New York, and drew up a petition asking him to come. At about the same time the New York Protestant Council also asked the Graham team to come. After a long delay, Wyrtzen was turned down and the Protestant Council's invitation was accepted, reversing Graham's position in his May 29, 1951 letter to the committee of eighty-seven. These maneuvers, however, were still behind-the-scenes and not public knowledge.

The year 1956 proved to be the year of unveiling for inclusive evangelism as Graham went public with his new policy and precipitated a final and complete break with separatist fundamentalists. Two principal events brought about the public disclosure: Graham's open support of the Cooperative Program of the Southern Baptist Convention in April, and an interview he gave in *Christian Life* magazine in June.

Liberalism proliferated in the Southern Baptist Convention's schools, denominational machinery, and some churches. The fundamentalist response inside the Convention was either to withdraw or, more popularly, to withhold support for the Cooperative Program which funded the denominational machine, including the schools. John R. Rice, who himself had come out of the Convention in the 1930s but still had an affinity for and close friends within the Convention, counseled the latter tactic of not supporting the Cooperative Program. It was quite a blow to Rice, therefore, when Billy Graham openly announced his loyalty to the Convention and his support of the Cooperative Program. Rice, an evangelist with a heart for mass evangelism and personal soul winning, had been defensive of Graham in the face of seemingly incontrovertible evidence of the evangelist's straying from separatism into inclusivism.[134] But Graham's support of the Cooperative Program proved too much for Rice.

A letter over Graham's signature appeared in *The Baptist Standard* (April 7, 1956), an organ of the Texas Baptist Convention. It said in part:

---

[132]James E. Bennet, "The Billy Graham New York Crusade: Why I Cannot Support It," *A Ministry of Disobedience*, p.11.

[133]Ibid.

[134]For example, "Questions Answered About Billy Graham," Sword of the Lord (June 17, 1955), p. 1. See also Farley P. Butler, "Billy Graham and the End of Evangelical Unity," chapter 5, "The Sword and Billy Graham" (pp. 66-91) for an excellent chronicle and analysis of the relationship between Rice and Graham.

> I am proud to be a member of the State Baptist Convention of Texas....My heart was always with the convention....I have come to believe that it is nearer the New Testament church than any other denomination....Concerning the Cooperative Program, I believe it is the greatest means ever devised by the church for giving one's tithe....In private and public conversation I support the Cooperative Program without hesitation....I am proud of our convention and I take my stand with it with an undying loyalty.[135]

A public rift between Rice and Graham developed. Graham resigned from Rice's board, his name was removed from the masthead of the *Sword*, and Rice wrote a number of articles that were anti-new evangelical and anti-inclusivist. For all practical purposes, the *Sword* turned anti-Billy Graham as well, although Rice tried to give the impression that he was not against Graham personally nor his crusade message of salvation in Jesus Christ alone.[136] Butler observed correctly that when Billy Graham broke with John R. Rice over supporting the Cooperative Program, "Graham had severed his last tie with separatist fundamentalism." This was far more than a personal thing. "Graham would emerge as the chief public spokesman of the new evangelicalism, and the division of conservative evangelicalism would follow."[137]

In an interview with Billy Graham in *Christian Life*, the evangelist seemed to be making a public declaration of his new inclusive policy of ecumenical evangelism.[138] He noted the "full retreat" of "extreme liberalism" as well as the "fighting, feuding and controversies among God's people, even within evangelical circles in the United States and even abroad." He was determined "to stay out of these controversies and divisions among God's people and continue to preach Christ and him crucified to sinful men." In view of the New York Crusade the next year, Graham noted the "deep cleavages among Christians in New York City." When the interview finally came around to sponsorship of the upcoming crusade, the evangelist said, "What difference does it make who sponsors a meeting? It is the message that counts," and he went on to cite Paul at Mars Hill and Christ in the synagogues as examples of the inclusive policy. As to his policy on accepting speaking engagements, he answered, "I shall continue to go wherever I am invited and shall give priority to those groups that seem to need the Gospel most." While there may be a certain amount of cryptic language in the words, fundamentalists who had been following the crusades for five or six years knew what was being said. It was an open announcement of a change in evangelism policy.

That policy was made unambiguously clear the next year at the meeting of the NAE in Buffalo, NY, April 3, 1957. There Graham, in an address entitled "The Lost Chord of Evangelism," said bluntly:

---

[135]The letter was reproduced by Rice in "Which Way, Billy Graham?" *Sword of the Lord* (Nov 23, 1956), p. 2.

[136]This distinction by Rice that he would not separate from Graham because the evangelist was a Christian and was winning souls eventually led to the controversy within the fundamentalist camp in the 1960s of "degrees" of separation. Rice felt that he was not separating from Graham technically, but from the modernists in his inclusivist campaigns. Rice's position on ecclesiastical separation was that one should only separate from modernists, cultists, and infidels (i.e., 1st degree separation), not from fellow Christians who do not separate from modernists (2nd degree separation).

[137]Farley P. Butler, "Billy Graham and the End of Evangelical Unity," p. 160.

[138]"What's the Next Step?" *Christian Life* (June 1956), pp. 20-23.

Our New York campaign has been challenged by some extremists on two points. First, as to sponsorship, I would like to make myself quite clear. I intend to go anywhere, sponsored by anybody, to preach the Gospel of Christ, if there are no strings attached to my message. I am sponsored by civic clubs, universities, ministerial associations and councils of churches all over the world. *I intend to continue* (emphasis his).

Second, we have been challenged on what happens to the converts when the crusade is over. Apparently these brethren who make these statements have no faith in the Holy Spirit....The work of follow up is the work of the Holy Spirit....We do all we can in follow up, but ultimately they're in the hands of the Holy Spirit. *He is more than able* [emphasis his].

There is a great swing all over the world, within the Church, toward a more conservative theological position. The old terms fundamentalism and liberalism are now passé. The situation is radically changed, since the days of Machen, Riley and other defenders of the faith a generation ago.[139]

In so saying, Graham publicly articulated the inclusive policy of ecumenical evangelism followed in every Graham crusade thereafter and by all the new evangelical-type evangelists since. The address was especially timed to inform the public, notably the fundamentalist community, of the ecclesiastical infrastructure of the upcoming New York Crusade in May and of the new ongoing policy of sponsorship and convert referral. Granted, the new policy of convert referral is somewhat encoded in Graham's address, but it was easily deciphered by those who were knowledgeable (fundamentalist, evangelical, and liberal) of crusade evangelism.

According to plan, the steering committee for the crusade featured some well-known local evangelicals and fundamentalists such as Jack Wyrtzen of Word of Life Fellowship youth ministry; John Wimbish, pastor of the First Baptist Church; Daniel Poling, editor of *The Christian Herald*; John Bradbury, editor of the Baptist periodical *The Watchman Examiner*; Frank Gaebelein, headmaster of the Stoneybrook school; and William Ward Ayer, pastor of the Calvary Baptist Church. The committee also displayed a virtual "who's who" of prominent New York liberal/neo-orthodox churchmen such as Dan Potter, executive director of the Protestant Council; Jesse Bader, executive secretary of the Department of Evangelism of the National Council of Churches; John Sutherland Bonnell, pastor of the Fifth Avenue Presbyterian Church; Norman Vincent Peale, pastor of the Marble Collegiate [Methodist] Church; Robert J. McCracken, pastor of the Riverside [Baptist] Church; Henry Pitney Van Dusen, president of the Union Theological Seminary; and Ralph Sockman, pastor of the Madison Avenue Methodist Episcopal Church. Inquirers/converts were duly routed back to "the church of their choice." Marble Collegiate church reportedly received the highest number of decision cards (373) with the Riverside Church being second.[140]

---

[139]Billy Graham, "The Lost Chord of Evangelism," *Christianity Today* (April 1, 1957), p. 26.

[140]Reported by William Ward Ayer, "Aftermath of the Billy Graham Crusade of New York," and quoted by Dunzweiler, "Billy Graham: A Critique," p. 24. Ayer's review also noted that 159 clergymen reported a total of 3,997 referrals, 2,552 of which were already members of churches.

As William Martin observed:

> The New York crusade did not cause the division between the old Fundamentalists and the New Evangelicals; that had been signaled by the nearly simultaneous founding of the National Association of Evangelicals and McIntire's American Council of Christian Churches fifteen years earlier.[141]

The New York Crusade simply put in place permanently the old fissure that the new evangelicals created back in the 1940s. Fundamentalists could not pull in the harness with modernists and thus they could not collaborate with Billy Graham and the Graham-type of ecumenical evangelism.[142] Graham brought an end to evangelical unity. With the New York Crusade, Graham's position of working with unorthodox churchmen and churches was clear. "Some working relationship with the neo-orthodoxy that was dominant had been arranged, and the pattern of New York was followed in city after city."[143]

---

[141]William Martin, *A Prophet With Honor: The Billy Graham Story* (New York: William Morrow, 1991), p. 224.

[142]A few fundamentalists, such as Jack Wyrtzen and William Ward Ayer, did cooperate but did so on principles inconsistent with their fundamentalist separatism and previous concerns about having modernists on the crusade committee.

[143]Farly P. Butler, "Billy Graham and the End of Evangelical Unity," p. 13.

4

OTHER CONTRIBUTIONS

While the New York Crusade was the cap sheaf to the formation of the new evangelicalism's distinction from fundamentalism, other contributing phenomena should be mentioned at least briefly because they form part of the historical milieu from which emerged the new evangelical coalition. These phenomena are the various books and articles that had their influence in flavoring the fundamentalist/evangelical atmosphere of the 1950s. Attention has already been called to the publication of Bernard Ramm's *The Christian View of Science and Scripture* in 1954 and Carl Henry's *Evangelical Responsibility in Contemporary Theology* in 1957.

"THE NATURE OF EVANGELICALISM"

In 1956 Vernon Grounds, of the Denver Conservative Baptist Theological Seminary, wrote an article entitled, "The Nature of Evangelicalism." After showing how evangelicalism has some things in common with "the great faiths of humanity" (Buddhism, Hinduism, Taoism, Confucianism, Judaism, Mohammedanism), liberal Protestantism, neoorthodoxy, and Roman Catholicism, he concluded:

> Undeniably evangelicalism is fundamentalism, if by fundamentalism is meant a tenacious insistence upon the essential and central dogmas of historic Christianity. Yet as undeniably evangelicalism is not fundamentalism as fundamentalism is ordinarily construed. A thoroughgoing evangelical recognizes with a wry smile the truth in the liberal jibe: "Fundamentalism is too much fun, too much damn, and too little mental."[1]

In the opinion of one analyst, this article "contained the first sustained public attempt by an evangelical scholar to dissociate himself from fundamentalism."[2]

CHRISTIANITY TODAY

The creation of *Christianity Today* in 1956 proved to be another fortunate influence in the fundamentalist/evangelical struggles. The bi-monthly magazine delivered the new evangelical cause on intellectual and practical, as well as newsy, informative planes. It was designed to be "an evangelical *Christian Century* [the

---

[1]"The Nature of Evangelicalism," *Eternity* (Feb 1956), pp. 12, 13.

[2]Farley P. Butler, "Billy Graham and the End of Evangelical Unity," (Ph.D. dissertation, University of Florida, 1976), p. 116. He reiterated, "With the publication of this article by Vernon Grounds, the process of the division of evangelical orthodoxy into evangelicalism and fundamentalism came into the open" (p. 122).

leading liberal mouthpiece]."[3] Carl F. H. Henry was the first editor, and in his maiden editorial he outlined the purposes of the periodical. In forthcoming issues, a growing group of evangelical scholars "will expound and defend the basic truths of the Christian faith in terms of reverent scholarship and of practical application to the needs of the present generation." "*Christianity Today* will apply the biblical revelation to the contemporary social crisis, by presenting the implications of the total Gospel message for every area of life. This, Fundamentalism has often failed to do." The new publication "will set forth the unity of the Divine revelation in nature and Scripture," and will further "seek to supplement seminary training with sermonic helps, pastoral advice, and book reviews, by leading ministers and scholars."[4] Billy Graham, stirred by an early morning burst of inspiration, had suggested the new magazine. He recalled: "During 1953, I was beginning to be attacked from both the left and the right." At 2 a.m. one morning late in 1953, he was awakened and went to his desk and wrote out his ideas for "an evangelical counterpart to *The Christian Century*."[5] The editorial stance had to tread a middle road between the extreme left and extreme right. But while slanted toward evangelicalism, its editors understood that "the magazine would be useless if it had the old, extreme fundamentalist stamp on it."[6] With money from J. Howard Pew (board chairman of the Sun Oil Co.) and the Billy Graham Evangelistic Association, the magazine began. Harold John Ockenga served as chairman of the board of *Christianity Today* and continued in that role for twenty-five years (1956-1981).

"IS EVANGELICAL THEOLOGY CHANGING?"

Allusion has already been made to the watershed article, "Is Evangelical Theology Changing?" an evangelical symposium in the March 1956 issue of *Christian Life*. The article argued that evangelical theology definitely was changing; "fundamentalism has become evangelicalism."[7] Eight areas of change were listed. (1) "A friendly attitude toward science," (2) "a willingness to re-examine beliefs concerning the work of the Holy Spirit," (3) "a shift away from so-called extreme dispensationalism," (4) "an increased emphasis on scholarship," (5) "a more definite recognition of social responsibility," (6) "a re-opening of the subject of biblical inspiration," (7) "a more tolerant attitude toward varying views of eschatology," and (8) "a growing willingness of evangelical theologians to converse with liberal theologians."[8] As might be expected, numerous fundamentalists responded negatively.[9]

[3]George M. Marsden, *Reforming Fundamentalism: Fuller Seminary and the New Evangelicals* (Grand Rapids: Eerdmans, 1987), p. 157.

[4]Carl F. H. Henry, "Why Christianity Today?" *Christianity Today* (Oct 10, 1956), p. 20.

[5]"In the Beginning: Billy Graham Recounts the Origins of *Christianity Today*," *Christianity Today* (July 17, 1981), p. 26. For another of Graham's personal recollections of the origin of the magazine, see his *Just As I Am: The Autobiography of Billy Graham* (San Francisco: HarperSanFrancisco Zondervan, 1997), pp. 184-94.

[6]Graham, *Christianity Today* (July 17, 1981), p. 26.

[7]"Is Evangelical Theology Changing," *Christian Life* (March 1956), p. 17.

[8]Ibid., pp. 17-19. This article was followed by a similar one the next month, "Is Liberal Theology Changing?"

[9]Such as Richard V. Clearwaters, "The Bible: The Unchanging Evangelical Volume," *Sword of the Lord* (May 4, 1956), p. 1; Robert T. Ketcham, "A New Peril in Our Last Days," *Christian Beacon*

OCKENGA NEWS RELEASE

On December 8, 1957, Ockenga gave a news release stating that "the New Evangelicalism is the latest dress of orthodoxy as Neo-Orthodoxy is the latest expression of theological liberalism." He stressed the differences between the new evangelicalism and fundamentalism. New evangelicalism had "a willingness to handle the social problems which Fundamentalism evaded," a change of strategy "from one of separation to one of infiltration," a willingness to "face the intellectual problems and meet them in the framework of modern learning," and a "positive proclamation of the truth in distinction from all errors without delving into the personalities which embrace the error." New evangelicalism also had a united front, in Ockenga's opinion. He listed a series of entities representing the new movement including the National Association of Evangelicals, the World Evangelical Fellowship uniting national organizations in twenty-six countries into a world organization, a "stream of apologetic literature" expounding the movement's point of view, Fuller Seminary and other seminaries committed to orthodoxy, *Christianity Today* explaining the positions of the movement, and evangelist Billy Graham, "who on the mass level is the spokesman of the convictions and ideals of the New Evangelicalism." Some twenty-one years later, Ockenga formulated a slightly different wording for the emergence of the new group, putting more of an onus on fundamentalism than the news release had. He thought that "the fundamentalists were not Christian in their attitude toward defending the faith" and that the "strategy of the fundamentalists was wrong. He raised a shibboleth of having a pure church, both as a congregation and a denomination," and the "social theory of the fundamentalists was governed by eschatology."[10]

COOPERATIVE EVANGELISM

In 1958 a 100-page book entitled *Cooperative Evangelism,* an apologetic for inclusive evangelism of the Billy Graham variety, was sent free to thousands of ministers and ministerial students.[11] While there had been attempts to justify the new policy of sponsorship and convert referrals,[12] this was the first book-length endeavor

---

(May 17, 1956), p. 2; William F. Culbertson, *Sword of the Lord* (May 25, 1956), p. 5; John R. Rice, "Letter To the Editor," *Christian Life* (May 1956), p. 3; Bob Jones Sr, "Letter To the Editor," *Christian Life* (June 1956), p. 4; Chester A. Tulga, "Baptists Are More Than Evangelicals," *The Baptist Bulletin* (June, July, Aug 1956); "Is Evangelical Christianity Changing?" A symposium article edited by Charles L. Feinberg, *The King's Business* (Jan 1957), p. 23; Alva J. McClain, "Is Theology Changing in the Evangelical Camp?" *The Brethren Missionary Herald* (Feb 23, 1957), p. 123; and John F. Walvoord, "What's Right About Fundamentalism?" *Eternity* (June 1957), p. 6.

[10]Harold John Ockenga, "From Fundamentalism, Through New Evangelicalism, to Evangelicalism," in *Evangelical Roots* ed. Kenneth Kontzer (Nashville: Thomas Nelson, 1978), pp. 42, 43.

[11]Robert O. Ferm, *Cooperative Evangelism: Is Billy Graham Right or Wrong?* (Grand Rapids: Zondervan, 1958).

[12]Such as those by William K. Harrison, "General Harrison Answers Graham Critics," *Christianity Today* (Jan 21, 1957), p. 28; Paul S. Rees, "Billy Graham Crusades: What About the Criticism?" *Christian Life* (April 1957), p. 14; Carl F. H. Henry, "Opposition to Evangelism A Strange Phenomenon," *Christianity Today* (Feb 18, 1957), p. 23; Joe Bayly, "Editorial on the Billy Graham New York Crusade," *His* (Oct 1957), pp. 39-40; and Donald Grey Barnhouse, " Billy in Manhattan," *Eternity* (May 1957), p. 7.

to give the policy scholastic and intellectual respectability. The publication met unfavorable responses from fundamentalists and even some evangelicals.[13]

THE CASE FOR ORTHODOX THEOLOGY

In 1959 a book written by Fuller Seminary professor Edward John Carnell, *The Case For Orthodox Theology*,[14] landed like a bombshell in the evangelical and fundamentalist communities, creating great concern for fundamentalists and considerable anxiety for evangelicals. The book intemperately and caustically attacked fundamentalism. Westminster Press published a trilogy of "case" books, and Carnell allegedly presented the case for orthodoxy.[15] In many minds, Carnell not only did not make a case for orthodoxy, he did not even make a case. He was especially unclear on where he stood on the linchpin doctrine of fundamentalism and conservative orthodoxy—verbal inerrancy.[16] This ambiguity was the main problem that inerrantists (fundamentalist and evangelical) had with the book. So dissatisfied was Cornelius Van Til with Carnell's contribution that he wrote his own volume critiquing the trilogy of case books and presenting his own case for orthodoxy under the title, *The Case For Calvinism*.[17] Carnell's *Case* book stirred up enough controversy among evangelicals that in December 1959, Wheaton College hosted a roundtable discussion of the book consisting of George Ladd (Fuller Theological Seminary); Arthur Holmes, Robert D. Culver, and Samuel J. Schultz (Wheaton College); and John C. Whitcomb (Grace Theological Seminary), among others. Grace Theological Seminary's faculty had its own evaluation session of the book that same month, concluding that Carnell's work was inadequate and disappointing.[18] Other negative scholarly analyses of the book were also made.[19]

---

[13]Gordon H. Clark, "Letter To the Editor," *Christianity Today* (May 26, 1958), p. 18; John R. Rice, "Cooperative Evangelism," *Sword of the Lord* (June 20, 1958), p. 1; Phil Foxwell, "Book Review: Cooperative Evangelism," *Bible Presbyterian Reporter* (June-July 1958), p. 15; Gary G. Cohen, *Biblical Separation Defended: A Biblical Critique of Ten New Evangelical Arguments* (Philadelphia: Presbyterian and Reformed, 1966), and William Culbertson, "Review of *Cooperative Evangelism*," *Moody Monthly* (Aug 1958), pp. 54-55.

[14]Philadelphia: Westminster, 1959.

[15]The other two were *The Case For A New Reformation Theology* [neoorthodoxy] by William Hordern, and *The Case For Theology in Liberal Perspective* by L. Harold DeWolf.

[16]For example, he maintained that "orthodoxy has never devised an official view of inspiration" (p. 99), or "orthodoxy may never officially decide whether the Holy Spirit corrected the documents from which the Chronicler drew his information" (p. 111). This point was not lost on non-evangelical theologians. John B. Cobb Jr. noted it in his review of Carnell (*Interpretation* [June 1960], pp. 94-96). L. Harold DeWolf himself thought the new evangelicals were in a "noticeable, though indecisive change" on inspiration and biblical authority and cites Carnell's *Case* as evidence (*Present Trends in Christian Thought* [New York: Association Press, 1960] pp. 45, 55-56). More pointedly, DeWolf felt that with the *Case* book, Carnell "advanc[ed] to a new position which [had] brought him into opposition, not only to the self-declared fundamentalists but also to many of the more conservative representatives of the new evangelicalism. In fact he might not now care to be identified as a new evangelical at all" (letter to Pastor Vernon Lyons, Ashburn Baptist Church, Chicago, dated May 11, 1962). William Hordern observed: "It has been evident for some time that the new conservatives have had difficulties with their concept of inerrancy," citing Carnell, among others, as evidence (*New Directions in Theology Today* [Philadelphia: Westminster, 1966], pp. 80-89).

[17]Philadelphia: Presbyterian and Reformed, 1963.

[18]*The Brethren Missionary Herald* (Jan 23, 1960), pp. 59-62. See especially the analysis of John C. Whitcomb, "Present Trends in Evangelical Theology," pp. 61-62.

[19]Robert E. Nicholas, "Review of *The Case For Orthodox Theology*," *Westminster Theological Journal 22* (Nov 1959); J. Oliver Buswell, "Book Review: 'The Case For Orthodox Theology,'" *Bible Presbyterian Reporter* (Dec 1959, p. 16, and Jan 1960, p. 15); and John F. Walvoord, "A Trilogy of Theology," *Moody Monthly* (Feb 1960), p. 70.

DONALD GREY BARNHOUSE

Donald Grey Barnhouse figures largely in the emergence of the new evangelicalism in the 1950s. One historian/biographer noted that "theologically, Barnhouse will be remembered as one...who late in life contributed to the early development of twentieth century neo-evangelicalism."[20] Barnhouse pastored the Tenth Presbyterian Church, Philadelphia, from 1927 to his death in 1960 at age sixty-five. He studied at the Bible Institute of Los Angeles, the University of Chicago, Princeton Theological Seminary, the University of Grenoble (France), and the University of Pennsylvania. He was a Presbyterian fundamentalist of the vintage of J. Gresham Machen, though a non-separatist. In 1932 the Philadelphia Presbytery "admonished" him for breaking the ninth commandment about bearing false witness and for breaking his ordination vows by charging fellow clergymen with heresy without going through the designated ecclesiastical channels to register his protest.[21] Nevertheless, he retained a life-long affiliation with the Presbyterian Church in the USA.

Barnhouse's personality could be antagonizing. His intellectual genius made him appear arrogant and high-minded both to conservatives and liberals. However, in his early years he was a great defender of the faith. He showed support for Dr. Machen by having him preach at Tenth Church, ignoring the presbytery's edict against Machen.[22] He stood against liberalism in his preaching, as editor of *Revelation* (later *Eternity*) magazine, and on his national radio program, The Bible Study Hour. He opposed error and unbelief in his own denomination, and vocally opposed the liberal conciliar movements.

However, in 1953 he issued a "New Year's Resolution," and took a decided turn in his attitude and actions toward fundamentalists and liberals. He noted about his early ministry: "I conceived the idea that I must strike out against all error wherever I saw it." He now wanted to have "Christian fellowship with a much wider circle of people." He wanted to "make his circle of fellowship on the basis of the fact that a man is going to be in Heaven with me." He also confessed that he "did not recognize that some of the things that have been accomplished by the National and World Councils are truly magnificent achievements for the Lord Jesus Christ."[23] Barnhouse apologized to the Presbyterian Church in the USA and to the National Council of Churches for his past belligerence and bellicose attitude toward them. As a result the National Council offered to sponsor an opportunity for him to preach a series of national television messages.[24] He found fellowship with Seventh-day Adventists,[25] declaring them to be evangelical Christians. He

---

[20]C. Allyn Russell, "Donald Grey Barnhouse: Fundamentalist Who Changed," *Journal of Presbyterian History* 59 (Spring 1981), p. 54.

[21]Ibid., pp. 45-48.

[22]Ibid., p. 47.

[23]*Eternity* (Jan 1953), inside front and back covers.

[24]He as much as announced this forthcoming series in "Where Am I Going?" *Eternity* (June 1954), pp. 39-40. Later that year he accepted the invitation. See also his "One Church," *Eternity* (July 1958), p. 20.

[25]"Are Seventh-day Adventists Christians?: A New Look at Seventh-day Adventism," *Eternity* (September 1956), p. 6. Also his "Postscript on Seventh-day Adventism," *Eternity* (November 1957), p. 22, and "One Church," *Eternity* (July 1958), p. 20.

discovered a oneness with the Assemblies of God Pentecostals.[26] He defended the
National and World Councils of Churches.[27] He castigated fundamentalists' practice
of separation over Bible doctrine as completely unbiblical, Pharisaical, and sinful.[28]
He printed an article in *Eternity* by Vernon Grounds charging fundamentalists with not
believing in the great commandment to love.[29] Though a loner by instinct, Barnhouse's
influence in the changing evangelical scene in the 1950s increased dramatically.

THE CHRISTIAN CENTURY

By the end of the 1950s, the decade of turbulent struggles between the new
evangelicals and the fundamentalists, several articles by evangelicals began to
appear in the liberal *Christian Century*. The symbolism of the gesture and the
clear content of these announcements should not be overlooked. Nationally-
known evangelical leaders, through the mouth piece of liberalism, declared to
the liberal community through its own mouthpiece their change in status from
fundamentalism to a more progressive and irenic new evangelicalism. Carnell
noted that "through a series of subtle internal changes, fundamentalism shifted
from an affirmation to a negation. The result was a cunning pharisaism that confused
possession of truth with possession of virtue." "Fundamentalism often took on the
mannerisms of a pugnacious cult." "Fundamentalism made its crowning error when it
enlisted the doctrine of the church in its quest for negative status....It was by discovery
of this pompous theological error that I awoke from dogmatic slumber."[30]

Billy Graham, in the *Christian Century* series, "How My Mind Has Changed,"
noted seven areas where his mind had changed.[31] He began by stating, "How I
wish I could take back some of the statements made in those early days because of
immaturity or a lack of knowledge and experience." He listed some of the changes
as being the narrow limits of evangelism, the realistic results of mass evangelism,
and his "increasing confidence in the ultimate triumph of the kingdom of God."
Also his "belief in the social implications of the gospel [had] deepened and

---

[26]"Finding Fellowship With Pentecostals," *Eternity* (April 1958), p. 8. This was actually the first
celebrated new evangelical contact of fellowship with Pentecostals. While the Pentecostal-oriented
Assemblies of God was in the National Association of Evangelicals, Pentecostals were second class
citizens in the minds of some elements of the NAE. As late as 1967 Carl F. H. Henry lamented the
number of Pentecostals in the NAE (35%), and went so far as to suggest starting another movement
separate from the NAE (*Evangelicals At the Brink of Crisis: Significance of the World Congress on
Evangelicalism* [Waco, TX: Word, 1967], pp. 107-108). Pentecostals received formal welcome into the
new evangelical ranks when Oral Roberts was officially invited to the 1966 Berlin World Congress on
Evangelism and Billy Graham was the featured speaker at the dedication of Oral Roberts University
in 1967.

[27]"Evanston: What It Was," *Eternity* (Oct 1954), p. 8; "Who's Putting Religion Off the Air?" *Eternity*
(April 1957), p. 14; and Walter R. Martin, "Oberlin Report: The World Council of Churches and
Christian Unity," *Eternity* (Nov 1957), p. 14.

[28]"Twentieth Century Pharisaism," *Eternity* (Aug 1957), p. 6; "Thanksgiving and Warning," *Eternity*
(Sept 1957), p. 9; and "One Church," *Eternity* (July 1958), p. 20.

[29]Vernon Grounds, "Is Love In the Fundamentalist Creed?" *Eternity* (June 1954), p. 6. Grounds
wrote: "This supreme fundamental [to love one another] has been grossly ignored. And perhaps that
neglect explains to a large degree why fundamentalism in many quarters degenerated into a legalistic
Pharisaism, hard, frigid, ineffective, unethical and loveless."

[30]"Post-Fundamentalist Faith," *The Christian Century* (Aug 26, 1959), p. 971.

[31]"What Ten Years Have Taught Me," *The Christian Century* (Feb 17, 1960), pp. 186-89.

broadened....(Naturally, there are some statements that I made a few years ago on socio-political affairs that I would like to retract)." He also noted:

> My concept of the church has taken greater dimension. Ten years ago my concept of the church tended to be narrow and provincial,...I am now aware that the family of God contains people of various ethnological, cultural, class, and denominational differences. I have learned that there can even be minor disagreements of theology, methods and motives but that within the true church there is a mysterious unity that overrides all divisive factors....I have also come to believe that within every visible church there is a group of regenerated, dedicated disciples of Christ.[32]

The words in and of themselves may be interpreted as evangelical and right-sounding; but given the historical and literary context in which were written, a discerning reader, whether liberal or conservative, could not fail to hear the subtle voice of ecumenical inclusivism.

Carnell, in another bitter, parting shot at fundamentalism, wrote in the *Christian Century* an article entitled, "Orthodoxy: Cultic vs. Classical." Fundamentalism, he said, was "cultic." "A cult lives by mores and symbols of its own devising; it makes no effort to join fellowship with the church universal."[33] After criticizing fundamentalism for its view of a pure church and separatism, he closed with one of the most pompous and condescending diatribes in all the fundamentalist-new evangelical controversy.

> Perhaps the day will come when the fundamentalist will temper his separatism by the wisdom of the ages. Perhaps not. But in the meantime let us not be too disturbed by his vanity. The fundamentalist means well. He wants status in the church, but he errs in the way he goes about getting it. Having missed the way, he needs our pity, not our scorn.[34]

For twenty years, i.e., the 1940s and 1950s, fundamentalism endured the new evangelical agitations, its birth and subsequent spasms of childhood and adolescence. It had still to abide another four decades of tension, acrimony, and criticism from the new evangelical coalition. In the meantime new evangelicalism went through upheavals and convulsions that left it in a state of malaise and theological depletion. Measured by its own complaints against fundamentalism in the 1940s for not penetrating and capturing the general culture for Christ, the new evangelicalism at the end of the twentieth century appears to have drifted into irrelevancy. Fundamentalism has suffered setbacks in its struggles. It has witnessed pockets of diminished vitality and an overall diminution in numbers. But after fighting off the inroads of modernism in the 1920s and making a fresh start in the 1930s, and suffering the internal upheavals from the moderate evangelicals beginning in the 1940s, fundamentalism has managed to retain the integrity of its heritage.

---

[32]Ibid., p. 188.

[33]"Orthodoxy: Cultic vs. Classical," *The Christian Century* (March 16, 1960), p. 377.

[34]Ibid., p. 379.

PART 3: ECUMENISM

Of the multi-sided rationale for the formation of the new evangelical coalition in the 1940s, the most prominent and fundamental aspect was the issue of unity. The new evangelicalism began in protest against the separatism of fundamentalism and its militant exposure of and separation from the unbelief of modernism. Harold John Ockenga, a prime mover in the new coalition, said the technique of the new group was the "infiltration" of the ranks of the liberals and not separation from them.[1] The early new evangelicals were ambivalent toward liberalism and neo-orthodoxy. They aggressively opposed unbelieving theology and philosophy as a scholastic exercise but were unwilling to sever their denominational ties with the apostasy they academically opposed. Ockenga spoke for the new group when he said that their strategy in this regard was the "positive proclamation of the truth in distinction from all errors without delving in personalities which embrace the error."[2]

"Ecumenical" means world wide, and in professing Christian circles refers to the visible unity that certain churches, denominations, and religious endeavors seek to maintain. Doctrine, truth, and group distinctives are ignored or greatly minimized for the sake of a united front. Ecumenism refers to the efforts expended to implement such unity. In this chapter ecumenism will mean specifically the collaboration between evangelicals and non-evangelicals in promoting various religious and spiritual projects. New evangelical ecumenism has many aspects. Ecumenical activity occurs in the new evangelical participation in the conciliar movement, including the National and World Councils of Churches and the Consultation Church Union, among others. It has occurred in the field of publishing in which traditionally evangelical and orthodox publishing houses, such as Eerdmans, Revell, Tyndale House, and InterVarsity Press publish books written by non-evangelicals or extreme *avant garde* evangelicals. Evangelical periodicals such as *Christianity Today*, *Decision*, and *Eternity* published articles by liberal, neo-orthodox, and Roman Catholic writers in what may be called ecumenical journalism. Ecumenical pulpiteering, in which evangelical churches and college and seminary chapels invite non-evangelicals to speak, occurs regularly. Positive assessments of heretical writers and leaders is another form of evangelical ecumenism, to say nothing of the across-the-board cooperation between evangelicals, the charismatic movement, and Roman Catholicism.

---

[1] News Release, Dec 8, 1957.
[2] Ibid.

5

ECUMENICAL EVANGELISM

One of the most obvious forms of new evangelical ecumenism, and the one probably most productive for its cause, is cooperative or inclusive evangelism— the uniting of evangelicals and non-evangelicals in evangelistic crusades to reach the masses for Christ. Billy Graham's switch from separatism to inclusivism began the policy later followed by new evangelical evangelists, such as Cliff Barrows, Roy Gustafson, Grady Wilson, T. W. Wilson, Luis Palau, Leighton Ford, Franklin Graham, Ralph Bell, and John Wesley White. Today, youth groups, evangelistic associations, missions agencies, and endeavors of all varieties take the inclusive policy for granted, and anyone who questions it is looked upon as odd, disinterested in souls, and nostalgic for the old fundamentalism now considered passé.

ARGUMENTS IN FAVOR OF ECUMENICAL EVANGELISM
Many arguments justify the inclusive policy. Robert O. Ferm authored the first, and apparently only, book-length apologetic, *Cooperative Evangelism: Is Billy Graham Right or Wrong?*[3] Some of his arguments, among others, will be briefly presented and analyzed. An excellent analysis of Ferm's argumentation from the fundamentalist standpoint is Gary Cohen's, *Biblical Separation Defended: A Biblical Critique of Ten New Evangelical Arguments.*[4] Ferm's apologetic, Cohen's rebuttal, and other fundamentalist evaluations of Ferm's book will inform the following discussion.[5]

The Ministry of the Twelve
Making contemporary applications from Christ's commissions to the Twelve and to the Seventy, Ferm concluded that the disciples "were supposed to accept hospitality when it was offered. They were to leave only when they were positively rejected (Matt. 10:14)." Further, in the interests of evangelism, Christ instructed the disciples "to enter into any community or home that would receive them, but

---

[3]Grand Rapids: Zondervan, 1958.

[4]Philadelphia: Presbyterian and Reformed, 1966.

[5]John R. Rice, "Cooperative Evangelism," *Sword of the Lord* (June 20, 1958), p. 1. William Culbertson, *Moody Monthly* (Aug 1958), p. 54. Phil Foxwell, *Bible Presbyterian Reporter* (June-July, August 1958). Gordon H. Clark, "Letter to the Editor," *Christianity Today* (May 26, 1958), p 18.

on their own terms (Luke 10:5-10)."[6] Apparently Ferm posits two primary reasons to disassociate from inclusive endeavors: when limitations are imposed on the message or the message is rejected conclusively. The Twelve were to leave a house when definitely rebuffed, and the Seventy were to move on when their own terms were not met.

The argument fails for several reasons. One, the whole matter concerns a different dispensation. The Twelve and the Seventy were still on Old Testament grounds, living and operating under the Mosaic law covenant. The "commission" of the disciples, for example (Matt 10:5-7), is vastly different from the "great commission" for the church age (Matt 28:18-20). While some have tried to equate the two commissions in the interests of a continuity between Israel and the church, the discrepancies between the two mandates are patent. The recipients of the messages differed. One audience consisted of the lost sheep of the house of Israel (Matt 10:5-6), and the other was the world (Matt 28:20). The messages differed. One message announced the impending kingdom of heaven (Matt 10:7), and the other proclaimed repentance and forgiveness of sins based on the death and resurrection of Christ (Matt 28:19; Luke 24:46-48). Furthermore, the accompaniments of the preaching differed. One commission included healing the sick and raising the dead (Matt 10:8-14), and the other commanded water baptism and Christian instruction (Matt 28:19).

What is really overlooked in the argument is that Christ, in preparing His followers for His absence, later specifically *rescinded* the original mandate to the Twelve (Luke 22:35-36). Making a divinely-rescinded first-century mandate to the disciples become the basis of inclusive evangelism in the twentieth and twenty-first centuries constructs quite a hermeneutical conundrum! The commission of the Twelve commands them to seek the "worthy" (Matt 10:11); mere *willingness* of the audience to receive them was not the only criterion. This searching would at least exclude false prophets, pagans, profiteers, and unbelievers. As well, the Twelve and the Seventy did not seek the "cooperation" of those to whom they went. Those *to whom* the evangelist preaches are vastly different from those *with whom* he cooperates and seeks support in the effort. Bob Jones, Sr. put it plainly:

> It is one thing to preach to modernists who reject the virgin birth, the incarnation, the vicarious blood atonement, the bodily resurrection, and salvation by grace through faith; but it is another thing to be sponsored by such modernists and give to them the same Christian recognition that is given to born-again, Bible-believing preachers. The Bible is certainly clear in its teachings along this line.[7]

Non-opposition

Ferm contends that Christ accepted the cooperation of any who did not *oppose* Him. The disciples found a man casting out demons and tried to prevent him because he was not following along with them. Jesus, however, saw the man as an ally and remarked, "he who is not against you is for you" (Luke 9:49-50).

---

[6]Robert O. Ferm, *Cooperative Evangelism*, pp. 34-35.

[7]Bob Jones Sr., "Letter To a Friend," March 6, 1957, Fundamentalism Archives, Bob Jones University, Greenville, SC.

Ferm therefore concludes, "If Jesus accepted the cooperation of any who did not oppose him, even though they did not conduct their mission in precisely the same manner he conducted his, an evangelist can scarcely make more exacting demands."[8] "Oppose" is apparently limited to active, vocal, and public opposition. The assumption is that liberals and modernists do not openly oppose Christ and therefore should be permitted to participate in an evangelistic crusade.

Liberals and infidels are not neutral toward Christ. Liberalism and neo-orthodoxy, for example, have been systematically constructed in opposition to biblical Christianity. Scholars have given lifetimes of meticulous study in order to undermine and discredit New Testament Christianity. Educated unbelief is the worst kind of unbelief. Some of the early new evangelicals were incredibly naive on this point. J. Elwin Wright, an energetic promoter of the National Association of Evangelicals, said at the founding: "Some of us have been slow to realize that not all modernists are hopeless apostates. May God give to us the ability to discern that we may save, through our gentleness and brotherly kindness in dealing with them, some of these who are in a state of confusion."[9] In the 1950s Carl F. H. Henry, believing the era of controversy was over and that both fundamentalism and old liberalism had died, asserted that Karl Barth's doctrines "as far as they go, have an evangelical ring and rigor."[10] (James DeForest Murch, another early pioneer of the NAE, was one of a few that publicly distrusted the non-evangelicals.[11]) Donald Bloesch, a left-wing new evangelical, criticized J. Gresham Machen because he did not recognize that "liberals can still be men of deep personal faith despite the errors in their thinking."[12] Clark Pinnock said of liberals and evangelicals: "It is time we [evangelicals] left behind the attitude 'I have all the answers, you have all the problems' and begin to encounter one another with understanding and love in the spirit of the Gospel."[13]

Alva J. McClain, my mentor in theology in seminary, had it exactly right when he commented on the rapprochement and dialogue with unbelieving scholars taking place in early new evangelicalism:

> Hobnobbing too closely with the enemy has always cost the cause of Christianity much more that it ever gained. I understand the desirability of an acquaintance with the program and ideas of our opponents, *but we must never for one instant forget that they are deadly enemies with whom there can be neither truce nor compromise* (italics added).[14]

---

[8]*Cooperative Evangelism*, p. 38.

[9]"A Report of the [Chicago, 1943] Constitutional Convention," quoted in Farley P. Butler, "Billy Graham and the End of Evangelical Unity" (Ph.D. dissertation, University of Florida, 1976), p. 17.

[10]Carl F. H. Henry, *Evangelical Responsibility in Contemporary Theology* (Grand Rapids: Eerdmans, 1957), p. 54.

[11]"Dare We Renew the Controversy?" *United Evangelical Action* (Sept 15, 1957), pp. 17-18.

[12]Donald G. Bloesch, *The Evangelical Renaissance* (Grand Rapids: Eerdmans, 1973), p. 149.

[13]Clark H. Pinnock, "Time For Fruitful Dialogue," *Christianity Today* (Sept 15, 1972), p. 32.

[14]Alva J. McClain, "Is Theology Changing in the Evangelical Camp?" *The Brethren Missionary Herald* (Feb 23, 1957), p. 12.

The new evangelical argument from Luke 9:49-50 overlooks the fact that indifference and non-opposition are still unbelief. In Luke 11:23, Jesus said plainly: "He who is not with me is against me; and he who does not gather with me, scatters."

Even if liberals do not actively oppose a crusade or act overtly negative toward the cause of Christ, they are still in entrenched opposition. If they are not garnering for biblical Christianity, they are scattering. There is no half-way house in these matters. Even lukewarmness toward the things of Christ is cause for divine judgment (Rev 3:15-16). Enlisting the unorthodox and non-evangelicals in an endeavor as important as evangelizing and saving souls from eternal perdition betrays the uniqueness and exclusiveness of the Christian religion. The argument from Luke 9 betrays mystical thinking and sloppy reasoning. Furthermore, Luke reveals that the man in question was actually *for* Christ. He was doing a good work (casting out demons) in a right manner (in Christ's name) and not reproaching Christ or His cause. The attempt to use Luke 9 as a paradigm for ecumenical evangelism is baseless and false.

Neither Christ nor Paul accepted the testimony of unbelief as any kind of support for their ministries. Jesus rebuked a demon for declaring a most cherished truth (Luke 4:41: "You are the Son of God"). Paul at Philippi exorcised a demon from a slave girl who at least verbally gave accurate testimony to Paul's ministry (Acts 16:17: "These men are bond-servants of the Most High God, who are proclaiming to you the way of salvation"). In both cases, the unbelieving source of an accurate message met with rebuke.

Temple Attendance

Another argument supporting inclusivistic ministry originates with Christ's attendance at the temple. The temple lay under the oversight of those who erred theologically and were apostate (Luke 2:21-22, 49; et al.). The inference drawn is that Christ obtained a wider audience by this strategic technique, while at the same time not approving the leaders or their errors. "Had Jesus acted upon the general principle of separation as interpreted by the present-day separatist, he would not have visited the Temple, even to cleanse it."[15]

Christ's temple visits took place under the dispensation of law, and no alternative to the Hebrew temple in that economy existed. One could not start another center of worship or in any way rival the central altar. In Mosaism God had to be approached at the central shrine where He "placed His name" and through the God-appointed Levitical forms and personnel (Exod 29:42, 43; Lev 17:1-9; Deut 12:5, 11-14). Despite its corruption in Jesus' day, the temple still had some sanctifying power and thus had religious and spiritual significance (Matt 23:17, 19). Jesus' visits had purpose; His absence would have been construed as indifference toward Yahweh and would have caused some to stumble into apostasy (Matt 17: 24-27). What is more, Christ's visits to the temple often ended in *controversy* due to His forthright declaration against error and the open presentation of His Messianic claims. He overturned the tables of the merchandisers (John 2:13-17;

---

[15]*Cooperative Evangelism*, p. 37.

Matt 21:13). He had a confrontation with the Pharisees over His origin (John 8: 21-59). On another occasion, at the Feast of Dedication, the Jews took up stones to kill Him (John 10:22-39).[16] The analogy of Christ visiting the temple is totally irrelevant to ecumenical evangelism.

Closely connected to the temple visits are Christ's visits to the synagogues.[17] Though Jews with carnal misconceptions of the Messianic kingdom dominated the synagogues, Jesus did not consider that sufficient reason to withdraw. Billy Graham invoked a form of this argument in anticipation of the 1957 New York Crusade.[18] However, in the synagogues Jesus plainly and unambiguously presented His Messianic claims, and His visits often ended in conflict, offense, controversy, and even plots against His life (Luke 4:16-31; 6:6-11).[19] The message and methods of ecumenical evangelism have never paralleled those of Jesus, and the new evangelical mentality has been to avoid conflict with those of unorthodox belief and outright denial of the fundamental truths of Christianity.

Souls Are Being Won

A rather common justification for ecumenical inclusivism is that souls are being won to Christ. If people are saved from sin, the blessing of God must be on the endeavor. An example of this type of reasoning surfaced in Joe Bayly's editorial on the 1957 New York Crusade.[20] Incredibly, Bayly acknowledges that the Bible teaches that "the Lord's people are to carry on the Lord's work with the Lord's money." He discerns the fundamentalist criticism that "it is confusing to invite all shades of belief into an evangelistic effort—or any other distinctly Christian effort, for that matter." He concedes: "Now that argument is a strong one, and we must admit that most of the Christian work we carry on today assumes its truth, at least on a local level where work with individuals is actually carried on." He felt that one "must admit that the Bible does teach, by precept and example, that Christians are to do the work of the Lord without seeking the support or sponsorship of non-Christians." However, his spiritual perception of the evidence compels him to demur and give weight to "the obvious work of God's Spirit in New York City, at Yale, in India...the obvious sincerity of Billy Graham...he is not a double-minded man." If the evangelist is wrong, "it would be puzzling...to reconcile this with the evident work of God through His servant." Bayly then surrenders the whole point in a stunningly pragmatic about-face: "I believe the answer is to be found in another question: Is God Himself bound always to work in the manner He has commanded in His word?" In the end he justifies inclusivism as one of "God's omnipotent exceptions."[21]

---

[16]For a list of Jesus' visits to the temple and their outcomes, see Gary G. Cohen, *Biblical Separation Defended: A Critique of Ten New Evangelical Arguments* (Philadelphia: Presbyterian and Reformed, 1966), pp. 17-18.

[17]*Cooperative Evangelism*, p. 37.

[18]"What's the Next Step?" Interview with Billy Graham, *Christian Life* (June 1956), pp. 20-23.

[19]Gary G. Cohen lists Jesus' visits to the synagogues and the tenor of each. *Biblical Separation Defended*, p. 26.

[20]Joe Bayly, "Editorial on the Billy Graham Crusade," *His* (Oct 1957), pp. 39-40.

[21]To document further Bayly's ambivalence, note his skepticism and negative attitude toward inclusive sponsorship fourteen months earlier ("Letter to the Editor," *Christian Life* [Aug 1956], p. 4).

Bayly's argument rises from the unbiblical philosophy of pragmatism. Pragmatism holds that the good and the true are found in what is productive, that "the end justifies the means" in more colloquial terms. The empirical criteria of the evangelist's sincerity and the subjectively-determined "blessing" of God are totally intuitive and lack any objective limiting concept. Virtually no religious endeavors and their results could be ruled out on these pragmatic criteria. This is far different from Paul's dictum that Christian service and rewards have rules and parameters. "If anyone competes as an athlete, he does not win the prize unless he competes according to the rules" (2 Tim 2:5). Paul obviates "omnipotent exceptions" and related notions.

The pragmatic argument also denies the fundamental duty of a Christian—simple obedience to the will of God as revealed in the Word of God. Obedience to divine authority overrides even the doing of normally good and acceptable service. "To obey is better than sacrifice, and to heed than the fat of rams," were Samuel's words to Saul (1 Sam 15:22). "Full obedience to the Lord includes winning souls, but winning souls does not abrogate our duty of obedience to God."[22] In addition, positive results may be produced without being in the will of God.[23] When Moses struck the rock in disobedience to God's command to speak to the rock, the results were phenomenal and beneficial; water came forth in abundance (Num 20:7-13). But Moses paid a dear price for this rebellious and presumptuous act (Num 20:24, 27:14; Deut 2:51; Ps 106:32-33). When Balaam prophesied against Israel in disobedience to God's express command, some positive things came out of it. Some of the most far-reaching prophecies concerning Christ and His Messianic office were given by Balaam (Num 22-24)! But this hardly justifies Balaam's disobedience. Balaam was a Mesopotamian occultist (Josh 13:22) who had no saving relationship with nor obedience to the God of the covenant. Balaam's results appeared staggeringly successful, but the same could be said for modern healers, spiritists, and cultists. Anecdotal evidence supports the alleged validity of such practitioners.

Pragmatism also circumvents the true criterion for judging spiritual work—the Bible.[24] God, through the ancient prophet Isaiah, set the standard: "To the law and to the testimony! If they do not speak according to this word, it is because they have no dawn" (Isa 8:20). In a day when some Israelites sought the mediums and spiritists in violation of the first commandment, God rebuked them for not consulting Him through His covenant revelation. As far as the ecumenical evangelist is concerned, "*We are to judge Graham's campaigns as we are to judge everything else—by the Word of God, not by the results they produce*" (italics his).[25]

An evangelist's message is far more complex than the spoken words of the plan of salvation from a lectern or podium. The message includes the evangelist's associations, attitudes, and comments on other leaders and issues. What is done by example is also an integral part of a preacher's total "message."[26]

---

[22]Ernest Pickering, "Should Fundamentalists Support the Billy Graham Crusades?" (Minneapolis: Central Seminary Press, n.d.), p. 19.

[23]Ibid.

[24]Ibid.

[25]Ibid.

[26]Ibid., p. 20.

Judge Not

A favorite argument against separatism by supporters of ecumenical evangelism is that Christians are not to judge others—Matthew 7:1 ("Do not judge so that you will not be judged"). In Ferm's line of reasoning, the Lord forbad Christians to sit in judgment on other Christians. Further complicating the issue is the impossibility of accurately ascertaining the orthodoxy of every minister and church in the crusade. Judging is not only impossible, it is deemed unnecessary because the Holy Spirit will complete the work of salvation begun at the time of faith.

> It is the Gospel, not human association, that operates in the heart and converts the sinner. This same Holy Spirit must be trusted to perfect the work which he has begun....Any minister or church that willingly enters into a cooperative effort,... is certainly deserving of having converts who so desire join in the fellowship of that particular church. If later any are led astray, or spiritually starved, the responsibility rests squarely on those churches, not on the evangelist. To take any other course is to sit in judgment on other Christians, something against which our Lord specifically warns us....It would be impossible to set up a local committee that would agree on which churches are worthy and which are not.[27]

Closer examination reveals that Matthew 7:1 forbids censoriousness, not the duty to "try the spirits" found in such injunctions as Matthew 7:6 ("Do not give what is holy to dogs, and do not throw your pearls before swine"), 1 Corinthians 5:12 ("For what have I to do with judging outsiders? Do you not judge those who are within *the church*?"), John 7:24 ("Do not judge according to appearance, but judge with righteous judgment"), and Titus 3:10 ("Reject a factious man after a first and second warning").[28] Matthew 7:1 refers to a condemning, harsh, and unmerciful spirit, not to the act of judging or discerning. Luke's parallel to Matthew 7:1 speaks of being merciful and not condemnatory (Luke 6:37 "Do not judge, and you will not be judged; and do not condemn, and you will not be condemned; pardon, and you will be pardoned"). In Matthew 7:1 Jesus is addressing hypocrites and is thus *condemning* hypocrisy. The only alternative to using judgment and discernment is the abandonment of doctrinal investigation, church discipline, or moral inquiries. Having a clear doctrinal statement and requiring adherence without mental reservations would facilitate discerning the worthiness or orthodoxy of ministers and churches in a cooperative endeavor.

Texts

Bible passages urging separatism typically receive only cursory attention by new evangelicals. Others restrict the application of the texts so narrowly that it is nearly impossible for them to be applied in contemporary ministry. For example, Galatians 1:8-9 ("But even if we, or an angel from heaven, should preach to you a gospel contrary to what we have preached to you, he is to be accursed!...so I say again...") is narrowly interpreted to refer only to "Judaizers who were preaching a gospel of ceremonial works." Since Billy Graham is not a Judaizer, and "does not preach ceremonial works but a clear, straightforward presentation of the gospel

---

[27]*Cooperative Evangelism*, p. 19.
[28]*Biblical Separation Defended*, pp. 40-41.

message,"[29] the passage is dismissed for consideration. However, Paul is speaking of anyone who perverts the gospel. The objection to inclusivism is not that the evangelist preaches works or is a Judaizer, but that he knowingly consorts with those who pervert the gospel.

2 John 9-11 is also misunderstood ("Anyone who goes too far and does not abide in the teaching of Christ, does not have God....If anyone comes to you and does not bring this teaching, do not receive him into your house, and do not give him a greeting; for the one who gives him a greeting participates in his evil deeds"). The ecumenist responds, again artificially narrowing the application, that "these were people who denied even the historical fact of Christ. I seriously doubt if Billy Graham has ever knowingly had fellowship with a man who denied the historical fact of Christ."[30]

Very few deny the historical fact of Christ's existence. Even after the searches for the historical Jesus, no one but the most obtuse apostate denied His "thatness." John is clearly referring to more than mere existence, but to identity as the virgin-born God-man. Any who deny His absolute deity or His genuine and complete humanity are false prophets who are not to be recognized as messengers of truth. What would John say to enlisting such heretics as helpers in spreading the truth about Christ and sending converts back to unbelieving churches?

OBJECTIONS TO ECUMENICAL EVANGELISM

Fundamentalist objections to ecumenical evangelism fall into three categories: Interdenominationalism, Sponsorship, and Convert Referrals.

Interdenominationalism

Interdenominationalism represents the inability or refusal to agree on various doctrines, especially the tenets distinctive to different denominations or groups of Christians. For example, Interdenominationalism cannot agree on the number, meaning, and purposes of the church ordinances, the composition and polity of the local church, the Second Coming of Christ and related themes (tribulationism, millennialism, dispensationalism, covenant theology, et al.), eternal security and sanctification, and what is truly essential and what is non-essential or peripheral. Carl Henry said, "Surely denominational differences are often secondary and provide no real barrier to a larger fellowship and cooperation of believers." He does attach significance to "fundamental matters" that convey "revealed doctrine."[31] But what is the criterion here? Some of God's people have suffered and died for what others would take as peripheral or secondary, or as non-foundational.

Interdenominationalism is a way of doing God's work that may have some limited, qualified practical value in certain ecclesiastical pursuits. The biblical ideal, however, projects the primacy of the local church (1 Tim 3:15). The "household of God," the "church of the living God" is, in context of the Pastoral Epistles and 1 Timothy 3, the local church of the New Testament. It is the "pillar

---

[29]*Cooperative Evangelism*, pp. 44-45.

[30]Ibid., p. 46.

[31]Carl F. H. Henry, "The Unity That Christ Sustains," *Eternity* (Mar 1956), p. 19.

and support of the truth." To that institution has been committed the fate of revealed truth in this dispensation. This means that it is always best to do Christian work from a full biblical agenda in the context of the local church or an association of churches of like mind and practice. The ordinances can be determined and practiced freely; doctrines peculiar to the group can be emphasized without the charge of intolerance, bigotry, insensitivity, or lack of love; the maturity of new converts can be effected with confidence; outlets of Christian service can easily be provided and mentored; and fellowship can be fully enjoyed without dancing around others' ideologies and distinctives.

Sponsorship

The question of sponsorship raises a second objection to inclusive evangelism. This issue has been dealt with in previous contexts in this work so that repetition will be minimized at this point. The titular head of evangelism since the mid-1940s has been Billy Graham. Originally, he sought sponsorship by fundamentalists. Ecumenism in the contexts out of which Graham came was non-existent (i.e., southern revivalism, Bob Jones University, Florida Bible Institute, Wheaton College, and Youth for Christ). In the mid-1950s that policy was deliberately changed to one of inclusivism wherein evangelical and non-evangelical ministers and groups united to sponsor city-wide crusades. The 1957 New York Crusade was the official public launching of ecumenical evangelism. On this occasion the split between fundamentalists and new evangelicals became irrevocable.

As early as June 1956, in a *Christian Life* interview, Graham publicly outlined his strategy. Due to his success and rising popularity, he dismissed his critics by condemning the "fighting, feuding, and controversies among God's people, even within evangelical circles in the United States."[32] Graham never answered specific charges; he could always stay on the lofty plane above the "feuding and fighting" and ride the crest of his popularity and God's "blessing" on his ecumenical, inclusive policy. Inclusive evangelism became the pattern of every Graham crusade and of every new evangelical, Graham-type evangelist thereafter.[33]

---

[32]"What's the Next Step?" p. 21.

[33]Source material on the subject of ecumenical evangelism, including sponsorship, convert referral, and related themes would include (an asterisk indicates a source critical of cooperative evangelism): *William E. Ashbrook, *Evangelicalism: The New Neutralism*, 8th printing (Columbus, OH: Wm. E. Ashbrook, n.d.); *John E. Ashbrook, *New Neutralism II* (Mentor, OH: Here I Stand Books, 1992); *Billy Graham: Performer, Politician, Prophet? A Chronological Record Compiled from Public Sources* (Wheaton, IL: Church League of America, n.d.); *Gary G. Cohen, *Biblical Separation Defended*; *Farley P. Butler, "Billy Graham and the End of Evangelical Unity"; *Robert Dunzweiler, *Billy Graham: A Critique* (Philadelphia: Faith Theological Seminary, n.d.); Robert O. Ferm, *Cooperative Evangelism*; Billy Graham, *Just As I Am: The Autobiography of Billy Graham* (San Francisco: Harper Collins, 1997); *Brad K. Gsell, *The Legacy of Billy Graham: The Accommodation of Truth to Error in the Evangelical Church*, revised and expanded edition (Charlotte, NC: Fundamental Presbyterian Publications, 1998); Carl F. H. Henry, *Evangelicals At the Brink of Crisis* (Waco, TX: Word, 1967); *Erroll Hulse, *Billy Graham: The Pastor's Dilemma* (Hounslow, Middlesex, UK: Maurice Allen Ltd., 1966); *Carl McIntire and James Bennet, *A Ministry of Disobedience* (Collingswood, NJ: Christiana Beacon, n.d.); *Carl McIntire, *Outside the Gate* (Collingswood, NJ: Christian Beacon, 1967); *Ernest Pickering, "Should Christians Support the Billy Graham Crusades?"; John Pollock, *Billy Graham: The Authorized Biography* (Grand Rapids: Zondervan, 1966); John Pollock, *Crusades: Twenty Years With Billy Graham* (Minneapolis: World Wide Publications, 1966); John Pollock, *Billy Graham: Evangelist To the World* (Minneapolis: Worldwide Publications, 1979); Jack Van Impe, *Heart Disease in Christ's Body* (Royal Oak, MI: Jack Van Impe, 1984).

The evangelist sidestepped the problem of liberal and unorthodox sponsorship by saying that he would "go anywhere, sponsored by anybody, to preach the Gospel of Christ, if there are no strings attached to my message."[34] But the ecumenical evangelist attaches strings to his own message by accepting liberal and other non-evangelical sponsorship. As a matter of ethics, he must *not* denounce their apostasy, warn against their churches and false teaching, refuse to have them on the public platform participating in the services, nor refuse to send them convert referrals.[35] Nor can the ecumenical evangelist preach on topics or doctrines that may be offensive to his non-evangelical supporters. As a result, a number of truths have been neglected, avoided, or blurred because of these self-attached restrictions that come with the inclusive policy.

As an example, the *United Church Observer*, the official organ of the United Church of Canada, featured an article entitled, "Billy Graham Answers 26 Provocative Questions."[36] The evangelist left unanswered the question, "Do you believe that we who teach that Christ is the word of God and that the Bible bears witness to God's revelation in him—but that the Bible is full of parable, myth, allegory and is often quite unhistoric and inexact—are 'false teachers?'" Another question was, "Do you think that churches such as The United Church of Canada and the great liberal churches of the United States that are active in the ecumenical movement and whose ministers study and respect the work of Paul Tillich and other great modern teachers are 'apostate?'" The evangelist said, "I could not possibly pass this type of judgment on individual churches and clergymen within The United Church of Canada—my knowledge of the United Church of Canada is too inadequate and my ability to make such discernment is too limited."

In another instance in the interview, a question that was asked concerned the virgin birth of Christ.

> Q. Do you think a literal belief in the Virgin birth—not just as a symbol of the incarnation or of Christ's divinity—as an historic event is necessary for personal salvation? A. While I most certainly believe that Jesus Christ was born of a virgin, I do not find anywhere in the New Testament that this particular belief is necessary for personal salvation.

The evangelist's answer here may be formally true in that the virgin birth is not made a specific article of saving faith. Yet the reply is evasive and incomplete. In general, Graham answered most of the questions ambiguously and with circumlocution when they clearly should have been covered more forthrightly. Obviously he was painfully sensitive to the theology of his liberal supporters in the United Church.

---

[34]"The Lost Chord of Evangelism," *Christianity Today* (April 1, 1957), p. 26.

[35]Robert Dunzweiler, *Billy Graham: A Critique*, pp. 19-20. In a letter, dated Jan 30, 1964, under the letterhead of the Billy Graham Evangelistic Association, Minneapolis, Associate George L. Edstrom responded to an inquiring letter. "Many of Mr. Graham's critics do not know that our Follow-Up Department here sends every convert a series of letters urging them to get into a Bible believing church and unite in a church where there is real Christian fellowship. *It would be discriminatory for Mr. Graham to tell people which church to go to. He could not do this* and if he did, he would be criticized on this issue" (italics added).

[36]Kenneth Bagnell, managing editor (July 1, 1966), reprinted in the *Christian Beacon* (Aug 18, 1966).

When attempting to define a theological basis of Christian separation, Graham demurred on the doctrine of the verbal inerrancy of Scripture as a criterion. With somewhat circuitous logic he stated:

> I do not believe that the ground of our fellowship is to be the inerrancy of Scripture but, rather,...the deity of our Lord Jesus Christ. I myself hold to the verbal inspiration viewpoint; I think any other position is fraught with danger. However, many of the leading evangelicals, and even fundamentalists when pinned down, do not hold to the verbal inspiration of Scripture....Yet I know devout men of God who believe in the virgin birth...atonement...resurrection...have strong evangelistic zeal...who do not hold to this particular theory of inspiration.[37]

A correspondent asked Graham why he did not preach on the blood of Christ in his crusades. On behalf of Graham, W.H. Martindale, a counselor for Graham's ministry, responded:

> There are many facets of the Christian life that Mr. Graham does not touch upon because he does not believe that they are the duty and responsibility of the evangelist. Mr. Graham believes that we are saved through the blood of Christ, however, this aspect of Christian doctrine he does not emphasize in his messages. This is the duty and prerogative of the pastors.[38]

Martindale did not offer an opinion as to how the sponsoring pastors who do not believe in the atoning blood of Christ could preach on it truthfully. The offense of "this aspect of Christian doctrine" to his liberal friends and backers is undoubtedly reason enough why the evangelist himself did not preach on it.

Mr. Graham has been a Baptist all his life and presumably believes in the immersion baptism of believers. In 1961 a flap arose over an interview he gave with Wilfred Bockelman, editor of the *Lutheran Standard,* in which he clearly affirmed paedobaptism (infant baptism) to be spiritually efficacious. The Graham office later said the evangelist was misquoted, a common response that was given during controversies of this sort. In the interview, Graham said:

> I have some difficulty in accepting the indiscriminate baptism of infants without a careful regard as to whether the parents have any intention of fulfilling the promises they make. But I do believe that something happens at the baptism of an infant, particularly if the parents are Christians and teach their children Christian truths from childhood.[39]

The editor went on to write that "Graham fully granted that not every Christian need have a violent emotional experience to which he can point as the beginning of his Christian life. He grants that there are many who were made Christians in infant baptism and who because of the Christian training in their homes never have known a time when they were not Christians."[40]

Perhaps the greatest shocker by Billy Graham came in recent years. In an appearance at Robert Schuller's Crystal Cathedral (May 31, 1997), Schuller asked,

---

[37]"Billy Graham on Separation," a personal letter released to *Eternity* (Nov 1958), pp. 18-19.

[38]Letter written by W. H. Martindale, dated Feb 29, 1968, under the letterhead of the Billy Graham Evangelistic Association, Minneapolis, MN. Fundamentalism Archives, Bob Jones University, Greenville, SC.

[39]"A Lutheran Looks at Billy Graham," *Lutheran Standard* (Oct 10, 1961), p. 12.

[40]Ibid.

"Tell me, what do you think is the future of Christianity?" Graham replied in part,

> I don't think we're going to see a great sweeping revival, that will turn the whole world to Christ at any time....James said that God's purpose for this age is to call out a people for His name. And that's what God is doing today, He's calling people out of the world for His name, whether they come from the Muslim world, or the Buddhist world, or the Christian world or the non-believing world, they are members of the Body of Christ because they've been called by God. They may not even know the name of Jesus but they know in their hearts that they need something that they don't have, and they turn to the only light that they have, and I think that they are saved, and that they're going to be with us in heaven."[41]

As if he couldn't believe his ears, Schuller then asked, "What, what I hear you saying that it's possible for Jesus Christ to come into human hearts and soul and life, even if they've been born in darkness and have never had exposure to the Bible. Is that a correct interpretation of what you're saying?" Graham replied:

> Yes, it is, because I believe that. I've met people in various parts of the world in tribal situations, that they have never seen a Bible or heard about a Bible, and never heard of Jesus, but they've believed in their hearts that there was a God, and they've tried to live a life that was quite apart from the surrounding community in which they lived.[42]

The article goes on: "[R.S. trips over his tongue for a moment, his face beaming, then says] I'm so glad to hear you say this. There's a wideness in God's mercy. GRAHAM: There is. There definitely is."[43] If his words mean anything, the evangelist is denying the patent New Testament truth that Jesus Christ is the only way to God and salvation.

While a formal link may be impossible to prove, it is hardly deniable that Graham's long associations with those who hold to these heretical ideas finally caused him to believe them also, or at least to feign belief in them. So in forty years, from the declaration in 1957 to go anywhere as long as "no strings" were attached, to the Schuller incident in 1997, the disastrous naivete of such a policy was being played out on the national and international stage of ecumenical evangelism.

Bob Jones Sr., a seasoned evangelist who was at the height of his ministry during World War I, said with near prescience of the new evangelical inclusive policy:

> If Billy Graham is right in his evangelistic approach, then all of the great evangelists who have lived for fifty years have all been wrong. I am sure that Billy Graham is sacrificing the cause of evangelism on the altar of a temporary convenience. All of the evangelists who have lived for fifty years have made mistakes....But not one of them ever made the fatal mistake that Billy Graham is making. Billy Graham is the only evangelist I have ever known who is doing the type work that is destroying the foundation upon which the evangelistic house is built.[44]

---

[41]Robert E. Kofahl, "Graham Believes Men Can Be Saved Apart From Name of Christ," *Christian News* (Oct 20, 1997), p. 15.

[42]Ibid.

[43]Ibid.

[44]"Letter To a Friend," March 6, 1957.

The doctrine of ecclesiastical separation, the biblical antidote and answer to inclusivism, will be defended in due course, but it can be noted here that the New Testament has a pattern of sponsorship and cooperation that is in clear opposition to the new evangelical practice (2 John 9-11; Gal 1:8-9; 1 Tim 6:3-5; Rom 16:17).

Convert Referrals

A third objection against ecumenical evangelism has to do with convert/ decision card referrals. Ecumenical evangelism refers inquirers to the church of their choice, and if there is no preference, a committee of local ministers selects one.[45] Consequently inquirers are routed to all sorts of places.[46] For example, from the Greater London (Harringay) Crusade (1954), only 10% expressed no preference.[47] Other early statistics tell the same story.[48] This means that nearly all the converts go back to the churches they once attended or knew about while still unsaved. Liberal Protestant churches, Greek Orthodox churches, and Roman Catholic churches were all sent the names of inquirers from the ecumenical crusades.

A special handling of those of the Jewish faith developed because of complaints by Jews of being proselytized or evangelized by the evangelicals. In an interview by Rabbi Arthur Gilbert (of the New York staff of the Anti-Defamation League) with Graham, the rabbi reported the following: "When Jews step forward at his crusades, [Graham] makes no special missionary appeal for their conversion. He urges that they study Hebrew Scripture, certain, he said, that they will find the Messiah in the words of the Old Testament." He quotes Graham: "Jews have a right to be respected for what they are—a people who live still by the light of God in the Old Testament." The evangelist went on: "It is my conviction that Christ is the only way to God's forgiving love, but it ill behooves me to judge Jews as a people lost to salvation. God, in His own time and way, will judge all men by the light according to which they live." The rabbi concluded by saying, "I left Montreat [Graham's home] satisfied that our dialogue would continue, encouraged that evangelicals are no longer inaccessible. I left Montreat respectful of Christianity—and strengthened in my Judaism."[49] During the Key 73 effort (an evangelical program to evangelize the North American continent in 1973), Jews were upset that they would be proselytized into faith in Jesus Christ. Graham, in a verbal circumlocution, virtually assured them that there would be no disturbance of Jews.[50] At least that is how Rabbi Marc Tannenbaum interpreted the evangelist's words.[51]

---

[45]John Pollock, *Billy Graham: The Authorized Biography*, p. 198.

[46]Robert Dunzweiler, *Billy Graham: A Critique*, pp. 20-24.

[47]"Billy Graham's Story: New Crusade in Europe," *U.S. News and World Report* (Aug 27, 1954) p. 89.

[48]Robert Dunzweiler, quoting William G. McLoughlin, Jr., *Billy Graham—Revivalist in a Secular Age*, relates that 87% of seekers in Detroit (1953), 95% in Nashville (1954), and 94% Oklahoma City (1956) gave a church preference.

[49]The interview appeared in the Anti-Defamation League Bulletin (Dec 1967) and was quoted in the *Fundamental Baptist Information Bulletin* (May-June 1968).

[50]"Billy Graham on Key 73," *Christianity Today* (Mar 16, 1973), p. 29.

[51]"Tannenbaum: Response and Rejoinder," *Christianity Today* (Mar 30, 1973), p. 48. A UPI dispatch noted: "Rabbi Marc Tannenbaum said Graham's remarks would encourage other Christian leaders to 'make clear that Key 73 is aimed at reaching uncommitted Christians and has no intention of

In an interview in *McCall's* that caused considerable controversy and denial, the interviewer reported this:

> In recent years Graham has shown particular affection for Jews. Like most Christian Fundamentalists, Graham once believed that Jews, too, were lost if they did not convert to Christianity. Today Graham is willing to leave that up to God. "God does the saving," Graham asserts. "I'm told to preach Christ as the only way to salvation. But it is God who is going to do the judging, not Billy Graham."[52]

The effectiveness of the ecumenical convert referral system was questioned quite early on. Erroll Hulse, a pastor in England, and his wife followed up twenty-six seekers from the Wembley Crusade (1955). They found that two or three, who had been in church before, were still there. A pastor friend followed up on ninety decisions from the Harringay Crusade (1954), and he knew of only two that had stood.[53] James E. Bennet, a New York attorney, reported of the New York Crusade (1957):

> A pastor in one of the churches told me that he had received 33 cards from the Crusade office and 32 of them were useless and the one remaining might possibly prove to be a convert. Another pastor reported to his congregation that out of 30 cards received, none were prospective "deciders" for Christ. Another said that he had received 5 cards, 4 of which represented people already in the church and the other he could not locate.[54]

From the San Francisco Cow Palace Crusade (1958) came this report:

> The Billy Graham crusade in the Cow Palace stirred up the faithful and the backsliders but had only a negligible impact on those with no prior church affiliation. Approximately 1300 people made decisions at the Cow Palace who had not frequented a church before. Less than one per cent of this number have become church members. These findings along with other statistics and evaluations of the Cow Palace crusade were announced yesterday by Dr. Charles Farrah of the crusade follow-up team. He has been gathering data since June on the crusade's effectiveness.[55]

Farrah went on to report that the percentage of follow-up of decision cards in the Bay Area was very high. Of the 26,696 people who made decisions, 96% were personally contacted, compared with New York where only 36% were contacted. While the poor follow-up in New York may not be directly the fault of

---

proselytizing the Jewish community'" (Mar 30, 1973). For other material on Key 73 and the Jews, see Solomon S. Bernards, "Key 73—A Jewish View," *The Christian Century* (Jan 3, 1973), pp. 12-19; Leslie K. Tarr, "Key 73: No Violation," *Christianity Today* (Mar 16, 1973), p. 39; Andre Lacocue, "Key 73, Judaism, and the Tragedy of Triumphalism," *The Christian Century* (May 30, 1973), pp. 629-31; Susan Pearlman, "Furor Over Jewish Evangelism," *Eternity* (April 1973), pp. 20-23, 47; and the *Key 73 Congregational Resource Book* (St. Louis: Concordia Publishing House, n.d. [1972]). A good overall look at Key 73 from the fundamentalist position is M. H. Reynolds Jr., *Key 73: An Appraisal* (Los Angeles: FEA Press, 1972).

[52]James Michael Beam, "I Can't Play God Any More," *McCall's* (Jan 1978), p. 158.

[53]Erroll Hulse, *Billy Graham—The Pastor's Dilemma*, pp. 11-12. Iain H. Murray gave similar reports on the 1954 Harringay Crusade and the 1966-67 Greater London crusades. *Evangelicals Divided: A Record of Crucial Change In the Years 1950-2000* (Carlisle, PA: Banner of Truth Trust, 2000), pp. 56-57.

[54]*Christian Beacon* (Aug 1, 1957).

[55]Bill Rose, "Effectiveness of Graham Visit Studied," *Oakland Tribune* (Dec 17, 1958), p. 6S.

the ecumenical evangelist, it is still a most undesirable element in the wake of the ecumenical crusade. Farrah also noted that "approximately 5 percent of those making decisions here were Roman Catholic....Nearly all of this number have remained Roman Catholic.[56] Farrah's conclusion in 1958 was quite apt and is applicable to twenty-first century evangelistic inclusivism as well: "Very few churches were able to gain new adherents by contacting those whose decision cards were assigned to the church but who had no previous contact with the particular church."[57]

Sherwood Wirt, a friend of ecumenical evangelism, in writing a book on the San Francisco Crusade (1958), said of the "decisions" being counted in the meetings:

> Human nature being what it is, there were undoubtedly twenty-eight thousand reasons why the twenty-eight thousand people came forward at the San Francisco Crusade. Some came admittedly just for kicks. Some came out of the curiosity to find out what went on in the counseling room. Some went down because girl friends or boy friends did, and it was less conspicuous (so it seemed) to go than to remain behind. Some were really confused. Some were Roman Catholic, and went forward as one would go to light a candle in an act of devotion. Some little children went along because they had to accompany their older brothers and sisters. Some adults were seeking background material for a term paper on religion. Some simply wanted a closer look at Billy Graham. At least one man went forward in an attempt to restore his sanity.[58]

A report from the Oakland, CA, Crusade (1971) said that

> ministers evaluating the July Billy Graham crusade in Oakland have estimated that about one third of the 21,670 who registered "decisions for Christ" gave false names and addresses....The ministers, attending a meeting of the Eastbay Fellowship of the NAE, also noted that very few of the "unchurched people" referred to them for follow-up are responsive to invitations to attend their churches. "Many of these contacts give you the 'don't-call-me, I'll-call-you' business when you visit them," reported the Rev. Dan Seagren of the Berkeley Covenant Church.[59]

The Institute For American Church Growth in Pasadena, CA, conducted an intensive research of the 1976 Seattle Crusade. This crusade was chosen because Graham's *Decision* magazine said it was the most successful up to that point in the evangelist's crusade history.[60] Twelve hundred participating pastors were contacted.

> The study found that 53% of the registered decisions were made by church members rededicating their lives to Christ. Of the non-churchgoers who made decisions, 85% had not joined any church within a year after the crusade. Of those who did join a church, 80% had friends or relatives attending the church they joined. Of the total number who attended the crusade, only 4.2% made decisions for Christ and only .3% were incorporated into a local church body.[61]

---

[56]Ibid. In today's ecumenical crusades, where Roman Catholics are given full participation in sponsorship, singing in the crusade choir, appearing on the public platform with the evangelist, counseling inquirers, and receiving decision cards, this sort of statistic is ho-hum. But in 1958 it was an alarming concern and omen in the minds of fundamentalists who uniformly opposed the inclusive policy.

[57]Bill Rose, "Effectiveness of Graham Visit Studied," p. 6S.

[58]Sherwood Eliot Wirt, *Crusade At the Golden Gate* (New York: Harper, 1959), pp. 148-49.

[59]"Crusade Aftermath," *The Baptist Bulletin* (Jan 1972), p. 6.

[60]"Graham Crusade Gets Church Growth Study," *Eternity* (April 1978), p. 11.

[61]Ibid.

The institute conducted a similar study of the Here's Life America campaign (1976) organized by Campus Crusade for Christ. "Like the Graham crusade, Here's Life was found to be ineffective in terms of church growth. In the several cities under study, less than 4 of every 10 decisions (3.3%) resulted in new church members, and of these, 42% had transferred from another church."[62]

The opinion and informed evaluation of inclusive evangelism by Bob Jones, Sr. is almost prophetic. In view of the 1957 New York Crusade, Jones foretold:

> I am convinced that when you consider the publicity, the way the work is headlined, the crowds that are being drawn, and the money that is being spent, Billy Graham is having possibly the smallest percentage of conversions of any evangelist who has lived for fifty years or any evangelist who is living today and is being sponsored by orthodox, Bible-believing pastors and churches. When the returns come in, we are going to find that some of these "little" men you have never heard of and whose budgets are not heavy and who never make the headlines have led more people to Jesus Christ than Billy Graham is doing.[63]

> Some people say that if an evangelistic campaign produces one convert, the crusade has been worth it. That is not true. The evangelist…is given to the Body of Christ. The real test of an evangelistic campaign is not how many people are converted but in what kind of spiritual condition does it leave a community.[64]

The New Testament method is for new converts to be baptized in water as a public testimony of faith, to become a member of a local New Testament church and come under its discipline for instruction and learning, and to fulfill the Great Commission within the ministry and outreach of that local church (Matt 28:18-20; Acts 2:41-42; 2 Tim 2:2). The evangelist definitely has the responsibility of spiritually nurturing converts, including warning them against false teachers and false churches. To do otherwise is to tempt God concerning His keeping power. William K. Harrison defended sending converts back to modernist churches by saying, "Who knows that converts going to a modernist church may not be God's witness in that church until such time as they leave or are expelled."[65] Billy Graham also absolved himself from the responsibility of the converts.[66] However, the New Testament instructs both the mature and the immature in spiritual things, including warnings against false doctrine and teachers—Matthew 7:15 ("Beware of false prophets who come to you in sheep's clothing, but inwardly are ravenous wolves"); John 21:15, 16, 17 ("tend My lambs," "shepherd My sheep," and "tend My sheep"); Acts 20:26-30 ("Be on guard for yourselves and for all the flock," "savage wolves will come in," and "from among yourselves men will arise, speaking perverse things"); Colossians 1:28 ("admonishing every man and

---

[62]Ibid.

[63]"Letter to a Friend," March 6, 1957.

[64]Ibid.

[65]"General Harrison Answers Graham Critics," *Christianity Today* (Jan 21, 1957), p. 33.

[66]"The Lost Chord of Evangelism," p. 26. This was the address he gave before the National Association of Evangelicals in Buffalo, NY, April 3, 1957, in which he formally put forth his inclusive policy for the upcoming New York Crusade in September.

teaching every man with all wisdom"); and 2 Timothy 2:2 ("The things you have heard from me...entrust to faithful men who will be able to teach others also").

THE FAILURE OF ECUMENICAL EVANGELISM

The inclusive policy of new evangelical evangelism turned out to be, as fundamentalists feared and warned, a colossal failure. The ecumenical evangelist puts himself into the position where he is unable to speak against apostasy because he has apostate ministers in his sponsorship, and he is unwilling to speak against unorthodox denominations and institutions because he believes there are many fine Christians still in them. (Carl Henry once said that sixty percent of the clergy and members of the National Council of Churches was evangelical.[67]) The evangelical ecumenist's ignorance, naivete, or deliberate planning played into the liberals' hands. Post-Enlightenment liberal/neo-orthodox Christianity soon turns sterile and unable to reproduce itself. Consequently those churches empty out because all there is to hear is pious-sounding God-talk—empty, banal rhetoric that has nothing of substance to satisfy the human spirit. Denominational Protestantism in the USA and abroad in the post-World War II years of the 1940s and 50s illustrated this anemic condition. Meanwhile the post-war evangelical/fundamentalist coalition was experiencing remarkable results in mass evangelism. The liberals sought to catch this swelling tide of evangelism and thus fill their empty churches. By the technique of ecumenical inclusivism they were able to join the evangelicals in cooperative evangelism and share the amazing numerical success that it brought. For example, the Greater London Crusade (1954) provided this service for the liberals. The liberal Bishop of London, J. W. C. Wand, said, "Dr. Graham served us well by carefully handing on the names and addresses of enquirers to the ministers and parochial clergy of all denominations."[68] Geoffrey Fisher, then the Archbishop of Canterbury, in the *Canterbury Diocesan Notes*, commended the ecumenical evangelist: "One striking feature was the elaborate steps that were taken to pass on all enquirers to the particular Christian body to which each had been in the past or now desired to be attached."[69] Leslie Weatherhead, liberal pastor of City Temple, London, in *City Temple Tidings*, noted:

> What does fundamentalist theology matter compared with gathering in the people we have all missed, and getting them to the point of decision? Theology comes much later....[Graham] offered them the good news of Christ, and I should have thought that any Minister who frequently preaches to small congregations might rejoice that Billy Graham is helping to fill our churches for us. We can teach theology when we have got somebody to teach.[70]

Ecumenical evangelism resided in the minds of the liberals years before it was in the minds of the evangelicals. Monroe Parker, a fundamentalist evangelist and an assistant to the president, Bob Jones Sr., at Bob Jones University, recalled taking summer school work at Princeton Seminary in 1945. Princeton president,

---

[67]Carl F. H. Henry, *Evangelicals At the Brink of Crisis* (Waco: TX: Word, 1967), p. 104.

[68]Quoted by Michael Boland, "Co-operative Evangelism at Harringay," *The Banner of Truth* 42 (May/June 1966), p. 9.

[69]Ibid.

[70]Ibid., p. 10. A similar report is given by Iain H. Murray, *Evangelicalism Divided*, pp. 35, 55.

John MacKay, had returned from Amsterdam and gathered the faculty and students on the lawn at Princeton. He said [paraphrased by Parker], "There are several great denominations coming together [in the World Council of Churches]. The Greek Catholics will likely join, the Roman Catholics are observing, the Pentecostals are interested, but we're going to need the evangelicals—*but there must be a new evangelicalism*" (emphasis added).[71] In the summer of 1946 Parker was studying at Columbia University where he heard Paul Scherer say [paraphrased],

> We modernists have led the world astray. We have preached our humanism and our pacifism, and we have told the people that humanity is too good to wage war anymore. We are responsible for the war through which we have just passed. We stand with our hands dripping with the life blood of the nations. We need to retrace our footsteps back toward the old orthodox position of our fathers. But shall we go back to that position? NO! NO! NO! We need to go back in that direction until we can strike a synthesis with the evangelicals. *What we need is a new modernism*" (emphasis added).[72]

In September 1950, Parker heard John MacKay at Princeton Seminary relate the following:

> This past summer I passed through Portland, Oregon, at a time when evangelist Billy Graham was being listened to by crowds of over one hundred thousand. I learned that churches in the great Oregon city were getting behind that simple, non-college trained young man,[73] an intimate friend of our own Charles Templeton. The churches cannot ignore the phenomenon which this young man presents. And then there's the Youth For Christ movement, and the Inter-Varsity movement, the Pentecostals—all of whom are doing an amazing work in many parts of the world. These groups are often frowned upon as Christianity's "lunatic fringe" because of certain objectionable features which they manifest. Yet according to the clear evidence of spiritual results, they are doing a great work in which God is present. As to the fruits that may be garnered into the storehouse of the Christian Church, that will depend upon the sympathy, the good judgment, and the statesmanship of Christian churchmen. Among the things which I have learned in my lifetime, both by experience and observation, is this: Never to be afraid of the young fanatic or of what appears to be a fanatical movement, if Jesus Christ appears to be the supreme object of devotion....The young fanatic, if wisely dealt with, can be toned down and mellowed.[74]

To show further how the new evangelical inclusive policy was engineered by liberals who reaped great benefits from it, consider the astute churchmanship of neo-liberal Walter Marshall Horton in 1953:

---

[71]"Backgrounds to New Evangelicalism," chapel message by Monroe Parker containing reflections, recollections, and reminiscences of his experiences during the formative years of the new evangelicalism, Detroit Baptist Theological Seminary, Allen Park, MI (Dec 6, 1985).

[72]Ibid. See also a terse summary of this quote in Monroe Parker, *More Precious Than Gold* (Long Prairie, MN: Hart Press, 1963), p. 40. Paul Sherer was pastor of the Evangelical Lutheran Church of the Holy Trinity in New York City and professor of preaching at Union Theology Seminary (NY) in 1946.

[73]Either Parker or MacKay is in error here. Seminary training is probably meant; Graham was in fact college trained.

[74]Monroe Parker, *More Precious Than Gold*, pp. 40-41. Parker notes: "Remember, that statement was made in 1950 at Princeton. In 1957 Dr. Mackay was among the sponsors of Billy Graham's New York Campaign" (p. 41).

I do not believe the leaders of the ecumenical movement are going to be able to change the feelings or allay the suspicions of the Conservative Evangelicals sufficiently to bring them fully into the I.M.C. [International Missionary Council] or the World Council in the near future; but they can do two things which may make future reconciliation possible; one, keep in personal touch with the evangelical leaders, answering their sometimes captious criticisms with patience and not with scorn; and, two *conduct evangelistic campaigns and world missions with an earnestness which their rivals cannot fail to respect and a constant willingness to collaborate on particular evangelistic projects.*

A generation of such tolerant, respectful relations might actually lead to unity, since there is an almost invariable historic law that evangelistic movements become less separatistic in the second generation (italics added).[75]

E. Stanley Jones, a neo-orthodox Methodist missionary to India, in the mid-1950s saw Billy Graham and ecumenical evangelism as a "synthesis" between conservatism and liberalism, all to the benefit of the non-evangelical.

If there is truth in Hegel's dictum, and I believe there is, that thought moves from thesis to antithesis to synthesis, then it seems to be applicable to the controversy regarding the Graham crusade going on in your pages....The thesis in this controversy in its larger aspects is conservatism, and it has produced its opposite, liberalism....Out of this struggle of thesis and antithesis there is emerging a something which seems to be gathering up the truth in each in a higher synthesis. The Graham crusade is a symptom of that emerging synthesis....The synthesis is emerging at a very important place—at the place of evangelism. There conservative and liberal could join in the only place they could get together—at the place of making Christ known to people inside and outside the churches who need conversion....After talking personally with Billy Graham I am persuaded that he is more or less consciously one of the meeting places of this movement toward synthesis....[76]

Neo-liberal/neo-orthodox Protestantism, through its shrewd use of diplomatic churchmanship and the eager but naive complicity of evangelical revivalists, turned the tide of its near collapse after World War II. These Protestants hoped to see their empty pews filled, thanks to the multiplied thousands referred to them by the new evangelical evangelists. And they could again see their theologians, preachers, and denominational executives being featured as great spiritual and ecclesiastical leaders before the enormous crowds and in the publicity of the ecumenical crusades. The non-evangelicals had nothing to lose in yoking up with the evangelicals; for the evangelicals, it was just the reverse.[77]

---

[75]Walter Marshall Horton, *Toward A Reborn Church* (San Francisco: Harper, 1953), pp. 30-31.

[76]E. Stanley Jones, "Letter To the Editor," *Christianity Today* (Aug 14, 1957), p. 970. The letter is titled by the editor, "Higher Synthesis?"

[77]These optimistic hopes of the liberals, in England at least, were found to be illusory in succeeding years as lasting results from the crusades did not materialize. See Iain H. Murray, *Evangelicalism Divided*, pp. 57-58.

6

ECUMENICAL
CHURCH COUNCILS

The conciliar movement, as used here, is composed of groups of contemporary cooperative ecumenical agencies united around minimal religious tenets in order to promote social, political, spiritual, or ecclesiastical goals. Various "councils" have arisen to further these ends. These groups, in power structure and motif, have always been liberal, neo-orthodox, or at least unorthodox or non-evangelical, and definitely anti-fundamentalist. Fundamentalism has always stood against this movement. At first new evangelicalism was negative toward this movement but eventually it became sympathetic, then positive. Finally new evangelicalism promoted conciliarism.

THE NATIONAL COUNCIL OF CHURCHES
The National Council of Churches of Christ in the USA (NCC) arose in 1950 as a coalition of interdenominational agencies. It favored the structure, ecumenical goals, and social gospel ideals of the Federal Council of Churches established in 1908. While its purpose statement sounded evangelical ("Jesus Christ as the divine Lord and Savior"[1]), the ultimate purposes, goals, and strategies of the NCC were not. The premier new evangelical coalition, the National Association of Evangelicals (NAE), from its beginning (1942) postured itself ambivalently toward the National Council (then called the Federal Council). The founding fathers and leadership of the NAE opposed the NCC in principle, often voicing concerns publicly; however they were quite unwilling to go on record in any formal way as opposing the Federal Council for fear of alienating any would-be evangelicals who were sympathetic to the Council.[2]

The majority of new evangelicals, especially the leadership, favored participation in the National Council. The anti-separatist new evangelical

---

[1]*Dictionary of Christianity in America*, s.v. "National Council of Churches of Christ in the U.S.A.," by P. A. Crow, pp. 798-99.

[2]The ecclesiastical separation issue, the crux of which was the attitude toward the Federal Council, divided the NAE from the fundamentalist American Council of Christian Churches begun by Carl McIntire in 1941. See chapter three, "The Unity/Separation Issue: The National Association of Evangelicals (1942)," pp. 16-22, 30-34.

philosophy of "infiltration" of the mainline denominations encouraged involvement, but it was not until the early 1960s that wider new evangelical interest in the NCC became obvious.

Collaboration with the NCC quite naturally rose out of the milieu of ecumenical evangelism led by its titular head, Billy Graham. The NCC promoted its local agenda and functioned through state and city-wide councils. Such was the case with the Graham 1957 New York Crusade. The Protestant Council of New York was "the No. 1 local council affiliated with the National Council of Churches,"[3] and it was also the primary sponsor and promoter of the Crusade. In addition, various NCC executives or department heads staffed the crusade organizational committee and wielded influence on behalf of the Council and liberal churches in general. The Graham crusade left nearly $68,000 with the Protestant Council for further evangelism and follow-up.[4] By 1960 cozy relations between the NCC and new evangelical evangelism had become apparent. In December, 1960 Graham formally addressed a crowd of 1800 sponsored by the Christian Men's Assembly in connection with the opening of the third triennium convention of the NCC meeting in San Francisco. This address was from the pulpit of the Grace Cathedral at Bishop James A. Pike's invitation. "In his closing prayer, Dr. Graham offered a special petition for the success of the current assembly of the National Council of Churches, and prayed that 'out of this meeting there may come a great message to the Christian world.'"[5] At the 1966 Miami meeting of the NCC Graham again anchored the key note speakers. Graham told the group: "I am honored and privileged to be here to participate with you, and I would like to put it in those terms, to participate with you—in finding answers to some of the great problems that are faced in the field of evangelism today."[6]

In 1988 the National Council of Churches sponsored a conclave in Arlington, TX, "A Gathering of Christians—Pentecost 1988: No Longer Strangers." In a firsthand report, fundamentalist Dennis Costella summed up the conclave's purpose: "This gathering was designed to offer groups and individuals outside the official membership of the NCC an opportunity to experience the supposed joys of ecumenism in a non-threatening, non-judgmental, 'anything goes' context."[7] Ron Sider, a prominent new evangelical social activist, encouraged evangelicals to participate in the National Council programs. "It is long past time," he said, " when any Christian dare refuse to listen, share and worship with other Christians who confess Jesus Christ as God and Savior according to the Scriptures."[8] He also noted

---

[3]Carl McIntire, *The National Council of Churches, 1957* (Collingswood, NJ: Christian Beacon Press, 1957), p. 36.

[4]Ibid.

[5] NCC news release, *San Francisco Examiner* (Dec 5, 1960) as quoted by G. Archer Weniger, "The National Council of Churches," *Conservative Baptist Fellowship Information Bulletin* (Dec 1960-Jan 1961), p. 6.

[6]G. Archer Weniger, "Dr. Billy Graham and the National Council of Churches," *Sword of the Lord* (Sept 19, 1969), p. 12.

[7]Dennis W. Costella, "A Gathering of Christians," *Foundations* (Apr-June 1988), p. 11.

[8]Ron Sider, "Plenaries, Workshops, Forums Take Shape for May 1988 'Gathering of Christians,'" *The Christian News* (Apr 4, 1988), p. 1.

that "the Gathering of Christians is one of the first major church events where Catholics, Evangelicals, Protestants and Orthodox Christians join together in a celebration of their common faith in Christ. I hope this Gathering is the beginning step on the road to increased dialogue, fellowship, and common action."[9] Richard Lovelace, church history professor at Gordon-Conwell Theological Seminary, speaking as an evangelical, said, "You can't be really spiritual without being radically ecumenical, and you can't be truly ecumenical unless you are radically spiritual."[10] Evangelical educator, Tony Campolo, professor of sociology at Eastern Baptist College, addressed a plenary session on "Beholding the New" in which he stressed a pacifism of positive love gained through sacrifice as the way to minister in today's world. Love and power are inversely related, he averred; if one loves, he cannot dominate the one he loves, and vice versa. Campolo used Mother Teresa as a paradigm of this positive love, an authority she gained through sacrifice on the streets of Calcutta.[11]

The anomaly of this evangelical fraternization with the NCC in the 1980s is that the NCC had been suffering financially. By the late 1980s the funding crisis had become visible, mostly due to the fact that the NCC had become more politically liberal than the members of its constituent churches.[12] Funding dried up.[13] To prop up the ailing finances, Graham met with NCC leaders at their headquarters in New York in August 1991 to discuss ways to broaden the NCC's base. The NCC press released (Aug 27, 1991) the following:

> Focusing on the need for unity among all Christians, Graham and NCC General Secretary Joan Brown Campbell pledged to increase understanding and fellowship between conservative evangelicals and mainline Protestants....Graham responded... "There's no group of people in the world I'd rather be with right now than you," he told NCC staff members and other religious leaders. "I think of you, I pray for you [and] follow with great interest the things you do....The world looks on us and sees our divisions and our problems, and they're turned off," he said. "But if they could just see that we love each other and we work together because we believe in Jesus Christ, that would be one of the greatest things that could happen."[14]

During the decade of the 1990s the National Council's financial troubles continued with a budget shortfall of nearly $6.4 million by 1999. Due to the Council's poor business practices, unwise investments, and overall fiscal irresponsibility, the largest member denomination, the United Methodist Church, "not only declined in October [1999] to consider giving an emergency gift to the Council, but voted to suspend all financial support of the NCC, citing

---

[9]Quoted by Costella, "A Gathering of Christians," p. 12.

[10]Ibid., p. 13.

[11]Ibid. See also "Plenaries, Workshops, Forums," p. 23.

[12]Even a secular sociologist deplored the NCC "supporting revolution instead of religion." Rael Jean Isaac, "Do You Know Where Your Church Offerings Go?" *Reader's Digest* (Jan 1983 reprint).

[13]Randy Frame, "The National Council of Churches in Crisis," *Christianity Today* (Jan 13, 1989), pp. 49-50.

[14]"The Graham Touch: Salvation and Unity," *The American Baptist* (Jan/Feb, 1992), p. 11, quoted in George Houghton, "Some Thoughts on Ecumenical Evangelism—A Case Study," *Faith Pulpit* (April 1995).

uneasiness with the NCC's debt load and financial operations."[15] However, the UMC reconsidered its stance and in November gave the NCC an emergency grant of $400,000 to keep its doors open. To further exacerbate the NCC's woes, the influential Church World Service, a relief organization under the auspices of the National Council, voted in 1999 to break away from the Council. To keep itself afloat, the NCC aggressively reached out to conservative Protestants, Roman Catholics, and charismatics. As the NCC general secretary put it: "It is time for the Christian community to kiss and make up....It is time to risk ourselves and examine what a national ecumenical organization could look like in a new century."[16] The National Association of Evangelicals, always ambivalent toward the National Council, took a "landmark step of its own [by changing] its bylaws to allow NCC members to join the NAE if they commit to NAE's statement of faith and mission."[17] A spokesman for the Reformed Church in America optimistically opined: "I trust that we can build bridges between divided parts of the Christian community for the sake of our common witness to the world."[18]

In retrospect, ironically, rather than allow an apostate organization like the NCC to meet an appropriate and well-earned demise, the new evangelicals, as professing Bible believers, have been trying to do as much as non-evangelicals to keep the Council on ecclesiastical life support.

THE WORLD COUNCIL OF CHURCHES

The World Council of Churches is a twentieth-century confluence of three tributaries, some of whose headwaters reach back into the eighteenth- and nineteenth-centuries' missionary movements.[19] The first tributary is represented by the Universal Christian Council on Life and Work, organized in meetings in 1920 (at Geneva), 1925 (at Stockholm), and 1937 (at Oxford) to handle urgent social problems worldwide. Similarly, the World Conference on Faith and Order organized meetings in 1920 (at Geneva), 1927 (at Lausanne), and 1937 (at Edinburgh) to deal with theology and liturgy. These two tributaries agreed to form the World Council of Churches in 1938 (at Utrecht) but encountered delays until 1948 (at Amsterdam) because of World War II. The International Missionary Council, rising from a gathering of missionary leaders in Edinburgh in 1910 and formally organized in 1921, formed the final stream. The IMC and the WCC merged at the WCC Assembly in New Delhi in 1961.

On paper, the WCC sported an evangelical trinitarian doctrinal basis and a commitment to spread the gospel of Jesus Christ; however, the WCC has never

---

[15]Jean Caffey Lyles, "The National Council of Churches: Is There Life after 50?" *The Christian Century* (Nov 10, 1999), p. 1086.

[16]Jody Veenker, "Time to Kiss and Make Up?" *Christianity Today* (Aug 7, 2000), p. 21.

[17]Ibid.

[18]Ibid.

[19]The following historical data was gleaned from "The Russians Join the World Council," *Time* (Dec 1, 1961), p. 61; John H. Piersma, "The Historical Background of the World Council of Churches," *Torch and Trumpet* (Feb 1962), pp. 14-17; and *Dictionary of Christianity in America*, s.v. "World Council of Churches," by P. A. Crow, pp. 1273-75.

produced a consensus definition of its theological language. In reality, the Council has heavily embraced liberal theology, the social gospel, and an unwavering commitment to the ecumenical movement. Between 1961 and 1968, social and political activism dominated the WCC's agenda. Doctrine and true missionary enterprises receded into the background. After 1968, doctrinal issues disappeared.[20]

Donald Grey Barnhouse in 1953 began searching for an expanded circle of Christian fellowship based on minimal doctrinal considerations. "I want to make my circle of Christian fellowship on the basis of the fact that a man is going to be in Heaven with me...but with whom I have disagreed on denominational emphasis."[21] He attended the 1954 World Council meeting in Evanston, IL and generated favorable impressions and evaluations of the Council. He testified that the WCC was not a super-church and that "in spite of an apparent inconsistency the majority of leaders do not seek the uniting of all denominations in a world church."[22] Barnhouse commended, however, the formation of the Church of Christ of South India out of the five major missionary agencies that worked there—the Church of England, American Congregationalists, Northern Baptists, Southern Methodists, and Scotch Presbyterians.[23] In 1957 Barnhouse's protégé, Walter R. Martin, testified favorably of the World Council. He admitted that "true unity in the Christian Church can never be achieved this side of Heaven," but he appreciated the ecumenical efforts of the World Council:

> The World Council of Churches is making such an attempt, though there are still elements within it that are hostile to the historic faith of Christianity and which, although weakened over the past decade, continue as a threat to true Christianity....Unless [the World Council's] sincerity be doubted, theirs is a praiseworthy attitude in the tradition of Christian unity and understanding.[24]

Beginning in the early 1960s the new evangelicals appeared as enthusiastic, if not more so, about the World Council than they had been about the National Council of Churches. Shortly after the 1961 New Delhi merger of the IMC with the WCC evangelicals encouraged evangelical participation in the World Council. Russell T. Hitt, editor of *Eternity* magazine, criticized the evangelicals for displaying aloofness from the WCC and criticized the WCC for its liberal constituency. He noted that many dedicated Christians were working in New Delhi.[25] Later he reported that some evangelicals in the WCC Faith and Order Committee welcomed Roman Catholics because they had more in common with them than with many liberal Protestants.[26] Similarly, Paul S. Rees, reporting on the Uppsala Assembly of the WCC (1968), said that evangelicals had many Christian brothers in the WCC and

---

[20]Harold O. J. Brown, "The World Council of Churches: Community or Conspiracy?" *Fundamentalist Journal* (April 1983), p. 29.

[21]Donald Grey Barnhouse, "New Year's Resolution," *Eternity* (Jan 1953), inside back cover.

[22]Donald Grey Barnhouse, "Evanston: What It Was," *Eternity* (Oct 1954), p. 8.

[23]Ibid.

[24]Walter R. Martin, "Oberlin Report: The World Council of Churches and Christian Unity," *Eternity* (Nov 1957), p. 43.

[25]Russell T. Hitt, "The World Council/New Delhi," *Eternity* (Feb 1962), pp. 10-12.

[26]Russell T. Hitt, "On Christendom—A Report From Uppsala," *Eternity* (Sept 1968), p. 9.

that he was not ashamed to sit with them. He named David Allan Hubbard, John R. W. Stott, G. C. Berkouwer, Leighton Ford, and others.[27] Hubbard, president of Fuller Seminary, defending his own presence at Uppsala, said: "Participation in theological councils of the church by conservative evangelicals is essential."[28]

Harold Lindsell took a middle-of-the-road stance toward the WCC, leaving open the question of whether evangelicals should stay in or pull out.[29] In a later article generally unfavorable toward the WCC, Lindsell still refused to advise evangelicals not to participate. Lindsell also reported that neither the Uppsala Assembly nor the WCC-sponsored World Conference on Salvation Today (Bangkok, 1973) "produced any full-orbed statement about salvation, conversion, evangelism, or the mission of the Church that is biblically sound and therefore acceptable to evangelicals. Indeed their statements are inimical to the evangelical viewpoint." He went on to say: "Evangelicals should say to those who truly believe that salvation is deliverance from political, economic, and social oppression: 'You do your thing and we'll pray for you; we'll do our thing and you pray for us.'" He closed the article with a conciliatory couple of paragraphs.[30]

Graham made it clear at a press conference that his Berlin Congress on Evangelism (1966) did not oppose the World Council of Churches. He claimed the WCC's officers and executives read Scripture and had participated in his 1969 New York Crusade.[31] At the Lausanne Congress on Evangelism (1974), Graham said,

> We have had, as far as I know, nothing but the warmest relationship with the World Council. In fact, I think that in their meeting in Bangkok, they voted to help in any way that they could. Bishop Dain [Anglican churchman from Australia, chairman of the Congress executive committee] has been in touch with them more than I have and perhaps he might add to that."[32]

Evangelical Peter Beyerhaus, commenting on the 1973 Bangkok World Conference on Salvation Today, sponsored by the WCC Commission on World Mission and Evangelism, noted with alarm that the concept of "salvation" in the WCC depicted any "liberating experience" under "a seemingly biblical cover," robbing the word of "its Christian distinctiveness." Nevertheless, he would not even hint that evangelicals should withdraw from the WCC. Beyerhaus' only commentary blandly appealed to evangelicals: "We [evangelicals] are now challenged to present the biblical alternatives by articulating our faith and by acting accordingly in obedience to Christ's Great Commission."[33]

In the 1980s and 90s strong calls from evangelicals to get involved in the World Council continued. Concerning the 1983 WCC Assembly in Vancouver, Richard Lovelace, professor of church history at Gordon Conwell Theological Seminary, reported:

---

[27]Paul S. Rees, "Influencing a Conglomerate," *World Vision Magazine* (Oct 1968), p. 47.

[28]Reported by Paul S. Rees, "Uppsala Reflections," *World Vision Magazine* (Nov 1968), p. 47.

[29]Harold Lindsell, "Uppsala, 1968," *Christianity Today* (Aug 6, 1969), pp. 3-7.

[30]Harold Lindsell, "Dateline: Bangkok," *Christianity Today* (Mar 30, 1973), p. 9. Interestingly, evangelical theologian J. I. Packer finally quit working with the WCC as a result of the Assembly at Bangkok ("Why I Left," *Christianity Today* [April 5, 1993], pp. 33-34).

[31]As reported by John R. Rice, *Sword of the Lord* (Sept 19, 1969), p. 12.

[32]As reported by D. A. Waite, "What's Wrong With the ICOWE?" Pt. II, p. 157 (mimeographed, 1969).

[33]Peter Beyerhaus, "The Theology of Salvation in Bangkok," *Christianity Today* (Mar 30, 1973), p. 17.

The majority of evangelicals who caucused at the [Vancouver, 1983] assembly were also enthusiastic, so much so that they produced a statement commending the World Council and inviting evangelicals to add their gifts to its process.

Emilio Castro, head of the WCC Division of Mission and Evangelism, was ecstatic about the support provided for evangelical concerns in the Council and predicted that the open letter would turn out to be the most important event at the Sixth Assembly. More than 200 persons signed the document.[34]

Castro also noted:

A substantial number of Christian brothers and sisters of evangelical persuasion are open to the ecumenical movement and willing to participate in it with their testimony....I see signs everywhere of a wider participation of evangelicals in the forum that is the World Council of Churches.[35]

Incidentally, at the Vancouver meeting, for the first time, the delegates heard from a theological atheist, Dorothee Soilee. Leading representatives of non-Christian religions also addressed the assembly.[36] Amazingly, the theme chosen for the Vancouver assembly was "Jesus Christ the Life of the World."

Probing questions come to mind. How could a gathering with such a lofty theme digest the oration of an *atheist*? How could evangelicals participate in such a mixed multitude of belief and practice without prostituting their heritage? And what could non-Christian religions possibly contribute to Jesus Christ being the life of the world?

The new evangelicals kept raising questions about the WCC's liberal theology and practice of the social gospel. Sadly, the evangelicals never demanded or provided answers. Queries and commentaries abounded, but nothing of substance ever came of them. Scholarly analyses, erudite replies, learned questions, evasive comments, and cautious complaints recurred with nearly every WCC Assembly or major event. Examples of WCC events include: "Facing New Delhi: Crisis of the Ecumenical Movement,"[37] "The 'Super Church' Charge,"[38] "The World Council/New Delhi,"[39] "New Delhi in Retrospect,"[40] "Evangelicals and the World Council,"[41] "Influencing a Conglomerate,"[42] "Uppsala: Awkward Ecumenical Timing,"[43] "Uppsala 1968,"[44] "On Christendom—A Report From Uppsala,"[45]

---

[34]Richard Lovelace, "Are There Winds of Change at the World Council?" *Christianity Today* (Sept 16, 1983), pp. 33, 34. The "open letter" referred to by Castro was drawn up by Arthur Glasser and other evangelicals.

[35]*One World* [a WCC publication] (Jan 1986) as reported in *The Baptist Bulletin* (April 1987), p. 9.

[36]Ibid., p. 34.

[37]Hermann Sasse, *Christianity Today* (April 10, 1961), p. 3.

[38]*Christianity Today* (Mar 16, 1962), p. 35.

[39]Russell T. Hitt, *Eternity* (Feb 1962), p. 9.

[40]J. D. Douglas, *Christianity Today* (May 25, 1962), p. 29.

[41]Elmer Smith, *Christianity Today* (Aug 30, 1963), p. 55.

[42]Paul S. Rees, *World Vision Magazine* (Oct 1968), p. 47.

[43]*Christianity Today* (Aug 16, 1968), p. 43.

[44]Harold Lindsell, *Christianity Today* (Aug 16, 1968), p. 3.

[45]Russell T. Hitt, *Eternity* (Sept 1968), p. 9.

"Uppsala Reflections,"[46] "WCC Central Committee: Fellowship Adrift,"[47] "The Theology of Salvation in Bangkok,"[48] "Dateline: Bangkok,"[49] "Nairobi: Crisis in Credibility,"[50] "The WCC: Words in the Wilderness,"[51] "The World Council of Churches: Community or Conspiracy?"[52] "Are There Winds of Change At the World Council?"[53] "World Council Defies Critics in Vancouver,"[54] "Conflicting Forces at WCC Vancouver Assembly,"[55] "Winds of Change In the World Council?"[56] "An Evangelical at the WCC,"[57] "WCC: Evangelicals Find Inroads, Remain Cautious,"[58] "Has the WCC Kept the Faith?"[59] "Evangelicals Seek to Refocus WCC,"[60] and "Orthodox, Evangelicals Push for WCC Reforms."[61]

For all the high-sounding articles and the cerebral energy expended in them, virtually no one of the new evangelical camp explicitly declared that evangelicals should *not* cooperate with the World Council with the exception of Francis Schaeffer.[62] Interestingly, secular analyses of the World Council spawned more negative feedback than did the evaluations of the new evangelicals.[63]

Despite the miserable track record of the WCC since 1948, new evangelicals still continue to call for participation. The justifications for doing so are the evangelical tone of the simple WCC doctrinal base, the opportunity for evangelism, the concern for the unity of the Body of Christ and the overriding need for a united front in Christendom, the outlet that the WCC provides for social activism, and the benefits of mutual learning and understanding from continuing dialogue between the evangelicals and non-evangelicals.

---

[46]*World Vision Magazine* (Nov 1968), p. 47.

[47]Edward A. Plowman, *Christianity Today* (Sept 15, 1972), p. 45.

[48]Peter Beyerhaus, *Christianity Today* (Mar 30, 1973), p. 11.

[49]Harold Lindsell, *Christianity Today* (Mar 30, 1973), p. 4.

[50]Harold Lindsell, *Christianity Today* (Jan 2, 1976), p. 10.

[51]Arthur H. Matthews, *Christianity Today* (Jan 2, 1976), p. 31.

[52]Harold O. J. Brown, *Fundamentalist Journal* (April 1983), p. 28.

[53]Richard Lovelace, *Christianity Today* (Sept 16, 1983), p. 30.

[54]*Eternity* (Oct 1983), p. 12.

[55]Richard J. Mouw, *Christianity Today* (April 22, 1983), p. 52.

[56]Kenneth Kantzer and V. Gilbert Beers, *Christianity Today* (April 20, 1984), p. 10.

[57]Interview with James Van Hoeven, *Christianity Today* (Jan 13, 1989), p. 51.

[58]*Christianity Today* (April 8, 1991), p. 68.

[59]*Christianity Today* (April 5, 1993), pp. 31-40. Essayists were: Peter Beyerhaus, "Defining Moments"; J. I. Packer, "Why I Left"; Tokunboh Adeyemo, "What Ever Happened to Evangelism?"; Wesley Granberg-Mickaelson, "Should Evangelicals Come On Board?"; Thomas Giles, "Five Reasons to Cooperate"; James Stamoolis,"What Can We Learn From the Orthodox?"; and Thomas C. Oden, "How Should Evangelicals Be Ecumenical?"

[60]*Christianity Today* (Dec 7, 1998), p. 23.

[61]Tom Finger, *Christianity Today* (Jan 11, 1999), p. 22.

[62]Francis Schaeffer, "To the Editor," on the question: "Should Evangelicals Cooperate with the World Council of Churches?" *Eternity* (Nov 11, 1983), p. 82. A vigorous statement for the affirmative was made by Arthur Glasser, dean emeritus of the School of World Mission, Fuller Theological Seminary (ibid.).

[63]For example, Joseph A. Harriss, "Karl Marx or Jesus Christ: Which Master is the World Council of Churches Serving?" *Reader's Digest* (Aug 1982 reprint), and Joseph A. Harriss, "The Gospel According to Marx," *Reader's Digest* (Feb 1993), pp. 68-73.

7

ECUMENICAL ACCOLADES AND ECUMENICAL JOURNALISM

ACCOLADES

Many early new evangelicals acknowledged and positively assessed the influence of heretical leaders and churchmen on their thinking. For example Donald Bloesch considers Jacques Ellul, Helmut Thielcke, D. Elton Trueblood, John MacKay, Karl Barth, and E. Stanley Jones to be evangelicals, along with Carl Henry, Edward Carnell, Vernon Grounds, Harold Lindsell, and many other mainline evangelicals. Other scholars who figured prominently in the writings of the new evangelical renewalists included Soren Kierkegaard, P. T. Forsythe, Emil Brunner, and Dietrich Bonhoeffer.[1]

Fuller Seminary published a series of faculty portraits in which each faculty member named those who had most influenced them, beyond their fathers and mothers. The majority of names listed found their homes in the neo-orthodox/neo-liberal camp (i.e., Soren Kierkegaard, T. F. Torrance, Dietrich Bonhoeffer, Alan Richardson, Karl Barth, Robert McAfee Brown, E. Stanley Jones, Russel Spittler, Samuel Terrien, Otto Piper, John MacKay, Leslie Newbigen, and John Bright).[2] Is it any wonder that Fuller had increasing theological woes during its transition from evangelicalism to the theological left?

Of all the non-evangelical scholars, Karl Barth seems to have wielded the most influence on the thinking of the new evangelical theological community. As early as 1957 Paul Edwards declared in *Eternity* magazine that neo-orthodox theologians Karl Barth and Emil Brunner were "Christian scholars in every sense of the word." Barth, Brunner, and the neo-orthodox are said to have believed in the deity of Christ and that man is a sinner saved only by Jesus Christ who earned

---

[1]Donald G. Bloesch, *The Evangelical Renaissance* (Grand Rapids: Eerdmans, 1973), pp. 30-33, 38, 81. Bloesch dedicates the book to John MacKay "for his loyalty to the faith once delivered to the saints." Bloesch considers MacKay an evangelical (p. 81), but it was MacKay, who as president of Princeton Seminary (1936-1959), presided over the demise of the evangelical faith at that school after it had capitulated to the liberal/neo-orthodox forces in the aftermath of the reorganization of 1929.

[2]*Theology News and Notes* (Published by Fuller Theological Seminary, Nov 1987), whole issue.

salvation by His life, death, and resurrection. "This is what makes a person a Christian, and this is what Barth, Brunner, and neo-orthodoxy believe."[3] In 1960 E. M. Blaiklock declared, "The neo-orthodox should be welcomed by conservatives as friends and brethren."[4]

Edward John Carnell characterized Barth as an "inconsistent evangelical" rather than an "inconsistent liberal."[5] He seems to have been mesmerized when Barth lectured at the University of Chicago in 1962. While mildly finding fault with Barth's rejection of natural theology and his seeming disdain for ordinary logic in theological formulations, Carnell effusively praised Barth's having risen to "classical stature" on the doctrines of the Trinity, justification by faith, and the person and work of Christ. He glosses over Barth's errors and heresies by noting: "Whatever Barth may lack in the way of doctrinal consistency he compensates for by his Christian graciousness." He concurred with an onlooking journalist who said, "Merely to watch Karl Barth walk into the auditorium is a religious experience." Carnell then unleashed his typical invective against fundamentalists:

> I am utterly ashamed of the manner in which extreme fundamentalists in America continue to attack Barth. I felt actual physical pain when I read in *Time* magazine that Cornelius Van Til, one of my former professors, had said that Barthianism is more hostile to the Reformers than is Roman Catholicism. I propose that Van Til ask God to forgive him for such an irresponsible judgment....To the extreme fundamentalists I would say: Awaken from slumber! If you try to upgrade your own estate by downgrading the estate of others, God will see to it that you become a victim of your own cruel standard. Scripture is clear: "Judge not, that you be not judged...."[6]

The context of Carnell's extreme statements must be kept in mind. He formerly presided over the new evangelical flagship school—Fuller Theological Seminary—and represented the evangelical viewpoint on a panel that questioned Barth on some of his views. On the panel, he spoke in a quasi-official way for the new evangelical theological community. Further, Carnell could address his former professors and fundamentalists in general through the liberal *Christian Century*. However unintentional it may have been, he did send a clear message that, except for a few points that he could not personally accept, Barth's neo-orthodox theology was compatible with evangelicalism. There is no way to gauge Carnell's overall impact on new evangelicalism's theological fortunes but, judging from the later inroads of Barthianism into the movement, it must have been greater than anyone could imagine at the time.

Carnell had not always been that charitable to Barth. Reviewing Barth's *The Word of God and Word of Man*, he suggested concerning Barth's essential theology:

> Barth represents an extreme position. And extremes always falsify while they correct. No one can read this book without concluding that Barth's theological

---

[3]Paul R. Edwards, "Some Thoughts on Fundamentalist Infallibility," *Eternity* (Sept 1957), p. 6.

[4]E. M. Blaiklock, "Conservatism, Liberalism, and Neo-Orthodoxy," *Eternity* (Aug 1960), p. 33.

[5]Edward John Carnell, "Barth as Inconsistent Evangelical," *The Christian Century* (June 6, 1962), p. 714.

[6]Ibid.

imagination often outruns the precise lines of Scripture....Barth's theology is not evangelical—not consistently evangelical at any rate. His system is a strange composite of Scripture, Kierkegaardian existentialism, and a fertile imagination.[7]

What caused a turn-around in Carnell's thinking about Barth is anyone's guess, but in all likelihood it had to do with such things as the need for scholastic prestige among fellow evangelicals, peer acceptance in the non-evangelical community, the emotional impact of facing one of the world's most prominent theologians, and his continuing vendetta against fundamentalism and against his own fundamentalist background.

Another influential new evangelical theologian who became enamored with and eventually capitulated to Barthian neo-orthodoxy was Bernard Ramm. Ramm studied under Karl Barth in Basel in the late 1950s and was highly influenced by those studies.[8] He came to believe that the Enlightenment had precipitated a crisis in evangelical theology and that evangelicals had not "developed a theological method that enables them to be consistently evangelical in their theology and to be people of modern learning."[9] Ramm confessed: "I did not have a theology whose methodology was scientifically ascertained, nor doctrines scientifically inter-related, nor properly defended."[10] Over and again he stresses the need to "come to terms with the Enlightenment and its children."[11] He concluded that Barth's theology was the only paradigm that could bridge the gap between evangelical theology and modern scientific/philosophical thought.

Ramm's journey from evangelicalism to neo-orthodoxy progressed somewhat cautiously, extending more than twenty years from his tutelage under Barth in the late 1950s to his delineated paradigm in *After Fundamentalism* in 1983. Soon after his Basel experience, Ramm criticized fundamentalism's concept of propositional special revelation as "a transcript without mystery"[12] and for not seeing it as "the divine Person in *conversation* with sinners" (italics his),[13] criticisms heavy with Barthian overtones. His indebtedness to Barth is seen in his numerous citations of Barth in *Special Revelation and the Word of God,* slightly fewer than the one he quotes most often—Abraham Kuyper.[14] In *After Fundamentalism* Ramm speaks of the "interval" between the text of Scripture and the Word of God,[15] a clearly neo-orthodox dichotomy that refuses to identify the Bible as itself, the objective Word of God, although Ramm protested to the contrary.

---

[7]Edward John Carnell, "Understanding Karl Barth," *Eternity* (Feb 1958), p. 43.

[8]Bernard Ramm, *After Fundamentalism: The Future of Evangelical Theology* (San Francisco: Harper and Row, 1983), pp. 1-28.

[9]Ibid., p. 27.

[10]Ibid., pp. 1-2.

[11]Ibid., pp. 8, 14, 18, 19, 27, 101, 114, 136, 142.

[12]Bernard Ramm, *Special Revelation and the Word of God* (Grand Rapids: Eerdmans, 1961), p. 24.

[13]Ibid., p. 26.

[14]Ibid., pp. 216-17.

[15]*After Fundamentalism*, pp. 88-100.

Ramm alleged that "the modern [i.e., post-Enlightenment] world will only hear of a theology of freedom,"[16] and thus he opted for Barth's concept of the freedom of God, the "freedom of unlimited possibility."[17] But it is apparent that this idea of freedom is not that of the biblical apostles and prophets; it is that of autonomous human intellectual imagination, particularly secular philosophical existentialism with a religious veneer. Ramm's Barthian paradigm makes peace with this modern notion of and demand for freedom by giving it both a deity and a theology of freedom. But this deity-figure is not the God of the Bible and its doctrinal surrounding is nothing but sophisticated unbelief.

In the 1970s a radical, left-wing offshoot of the new evangelical movement surfaced under the various names of "young evangelicals,"[18] "worldly evangelicals,"[19] or "green grass evangelicals."[20] Their chief spokesman, Richard Quebedeaux, gladly acknowledged the influence of neo-orthodoxy in the following wishful and almost prescient words:

> Indeed, the new theological heroes of the evangelical left are Karl Barth, Emil Brunner, and Dietrich Bonhoeffer, while they were living the foremost spokespersons of neo-orthodoxy on the Continent. Reinhold Niebuhr, its most articulate American representative, has also become popular among many left evangelicals....The early demise of neo-orthodoxy in ecumenical circles may have been due to the fact that it had been born in liberalism. Neo-orthodoxy, carried and nurtured by *evangelical theology*, may prove to be stronger and more durable (italics added).[21]

By 1985 Donald Dayton recognized "a special affinity between 'evangelicals' and Barth [that] has, for example, recently swelled the ranks of the Karl Barth Society with newcomers from a variety of 'evangelical' traditions."[22]

Evangelicals had been clearly warned about the errors of Barth and neo-orthodoxy. In 1928 J. Gresham Machen puzzled over Barth's absolute dualism between "time" and "eternity," the virtual centerpiece of neo-orthodoxy, a dualism not based on the biblical Creator-creature distinction, but a radical dichotomy due to *sin*.[23] Machen found Barth's dialectic "strange," and confessed: "I cannot explain it; for I should find it difficult to explain what I do not understand."[24] He also found Barth's commentary on Romans "a very strange book" and a "strange exposition

---

[16]Ibid., p. 142.

[17]Ibid., p. 137.

[18]Richard Quebedeaux, *The Young Evangelicals: Revolution in Orthodoxy* (San Francisco: Harper and Row, 1974).

[19]Richard Quebedeaux, *The Worldly Evangelicals* (San Francisco: Harper and Row, 1978).

[20]Bernard Ramm, "Welcome 'Green Grass' Evangelicals," *Eternity* (March 1974), p. 13.

[21]*The Worldly Evangelicals*, p. 100.

[22]Donald W. Dayton, "Karl Barth and Evangelicalism: The Varieties of Sibling Rivalry," *TSF Bulletin* (May-June 1985), p. 18.

[23]"Karl Barth and 'The Theology of Crisis,'" a paper read to a small group of ministers in Philadelphia, April 23, 1928, *Westminster Theological Journal* 53 (1991), p. 198.

[24]Ibid., p. 200.

of the Apostle's words."[25] Machen concluded that "it would indeed be a great mistake to regard the Barthian teaching as a real return to the gospel of the Lord Jesus Christ."[26] D. G. Hart, a biographer of Machen and a student of his thought, summarized Machen's attitude: "Machen's early reaction to Barthianism suggests that he regarded neo-orthodoxy, in both its American and European varieties, as an extension rather than a repudiation of liberal Protestantism."[27]

In 1947, before the new evangelical fascination with Barth and Brunner, Cornelius Van Til of Westminster Seminary wrote an extensive critical analysis of the theology of Karl Barth and Emil Brunner, entitled *The New Modernism*.[28] Van Til's monumental work still stands as one of the most scholarly theological and philosophical blows to the neo-orthodox experiment. Van Til authored a second indictment, entitled *Christianity and Barthianism*,[29] reminiscent of J. Gresham Machen's *Christianity and Liberalism*. Here Van Til, like Machen, demonstrated that however religious and full of God-talk a theological system may be, if it is not based on the inerrant Scriptures, especially the teachings of Jesus Christ and His apostles, it is not Christian in the New Testament sense of the term; it is humanistic. Van Til tirelessly points out that *both* modernism and neo-orthodoxy, and any non-biblical, unorthodox religious scheme, are cut out of the cloth of human intellectual autonomy.

Van Til's attitude toward Barthianism could be summarized by his conclusion in a 1959 article in *Eternity*:

> Thus the very foundations of historic Christianity, as well as its central facts, are destroyed in Barth's theology. Barth's activistic view of Scripture, his dynamic view of Christ, his dove-tailing of all the events of the life, death, resurrection, ascension and return of Christ into one *Event* in the realm of *Geschichte*, are all of a piece. They are the product of an attempted synthesis between Christianity and modern existentialist philosophy. In this synthesis-theology all the teachings of the Bible are maintained—verbally. But they have all received new meanings. And these new meanings are quite to the liking of the natural man....Surely this is a gospel which is *another gospel*. The Christ of Barth is no more able to save men from sin than is the Christ of Paul Tillich (italics his).[30]

In 1958 David Hedegard warned against Barthianism, summarizing his findings tersely: "Barth denies all the fundamental truths that the so-called 'old fashioned modernists' denied....Karl Barth, far from being a reformer, is a destroyer of the Christian faith."[31] In 1962 theologian Fred Klooster of the Calvin Theological Seminary wrote a scholarly theological critique of Barthianism from

---

[25]Ibid., p. 206.

[26]Ibid.

[27]D. G. Hart, "Machen on Barth: Introduction to a Recently Uncovered Paper," *Westminster Theological Journal* 53 (1991), p. 193.

[28]Cornelius Van Til, *The New Modernism* (Philadelphia: Presbyterian and Reformed, 1947).

[29]Cornelius Van Til, *Christianity and Barthianism* (Philadelphia: Presbyterian and Reformed, 1962).

[30]Cornelius Van Til, "What About Karl Barth?" *Eternity* (Sept 1959), p. 21.

[31]David Hedegard, "What Does Barthianism Really Teach?" *Moody Monthly* (July 1958), p. 80.

the perspective of Reformed orthodoxy.[32] In the 1980s, when new evangelical fascination with neo-orthodoxy was reaching its apogee, other theologians, some from within the new evangelical ranks, were negative toward Barth's theology, such as Peter DeJong,[33] Carl Henry,[34] Kenneth Kantzer,[35] and Richard A. Muller.[36] Most in the new evangelical movement did not heed these voices.

The theological journey from the doctrines of the old fundamentalist/ evangelical coalition of the 1920s, 30s, and 40s to the embracing of neo-orthodox notions and worse transpired over a short time. The defection is traceable to a number of factors, not the least of which was the spirit of ecumenism endemic to the new evangelical cause. This spirit expressed itself in different ways, one of which was the practice of "dialogue." In dialogue, evangelical theologians permitted orthodox and heretical religious options to be debated, contrasted, compared, and analyzed for mutual enrichment, learning, correction, and updating. The strategy of dialogue proved disastrous for new evangelical theology. Millard Erickson observed in 1968 that new evangelicalism had already been moving in the direction of neo-orthodoxy—his observation turned out to be a portend of no small dimension.[37]

JOURNALISM

Ecumenical/cooperative journalism encourages the publication of articles in new evangelical publications or the publishing of books by evangelical publishing houses by those of unorthodox or unbiblical theology. The blurring of truth and the confusion of ideas in the minds of the readers results. Ecumenical/cooperative journalism includes publishing conciliatory, irenic articles by new evangelicals in liberal publications. Ecumenical journalism is now so common, no one thinks much about it. It is part of the new evangelical break-out that characterized the 1960s, the aftermath of the new movement's psychological and numerical triumphs from ecumenical evangelism in the later 1950s.

---

[32]Fred Klooster, *The Significance of Barth's Theology* (Philadelphia: Presbyterian and Reformed, 1962). See also his "Karl Barth's Doctrine of the Resurrection of Jesus Christ," *Westminster Theological Journal* 24 (1962), p. 137. Reviewing Bernard Ramm's *After Fundamentalism*, Klooster concluded: "Following Ramm's interpretation of Barth as a paradigm would prove disastrous for evangelical theology"("Barth and the Future of Evangelical Theology," *Westminster Theological Journal* 47 [1985], p. 316).

[33]Peter DeJong, "Karl Barth: Leader or Misleader of Our Age?" *The Outlook* (Sept 1983), p. 112.

[34]Carl F. H. Henry's *magnum opus*, a prodigious six-volume theological treatise, *God, Revelation, and Authority* (Waco, TX: Word, 1976-1983), is predicated on a repudiation of the neo-orthodox idea of revelation as a non-propositional personal "encounter" with God in a supra-temporal, existential realm.

[35]Kenneth Kantzer, "Thank God For Karl Barth, But...," *Christianity Today* (Oct 3, 1986), pp. 14-15. Six years later Kantzer was far more charitable toward neo-orthodoxy when he noted that "so-called neo-orthodox theology was interpreted and battled against as the same old liberalism, only slightly disguised, and hence dubbed the "New Modernism. It was not" ("The Doctrine Wars," *Christianity Today* [Oct 5, 1992], p. 33). His mention of the "New Modernism" refers to Cornelius Van Til's criticism of neo-orthodoxy.

[36]Richard A. Muller, "The Place and Importance of Karl Barth in the Twentieth Century: A Review Essay," *Westminster Theological Journal* 50 (1988), pp. 127-56.

[37]Millard J. Erickson, *The New Evangelical Theology* (Westwood, NJ: Revell, 1968), p. 226.

In the vanguard of the new approach in journalism came *Decision* magazine, a publication of the Billy Graham Evangelistic Association in Minneapolis that began in November 1960. Graham felt the need for two publications, one on an intellectual level (which developed into *Christianity Today* in 1956), and one on a popular, practical level "to include articles with an evangelistic emphasis, as well as devotional messages, simple Bible studies, stories of conversions and changed lives, and news of our Crusades."[38] This magazine was called *Decision*.

A random check of the five-year index of *Decision* (Dec 1965) reveals the following contributors: John Baillie, Henry Ward Beecher, Dietrich Bonhoeffer, John Bright, Walter Marshal Horton, and Horace Bushnell. The next few included Elmer Homrighausen, Helmut Thielicke, Emilio Castro, Bishop Gerald Kennedy, and John Mackay. Each of these men are either liberal, neo-liberal, or neo-orthodox. None could be considered evangelical in any meaningful sense of the term.

> A basic fault of *Decision* is the honor it gives to men who are apostate from the Christian faith....People can be expected to regard those so honored in *Decision* as leaders worthy of trust, support, and fellowship, when the truth is they may be some of the most dangerous leaders of modern religion.[39]

Note the contrast between the policy of *Decision* with the earlier attitude of Graham when he was president of Northwestern Schools and editor of *The Northwestern Pilot* in 1951.

> A SPECIAL WORD We sincerely regret that the ad on the back cover of the March issue of the *Pilot* carried an advertisement of a book by Dr. Harry Emerson Fosdick. This completely slipped the attention of our Advertising Department. The *Pilot* represents the orthodox, conservative, fundamental, theological position. We do not condone nor have fellowship with any form of modernism. Dr. Fosdick's position is well known as that of an extreme modernist. We do not commend his writings to our reading public. {Signed} Billy Graham, President.[40]

Christianity Today likewise has carried a pluralistic roster of contributors. A list of authors recommended in 1965 for devotional reading by W. N. Kerr, professor at Gordon Divinity School, included Dietrich Bonhoeffer, Helmut Thielicke, John Baillie, and Soren Kierkegaard.[41] Other issues throughout the 1960s and 70s carried numerous articles by John Sutherland Bonnell, John MacKay, D. Elton Trueblood, Oscar Cullman, and Martin Marty. Again, none of these is remotely evangelical.

Breaking new ground in ecumenical journalism, *Eternity* published an article by a Roman Catholic.[42] Early new evangelicals wrote numerous articles in the

---

[38]Billy Graham, *Just As I Am: The Autobiography of Billy Graham* (New York: HarperSanFrancisco & Zondervan, 1997), p. 295.

[39]G. Archer Weniger, "Billy Graham's *Decision* Magazine," *Sword of the Lord* (June 7, 1968), p. 1.

[40]*The Northwestern Pilot* (April 1951), p. 222.

[41]William Nigel Kerr, "Suggestions For Devotional Reading," *Christianity Today* (May 7, 1965), pp. 14-15.

[42]Neil J. McEleney, "The Roman Catholic Rediscovery of the Bible," *Eternity* (June 1962), pp. 21-23. A few years later *Eternity* published an even more provocative article by Paul Witte, "But can a Catholic Really be a Christian?" (June 1969), pp. 22-24.

liberal *Christian Century.*[43] Eerdmans Publishing Company has been especially lax in what it publishes. No longer can one assume that an author is evangelical if Eerdmans publishes his work. Decades ago *The Christian Century* threw Eerdmans a bouquet: "Wm. B. Eerdmans, it seems to us, has done particularly well at bridging from a confining conservative market to a pluralist one, with high standards of quality."[44] Tyndale House reprinted a book written by Malcolm Muggeridge, a European liberal, entitled *Jesus Rediscovered* (1969), in which he denies the deity of Christ, the virgin birth, and the resurrection.[45] Fleming H. Revell reprinted *The Power of Positive Thinking* by Norman Vincent Peale. An ad for the book read, "This is the book that will help you release your inner powers."[46] Peale was neo-orthodox at best.

Key '73 was an evangelical effort to evangelize the north American continent in 1973. The resource book had for its suggested reading authors including John Baillie, Karl Barth, Marcus Barth, John Bright, Horace Bushnell, Harry Emerson Fosick, Leslie Newbigen, H. Richard Niebuhr, Walter Rauschenbusch, Martin Marty, and D. Elton Trueblood,[47] none of which could be considered conservative or Bible-believing.

Weniger's conclusion about *Decision* magazine's pluralistic approach could be said of all those who practice ecumenical journalism. The practice holds up for emulation people who do not believe the Bible and whose lives, beliefs, and ministries are anti-evangelical and anti-fundamentalist. In addition, the practice blurs the clear distinction between the people of God and those who are not. In the 1960s Bethel Theological Seminary, St. Paul, MN had an array of neo-liberal and neo-orthodox chapel speakers. Robert Mounce was quite optimistic about the worth of such a practice. "When we walk with great men we seek almost unconsciously to match their stride."[48] Fundamentalists contended at the time, and history has confirmed, that such a statement has the hiss of the serpent in it.

---

[43]For example: Billy Graham, "What Ten Years Have Taught Me" (Feb 17, 1960); and Edward John Carnell, "Post-Fundamentalist Faith" (Aug 26, 1959) and "Orthodoxy: Cultic vs. Classical" (Mar 16, 1960).

[44]*The Christian Century* (April 28, 1971), p. 529, as reported in *Inklings*, an Eerdmans trade publication (May-June 1971), p. 4.

[45]See a brief review in William E. Ashbrook, *Evangelicalism: The New Neutralism* (Columbus, OH: Published by the author, 8th printing, ca 1975), pp. 115-116.

[46]"Spire Books, distinguished paperbacks at popular prices" (nd).

[47]*Key '73 Congregational Resource Book: Calling Our Continent to Christ* (St. Louis: Concordia Publishing House, nd), pp. 214-22.

[48]Mounce, in a publicity folder, was referring specifically to the upcoming lecture of D. Elton Trueblood, reported by G. Archer Weniger, "Bethel Seminary Entertains a Neo-Liberal Preacher," *Sword of the Lord* (Jan 7, 1966), p. 4.

8

THE CHARISMATIC
MOVEMENT

Old Pentecostalism is generally said to have begun in 1901 when Agnes Osman, a student in a newly-formed Bible institute in Topeka, KS, spoke in tongues. She appears to have been the first person to speak in tongues in response to definitely seeking the "baptism of the Holy Spirit." The charismatic movement, on the other hand, refers primarily to the neo-Pentecostal movement that began in 1960 when Dennis Bennett, an Episcopal priest in Van Nuys, CA, spoke in tongues and brought Pentecostalism into the mainline denominations.

Old line Pentecostalism remained fairly contained within the holiness movement. While fundamental in doctrine, the Pentecostals rarely, if ever, had interaction, much less fraternal cooperation, with early fundamentalists. The Assemblies of God participated in the National Association of Evangelicals, but old Pentecostalism did not have the ecumenical, non-doctrinal stance that the later charismatic renewal movement quickly assumed. Eventually the charismatic movement swallowed up Pentecostalism, and the two have become synonymous. Pentecostalism's inroads into evangelicalism appeared in the famous *Christian Life* article, "Is Evangelical Theology Changing?" The call for "a willingness to re-examine beliefs concerning the Holy Spirit,"[1] widely interpreted as a modified feeling toward the tongues and healing movement, represented a significant change.

Donald Grey Barnhouse probably spawned the rapprochement between the new evangelicals and the modern tongues and healing movement in 1957. In the early 1950s he had embarked on a quest to find true Christian unity wherever possible.[2] Accordingly, he and other evangelical churchmen spent a few days in Springfield, MO, with the twelve top leaders of the Assemblies of God denomination. His impressions and later comments were effusive and favorable. He noted that the "Pentecostal leaders express 95 per cent agreement with the editors [of *Eternity*]."[3] All concerned felt "that marvelous unity that comes only

---

[1] "Is Evangelical Theology Changing?" *Christian Life* (Mar 1956), p. 17.

[2] Barnhouse, "New Year's Resolution," *Eternity* (Jan 1953), inside back cover.

[3] Barnhouse, "Finding Fellowship with Pentecostals," *Eternity* (April 1958), p. 8.

from the Holy Spirit."[4] The agreement between the Pentecostals and Barnhouse eventuated in an invitation for him to hold a week of meetings in the Assemblies' Central Church in Springfield. Barnhouse seemed to understand the uniqueness of the moment: "It is good for the whole body of Christ to notice that a Presbyterian minister who adheres to the Westminster Confession is an acceptable guest in a Pentecostal Assembly."[5] However, it was not until the advent of the modern charismatic movement in the early 1960s that the new evangelical-charismatic brotherhood escalated.

The charismatic penetration of the new evangelicalism in the 1960s changed the direction of the evangelical periodical *Christian Life*. Under the editorship of Bob Walker, the magazine began featuring Pentecostal writers like Howard Ervin and Dennis Bennett. The subscriptions from traditional, non-Pentecostal evangelicals fell off, but new subscribers from Pentecostal/charismatic circles enrolled. In 1987 the magazine merged with *Charisma* to become *Charisma and Christian Life*.[6]

In 1963 the editor of *Eternity* wrote a favorable article appraising the new Pentecostalism. His closing sentence echoed the growing tolerance of Pentecostals: "Perhaps, God in His mercy, will use this strange stirring in the Church to call His people back to a higher level of both faith and practice."[7] In the same issue an article chiefly of a historical and biographical nature closed with similar words: "While we may disagree with many aspects of this movement, God seems to have worked through it, touching men, ministries and churches."[8] This issue reportedly netted *Eternity* 12,000 new subscriptions (no doubt mostly from charismatics). *Christianity Today* likewise weighed in with a factual analysis, concluding with words of encouragement that suggest acceptance of the charismatic phenomenon:

> Probably most evangelicals who are informed on the subject are sympathetically waiting to see the fruit of the new movement, not wishing to quench the Spirit, but sensing a need to try the spirits. They generally believe God is working in and through the movement but are questioning how close it may be to the biblical idea. They are grateful for spiritual awakening.[9]

The Berlin World Congress on Evangelism (1966) was the first occasion that a recognized leader of the modern tongues and healing movement, Oral Roberts, participated in a major new evangelical function. (The Congress refused to admit Anti-communist Richard Wurmbrand and fundamentalist Carl McIntire.[10]) Roberts understood the significance of his presence in Berlin. Speaking to a reporter, he confided his thoughts:

---

[4]Ibid., p. 9.

[5]Ibid., p. 10.

[6]*Dictionary of Pentecostal and Charismatic Movements*, s.v. "Publications," by W. E. Warner, p. 749.

[7]Russell T. Hitt, "The New Pentecostalism: An Appraisal," *Eternity* (July 1963), p. 16.

[8]James W. L. Hillis, "The New Pentecostalism: Its Pioneers and Promoters," *Eternity* (July 1963), p. 18.

[9]Frank Farrell, "The Outburst of Tongues: The New Penetration," *Christianity Today* (Sept 13, 1963), p. 7.

[10]G. Archer Weniger, "World Congress of New Evangelicals," *Sword of the Lord* (Dec 30, 1966), pp. 8-9.

For the first time in my ministry I have felt a full acceptance of myself as an evangelist by the mainstream of evangelical Christianity. And this may be the first time I have ever fully accepted all of them—mainstream evangelicals. This is also the first time that the healing ministry, as it has been given to me by God, has been so well understood and accepted by these leaders of Christian evangelicals.[11]

In return, Billy Graham was the featured speaker at the dedication of the Oral Roberts University in Tulsa, OK, April 2, 1967.[12]

An element of Pentecostalism lodged in the National Association of Evangelicals from the beginning, namely the participation of the Assemblies of God. However Pentecostals/charismatics were more or less second class citizens until their recognition and implied approval by the new evangelicals in the early 1960s. Their presence became so influential in the NAE and in the new evangelical movement as a whole that Carl Henry complained:

The NAE has acquired an image of being not only largely independent of mainstream churches, but also notably oriented to Pentecostal participation (about 35% of its membership is Pentecostal oriented). Consequently it has gained little enlistment from within such predominantly conservative bodies as the Southern Baptist Convention and the Lutheran Church—Missouri Synod.[13]

Henry's radical solution to the problem involved establishing another evangelical fellowship to attract evangelicals disillusioned with conciliar ecumenism and, by implication, who did not want to join the NAE because of its increasing Pentecostal influence.[14] Nothing came of Henry's suggestion, and the NAE continued to have about a 35% Pentecostal constituency with several Pentecostal leaders serving as president.

Meanwhile other prominent evangelical scholars lent their influence in favor of the charismatic movement. Clark Pinnock and Grant Osborne delighted to see the cooperation between Pentecostals and non-Pentecostals. While expressing some concerns about the tongues-speakers, Pinnock and Osborne anxiously desired that tongues be received as a legitimate gift of the Spirit and that tongues-speakers be accepted into Christian fellowship and other forms of cooperation between evangelicals.[15] They concluded that tongues "is not the best gift with which to edify the Church. Nevertheless, it has validity and should be gratefully received by all Christians as coming from God."[16] Two years later (1973) Pinnock endorsed the charismatic movement more enthusiastically, saying "the Church needs nothing

---

[11]Bill Rose, *Oakland* [CA] *Tribune* (Nov 20, 1966) as cited by Weniger, Ibid., p. 9.

[12]*Oral Roberts University Outreach* (Spring 1967). The whole issue was given to the dedication of the university and the investiture of Roberts as president. While there were numerous pictures of the day, by far the preponderance was of Graham and Roberts in various aspects of the ceremonies.

[13]Carl F. H. Henry, *Evangelicals At the Brink of Crisis: Significance of the World Congress of Evangelicals* (Waco, TX: Word, 1967), pp. 107-08.

[14]Ibid., pp. 108-09.

[15]Clark H. Pinnock and Grant R. Osborne, "A Truce Proposal for the Tongues Controversy," *Christianity Today* (Oct 8, 1971), pp. 6-9.

[16]Ibid, p. 9.

more than it needs a supernatural visitation of the Spirit of God," and he was sure that "the new Pentecostalism has arisen to meet this need."[17] Pinnock's appeals to empirical evidence to show that God is blessing the charismatic movement, and the evidence, he contends, must be appreciated by evangelicals. Experience trumps exegesis in Pinnock's approach, as is seen in his incredible, theologically naive assertion:

> Even if it could be established (which it cannot) that the supra-normal gifts were withdrawn, we could not safely conclude that the Spirit is incapable of bestowing them again should the need for them arise.[18]

Based on empirical evidence, Pinnock challenges evangelical leaders to "begin to think about how to integrate the charismatic movement into the life of the Church, and stop treating its members as spiritual lepers."[19] Within ten years, Pinnock's appeal had borne fruit in the "signs and wonders" movement. Whether his article had much to do with it is impossible to know. In 1973 *Eternity* magazine proclaimed that "the new Pentecostalism, with its controversial tongues-speaking and healing, is more popular than ever."[20] Again, empirical evidence suggesting God's blessing elicited counsel for the movement to be embraced by evangelicals.

Perhaps the greatest impetus to new evangelical acceptance of charismatic belief and practice arrived in the "signs and wonders" movement or so-called "third wave" of the Spirit's working. The first wave was the old Pentecostal movement which began in 1901; the second was the post-1960 charismatic renewal in denominational Protestantism and Roman Catholicism; and the third was the outpouring of healings, prophecies, exorcism, and other gifts of the Spirit, beginning in about 1980. The third wave "is composed largely of evangelical Christians who, while applauding and supporting the work of the Holy Spirit in the first two waves, have chosen not to be identified with either."[21] The signs and wonders movement received significant evangelical support through Fuller Theological Seminary.

C. Peter Wagner, professor of church growth at Fuller Seminary, received the power of God in a Pentecostal experience after having been on the mission field in Bolivia for sixteen years and after having taught at Fuller for several years. Working with John Wimber, a former student of Wagner's who had turned Pentecostal and had founded the Vineyard Christian Fellowship, Fuller established a course of study in 1982 at Fuller's School of World Wide Mission to teach and experience the miraculous power of God. This course focused on accelerated church growth. The course had to be canceled in 1986 due to its academic deficiencies and because of complaints from traditionalists both inside and outside of the Seminary.[22] Fuller

---

[17]Clark Pinnock, "The New Pentecostalism: Reflections by a Well-Wisher," *Christianity Today* (Sept 14, 1973), p. 6.

[18]Ibid., p. 8.

[19]Ibid., p. 10.

[20]Russell T. Hitt, "Tongues: Updating Some Old Issues," *Eternity* (Mar 1973), p. 8.

[21]*Dictionary of Pentecostal and Charismatic Movements*, s.v. "Third Wave," by C. Peter Wagner, p. 843.

[22]George M. Marsden, *Reforming Fundamentalism: Fuller Seminary and the New Evangelicalism* (Grand Rapids: Eerdmans, 1987), pp. 292-95. See also Marjorie Lee Chandler, "Fuller Seminary Cancels Course on Signs and Wonders," *Christianity Today* (Feb 21, 1986), pp. 48-49.

reinstated the course in 1987 under several scholastic restraints. But the genie was out of the bottle as far as charismaticism among the new evangelical community was concerned. By the mid-1980s the third wave/signs and wonders/charismatic movement had invaded evangelical parachurch organizations as well as the Presbyterian, United Methodist, Anglican, and Lutheran denominational bodies.[23] Campus Crusade, for example, had prohibited its staff to speak in tongues in the mid 1960s, but that policy changed in 1983.[24] Gordon-Conwell Theological Seminary in the mid-1980s had a president, Richard Cooly, and a professor of New Testament, Gordon Fee, who were charismatics. Another professor, John Jefferson Davis, noted that Reformed Christians have much to learn from Wesleyan, holiness, and Pentecostal experience of the Spirit, including healing, exorcism, and "free and joyful praise of the risen Christ." Davis was sympathetic to "power evangelism" although he was not a charismatic.[25] Having cited in 1973 what he thought were the positive contributions of Pentecostalism, Clark Pinnock had grown more certain of them by 1986. In a forward to charismatic Roger Stronstad's book, *The Charismatic Commentary of St. Luke*, Pinnock warned: "Watch out, you evangelicals, the young Pentecostal scholars are coming! We are going to have to take them seriously in the intellectual realm."[26]

No less an urbane Reformed evangelical theologian with a strong Anglican hue than J. I. Packer seems a bit confused by the charismatic phenomena among evangelicals. He never criticizes the charismatic movement or charismatic experiences as heretical or not from God. To the contrary, he is open to and allows for such experiences as being beneficial, thus ultimately encouraging charismaticism. He concludes: "I confess myself to be one among the many whom the features of the movement [i.e., mistaken experience, mishandling of Scripture, etc.] bother. Nonetheless, I think I see God's touch in charismatic experience, and therefore I venture upon a second course [instead of writing it off as delusive and dangerous]— that of retheologizing."[27] How an evangelical theologian can "retheologize" on the basis of an empirical/emotional sense of "God's touch" is a good question.

Jerry Falwell, an opportunistic would-be fundamentalist turned new evangelical, became embroiled in an incident involving the charismatic PTL organization. When Jim Bakker resigned as head of PTL in March 1987 because of his admitted involvement in a sex scandal, Falwell took over the organization. He immediately formed a new board consisting of Pentecostals and new evangelicals: Baily Smith (Southern Baptist), James Watt (Pentecostal; former Secretary of the Interior), Rex Humbard (Pentecostal; Cathedral of Tomorrow), Ben Armstrong

---

[23]Julia Duin, "What Does the Future Hold for Charismatic Renewal?" *Christianity Today* (May 16, 1986), p. 38f.

[24]Ibid., p. 40.

[25]John Jefferson Davis, "Future Directions for American Evangelicals," *Journal of the Evangelical Theological Society* (Dec 1986), pp. 461-67.

[26]"In Search of a Charismatic Theology," *Christianity Today* (May 16, 1986), p. 44.

[27]J. I. Packer, *Keep in Step With the Spirit* (Old Tappan, NJ: Revell, 1984), p. 201. See the numerous references to the subject on pp. 79-80, 190, 197, 201, 222, 224-25, 229-30, 232.

(National Religious Broadcasters), Richard Dortch (Bakker's assistant at PTL), Jerry Nims (staff of Falwell's Thomas Road Baptist Church), and Sam Moore (Thomas Nelson Publishers). Falwell's cooperation with Pentecostals and other non-fundamentalists caused a great outcry from separatist fundamentalists and others. Falwell justified his entanglement with PTL in the May 1987 issue of his publication, *The Fundamentalist Journal*. In October 1987 he resigned from PTL.[28]

The charismatic/Pentecostal element is now firmly entrenched within the new evangelical movement, a prime example being the popular Promise Keepers organization. Promise Keepers began in 1990 under Bill McCartney, an ex-coach at the University of Colorado and a member of a charismatic Boulder Valley Vineyard church. He and other Vineyard friends began Promise Keepers, a men's movement stressing the role of Christian husbands and fathers in strong nuclear families. In the decades of the 1990s their conferences attracted huge crowds. Promise Keepers has many strata of belief and practice, one stratum of which is charismaticism, as seen in the charismatic conference speakers and their writings (such as Greg Laurie, Chuck Smith, and Jack Hayford), the conduct of the public gatherings (including the music and hand lifting/waving), and the composition of its governing board.

The vast majority of new evangelicals and fundamentalists, had been cessationists in regard to the spiritual gifts (i.e., they held that the miraculous gifts had ceased in the first century AD). Until the rise of the charismatic and third wave movements, the majority opinion was that of B. B. Warfield as defined in his *Counterfeit Miracles*.[29] Warfield asserted that the miraculous gifts authenticated the New Testament apostles and their message of the grace and truth that came by Jesus Christ (John 1:17). They were "the signs of a true apostle" (2 Cor 12:12). Miracles served a foundational purpose in the transition from Law to Grace, or from Old Testament Mosaism to the New Testament finality of the cross work of Jesus Christ and the ushering in of the new age of the Holy Spirit.[30] The foundation of the new dispensation and its centerpiece, the church of Jesus Christ, was laid by the apostles and prophets (Eph 2:20). Foundationalism in this sense is by definition and function temporary.

The charismatic/Pentecostal presence in the new evangelical ranks has contributed to the deterioration of evangelical theology as a whole and has fostered an experience-oriented Christianity.[31] Without a solid foundation in theology, it is

---

[28]"Gospelgate II: Target Falwell," *Newsweek* (Jun 1, 1987), pp. 56-59; "Stones Fly in the TV Temple," *US News and World Report* (June 8, 1987), pp. 10-11; "A Crackdown at PTL," *Christianity Today* (June 12, 1987), pp. 51-53.

[29]Carlisle, PA: Banner of Truth Trust, reprint 1972.

[30]See the treatment by John C. Whitcomb, *Does God Want Christians To Perform Miracles Today?* (Winona Lake, IN: BMH Books, 1979). Also note the exegetical/theological analysis by Ken L. Sarles, "An Appraisal of the Signs and Wonders Movement," *Bibliotheca Sacra* 145 (1988), pp. 57-82.

[31]Strangely, David F. Wells, in his otherwise excellent tracing of the loss of theology in the new evangelicalism, does not mention the role of Pentecostalism/charismatism. He cites the inroads of Arminianism and the self movement, among other trends, but has no word about the charismatic movement (*No Place For Truth: Or Whatever Happened to Evangelical Theology?* [Grand Rapids: Eerdmans, 1993], pp. 140, 172). He only lightly criticizes charismatics in the sequel, *God In the Wasteland: The Reality of*

impossible to challenge successfully anyone's religious experience of tongues and other such manifestations. Theological discussion gets lost in the ooze of verbal pietism, emotionalism, and *ad hoc* interpretations of Scripture. Fundamentalists in general observe Pentecostalism/charismaticism as giving an enormous boost to the ecumenical movement.[32] Widely disparate religious groups within Protestantism and Roman Catholicism can now unite in many different ways because doctrine is not a factor. The glue is the experience of the baptism of the Spirit, in whatever way it may be understood or interpreted.

Truth In a World of Fading Dreams (Grand Rapids: Eerdmans, 1994), pp. 182, 194-95. Mark Noll, on the other hand, blames fundamentalism and its three main "innovations," one of which is Pentecostalism, for the destruction of the life of the mind among evangelicals. The other two are second blessing holiness and premillennial dispensationalism (*The Scandal of the Evangelical Mind* [Grand Rapids: Eerdmans, 1994], p. 115).

[32]For example, *Foundations* magazine, a publication of The Fundamental Evangelistic Association, gave the July-August 1996 issue to warning about the charismatic movement with articles such as Dennis Costella, "The Charismatic Movement is Dangerous—Watch Out for It!" and "Strange Fire on the Altar"; Franklin G. Harding, "Pentecostalism—Not Scriptural"; and M. H. Reynolds, Jr., "Where Is the Charismatic Movement Headed?"

9

ROMAN
CATHOLICISM

EARLY CONTACTS: 1950s

One of the tragic anomalies of the evolution of the new evangelicalism is its complete about-face toward Roman Catholicism. In the early 1940s, evangelicals faced what were called "The Big Three"—Liberalism/modernism, secularism, and Roman Catholicism.[1] In the 1950s Catholicism was still thought to be one of the "satanic ideologies" opposed to evangelical Christianity, as noted by the NAE president.[2] Carl Henry, editor of *Christianity Today*, noted the evident rise of Roman Catholicism in America:

> There is little doubt but that America is gradually becoming a Roman Catholic Country....She [Rome] adapts her strategy to every situation. When her interests are at stake, she is cruel. When they are not, she is gentle....The Pope must look to his legions because he can no longer look to the gospel.[3]

As late as 1958 Edward John Carnell spoke warningly of the Roman Catholic Church.[4]

While convert referrals were routed to Roman Catholic churches from the ecumenical evangelistic crusades, fraternal and cooperative relationships with Rome developed more slowly. But, the 1960s witnessed the formal beginnings of a new attitude toward Romanism that has only escalated since. At the center of this new relationship stood the visible, titular head of the new evangelical movement—Billy Graham, and the technique of rapprochement with Rome was again, inclusive evangelism. Ernest Pickering concluded correctly: "Much of the current [ca. 1994] theological confusion with regard to the Roman

---

[1]Harold John Ockenga, "The Unvoiced Multitudes," *Evangelical Action! A Report of the Organization of the National Association of Evangelicals for United Action*, compiled and edited by the Executive Committee (Boston: United Action Press, 1942), pp. 26-31. See also William Pettingill, *Christian Life and Times* (Oct 1947), p. 101.

[2]H. H. Savage, "United Evangelical Action," *United Evangelical Action* (May 1, 1955), p. 3.

[3]Carl F. H. Henry, "Billy Graham and the Pope's Legions," *Christianity Today* (July 22, 1957), pp. 20-21.

[4]Edward John Carnell, "Orthodoxy and Ecumenism," *Christianity Today* (Sept 1, 1958), p. 15.

Catholic Church can be laid at the feet of one man—Billy Graham."[5] Richard Quebedeaux noted that Graham was the first major revivalist to attract and use Roman Catholics in evangelistic crusades.[6]

While most early new evangelical leaders feared and condemned Rome, a naive fascination with Romanism eventually grew to outright acceptance and brotherhood. The early fascination either willfully ignored or simply failed to understand the doctrines and practices of Rome and the significance of the Protestant Reformation. Courtship of Romanism possessed all the familiar earmarks of the new evangelical pragmatism that characterized Graham and his advisors almost from the beginning.

The trend to embrace Rome seemed to begin in 1952 when the *Pittsburgh Sun-Telegraph* noted:

> "He [Graham] said he hoped to hear Bishop Fulton J. Sheen at one of the Masses at St. Paul's Cathedral tomorrow." He added, "Many of the people who reach a decision on Christ at our meetings have joined the Catholic Church and we have received commendations from Catholic publications for the revived interest in their Church following our campaigns. This happened both in Boston and Washington. After all, one of our prime purposes is to help the churches in a community. If after we move on, the local churches do not feel the effects of these meetings in increased membership and attendance, then our crusade would have to be considered a failure."[7]

A couple of years later, other announcements of the same nature followed.[8] On December 29, 1955, "Billy Graham met in his hotel suite with fundamentalists James Bennet and Jack Wyrtzen and confirmed his intention of sending converts back to the Roman Catholic Church."[9] In 1956, at a rally banquet of 1,100 people at the Commodore Hotel in New York, Graham said, "We're coming to New York, not to clean it up, but to get people to dedicate themselves to God and then send them back to their own churches—Catholic, Protestant, or Jewish."[10] Officially, the Roman Church opposed the 1957 New York Crusade. Cardinal Francis Spellman and Father John E. Kelley of the Bureau of Information voiced the opposition. Kelley had invoked the long-standing Catholic stricture against worshiping with heretics, especially in Protestant gatherings not approved by a Roman Catholic bishop.[11]

---

[5]Ernest D. Pickering, *Holding Hands With the Pope: The Current Evangelical Ecumenical Craze* (Decatur, AL: Baptist World Mission, n.d.), pp. 2-3.

[6]Richard Quebedeaux, *By What Authority?* (San Francisco: Harper and Row, 1982), p. 36.

[7]*Pittsburgh Sun-Telegraph* (Sept 6, 1952) as cited in Wilson Ewin, *Evangelism: The Trojan Horse of the 1990s* (Bible Baptist Church, Nashua, NY, n.d.), p. 3.

[8]"Billy Graham Story: New Crusade in Europe," *U.S. News and World Report* (Aug 27, 1954), p. 89. George Burnham, *Billy Graham: A Mission Accomplished* (Westwood, NJ: Revell, 1955), p. 113.

[9]Wilson Ewin, *Evangelism: The Trojan Horse of the 1990s*, p. 3.

[10]Interview with Graham representative Walter Smyth, *San Francisco News* (Sept 21, 1957), as cited by Ian Paisley, *Billy Graham and the Church of Rome* (Greenville, SC: Bob Jones University Press, 1972), p. 15.

[11]Father Richard Ginder, "Billy Graham: Do We Approve?" *Our Sunday Visitor* (June 23, 1957), as photographically reproduced in Ian Paisley, *Billy Graham and the Church of Rome*, Document No. 23a. See also *Time* magazine (May 6, 1957).

CONTACT IN THE 1960s

The 1960s saw the mutual fascination between new evangelicals and Roman Catholics blossom. A Roman Catholic bishop stood beside Graham and blessed converts as they came forward during the 1962 Sao Paulo Crusade.[12] In late 1963, Billy Graham accepted his first-ever invitation to a Catholic institution, speaking to 1500 nuns, monks, priests, students, and Catholic laymen at Belmont Abbey College, Belmont, NC. Both sides took a certain amount of pride in each's "firstness."[13] Graham noted that the ecumenical movement "is the beginning of something so fantastic it could change all Christendom." The initiation of the Second Vatican Council and other reforms of Pope John XXIII, he said, "brought a new dialogue, and a new understanding that might bring a great Christian revolution.... This is the beginning of something so great that it could change all of Christendom and will affect you, your children and their children."[14] The evangelist also received a Benedictine medal from the school. The executive vice-president of Belmont Abbey College wrote an appreciative summary of Graham's ministry there:

> Billy Graham gave an inspiring and a theologically sound address that may have been given by Bishop Fulton J. Sheen or any other Catholic preacher. I have followed Billy Graham's career and I must emphasize that he has been more Catholic than otherwise, and I say this not in a partisan manner but as a matter of fact....I would state that he could bring Catholics and Protestants together in a healthy ecumenical spirit.[15]

In October 1964 Billy Graham had a much-publicized meeting with Cardinal Richard Cushing of Boston. The meeting came at Graham's request to thank the Cardinal for his support of the two Boston Crusades. In the meeting Graham noted: "I feel much closer to the Roman Catholic tradition than to some of the more liberal Protestants." Referring to their discussion, Cushing later said: "No Catholic can do anything but become a better Catholic on hearing Dr. Graham. I am 100% for the evangelist."[16]

In 1965 the editor of *The Catholic World* enthusiastically encouraged the brotherhood with the new evangelicals and what it meant for ecumenical relationships between the two faiths.

> Billy Graham is...a conservative Protestant who is responsive to new ideas and movements, anxious to make the word of God relevant to 1965. We can divide conservative evangelicals into fundamentalists and "new evangelicals," the latter being more ecumenically minded. With these new evangelicals Roman Catholics can engage in fruitful dialogue....We [Catholics] have neglected conservative evangelicals and it is time that we made a sincere effort to cultivate better

---

[12]*New York Times* (Oct 25, 1963) as reported in Wilson Ewin, *Evangelism: The Trojan Horse of the 1990s*, p. 4.

[13]"Billy Graham at Belmont Abbey," *Christianity Today* (Dec 6, 1963), p. 30.

[14]"Graham: 'It's Fantastic,'" *Greenville* [SC] *Piedmont* (Nov 19, 1963).

[15]Cuthbert E. Allen, O.S.B., Letter to Mr. Julius C. Taylor, Taylors, SC, March 19, 1965. Fundamentalism Archives, Bob Jones University, Greenville, SC.

[16]James Daane, "From Warring to Wooing," *Christianity Today* (Oct 23, 1964), p. 40. See also John R. Rice, "Dr. Billy Graham Pleases Catholics," *Sword of the Lord* (Dec 4, 1964), p. 6; Erroll Hulse, *Billy Graham— The Pastor's Dilemma* (Hounslow, Middlesex, Great Britain: Maurice Allen, 1966), pp. 41-42.

relations with them. We have much in common with them and there is every reason why we should be friendly....The new evangelicals believe strongly in regeneration through baptism, insisting on the absolute need for baptismal rebirth and representing the experience of being saved through baptism as an emotional and spiritual experience that shakes the convert to the roots of his personality.[17]

While this Catholic editor may have been misled concerning baptismal rebirth by some apparently unwise and incautious statements by Graham himself,[18] he could clearly see the coming wave of new evangelical/Roman Catholic cooperative syncretism.

At the Zagreb, Yugoslavia crusade, at the benediction of one service Billy Graham, a Roman Catholic priest, a Lutheran minister, two Orthodox, and a Presbyterian held hands on the platform and sang "Blest Be the Tie That Binds."[19] Concerning the Graham-sponsored World Congress on Evangelism (1966), the Roman Catholic *Our Sunday Visitor* said: "The total isolation of conservative Protestant evangelicals and the Roman Catholic Church may be broken down as the result of an Evangelical Congress held recently in Berlin and the positive leadership of U.S. evangelist, the Rev. Billy Graham."[20]

The new evangelical/Roman Catholic accord reached a peak in 1967 with Graham's receiving an honorary degree from Belmont Abbey College. Graham noted the significance of the occasion, saying it was "a time when Protestants and Catholics could meet together and greet each other as brothers, whereas ten years ago they could not." In his sermon on things that will not be shaken in a shaking world, the evangelist concluded, "Finally, the way of salvation has not changed. I know how the ending of the book will be. The gospel that built this school and the gospel that brings me here tonight is still the way to salvation."[21] Only extreme naivete or simple exaggeration meant for public consumption could equate the gospel according to Rome with the gospel of the apostle Paul. The honorary degree citation to Graham said in part: "In this small company—the company of Picasso and Einstein, of Schweitzer, Churchill, and John XXII—will certainly be found the figure of William Franklin Graham."[22] In probably the best fundamentalist assessment of the Belmont Abbey exchange, William P. Thompson, a professor

---

[17]John B. Sheerin, C.S.P., "Dialogue with Evangelicals Like Billy Graham," *The Catholic World*, photostatically reproduced by the *Fundamental Baptist Information Bulletin* (Sept-Oct, 1965).

[18]The idea of baptismal regeneration may have been taken from an interview between Billy Graham and Wilfred Bockelman, associate editor of the *Lutheran Standard*. In that article Graham affirmed his belief in baptismal regeneration (his own children were sprinkled as infants): "I have some difficulty in accepting the indiscriminate baptism of an infant,....But I do believe that something happens at the baptism of an infant, particularly if the parents are Christians and teach their children Christian truths from childhood. We cannot fully understand the mysteries of God, but I believe a miracle can happen in these children so that they are regenerated, that is, made Christian, through infant baptism. If you want to call that baptismal regeneration, that's all right with me" ("A Lutheran Looks at Billy Graham," *Lutheran Standard* [Oct 10, 1961], p. 12). In typical fashion, the evangelist later said he was misquoted.

[19]"Graham's Rousing Red Welcome," *Christianity Today* (Aug 18, 1967), p. 45.

[20]James C. O'Neill, "Operation Understanding," *Our Sunday Visitor,* as cited in "World Congress of New Evangelicals," by G. Archer Weniger (*Sword of the Lord* [Dec 30, 1966], p. 8).

[21]Paul Smith, "Belmont Abbey Confers Honorary Degree," *The Gastonia* [NC] *Gazette* (Nov 22, 1967).

[22]"Catholic College Says Billy Graham One of the Greats," *The* [Jacksonville] *Florida Times* (Nov 25, 1967), p. A12.

at Piedmont Bible College, Winston-Salem, NC, noted that "the drift away from fundamentalism which began some years ago when the Evangelist first began his close association with theological liberals has now perhaps taken him farther afield than many of his supporters or even he himself ever anticipated."[23]

CONTACT IN THE 1970s AND 1980s

The 1970s and 80s saw greatly increased new evangelical and Roman Catholic relations, too numerous to document fully here. The November 1971 issue of *Eternity* magazine carried three articles positively disposed toward Catholicism. Robert Coote reviewed the new place of the Bible in Roman Catholic circles as a result of Vatican II and how evangelical youth organizations such as Youth for Christ, Young Life, and InterVarsity Christian Fellowship were working together with Catholics to reach out for Christ.[24] An editorial started out by noting that in upstate New York a nun is serving with Youth for Christ starting Bible clubs in local Roman Catholic high schools, and went on to describe the various groups within Roman Catholicism.[25] James Hefley entitled his article with an eye-catching "How I Lost My Protestant Prejudice," relating how his contact with certain Catholics in Chicago finally wore away his prejudices against Romanists. His conclusion to this experience: "Somehow, God seems bigger today, and the basics of Christianity much more important, than when I first started out as a prejudiced Protestant minister back in New Orleans."[26]

On April 21, 1972, Graham received the Franciscan International Award for True Ecumenism by the Conventual Franciscan Friars of Prior Lake, MN. The news release announced that "Dr. Graham was selected to receive the coveted award by the leading Catholic laymen and women in the Twin City area and delegates of the Franciscan Order for 'his sincerity and authenticity in presenting the Gospel of Christ.'"[27] *The Minneapolis Star* gave ample coverage to the event along with a five inch square photo of Graham receiving the plaque from the Very Reverend Robert Bayer, provincial of the Conventual Franciscan Friars.[28]

Two events of 1973 enhanced the new evangelical/Roman Catholic dialogue and organizational cooperation: The Billy Graham St. Louis Crusade and the Key 73 undertaking. St. Louis is a heavily Roman Catholic area, and visible Catholic participation exceeded any previous Crusade. About fifty Catholics, including some nuns, took the pre-crusade counseling-training course, and several nuns sang in the crusade choir. The percentage of Catholics who responded to the invitation and signed commitment cards rose to ten percent in heavily Catholic populated

---

[23]William P. Thompson, "Belmont—Triumph or Tragedy," *The Baptist Bulletin* (April 1968), p. 12.

[24]Robert T. Coote, "Revival and Renewal: Impact of the Bible on Roman Catholics Today," *Eternity* (Nov 1971), pp. 17-22.

[25]Russell T. Hitt, "Old Issues, New Directions," *Eternity* (Nov 1971), pp. 6, 8.

[26]James Hefley, "How I Lost My Protestant Prejudice," *Eternity* (Nov 1971), p. 16.

[27]News Release, Franciscan International Award Dinner Committee, Prior Lake, MN, n.d.

[28]"Rekindle Spiritual Values—Graham," *The Minneapolis Star* (Apr 22, 1972), p. 11.

communities such as St. Louis and Cleveland.[29] Msgr. John T. Byrne advised his constituents that "Catholics have little reason to disagree with Dr. Graham as far as the theology of his crusade is concerned....He is insistent that those who make a decision for Christ follow it up by membership in and attendance at some church."[30]

Key 73's massive new evangelical evangelistic effort to reach the North American continent with the gospel of Christ grew out of the Berlin Congress on Evangelism (1966). In addition, an article by Carl Henry, "Somehow Let's Get Together." influenced the effort.[31] Henry distilled the evangelist vision in an article, "I Had a Dream."[32] Forty church leaders met with Graham and Henry in September 1967 at the Key Bridge Motel in Washington, D.C., out of which later meetings arose, and the Key 73 structure emerged. Each group participating in the Key 73 outreach was to develop its own program of evangelism, a "do your own thing" methodology.[33] Roman Catholic support was solicited and received. The National Council of Catholic Bishops gave an implied endorsement of participation in Key 73 on a parish-by-parish basis, and early in 1973 forty dioceses in the United States and many others in Canada were involved.[34] Not all new evangelicals were happy about the Catholic presence in Key 73. For that reason, the National Association of Evangelicals tabled indefinitely a resolution urging its churches to participate in the endeavor, causing consternation and not a little acrimony among the new evangelical brethren.[35] Fundamentalists, of course, would have no truck whatever with the ecumenical Key 73 push despite the lofty aim of confronting everyone in North America with the claims of the gospel of Jesus Christ.[36] In retrospect, not even Carl Henry remained enthusiastic about the success of Key 73.[37]

John R. W. Stott, a leading evangelical in England, said that "he was delighted to be a part of the Evangelical-Roman Catholic Dialogue on Mission" in Venice

---

[29]David Kucharsky and Edward E. Plowman, "An Evangelical Awakening in the Catholic Church?" *Christianity Today* (Dec 7, 1973), p. 46. Harold Lindsell, editor of *Christianity Today*, was not certain whether a "world-wide breakdown of Roman Catholicism" was imminent or not, but he asserted that "it is clear that there is a tremendous hunger among tens of millions of Catholics today" ("Roman Catholics—Ready to Hear," *Christianity Today* [Dec 7, 1973], p. 31).

[30]John T. Byrne, "Dr. Graham in St. Louis," editorial in *St. Louis Review*, a Catholic archdiocesan weekly, reproduced in *Christianity Today* (Dec 7, 1973), p. 46.

[31]Carl F. H. Henry, "Somehow, Let's Get Together," *Christianity Today* (June 9, 1967), pp. 24-26.

[32]Carl F. H. Henry, "I Had a Dream," *Key 73 Congregational Resource Book*, p. 156.

[33]David E. Kucharsky, "Time To Do Your Thing," *Christianity Today* (Oct 27, 1972), p. 34.

[34]"Catholic Bishops: Key 73 Sounds Okay," *Christianity Today* (May 12, 1972), p. 35; Barrie Doyle, "Roman Catholics: Keyed Up for Key 73," *Christianity Today* (Feb 16, 1973), p. 52

[35]Wilmar Thorkelson, "Evangelism Campaign Spurned," *The Minneapolis Star* (Apr 22, 1972). Clyde W. Taylor, executive director of the NAE, tried to put the best possible spin on the negative vote ("three-fourths of the voting delegates were attending convention luncheons" when the resolution was passed) (ibid.). See also Edward Plowman, "NAE: Key 73 a Key Issue," *Christianity Today* (May 12, 1972), pp. 34-35, and G. Archer Weniger, "Key 73 and Roman Catholic Ecumenism," *Sword of the Lord* (Apr 6, 1973), pp. 4-5.

[36]See, among many others, Wilson Ewin, "Key 73 Comes to Quebec or Key 73 and the Roman Church," *The Gospel Witness* (Dec 18, 1972), pp. 3-6; Ewin, "Key 73 and Its Wafer God: Is Rome Now Evangelical?", *The Gospel Witness* (Feb 8, 1973), pp. 1-7; Jack Wyrtzen, "Key 73: Compromise and Confusion," *Sword of the Lord* (Mar 16, 1973), p. 1; "Key 73 Evangelism: Why True Believers Cannot Cooperate," pamphlet of the Fundamental Evangelistic Association, Los Angeles, n.d.; and G. Archer Weniger, "Key 73: The Prostitution of Evangelism," *Faith For the Family* (Mar/Apr 1973), p. 10.

[37]Carl F. H. Henry, "Looking Back at Key 73," *The Reformed Journal* (Nov 1974), pp. 6-12.

in April 1977. He reported that "although we came together with some fears and suspicions of one another, soon the caricatures were discarded, and through patient listening we came to know, respect, and love one another in the Holy Spirit."[38] Stott also concurred with the Statement of the second National Evangelical Anglican Congress in Nottingham, England (1977), that had as its goal the visible unity of all professing Christians and proposed that evangelicals join other Anglicans working toward full communion with the Roman Catholic Church.[39]

The 1980s saw continued escalation of evangelical/Roman Catholic cooperation in crusade evangelism. Also several irenic articles generally favorable to rapprochement between the two faiths appeared, especially in the early years of the decade.[40] Probably the bombshell of the decade was Thomas Howard's conversion to Romanism in 1985. Howard taught English at Gordon College. Howard claimed that he knew of other Christians "on the verge of converting to Catholicism, including some people 'well known to evangelicals.' However, he declined to name anyone."[41] When asked if he ceased being an evangelical on becoming a Catholic, Howard replied: "Quite the contrary. Evangelical and Catholic are, or ought to be, synonymous. I will never be anything but an evangelical."[42] Howard faulted evangelicalism because it did not have an infallible teaching office and because it did not meet his expectations of meaningful worship.[43] J. I. Packer, who co-authored a book with Howard, said of the conversion of his friend: "I don't think becoming a Catholic is anything like the tragedy of a person becoming a [theological] liberal and losing touch with objective authority altogether.... Catholics are among the most loyal and [spiritually] viral brothers evangelicals can find these days."[44]

"EVANGELICALS AND CATHOLICS TOGETHER" (ECT) 1990s and LATER
Phase 1

New evangelical and Roman Catholic friendliness and fraternity reached an earth-shaking crescendo in 1994 with the document "Evangelicals and Catholics Together: The Christian Mission in the Third Millennium."[45] This publication

---

[38]John R. W. Stott, "Evangelicals and Roman Catholics," *Christianity Today* (Aug 12, 1977), p. 31.

[39]Arthur Johnston, *The Battle For World Evangelism* (Wheaton: Tyndale House, 1978), p. 328; Iain H. Murray, *Evangelicalism Divided: A Record of Crucial Change in the Years 1950 to 2000* (Carlisle, PA: Banner of Truth Trust, 2000), p. 216.

[40]For example, Andrew T. LePeau and Noel Becchetti, "Understanding Roman Catholocism," *His* (April 1981), p. 22; Kenneth Kantzer, "What Separates Evangelicals and Catholics?" *Christianity Today* (Oct 23, 1981), p. 12; Thomas F. Stransky, "Catholics and Evangelicals: A Roman Priest Looks Across the Divide," *Christianity Today* (Oct 22, 1982); "More Catholic Evangelicals?", *Eternity* (May 1983), p. 56; and George Weigel [a Catholic theologian], "A New Ecumenism," *Eternity* (July/Aug 1985), p. 33.

[41]Randy Frame, "Well-known Evangelical Author Thomas Howard Converts to Catholicism," *Christianity Today* (Apr 17, 1985), p. 46.

[42]John D. Woodbridge, "Why Did Thomas Howard Become A Roman Catholic?", an interview, *Christianity Today* (May 17, 1985), p. 49.

[43]John D. Woodbridge, "Is Evangelical Faith Enough?" *Christianity Today* (April 17, 1985), p. 58.

[44]"Well-known Evangelical Author Thomas Howard Converts to Catholicism," pp. 46-47.

[45]*First Things* (May 1994), pp. 16-21.

was principally the result of the efforts of evangelical Charles Colson of Prison Fellowship and politically conservative Richard John Neuhaus, a Lutheran minister turned Roman Catholic priest. Other evangelicals who helped form and/or endorsed the document were Richard Land and Larry Lewis of the Southern Baptist Convention, Jesse Miranda of the Assemblies of God, Brian O'Connell of the World Evangelical Fellowship, John White of Geneva College and the National Association of Evangelicals, Bill Bright of Campus Crusade for Christ, Os Guiness of Trinity Forum, Nathan Hatch of Notre Dame University, Richard Mouw of Fuller Theological Seminary, Mark Noll of Wheaton College, and J. I. Packer of Regents College. A comparable number of Roman Catholic theologians, priests, and heads of organizations were also involved, such as Avery Dulles of Fordham University, George Weigel of the Ethics and Public Policy Center, and John Cardinal O'Conner of the Archdiocese of New York.[46]

The original 1994 ECT document began with the premise "there is a necessary connection between the visible unity of Christians and the mission of the one Christ. We [Evangelicals and Catholics] together pray for the fulfillment of the prayer of our Lord: May they all be one…(John 17)."[47] In the "We Affirm Together" section, they expressed doctrinal unity that Jesus Christ is Lord, believers are "justified by grace through faith because of Christ," and the Apostles Creed is "an accurate statement of scriptural truth."[48] Their common hope was that "all people will come to faith in Jesus Christ as Lord and Savior," and that the trust and understanding between the two communities of faith would "require an assiduous attention to truth."[49] The convergence of the two groups resulted from previous common efforts against abortion and the protection of the unborn. Their new joint contention would also include delving into education, market economy, family, pornography, and American foreign policy.[50] Their "witness together" would observe the ancient patterns of "different ways of being Christian," which carried with it a prohibition against "proselytizing among active adherents of another Christian community."[51] Noting the unresolved differences between Evangelicals and Catholics, there was a determination that

> those converted—whether understood as having received the new birth for the first time or as having experienced the reawakening of the new birth originally bestowed in the sacrament of baptism—must be given full freedom and respect as they discern and decide the community in which they will live their new life of faith in Christ.[52]

Numerous supportive comments appeared in new evangelical publications. John White, president of Geneva College, for example, optimistically stated that

---

[46]Ibid., p. 22.

[47]Ibid., p. 15.

[48]Ibid., p. 16.

[49]Ibid., p. 17.

[50]Ibid., pp. 19-20.

[51]Ibid., p. 21.

[52]Ibid., p. 22.

ECT "has the potential to recast all the ecumenical discussions that have gone on through the years....This is a new day. Our closest friends as evangelicals, in the cultural task and in the fundamental theological task, are the Roman Catholics."[53] Timothy George, dean of the Beeson Divinity School, Samford University, noted that ecumenism had too long been carried on by Catholics and Protestants of the theological left, and "for that reason alone, evangelicals should applaud this [ECT] effort and rejoice in the prospect it represents."[54] Charles Colson, one of the founding energies behind ECT, felt that today's culture war is going beyond political alliances and "is taking place at a level much deeper than politics. At root, it is a battle for truth—and to fight effectively we need a distinctive Christian presence and world view."[55] The editor of *Christianity Today* expressed concern over the fate of the doctrine of justification by faith in the ECT document, but still felt that many Catholics are genuine believers in Christ and are thus evangelicals, but "inconsistent evangelicals."[56]

Other antecedents to the 1994 collusion between evangelicals and Catholics not specifically mentioned in the ECT document included the decades of ecumenical evangelistic crusades by Graham and others, the broadening effect of the Second Vatican Council (1963-65) which admitted some non-Catholics to the category of genuine but imperfect Christians, the openness of Pope John Paul II, the pro-life movement as a whole, the evangelical-like charismatic movement among Roman Catholics, and the "co-belligerence" of the two communities against public social problems, including their cooperative relationship within the Moral Majority headed by Jerry Falwell. Groundwork for 1994 had thus been amply laid, unwittingly or otherwise, and, while somewhat surprising, the new fraternity between evangelicals and Romanists was easily understandable and explainable by fundamentalist leaders.[57]

Phase 2

The ECT document and what it represented did not go over very well in the new evangelical community, precipitating one of the most intense intramural doctrinal squabbles of the movement's history. J. I. Packer, one of the original endorsers of ECT, felt compelled to explain his reason for approval.[58] Even the liberal *Christian Century* took note.[59] This unfavorable reaction led to phase two of ECT.

On January 19, 1995 many dissatisfied evangelical scholars and leaders[60] met with Colson and two of the original signers, J. I. Packer and Bill Bright, at

---

[53]"Evangelicals, Catholics Urge More Cooperation," *Moody* (May 1994), p. 62.

[54]Timothy George, "Catholics and Evangelicals In the Trenches," *Christianity Today* (May 16, 1994), p. 16.

[55]Charles Colson, "Why Catholics Are Our Allies," *Christianity Today* (Nov 14, 1994), p. 136.

[56]Kenneth S. Kantzer, "Should Roman Catholics and Evangelicals Join Ranks?" *Christianity Today* (July 18, 1994), p. 17.

[57]See the excellent analyses, for example, of James Singleton, "Catholic Cooperation?", *Frontline Magazine* (Fall 1994), pp. 29-31, and Ernest D. Pickering, *Holding Hands With the Pope.*

[58]J. I. Packer, "Why I Signed It," *Christianity Today* (Dec 12, 1994), pp. 34-37.

[59]"Evangelical-Catholic Statement Criticized," *The Christian Century* (May 18-25, 1994), pp. 520-21.

[60]Such as John MacArthur, R. C. Sproul, John Ankerberg, Michael Horton, D. James Kennedy, Joseph Stowell, and John D. Woodbridge. Joe Maxwell, "Evangelicals Clarify Accord With Catholics," *Christianity Today* (Mar 6, 1995), pp. 52-53.

Colson's request. The points of contention consisted of the inadequate statement of the doctrine of justification and the prohibition of evangelization between the two groups, evangelicals and Catholics. The result was ECT II, a five-point statement of clarification.[61] Bill Bright rejoiced that the meeting displayed God's marvelous wisdom and grace in providing a face-saving instrument, "a final, unanimous accord that would not have the signer repudiate the ECT but would allow us to issue a clarifying statement."[62] Meanwhile a new group that was formed, the Alliance of Confessing Evangelicals,[63] came out in 1994 with a document drafted by Michael Horton and revised by J. I. Packer, "Resolutions for Catholic and Evangelical Dialogue." The alliance noted that engaging with Romanism in cultural, moral, political, and social endeavors is not tantamount to "common ecclesial action in fulfilling a common ecclesial mission." It went on to deny that "in its present confession [Catholicism] is an acceptable Christian communion, let alone being the mother of all the faithful to whom every believer needs to be related."[64] In April 1996 the Alliance drew up "The Cambridge Declaration," a document stressing the five "Solae"[65] of biblical, Reformation Christianity, and lamenting the sterility of ECT and the fact that the term "evangelical" had "become so inclusive as to have lost its meaning."[66]

Phase 3

A third phase, "The Gift of Salvation," an ECT document stating what evangelicals and Catholics mean by the gospel, came out in December 1997. In it they asserted "the binding authority of Holy Scripture," the absoluteness of Jesus Christ as the one mediator between God and men, the centrality of justification by faith, which is defined as "agreement with what the Reformation traditions have meant by justification by faith alone," the assurance of eternal life, the eternal lostness of those who "do not know the way of salvation," and the need to evangelize everyone, which means evangelicals speaking the gospel to Catholics and vice versa.[67] This consensus received a massive endorsement from mainline new evangelical theologians and leaders. Still, the Alliance of Confessing Evangelicals felt the document did not go far enough to define the Reformation

---

[61]Ibid. Also "Evangelicals Clarify Cooperation Statement," *Moody* (Mar 1995), pp. 67-68.

[62]Bill Bright, an open "Dear Friend" letter under the letterhead of the Campus Crusade For Christ International, n.d.

[63]Consisting of such evangelicals as James Montgomery Boice, Alister Begg, Roger Nicole, Tom Nettles, Albert Mohler, Jr., John Hannah, and David Wells, among others.

[64]"Resolutions for Roman Catholic and Evangelical Dialogue," http//www.alliancenet.org/pub/aticles/horton.ECTresolutions.html.

[65]Salvation encompasses the Scriptures alone (*Sola Scriptura*), by grace alone (*Sola Gratia*), through faith alone (*Sola Fide*), in Christ alone (*Solus Christus*), to the glory of God alone (*Soli Deo Gloria*).

[66]"The Cambridge Declaration of the Alliance of Confessing Evangelicals," http://www.aliancenet.org/intro/CamDec.html. See the short description by Ted Olson, "Return to Reformation Roots?" *Christianity Today* (June 17, 1996), p. 62. Timothy George had a negative assessment of the Alliance, noting that it was too Reformed and that the Wesleyans, Anbabaptists, and Pentecostals "were conspicuous by their absence" ("Promoting Renewal, Not Tribalism," *Christianity Today* [June 17, 1996], p. 14). See also the exchange between David Wells and Timothy George, "Letters To the Editor," *Christianity Today* (Aug 12, 1996), p. 8.

[67]"Evangelicals and Catholics Together: The Gift of Salvation," *Christianity Today* (Dec 8, 1997), pp. 35-38.

doctrine of justification by faith alone. As a result the Alliance issued "An Appeal to Fellow Evangelicals," a response to "The Gift of Salvation," concerning which the Alliance framers say, "we are profoundly distressed by ['The Gift of Salvation's"] assertions and omissions, which leave it seriously flawed." They maintained that the latest ECT document had nothing new from the Roman Catholic perspective in that it left open the question of infused or imputed righteousness, the meaning of "faith alone," and what the call to "evangelize" really means in Roman Catholic teaching.[68]

Phase 4

A 1999 fourth phase of the ECT controversy was "The Gospel of Jesus Christ: An Evangelical Celebration," a 3,400 word document endorsed by 125 evangelical Christian leaders including some who were for and some who were against the original endeavor of 1994.[69] This seemed to satisfy the Alliance of Confessing Evangelicals who welcomed the statement because it clarified "the central content of the evangelical understanding of the Gospel that was confused and obscured by such initiatives as *Evangelicals and Catholics Together* and *The Gift of Salvation.*"[70]

A few scholars on the left wing of new evangelicalism expressed dissent with the Celebration proposal. Roger Olson felt that the framers had gone farther than they intended in stressing the forensic nature of justification, the penal vicarious satisfaction of Christ's atonement, and the eternal lostness of the unevangelized. This would exclude too many from the pale of evangelical Christianity, he feared.[71] Similarly, Gabriel Fackre demurred over the "penal and personal" elements in the statement so that "other classical Christian teachings are muted or missing."[72] He complained that political, social, and economic principalities and powers were not being challenged by true resurrection faith, reflecting a failure to comprehend the fact that "a full-orbed understanding of the atonement affects ethics."[73] In other words, the Evangelical Celebration's view of the atonement was too simplistic. Also the document emphasized too much personal salvation and did not frame it enough in a context of awareness of religious pluralism. In Fackre's judgment, the Celebration statement had too much of an "imperial ring," and its soteriology and eschatology did not respond to the "ecological and political mandates of the day" and thereby ignored the expenditure of the energy of the End in order to prepare for the Finality to come.[74] In short, his assessment was that his evangelical peers had veered too often into a "fortress mentality" in their understanding of the gospel of Jesus Christ.[75]

---

[68]"An Appeal to Fellow Evangelicals: An Alliance Response To the New ECT Document, 'The Gift of Salvation,'" http://www.alliancenet.org/mont/98.08.appeal.html.

[69]The full text is in *Christianity Today* (June 14, 1999), pp. 51-56.

[70]"Response to 'The Gospel of Jesus Christ: An Evangelical Celebration,'" http://www.alliancenet.org/month/pr9901.EvangCelebration.html.

[71]Roger E. Olson, "Theology For the Post-Graham Era," *The Christian Century* (Aug 25-Sept 1, 1999), p. 816.

[72]Gabriel Fackre, "Ecumenical Admonitions," *The Christian Century* (Aug 25-Sept 1, 1999), p. 818.

[73]Ibid.

[74]Ibid.

[75]Ibid., p. 819.

Others on the left complained that the Celebration document spent too much time on justification and too little on sanctification, and that it reflected the exclusivist view that those who do not place personal faith in Jesus Christ are eternally lost. They summarized: "We are sorry, however, that it does not in fact represent adequately the evangelical consensus it purports to reflect."[76]

Despite all the revisions, clarifications, and restatements of ECT, the fact remains that certain fundamental, load-bearing doctrines have been overlooked or ignored. They have been obscured or lost in the optimism and heady atmosphere of evangelical/Roman Catholic inclusivism, undermining any true basis of ecclesial cooperation, including the proclamation of the good news of Jesus Christ and His provision for reconciliation with God. There is no genuine consensus between the two faiths on who actually is a Christian and precisely how one *becomes* and remains a Christian. The sacramentarianism of Rome has been papered over by the evangelicals. Is faith alone in Jesus Christ alone a very personal and volitional act or is baptism the sacrament of faith in the last analysis? It cannot be both. Is justification a once-for-all forensic imputation of Christ's merit to the sinner's account, or is it something that begins with a subjective "infusion" of merit and "increases" with the observance of the sacraments? In like manner, is justification an eternal standing with God, or is it something than can be lost because of a "mortal sin," thus necessitating a "re-justification" through penance, a parallel sacrament to baptism? There is no middle ground to be carved out here. Biblical faith and sacramental grace are mutually exclusive. The ominous note that there are "different ways of being Christian" in the 1994 ECT declaration has loomed since then as an ever-larger and ever-increasing obstacle between New Testament Christianity and Romanism. The Bible presents mankind in two unmixed categories: believers and unbelievers; Spirit people and non-Spirit people; those either in light or darkness, life or death.

There is no agreement in the evangelical/Catholic dialogue on who actually needs conversion to Christ. The designation "believing Catholics" is never used by Rome of is adherents.[77] Its institutional baptism makes one a believer and a Catholic simultaneously. The word "believing" is a totally unnecessary and contradictory qualifier to the word "Catholic." No other kind of Roman Catholic exists than "believing" because baptism is the sacrament of faith. Therefore "evangelizing" Catholics or "making believers" of them is completely oxymoronic in Romanist dogma. Hence the failure to genuinely come to terms with the evangelism issue in the dialogue, the affirmations and declarations to the contrary notwithstanding.

Evangelicals such as J. I. Packer seem confused and misguided on this point. It is said that evangelicals can indeed have authentic theological and cooperative rapport with Roman Catholics who "do not self-consciously assent to the precise definitions of the Roman Catholic magisterium regarding justification, the sole

---

[76]Cornelius Plantinga Jr., Alan G. Padgett, Nicholas Woltestorff, et al., Letter to the Editor, *Christianity Today* (Oct 4, 1999), p. 15.

[77]Iain H. Murray, "'Evangelicals and Catholics Together' — A Movement of 'Watershed Significance?'" *Banner of Truth* 393 (1996), p.13.

mediation of Christ, the relation between faith and the sacraments," and the like.[78] In other words, evangelicals can work with "believing Catholics." But "believing Catholics" is a meaningless term in Rome's doctrine and practice, as noted above. Furthermore, it is incredibly naive to think that the theologians, priests, and others of the Roman hierarchical clergy aboard ECT, such as Richard John Neuhaus and Avery Dulles, do not self-consciously subscribe to Romanist dogma.[79] To them, such a thought is unthinkable! In reality, the true common ground between the new evangelicals and the Roman Catholics is simply God-talk. Both are using the same words and affirming the same terms, but the propositional *understanding* between them is missing.

In truth, Romanist doctrine has not changed over the centuries. Rome's magisterium—the official teaching office of the church, which is undergirded and walled in by the notion of infallibility— precludes such change. Pickering again is quite insightful:

> Stray remarks by priests, cardinals, or other leaders of Rome do not constitute Rome's official position. Much has been made of the fact that the numerous charismatics now found within the Roman Catholic Church are "more like evangelicals," and have some views that may not be compatible with historic Romanism. This may be true, but individual communicants within the Catholic Church do not determine the doctrinal basis of the Church. Roman Catholicism does not accept, as do Protestants, the right of individual biblical interpretation. Authoritative teaching comes through the Church and is incorporated in the collective body of Roman Catholic dogma that has collected over the centuries.[80]

Ecumenism, then, has been the most productive and at the same time the fatal enginery of the new evangelical movement. Ecumenism as described here in Part 3 is precluded by the biblical doctrine of ecclesiastical separation. This doctrine, of course, was the first to be jettisoned by the plotters and leaders of the new coalition back in the 1940s. It is to this doctrine that we now turn in Part 4.

---

[78]J. I. Packer, *Evangelicals and Catholics Together: Towards a Common Mission* (Dallas: Word, 1995), p. 159, as cited in Murray, "Evangelicals and Catholics Together," p. 16.

[79]Iain Murray, "Evangelicals and Catholics Together," p. 16.

[80]Ernest D. Pickering, *Holding Hands With the Pope*, p. 4.

PART 4: ECCLESIASTICAL SEPARATION

Ecclesiastical separation takes place on the organizational level where religious groups operate and interact. Ecclesiastical separation is to be distinguished from personal separation which has to do with the individual believer and his personal relationship to the "world." Ecclesiastical separation is the refusal to collaborate in or the withdrawal from a working relationship with an organization or a religious leader that deviates from the standards of Scripture. It normally involves such things as local churches, other ecclesiastical institutions or bodies, and religious or quasi-religious endeavors of all kinds. Ernest Pickering defined ecclesiastical separation as it affects local churches, but the principles could be applied more broadly. In his words, ecclesiastical separation is

> the principle of separation as applied to the nature and associations of the visible churches. Biblical separation is the implementation of that scriptural teaching which demands repudiation of any conscious or continuing fellowship with those who deny the doctrines of the historic Christian faith, especially as such fellowship finds expression in organized ecclesiastical structures, and which results in the establishment and nurture of local congregations of believers which are free from contaminating alliances.[1]

Modern ecclesiastical separation for Bible-believers came to the forefront during the great fundamentalist-modernist controversy of the 1920s to the 1940s in North America. For the fundamentalists the 1920s was a period of controversy and battle with liberals and other assorted infidels and Bible-deniers, particularly in the Northern Baptist Convention and among the northern Presbyterians. The 1930s and 1940s represented a period of cohesion and building institutions and associations of various kinds around strong leaders. The hallmark of early fundamentalism was ecclesiastical separation despite the inconsistencies of a few.

In the early 1940s notes of dissatisfaction with fundamentalism began to be heard, particularly having to do with ecclesiastical separation. These expressions came from within the ranks of professing fundamentalism itself, or more properly from within the fundamentalist/evangelical coalition that had gone through the fundamentalist-modernist controversy. The National Association of Evangelicals, for example, was formed as a non-separatist organization in 1942, in distinction from the fundamentalist, separatist American Council of Christian Churches. The new evangelicals were caught in a bind, however, in that they wanted to distance themselves from separatism and reach out to evangelicals in the Federal Council

---

[1]Ernest Pickering, *Biblical Separation: The Struggle For a Pure Church* (Schaumburg, IL: Regular Baptist Press, 1979), p. 10.

of Churches and thus develop a broad-based Protestantism around the NAE. At the same time the fundamentalists, especially the ACCC led by Carl McIntire, were pressuring them to come out against the Federal Council, the most visible institution of ecumenical liberalism of the day. The NAE finally had to change its by-laws to prohibit dual membership in the Federal Council and the NAE.[2] Partial relief for the NAE ambivalence came through making a distinction between "independency" and "separatism." Carpenter suggests that mainline Protestants did not see much difference between the two terms, and thus did not discern much real distinction between the NAE and the ACCC on the subject of ecclesiastical separation.[3] The truth is that the new evangelicalism of the 1940s and 1950s had as its leading indicator a repudiation of ecclesiastical separation in favor of openness toward, infiltration of, and dialogue with non-evangelicals. Their activities in the 1940s and the inclusivistic ecumenical evangelism practiced and promoted by Billy Graham in the 1950s verify it.

The biblical principle of ecclesiastical separatism antedated the events of the 1920s. Its roots are traceable to the Old Testament and didactically presented in the New Testament. Pickering succinctly chronicles the ecclesiastical separation by the Montanists and Novatians, forerunners of the Donatist separation from the Catholic church in the fourth century, some Puritans and 18th century Separate Baptists in America, on the eve of post-Enlightenment religious liberalism. The historical separatists include the Albigenses, Bogomils, Paulicians, Petrobrusians, Bohemian Brethren, Waldensians, Lollards, Hussites, and Anabaptists. In addition to separatism, some held to questionable and/or unacceptable doctrines.[4]

The rise of liberalism/modernism and its clash with biblical Christianity further framed separatism's issues, forms, and controversies. The classic example early in the clash was Charles Haddon Spurgeon's controversy with liberalism in the Baptist Union in nineteenth-century England.

In the *Sword and Trowel* Spurgeon chronicled the doctrinal and spiritual decline of the churches in Great Britain, a process he called the "Down-grade." His reactions, warnings, and attempts at correcting the inroads of liberalism, and his eventual withdrawal from many good men in the Baptist Union, serve as an excellent model parallel to the struggle of Bible-believers in America with modernism and the inevitable necessity of separation when efforts at internal resolution fail.

Spurgeon traced the blame for the Down Grade to the Act of Uniformity in 1662, a decision that purged Calvinist Puritanism from the Church of England and effectively installed Arminianism in its place.[5] The Presbyterians fell first, Spurgeon

---

[2]Joel A. Carpenter, *Revive Us Again: The Reawakening of American Fundamentalism* (New York: Oxford Press, 1997), p. 153.

[3]Ibid.

[4]Pickering, *Biblical Separation*, pp. 11-73 (see p. 29 for a disclaimer on some of the doctrines of these groups). In fact, Pickering carries the history up through the new evangelical era of ecumenical evangelism.

[5]Charles Haddon Spurgeon, "The Down Grade," *Sword and Trowel* (March 1887), p. 122. Spurgeon was adamant that Arminianism was the culprit eventually responsible for the Down Grade. For example,

noted, primarily because their practice of infant baptism and church membership allowed many to grow up in the church unregenerate.[6] Behind the deterioration brought in by Arminianism lay a more foundational issue—the departure from the doctrine of the inspiration of the Scriptures. This was "the first step astray," and Spurgeon concluded, "let a man question, or entertain low views of the inspiration and authority of the Bible, and he is without chart to guide him, and without anchor to hold him."[7] He considered liberalism a new religion "which is no more Christianity than chalk is cheese," and he was incensed that "these enemies of our faith expect us to call them brethren, and maintain a confederacy with them!"[8] His critics suggested his concern was due to his deteriorating physical condition and recommended a vacation.[9] Spurgeon withdrew from the Baptist Union in October 1887, arguing that "it behooves us to see that we do not become accomplices with those who teach another gospel,"[10] and adding, "With deep regret we abstain from assembly with those whom we dearly love and heartily respect, since it would involve us in a confederacy with those with whom we can have no communion in the Lord."[11] Later he explained: "As soon as I saw, or thought I saw, that error had become firmly established, I did not deliberate, but quitted the body at once."[12]

Spurgeon perceived other factors in the Down Grade controversy. For one, he criticized the influential Philip Dodderidge, whom he considered "as sound as he was amiable," but who "sometimes mingled in a fraternal manner, even exchanging pulpits, with men whose orthodoxy was called in question. It had its effect on many of the younger men."[13] Furthermore, Spurgeon lamented the attempt at neutrality by those who "would rush in between the combatants, and declare that there was no cause for war but that our motto might continue to be 'Peace, peace!'"[14] Spurgeon wished to raise a protest against infidelity so that those who held to New Testament Christianity could join in and at least "free themselves of that complicity which will be involved in *a conspiracy of silence*" (italics added),[15] an apparent reference to the waffling "peace" faction. He saw three parties involved in the controversy with liberalism: the liberals, those who

---

he wrote, "Arminianism, which is only Pelagianism under another name, had, to a large extent, eaten out the life of the Church of England, and Arianism followed to further and complete the destruction" (*Sword and Trowel* [April 1887], p. 166), and "from facts too stubborn to be bent, and too numerous to be contradicted, Arminianism has been among them the common road to Arianism and Socinianism" (ibid., p. 169).

[6]*Sword and Trowel* (March 1887), p. 126.

[7]*Sword and Trowel* (April 1887), p. 170.

[8]*Sword and Trowel* (Aug 1887), p. 397.

[9]*Sword and Trowel* (Sept 1887), p. 461.

[10]*Sword and Trowel* (Oct 1887), p. 513.

[11]Ibid., p. 515.

[12]"The Drift of the Times, Sound the Alarm!", written in 1888 by Spurgeon and reprinted in *The Gospel Witness* (Jan 12, 1995), p. 5.

[13]*Sword and Trowel* (April 1887), pp. 166-67.

[14]*Sword and Trowel* (Oct 1887), p. 509.

[15]*Sword and Trowel* (Aug 1887), p. 400.

held to the Bible, "and a great mixed multitude who from various causes decline to be ranked with either of them."[16] He considered the "brethren in the middle [as] the source of this clinging together of discordant elements" [i.e., those who wanted peace and fellowship with both liberals and Bible-believers inside the Baptist Union].[17]

Since Spurgeon's day, the "Down-grade" controversy has been repeatedly replayed, and America would taste her share of the battles. The fundamentalists faced the same acrimony from liberals and heard the same arguments for non-separatism from their alleged friends in conservative evangelicalism. The arguments have been perpetuated by the new evangelicals to this day.

---

[16]"The Drift of the Times, Sound the Alarm!" p. 6.
[17]Ibid.

10

THE RATIONALE OF EVANGELICAL NON-SEPARATISM

A wide spectrum of new evangelical thought exists concerning the various facets of apostasy, cooperation, and separation. Taken together, the salient features of this spectrum form a rationale for the anti-separatism stance that characterized the new evangelical movement from the beginning. Indeed, it can be argued, as has been shown in chapter 3, that the unity/separation issue and the disdain for ecclesiastical separation was the underlying complaint that the new evangelicals had against their fundamentalist brethren in the original fundamentalist/evangelical coalition.

PRAGMATISM

Sometimes the question of separation is approached on pragmatic and philosophic grounds instead of biblical grounds. Ecclesiastical separation, Ronald Nash declared, "could possibly do more harm in the long run than good." (He disclaimed the idea that "separation is never justified" because there have been times when it was required: the Reformation, for example.)[18] On another note, J. D. Douglas opined: "Some pastors are called, not to sacrificial secession, but to sacrificial continuance in situations calling for steady preaching of the evangel amid heretics and apostates, publicans and sinners."[19] Neither Nash nor Douglas recognized a biblical norm for staying in the apostasy or coming out. Their only standard was pragmatism: not what is right or wrong, but what is productive. When the end justifies the means in ecclesiastical practice, the end soon sanctifies the means. The pragmatic argument has a conspicuous absence of biblical input. Nash devotes two chapters to the questions, "To Separate or Not to Separate" and "To Unite or Not to Unite," and not a shred of biblical evidence is in either one! Nor for that matter does Douglas bother to adduce any Scriptural data for his rubric. Others, such as Robert Ferm's attempt in his apologetic for inclusive evangelism, produce questionable applications from sloppy exegesis at dealing with the sacred text. The results are ludicrous.[20] This omission and/or inept handling of Scripture does not commend the new evangelical rationale against ecclesiastical separation.

---

[18]Ronald Nash, *The New Evangelicalism* (Grand Rapids: Zondervan, 1963), p. 87.

[19]J. D. Douglas, "Separated—or Guilty?" *Christianity Today* (Feb 2, 1968), p. 60.

[20]Robert O. Ferm, *Cooperative Evangelism: Is Billy Graham Right or Wrong?* (Grand Rapids: Zondervan, 1958).

INFILTRATION

The genius of the new evangelical thinking on this subject is a simple repudiation of ecclesiastical separation in favor of infiltration. Harold John Ockenga seems to be the originator of the idea of infiltration, at least in 1940s and 50s context,[21] and it has been picked up by many since. Ockenga reasoned that a militaristic "frontal attack" on liberalism no longer served a useful purpose and that the principle of infiltration used by the communists against the allies in the Far East would be more effective. In addition, the liberals had been infiltrating evangelicals for many years.[22] By this method, he figured, regaining control of the major denominations might be achievable. Nash echoes the same call of infiltration of liberal ranks by evangelicals.[23] L. Nelson Bell, Billy Graham's father-in-law and one of the first board members and supporters of *Christianity Today* lamented: "It's highly distressing that perhaps the greatest field for Christian witness today is *within* the Church (italics his)."[24] Weisiger's infiltration strategy proposed staying in corrupt denominations to "give a witness of generous stewardship,"[25] apparently not grasping that generously funding the apostate denomination practiced poor stewardship of Christian resources. The ecclesiastical executives probably considered Weisiger's "witness" as useful evangelical naivete, if not worse.

The "infiltrations" of the liberals and the evangelicals proceeded with differing ethics. The liberals did not hesitate to lie, steal, and cheat in their efforts to wrest control of the denominations, churches, seminaries, mission agencies, and other ministries, from the fundamentalists. Countering liberal strategy with rational dialogue, ecclesiastical politics, and pacific, loving pietism proved ineffective to recover denominational leadership. An illustration of the ineffectiveness of the tolerant approach occurred when the United Presbyterians replaced the historic Westminster Confession with a New Book of Confessions that included the new "Confession of 1967."[26] The New Book then served as the sole creedal authority for the ordination of elders in that communion. The following report by the editor of *Eternity* showed no alarm:

> Conservative evangelical reaction to the enactment of the new confessional structure has varied greatly. Some have branded the action as "a final step toward complete apostasy" while others have expressed widely ranging views from the apathetic stance of "I guess I can live with it" to those who are enthusiastic for its contemporaneity. *Many conservatives voted with the majority"* (italics added).[27]

---

[21]News Release, Dec 8, 1957.

[22]Harold Ockenga, "Resurgent Evangelical Leadership," *Christianity Today* (Oct 10, 1960), pp. 14-15.

[23]*The New Evangelicalism*, p. 96.

[24]L. Nelson Bell, "On 'Separation,'" *Christianity Today* (Oct 8, 1971), p. 26.

[25]Cary N. Weisiger III, "Denominational Giving: An Evangelical's Dilemma," *Christianity Today* (Mar 30, 1973), p. 39.

[26]Russell T. Hitt, "Presbyterians Adopt New Confession in Portland," *Eternity* (July 1967), p. 36. For an informative concise overview of the provisions of the new confession vis-a-vis the Westminster standards, see Frank Farrell, "The New Presbyterian Confession," *Christianity Today* (May 7, 1965), pp. 52-53.

[27]Russell T. Hitt, "Presbyterians Adopt New Confession," p. 36.

The editor missed a prime opportunity to note the failure of evangelicals to stand their ground. To have done so, would have highlighted the failure of the infiltration technique. In other words, the editor did not want to point out the obvious to his peers. By cooperating, the few evangelicals not only failed to carry the day for truth, they gave aid and comfort to the opposition.

Much more recently in the Presbyterian Church (USA), turmoil developed over ordaining homosexuals. At the 2001 General Assembly the denomination voted to overturn the 1978 ban on gay clergy; it also drew up a statement that failed to teach the only way to heaven is through Jesus Christ. As well, it voted to retract a 1997 requirement that Presbyterian ministers are to "live either in fidelity within the covenant of marriage between a man and a woman, or chastity in singleness."[28] This brought expressions of "great dismay" from conservatives, who in turn formed a Confessing Church Movement. Ironically, the PC USA elected an evangelical at its new moderator—Jack Rogers, a former theology professor at Fuller Seminary. According to the report, "Rogers says he is determined to keep the denomination together."[29] Instead of siding with the confessing church, Rogers sought peace and a continued presence of evangelicals in the PC USA—which is what one should expect from the new evangelical infiltration policy that had failed the cause of truth for sixty years.

In another arena, Thomas Oden is considerably up-beat over the prospects of the broad evangelical Confessing Movement's influence in the United Methodist Church. While claiming that Methodist evangelicals have pulled what was thought to be "an 'incurably liberal' denomination back toward the orthodox center," he also notes that "Evangelicals have been unable for the most part to gain positions on seminary faculties, influence church spending, or elect bishops."[30] The Confessing Movement is hoping to build on the efforts of the renewal group in the United Methodist Church, namely the Good News movement, founded in 1967, "to bring a more distinctly evangelical emphasis to the denomination."[31] From the previous track record, those efforts also offer very dismal prospects for the cause of God's truth.

W. B. Riley saw the same failed efforts in his struggles with liberalism in the Northern Baptist Convention in the 1920s, 30s, and 40s. He roundly castigated the "middle-of-the-road man":

> The middle-of-the-road man is the theological menace of the 20th century. He has been the danger-driver; to his influence may be attributed the triumph of infidelity in the denominational camps. His vote has been the balance of power, and it goes almost uniformly to the theological leftists....On that account, the middle-of-the-road-man is a greater menace to his denomination than is the modernist. Believers can meet the modernist in the intellectual forum and worst him in debate, but that fact avails little since the victory and the argument are wrested by the popular vote. That is why the middle-of-the-road man menaces the very life of the true church.[32]

---

[28]John W. Kennedy, "Presbyterians Void Ban on Gay Clergy," *Christianity Today* (Aug 7, 2001), p. 22.
[29]Ibid.
[30]Thomas Oden, "Mainstreaming the Mainline," *Christianity Today* (Aug 7, 2001), p. 59.
[31]Ibid., p. 61.
[32]W. B. Riley, "Middle-Of-The-Road-Men," reprinted in *The Projector* (Mar 1979), p. 11.

The new evangelical movement has resembled a middle-of-the-road evangelical corporate man, aiming to carve out an acceptable, middle position between the neo-liberal/neo-orthodox left and the separatist fundamentalist right. The liberal *Christian Century* lauded the NAE's spirit of "turning constructive" instead of becoming reactionary. Harold Fey based his praise on the conciliatory 1963 annual meeting of the NAE in Buffalo, NY.[33] NAE president, Robert A. Cook, announced that the organization would walk a middle path between the National Council of Churches and the American Council of Christian Churches.[34] This halfway stance earned them the dubious distinction of "bystanders of the faith."[35]

APOSTASY

Another factor in the new evangelical approach to separatism is the tendency to acknowledge times when separation has been justified (e.g., the Protestant Reformation), and may still be justifiable.[36] However, the bases for separating either remain unspecified or are reduced to one or two criteria so as to be functionally useless.

New evangelicals generally believe that apostasy is a legitimate reason for ecclesiastical separation. *Defining* apostasy proves much more difficult. From the beginning, the controlling leadership of the NAE wanted to steer a middle course between staying in and coming out of corrupt denominations. This mediating motif spawned more controversy after Harold Ockenga announced in 1947, almost offhandedly at Fuller Seminary's convocation, that the school was not a "come-outer" institution. His comment drew fire immediately from the separatists in the fundamentalist/evangelical coalition, and the NAE scrambled to carve out a half-way house between the sympathies of the non-separatists and the convictions of the separatists within the young organization. At a meeting of the Executive Committee of the NAE in June 1948, a statement drafted duly acknowledged that "the growing liberalism of the denominations sometimes reaches that final apostasy when the only proper course for Evangelicals is to withdraw in loyalty to the Scriptures." But the statement still avoided taking sides by adding: *"But the NAE does not presume to decide when that point has been reached, recognizing at this point the responsibility of the individual conscience"* (italics added).[37] Perhaps this statement is the most that could be said under the tension of the ecclesiastical politics of the moment, but it is considerably less than conclusive.

Carl Henry also listed apostasy as a basis for separation but did not define the term further.[38] Elsewhere he indirectly suggested that apostasy was practically

---

[33]Harold E. Fey, "N.A.E. Turns Constructive," *The Christian Century* (May 8, 1963), p. 607.

[34]Carl McIntire, "Down the Middle," *Christian Beacon* (May 9, 1963), p. 1.

[35]Robert Lightner, "The New Evangelicals—Bystanders of the Faith," *Sword of the Lord* (Aug 1, 1969), p. 1. This was Dr. Lightner's address to the 25th Spring Convention (1967) of the American Council of Christian Churches.

[36]For example, Ronald Nash, *The New Evangelicalism*, pp. 87, 91.

[37]Stephen Paine, "NAE and Separation," *United Evangelical Action* (Sept 15, 1948), p. 22. Paine, editor of the publication, noted about the matter of separation from apostasy: "This, and this alone, is the present issue between the American Council of Christian Churches and the National Association of Evangelicals."

[38]Carl F. H. Henry, "The Perils of Ecumenicity," *Christianity Today* (Nov 26, 1956), p. 20.

indefinable.[39] He noted that separatists have pressed 2 Corinthians 6:17 ("come out from their midst and be separate...") to mean that if a denomination is apostate, Christians sin against their consciences by staying in and supporting it. Henry disagreed totally with this interpretation (he thought it only referred to withdrawal from pagan idolatry). He also believed that "the problem of the separatist is of being certain when a church has become apostate."[40] He proposed an "intermediary position" between apostasy and separatism where there is room for a "distinctly evangelical witness and fellowship." His conclusion was not very reassuring. He left the problem dangling by saying: "The difficulty of this position...is that of locating the transition-line to apostasy."[41]

Carnell defined a state of apostasy as, when "a denomination removes the gospel from its creed or confession, or if it leaves the gospel but removes the believer's right to preach it." Such a group is no longer a church and the formation of a new fellowship is justified.[42] Carnell's definition stops short of an applicationally certain principle; i.e., just *how* is this to be practiced without offending what he held to be the inexorable law of love? Whatever the answer, Carnell insisted that it must pass muster with "the counsel of the brethren and the wisdom of classical theology."[43] He ruled out two possible ties: "Unfaithful ministers do *not* render the church apostate," and "wicked members do *not* make the church apostate."[44]

Perhaps the ultimate dilemma in the use of the apostasy rubric is posed by Vernon Grounds. He defines apostasy as "declension from the rebellion against a religion once professed."[45] He understands Christianity as "destined to terminate in a gross anti-Christianity" in the end times, though it will be something less than total apostasy.[46] His final proposition and conclusion leaves one in a fog of contradiction, uncertainty, and ambiguity. He concludes:

> The doctrine of an apostate Christendom need not promote a mood of judgmental Pharisaism or pessimistic defeatism. It is not for us to worry about when the epithet "apostate" may be properly applied. In my opinion, however, only under extraordinary circumstances and with the utmost circumspection are we ever in a position to condemn any particular fellowship as apostate. We may be distressed by tendencies and practices within it; we may conclude that it is impossible for us to retain membership within a certain group or denomination; *but I feel we have no sure Biblical criteria which permit us to pronounce the sentence of apostasy.* Within the most apparently apostate body there may still be a God-pleasing

---

[39]Carl F. H. Henry, "The Unity That Christ Sustains," *Eternity* (Mar 1956).

[40]Ibid., p. 19.

[41]Ibid.

[42]Edward John Carnell, *The Case For Orthodox Theology* (Philadelphia: Westminster, 1959), p. 137.

[43]Ibid.

[44]Ibid., pp. 115, 135.

[45]Vernon Grounds, "Christianity and Apostasy," *Seminary Study Series* (Denver: Conservative Baptist Theological Seminary, n.d.), p. 1.

[46]Ibid., pp. 3, 7.

remnant of genuine believers (Gen 18:23-33). In my opinion, furthermore, revival is never precluded by anything that Scripture teaches with respect to prophecy. *I see nothing which makes a drift toward apostasy irreversible* (italics added.)[47]

But what good is his rubric if there are no biblical standards to discern apostasy, and how can a drift toward apostasy be prophetically destined for Christendom and still be reversible by a small remnant who choose to remain in an apostate group? The concept of apostasy as a working principle is canceled by its inability to be defined and recognized, making the apostasy criterion self-destructive and useless.

Barnhouse understood apostasy to mean a denial of the deity of Christ.[48] Ockenga and Eenigenburg interpreted apostasy similarly.[49] Reuben Lores spoke of a deficient Christology (a denial of Christ's humanity) and a deficient doctrine of salvation (salvation by works).[50] While these definitions of apostasy are more specific than others, a sufficient ambiguity precludes a workable application.

On the other hand, some evangelicals consider eviction as an acceptable, even preferable, form of separation. Carnell compared the apostles' expulsion by the Jews and the Reformers from Romanism as examples, justifying forming a new fellowship.[51] Ockenga taught that evangelicals have a responsibility to stay in the mainline denominations unless expelled.[52] Eenigenburg contended that the Reformers never separated from the Roman church but were ejected;[53] therefore to him, separation is "the act of an express, voluntary rejection of one group of professing Christians in favor of another."[54] While being evicted for orthodoxy has biblical and historical precedent, it often tends to be a veiled invitation for evangelicals to stay in doctrinally deviant organizations. Ironically, eviction demands that those denying key doctrines should practice separation sooner than those who adhere to the Scriptures.

THE IMPOSSIBILITY OF A PURE CHURCH

Another defining ingredient in the new evangelical rationale of non-separatism is the conviction that a pure church is not possible. If a church free of heresy and false teaching is an unattainable ideal, then efforts to separate from such a church or denomination are counterproductive and wrong-headed. Augustine's attack on the Donatists for separating from the Catholic church seems to be the origin of this idea.[55]

---

[47]Ibid., p. 8.

[48]Donald Grey Barnhouse, "Thanksgiving and Warning," *Eternity* (Sept 1957), p. 9.

[49]Harold John Ockenga, "Resurgent Evangelical Leadership," p. 15. Elton M. Eenigenburg, "Separatism Is Not Scriptural," p. 22.

[50]Reuben Lores, "Ecumenism," *World Vision Magazine* (Nov 1967), p. 14.

[51]Edward John Carnell, *The Case For Orthodox Theology*, pp. 136-37.

[52]"Resurgent Evangelical Leadership," p. 15.

[53]"Separatism is Not Scriptural," p. 22.

[54]Ibid., p. 18..

[55]Ernest D. Pickering, *Biblical Separation*, pp. 21-24.

George Eldon Ladd, professor of biblical theology at Fuller Seminary spelled out this argument clearly,[56] positing that the unity of the church overrides the purity of the church.[57] Citing the example of Hymenaeus and Philetus, who taught a non-body resurrection (2 Tim 2:17) and denied an eschatological resurrection of the body, Ladd asserts they "were initiating an apostatizing movement."[58] Paul's counsel to Timothy that the presence of vessels of wood, earthenware, and dishonor alongside the ones of gold and silver (2 Tim 2:20) "can mean nothing less than that in the church we are to expect different kinds of ministers; and the point of reference is doctrinal purity. Nothing can be clearer than the statement of this verse that perfect doctrinal purity is an ideal which can never be obtained."[59] The apostle's directive to Timothy to "cleanse himself" from these dishonorable vessels is, in Ladd's view, that "the church is to be *warned* against these false teachings" (italics added).[60] His conclusion here is:

> Paul's over-all strategy in safeguarding the church against heretical teaching is not that of searching for and rooting out every vestige of error; it is rather the vigorous propagation of sound doctrine in the spirit of love as the means of protecting the church against error. The desire to recover dissident teachers is more important than the denunciation of their error.[61]

However, the idea of "cleansing" oneself from these false teachers means far more than the "warning" that Ladd counseled. Homer Kent saw the apostle's teaching more clearly. "The great house is a symbol of the professing church in its widest aspect." As wood and pottery vessels are unenduring and must be replaced, "So in the church, false teachers arise from time to time, but eventually their worthlessness is recognized, and they are removed."[62] As the contamination of the dishonored containers must not be allowed to soil the honored ones, "the true servant of God must purge himself from the company of the valueless ones. By doing so, he will have become separated from evil...and thus be of use...to the Master of the household."[63] In the analogy, the cleansing/purging is from the false teachers themselves and not just the uncleanness of their message, much less some sort of warning against their doctrine.[64]

Ladd goes on to explain Titus 3:10-11 ("reject a factious man...") by understanding the "heretick" (KJV) or factious man as not referring to a false teacher and his teaching

---

[56]George E. Ladd, "The Evangelical's Dilemma: Doctrinal Purity vs. Visible Unity," *Eternity* (June 1962), p. 7.

[57]Both the new evangelicals and the fundamentalists believed in and appealed to the purity of the visible church in their diverse formulations of separatism. After extensive research, Larry R. Oats concluded that neither side gave theological precision to their doctrine of ecclesiology, and this failure only furthered the division between the two groups. *The Relationship of Ecclesiology to the Doctrine of Ecclesiatical Separation Evidenced in the New Evangelical and Fundamentalist Movements of the Middle Twentieth Century* (Ph.D. dissertation, Trinity Evangelical Divinity School, 1999), p. iv.

[58]"The Evangelical's Dilemma," p. 9.

[59]Ibid.

[60]Ibid.

[61]Ibid.

[62]Homer A. Kent, Jr., *The Pastoral Epistles* (Chicago: Moody, 1958), p. 277.

[63]Ibid., p. 278.

[64]While not specifically commenting on this passage, Francis Schaeffer advocated a "discipline" of liberals in order to maintain the purity of the visible church (*The Church Before the Watching World* [Downers Grove, IL: InterVarsity, 1971], p. 67). In his Presbyterian polity this probably meant more

but to "divisive, disruptive conduct."[65] This passage says, "is a strong proof text against those who have little or no regard for the unity of the visible church. To him [i.e., Paul], the main concern in this passage is in fact the unity of the church."[66]

Concerning the factious man of Titus 3:10, the unity of the church is of course involved, but the ultimate question is: *What* is causing the disunity and division? In context it is false teaching about the Law of Moses (3:9); *truth* is the issue. The concept behind *hairetikos* (heretic, factious man) refers to making a choice, or making a choice pleasing to oneself.[67] In this case, division and schism are caused in the church by those who choose doctrine contrary to apostolic teaching. If there is no resolution after two warnings, a separation was to take place. *Paraitou* means to reject. While the unity of the body and the recovery of the person are important, the pure doctrine which creates the unity of the body[68] and to which the person is to be recovered[69] is what is normative finally. *Paraitou* can ultimately command the terminal extreme of excision. As Litfin put it: "Paul's thought here is similar to the Lord's instructions (Matt 18:15-17), when He taught that after giving an offender three chances to repent, he is then to be cut off (but cf. 2 Thes 3:14-15)."[70]

Some new evangelicals assert that the parable of the wheat and the weeds (Matt 13:24-30, 36-43) teaches that false teachers are not to be rooted out of the church but left there until the *eschaton* when only God Himself can and will make the final separation.[71] Again, the thought is that a pure visible church is not only an unattainable ideal, but the opposite should be expected. This view is a colossal misinterpretation. The field in the parable is *not the church but the world* (v.38), and only God knows infallibly who are the believers (wheat) and who are the pretenders (weeds) in the "world." Furthermore, He has chosen not to make this division between the two groups public until the end times. The parable therefore is cosmic not ecclesial; it bears no weight whatever on the subject of ecclesiastical separation. Buswell's commentary on this point is instructive and well taken: "God's longsuffering in the administration of cosmic affairs is no more an argument against the biblical doctrine of the purity of the visible Church than against the purity of the individual life."[72]

---

than simple exclusion from the membership of the local church, but he was quite tedious in parsing the difference between discipline and separation. To him, discipline "is not the principle of separatism. It is the practice of the principle of the purity of the visible church" (p. 72). "We are not practicing separation. Separation is a negative concept and builds a poor mentality. The Bible's emphasis is never on negation but on affirmation. The Bible's principle of the practice of the purity of the visible church is a positive concept" (p. 74). Whatever Schaeffer's reason, to some fundamentalists this semantic tedium appears to be no more than circumlocution.

[65]Ladd, "The Evangelical's Dilemma," p. 33.

[66]Ibid.

[67]Homer A. Kent, Jr., *The Pastoral Epistles*, p. 244.

[68]The believers in the early church "were continually devoting themselves to the apostles' teaching and to fellowship" (Acts 2:42), showing that doctrine precedes and structures fellowship and unity.

[69]In the Pastoral Epistles, Paul instructs that the minister must be "able to teach" so as to correct those in error, which in turn is to lead to their repentance and recovery of the truth, and thus to the restoration of the disrupted unity (2 Tim 2:24-25).

[70]A. Duane Litfin, "Titus," in *The Bible Knowledge Commentary, New Testament Edition*, John F. Walvoord and Roy B. Zuck, eds. (Wheaton, IL: Victor, 1983), p. 767.

[71]Elton M. Eenigenburg, "Separatism Is Not Scriptural," *Eternity* (Aug 1963), p. 20.

[72]"J. Oliver Buswell, Jr., "The American and International Councils of Christian Churches," *Christianity Today* (Jan 29, 1965), p. 9.

11

THE BIBLICAL IDEA OF ECCLESIASTICAL SEPARATION

THE BIBLICAL DOCTRINE OF SEPARATION

God wants His people to be distinct from the rest of the world as a special people set apart for His purposes. Israel, the Old Testament people of God, was God's own "possession" or special treasure (KJV, "peculiar treasure") (Exod 19:5; Deut 4: 20; 7:6;14:2; 26:18; Ps 135:45). The New Testament church is designated likewise (Titus 2:14; 1 Pet 2:9). The Old Testament word (*segulah*) denotes private possession or personal property, vis-a-vis those things which belonged to a larger community (cf. 1 Chron 29:3).[1] The New Testament expression (*periousion*) also contains the idea of uniqueness, being chosen, specialness, that which in a special sense belongs to oneself.[2] This special relationship to God meant that He had unquestioned right to first place in all things in their experiences and could demand absolute obedience. In the case of Israel, this relationship was due to the nation's unconditional national election by God (Deut 7:7-8), exemplified in the exodus of the nation from Egyptian servitude in undoubtedly the most colossal miracle of God in the Old Testament on behalf of His people (Exod 19:4). For the church, this treasured relationship to God is traced to the cross work of Jesus Christ, validated by the most stupendous miracle of all time—His bodily resurrection from the dead by which the believer is redeemed, freed from the tyranny of the guilt of sin (Titus 2:14a). In either case, whether the bond is national and political or spiritual and personal, people can be God's in some special, loving, and unique sense, and they have a unique, separated status with Him.

The direction, mind-set, values, philosophies, and destiny of His people are not only different from those who are not, they are diametrically opposed to them in an inevitable conflict. God Himself unilaterally instituted the enmity between His people and Satan's people (Gen 3:15) (Heb, *ebah*—hatred, hostility[3]), and will

---

[1]*Theological Wordbook of the Old Testament*, s.v. *segulah,* by Robert D. Patterson, II, p. 617. See also W. H. Gispen, *Exodus*, Bible Student's Commentary (Grand Rapids: Zondervan, 1982), p. 180.

[2]BDAG, s.v. "*periousios*," p. 802; Homer A. Kent, Jr., *The Pastoral Epistles* (Chicago: Moody, 1958), p. 236; Donald Guthrie, *The Pastoral Epistles*, Tyndale New Testament Commentaries (Grand Rapids: Eerdmans, 1957), p. 201.

[3]*Theological Wordbook of the Old Testament*, s.v. *ebah,* by Thomas McComiskey, II, p. 36.

not cease until the day of final eschatological judgment when all sin and sinners are eliminated forever. This radical, current, day-to-day discord is simply an extension of the long war between God and Satan. Two things are plainly mandated in this war: separation from the enemy's minions and their message, and an active participation in the fight against them; in other words, a militant defense and attack—separation and assault.

In its core genius and practice, fundamentalism has always been "separatistic." David Beale has correctly distinguished between "non-conformist fundamentalism" and "separatist fundamentalism."[4] The former was principally the pre-1930s fundamentalism in the great controversy with modernism. The latter was what grew out of the fierce struggles of the modernist controversy, beginning with the regrouping and consolidation efforts of fundamentalists in 1930. Even the non-conformists were separatistic at heart in that they attempted to purge their denominations and institutions of unbelief; i.e., they tried to separate the liberals from their midst. When their efforts did not prove successful, they began disjoining themselves from the liberals in a formal practice of ecclesiastical separation.

Broadly speaking, ecclesiastical separation is the refusal to collaborate with or the withdrawal of a working relationship from an ecclesiastical organization or religious leader that deviates from the standard of Scripture or that does not believe and obey the word of God in doctrine or practice. Separation is the refusal to join hands or make common cause with those who deny or disobey the Scriptures. Separation is an unwillingness to become associated or involved in any kind of ecclesiastical relationship that breaks down the divinely-ordained enmity between God and Satan, truth and error, light and darkness, good and evil, or obedience and disobedience to the Word of God. Separation requires a hatred of evil, and as a necessary correlate, a separation unto holiness, righteousness, godliness, purity, truth, and Christlikeness in all its forms and expressions—an embrace of what is good (Rom. 12:9).

The Basis of Separation

The basis of biblical separatism is the holiness of God. Holiness in both the Old and New Testaments carries the fundamental idea of separation, apartness, differentness, or a distinctness from that which is common, profane, or ordinary. Ecclesiastical separation is grounded in the character of God Himself; it is an expression of His eternal holiness. The call to separate is not the fiat of a far-off deity, or the decree of a church council or ecclesiastical executive; instead it is based on commands of God rooted in His eternal character. To "sanctify" (a verb form of the word holy) means to consecrate, set apart, or separate for God's special purpose. God's holiness is seen theologically along two lines. One is His apartness from all that is created and finite, a holiness of majestic transcendence. This is holiness in a pre-ethical sense.[5] In this respect God is the One "lofty and exalted"

---

[4]David O. Beale, *In Pursuit of Purity: American Fundamentalism Since 1850* (Greenville, SC: Unusual Publications, 1986), p. 5.

[5]Gordon Lewis and Bruce Demarest, *Integrative Theology* (Grand Rapids: Zondervan, 1987), 1:233.

(Isa 6:1), the "high and exalted one who lives forever," who dwells on a "high and holy place," and "whose name is Holy" (Isa 57:15). God is "enthroned above the cherubim," "exalted above all the peoples," whose name is "great and awesome" because He is holy (Psa 99:1-3). This aspect of God's holiness forms one of the most elementary yet far-reaching truths of theology—the Creator-creature distinction. This distinction is absolutely fundamental to man's relationship with God, and the very essence of sin is to destroy it by elevating some facet of creation over the Creator (Rom 1:25).

Second, and more to the point in this discussion, God's holiness is His apartness from all that is ethically unclean or sinful; a holiness of moral purity. Isaiah was impressed with the thrice-holy God and reacted by acknowledging his own moral uncleanness (Isa 6:3, 5). God is holy Light intrinsically (1 John 1:5), and He dwells in unapproachable holy light (1 Tim 6:16). In theology, this aspect of God's holiness is defined as His self-affirming purity[6] wherein His being and His will eternally conform to each other. God's ethical holiness is active not passive; it is not static like pure marble, but is dynamic, the energy of will. It is not merely the absence of sin and uncleanness, but the self-affirmation of holy Being. As a personal being God *expresses* His holy nature, not causes it, for He is completely uncaused. God's holiness affirms and asserts itself as the highest motive and end. In a meaningful sense, holiness is the moral attribute that governs all God's attributes.

God, therefore, has a constitutional reaction against anything that contradicts His holiness or that is ethically unlike Himself in any way. Sin, and only that, excites God's holy wrath or His judicial anger and revulsion. God demands that people be like Him in character and conduct (Matt 5:48; Rom 12:1; 1 John 2:1). Biblical separation, then, is not an ambiguous theory concocted by maladjusted fundamentalists,[7] nor was it pragmatically devised during the heat of controversy. Being separatistic is of God's very nature, and the demands He makes on His people arise out of His intrinsic Being.

The Background to Separation

While the Old Testament does not directly assert truth distinctive to the New Testament church, it nonetheless has principles and illustrations that set forth transdispensational guides and directives for all God's people. We learn that God chose Israel as a nation by His sovereign grace and loving good pleasure. The people had nothing with which to attract His benevolent attention or to commend themselves to Him (Deut 4:37; 7:6-8). Because of this divine choice, Israel was a "holy nation" (Exod 19:6), set apart and separated from the other nations as especially belonging to God. They were therefore to be different from the other people and thus exhibit their God-ordained distinctiveness. As a reminder of their separate status, God established prohibitions relative to some ordinary things in life, proscriptions that dealt with their occupation, clothing, worship, and diet. For

---

[6]Augustus H. Strong, *Systematic Theology* (Valley Forge, PA: Judson, 1907), pp. 173-75.

[7]This is the implicit charge, for example, of Edward John Carnell, *The Case For Orthodox Theology* (Philadelphia: Westminster, 1959), pp. 117, 119.

instance, they could not cultivate their fields with an ox and a donkey yoked to the same implement (Deut 22:10); they could not wear clothes that had mixed threads (Deut 22:11); and they were prohibited from having certain animals and insects in their diet (Lev 11:1-23, 41-47). Naturally, God also forbade their engaging in any worship other than of the one true and living covenant God of the nation (Exod 20:2). Yahweh-worship was the official state religion of Israel, and idolatry and all false worship warranted capital punishment (Deut 6:4-5; Lev 20:3-6).

God's underlying reason for the separation laws stemmed from His national separation of Israel from other nations. He required the Jews to demonstrate their separated status in their own personal lives. God said,

> For I am the Lord your God. Consecrate [separate] yourselves, and be holy, for I am holy....You shall not make yourselves unclean with any of the swarming things....For I am the Lord who brought you up from the land of Egypt to be your God; thus you shall be holy, for I am holy....This is the law...to make a distinction between the unclean and the clean (Lev 11:44-47).

> Moreover you shall not follow the customs of the nations which I will drive out before you,....I am the Lord your God, who separated you from the peoples. You are therefore to make a distinction between the clean animal and the unclean,...Thus you are to be holy to Me, for I the Lord am holy; and I have set you apart from the peoples to be Mine (Lev 20:23-26).

Separation was a way of life under the covenant; it was not simply a matter of food, seed, animals, and clothing. Israel's unique relationship to God found graphic visible portrayals in everyday life; God wove reminders of His special relationship with them into every aspect of their lives. The principle of separation was woven by God into their social structures and into the very fabric of daily life.

God imposed other separation laws on His people that provide a backdrop for the New Testament teaching. A proscription against intermarriage with the heathen provides a good illustration. Because of their separated covenant status as an ethnic group due to the promise of an enduring posterity through Abraham (Gen 12:3; 13:16; 15:5), God forbad the Jews to intermarry or to enter into any treaties with the surrounding Canaanite nations (Exod 34:10-16; Deut 7:3-5). God expressed the basis plainly and simply: Israel was "holy," that is separated unto God, and their separation laws were predicated on that significant fact (Deut 7:6). To intermarry would pollute the genetic Messianic line as well as lead Israel into pagan idolatry, both of which were apostasies that would bring the covenant into dissolution. Intermarriage with the heathen was rife during the post-exilic restoration. Ezra established a three-month divorce court to dissolve the illicit unions (Ezra 10). The same problem cropped up twice again a decade or two later (Neh 10:30: 13:23-29). These separation proceedings were based on the Law covenant (Ezra 10:3), and the proceedings seemed to communicate that the apostasy that permitted the unbiblical marriages could not be prolonged.

The principle of separation lies behind other relationships and alliances prohibited by God. Good king Jehoshaphat, for example, was troubled over the division between

Judah and the northern kingdom of Israel, so he took steps to close the breach. No doubt he rationalized that Judah and Israel were brethren and ought to be displaying a united front before the pagan nations. God warned Jehoshaphat that common cause would be disastrous because in these compromises he would "help the ungodly, and love them that hate the Lord" (2 Chron 19:2). Nevertheless, Jehoshaphat entered into a series of alliances with the northern kingdom. He united with Ahab against the Arameans at Ramoth-Gilead (1 Kgs 22; 2 Chron 18), he gave his son Jehoram in marriage to Athaliah, the daughter of Ahab and Jezebel (2 Kgs 8:18), he joined in a military coalition with Joram against the Moabites (2 Kgs 3:7ff), and he had a joint commercial shipping fleet with Ahaziah that God literally sank (2 Chron 20:35-37). The author of the Book of Kings, in what must surely be an understatement, tersely noted in the obituary: "Jehoshaphat also made peace with the king of Israel" (1 Kgs 22:44). Imbued with good intentions, Jehoshaphat's policy of inclusivism became one of prolonged entanglement that undid his positive contributions after his death, a legacy he never intended to leave. Evidently it is possible to "love" the wrong people the wrong way (2 Chron 19:2).

Israel's separated status had become well entrenched by the time of Christ's ministry. Some perverted this separatist mode by apostate interpretations (Matt 9:11; 15:2-9). However, the incarnation of meekness and love Himself, Jesus Christ, upheld the divine intent of the covenant by confronting false teachers and calling the nation back to its true separatist roots in Old Testament revelation (Matt 7:15; 12:1-8; 22: 39; 23:1-33; John 8:31-59). Until the inauguration of the dispensation of grace, the outward approach to God was confined to the central shrine where God had placed His name (Ex. 29:42-43). There was no alternative to the central altar in the dispensation of law under which those in the era of the Gospels lived. One could not start a rival worship service. As the reality and superiority of Christ's work became apparent to the believing Jews, some of the Old Testament separation laws were rescinded (Mark 7: 19b; Acts 10:1-16, 34-43). Although a one-for-one example of ecclesiastical separation is not found in the Gospels, the principles of separation remain, such as identifying and denouncing false teachers and their spurious doctrines (Matt 7:15; 23:1-33).

The Categories of Separation

The New Testament epistolary literature is unambiguous about the grounds for and practice of ecclesiastical separation. The same principle of separation that predicated Israel's life as an elect people is applied to New Testament believers (1 Pet 1:16). Church saints, individually and corporately, are a separated people unto God, and He requires them to be a distinct people as well.

Different methods of classifying the groups with whom a working fellowship is not biblically sanctioned have been suggested; this study will focus on four classifications.

Heresy

Heresy is an elastic word, as any worthwhile dictionary will attest; therefore it is necessary to distinguish between error and heresy.[8] Error exists when there is

---

[8]Robert Delnay broached this distinction as a factor in implementing separation. "Ecclesiastical Separation," *Faith Pulpit* (June-August 1987). *Faith Pulpit* is a publication of the Faith Baptist Theological Seminary, Ankeny, IA.

a doctrinal discrepancy between two Christians or organizations in which case one or both may be wrong, but both cannot be right. Error may or may not be grounds for ecclesiastical separation, depending on the nature of the error and one's philosophy of ministry. Heresy, however, "strikes at the very roots of the faith, and heresy is always ground for breaking fellowship."[9]

Galatians 1:8-9 identifies the heresy of a different gospel, in this case salvation by works, a legalistic soteriology; but any other heterodox plan of redemption would also come under the apostle's wrath.

> But even if we, or an angel from heaven, should preach to you a gospel contrary to what we have preached to you, he is to be accursed! As we have said before, so I say again now, if any man is preaching to you a gospel contrary to what you received, he is to be accursed!

In this context, Paul anathematizes anyone who would preach contrary to his gospel, referring to those who suspend justification on law-keeping instead of anchoring it in the grace of God through personal faith in Jesus Christ. Law-keeping meant deserting Christ for a different gospel (1:6), and it was intolerable. Sidwell notes J. Gresham Machen's observation that Paul could endure people who preached the true gospel for bad motives (Phil 1:15-18), but he could not abide anyone who preached a "bad gospel" even with good intentions.[10] Elsewhere Paul speaks of a "different gospel" that was antithetical to his message (2 Corinthians 11:4) and, while there is considerable irony in the context of 2 Corinthians 11, the apostle contends that those who preach this false gospel are imposters.

Some might propose that Paul in 2 Corinthians 11 and Galatians 1 does not state ecclesiastical separation in formal, didactic words; therefore it is only an inference or a logical deduction and not the express teaching of the apostle. However, this would be true in only the most extremely pedantic sense. Separation is a correlate of the anathema and not simply an inference or corollary; it is clearly contained in, parallel with, or is tethered inextricably to the curse. To disassociate the two components is artificial and suggests a preconceived agenda imposed on the text.

In Romans 16:17-18, Paul gives clear direction concerning the response to false teachers and their propaganda:

> Now I urge you, brethren, keep your eye on those who cause dissensions and hindrances contrary to the teaching which you learned, and turn away from them. For such men are slaves, not of our Lord Christ but of their own appetites; and by their smooth and flattering speech they deceive the hearts of the unsuspecting.

The doctrine of the apostles establishes the norm, and the church is commanded to note those who teach contrariwise. False doctrine is the cause of division in the local body and the cause of "offenses" ("hindrances" in NASB), a word denoting serious backsliding or apostasy.[11] The naive are especially vulnerable to the self-

---

[9]Ibid.

[10]Mark Sidwell, *The Dividing Line: Understanding and Applying Biblical Separation* (Greenville, SC: Bob Jones University Press, 1998), p. 44.

[11]Trivial understandings of "offense" (*scandalon*: stumblingblock) as hurt feelings, diminished self-esteem, or a simple garden variety miff fall wide of the mark. The Old Testament milieu of the word can suggest idolatry itself (Zeph 1:3, Heb). The gravity of what an "offence" is should not be underestimated.

serving flattery and deception of divine predators. Murray describes the offense and offenders, and what to do about them.

> The stumbling is that caused by false doctrine and falls into the category of the error anathematized in Galatians. The injunctions comport with an error of such character: they are to 'mark' the proponents so as to avoid them and they are to 'turn away from them.'[12]

Pickering's understanding of the apostle's injunction challenges the non-separatist position: "To remain, therefore, in whatever kind of a religious organization with such persons seems in direct contradiction to the command of the apostle."[13]

The few new evangelicals who chose to separate from an apostate denomination considered the effects that staying in would have on church members. For example, Frank Barker led the Briarwood Presbyterian Church, Birmingham, AL to separate from the Southern Presbyterian Church in 1973. Of the four principles on which the church proceeded,[14] one principle emphasized the protection of the flock.[15] A godly pastor could hardly fulfil Paul's command to guard the flock against the savage wolves that would prey on a church if he did not separate from false teachers (Acts 20:28-30). Of course, deviant teachers must be rebuked (Titus 1:13), but rebuke is not enough in some cases, and the separation of the flock is the only certain means to protect the sheep.

The apostle John sets forth heretical Christology as grounds for separation in 2 John 9-11.

> Anyone who goes too far and does not abide in the teaching of Christ, does not have God; the one who abides in the teaching, he has both the Father and the Son. If anyone comes to you and does not bring this teaching, do not receive him into your house, and do not give him a greeting.

The "teaching of Christ" refers to the full biblical teaching about Jesus of Nazareth, the Christ of God, especially the inseparable union of the fully human and fully divine natures in the one indivisible Person of the God-man. The Gnostic heresy that forms the background for John's writing, denied on Platonic grounds that deity and humanity, God and man, could ever exist on the same continuum or in the same person. Gnosticism's view of Christ destroyed the basis of atonement through penal satisfaction, eroding the foundation for eternal salvation. If Christ were not fully and genuinely human, He could not pay the penalty, the divine death sentence, for human sin. If He were not also fully and genuinely deity, His death could not have infinite value and therefore was incapable of being a surety for human sin. A denial or denigration of either of Christ's natures is a slur on His Person and nullifies

---

[12]John Murray, *The Epistle to the Romans*, The New International Commentary on the New Testament, Ned B. Stonehouse, ed., 2 vols. in one (Grand Rapids: Eerdmans, 1968), 2:236.

[13]Ernest Pickering, *Biblical Separation: The Struggle For a Pure Church* (Schaumberg, IL: Regular Baptist Press, 1979), pp. 175-76.

[14]Frank Barker, "Why We Left," *Eternity* (April 1980), pp. 17-21.

[15]Ibid., p. 18. The other principles were the preserving of the truth, the purity of the church, and the avoidance of partaking of another's sins.

His redemptive work. No gospel remains because no salvation is possible. John's stricture condemns recognizing a Christological heretic as a messenger of truth, or as a Christian for that matter (he "does not have God"), even if it means excluding him from common hospitality or not extending to him a courteous "God bless you." To do so makes one an accessory in the apostasy. Certainly, excluding a heretic from personal interaction would preclude any ministry fellowship with him.

Other texts speak of separating from false teachers and their erroneous teachings. In 1 Timothy 6:3-5 Paul denounces those who "advocate a different doctrine" inconsistent with the words of Christ and the promotion of godliness. Jesus criticized the church at Pergamum for tolerating those who held to "the teaching of Balaam" and "the teaching of the Nicolaitans" (Rev 2:14-15). What constituted these heresies need not be examined in order to perceive that Christ held the church accountable to excise false teaching. When false preachers ignore the warnings, new evangelicalism tends to tolerate their heresies until the official creeds or confessions eventually become contaminated; sadly, the formal change of doctrinal positions typically means the error has become pervasive and any resistance is token.

Unequal Alliances

A warning against unequal alliances with unbelievers appears in 2 Corinthians 6:14-7:1.

> Do not be bound together with unbelievers; for what partnership have righteousness and lawlessness, or what fellowship has light with darkness? Or what harmony has Christ with Belial, or what has a believer in common with an unbeliever? Or what agreement has the temple of God with idols? For we are the temple of the living God; just as God said, "I will dwell in them and walk among them; And I will be their God, and they shall be My people. Therefore, come out from their midst and be separate," says the Lord. "And do not touch what is unclean; and I will welcome you. And I will be a father to you, and you shall be sons and daughters to Me," says the Lord Almighty. Therefore, having these promises, beloved, let us cleanse ourselves from all defilement of flesh and spirit, perfecting holiness in the fear of God.

New evangelicals consistently have narrowly interpreted the above passage, applying it only to separation from pagans or from the pagan temples. They do not make it applicable to ecclesiastical separation. Since pagan idol temples are rare in the United States, the force of this passage, in the hands of the new evangelicals, is entirely lost for contemporary contexts. Fundamentalists have challenged the narrow understanding of Paul's admonition. There is nothing in the immediate or remote contexts that would limit the apostle's intention only to pagan idol worship. The subject is simply the separation of Christians from non-Christians based on the systemic incompatibility of the two groups as illustrated in the five antitheses in verses 14 to 16. Worship of idols by a believer is simply one of the five (v. 16a), and good interpretation does not substitute a part for the whole. While Paul does not state specifically what it means to be unequally bound with unbelievers, a number of things from his first epistle supply some clues, namely marriages between believers and unbelievers (1 Cor 7:12-15), eating idol meat in the home of an unbeliever (10:27ff), speaking in tongues in the assembly when unsaved people are present (14:24), and settling disputes before unbelievers (6:5ff).[16]

The binding together or the "yoke" is analogous to the Old Testament prohibition against yoking an ox and a donkey together (Deut 22:10). A working relationship[17] or a pulling together in the harness is depicted. The working relationship may take a variety of forms and still fall within the purview of the apostle's intention. Fundamentalists have historically seen a parallel between the passage and the inclusive policy that encourages evangelicals and apostates to unify for ministry opportunities. Tasker suggests that the yoke figure refers to compromise with unbelievers.[18] Unless one is prepared to argue that liberal and neo-orthodox apostates, for example, are actually true believers, the apostle's proscription of evangelical ecumenism is patently clear.

Charles Hodge, the old Princetonian, saw the legitimate application of Paul's term ("unbelievers") to extend beyond the heathen:

> It is no doubt true that by unbelievers Paul means the heathen (see 1 Corinthians 6:6). But it does not follow from this that intimate association with the heathen is all that is forbidden. The principle applies to all the enemies of God and the children of darkness.[19]

Organized Apostasy

Organized apostasy is seen in Revelation 18:4:

> I heard another voice from heaven, saying, "Come out of her, my people, so that you will not participate in her sins and receive of her plagues."

The context is eschatological Babylon, an entity that includes "Babylon the mother of harlots and of the abominations of the earth" (Rev 17:5). This is "Ecclesiastical Babylon" according to some scholars, that represents the ecumenical umbrella of all false religions and religious leaders united behind the Antichrist of the end times.[20]

> This great ecclesiastical organization of the end times is universal in scope and includes all segments of Catholicism: Roman, Russian, and Greek; it includes all segments of liberal and apostate Protestantism together with the vast array of cults; it includes apostate Judaism and the great pagan religions of the world.[21]

While the immediate context refers to the tribulation period of the *eschaton*, the *principle* of separation from organized apostasy whenever and wherever it occurs is not lost in this text. The wording is reminiscent of 2 Corinthians 6:17 ("do

---

[16]Philip Edgcumbe Hughes, *Paul's Second Epistle To the Corinthians*, in NICNT, p. 245.

[17]Fred Moritz, *"Be Ye Holy"* (Greenville, SC: Bob Jones University Press, 1994), p. 51.

[18]R. V. G. Tasker, *The Second Epistle of Paul to the Corinthians*, Tyndale New Testament Commentaries, R. V. G. Tasker, ed. (Grand Rapids: Eerdmans, 1979), p. 98.

[19]Charles Hodge, *An Exposition of the First Epistle to the Corinthians* (Grand Rapids: Eerdmans, 1950), p. 166.

[20]John F. Walvoord, *The Revelation of Jesus Christ* (Chicago: Moody, 1966), pp. 243-57.

[21]Herman A. Hoyt, *An Exposition of the Book of Revelation* (Winona Lake, IN: The Brethren Missionary Herald Co, 1966), p. 83.

not be bound together with unbelievers"), Isaiah 52:11 ("depart, depart, go out from there, touch nothing unclean"), and Jeremiah 50:8; 51:6 ("flee from the midst of Babylon"), 9 and 45 ("come forth from her midst, My people"). The prophetic milieu of the Old Testament references is Israel's return from apostate Babylon, either in the restoration period or in the eschaton, depending on context. But John's point is clear: God's people must disassociate from apostate surroundings, and if it is God's determination that His people separate from apostasy in history and prophecy, no legitimacy in denying the need for separation in the present age can be claimed.

Organized apostasy has included some of the following activities: (1) participating in ecumenical evangelistic crusades; (2) belonging to a denomination or association of churches that has false doctrine in its seminaries, pastors, and churches (such as the United Methodist Church, the American Baptist Churches, the Southern Baptist Convention, the Evangelical Lutheran Church, the Presbyterian Church in the USA, and many others); (3) affiliating with the conciliar movement (e.g., National Council of Churches, World Council of Churches, Baptist World Alliance); (4) giving financial aid or support to these types of groups or individuals; (5) speaking for any of these groups and sponsoring any of their speakers and representatives; or (6) appear on the same platform or participating in a program with these groups or individuals.

A separated response declares: We will not associate our name or the name of our organization (church, school, association of churches, mission agency, etc.) with any church, ecclesiastical organization, or religious leader which does not believe and obey the word of God in doctrine or practice.

Disobedient Christians

A final category of organizational separation calls for separation from disobedient Christians, a practice commonly called "secondary" or "second degree" separation. Primary separation is the withdrawal of organizational cooperation with apostates, liberals, cultists, and other deviants from New Testament Christianity. Many new evangelicals rejected even this, although some would theoretically allow complete apostasy as grounds for separation. Secondary separation is the refusal to cooperate with erring and disobedient Christians who do not adhere to primary separation and other vital doctrines. The new evangelicals almost unanimously assert that it is wrong to separate from fellow members of the body of Christ in any ecclesiastically organizational sense. Carnell was unambiguous in his declaration: "Christian fellowship repudiates *any* separation of brother from brother in the community of faith" (italics his).[22] Barnhouse's words also reflect the thinking of many of his colleagues in new evangelicalism: "And I wish I could put before you to the utmost that second degree separation is a sin." Putting it even more forcefully, he stated: "And God says, 'I will judge you if you are separatist. I will judge you if you separate from any member of the Body of Christ.'"[23] He and others

---

[22]Edward John Carnell, *The Case For Orthodox Theology*, p. 130.

[23]Donald Grey Barnhouse, "One Church," *Eternity* (July 1958), pp. 20, 22.

allowed morals to be grounds for separation between brethren but never doctrinal differences.[24] Nearly all new evangelicals would understand church discipline of disobedient Christians for scriptural reasons to be a legitimate form of separation, but church discipline and ecclesiastical separation apply the "degree" issue differently.

Separation from brethren has caused unrest in the fundamentalist camp going back especially to the 1950s' controversy over inclusive evangelism. Separation from apostates and unbelieving organizations constituted an article of fundamentalist faith, but with the evangelism issue fundamentalists encountered the need to articulate a separatist position with reference to their own brethren and fellow churchmen. Some fundamentalists' separation was not to be from other Christians but only from unbelievers. For them there was no justification of organizational separation, for example, (1) from other believers in general (church discipline excepted), or (2) from new evangelical organizations and leaders, or (3) from Christian institutions and leaders still organizationally affiliated with liberals and others who do not believe and obey the word of God, or (4) from Christians who compromise on separation itself and blur the distinction between truth and error, right and wrong, God's cause and Satan's cause. Because of their antipathy toward separation from erring brethren, certain leaders feel comfortable having fellowship with a pastor or a church that is evangelical but belongs to a denomination whose schools and churches are infected with doctrinal infidelity (such as the Southern Baptist Convention), or with those who are involved in some way with the National Council of Churches. Sometimes a smoke screen is raised, such as a caricature of "degrees" of separation. But this is willfully to ignore the plain teaching of separation and its principles. Their arguments against separation from disobedient Christians have been referenced, analyzed, and answered by other fundamentalists.[25]

Ecclesiastical separation does not really admit of "degrees."[26] Separation is directed to the other person because of *his* deviations from Scripture in whatever ways he may express them. If the erring brother runs with the wrong crowd, separation at this point is from *him* as well as from the unbiblical company he is keeping. The reason for separating may well involve someone's unscriptural involvements, but in reality this is no more "secondary" than a "primary" separation from apostasy.

---

[24]Donald Grey Barnhouse, "Thanksgiving and Warning," *Eternity* (Sept 1957), p. 9.

[25]John Ashbrook, "Separation from Brethren," *The Ohio Bible Fellowship Visitor* (Aug-Sept 1975); Ernest Pickering, *Biblical Separation*, p. 217ff, and *Should We Ever Separate From Christian Brethren?: An Examination of the Issue of So-Called "Secondary Separation"* (Decatur, AL: Baptist World Mission); Fred Moritz, *"Be Ye Holy,"* pp. 71-87; Mark Sidwell, *The Dividing Line*, pp. 55-68; Paul R. Jackson, "The Position, Attitudes, and Objectives of Biblical Separation," Literature Item Number 12, p. 10, and "The Position of the General Association of Regular Baptist Churches on Separation," Literature Item Number 6, p. 6 (both published by the General Association of Regular Baptist Churches, Chicago, n.d.); Bob Jones, "Scriptural Separation: 'First and Second Degree'" pamphlet (Greenville, SC: Bob Jones University Press, 1971); and Charles Woodbridge, *Bible Separation* (Halifax, NS: The Peoples Gospel Hour Press, 1971), pp. 11-20.

[26]Bob Jones, "Scriptural Separation: 'First and Second Degree.'"

Sometimes a church, or a pastor's fellowship, or a missionary organization, or a church association, or a Christian school will tolerate certain new evangelicals, or inclusivists, or those who fellowship with new evangelicals, or those who engage in entangling unbiblical alliances of various sorts, or whose standards of personal deportment and music are intolerable. The group itself may have a strong fundamentalist (and even separatist) statement of faith and practice, but overlooks or refuses to deal with its problems. If, after the passing of reasonable time, and appropriate biblical confrontation, it is apparent that the organization is unable or unwilling to put its house in order, then the Bible-believing separatist has no recourse but to withdraw. Nevertheless, the hope is for the erring organization to be restored, and that in the interim others will take a similar stand against the compromise and will also withdraw as a testimony to the truth of ecclesiastical separation and of the original position of the organization's founders.

Within the fundamentalist ranks there is a difference over the classification of separation from brethren. Some, myself included, consider it a form of ecclesiastical separation, while others do not, terming it "familial separation."[27] The intramural difference in terminology is not great since both groups have the same general *practice* in most cases.

The Bible teaches separation from Christian individuals and organizations that are doctrinally deviant, that affiliate with those who deny the faith, or that are content to walk with those who compromise the doctrine and practice of Scripture. Sidwell has an excellent definition of a "disobedient brother" and outlines the principal differences in separation from him and separation from an apostate or false teacher:

> A professing Christian who deliberately refuses to change some aspect of his conduct to conform to the clear teaching of Scripture is a disobedient brother. Our attitude will differ from that we would take with a false teacher because the disobedient brother has, we presume, faith in Christ's saving work. However, he refuses to cease from his disobedient practice.[28]

The main biblical passage on separation from erring brethren is 2 Thessalonians 3:6-15, especially verses six and fourteen:

> Now we command you, brethren, in the name of our Lord Jesus Christ, that you keep away from every brother who leads an unruly life and not according to the tradition which you received from us.

> If anyone does not obey our instruction in this letter, take special note of that person and do not associate with him, so that he will be put to shame.

The object of the separation is a "brother." Many confuse the problem here with its manifestation. The brother's disobedience to the word of God revealed in apostolic teaching is the problem. The local manifestation of the problem was

---

[27]For example, Douglas R. McLachlan, *Reclaiming Authentic Fundamentalism* (Independence, MO: American Association of Christian Schools, 1993), p. 125ff.

[28]Mark Sidwell, *The Dividing Line*, p. 56.

that of being "unruly" (*ataktos*), meaning idle, lazy, selfish, and irresponsible, including being a busybody (v. 14) or a meddler in others' affairs of which he had no legitimate interest. The erring brother may also have been sponging off the local church in some way since he had no gainful livelihood. The "tradition" (*paradosis*) of verse 6 is not of the rabbinic or ecclesiastical variety of extra-biblical religious opinions or customs handed down through the generations that have become encrusted with some kind of human authority. In context, the tradition is divinely authoritative instruction, including the example of Paul and his company (vv. 7-9), his current word to them (v. 12, "we command and exhort"; v. 14, "in this letter"), his specific oral teaching to them earlier (v. 10, "we used to give you this order"), and his previous written revelation (1 Thess 4:11-12) that commanded believers in the church to warn these people (1 Thess 5:14). Paul's education of them, then, was not only about honest employment and compensation but also about the Christian life in general since their disobedience was against the apostle's commands concerning idleness, leeching, meddling, and selfishness. Furthermore, the plural (traditions) in 2 Thessalonians 2:15 would tend to expand the apostle's intention of his use of the singular in 3:6. "Paul uses the plural 'traditions' in 2:15 to refer to the bulk of his communication to them. By application, any conscious violation of a specific command given to them by the apostle would qualify the offender for the same discipline as directed in verse 6."[29]

> The sin of these brothers then was the leading of an unruly and disobedient lifestyle. It entailed laziness, freeloading, and meddling in the lives of others. Those involved in it were fully aware of their wickedness, and though they had been continually challenged to alter their lifestyle, were content in their sin. They were living in total disregard of the exhortations of the apostle Paul, his company, and the other believers in the assembly.[30]

Note also that the apostle's directive here is authoritative (v. 6, "we command") and affectionate (v. 6, "brethren"). The sin of the brother is not an isolated event or a single failure; it is a pattern of willful misconduct as seen in the present tenses of "leads" (v. 6) and "does not obey" (v. 14). Moreover, the separation is intended to be remedial—that he would be "ashamed" yet not regarded as an "enemy" (vv. 14-15).

Paul instructs the church at Thessalonica to "withdraw" (*stello*) from the person. The verb carries the thought of keeping away, avoiding, or standing aloof.[31] In verse 14 this action is interpreted as not associating with the brother. While the specifics of this action are not spelled out by Paul, it seems that a minimum understanding would be excommunication from membership, or church discipline. It may be objected that it could not be such because this one is not to be regarded as an enemy whereas a disciplined member is to be considered a Gentile and a tax collector (Matt 18:17). However, this distinction appears a little over solicitous of

---

[29]R. Bruce Compton, "2 Thessalonians 3:6-15 and Biblical Separation," *The Sentinel* (published by the Detroit Baptist Theological Seminary, Allen Park, MI), 5 (1988).

[30]Scott A. Williquette, "2 Thessalonians 3:6-15: A Case for Secondary Separation?" (Term paper for the course "History of Neo-Evangelicalism," Detroit Baptist Theological Seminary, Dec 8, 1993), p. 12.

[31]BDAG, s.v. "*stello*," p. 942.

the word "as" in both cases. Christ said the one in His teaching was also a "brother" (Matt 18:15). "The church is to regard him [the person in Matt 18:17] as if he were not a believer, although in fact he is."[32] It appears that the two scenarios (i.e., Matt 18 and 2 Thess 3) are comparable.

The question still remains: Is ecclesiastical separation in view here? If the local church excludes this person, is there any warrant in this passage for a local church itself to withdraw from an association of churches or from an organized Christian endeavor of some kind? If there is such authority, is this merely an inference or logical deduction from the text and not the actual teaching of the text?

It is clear that the local church at Thessalonica needed to carry out the apostle's mandate by withdrawing from and severing association with the erring brother. But other local churches and leaders—those who read Paul's words in this epistle—were likewise to take warning and not collaborate with the disobedient one. These injunctions apply to the churches of every century, including our own. They cannot be buried in the decades of the early church or restricted simply to present-day identical replications of first-century disobedience to a command of the word of God.

If disregard for the word of God qualified people for dismissal from the fellowship of a local church, on what basis could there be broader organizational fellowship with them, even in a worthy project such as winning others to Christ? The polity that regulates local church fellowship also in principle regulates ecclesiastical connections and associations that may transcend the affairs of a local church. Paul explicitly named two Christian leaders who had deviated in doctrine and conscience and who were consequently "handed over to Satan" (1 Tim 1:20). This means at least excision from the local assembly, but a warning for all other pastors and churches is implicit. In other words, if the local church at Ephesus had separated itself from these deviants, the same principle was to be observed by the other churches and their leaders. The same principle transcends Ephesus to include all local churches and leaders to whom the epistle of 1 Timothy and the New Testament come.

In 1 Timothy 5:22 Paul states,

> Do not lay hands upon anyone too hastily and thereby share responsibility for the sins of others; keep yourself free from sin.

The context here concerns a local church's responsibility toward the pastoral office. There is a protection of the office that the church must uphold (v. 19); an accusation against the pastor must not be entertained in any form except there are corroborating witnesses of the alleged sin (Deut 19:15). There is also a duty for the church to discipline pastors who are not godly and whose excision from the office will cause others to fear (v. 20). These things demonstrate the seriousness of choosing someone with good character for the pastoral office; hence the need to take time for careful inquiry to determine this in advance of the call to the pastoral office (vv. 24-25). Paul warns Timothy to be deliberate; to be hasty may place the church or ordaining pastor in blame if there is misconduct later.

---

[32] R. Bruce Compton, "2 Thessalonians 3:6-15."

Commonly understood to refer to ordination, or at least the call and installation of a new pastor, there is also the principle here that recognition of someone as a genuine Christian leader must be preceded by cautious and wise investigation. Otherwise one could share responsibility for his sins. The injunction to "keep yourself free from sin" has strong overtones of ecclesiastical separation. Pedantic exegesis may wish to restrict the apostle's instruction here to the first century, or simply to the calling of a new pastor to a local church. But modern Christian pastors and leaders cannot be absolved of their obligation to biblical separatism that easily.

Separation from erring brethren means that we will not associate our name or the name of our organization with any church, ecclesiastical organization, or religious leader *which maintains connections* with those who do not believe and obey the word of God in doctrine and practice. Spurgeon's example from the nineteenth-century struggle between the separatists and liberals and their sympathizers in the Baptist Union in England is entirely appropriate for the twenty-first century. He explained:

> Complicity with error will take from the best of men the power to enter any successful protest against it....Fellowship with known and vital error is participation in sin....As soon as I saw, or thought I saw, that error had become firmly established, I did not deliberate, but quitted the body at once....No protest could be equal to that of distinct separation from known evil....That I might not stultify my testimony I have cut myself clear of those who err from the faith, *and even from those who associate with them* (italics added).[33]

Certain pockets of professing fundamentalism, unfortunately, have become inured to this aspect of ecclesiastical separation. Incidents of working relationships between fundamentalists and new evangelicals and those who have associations with unorthodox and non-evangelical groups and leaders continue to increase. For example, Jerry Fawell's fraternity with the Southern Baptist Convention, his numerous connections with new evangelical leaders and institutions, and with others far to the left of either in the Moral Majority is well documented.[34] Yet he is accepted in many fundamentalist contexts with little or no concern.

John Piper, pastor of the Bethlehem Baptist Church (Baptist General Conference) in Minneapolis is another example. Piper has many admirable personal qualities as well as considerable preaching and writing skills. But his speaking schedule finds him in quasi-charismatic company, and the Bethlehem Conference for Pastors roster includes new evangelicals such as R. Albert Mohler of the Southern Baptist Seminary in Louisville, KY, David Wells of Gordon Conwell Seminary, D. A. Carson and Wayne Grudem of the Trinity Evangelical Divinity School, Daniel Fuller of Fuller Theological Seminary, and others of unbiblical associations and ideas such as Larry Crabb, Os Guiness, Roger Nicole, and J. I. Packer.[35]

---

[33]Quoted by Jerry Huffman, *The Calvary Contender* (Mar 1, 1994).

[34]See chapter 18: New Evangeliocal Social Activism. See also the website of *The Calvary Contender*, http://home.hiwaay.net/~contendr/.

[35]http://www.desiringgod.org/ or http://bbcmpls.org/.

The Baptist General Conference recently went through an internal controversy over the propagation, by writing, speaking, and classroom, of open or free-will theism by Gregory A. Boyd of the group's school, Bethel College of Arden Hills, MN. Piper has denounced this theology as one that "dishonors God, distorts Scripture, damages faith, and would if left unchecked, destroy churches and lives. Its errors are not peripheral but central."[36] Despite the presence of this unbiblical teaching, Piper gives nine reasons to remain in the Baptist General Conference, the last of which states:

> Our Conference is fundamentally orthodox. It has taken a terrible step away from orthodoxy in the willingness to define ourselves as inclusive of this non-Christian view of God's foreknowledge. But a step away from orthodoxy is not yet the abandonment of orthodoxy. We should watch and pray and work that more steps not be taken. When and if the BGC becomes so attached to a mindset of indifference to orthodox doctrine or explicitly abandons crucial doctrines in what it affirms and denies, then we may, with more warrant, consider removing our membership from the Conference.[37]

While caution is always commendable in such cases, one wonders just how much more non-Christian, God-dishonoring, faith-damaging, Scripture-distorting, church-devastating, and lives-destroying doctrine it will take before membership is removed from the Baptist General Conference. The most distressing upshot of all this is that a professing fundamentalist mission agency, the Evangelical Baptist Mission, scheduled Piper for a Midwest Missions Forum in Indianapolis, IN, for May 20-21, 2002.[38]

John MacArthur is the pastor of a very large and responsible ministry and a well-known speaker. His influence is quite pervasive by means of his books, tapes, radio program, preaching, and teaching throughout the world. He is considered a fundamentalist by many, and he speaks before numerous professing fundamentalist groups and ministries such as the General Association of Regular Baptist Churches and its related schools and agencies, for one example. While many professing fundamentalists are uneasy about his connections and speaking engagements, they are not quite willing to regard him as a new evangelical. MacArthur himself has disavowed militant fundamentalism in some incautious if not intemperate charges.[39] From his and his father's fundamentalist backgrounds, he knows what the movement is about and wants no part of it. His doctrine and practice of ecclesiastical separation is unclear at best. He counsels Christians that they should keep "spiritually separate," not have any "spiritual union," and not forge any "spiritual bonds" with those who corrupt the gospel.[40] But this advice

---

[36]John Piper, "What are John Piper's views on God's foreknowledge and openness theology?", http://www.desiringgod.org/About_DGM/DGMFAQs/TheologyFAQs/Foreknowledge.htm.

[37]John Piper, "What denomination is [Bethlehem Baptist Church] a part of and why?", http://www.desiringgod.org/About_DGM/DGMFAQs/BBCDenom.htm.

[38]http://www.desiringgod.org/conferences/PiperEvents/jpspeaksched.htm.

[39]John F. MacAarthur, *Reckless Faith* (Wheaton, IL: Crossway, 1994), pp. 67-68, 95-96.

[40]Ibid., pp. 107, 108, 116.

is ambiguous and lacks any practical content for ecclesiastical separation from unbelief. What does "spiritual" mean and how does this translate, if at all, into the real world of ecclesial struggles? His antipathy toward Roman Catholicism and the Evangelicals and Catholics Together coalition suggests he would not cooperate with Romanists, but he has no problem working with Southern Baptists, for example, nor with Conservative Baptists, the Baptist General Conference, and elements of the Billy Graham Evangelistic Association, all avowed new evangelical groups at best. He has spoken regularly for the Founder's Week of the Moody Bible Institute which always features a roster of new evangelicals. While MacArthur is militant about certain aspects of biblical doctrine, he appears apathetic and lethargic about the doctrine of ecclesiastical separation; giving him a new evangelical profile and making anomalous his appearance in would-be fundamentalist conclaves.

THE IMPLEMENTATION OF ECCLESIASTICAL SEPARATION

Investigation

Four factors relative to the actual practice of the doctrine of ecclesiastical separation must be considered. First, separation begins with adequate investigation of the other parties or participants involved in the proposed collaboration. This means being knowledgeable of their beliefs, testimony or image that is projected, comments on current issues and leaders, and attitudes toward fundamentalism and separatism, among other things. For example, where do they stand on some points of crucial doctrine other than the "five fundamentals" of the faith, such as the Baptist distinctives, or the doctrines of grace and salvation? Investigation would also include the others' influence, associations, reputation (for what are they really known?), and what they condone. Also to be asked: What is the real intent behind the proposed endeavor or fellowship? Such an investigation will take time and effort but it will prevent embarrassment later, or worse, an unbiblical entanglement.

Identification

Separation considers the matter of identification. What will happen to one's testimony and image in the contemplated association? What will the proposed union do to the spirituality of one's church and himself. While some may debate whether there is a legitimate "condemnation by association," there is certainly a *corruption by association* to be feared (1 Cor 15:33, "Bad company corrupts good morals").

Promotion

Separation considers the matter of promotion. If one recognizes or has fellowship with those whose alliances and positions are unscriptural, then influence is given to their compromise and one ends up promoting things that are unbiblical and against which he would otherwise take a stand. As did Jehoshaphat, one may "love those that hate the Lord" (2 Chron 19:2) and became an accessory to the promotion of their agendas. When professing fundamentalist preachers and churches publicly link arms with Roman Catholics, Jews, and Mormons on a common moral or political issue, they give the appearance of tacit approval of the doctrines and practices of these groups. The Bible-believers end up promoting them directly or indirectly, which would not be done under any other circumstances.

Levels

Separation considers the question of levels; it is not a one-size-fits-all.[41] There are different and varying tiers of cooperation and association in religious endeavors, and these levels carry their own doctrinal and practical requirements. The first level, the personal, may not necessarily be ecclesiastical in context. All Christians have certain things in common—the new birth, the indwelling Spirit, a positive attitude toward the Bible, a kinship for the Lord's house and His people, and much more. The doctrinal requirements for two Christians having a cup of coffee and enjoying that level of fellowship are minimal. Arminians and Calvinists, premillennialists and amillennialists, and tribulationists of multiple stripes should all be able to enjoy a mutual Thanksgiving dinner and rejoice in the goodness of their God even though they would not collaborate in other projects. The only common ground they share is their fear of God and love of His precepts (Psa 119: 63), but their fellowship on that level is genuine and commendable.

Next there is the local church level. Conditions and requirements for church membership significantly exceed the coffee cup level. Even within the membership, a local church may establish leadership standards for those who serve in public (e.g., ushers), and even higher standards for Sunday school teachers, deacons, and the like.

Last, there is the organizational level. (This level is not necessarily to be construed as greater or more important than the previous level, only different.) Different doctrinal requirements are met here than on previous levels. Even within this stratum there may be gradations or variations of cooperation, such as in Christian college sports competition, academic societies, or scholastic projects promoting mutual standards for accreditation, transfer of credits, and recognitions of that sort. Would pretribulationism be a criterion for an intercollegiate soccer game? Or a no-divorce-under-any-conditions for a football league? Or immersion baptism for a violin competition? A theological society may have a simple doctrinal statement affirming the inerrancy of Scripture and the triunity of God whereas a missionary agency or an association of churches would want far more detailed doctrinal requirements for participation. However, it must still be remembered that doctrinal statements alone do not guarantee the soundness of an organization's reputation and influence.

In working through the various levels and their principles and internal requirements, there is obviously the need for a great deal of Christian charity in some cases when determining the extent of one's working relationship with various people and groups, and when evaluating others' practice of separation.

God's means of preserving the truth of the gospel and of all His word has been that of separation. Otherwise a gradualism sets in that eventually will leave a person or institution with no pure doctrine left to preserve, much less any vitality with which to maintain and defend it. The new evangelicalism since the 1940s has been a moving picture of the process of gradual erosion to the point where it has no doctrine of separation anymore and no energy to pursue such belief and practice.

---

[41]The concept of "levels" was introduced by Ernest Pickering, *Biblical Separation*, p. 218.

PART 5: THE BIBLE AND AUTHORITY

A ny new movement in Christianity and Christian theology faces the question of religious authority, particularly the Bible's authority—typically the first area where rethinking, adjustment, and eventual compromise occur. An ominous note sounded for the new evangelicalism when the re-opening of the subject of biblical inspiration appeared in a *Christian Life* article in March 1956.[1]

Some new evangelicals have been willing to concede divine verbal revelation and the full inspiration and inerrancy of the Bible. The concessions rose out of an attempt to meet unbelieving scholarship on its own ground or from a sense that true scholarship or acceptance by academia necessitated capitulation. Bernard Ramm sought to "come to terms" with Enlightenment thought, fearful of being charged by scholars with fundamentalist obscurantism.[2]

The influence of neo-orthodoxy appeared early in new evangelical theology, especially in the doctrines of revelation and inspiration. The spectrum of doctrines infected only widened through the decades despite the warnings and analyses put forth by fundamentalists and a few new evangelicals. Twenty-first century *avant garde* new evangelicals, sometimes called post-conservative, post-modern, or younger evangelicals, have now abandoned the issues of revelation and inspiration in favor of discussing hermeneutics and authority. The orthodox, traditional doctrines of propositional revelation and verbal inspiration/inerrancy have been conceded to non-evangelical thought. The current debate attempts to define how an errant Bible can be interpreted so to speak to contemporary, post-modern cultural relativism, with any sense of religious authority.[3]

---

[1]"Is Evangelical Theology Changing?" *Christian Life* (Mar 1956), pp. 18-19.

[2]Bernard Ramm, *After Fundamentalism: The Future of Evangelical Theology* (San Francisco: Harper and Row, 1983), pp. 8, 14, 18, 19, 27, 99, 101, 114, 136, and 142.

[3]Douglas Jacobsen, "From Truth to Authority to Responsibility: The Shifting Focus of Evangelical Hermeneutics, 1915-1986 (Part II)," *TSF Bulletin* (May-June 1987), pp. 10-14.

12

BIBLICAL REVELATION

Propositional revelation has always been attacked by critical scholars as reducing the idea of the ineffable and essentially unknowable God to truth-statements, words, and sentences. Allegedly, men were attempting to confine God by limiting Him to human language and to a book of human languages—the Bible. Critical scholarship asserted that propositional revelation sacrificed the transcendence of God. As a result, revelation must be personal rather than propositional and, furthermore, a human response is required or divine revelation can never occur. Revelation can never be objectified or identified directly with words on a page; it can never be limited in a form that has any human contribution or control. Therefore, revelation is an "act" or "event" (notably the "Christ event"), and the Bible is a "witness" to the revelation-event. What God reveals is *Himself,* not ideas about Himself.

Ralph Earle, one of the first new evangelical scholars to deny the traditional, orthodox doctrine of revelation, taught at Nazarene Theological Seminary. Finding truth in all theories of inspiration and in all theories of atonement, Earle thought Karl Barth's idea of two phases of inspiration, one of the writer and one of the reader of Scripture, was needed in evangelicalism. He wanted revelation to be subject-object-subject (i.e., God-Scripture-man). "Without disparaging the authority of the Bible as itself a divine revelation—as Barth does—we yet need to recognize that revelation is not complete unless and until God's Word actually reaches me through the help of the Holy Spirit."[4] However, for Earle, whatever objectivity revelation may have is swallowed up in subjectivity. His reference to Barth's contribution takes him beyond the orthodox position, and if that is not his intent, his appeal to Barth is gratuitous.

The first comprehensive new evangelical rejection of propositional revelation appeared at the same time from the pen of Dewey Beegle, a professor at Biblical Seminary in New York.[5] He interpreted divine revelation in terms of the human response elicited, a direct concession to neo-orthodoxy. "Scripture must have the

---

[4]Ralph Earle, "Further Thoughts on Biblical Inspiration," *Bulletin of the Evangelical Theological Society* 6 (1963), p. 14.

[5]Dewey M. Beegle, *The Inspiration of Scripture* (Philadelphia: Westminster, 1963). Ten years later he produced an expanded edition entitled *Scripture, Tradition and Infallibility* (Grand Rapids: Eerdmans, 1973).

response of the hearer or reader. It is beyond question, therefore, that revelation must be defined subjectively if the term is to be in accord with the facts."[6] For Beegle, revelation, like communication, must have three ingredients: a communicator, the message, and the receiver's response. "If any one of the three is missing, there is no revelation or communication."[7] Revelation is subject to subject, a *personal* self-disclosure. What God reveals is Himself, not information about Himself, although at the end of the book he concedes that "some minimal amount of objective truth" is necessary for subjective truth to occur.[8] This rather offhanded remark, however, did not recover the propositional, objective revelation surrendered everywhere else in the book.

Daniel Stevick, an erstwhile evangelical, forthrightly states the need to begin with God, not revelation. "Revelation is incomplete until it is consummated in human faith....The relationship is personal—like a meeting or an encounter."[9] "'Reveal' as a biblical term has little to do with communication of information or true propositions....God, not information about God, is what is given in revelation....The soul is the ultimate place where authority becomes authoritative and where revelation becomes revelatory."[10]

George Eldon Ladd wrote a masterful article setting forth the orthodox doctrine of propositional revelation and defending it against the subjective, human response view of neo-orthodoxy.[11] Later, Ladd reversed himself and concluded in a lengthy treatise, "I cannot assent to the older orthodox view, which still has its adherents, that 'Revelation, in the biblical sense of the term, is the communication of information.'"[12] He did not want to deny all truth content to divine revelation but, with an eye to neo-orthodoxy, wanted to minimize it and say that revelation's dimension was personal encounter.

Likewise, Bernard Ramm once championed propositional special revelation, saying rather uniquely, "The knowledge *of* God must be a knowledge *from* God and the pursuit of this knowledge must be governed by the nature of God and of his self-revelation....*Revelation is the autobiography of God*" (italics his).[13] Revelation is concrete and conveys a cognitive knowledge of God, and "from the perspective of religious theory of knowledge special revelation is the most important doctrine of the Christian faith."[14] After a year of study under Karl Barth, his orientation changed completely. He then felt that Barth's theology was the only

---

[6]*The Inspiration of Scripture*, p. 126.

[7]Ibid., p. 131.

[8]Ibid., p. 191.

[9]Daniel B. Stevick, *Beyond Fundamentalism* (Richmond, VA: John Knox, 1964), p. 67.

[10]Ibid., p. 68.

[11]George E. Ladd, "Revelation, History and the Bible," *Christianity Today* (Sept 30, 1957), pp. 5-8.

[12]George E. Ladd, "The Search For Perspective," *Interpretation* 25 (1971), p. 62. His quote, to which he is taking exception, is of Edward J. Young, *Thy Word is Truth* (Grand Rapids: Eerdmans, 1957), p. 41.

[13]Bernard Ramm, *Special Revelation and the Word of God* (Grand Rapids: Eerdmans, 1961), pp. 16-17.

[14]Ibid., p. 19.

answer to the demands of the Enlightenment and its children, and the only way for evangelical thought to come to terms with current theological/philosophical scholarship.[15] Special revelation was no longer the most important doctrine for Christianity; it was "the person of Christ and his Gospel," the content of the Gospel not its verbal revelatory form.[16] From P. T. Forsyth Ramm learned that one cannot go from revelation to inspiration to theology; one must come to Christianity first through its content—Christ and his Gospel. From Barth he learned that there is a "distance" between the Word of God and the text of Scripture, the distance coming at two points: human language and the human mind. Because of this interval, there is at best an *indirect* identity between the Word of God and Scripture, and the Bible is a "witness" to that Word.[17]

In a similar journey from evangelical orthodoxy to the outer fringes of neo-orthodoxy, Clark Pinnock originally articulated a biblically and theologically well-reasoned position on revelation. He pointedly inveighed against the neo-orthodox idea of revelation: "The dialectical notion that revelation becomes valid only in subjective response threatens the reality of revelation itself."[18] Later Pinnock gave equal if not more stress to the human response. Revelation was "bipolar" in structure—objective and subjective. In his judgment, he escaped, and thus corrected, the erroneous over-emphases of both orthodox objectivism (biblical truth content) and liberal subjectivism (existential encounter with God). In his middle position, he felt he had "propositional communication as well as personal communion," the best of both worlds.[19] Theologically he came to the inevitable neo-orthodox conclusion that "the Bible is a witness, although a primary one, to the revelation of God in the face of Jesus Christ. Christology, not Bibliology, occupies the center stage in Christianity."[20] One cannot equate the human words of the Bible with the words of God.[21]

In the neo-orthodox approach, the Word of God exists "in, with, and under" the sacred text, as it were, a text which is thoroughly conditioned by human culture and error. But the Word of God never *is* the text itself. Through the Bible the authentic voice of God is heard, or God's living Word breaks through the written words of Scripture in an indirect way, and one then has revelation and meets God in that magic moment.[22] Fortunately, not all new evangelicals by any means held to these non-evangelical, neo-orthodox deviations from the doctrine of divine

---

[15]*After Fundamentalism*, pp. 8-9, *passim* (see footnote # 2).

[16]Ibid., p. 9.

[17]Ibid., pp. 89-91.

[18]Clark H. Pinnock, *Biblical Revelation: The Foundation of Christian Theology* (Chicago: Moody, 1971), p. 44.

[19]Clark H. Pinnock, *The Scripture Principle* (San Francisco: Harper and Row, 1984), p. 5.

[20]Ibid., p. 16.

[21]Ibid., p. 143.

[22]For a good description of this approach, see D. W. Anderson, "Revelation and Differences Within the Church," *Torch and Trumpet* (May-June 1966), pp. 29-31.

revelation.[23] But this unbiblical, unorthodox undertow constantly influenced new evangelicalism and eventually led to significant drift.

The Bible teaches of itself that it is objective, special revelation from God regardless of any human response, and therefore has inherent objective force. It claims for itself absolute, indefectible divine authority (Isa 8:20; 1 Cor 14:37; 2 Thess 3:14; Rev 22:18-19). The Scriptures are self-authenticating and self-attesting. One cannot delegate authority to divine revelational truth; it can only be recognized and received with thanksgiving. The Bible is authoritative because God is the author, and He is the author by the miracle of inspiration (2 Tim 3:15-16). The Bible's own infinite perfections make it authoritative. It came from God propositionally in history through human instruments (2 Pet 1:21). It has a genuine historical nexus and a permanent standing authority unaffected by human response (Matt 5:18-19; 24:35; 1 Pet 1:24-25).

Historical, objective, self-attesting revelation of God in the Bible is perceived and personalized savingly by the illumination of the Holy Spirit. Biblical authority is based on inspiration; *certainty* of that authority comes by illumination. This is sometimes called by theologians the internal testimony of the Holy Spirit. It answers the question of how the Bible can be known to be true. Illumination is the regeneration of the mind that removes the hostility of depravity to Scripture and conveys an intuitive certainty and welcome that the Bible came from God and is true and authoritative (1 Cor 2:4-5, cf. v. 14; 1 Thess 1:5; 2:13; 1 John 2:20, 21, 27). The Bible retains its divine authority in the absence of any human, internal testimony. "The Scripture is not bereft of its intrinsic authority and power when this inward witness is not savingly operative. There are functions which Scripture as the living Word of God performs outside the orbit of salvation, and these we must not underestimate."[24]

A profound difference separates the orthodox, biblical doctrine of the internal testimony of the Holy Spirit and the neo-orthodox/neo-liberal view that the Bible is only an indirect "witness" to the revelation of God aided by the Spirit or through an existential "encounter" with God. Barthian, dialectical theology rejects any genuine historical nexus. The Word of God is not a revelation/inspiration process accomplished inside the historical, calendrical process. It is not an event within the public domain. The encounter is not connected with any past action of God in history. It occurs in the existential realm of "supra-history." Barthianism teaches a personal confrontation between man and God *Himself* in revelation. In this scheme, God does not exist independently of His revelation; He is identical to His revelation. He reveals Himself wholly in the existential encounter. As one

---

[23]For early new evangelical responses see the early George Ladd, "Revelation, History, and the Bible," *Christianity Today* (Sept 30, 1957), p. 5; G. C. Berkouwer, "Revelaton: The Christian View" (part one), *Christianity Today* (Oct 13, 1958), p. 15; James I. Packer, "Contemporary Views of Revelation" (parts one and two), *Christianity Today* (Nov 24, 1958, p. 3; Dec 8, 1958, p. 15); and David Barker, "The Controversy Is Not New," *Christianity Today* (Nov 21, 1960), p. 14. In the eye of the new evangelical storm over inerrancy in the later 1970s, Ronald Nash clearly debunked the human response, revelation-as-event view ("Truth By Any Other Name," *Christianity Today* [Oct 7, 1977], p. 17).

[24]John Murray, "Review of Bernard Ramm, *Special Revelation and the Word of God*," *Westminster Theological Journal* 24 (1962), p. 207.

orthodox scholar describes this neo-orthodox idea: "Revelation is always a non-verbal *direct theophany* outside of ordinary history, and religious truth is always personal, or existential truth."[25]

The biblical view, however, is that God is distinct from His revelation in Scripture, that the Bible is not an extension of the divine essence. The Bible is a mediatorial book, not an extension of deity. The Scripture is identical to God's *revelation*, but it is not identical to God's *essence*. A further difference between the internal testimony of the Spirit to an objective revelatory Bible and Barthian existentialism is that the latter rejects the inherent and qualitative revelatory authority of the *text* of Scripture. In neo-orthodoxy, the Bible is a "pointer" or a witness to revelation but is not revelation. The Bible "becomes" the Word of God and revelation is an ever-recurring act of God in some sort of a supra-temporal realm.

Some new evangelicals have gravitated to Barth's view.[26] According to them, since the Spirit of illumination infallibly testifies to redemptive truth in Scripture, it does not matter if there is an infallible Bible or not. Essential truth is borne home by the Spirit overriding the cultural conditioning and human errors of the text. Unwittingly, such a position confounds the doctrine of revelation. The internal testimony is dependent on the inherent perfection of Scripture; it is a perfection to which the Spirit bears witness and of which He convinces the individual. The inerrancy of Scripture in part is what makes the internal testimony possible. The Spirit's illumination is not some sort of irresistible stream that convinces one of the divine authority of the Bible, errors and all![27]

The new evangelical/neo-orthodox human response position on revelation also betrays an unbiblical view of the nature of truth.[28] There are not actually two different kinds of truth, personal and propositional. Truth is that which corresponds to the mind, character, and will of God. It is what God could say about anything. Truth consists of propositions that correctly represent an actual state of affairs. By definition, truth is propositional. It is subject and predicate material—ideas, concepts, and information. All "personal" truth is propositional. Truth may have an intellectual and/or a personal *apprehension*, but ultimately is still in propositions. Non-propositional, non-cognitive truth is unthinkable!

[25]Robert L. Reymond, *Preach the Word* (Edinburgh: Rutherford House, 1988), p. 4.

[26]Dewey M. Beegle, *The Inspiration of Scripture*, pp. 176, 178, 181, 182, 187, 192, 193. Clark H. Pinnock, *The Scripture Principle*, pp. 103-104, 156. Donald G. Bloesch, *Essentials of Evangelical Theology*, 2 vols. (San Francisco: Harper and Row, 1978), 1:65. David Allan Hubbard, "The Current Tensions: Is There A Way Out?" in *Biblical Authority*, ed. Jack Rogers (Waco, TX: Word, 1977), p. 165.

[27]Concerning the internal testimony, one may consult John Calvin, *The Institutes*, Henry Beveridge, trans. (Grand Rapids: Eerdmans, 1964), Book 1, chap. 7, par. 8; John Murray, "The Attestation of Scripture," in *The Infallible Word*, Ned B. Stonehouse, ed. (Philadelphia: Presbyterian and Reformed, 1946), chapter 1; Cornelius Van Til, "Introduction," in B. B. Warfield, *The Inspiration and Authority of Scripture* (Philadelphia: Presbyterian and Reformed, 1948); J. I. Packer, *Fundamentalism and the Word of God* (Grand Rapids: Eerdmans, 1958), pp. 118-25; John M. Frame, "God and Biblical Language," in *God's Inerrant Word: An International Symposium on the Trustworthiness of Scripture*, John Warwick Montgomery, ed. (Minneapolis: Bethany Fellowship, 1974), chapter 7; R. C. Sproul, "The Internal Testimony of the Holy Spirit," in *Inerrancy*, Norman Geisler, ed. (Grand Rapids: Zondervan, 1979), pp. 337-54; Wayne A. Grudem, "Scripture's Self-Attestation and the Problem of Formulating a Doctrine of Scripture" in *Scripture and Truth*, D. A. Carson and John D. Woodbridge, eds. (Grand Rapids: Zondervan, 1983), pp. 19-59; and Bernard Ramm, *The Witness of the Spirit* (Grand Rapids: Eerdmans, 1959).

[28]For example, Dewey M. Beegle, *The Inspiration of Scripture*, pp. 153-64.

What defines the content of divine verbal revelation? What is the ultimate purpose of Scripture? To what does the Bible "witness" in the human response view, or what kind of information is true and authoritative in the Bible? Daniel Fuller asserted that the purpose of Scripture is to "make us wise unto salvation." "The Biblical writers make it clear that their purpose was to report the happenings and meaning of the redemptive acts of God in history so that men might be wise unto salvation."[29] Fuller had earlier propounded this idea in terms of the "revelational" vis-a-vis "non-revelational" verses in Scripture. Truth that concerns salvation is revelational, or "doctrinal"; other biblical material is non-revelational.[30] "When the Bible teaches its authority, the emphasis is on what makes a man wise unto salvation."[31]

There are at least two problems with Fuller's understanding. One, the revelational and the so-called non-revelational material are so intertwined in Scripture that the dichotomy cannot stand. The Bible's *entire teaching authority* performs its purpose and not just the authority of the revelational or doctrinal texts. Two, Fuller's bifurcation has no workable way to determine what is revelational and what is not. He has no criteria, and worse, he has no method even to determine what the criteria are or should be, in terms of the purpose for the Bible's revelation. Fuller holds up 2 Timothy 3:15 (Scripture makes us wise unto salvation) as the absolute standard to judge what is revelational and what is not. But by what standard can he create such a litmus test? How does he judge even 2 Timothy 3:15 to be "revelational?" His procedure is therefore self-defeating and useless. It rests on a baseless presupposition of some sort if not sheer dogmatism. Subjectivism and skepticism govern in such a dichotomy. In any case, the ultimate criterion is the human intellect.

The purpose of God's special revelation in Scripture is intertwined with a greater question of what is God's ultimate purpose in all things external to Himself? The purpose of the two must be one and the same. God must be *doing* what He is *saying* in Scripture and, of course, must be saying what He is doing. The two are correlative; this leads us to what is called the unifying center of God's activity. What principle can account for all of God's activity external to Himself and which He describes in His verbal revelation? The principle most commonly put forth is redemption, as noted in Fuller's approach. The Scriptures are designed to make us wise unto salvation in this view. God's activity and thus the Bible's central message is soteric.

But there are some problems with this approach. One, it is man-centered. God's focus is on the creature. This is bad theology, philosophy, and biblical understanding. God's activity must center on *Himself*. Everything He does is self-referential. There is no higher standard for God to set or goal to reach than pleasing Himself. Second, it is sin-oriented. It takes its starting point at the fall of man into sin. Sin is allowed to set the agenda for what God does in and with His universe.

---

[29]Daniel P. Fuller, "The Nature of Biblical Inerrancy," *Journal of the American Scientific Affiliation* 24 (1972), pp. 47, 50.

[30]Daniel P. Fuller, "Benjamin B. Warfield's View of Faith and History," *Bulletin of the Evangelical Theological Society* 11 (1968), pp. 80-81.

[31]Daniel P. Fuller, "Biblical Infallibility," *Fuller Seminary Bulletin* (March 1968).

Third, it gives no coherent rationale for God's activity prior to the fall. Beginning as it does with Genesis 3:15 and the first redemptive news, a redemption-oriented approach cannot account for God's activity in Genesis 1 and 2. It cannot account for the original creation and all pre-redemptive special revelation. It fails to explain *all* of God's work outside His self-contained tri-unity.

A better understanding is to see that God's ultimate goal in everything is to glorify Himself, to employ the best means in order to achieve the highest end of His own maximum self glory. He exists both *from* Himself and *for* Himself (Rom 11:36; 1 Cor 15:28b; Col 1:16). God's goal for all His external activity is for it to be initiated and consummated on the historical level; that is, beginning with creation and culminating in the *eschaton*. That goal is to establish a sovereign relationship of fellowship/responsibility with creatures in His image and to dwell with them everlastingly; a relationship of "I will be their God and they will be my people, and I will dwell among them" (Gen 1:26-27; 3:8; Rev 21:3). For this purpose God created man in His image, and He made the rest of the universe to be subservient to man as the vice-regent of his Creator. To forward in history this relationship, God parceled out His special revelation and established various stewardships of this revealed light. The Scriptures are the depository of this information and the "blueprint" of God's activity. All that it affirms, asserts, or informs, on whatever subject, is true and therefore relevant to God's ultimate purpose. Singling out some parts of the Scripture as germane and others as not is to trivialize God's infinite character and the unity of His comprehensive plan for all that comes to pass. There are no unplanned loose ends in God's universe. All revelation is truth (although not all truth is revelation), truth is interlocking, and the Bible is an indivisible and unbreakable divine truth deposit.

13

BIBLICAL INSPIRATION AND INERRANCY

Concessions concerning inspiration and inerrancy, especially inerrancy, are where the principal departures of some new evangelicals lie and where the deviations are most visibly pronounced, and destructive. Non-evangelicals have been quick to notice the concessions. L. Harold DeWolf, a liberal from Boston University, in 1960 noted "revisions" in the "fundamentalist" view of inspiration, as did John B. Cobb and William Hordern (neo-orthodox).[1] Fortunately, voices within new evangelicalism itself sounded alarms about the drift and manifest destiny of concessions on inerrancy. Frank Gaebelein, for example, warned: "We must not blink at the evidence that there is current among some evangelicals a subtle erosion of the doctrine of the infallibility of Scripture that is highly illogical as well as dangerous."[2] Gaebelein's red flag went unheeded and inerrancy suffered the fate Gaebelein envisioned. Interestingly, the "subtle erosion" sailed under different mastheads, rationalizing the concessions in a variety of ways, though most included calls for higher scholarship. Some of the rationalizations will be analyzed below.

INSPIRATION IS OF THE WRITER NOT THE WRITINGS

Dewey Beegle argued that the human author of Scripture partook of inspiration,[3] therefore, degrees of inspiration within the Bible exist; i.e., degrees of "inspiredness" of the writers. Beegle even insists that the inspiration of the biblical writers is no different in kind than that of hymn-writers of the church; the difference is in degree.

---

[1] L. Harold DeWolf, *Present Trends in Christian Thought* (New York: Association Press, 1960), pp. 45, 55-56. John B. Cobb, Review of *The Case for Orthodox Theology*, by E. J. Carnell, *Interpretation* 14 (1960), pp. 94-96. William Hordern, *New Directions in Theology Today* (Philadelphia: Westminster, 1966), pp. 80-89. See also the assessment of James Davison Hunter, a sociologist who interviewed students from several evangelical educational institutions (*Evangelicalism: The Coming Generation* [Chicago: University of Chicago Press, 1987], p. 31).

[2] Frank E. Gaebelein, "The Word of God in Education," *Christianity Today* (May 9, 1960), p. 7.

[3] Dewey Beegle, *The Inspiration of Scripture* (Philadelphia: Westminster, 1963), p. 71.

Some of the great hymns are practically on a par with the psalms, and one can be sure that if Isaac Watts, Charles Wesley, Augustus Toplady, and Reginald Heber had lived in the time of David and Solomon and been *no more inspired than they were in their own day*, some of their hymns of praise to God would have found their way into the Hebrew canon (italics his).[4]

Undoubtedly, God's Spirit spoke in this vital way to the troubled soul of George Matheson. This is the kind of inspiration of which the psalms were made. There is no difference in kind. If there is any difference, it is a matter of degree.[5]

Ralph Earle likewise notes: "Recognition should be given to the idea of 'degrees of inspiration.'"[6] Millard Erickson clearly identifying the writers of Scripture as inspired, says: "The inspiring by the Holy Spirit was, to be sure, properly the inspiration of the writer, and can only derivatively be predicated on his writings as the result he produced under the Holy Spirit's influence."[7]

The only text of Scripture that deals specifically with the object of inspiration is 2 Timothy 3:16: ("All Scripture [*graphe*] is inspired by God [*theopneustos*]." Scripture, not the writers, is inspired. *Graphe* is writing, script, something written down. The writings are the product of the creative breath of God. While one cannot divorce the writer from his produced writing, theologically it is the writing that is supernaturally generated and bears the inherent divine perfections of sacred Scripture. Writing consists of words. Inspired Scripture is therefore the inspiration of words. "Scripture and the words of Scripture are identical. The words go to make up the Scripture."[8]

The dispute over the object of inspiration is not a minor theological quibble; the answers bear direct debate, specifically regarding the subjectivistic influence rooted in neo-orthodoxy. Once human subjectivism has been introduced into the meaning of inspiration, little or no divine control is left, and biblical inspiration becomes captive to anyone's concept of the degree of the biblical author's spiritual afflatus. Psychology, not theology and exegesis, becomes authoritative. Beegle, James Orr, and others led evangelicals down a treacherous path by introducing the subjective idea of the inspiration of the writer instead of his writing.[9] Notions of varying degrees of inspiration and authority within the Bible, levels of truth and error within Scripture, decisions of what is revelational and non-revelational, and the inevitable search for the "canon within the canon" all have their illegitimate parentage in a subjective view of inspiration.

INERRANCY IS NOT A TEST OF ORGANIZATIONAL FELLOWSHIP

In the immediate aftermath of the formal announcement of Billy Graham's ecumenical evangelism, justification of organizational ties with non-evangelicals

---

[4]Ibid., p. 140.

[5]Ibid., p. 141.

[6]"Further Thoughts on Biblical Inspiration," *Bulletin of the Evangelical Theological Society* 6 (1963), p. 15.

[7]*The New Evangelical Theology* (Westwood, NJ: Revell, 1968), p. 63. The same is asserted in his *Christian Theology*, 2nd ed. (Grand Rapids: Baker, 1998), pp. 224, 244.

[8]Edward J. Young, "God's Infallible Word" (A lecture given at Oak Glen, IL, under the auspices of the Layman's League of Illiana, unpublished, n.d.), p. 4.

[9]James Orr, *Revelation and Inspiration* (Grand Rapids: Baker reprint, 1969), pp. 162-63.

appeared in numerous quarters. Questions circulated, probing the definition of a true evangelical, the bases of religious endeavors with liberals, and what doctrines should determine the parameters of cooperation. Some argued that biblical inspiration/inerrancy factors should have no bearing: "If our Lord and Savior has received anyone with open arms, we dare not reject him." Biblically centered and consistent theology "must never be made the criterion for Christian fellowship.... A faulty, imperfect theology will not keep anyone out of heaven."[10] Another objected to those who "have insisted on making the doctrine of plenary inspiration the basis for Christian fellowship."[11] Bernard Ramm disagreed with the "purist" view that says "if a theologian does not hold to a certain view of Scripture, then all is lost....Orthodoxy does not depend upon a certain theory of inspiration."[12] Billy Graham concluded that the deity of Jesus Christ, not biblical inerrancy, should be the ground of fellowship.[13] Harold Lindsell contended that since the logical conclusions of one's theology are not always pressed, one could deny inerrancy without giving up other cardinal doctrines. "It is for this reason that those who accept biblical inerrancy should not break with those who disagree with them unless the divergence includes a further departure from other major doctrines of orthodoxy." He went on to note that continued close contact may convince those who reject inerrancy of the logical outcome of their position.[14]

Other prominent new evangelicals voiced their concern that inerrancy not become a litmus test for fellowship.[15] Paul S. Rees practically dismissed the whole inerrancy issue by saying that it was not a matter of the infallibility of the Scriptures but rather "the infallibility of the word 'inerrancy' to describe the total authority and credibility of the Bible in its original form."[16] For him, the whole controversy could be reduced to an intramural squabble over semantics.

In the later 1970s Harold Lindsell rocked the new evangelical community by exposing the duplicity and hypocrisy of those who gave lip service to verbal inerrancy, even signing doctrinal statements affirming it, but who did not believe and teach it. He took a tenuous position by reaffirming that inerrancy should not be a test of fellowship while insisting that one could not be an evangelical without affirming inerrancy.[17] The latter position elicited strong negative reaction from fellow

---

[10]Paul R. Edwards, "Some Thoughts on Fundamentalist Infallibility," *Eternity* (Sept 1957), p. 48.

[11]C. Peter Wagner, "Bibliolatry," *Eternity* (Oct 1958), p. 11.

[12]Bernard Ramm, "In Defense of Scripture," *Eternity* (March 1959), p. 40. Ramm is reviewing *Fundamentalism and the Word of God* by J. I. Packer (Grand Rapids: Eerdmans, 1958).

[13]Billy Graham, "Billy Graham on Separation," *Eternity* (Nov 1958), p. 18.

[14]Harold Lindsell, "A Historian Looks At Inerrancy," *Bulletin of the Evangelical Theological Society* 8 (1965), p. 10.

[15]Ralph Earle, "Further Thoughts on Biblical Inspiration," p. 15; Roger Nicole, Letter to the Editor, *Christianity Today* (Dec 23, 1966), p. 17.

[16]Paul S. Rees, "Embattlement or Understanding: A Forward," in *Biblical Authority*, Jack Rogers, ed. (Waco,TX: Word, 1977), p. 9.

[17]Harold Lindsell, *The Battle For the Bible* (Grand Rapids: Zondervan, 1976), pp. 139-40, and its sequel, *The Bible In the Balance* (Grand Rapids: Zondervan, 1979), pp. 313-15.

new evangelicals. Carl Henry, a former colleague of Lindsell, criticized Lindsell, accusing him of promoting a division in evangelicalism over inerrancy.[18]

Bernard Ramm thought Lindsell reduced inerracy to a simplistic test that divided the sheep from the goats, saints from heretics.[19] Another contended that Lindsell had defined his terms so narrowly that only a small minority of Christendom would qualify as evangelicals and maybe as believers.[20] Evangelical Donald Dayton claimed that an increasing number of evangelicals were not holding to inerrancy and concluded inerrancy could not, therefore, be a legitimate test of evangelical fellowship. Many viewed inerrancy simply as a product of B. B. Warfield and A. A. Hodge's "Princeton Theology" and believed biblical criticism had discredited it. Others placed a premium on inerrancy because it diminished attention to social concerns. The inerrantists' claim to have a timelessly accurate Bible aggravated the aggressively social minded who considered the Bible to be "historically conditioned" and either irrelevant or oppressive for contemporary social concerns.[21] Clark Pinnock considered Lindsell's work intellectually superficial and too militant and controversial.[22] Even Roger Nicole, a champion of the high view of Scripture, declined to make inerrancy an article of faith for evangelicals. "I feel that in all fairness those who prefer to avoid its use [the term inerrancy] ought not necessarily to be denied recognition as thoroughgoing evangelicals....I doubt that we can make this term a shibboleth by which evangelicals should be separated from non-evangelicals."[23]

Tolerating those who deny inerrancy is a practice that must be tested scripturally. The Bible clearly condemns collaboration with an erring brother (Rom 16:17; 2 Thess 3:6). Deviations from apostolic doctrine (the "tradition") certainly must include the doctrine of Scripture. Furthermore, if part of the essence of being an evangelical is belief in verbal inerrancy, then it must also become part of the irreducible minimum of beliefs in order for one to cooperate in an organized, ecclesiastical manner. Lindsell subverted his argument on this point. He cogently related how the inroads (the "new leaven") of unbelief affected the new evangelicals, and how the opponents of Christianity influenced the movement, including its views of inspiration and the authority of the Bible. He even demonstrated how this infects other doctrines. But it is incredibly problematic that he could turn around and claim that inerrancy should not cause a breach of fellowship among evangelicals.[24]

---

[18]Carl F. H. Henry, "The War of the Word," *New Review of Books and Religion* (Sept 1976), p. 7. His disagreements with the book also were noted in an interview with *Eternity* magazine ("The House Divided," *Eternity* [Oct 1976], p. 38). He was especially upset that Lindsell's criterion would exclude F. F. Bruce and G. C. Berkouwer from being "authentic evangelicals." Lindsell wrote a lengthy reply to and an exposure of Henry on this point in *The Bible In the Balance*, pp. 31-36.

[19]Bernard Ramm, "Misplaced Battle Lines," *The Reformed Journal* (July-Aug 1976), pp. 37-38.

[20]Bill Blackburn, "Review of *The Battle For the Bible*," *The Review and Expositor* 74 (1977), pp. 105-07.

[21]Donald W. Dayton, "'The Battle for the Bible': Renewing the Inerrancy Debate," *The Christian Century* (Nov 10, 1976), pp. 976-80.

[22]Clark H. Pinnock, "Acrimonious Debate On Inerrancy," *Eternity* (June 1976), pp. 40-41.

[23]Roger Nicole, "Letter to the Editor," *Christianity Today* (Dec 23, 1966), p. 17. Granted, Nicole is referring to the "term" inerrancy, but the context of the Wenham Conference on Biblical Inspiration (June 1966) and the controversy among the evangelicals at the time take the matter far beyond a choice of terms.

[24]"A Historian Looks At Inerrancy," pp. 10-11.

The Bible is the basis of any other doctrine that may be construed as essential to fellowship. One cannot hold to the deity of Christ as fundamental, for example, and ignore the *only* source of the knowledge of that deity. If "evangelical" is given its simplest definition as a belief in the evangel or the gospel of saving grace in Jesus Christ (the *euaggelon*), then one must include the inerrancy of Scripture as an indispensable item. There is no gospel apart from Christ and His work, and there is no knowledge of Christ and His work apart from an inerrant Bible (1 Cor 15:1-11 ["according to the Scriptures"]; Heb 10:7 ["in the scroll of the book it is written of me"]).

ERRANT SOURCES WERE COPIED BY BIBLE WRITERS

Some new evangelicals contend that errors inadvertently crept into the Bible when Bible writers used non-inspired sources. Everett F. Harrison, a professor at Fuller Seminary, raised the question, "Does inspiration require that a Biblical writer should be preserved from error in the use of sources?" His answer is ambiguous, but he as much as said that inspiration does *not* so require.[25] Harrison's query did not raise much notice, but the outright assertions of Edward John Carnell certainly did. He desired to speak for orthodoxy and posited his conclusion almost as an article of evangelical faith:

> Orthodoxy may never officially decide whether the Holy Spirit corrected the documents from which the Chronicler drew his information. But this irresolution does not affect the theology of the church, for Paul received his theology directly from Jesus Christ (Gal 1:11-12). He did *not* draw on existing documents (italics his).[26]

Carnell quotes approvingly of Matthew Henry's understanding: "This holy man [the Chronicler] wrote as he was moved by the Holy Ghost; but there was no necessity for the making up of the defects, no, nor for the rectifying of the mistakes, of these genealogies by inspiration."[27] More recently, Millard Erickson noted his agreement with Harrison.[28]

A major problem here is that this view ends up questioning all the historical books of the Bible and the historical sections of numerous other biblical books. Clearly, some of the biblical authors used non-inspired sources. Moses drew material from the "Book of the Wars of the Lord" (Num 21:14); Joshua quoted the "Book of Jasher" as did David (Josh 10:13; 2 Sam 1:18); the Chronicler used the diaries of prophets to put together his history (1 Chron 29:29); Luke testified to his investigation into the life of Christ and used his research to assure Theophilus of the accuracy of his account (Luke 1:1-4); Paul cited approvingly certain Greek poets (Acts 17:28); Titus quoted a Cretan "prophet" (Tit 1:12); and quite possibly Jude drew from the pseudepigraphical book of Enoch (Jude 14). The question is, do quotations from these sources compromise verbal inerrancy?

---

[25]Everett F. Harrison, "The Phenomena of Scripture," in *Revelation and the Bible*, Carl F. H. Henry, ed. (Grand Rapids: Baker, 1958), p. 249.

[26]Edward John Carnell, *The Case For Orthodox Theology* (Philadelphia: Westminster, 1959), p. 111. Note his discussion of the problem on pp. 102-10.

[27]Ibid., p. 107, quoting Matthew Henry's *Commentary on the Whole Bible* at 1 Chron 8:1-32.

[28]Millard J. Erickson, *Christian Theology*, p. 258.

Carnell's solution that Paul got his theology from Jesus and did not use existing documents is a serious misunderstanding and deprecation of "plenary" inspiration, which is the inspiration/inerrancy of the *entire* Bible. Paul's assertion in 2 Timothy 3:16 (*all* Scripture is God-breathed) negates any notions of differing levels of authority, trustworthiness, and truth and error in the Bible. In addition, even the Apostle Paul demanded recognition of the authority of his writings equal to that of Jesus Christ Himself (1 Cor 14:37—"If anyone thinks he is a prophet or spiritual, let him recognize that the things which I write to you are the Lord's commandment"). The Son of God placed full divine authority on the Old Testament where these errors supposedly crept in (John 10:35). The doctrine of divine inspiration/inerrancy guarantees that no error inadvertently slipped into the sacred text. Just *how* the Spirit superintended the use of non-inspired sources is not revealed in the Bible and, furthermore, is not germane to the fact of inerrancy.

INERRANCY IS NOT NECESSARY IN "PERIPHERAL MATTERS"

Some evangelicals have argued that the purpose of Scripture is to create life, not to reveal truth. As Carnell put it, "The communication of *life*, not knowledge, is the goal of inspiration" (italics his).[29] That is, the salvation of sinners is not dependent on accuracy in obscure chronologies or passages not directly bearing on redemption from sin. Inerrancy inheres only in the parts intended to make us wise unto salvation (2 Tim 3:15). Beegle, who denies inerrancy, seems dubious as to how far Carnell's life/truth dichotomy could be pushed. Using induction, he concludes:

> But in spite of errors scattered throughout [translations], enough of the truth was retained to bring the readers under the convicting power of the Holy Spirit. As a result, lives were transformed and whole churches came into being. When one observes God working his purpose through such imperfect means, has one the right to exclude such a translation from the category of inspired writings?[30]

Clarence Bass of Bethel Theological Seminary, St. Paul, suggested that infallibility be defined in terms of God's purpose for Scripture. "Infallibility can only be dogmatically asserted in the accomplishing of the purpose of Scripture," and that purpose is to "exhibit Christ." He concludes, "Since the true purpose of Scripture is to give a true revelation of Christ, and not necessarily give accurate facts about other incidentals, then the important belief that must be held is that it is infallible in its teaching about Him."[31] Bass later explained: "Many of us admit that the Bible unquestionably contains factual errors,...but we still maintain that it is inerrant in divine purpose."[32]

---

[29]*The Case For Orthodox Theology*, p. 100.

[30]*The Inspiration of Scripture*, p. 40. His argument here is that there is no theological difference between autographs and translations, that if translations can have error, so may the originals. But errors are an irrelevant factor in either case, in his opinion, since people have been saved through errant translations.

[31]Clarence B. Bass, "The Relationship of Inerrancy to Infallibility in the Scripture" (A paper presented at Bethel Seminary, Dec 9, 1964, unpublished), pp. 17-18.

[32]Interview with Jim Huffman, "Conservative View of Theology is Changing," *Minneapolis Tribune* (Jan 22, 1966).

Bernard Ramm testified:

> I find the Holy Scripture is functionally the Word of God to me because of its divine authority, its sufficiency (or 'perfection' in the sense that it teaches all we need to know in this life for salvation, Christian living, and the hope to come), its clarity, and its efficacy. These are the qualities whereby we really are actually and effectively held to Holy Scripture, for in these matters the Scriptures do function as the written Word of God."[33]

William Sanford LaSor, while discussing the infallibility of the Bible "in faith and practice," made clear what the phrase meant to him: "I submit that the primary—if not only—purpose of the Bible is to bring men to know the redeeming love of God in Christ Jesus and to know the full implications of salvation. This is 'faith and practice.' Anything else is less than fully biblical."[34] After discussing the number of angels at Jesus' tomb and to whom they appeared on resurrection morning, LaSor states, "Whether there were one, two, or even three angels at the tomb is of no great moment; what is of eternal significance is the fact that the body of Jesus was not there, he had risen from the dead, and by this fact God had placed his seal on all that Jesus had taught and done for man's salvation (Romans 1:4)."[35]

A variation of the above argument claims that biblical passages dealing with geology, biology, botany, meteorology, etc., are not to be considered necessarily inerrant but are actually the cultural framework to which Jesus and others accommodated themselves in order to convey the essential gospel. Daniel P. Fuller articulated this view:

> But why is it not at least as reasonable to infer from inspiration that the God who lovingly willed to communicate revelational truth to men deliberately accommodated his language in non-revelational matters to the way the original readers viewed the world about them, so as to enhance the communication of revelational truth, by which alone men could be saved?[36]

Fuller cites Jesus' references to the mustard seed being the smallest of seeds (Matt 13:32; 17:20). However, Fuller believes Jesus accommodated Himself to this error in order to convey the truth of the efficacy of faith. Later Fuller considerably elaborated the point:

> A communication can be in error only if it fails to live up to the intention of its author....The Bible writers make it clear that their purpose was to report the happenings and meaning of the redemptive acts of God in history so that men might be made wise unto salvation....Thus the Bible is inerrant, because, being

---

[33]Bernard Ramm, "The Relationship of Science, Factual Statements and the Doctrine of Biblical Inerrancy," *Journal of the American Scientific Affiliation* 21 (1969), pp. 103-04.

[34]William Sanford LaSor, "Life Under Tension," *Theology News and Notes* (Published by Fuller Theological Seminary, special issue, 1976), p. 8.

[35]Ibid., p. 25.

[36]Daniel P. Fuller, "Benjamin B. Warfield's View of Faith and History," p. 81.

verbally inspired, it fulfills its intention to recount and give the correct meaning of God's redemptive acts in history....Consequently the Biblical writers are to be judged only on the terms of the revelational teachings they intended to communicate, for revelation concerns what eye cannot see or ear hear by itself. Thus since the Bible declares that its purpose is to impart revelation, we run no risk of distorting its message as we credit its revelational teachings and admit the possibility that its non-revelational statements and implications are a reflection of the culture of the writer and his original readers.[37]

Bernard Ramm had expressed a similar conclusion:

I think it is possible to make a distinction between the structural and cultural forms that revelation comes through, and the revelation itself. The revelation does not dignify the structure into the category of the revelational....Therefore it is valid to make a distinction between the structural or literary forms in which a revelation comes and what the revelation itself teaches.[38]

Ramm was unsure, however, how far this could be taken. He suspects that "if a pre-scientific world view were strongly animistic or polytheistic or mythological, it could not serve as a structural form through which a true revelation could come."[39] This is to say that God simply could not communicate His message of salvation to some cultures despite His universal love for all (John 3:16), His provision of an infinite redemption and its objective availability to all (Rev 22:17), and His express wish for all to come to repentance (2 Pet 3:9).

Donald Bloesch, an evangelical on its port side, spoke of the infallible message of Scripture being "hidden" in the cultural baggage of the biblical writers.

They did not err in what they proclaimed, but this does not mean that they were faultless in their recording of historical data or in their world view, which is now outdated. The Scriptures are entirely trustworthy in what they purport to give us, but this trustworthiness is a property not simply of the letter of the Bible but of the Spirit, the primary author of the Scripture.[40]

The assertion that inerrancy does not inhere in "peripheral matters" and that such areas are best understood as a divine accommodation to cultural error in order to communicate truth has serious problems. For one, no human standard exists by which redemptive verses can be declared inerrant and others not. Omniscience would be required. No human is competent to judge God's work as to truth or error. The accommodation view denies the plenary inspiration and inerrancy of Scripture, which says that *all* of Scripture, the Bible in its entirety, in the whole and the parts, partakes equally and totally of divine inspiration. We are as dependent on the same writers to tell us of an empty tomb as we are to learn of the number of angels at the tomb. The so-called revelational and non-revelational, the soteriological and the botanical/meteorological/biological are so thoroughly integrated that the distinction cannot be discovered short of divine omniscience.

---

[37]"The Nature of Biblical Inerranacy," pp. 47, 50.

[38]"The Relationship of Science, Factual Statements and the Doctrine of Biblical Inerrancy," p. 101.

[39]Ibid.

[40]Donald G. Bloesch, *Essentials of Evangelical Theology*, 2 vols. (Peabody, MA: Prince Press, 1998), 1:65.

The most obscure passage in the canon may well have a bearing on the Lord Jesus Christ and His mission in the world. Finitude and original sin prevent one from seeing the full implication of Scripture. If Jesus could see clearly the doctrine of resurrection from the incident of the burning bush (Matt 22:29), how much more is there to be seen in Scripture if only there were the ability? If Christ could upbraid the theologians of His day for missing this important truth from an Old Testament narrative, dare any mortal presume to declare what is revelational or non-revelational, and on that basis decide what is inerrant and what is possibly not in Scripture?

The new evangelical argument also creates an ambivalence to authority within the Bible itself. Some verses have *no* divine authority because they contain error. Only the salvation texts, called "revelational" or "doctrinal," have real, binding authority. The selective process creates a "canon within the canon," and one is forced to weed through the Scripture searching for truth in the midst of error hoping to find the genuine canon and save his soul from eternal perdition. This is hopeless. Further, the argument shifts the real authority to the human mind and away from the Bible's own testimony concerning its origin, nature, and authority (2 Tim 3:16-17; 2 Pet 1:21; et al.). Intellectual autonomy is the scarlet sin of theologians and philosophers.

A proper concept of accommodation has been used for centuries to denote the simple fact that God condescended to human finitude to speak His revelation in human languages. Calvin likened it to God "lisping" so as to "accommodate the knowledge of him to our feebleness. In doing so, he must of course stoop far below his proper height," referring especially to biblical anthropomorphisms.[41] But it is quite another matter, and an impossibility, for Jesus Christ, the incarnation of truth (John 14: 6), to appropriate *error* in conveying the truth. Warfield stated the matter cogently: "It is one thing to adapt the teaching of truth to the stage of receptivity of the learner; it is another thing to adopt the errors of the time as the very matter to be taught."[42]

The new evangelical form of the accommodation view casts serious reflection on Christ's person and on His position as the supreme Master Teacher of all time. As such a Teacher, He put His full authority on the written Word of God (Matt 5: 18; John 10:35; 17:17). He also pre-authenticated the forthcoming New Testament (John 14:26; 16:13-15) and could not have been ignorant of these so-called allowable errors in people's understanding. If He were, His omniscience would be impugned and compromised. For Him to stamp an error-filled Bible with eternal trustworthiness would impeach His own truthfulness and integrity. Also, the Holy Spirit, whom LaSor says was "wisely allowing"[43] this accommodation, is Himself truth (1 John 5:6; 2:27; John 14:17; 15:26), and He could not have participated in accommodating error.

---

[41]John Calvin, *The Institutes of the Christian Religion*, Henry Beveridge, trans. (Grand Rapids: Eerdmans, 1964), I, xiii, 1.

[42]B. B. Warfield, *The Inspiration and Authority of the Bible* (Philadelphia: Presbyterian and Reformed, 1948), p. 195.

[43]"Life Under Tension," p. 27.

Wayne Grudem, also a new evangelical, articulates six objections to accommodationism. As to the purpose of Scripture, his conclusion is appropriate: "It is better to say that the whole purpose of Scripture is to say everything it does say, on whatever subject."[44]

INERRANCY IS NOT POSSIBLE FROM A PHILOSOPHICAL STANDPOINT

Some evangelicals conjecture that human language is incapable of conveying absolute truth because, being symbolic or metaphorical in nature, language is relative. No two people understand exactly the same thing by a given word, concept, or sentence. Eugene Nida, for example, says:

> The only absolute in Christianity is the triune God. Anything which involves man, who is finite and limited, must of necessity be limited, and hence relative. Biblical relativism is an obligatory feature of our incarnational religion, for without it we would either absolutize human institutions or relativize God.[45]

Richard Curtis, a professor at Bethel College and Seminary, St. Paul, developed Nida's argument further. Beginning with the idea that "no two people see anything alike in every respect," Curtis says that "with most of our value judgments there is a continuum of gray between the black at one extreme and the white at the other." Shifting this line to the Bible, he reasons that "the Scriptures in our possession are, at best, accurate representations *to a high degree of probability* (and not *absolute* as some have stoutly maintained, and others have unconsciously assumed, even though a cursory look at the evidence would have quickly disproved it)" (italics his). He concludes:

> The most we can truthfully say is that our present translations represent the original revelation (which we believe *by faith* to have come from God) to a high degree of probability (such degree varying with the translation-interpreter relationship) (italics his).[46]

Curtis is not talking about manuscript reliability or the probabilities of correspondence to the autographs; he is referring to the ability of language itself to communicate divine verbal revelation. Ralph Earle came to the same position. Building on Nida's assertions that people using human language symbols communicate only about 80%, he concludes that "what we should look for in the Scriptures is not a formal equivalence but a dynamic equivalence. The words are not the ultimate reality, but the thoughts which they seek to convey."[47] Earle is not referring to translation theories but to the impossibility of human language being a vehicle to communicate divine, inerrant revelation.

---

[44] Wayne A. Grudem, "Scripture's Self-Attestation and the Problem of Formulating a Doctrine of Scripture," p. 57.

[45] Eugene Nida, *Customs and Cultures: Anthropology For Christian Missions* (New York: Harper, 1954), p. 282.

[46] Richard K. Curtis, "Language and Theology: Some Basic Considerations," *Gordon Review* (Sept 1955), pp. 97-109.

[47] "Further Thoughts on Biblical Inspiration," p. 16.

A variation of this argument is that there is a necessary gap or interval between God and man in the area of human language so that the very concept of propositional revelation as well as inerrancy is called into question. This is the neo-orthodox view put forth by Karl Barth and recommended as needful for evangelicals by Bernard Ramm.[48]

There are several objections to the idea that human language itself precludes inerrancy.[49] The argument fails to have a truly theistic view of human language. Language is a part of the image of God in man that enables him to receive divine verbal revelation and to communicate with his Maker. God gave language for theological expression. God created human language and created man as a linguistic being. He is the sovereign God; therefore, human language can never successfully frustrate or resist His purposes to communicate inerrantly in human language.

Finitude is an important factor in language barriers and difficulties. God cannot be *fully* known by the human mind; a complete understanding of God and His ways is not possible for a finite intellect. But it is not clear theologically (or logically) how human finitude *necessitates* error in verbal revelation. Jesus Christ was fully human (as well as fully God), and He spoke human language. Any questioning or denial of verbal inerrancy because of philosophical problems in linguistics ultimately reflects on God's supreme revelation in human form—the incarnation. If the human aspect of the Bible inevitably involves error and precludes inerrancy, serious questions arise concerning the person of Christ who also was human.

The "gap" proposed by Barth and Ramm is simply a form of the old Platonic, Kantian dualism that has cursed theology more than is realized. Platonism stressed the absolute dichotomy between matter and spirit, body and soul, God (or the gods) and man, universals and particulars, etc. Kant proposed an absolute distance between the phenomenal realm (the real empirical world) and the noumenal realm (the unknowable ideal world of God and perfection). Plato and Kant have been used by theologians and philosophers to deny the incarnation of Christ, the material-immaterial composition of man, and even a literal, earthly millennial kingdom of God in the *eschaton*. Neo-orthodoxy and liberalism have not hesitated to deny the deity of Christ with the same Platonic/Kantian reasoning by which they rejected propositional revelation, verbal inspiration, and inerrancy. Richard Gaffin expressed it crisply:

> To call into question the inerrancy of the Bible is to call into question the infallibility of Christ. To put the matter simply: the abandonment of the infallibility of Scripture and of the conviction that it is the very words of God is the abandonment of evangelical theology.[50]

---

[48]*After Fundamentalism: The Future of Evangelical Theology* (San Francisco: Harper and Row, 1983), pp. 89-93.

[49]An excellent analysis of Curtis' article is by Roger Nicole, "A Reply to 'Language and Theology,'" *Gordon Review* (Dec 1955), pp. 143-51. Some of my objections reflect his analysis. See also Gordon H. Clark, "Logic and Language," *Gordon Review* (Feb 1956), pp. 3-9.

[50]Richard B. Gaffin, Jr., "Review of Dewey M. Beegle: *The Inspiration of Scripture*," *Westminster Theological Journal* 6 (1964), p. 235.

The argument that human language cannot convey inerrant information is self-defeating. If language cannot convey absolute truth, then the dictum itself is not true. If language is inherently relative, then the principle of the relativity of language is itself relative, i.e., a relative relativism elevated to an absolute relativism by sheer cerebral fiat! Or if no two people understand words exactly alike and this fact precludes errorlessness, then the argument is itself erroneous. All truth statements about anything are questionable—a hopeless conclusion. Packer has answered the matter of the adequacy of human language to convey divine revelation.[51] Clark Pinnock once did also, but he later used the humanity of Scripture to argue against biblical inerrancy.[52]

The men who wrote under inspiration or who gave the Word of God under prophetic consciousness[53] claimed absolute authority for their words. This was true of David (2 Sam 3:2), Isaiah (Isa 1:20), Jesus Christ (Matt 24:35; John 17:8, 14), Paul (Gal 1:8), and John (Rev 22:19), among others. The Bible writers regarded the inspired works of others as absolute and authoritative (Ps 19:7; 119:89, 128; Isa 8:20; Matt 5:18; John 10:35; Acts 7:38; 2 Tim 3:16; 2 Pet 1:21). The interesting interchange of "God" and "Scripture" is also instructive (Rom 9:17; Gal 3:8). No error between God and His verbal revelation in Scripture is possible.

SCRIPTURAL ACCURACY CANNOT BE JUDGED BY PRESENT STANDARDS

It is alleged that "missile-launching accuracy" cannot be predicated of the Bible in all its parts. For example, with the value of *pi* (3.14159), Solomon's "molten sea" could not have had a diameter of 10 cubits and circumference of 30 (2 Chron 4:2). Robert Mounce, a professor at Bethel College, St. Paul, asks, "Are we to argue deductively that inspiration logically necessitates Cape Kennedy accuracy, or shall we adopt the inductive approach and ask Scripture to define its own terms?" His answer: "Our concern that the Bible be held in high esteem does not allow us the prerogative of propounding a level of missile-launching accuracy, especially when the Word of God itself does not support such a position."[54] Jack Rogers, a theologian from Fuller Seminary, wrote: "I believe it is wrong to impose our changing twentieth-century standards of science on the Bible in an attempt to make it conform to secular standards."[55]

In the aftermath of Lindsell's *Battle For the Bible* (1966), a collective response appeared entitled *Biblical Authority*, edited by Jack Rogers.[56] One of

---

[51]J. I. Packer, "The Adequacy of Human Language," in *Inerrancy*, Norman Geisler, ed. (Grand Rapids: Zondervan, 1979), pp. 197-226.

[52]Clark Pinnock, *Biblical Revelation*, p. 17. Compare his "This Treasure In Earthen Vessels," *Sojourners* (Oct 1980), p. 18.

[53]A theological term denoting the awareness of the person giving divine revelation under the power of the Holy Spirit, that he was speaking infallibly for God.

[54]Robert H. Mounce, "Clues To Understanding Biblical Accuracy," *Eternity* (June 1966), pp. 17-18. Ten years later he reiterated his position during the "Battle For the Bible" controversy within new evangelicalism ("Does the Bible Contain Errors?" *Eternity* [Aug 1976], p. 49).

[55]Jack Rogers, Letter to the Editor, *Christianity Today* (Mar 5, 1982), p. 10.

[56]Waco, TX: Word, 1977.

the respondents, Fuller president David Hubbard concluded: "Modern standards of accuracy have been imposed on books that God was pleased to inspire in ancient Oriental contexts, with their very different standards of accuracy." He was concerned that error be "defined in theological terms derived from and limited to the Bible itself," but he observed that inerrancy arguments usually contain "an appeal to Webster's Dictionary for support." "Error theologically must mean that which leads us astray from the will of God or the knowledge of his truth." That is, the biblical understanding of error has solely to do with willful deception, not with correspondence to an actual state of affairs. On such a basis one could argue for "inerrancy" but still maintain the presence of factual errors in the Bible. Hubbard says, "We break with the basic Reformed teaching on the sufficiency of the Bible both when we claim it to be inerrant on the basis of minute details of chronology, geography, history, or cosmology or when we attack its authority by pointing to alleged discrepancies."[57] Donald Bloesch likewise argues for biblical inerrancy only in the sense of its indeceivability, meaning that there is no intention to deceive.[58]

The new evangelical objection to inerrancy on this point rests on a faulty view or definition of truth. As noted earlier, truth is an expression of the mind of God, that which God could say about any and all reality or states of affairs. Intentionalism is not in itself a valid definition or criterion of truth. John Feinberg correctly notes that Hubbard and others have arrived at a meaning of truth by studying the words "truth" and "error" in the Bible and not facing the biblical *concept* of truth. The latter defines what sort a thing truth really is.[59] A concept or theory of truth is not captured by the study of one word and its antonym.

The intent to deceive is too subjective and elusive a criterion to apply to biblical inerrancy. While all would agree that volition and intention affect the definition of error, errors can be made with or without the intent to do so. Intent cannot be the sole, nor prime, ingredient in defining error. Such a definition is more psychological and subjective than objective. The biblical idea of truth rests on a correspondence foundation, that which corresponds to God's declaration concerning a state of affairs. Truth and error are theistically determined. Any truth or error is what it is in relation to the self-contained triune God of the Scriptures, that is, in relation to His comprehensive plan, original creation, and present exhaustive preservation and absolute control of the universe.

---

[57]David Allan Hubbard, "The Current Tensions: Is There A Way Out?" in *Biblical Authority*, pp. 160, 167-68. Jack Rogers also defined error as intent to deceive. He concluded: "To confuse 'error' in the sense of technical accuracy with the biblical notion of error as willful deception diverts us from the serious intent of Scripture" [which is to inform us of salvation] ("The Church Doctrine of Biblical Authority," ibid., p. 46).

[58]*Essentials of Evangelical Theology*, 1:67-70.

[59]John S. Feinberg, "Truth, Meaning, and Inerrancy," *Journal of the Evangelical Theological Society* 26 (1983), p. 26. For the whole question of the meaning of truth and its role in the inerrancy debate, see further his "The Meaning of Inerrancy," in *Inerrancy*, pp. 267-304, and "Truth: Relationship of Theories of Truth to Hermeneutics," in *Hermeneutics, Authority and the Bible*, Earl D. Radmacher and Robert D. Preus, eds. (Grand Rapids: Zondervan, 1984), pp. 3-50. See also Norman Geisler, "The Concept of Truth in the Inerrancy Debate," *Bibliotheca Sacra* 137 (Oct-Dec 1980), pp. 327-29, and a similar essay in *The Living and Active Word of God: Essays in Honor of Samuel J. Schultz*, Morris Inch and Ronald Youngblood, eds. (Winona Lake, IN: Eisenbrauns, 1983), pp. 225-36.

To deprecate ancient cultures as not having mathematical precision approaching modern standards is to underestimate their advances and abilities. For example, the Great Pyramid of Giza and other structures show a fantastic precision even to this day. After millennia, they still defy a consensus of opinion as to how they were so accurately constructed. In certain technical calculations in the Bible, there are many variables in computation which, if known, would uphold the doctrine of the inerrancy and complete accuracy of the biblical data. This has been the orthodox view from the beginning.[60]

Finally, it needs to be repeated that Jesus stamped the whole Old Testament as authoritative in all its parts (even an apparently obscure part) (John 10:35). Tedious distinctions on what constitutes accuracy and error in the biblical cultures are simply quibbles designed to evade the clear testimony of Scripture in the interests of agendas alien to the teaching of our Lord. It is the testimony of Scripture to itself through the lips and pens of Jesus Christ and His (Old and New Testament) prophets and apostles that is being impugned.

ARGUMENTS FOR INERRANT NON-EXISTENT AUTOGRAPHS ARE USELESS

Some new evangelicals consider it an exercise in futility to argue for the inerrancy of the original manuscripts of Scripture when they are lost and presumably unable to be retrieved. Mounce asserted: "The concept of an infallible original—infallible in the sense of perfect conformity to an arbitrary standard which we humans set up—is an unreal and ill-advised haven for those who are over-solicitous for the Word of God."[61] Paul S. Rees, former pastor of First Covenant Church, Minneapolis, replied to a newspaper reporter's question about the accuracy of the Bible: "We say this phrase [inerrancy] refers only to the original manuscripts of the writers, but no such manuscripts are available. So you can't apply this meaning to any existing part of the Bible."[62] In response to Lindsell's *Battle For the Bible*, one reviewer attempted at length to debunk the value of inerrant autographs:

> But I do not regard the doctrine of inerrancy helpful or relevant. Lindsell, in common with all who argue for inerrancy, acknowledges that it is only the "autographs" (original manuscripts) which are without error. He knows that there are no errorless copies of these documents in existence....The point is that [the existence of errors] in all the Bibles we use raises a question concerning the relevance of the contention that once there was an inerrant original.[63]

An additional aspect of this type of argument says that there is no need to argue for the inspiration of the original manuscripts only, because there is fundamentally, theologically, and practically no difference between the autographs and the

---

[60]See for example, Anton Kronstedt, "Pi: 3.141593," *Bible-Science Newsletter* (Nov 1972), p. 5; Henry Morris, "Alleged Scientific Mistakes," *Bible-Science Newsletter* (Nov 1972), p. 5; and Albert Zuidhof, "Solomon's Molten Sea and the Value of Pi," *Bible-Science Newsletter* (May 1973), p. 6.

[61]Robert H. Mounce, "Clues to Understanding Biblical Inerrancy," p. 18.

[62]Interview with Jim Huffman, "Conservative View of Theology is Changing," *Minneapolis Tribune* (Jan 22, 1966).

[63]Fred P. Thompson, Jr, "At Issue—The Wrong War," *United Evangelical Action* (Winter 1976), pp. 8-10.

apographs (copies). Therefore, since the copies contain errors, so must the originals; since the originals were inspired, so are copies. Beegle championed this position with clear explication. Holding that the purpose of Scripture is to bring about salvation, which occurs regularly through translations, he then asks, "Since God has seen fit to work through errant copies of Scripture, is one justified in claiming that God *had* to give the autographs inerrantly" (italics his)? He asks again, "Is it not valid to acknowledge that the autographs also had some inconsequential errors and were to all intents and purposes the pure, authoritative Word of God."[64] He also points to the authority of the Septuagint used by Jesus, Paul, and others as proof that autographs and apographs are essentially indistinguishable.[65]

Others contend that the infallibility of the autographs is a nineteenth-century invention of the "Old Princeton" theology of Alexander Hodge principally, as well as B. B. Warfield. Allegedly, appealing to inaccessible originals aimed to put the Scriptures beyond the reach of higher criticism and Darwinian evolutionism. The "retreat to the original autographs" was precipitated by the need for an apologetic against heretical presuppositions and conclusions of scholastic unbelief. [66]

As to the absence of the autographs, any view of inspiration faces the problem. It is just as difficult to demonstrate that the autographs had error. Empirical certainty is impossible in any case, and the available empirical (manuscript) evidence as such is inconclusive. Nothing therefore is established by saying that the inaccessibility of the autographs makes an appeal to them useless and/or precludes belief in inerrancy. Furthermore, the argument that there is no difference between originals and copies is based on unsupported assumptions. For example, some assume that the character of God does not *necessitate* the infallibility and inerrancy of His Word; however, the biblical view of the true God *demands* that His verbal revelation must be perfectly true in its whole and in its parts. The Scripture is as incapable of teaching error as it is incapable of propounding nonsense because God is infinite truth, knowledge, and wisdom. The old dictum is true that the kind of Bible one believes in reflects the kind of God one believes.

Cogent theological reasons for maintaining a fundamental distinction between autographs and apographs are available. Error in a copy reflects on a scribe or copyist; error in an original manuscript reflects on the author. With the God of truth as the author of Scripture, an erroneous verbal revelation is contradictory, impossible, and unthinkable. Errors in transmission are theoretically detectable and thus correctable; errors in originals lost forever are neither detectable nor correctable. An inerrant original text to which errors have been added in transmission can be approached through textual criticism. But an errant, corrupted original is hopelessly flawed.[67]

---

[64]Dewey M. Beegle, *The Inspiration of Scripture*, pp. 24-25. His discussion is from pp. 17-40.

[65]Ibid., p. 37. He does acknowledge that "there is a sense" in which a distinction can be made between autographs and copies. He understands the difference to be merely the "degree" of inspiration between them.

[66]Jack B. Rogers and Donald K. McKim, *The Authority and Interpretation of the Bible: An Historical Approach* (New York: Harper & Row, 1979), pp. 298, 300, 301. This idea is more fully developed on pp. 298-310.

[67]Paul D. Feinberg, "The Meaning of Inerrancy," in *Inerrancy*, p. 297. See also Greg L. Bahnsen's excellent article, "The Inerrancy of the Autographa," in *Inerrancy*, p. 183, and John Wenham, *Christ and the Bible* (Downers Grove, IL: InterVarsity, 1972), p. 186.

The argument against inerrancy from lost autographs fails to comprehend the *providence* of God (i.e., secondary causation) in the preservation of the text of Scripture; He did not choose to use *miracles* (a direct intrusion of His power) for that purpose. Thus there is a great difference between the original inspiration of the text (direct miracle) and its preservation (indirect providence)—a difference important for distinguishing originals and copies as to inerrancy and authority. Rather than positing "degrees" of inspiration to distinguish the two, as Beegle propounded, copies and translations partake of derivative inspiration from the autographs insofar as they reproduce the autographs. This derivative inspiration is linear in fashion; copies derive inspiration from previous copies, going back to the autographs. In that sense the original inspiration, inerrancy, and authority of the Bible appears in the copies, but total inerrancy is not argued for copies and translations. The argument against inerrancy from lost autographs also fails to realize that while the original manuscripts have been lost, the original words have not. While we do not possess the original *codex* (manuscript), we do possess the original *text* (words) in the many manuscripts, copies, translations, and versions of Scripture.

As to the charge that an appeal to inerrant autographs is rather recent, the Rogers and McKim proposal has been shown to be inadequate, prejudicial, selective in choice of evidence, and overall a sloppy piece of work.[68] Augustine, in the early fifth century A.D., wrote: "I have learned to yield this respect and honor only to the canonical books of Scripture: of these do I most firmly believe that the authors were completely free from error."[69] Erasmus himself believed in infallible originals.[70] Others in the sixteenth and early seventeenth centuries agreed, William Ames being a prime example.[71] After extensive documentation, Woodbridge concludes:

> The "authentic originals" concept played an important role in the controversies of some but not all Roman Catholics and Protestants in the sixteenth and seventeenth centuries. Those scholars who suggest that the idea of a completely infallible Bible in the original autographs is a late nineteenth-century construction would do well to reconsider these controversies.[72]

Nineteenth-century Reformed scholars prior to Hodge and Warfield held to the infallibility of the autographs.[73] Woodbridge's conclusion is apt: "Nor should scholars continue to assert with assurance that B. B. Warfield and A. A. Hodge

---

[68]John D. Woodbridge wrote a scholarly, well-documented refutation of the Rogers and McKim theory entitled *Biblical Authority: A Critique of the Rogers/McKim Proposal* (Grand Rapids: Zondervan, 1982). His conclusion concerning their work: "Because they desired so strongly to plead a certain case, they generally sacrificed their claims to even-handed scholarship by discounting out-of-hand contrary evidence, by neglecting a world of technical scholarship bearing on their broad subject, by fixing too uncritically upon a neo-orthodox historiography, and by relying too heavily upon secondary literature rather than examining primary sources for themselves. As a result, their volume lacks that quality of reliability that gives good historical surveys their endurance" (p. 155).

[69]*The Letters Augustine*, 82.3, quoted by Woodbridge, *Biblical Authority*, p. 167.

[70]Erasmus complained that "often the authentic and true text has been corrupted by ignorant copyists," cited by Woodbridge, *Biblical Authority*, pp. 51; also see his footnote 10 on p. 175.

[71]Ibid., pp. 74, 81-83.

[72]Ibid., p. 83.

[73]Ibid., pp. 115, 122-28, 130-33.

innovated in the Reformed tradition when they spoke of the biblical infallibility of the original autographs (1881)."[74]

INSPIRATION AND INERRANCY ARE NOT TANTAMOUNT TO EACH OTHER

Some new evangelicals assert that the Bible does not teach its inerrancy, but that inerrancy is implied or derived from inspiration—that technically inspiration does not necessarily entail inerrancy or absolute truth. E. F. Harrison noted: "Inerrancy is a conclusion to which devout minds have come because of the divine character of Scripture." And, "Unquestionably the Bible teaches its own inspiration. It is the Book of God. It does not require us to hold inerrancy, though this is a natural corollary of full inspiration."[75] In a review of Beegle's *Inspiration of Scripture*, another said that the link between inspiration and inerrancy "lacks the ring of honesty and it does not commend the Bible to the unbelieving mind."[76] Clarence Bass said that inerrancy may be "logically expected" from a perfect God, and that a revelation from God may be "logically inferred" to conform to His character. Also an inerrant revelation from God may be "inferred" because of "man's need for an accurate record." From the considerations of a perfect God and man's need for an accurate record, "it may be logically concluded that the revelation given to man in objective form would be perfect and infallible to the point of being inerrant."[77] Carl Henry shares the same opinion. "Evangelical theologians acknowledge that inerrancy is not formally claimed by the biblical writers. But they assert that it is a proper inference from the Bible's teaching about its own inspiration, and from the character of the self-revealing God."[78] Millard Erickson put it in similar words: "So while the Bible does not explicitly claim freedom from error, this is a corollary, or an implication, of its view of inspiration."[79] Clark Pinnock wrote that the inference that if God is the author of Scripture then it must be infallible, is invalid. "God uses fallible spokesmen all the time to deliver his word, and it does not follow that the Bible *must* be otherwise" (italics his).[80] More recently, Paul Feinberg noted: "Some, like B. B. Warfield, have argued that this doctrine [inerrancy] was *explicitly* taught in Scripture. I seriously doubt it. I think that the doctrine is *implicit* in Scripture" (italics his).[81]

A further refinement of this line of reasoning is the new meaning or connotation attached to the word "infallibility." In theology heretofore infallibility

---

[74]Ibid., p. 115. Consult the well-documented and well-written article by John D. Woodbridge and Randall H. Balmer, "The Princetonians and Biblical Authority: An Assessment of the Ernest Sandeen Proposal," in *Scripture and Truth*, pp. 251-79. See also Randall H. Balmer, "The Princetonians and Scripture: A Reconsideration," *Westminster Theological Journal* 44 (1982), pp. 32-65, and Richard B. Gaffin, Jr., "Old Amsterdam and Inerrancy," *Westminster Theological Journal* 44 (1982), pp. 250-89.

[75]E. F. Harrison, "The Phenomena of Scripture," pp. 238, 250.

[76]Harold Englund, "Review of *The Inspiration of Scripture*," *Eternity* (July 1963), pp. 42-43.

[77]Clarence B. Bass, "The Relation of Inerrancy to Infallibility in Scripture," pp. 1, 3, 5.

[78]"Yea, Hath God Said…?" *Christianity Today* (April 24, 1963), p. 26. He reiterated the point in, among other places, "A House Divided," *Eternity* (Oct 1976), p. 39.

[79]*The New Evangelical Theology*, p. 74. He made the same claim in his *Christian Theology*, pp. 246, 251, 255, 257.

[80]"Three Views of the Bible in Contemporary Theology," in *Biblical Authority*, p. 64.

[81]"Infallibility and Inerrancy," *Trinity Journal 6* (1977), p. 121.

meant incapable of error. Now it is used in the narrow and restricted sense of "infallibility as to purpose" and no longer "infallibility as to content." That is, Scripture will infallibly lead one to salvation in Christ and a right knowledge of God because that is its purpose, but it is not necessarily without error in some of its content. Bass reflected this new meaning when he said, "Infallibility can only be dogmatically asserted in the accomplishing of the purpose of Scripture. There is little doubt as to what this purpose is, though there may be varying interpretations as to the response required." That purpose is to "exhibit Christ."[82]

Stephen Davis, a self-confessed evangelical with neo-orthodox tendencies, testified, "I can affirm, as I did at my ordination to the ministry in 1965, that the Bible is 'the only infallible rule of faith and practice.' By that I mean that I find the Bible entirely trustworthy on matters of faith and practice."[83] He later refines his idea of infallibility/trustworthiness as a "notion that says that the Bible is fully trustworthy and never misleads us on matters that are *crucially relevant* to Christian faith and practice" (italics added). As to whether his definition can guarantee the truthfulness of the major doctrines of Scripture, he says in one sense yes, "but in another sense the answer is no, for I affirm Biblical infallibility not as a theological *a priori*—i.e., because the doctrine is needed for some theological or apologetic reason—but simply because *this seems to be a good way to describe the Bible*" (italics mine).[84]

Is biblical inerrancy only a deduction or inference made from the doctrine of inspiration? When the Bible teaches that God, who inspired Scripture, is truth and cannot lie (John 3:33; Titus 1:2), and that Jesus Christ, the enfleshment of truth (John 14:6), pronounced the Word of God as truth (John 17:17), is it mere pious logic that sees the God-breathed Book as inerrant? Hardly. Or consider the divine agent in inspiration, the Holy Spirit; He is called the Spirit of truth (John 14:7; 15: 26; 16:13). John later says explicitly, "the Spirit is the truth" (1 John 5:6). Since Satan is the source of error (1 John 4:6), we are then faced with the nonsensical anomaly that somehow the Bible is the product of the cooperative efforts of the Spirit of truth and the spirit of error. Gaffin correctly observes that "even a most cursory examination will be enough to impress upon the reader that in the New Testament the person and work of the Holy Spirit and truth are brought in the closest possible conjunction....The very least that is in view is the congruence of the work of the Holy Spirit and the communication of truth."[85] He further notes that Paul equates the Spirit and "spiritual" with that which is flawless; for example, the eschatological state of the believer's body is "spiritual" (1 Cor 15:44) and thus perfect. "For Paul, then, that which is spiritual is inherently synonymous with that which is perfect and perpetual, in contrast to the natural which after the fall is flawed and made transient by sin."[86]

---

[82]"The Relation of Inerrancy to Infallibility in the Scripture," p. 17.

[83]Stephen T. Davis, *The Debate About the Bible* (Philadelphia: Westminster, 1977), p. 15.

[84]Ibid., pp. 118, 121.

[85]Richard B. Gaffin, "Review of Dewey M. Beegle, *The Inspiration of Scripture*," p. 231.

[86]Ibid.

Edward J. Young is scathing in his analysis of the new evangelical dichotomy between inspiration and inerrancy. He notes that the Ten Commandments are preceded by "and God spoke all these words, saying," and it is much more than a "tremendous deduction" that we understand that these words from God are true. "To say that Scripture is God-breathed is the same as saying that Scripture is spoken by God....To talk of a God-breathed Scripture that is not infallible is to say a meaningless thing. If Scripture is God-breathed, it is also infallible; the two cannot be separated."[87]

The new evangelical disjunction between inspiration, inerrancy, and infallibility is purely a philosophical if not simply a semantic quibble, and has no basis in theology or exegesis. It is manifestly designed to avoid the clear teaching of Scripture concerning its own inspiration and inerrancy.

PHENOMENA NOT PROOFTEXTS FORM THE BASIS OF INSPIRATION

The "phenomena" in this argument include all the data, facts, evidences of what inspiration is, how the Bible was used by other Bible writers, prophets, and apostles, etc. It is argued that the doctrine of inspiration must be based on all these phenomena of Scripture, *including* the alleged contradictions, discrepancies, and factual errors. These problematic data must not be explained away by a predetermined doctrine based on proof texts, so the assertion goes. Instead man must examine all Scripture in an inductive, unprejudiced manner and thus extract a doctrine of inspiration.

E. F. Harrison was one of the first new evangelicals to postulate the "phenomena" theory. Dealing with the question of errant sources used by the Bible writers, he notes, "if the inductive study of the Bible reveals enough examples of this sort of thing to make the conclusion probable [that errors were thus incorporated], then we shall have to hold the doctrine of inspiration in this light."[88] This follows his earlier conclusion:

> It would seem that the only healthy attitude for conservatives is to welcome criticism and be willing to join in it. No view of Scripture can indefinitely be sustained if it runs counter to the facts. That the Bible claims inspiration is patent. The problem is to define the nature of that inspiration in the light of the phenomena contained therein.[89]

Beegle predicates his whole idea of inspiration on the phenomena of Scripture and the inductive method of learning.[90] He begins by saying that he has no intent to "parade the difficulties of Scripture,"[91] but goes on to list ten such difficulties "that by no means exhaust the difficulties that Biblical phenomena present to Christians."[92] He concludes that in each case but one, factual errors exist in the

---

[87]"God's Infallible Word," p. 4.

[88]Everett F. Harrison, "The Phenomena of Scripture," p. 249.

[89]Ibid., p. 239.

[90]Dewey M. Beegle, *The Inspiration of Scripture*, pp. 41-69.

[91]Ibid., p. 41.

[92]Ibid., p. 60.

autographs. He sees as a "peril" of the inerrancy position its "rigidity and all-or-nothing character."[93] The solution is an inductive method that converges on the phenomena of Scripture, the employment of "our reason objectively with respect to all the evidence, Biblical and otherwise."[94] This use of the phenomena is advocated also by Mounce and Ramm.[95]

Pinnock once had the right view (in 1967 and 1971) of the relation of the phenomena and the Bible's own testimony to itself.[96] Years later, however, he wrote: "Today there is a group of evangelicals trained in biblical studies and open to new ideas who cannot pull the rug over objective biblical phenomena and insist on either broadening the inerrancy category to accommodate them or on eliminating the term inerrancy itself." The reason that most new evangelical scholars were opting for a more elastic inerrancy view was to him simple: "The biblical text [i.e., the phenomena] forces it upon us. Unqualified inerrancy makes good rhetoric, but impossible exegesis."[97] While not holding to the old orthodox, fundamentalist view of inerrancy, he still thought the term was a good "metaphor" that depicts a determination to trust the Bible completely.[98]

The Wenham Conference on Biblical Inspiration (June 1966) quickly became polarized over inerrancy as a result of some wanting to begin with the phenomena rather than the Bible's express claims for itself.[99]

In response to the "phenomena" argument, the phenomena themselves must include the express teaching of Scripture concerning its own inerrancy, in other words, the "proof texts." Beegle, the champion of the phenomena argument, acknowledges this obvious point. "The proper use of the inductive method demands observation of the…claims of Scripture along with the data that fit into the so-called scientific category of human, nontheological history."[100] However, this rather self-evident discovery is virtually ignored in his procedure to construct a doctrine of biblical inspiration. A major ingredient in the process of formulating theology simply vanishes in practice. To frame a doctrine around the difficulties and logical extensions it may have is a fallacious means of theological construction. Only with the stability of an established doctrine can its phenomena be meaningfully studied. In the case of inspiration/inerrancy, good theology takes what the Bible says explicitly about itself. On that basis alone can the phenomena be properly evaluated and studied.

---

[93]Ibid., p. 62.

[94]Ibid., p. 63.

[95]Mounce, "Clues to Understanding Biblical Accuracy," p. 17. Ramm, "The Relationship of Science, Factual Statements and the Doctrine of Biblical Inerrancy," p. 102, and his "Scripture as a Theological Concept," *Review and Expositor* 71 (1974), pp. 150, 153, 154. Millard Erickson, as usual, tries to carve a middle position for the new evangelicalism on the issue (*The New Evangelical Theology*, pp. 75-76).

[96]Clark H. Pinnock, *A Defense of Biblical Infallibility* (Philadelphia: Presbyterian and Reformed, 1967), pp. 18-32, and "The Phenomena of Scripture," in his *Biblical Revelation*, pp. 175-207.

[97]Clark H. Pinnock, "The Ongoing Struggle Over Biblical Inerrancy," *Journal of the American Scientific Affiliation* (June 1979), p. 70.

[98]*The Scripture Principle*, p. 225.

[99]Kenneth S. Kantzer and Edward J. Young, "Letter to the Editor," *Christianity Today* (Sept 16, 1966), p. 18.

[100]Dewey M. Beegel, *Scripture, Tradition and Infallibility*, p. 18.

The phenomena argument assumes that fallen man can sit in judgment on the Bible. This assumption in turn denies the total inability of man, especially noetic sin—the depravity of the human intellect. The unaided mind of man simply does not have the right or capacity to pass judgment on the truth-claims of the Bible. This point is really encroaching on the next chapter, having to do with apologetics, but the answer of Beegle is typical. He contends that the human mind does not create the evidence it handles; all it can do is "function properly" with the data given in it.[101] But the mind's native inability to function properly is what renders pure induction in theology and moral matters unattainable. Unbiased and unprejudiced thought does not exist in any area, much less in the area of God and His self-disclosed demands and truth-claims. Here the human intellect's hostility and depravity are most pronounced, even in professing Bible-believing scholars.

Furthermore, the new evangelical argument here assumes that the "phenomena," "facts," or "evidences" are self-derived, self-interpreting, self-fulfilling, and independent. They just "are"; they have ultimacy in themselves. The biblical view is that all truth comes from the triune God, all reality external to God is created reality, and humans can know truth and reality only as they think their Creator's thoughts after Him, as it were. The first requirement, therefore, if man would know absolute truth on any subject, including inspiration, is a mind that has been regenerated and is in submission to God (cf. 1 Cor 2:14; Rom 8:7). A regenerated mind accepts the witness of Scripture about itself instead of assuming an autonomy of the mind in an open court of inductive investigation. This use of induction virtually rules out inerrancy at the outset. "It appears then that the fundaments of the method with which Beegle approaches the Bible are such that the possibility of the recognition of its infallibility is excluded before the investigation begins."[102]

INERRANCY IS DENIED BY HERMENEUTICAL METHODOLOGY

By the use of redaction criticism principally, which deals with the way a gospel writer edited his material, inerrancy is denied in practice although it may be affirmed as a theological tenet. J. Ramsey Michaels, for example, departed from the faculty of Gordon-Conwell Seminary in 1983 over the inerrancy question, especially as it affects the documents used in the composition of the gospels. In a book on Christ, Michaels stated arguments that imply that certain things appearing to be historical in Scripture actually never happened, or never happened in the manner represented in the gospels. In his view, the gospel writers were attempting to get a message to their audiences and were not overly concerned about original sayings and events and their historical contexts. Concerning the baptism of Jesus recorded in John 1:32-34, Michaels concludes that, contrary to the text, John the Baptist did *not* see the Spirit descending like a dove on Christ. "If John the Baptist actually had received such an unmistakable personal revelation, it would likely be reflected in the Gospel tradition more than it is."[103] "Does the Evangelist

---

[101]*The Inspiration of Scripture*, pp. 63-64.

[102]Richard B. Gaffin, Jr., "Review of *The Inspiration of Scripture*," p. 236.

[103]J. Ramsey Michaels, *Servant and Son: Jesus in Parable and Gospel* (Atlanta: John Knox, 1981), p. 33.

intend to describe an actual vision *at all*, or is this a highly theological account of something the Baptizer at some point *realized* to be true and to which he now bears his testimony" (italics his)?[104] "It is therefore precarious to use this passage, which does not, after all, claim to be a baptismal account, as conclusive evidence that John the Baptist saw the sign of the dove and confessed faith in Jesus at His baptism....Jesus and Jesus alone saw the Spirit in the form of a dove at his baptism, and only Jesus heard the voice of God."[105]

In similar fashion, Robert H. Gundry made use of redaction criticism to the extent that he denied biblical inerrancy in practice. Gundry concluded that Matthew used the Jewish literary genre of "midrash" which freely changes stories and events in order to get across a message. By this method Matthew changed the story of the shepherds at Jesus' birth into the wise men who came from the east. In actuality no wise men visited Jesus, but Matthew redacted or edited his source so as to make the shepherd incident tell the message about the birth of Israel's king in terms of wise men.[106] In 1984 Gundry was pressured to resign from the Evangelical Theological Society because his commentary violated the simple doctrinal statement affirming the inerrancy of the original manuscripts of the Bible.[107]

What is to be said in the face of the problem of hermeneutics vis-a-vis inerrancy? Biblical inerrancy demands a hermeneutic that will not undermine or deny the complete inerrancy and the total trustworthiness of Scripture. A method of interpretation that says the gospel writers reshuffled and modified their sources in such a way as to deny or change the historical setting does in fact undermine the trustworthiness of Scripture. What the Bible presents as historical event cannot be denied its actual historicity without denying biblical inerrancy. Confessional orthodoxy ("I believe in the inerrancy of Scripture") is not sufficient in itself because mere conscientious sincerity in affirming a doctrine is not enough. The doctrine's integrity must be maintained throughout scholarly processes and conclusions. Any exegetical or hermeneutical method or conclusion that destroys a clear doctrine nullifies the affirmation of that doctrine regardless of how conscientiously it may have been made originally.

---

[104]Ibid., p. 34.

[105]Ibid., p. 36. For further on the Michaels incident, see "The Issue of Biblical Authority Brings a Scholar's Resignation," *Christianity Today* (July 15, 1983), p. 35ff, and "Two Seminaries Face Doctrinal Difficulties," *Eternity* (July-Aug 1983), p. 9ff.

[106]Robert H Gundry, *Matthew: A Commentary on His Literary and Theological Art* (Grand Rapids: Eerdmans, 1982), p. 27.

[107]See D. A. Carson, "Gundry on Matthew: A Critical Review," *Trinity Journal* 3 (1982), p. 71; Leslie R. Keylock, "Evangelical Scholars Remove Gundry for His Views on Matthew," *Christianity Today* (Feb 3, 1984), p. 36; "Gundry Resigns ETS in Inerrancy Debate," *Eternity* (May 1984), p. 6; and Charles R. Smith, "On Current Concerns," *Grace Seminary Spire* (Spring 1984), back page. Nearly the whole issue of the *Journal of the Evangelical Society* 27 (1984) is given over to the Gundry problem. Joseph Bayly made a pietistic response to the Gundry episode, charging those who wanted Gundry removed with a deficiency of love, prayer, and peace-making ("Emptied Truth," *Eternity* [April 1984], p. 76).

14

FURTHER ISSUES, EVENTS, AND PUBLICATIONS RELATED TO INERRANCY

THE WENHAM CONFERENCE

On June 20-29, 1966 the Wenham Seminar On the Authority of the Bible convened on the campus of Gordon College, Wenham, MS. Fifty-one scholars met to discuss and debate various issues related to biblical inerrancy.[1] The standard evangelical press reports were either innocuous or optimistic and favorable. *Christianity Today* reported that "much of the wide-ranging discussion was on inerrancy. Some held this to be an essential biblical doctrine, while others preferred to speak of Scripture as infallible." There was "a consensus on the complete truthfulness of the Bible and its authoritativeness as the only infallible rule of faith and practice." The report stated with an overtone of triumph, "No participants affirmed the errancy of the Bible."[2] But the above affirmations about truthfulness and infallible authority for faith and practice were more than a little negated when "certain questions were found to require further study and consultation," among which were "the concept of inerrancy, whether and in what sense it is a biblical doctrine, and its relation to biblical authority."[3] *Eternity* magazine's report also spoke positively of the "warmhearted fellowship" and noted more than once the "substantial agreement" of those present.[4]

The *Christianity Today* coverage drew forthright negative reactions from some evangelical stalwarts. J. Barton Payne noted that the conference "made public what some have known for a considerable time, that certain leaders within conservative theological seminaries are no longer willing to affirm the inerrancy of Scripture." Referring to the apparent anomaly of strongly affirming the truthfulness of Scripture and yet acknowledging the need to explore inerrancy

---

[1]See the description of the conference in "Ten Days At Wenham: Seminar on Scripture," *Christianity Today* (July 22,1966), p. 41, and "Scholars Discuss Authority of Scripture," *Eternity* (Sept 1966), p. 8.

[2]"Ten Days At Wenham," p. 41.

[3]Ibid.

[4]"Scholars Discuss Authority of Scripture," p. 8.

to see if it is a biblical doctrine, Payne asks, "Must evangelicalism now therefore face the unhappy task of having to cross examine the profession of some of its leaders?"[5] Kenneth Kantzer and Edward J. Young sent a joint letter saying *Christianity Today's* coverage of Wenham was "a somewhat incomplete picture. It would be wrong to deny or to obscure the fact that serious differences of opinion about the Bible were present. Two mutually exclusive approaches to the Bible seemed to undergird much of the discussion." They go further and ask: "Are there elements in the Bible which are to be set apart from the teaching of the Bible? We would answer this question with an emphatic negative....To maintain otherwise, we believe, is to fall into serious doctrinal error; and yet in the discussions at Wenham this erroneous view was vigorously defended."[6]

Edward John Carnell, referring to the polarization between the phenomena and direct biblical assertion, recalled that "Warfield clearly perceived that a Christian has no more right to construct a doctrine of biblical authority out of deference to the (presumed) inductive difficulties in the Bible," than he has to formulate a doctrine of salvation from deference to the mysteries of the incarnation. "This means that whether we happen to like it or not," he says, "we are closed up to the teaching of the Bible for our information about *all* doctrines in the Christian faith, and this includes the doctrine of the Bible's view of itself."[7]

J. I. Packer described the historical context of Wenham in more forthright terms.

> The conference was called in hope of healing a breach that had developed between some faculty members and trustees of Fuller Seminary and the rest of North America's evangelical academic world....Those who organized and funded Wenham wanted it to be a peace conference,...but all were not agreed, and peace was impossible.[8]

George Marsden has a more extended but similar description of the background of the Wenham Seminar.[9]

As noted earlier, it was an ill wind that blew through the March 1956 article in *Christian Life* which called for a reopening of the subject of biblical inspiration. In a relatively few years, certain new evangelicals had begun to waver over and to concede the doctrine of inerrancy in the classroom and hallway, but ten years after the article, the division broke out into the open at Wenham. The theological fissure has only widened and the polarities hardened, and today the inerrancy issue is both lost and dead in new evangelicalism.

---

[5]"Letter to the editor," *Christianity Today* (Sept 2, 1966), p. 19.

[6]"Letter to the editor," *Christianity Today* (Sept 16, 1966), p. 18.

[7]"Letter to the editor," *Christianity Today* (Oct 14, 1966), p. 23.

[8]"Thirty Years' War: The Doctrine of Holy Scripture," in *Practical Ministry and the Ministry of the Church: Essays in Honor of Edmund P. Clowney*, Harvie M. Conn, ed. (Phillipsburg, NJ: Presbyterian and Reformed, 1990), pp. 30-31.

[9]*Reforming Fundamentalism* (Grand Rapids: Eerdmans, 1987), p. 228. He characterized the conference as a match between the Fuller Seminary ideas, especially those of Daniel P. Fuller, and those of "the party that coalesced around Trinity Evangelical Divinity School," where for ten days the scholars "had it out." Though peace was the goal, "the issues had become too hot to keep at the dispassionate level."

THE "BATTLE FOR THE BIBLE" CONTROVERSY

The ten years after Wenham were filled with unrest and further division over biblical inerrancy in new evangelicalism. By 1976 inerrancy was a hot issue. Harold Lindsell's *Battle For the Bible*[10] came as the greatest bombshell dropped on the new evangelical community in many years, and it came from within its own ranks. In this book Lindsell unmasked the hypocrisy of many new evangelicals who publicly affirmed inerrancy but inwardly did not. He set forth the orthodox doctrine of verbal inerrancy and showed that it is the historic faith of the Christian church. He also exposed the duplicity on this doctrine within the Lutheran Church—Missouri Synod, the Southern Baptist Convention, Fuller Theological Seminary, and other groups. Unfortunately Lindsell did not consider inerrancy a test of fellowship, although he considered it a test of orthodoxy.

Reaction to the book ran along predictable lines. Fundamentalists on one hand sympathized with Lindsell's position on inerrancy and efforts to expose the departure of individuals and institutions. Lindsell's warnings echoed the ones Fundamentalists had stated for over twenty years. On the other hand, Fundamentalists were saddened to see Lindsell affirm the old anti-separatist stand that had helped bring the new evangelical movement to its current impasse. In other words, while Lindsell had correctly diagnosed the malady of the new evangelicalism, he was still prescribing the same medicine that was killing the patient in the first place.

Evangelicals—new, young, social, feminist, right, left, middle-of-the-road—gave mixed reactions. Some praised the book as a necessary corrective to a serious drift in doctrine. Others tried to stay neutral and "irenic." Still others took a vehement stand against the book for a number of reasons, mostly the factors analyzed in the previous chapter. The overwhelming attitude was that the book was too conservative, too much like fundamentalism, too narrow, unkind, and destructive of evangelical unity at a time when it was needed the most. There was also a great deal of personal attack against the author, mainly from Fuller Seminary where Lindsell served for seventeen years as a faculty member. Lindsell had severely criticized Fuller for its departure in doctrine and ethics.[11]

---

[10]Grand Rapids: Zondervan, 1976.

[11]Unfavorable responses to Lindsell can be found in the following selected sources: *Theology, News and Notes* (Published by Fuller Seminary, special issue, 1976); Bill Blackburn, "Review of *The Battle For the Bible*," *The Review and Expositor* 74 (1977), pp. 105-107; Richard J. Coleman, "Another View: The Battle For the Bible," *Journal of the American Scientific Affiliation* (June 1979), pp. 74-79; Carl F. H. Henry, "The War of the Word," *The New Review of Books and Religion* (Sept 1976), p. 7; Robert Mounce, "Does the Bible Contain Errors?" *Eternity* (Aug 1976), pp. 49, 51; Clark Pinnock, "Acrimonious Debate On Inerrancy," *Eternity* (June 1976), p. 40; Bernard Ramm, "Misplaced Battle Lines," *The Reformed Journal* (July-Aug 1976), pp. 37-38; Donald Shriver, "Review of *The Battle For the Bible*," *Interpretation* 32 (1978), pp. 215, 218; and Fred Thompson, Jr., "The Wrong War," *United Evangelical Action* (Winter 1976), pp. 8-10.

Some favorable responses were: Hudson T. Armerding, "Review of *The Battle For the Bible*," *United Evangelical Action* (Summer 1976), pp. 22-23; Marshal Neal, "The Pastor's Bookshelf," *Biblical Viewpoint* (Nov 1976); Jack Murray, "The Battle For the Bible," *Voice* (July-Aug 1977), pp. 7-9; Francis R. Steele, "Inerrancy is Indispensable," *Christianity Today* (April 9, 1976), p. 35; Charles J. Woodbridge, "Reaping the Whirlwind," *Christian Beacon* (April 21 and 28; May 5 and 12, 1977); and Rolland D. McCune, "Review of *The Battle For the Bible*," *Central Bible Quarterly* (Summer 1976), pp. 34-36.

In 1979 Lindsell published a sequel, *The Bible in the Balance*,[12] that interacted with the negative criticism of his first book. He proved that his assertions in *The Battle For the Bible* were well-founded and correct and added further evidence to his views.

The *Battle For the Bible* controversy left the new evangelicalism in division and malaise. It sapped the doctrinal strength of the movement in a way from which it never recovered. Thirty-five years after its inception, the new coalition had reached its apogee and began a slide toward irrelevancy. Carpenter observed that "by the late 1960s the new evangelicalism began to break apart....By the 1970s and early 1980s, while evangelicals of many kinds flourished, the aging champions of the new evangelicalism spoke sadly of their failed dreams."[13] Lindsell himself felt the movement peaked in the 1970s, succumbing to pluralism and the total elasticizing of the word "evangelical."[14] The latest dress of new evangelicalism, the postconservative, postmodern, or younger evangelicals, considers the original movement to have been slipping down the slope toward fundamentalism since *The Battle For the Bible*.[15] To them, the old guard has not kept pace with the changing world and the need to meet it with a changed, or continually changing, theology.

---

[12]Grand Rapids: Zondervan, 1979.

[13]*Evangelical Dictionary of Theology*, s.v. "New Evangelicalism," by J. A. Carpenter.

[14]Harold Lindsell, "Evangelicalism's Golden Age," *Moody Monthly* (Dec 1985), p. 113.

[15]Roger E. Olsen, "Postconservative Evangelicals Greet the Modern Age," *The Christian Century* (May 3, 1995), p. 480.

15

THE AFTERMATH OF "THE BATTLE FOR THE BIBLE"

Three items of historical and theological interest followed in the aftermath of *The Battle For the Bible* and continued the debate set off by the book: the controversy over the historicity of inerrancy, the formation of the International Council on Biblical Inerrancy, and the rise of postmodern evangelicalism.

HISTORICAL THEOLOGY

The debate in the area of historical theology began with the charge that verbal inerrancy is a recent development in the history of doctrine. One asserted early on in the inerrancy debate that "those of us who staunchly believe in the verbal, plenary inspiration of the Scriptures will find it impossible to prove that such a view of inspiration received any dominance before John Calvin in the sixteenth century." Claiming that "our doctrinal position is not so obviously and clearly reflected in the Bible as we think," he went on to conclude that "our convictions about such things have not come to us directly from the Scriptures; rather they have been acquired directly from church history."[1] Many claim that the inerrancy doctrine held by orthodox believers goes no further back than the nineteenth century to the "Princeton Theology" of A. A. Hodge and B. B. Warfield. Inerrantists insist that verbal inerrancy is the doctrine of Christ and the apostles and prophets, and has been the common faith of the church since. The only exceptions have been the innovations and inroads at times of unbelief.

The recency idea's primary spokesman was Jack Rogers.[2] His understanding of historical theology drew a voluminous response from various evangelical scholars who understood the evidence completely differently. They pointed out the fallacies and prejudicial use of evidence in the Rogers/McKim proposal and unearthed a wealth of material that showed inerrancy to be the historic church doctrine.[3]

---

[1] Paul R. Edwards, "Fundamentalist Infallibility," *Eternity* (Sept 1957), p. 7.

[2] "The Church Doctrine of Biblical Authority," in *Biblical Authority*, ed., Jack Rogers (Waco, TX: Word, 1977), pp. 15-46, and Jack B. Rogers and Donald K. McKim, *The Authority and Interpretation of the Bible: An Historical Approach* (New York: Harper & Row, 1979), a massive appropriation of evidence that was interpreted against the idea that the Reformers and others believed in inerrancy.

[3] John H. Gerstner, "The Church's Doctrine of Biblical Inspiration," in *The Foundation of Biblical Authority*, James M. Boice, ed. (Grand Rapids: Zondervan, 1978), pp. 23-58. L. Russ Bush and Tom

THE INTERNATIONAL COUNCIL ON BIBLICAL INERRANCY

A second direct response to the rising non-inerrantist element in new evangelicalism and its vocal resistance to the position advocated in *The Battle For the Bible* was The International Council on Biblical Inerrancy. A group of thirty evangelical scholars met in Chicago in September 1977 to discuss the doctrine of biblical inerrancy. Spearheaded by James Montgomery Boice, pastor of Tenth Presbyterian Church, Philadelphia, the first and only chairman of the resultant group, the Council constituted a non-separatist, non-militant ("irenic") group of evangelical scholars fully committed to verbal inerrancy and its implications. A proposed organizational structure and a ten-year strategy of writing, speaking, and holding conferences on behalf of inerrancy received support. The Council held Summit I (Chicago 1978) on the subject of biblical inerrancy, Summit II (Chicago 1982) dealt with biblical hermeneutics, and Summit III (Chicago 1986) dealt with biblical application. Each summit produced a "Chicago Statement" on its particular theme.

The International Council also published scholarly volumes in keeping with its mission and overall theme: *The Foundations of Biblical Authority* (1978),[4] *Can We Trust the Bible?* (1979),[5] *Does Inerrancy Matter? (1979),*[6] *Explaining Inerrancy: A Commentary* (1980),[7] *Inerrancy* (1980),[8] *Freedom and Authority* (1981),[9] *Biblical Errancy: An Analysis of its Philosophical Roots* (1981),[10] *Biblical Meditation: A Transforming Discipline* (1982),[11] *Encyclopedia of Bible Difficulties* (1982),[12] *Hermeneutics, Inerrancy, and the Bible* (1984),[13] *Challenges to Inerrancy* (1984),[14] *Inerrancy and the Church* (1984),[15] and *Applying the Scriptures* (1987).[16]

J. Nettles, *Baptists and the Bible* (Chicago: Moody, 1980), show that the overwhelming majority of Bible-believing Baptists have held to inerrancy, exceptions coming basically in the 19th century and the rise of liberalism. Randall H. Balmer, "The Princetonians and Scripture: A Reconsideration," *Westminster Theological Journal* 44 (1982), pp. 352-65 (note his conclusion on pp. 364-65). John D. Woodbridge, *Biblical Authority* is insightful and penetrating research into the history of inerrancy, showing that it was the faith of true believers from the beginning; it also shows the Rogers/McKim book to be prejudiced, poorly researched and unreliable in many of its conclusions. There are numerous essays in historical theology on this subject by Philip Edgcumbe Hughes, Geoffrey W. Bromiley, W. Robert Godfrey, John D. Woodbridge, and Randall H. Balmer in *Scripture and Truth*, D. A. Carson and John D. Woodbridge, eds. (Grand Rapids: Zondervan, 1983). See also Mark Noll, *The Princeton Theology: 1812-1921* (Grand Rapids: Baker, 1983). *Inerrancy and the Church*, John D. Hannah, ed. (Chicago: Moody, 1984) contains essays in historical theology.

[4]James M. Boice, ed. (Grand Rapids: Zondervan, 1978).

[5]Earl D. Radmacher, ed. (Wheaton: Tyndale House, 1979).

[6]James M. Boice (Wheaton: Tyndale, 1981).

[7]R. C. Sproul (Oakland, CA: International Council on Biblical Inerrancy, 1980).

[8]Norman L. Geisler, ed. (Grand Rapids: Zondervan, 1979).

[9]J. I. Packer (Oakland, CA: International Council on Biblical Inerrancy, 1981).

[10]Norman L. Geisler, ed. (Grand Rapids: Zondervan, 1981).

[11]Ronald A. Jensen (Oakland, CA: International Council on Biblical Inerrancy, 1982).

[12]Gleason L. Archer (Grand Rapids: Zondervan, 1982).

[13]Earl D. Radmacher and Robert D. Preus, eds. (Grand Rapids: Zondervan, 1984).

[14]Gordon Lewis and Bruce Demarest, eds. (Chicago: Moody, 1984).

[15]John D. Hannah, ed. (Chicago: Moody, 1984).

[16]Kenneth S. Kantzer, ed. (Grand Rapids: Zondervan, 1987).

The Council dissolved in 1987, having achieved its ten-year objectives.[17] Since that time the inerrancy controversy within the new evangelicalism has dissipated considerably.

POST-MODERN EVANGELICALS

A third element in the fallout of *The Battle For the Bible* was the rise and development of a left-leaning coterie of would-be evangelicals known as post-conservative, postmodern, post-classical, or younger evangelicals. These *avant garde* thinkers quit talking about inerrancy and began exploring how post-modern liberalism could help them craft a theology that would present to postmodern culture a believable message. In true Hegelian fashion, this was a middle road—a synthesis—between the old evangelical position of Carl Henry and the postmodern liberalism of Hans Frei and the "Yale theology." It was a half-way house between a "literal" hermeneutic of the Bible based on the authority of inerrant propositional revelation and the "narrative" hermeneutic of Scripture backed by the consensus authority of the visible church. It was a repudiation of objective "foundationalism" (the absolute authority of an inerrant Bible) in favor of an irenic, pacifistic, subjective "living" of the gospel amid a non-absolutist culture.[18] This new approach to authority was woven together from various strands of postmodern theology and philosophy.[19]

As these scholars continue to search for a non-absolutist authority with which to convey the evangelical message to a rootless, non-absolutist age, the idea of an inerrant, authoritative Bible has long since been abandoned by them. The postmodern evangelicals consider such a view of Scripture an encrusted barnacle of a fossilized evangelical/fundamentalist era. The authority of choice now is the pluralistic opinion of the believing community, the responsible understanding of biblical Christianity forged by an acceptable cadre of interpreters. How such a flat, relativistic standard can even bear the weight of the word "authority" is a mystery, much less the kind of authority that has eternal consequences if it is not heeded. In truth it is no authority at all beyond that of the simple God-talk of some religiously sincere people. Such is the current legacy of the innocuous-sounding "re-opening of the subject of biblical inspiration" in 1956.

Many new evangelicals have capitulated to neo-orthodoxy and worse in the areas of bibliology in general and inerrancy in particular. Warnings were raised

---

[17]Kenneth S. Kantzer, "For Once We Knew When to Quit," *Christianity Today* (Nov 6, 1987), p. 11. In addition to the publications of the Council, one may consult "A Campaign For Inerrancy," *Christianity Today* (Nov 4, 1977), pp. 51-52; "Council Maps 10-Year Push for 'Historic, Verbal' Inerrancy," *Eternity* (Nov 1977), pp. 10-11, 90; Bob Jones, "Uncertain Trumpets," *Faith For the Family* (Feb 1978), p. 5; "Proinerrancy Forces Draft Their Platform," *Christianity Today* (Nov 17, 1978), pp. 36-37; "Inerrantists On the March," *The Christian Century* (Nov 22, 1978), p. 1126; G. Archer Weniger, "Inconsistency Revealed At Recent Congress," *Faith For the Family* (July-Aug 1982); J. I. Packer, "Thirty Years' War: The Doctrine of Holy Scripture," pp. 31-32; John A. Witmer, "The International Council on Biblical Inerrancy," *The Christian Librarian* 34 (1991), pp. 76-79.

[18]See the Addendum, a review article of Robert E. Webber, *The Younger Evangelicals: Facing the Challenges of the New World* (Grand Rapids: Baker, 2002).

[19]This post-classical evangelical hermeneutic actually takes the discussion into the field of philosophy and apologetics, the subject of the next chapter.

here and there by fellow new evangelicals but to no avail. (Fundamentalists issued warnings from the very beginning but of course were ignored because fundamentalism allegedly was obscurantist and had "bad manners.") New evangelicalism has only itself to blame for the departure of some of its children on the doctrine of Scripture. The warnings and lamentations being raised within the new evangelical community over the direction the movement has taken appear to fundamentalists to be so much hand wringing and a classic example of the old equine jibe of trying to lock the barn door after the horse has bolted.

Internal squabbles have arisen within the new evangelicalism over the doctrine of eternal punishment and related themes (such as the lostness of the heathen). There is an acceptance and promotion of homosexuality among certain new evangelical persons and groups. One of the greatest controversies to divide the new evangelical constituency since the inerrancy debate is the issue of feminism in its various forms (man-woman egalitarianism, ordination of women, etc.). Whether there is a linear descent of these problems from the denials of verbal inerrancy may be difficult to know or prove. But it seems more than coincidental that these and other doctrinal and practical divisions arose principally from those who had first shifted away from the fundamentalist, orthodox position of verbal inspiration, inerrancy, and authority. The late Harold Lindsell was patently correct when he said, "Once biblical authority is surrendered it leads to the most undesirable consequences. It will end in apostasy at last. It is my opinion that it is next to impossible to stop the process of theological deterioration once inerrancy is abandoned."[20]

---

[20]*The Battle For the Bible*, p. 142.

PART 6: APOLOGETICS

Apologetics generally has to do with the defense of the truth-claims of Christianity. The word apologetics comes from the Greek *apologia*, a term from criminal law and the courts meaning to make a speech of defense, a verbal defense, a reply to a formal charge—an answer or a vindication. The word *apologia* is used as a verb, noun, or adjective twenty times in the New Testament.[1]

One of the definitive complaints of the new evangelicals that precipitated their break with fundamentalism in the 1940s, accused fundamentalism of intellectual deficiency and credibility. The dissatisfaction behind the accusation eventually led to the formation of the Fuller Theological Seminary in 1947, one purpose of which was to create an academic center and think tank for evangelical apologetics and philosophy of religion. The new evangelicals were annoyed by fundamentalism's apparent penchant for proof-texting in evangelism and tendency to emphasize personal experiences. The truth-claims of Christianity would never achieve intellectual respectability and penetrate the culture for Christ while these means predominated.

This section will note some of the various apologetic methodologies, describing and analyzing the system championed among early new evangelicals and put forth as the "official" position of the movement.

At the center of any defense and propagation of the truth-claims of Christianity stands the matter of ultimate and absolute authority, an authority for which no greater authorization can be given. This in turn will control the apologetic method from starting point to conclusion and will have long-range ramifications for the future of the movement it characterizes. It will be seen that the leaders of the new evangelicalism in fifty years have abandoned the sense of an absolute and infallible religious authority, and today the evangelical movement is groping to find some kind of a basis or an authority to meet a rootless, non-absolutist, relativist culture on the culture's own terms with the claims of the living and true God. On the surface this appears to be an utterly impossible task.

---

[1]Robert L. Reymond, *The Justification of Knowledge* (Phillipsburg, NJ: Presbyterian and Reformed, 1979), p. 1; BDAG, s.v. "*apologia*," p. 117; U. Falkenroth, "Punishment," *The New International Dictionary of New Testament Theology*, Colin Brown, ed., 3 vols. (Grand Rapids: Zondervan, 1978), 3:97.

16

THE DEVELOPMENT OF NEW
EVANGELICAL APOLOGETICS

Different classifications of apologetics and ascertaining divine authority punctuate apologetic literature. In addition, some disagreement continues among evangelicals and fundamentalists over the exact role of Christian apologetics. Some argue that apologetics is either solely or primarily defensive in character, i.e., how to defend the faith from its detractors. Edward John Carnell said that Christian apologetics "is that branch of Christian learning devised to assist a person in the defense of his faith....Apologetics is simply Christianity defensively stated."[2] Others contend that apologetics is propagational or evangelistic in motif as well as defensive. However, for purposes of this chapter, this distinction will not prove significant.

In my understanding, Christian apologetics consists of both a defense and a propagation of the Christian faith. It is a methodology dealing with a message— how to defend and present the biblical message or the truth-claims of biblical Christianity. It can be argued that all apologetic systems would either fit one of three apologetic approaches or a combination of them.[3] The first method, called total rationalism or non-presuppositionalism, assumes an epistemology (a method of knowing) by which one can proceed from the ground up in arriving at and defending a comprehensive philosophy without having any prior commitment to a world view. Stuart Hackett is an example of the total rationalism motif.[4] His approach is based on two fundamental ingredients: a mind that is latent with "categories" or a structure of thought by which one comes to the world of

---

[2]Edward John Carnell, "How Every Christian Can Defend His Faith," *Moody Monthly* (Jan 1950), p. 312.

[3]Gordon R. Lewis presented six apologetic systems (*Testing Christianity's Truth Claims* [Chicago: Moody, 1976]). More recently James Emery White used five evangelical apologists as a paradigm of the field (*What is Truth? A Comparative Study of the Positions of Cornelius Van Til, Francis Schaeffer, Carl F. H. Henry, Donald Bloesch, Millard Erickson* [Nashville: Broadman, 1994]). Norman Geisler listed five types of apologetic systems ("Apologetics, Types of," *Baker Encyclopedia of Christian Apologetics* [Grand Rapids: Baker, 1999], pp. 41-44. Steven B. Cowan edited *Five Views on Apologetics* (Grand Rapids: Zondervan, 2000), also suggesting that there are basically five different apologetic methodologies.

[4]Stuart C. Hackett, *The Resurrection of Theism* (Chicago: Moody, 1957). See also his *The Reconstruction of the Christian Revelation Claim* (Grand Rapids: Baker, 1984).

experience (categories such as quantity, quality, relation, etc.), and data upon which this mental grid can terminate. Thus by using the Kantian rational categories and the pure reasoning powers of the unaided human intellect, Hackett attempts to build a bridge from man to God resting on a purely natural theology apart from the Bible or any presupposition of special divine revelation. As such this methodology is akin to Roman Catholic (Thomistic) philosophy and apologetics, and its attempt to prove the existence of God by using the "first principles" or the various "ways" of reasoning (such as from effect to cause to First Cause, etc.). Other evangelicals, without the overt dependence on Kant and Thomas Aquinas, also developed a non-presuppositional approach to apologetics, such as Norman Geisler,[5] R. C. Sproul,[6] and John Warwick Montgomery.[7]

A second methodology is termed semi-rationalism or semi-biblicism. This view postulates biblical Christianity and theism as a world view but subjects it to analytical testing and verification by one means or another. The foundational presupposition is drawn from the Bible, but it is immediately subjected to rational investigation and analysis to determine its veracity. The contention is that the biblical world view passes all tests with highest honors. This system is often called presuppositionalism, but it is not a consistently presuppositional method. It is a blend of a purely rational approach and a purely biblical approach; hence the terms semi-rationalism or semi-biblicism. It forms a modified Aquinas/Butler methodology that has achieved continued popularity in fundamentalism[8] and was carried over into the new evangelicalism. It may legitimately be called, "the new evangelical view." The leading proponents of this approach are Carnell,[9] Bernard Ramm,[10] Carl Henry,[11]

---

[5]Norman Geisler, *Christian Apologetics* (Grand Rapids: Baker, 1976) and *Philosophy of the Christian Religion* (Grand Rapids: Zondervan, 1976). See also Norman Geisler and Ronald Brooks, *Come, Let Us Reason* (Grand Rapids: Baker, 1990).

[6]R. C. Sproul, *Reason to Believe* (Grand Rapids: Zondervan, 1978), and R. C. Sproul, et al., *Classical Apologetics* (Grand Rapids: Zondervan, 1984). This non-presuppositional approach was brought into Protestantism from Roman Catholicism by the Anglican bishop, Joseph Butler, in the eighteenth century, principally in *The Analogy of Religion* (1736), and William Paley's *Natural Theology* (1802). Thomas Reid adapted some of the Thomistic "first principles" of Paley and Butler, namely, intelligent design and cause-effect, and forged the natural theology philosophy of Common Sense Realism. This in turn was adapted by many Reformed apologists including Charles Hodge and B. B. Warfield of old Princeton Seminary. See George Marsden, "The Collapse of American Evangelical Academia," in *Reckoning With the Past*, D. G. Hart, ed. (Grand Rapids: Baker, 1995), pp. 221-66.

[7]John Warwick Montgomery, *History and Christianity* (Downers Grove, IL: InterVarsity, 1975) and *Faith Founded on Fact* (Nashville: Thomas Nelson, 1978).

[8]As evidenced, for example, by the gospel song, "The Bible stands *every test we give it*, for its author is divine; By grace alone I expect to live it, and *to prove it* and make it mine" (italics added).

[9]Edward John Carnell, *An Introduction to Christian Apologetics* (Grand Rapids: Eerdmans, 1948) and *A Philosophy of the Christian Religion* (Grand Rapids: Eerdmans, 1952), among others that will be referred to and analyzed later.

[10]Bernard Ramm, *Problems in Christian Apologetics* (Portland, OR: Western Baptist Theological Seminary, 1949), *Protestant Christian Evidences* (Chicago: Moody, 1953), *Types of Apologetic Systems* (Wheaton, IL, Van Kampen, 1953), and *Varieties of Christian Apologetics* (Grand Rapids: Baker, 1965).

[11]Carl F. H. Henry, *Remaking the Modern Mind* (Grand Rapids: Eerdmans, 1948), *The Drift of Western Thought* (Grand Rapids: Eerdmans, 1951), and *God, Revelation and Authority*, 6 vols. (Waco, TX: Word, 1976-1983).

Clark Pinnock,[12] and Gordon Lewis.[13] The main precursor of the new evangelical apologetic methodology is Gordon Clark.[14]

The third method of apologetics is that espoused by Cornelius Van Til and is called total biblicism or total presuppositionalism.[15] In this methodology the revelation-claims of the Bible are not merely hypothetically assumed and later rationally validated, much less arrived at by independent reasoning. Instead, divine authority is accepted unconditionally and wholeheartedly by supernaturally-endowed faith. This system rejects all attempts to verify the Christian truth-claims independently of scripture because sinful, rational man has no legitimate canons by which to test God and His revelation. The Christian message is to be accepted on the basis of the authority of the living God, and divine authority ceases to be such when poured through the funnel of creaturely validation or arrived at through purely human cognitive processes. The controlling presupposition of the total biblicist is that the one living and true God, eternally existing in self-contained tri-unity, has revealed Himself inerrantly in the self-attesting Scriptures of the Protestant canon. This foundational axiom is drawn from the canon itself, that is, it is the underlying claim and overt testimony of Scripture to itself and to God the author of the Bible, who is also the source, maker, sustainer, and controller of all things in the universe. Furthermore, without this presupposition, nothing anywhere has an explanation;[16] all is bereft of meaning because the only alternative is blind, irrational chance as the ground of all being. Biblical presuppositionalism recognized that all thinking about ultimate reality and a comprehensive world view is in the last analysis circular. Reasoning is impossible without it. The concept of an open universe where genuine novelty, pure contingency, and free-from-God "facts" exist is apostate thinking.

---

[12]Clark H. Pinnock, *Set Forth Your Case* (Nutley, NJ: Craig, 1968); *Biblical Revelation* (Chicago: Moody, 1971), chapter 1, "The Pattern of Divine Revelation," especially pp. 37-52; and *Reason Enough* (Downers Grove, IL: InterVarsity, 1980).

[13]Gordon R. Lewis, *Testing Christianity's Truth Claims*.

[14]Gordon H. Clark, *A Christian View of Men and Things* (Grand Rapids: Eerdmans, 1952); "The Wheaton Lectures," in *The Philosophy of Gordon H. Clark*, Ronald H. Nash, ed. (Philadelphia: Presbyterian and Reformed, 1968); *Religion, Reason, and Revelation* (Philadelphia: Presbyterian and Reformed, 1961), among many others. Clark taught philosophy at Wheaton College when some of the early thinkers of the new evangelicalism were there as students. Clark's philosophy and apologetics underwent a transformation later in his life. Apparently in the 1960s he shifted away from his early self-styled presuppositional position which was actually semi-rational; but his early views seem to have set the pace for the new evangelical apologetics.

[15]Among the scores of publications of Cornelius Van Til, probably the most definitive is *The Defense of the Faith* (Philadelphia: Presbyterian and Reformed, 1955). This work was revised and abridged by the publisher in a second (1963) and third (1979) edition. Others of the Van Tillian methodology are Greg Bahnsen (*Always Ready—Directions For Defending the Faith*, Robert R. Booth, ed. [Texarkana, AR: Covenant Media, 1996]); Bahnsen's, *Van Til's Apologetic* (Phillipsburg, NJ: Presbyterian and Reformed, 1998); Jim S. Halsey, *For Such a Time As This: An Introduction to the Reformed Apologetic of Cornelius Van Til* (Phillipsburg, NJ: Presbyterian and Reformed, 1976); John C. Whitcomb, "Contemporary Apologetics and the Christian Faith," *Bibliotheca Sacra* 134 (Apr-Jun 1977 through Jan-Mar 1978); and Richard L. Pratt, Jr., *Every Thought Captive: A Study Manual for the Defense of Christian Faith* (Phillipsburg, NJ: Presbyterian and Reformed, 1979).

[16]This is known in apologetics as the transcendental method, or reasoning from the impossibility of the contrary.

Identifying apologetic methodologies raises the question of ultimate authority in Christian apologetics. Methodology and authority are closely intertwined; the ultimate authority determines and controls an apologetic methodology. It is not an oversimplification of things to say that *all* methodologies can be classified in one of two groups, depending on the ultimate or most primitive starting authority. The first includes those who accept the Scriptures as the constant sole authority; the other includes all those who substitute something other than the Bible as ultimate authority. The latter may appeal logic, philosophy, science, or the decrees of the church, each a form of *human reasoning*. In simplest language, ultimate authority in theology and apologetics is either God or man; either the self-contained triune God and His self-attesting witness to a self-identifying Christ in the Scriptures is the final court of appeal, or else man pronounces the final verdict, if only to *verify* the truth-claims of Christianity.

The new evangelical apologetic method began as a mediating position between a totally non-presuppositionalism and consistent presuppositionalism. Though the hybrid method adopted the name of presuppositionalism, its methodology proved inconsistent, making important concessions to rationalistic thinking with a corresponding discount and/or denial of the noetic effects of sin, i.e., the effects of depravity on the human mind.

PURPOSE

The new evangelical apologetic methodology had a twofold purpose: to remove intellectual doubts about the claims of Christianity and in so doing to make way for a free-will choice between faith and unbelief or between Christianity and other religious options. As Carnell put it:

> The sole purpose of any skilled refutation...is to prepare the ground so that the seed of the gospel can find good soil. This means that your aim should be twofold: first prayerfully seek to answer intellectual difficulties on the part of the unbeliever; then, when these have been met and the way is open, proceed swiftly with the sowing of the gospel seed. Preach Christ![17]

Carnell understood faith to be a resting of the mind in the sufficiency of the evidences; that unless the debris of doubt, uncertainty, and intellectual objections was removed, saving faith could not operate. In a real sense, the credibility of the Christian message must be demonstrated objectively *before* the simple gospel can be preached. For Carnell the Christian world view must be open to rational investigation before any specific claims from special revelation can be made.[18]

Pinnock noted that the aim of apologetics is to strive at "laying the evidence for the Christian gospel before men in an intelligent fashion, so that they can make a meaningful commitment under the convicting power of the Holy Spirit."[19] "Meaningful commitment" is possible because the gospel pleases both the head and the heart. In Pinnock's view, the good news cannot be presented on the spur of the

---

[17]Edward Carnell, "How Every Christian Can Defend His Faith," p. 312.

[18]Gary Dorrien, *The Remaking of Evangelical Theology* (Louisville: Westminster John Knox, 1998), pp. 64-65.

[19]*Set Forth Your Case*, p. 3.

moment by "spouting proof texts and an appeal to religious excitement in the soul. There is need for more serious regard for the philosophical and factual content of the gospel, so that a bolder and more imaginative witness can be undertaken in this critical hour."[20] He explained further that "the intent of Christian apologetics and evidence is not to coerce people to accept the Christian faith, but to make it possible for them to do so intelligently."[21] Like Carnell, Pinnock defined faith as a resting of the heart in the sufficiency of the evidences; it is trusting what you believe to be true based on credible testimony. In this case it is the testimony of evidence that forms the sure basis of faith. Otherwise, he feels, one could believe anything on sheer credulity and gullibility, and this would be intellectual suicide.[22]

Gordon Clark asserted boldly that every Christian is under obligation to defend the claims of Christianity in the face of consistent rejection.[23] Bernard Ramm understood that apologetics and evidences are not the gospel, "but if a man has a prejudice against the gospel it is the function of apologetics and evidences to remove that prejudice. The value of apologetics and evidences for evangelistic purposes…is too frequently underrated usually on the grounds that people are won by preaching of the Word alone." For him, it is quite evident that "no man will give the necessary credence to the Word if he has certain mistaken notions and biased opinions about the facts and nature of the Christian religion. Apologetics and Christian evidences cut down these objections to enable the gospel once again to directly confront the consciousness of a man."[24] Buswell, of the non-presuppositionalism camp and somewhat a precursor of the new evangelical apologetics, assigned evangelistic value to rational arguments.

> What is the value of the arguments? They have indeed great value. According to the Bible, and according to Christian experience, we know that the Holy Spirit is pleased to use the arguments in the process of producing conviction and conversion. The arguments themselves never regenerated anyone but they have been instrumental in the process of evangelism, and this is all that is rightfully claimed for them.[25]

The search for Noah's ark provided ripe opportunity for credible apologetic evidences. Though search teams encountered inclement weather, disagreeable Turkish authorities, and other perennial setbacks, the teams forged ahead year after year optimistically. As one summed it up: "We couldn't stand the strain of Ararat if the winds of unbelief in the authority of God's Holy Word didn't impel us to do all that is possible to confirm its entire trustworthiness."[26] Another observed, "Ark hunters say they search to find conclusive proof that the story of Noah, often disputed

---

[20]Ibid., p. 2.

[21]Ibid., p. 44. See also pp. 4, 5, 8, and 45 for the purpose of apologetics.

[22]Ibid., pp. 48, 49.

[23]Gordon H. Clark, "How May I Know the Bible is Inspired?" in *Can I Trust My Bible?* (Chicago: Moody, 1963), p. 22. He went further: "Anyone who is unwilling to argue, dispute, and reason is disloyal to his Christian duty" (p. 29).

[24]*Protestant Christian Evidences*, pp. 15-16.

[25]J. Oliver Buswell, Jr., *A Systematic Theology of the Christian Religion*, 2 vols. (Grand Rapids: Zondervan, 1962), 1:73.

[26]John Warwick Montgomery, "Arkeology 1971," *Christianity Today* (Jan 7, 1972), p. 51.

by non-inerrantists and non Christians, is true. Cornuke, an ark hunter, believed the discovery of Noah's ark would help convince some people of the authenticity of the whole Bible, including the life, death, and resurrection of Jesus Christ."[27] Just how the discovery of the ark would verify the truth-claims and trustworthiness of the whole Bible and the person and work of Christ is anything but clear, but such is the implication of this methodology's purpose.

FOUNDATION

The new evangelical apologetic methodology is erroneously called presuppositionalism. While the claims of Scripture are presupposed to be reliable truth-content for initial saving faith, the presupposition of the Bible as true still needs objective validation. Though the basic assumptions about God and revelation are incapable of formal proof, they can be indirectly verified because man is capable of conducting a rational investigation into the implications of every basic assumption to determine which is more probably true. If a choice must be made between two antithetical first principles, the advice is to choose the one which when applied to the whole of reality gives the most coherent picture and has the fewest difficulties. Clark makes a strong case for the idea of a presuppositional first principle and its necessity in dealing with God and His eternal truth-claims. However, he does not argue for the presupposition of an inerrant Bible, but the governance of the law of contradiction, or simply logic, in constructing a world view.[28] The laws of logic become the ultimate and absolute authority in the verification process.

"Probability" is the acme of this methodology; it is as high as human reason can ascend to subject God and his revelation-claims to an outside authority. The probability standard is external both to God and man and is a tool for ascertaining if truth has been found in Scripture after all. Buswell therefore says, "There is no argument known to us which, as an argument, leads to more than a probable (highly probable) conclusion."[29] He adds: "Concluding then the inductive arguments for the existence of God, we hold that these arguments do establish a presumption in favor of faith in the God of the Bible."[30] Henry contends that revelational philosophy is "an all-inclusive explanation of reality which answers the most problems and leaves the smallest residue of unsolved problems."[31] Likewise, Carnell states: "Let us establish securely the fact that proof for the Christian faith, as proof for any world-view that is worth talking about, cannot rise above rational probability. Probability is that state of coherence in which more evidences can be corralled for a given hypothesis than can be amassed against it."[32] Indeed, probability "is the guide of life."[33]

---

[27]Louis Moore, "Still Searching For the Lost Ark," *Moody Monthly* (Mar 1989), p. 33.

[28]*A Christian View of Men and Things*, pp. 26-31.

[29]*A Systematic Theology of the Christian Religion*, 1:72.

[30]Ibid., 1:100.

[31]*Remaking the Modern Mind*, p. 237.

[32]*An Introduction to Christian Apologetics*, p. 113. Carnell tries to demonstrate that probability is not incompatible with subjective moral certainty and assurance (pp. 113-21).

[33]Ibid., p. 106.

For those espousing the need to verify Bible statements, saving faith is a tentative acceptance of and trust in something not initially proven, that needs to be rationally verified or inductively vindicated so that the initial assumption does not turn out to be irrational and baseless.

> While the Bible not only states what is true, but also that its content is true, one cannot utilize it as his authority in this latter sense. He must decide on the basis of the evidence whether the claimed revelation is genuine. He is forced to do so on the basis of reason, whether he wishes to or not. In actual practice, all men do this, regardless of how naively or simply it may be done.[34]

Holding that "it is possible to exhibit the truthfulness of the Biblical view by appealing to evidence drawn from the created space-time universe,"[35] Erickson ironically posits that this process is "not in conflict with the Bible's authoritative function....It is simply determining whether the Bible is what it claims to be."[36] With this in mind,

> Faith...is for the new evangelicals...a *provisional acceptance* of the world and life view revealed in Scripture. This means that while it cannot be proven antecedently to belief, once one has been willing to take the revelation at face value and consider the *possibility* that it is actually true and is the revealed Word of God, evidence may then be offered to that effect (italics added).[37]

> One must begin with faith, then. Without reliance upon the knowledge of God as revealed in the Bible, at least by a *tentative acceptance*, one would never really come to know Him. Yet faith in the sense of a *provisional acceptance* of something not initially proved need not remain on this level. It can go on to be verified, or at lease vindicated, so that the assumption is not irrational (italics added).[38]

Pinnock is even more tentative about the basis of initial saving faith, at least as far as the existence of God is concerned. For him the reason for the rational arguments is "to test rationally what we already *suspect* and are concerned about" (italics added).[39]

What then are the bases for verifying the truthfulness of basic assumptions, in this case the provisionally held revelation-claims of God in Scripture? How is this new evangelical "interpretative hypothesis"[40] validated? What criteria can eventually exonerate Scripture from its probationary status? Carnell would say that the standards are fundamentally two: logical consistency and empirical correspondence to "facts."[41] Nash expands them to four criteria: consistency, coherence, applicability, and adequacy.[42]

---

[34]Millard J. Erickson, *The New Evangelical Theology* (Westwood, NJ: Revell, 1968), p. 202.

[35]Ibid., p. 200.

[36]Ibid., p. 202.

[37]Ibid., p.130.

[38]Ibid., p. 132.

[39]*Reason Enough: A Case For the Christian Faith*, p. 69.

[40]Gary Dorrien, *The Remaking of Evangelical Theology*, p. 71.

[41]*An Introduction to Christian Apologetics*, pp. 108-13.

[42]Ronald H. Nash, *The New Evangelicalism* (Grand Rapids: Zondervan, 1963), pp. 116-20.

First, consistency is the application of the law of contradiction (logic) to determine internal self-consistency. This is a negative test for truth in that it does not guarantee truth since the premises may be invalid; but inconsistency does reveal when there is *not* truth. Consistency determines if a system is free from internal self-contradictions. Clark held that all false systems can and must be reduced to rational absurdity through the rigorous use of logic.[43] Second, coherence is a use of logic to determine if the would-be revelation sticks together. Clark proposed that logic as a negative test is not enough; logic must also exhibit the internal *consistency* of the Christian revelation-claim, a process he calls axiomatization.[44] Third, applicability is an empirical test to determine if a world-view claimant is relevant to experience. Such a system must be able to explain experience better and more thoroughly than any other. Fourth, adequacy is also an empirical test to see if the would-be revelation is adequate to all possible experience. These four criteria yield the hypothesis or presumptive first principle, in this case the Bible as a provisional object of faith, which is more probably true vis-a-vis other systems of truth-claims.

COMMON GROUND

Common ground is an area constituted of supposedly neutral facts, objectively accessible to all, by which the claims of Christianity can be proven. The fundamentalist forbearers of new evangelicalism adopted the common ground principle and thus were not wholly biblical themselves. For example, the great evolution debates and other argumentation were generally attempts to meet and refute evolutionists, liberals, and infidels by their own rules on their own ground. Sermons or lectures by fundamentalists on "Why I Believe in God" or "Why I Believe the Bible Is the Word of God" consisted of Christian evidences as independent empirical criteria to bolster, confirm, establish, or verify the Bible's self-validation. In so doing fundamentalist apologists inadvertently diluted the integrity of the Christian faith, as does the new evangelical methodology.[45]

Carnell, more than any other new evangelical apologist, worked out the strategic use of common ground in his principal writings. He intended to reach as many people as possible with the Christian message, and he always placed himself in the tradition of the Reformers as against Romanists, liberals, neo-orthodox, cultists, and all other forms of essentially pagan philosophy. In each of his major publications, Carnell sought to find a meaningful and different point of contact with the general culture. It was from this point of common ground that he developed his apologetic, giving a rational presentation of the Christian revelation-claim and defending it against the rational attacks of others.

Logic

In *An Introduction to Christian Apologetics,* Carnell appeals to logic or the law of contradiction. He assumes the truth of the biblical witness and proceeds to show that it is not incompatible with the law of contradiction but is actually

---

[43]Gordon H. Clark, *Karl Barth's Theological Method* (Philadelphia: Presbyterian and Reformed, 1963), p. 85.

[44]Ibid., p. 95.

[45]Donald G. Bloesch, *The Evangelical Renaissance* (Grand Rapids: Eerdmans, 1973), p. 143.

established by it. Appealing to empiricism, he says, "the true is a quality of that judgment or proposition which, when followed out into the total witness of facts in our experience, does not disappoint our expectations."[46] Refracting it a bit, he defines truth *for the Christian* as "correspondence with the mind of God."[47] However the empirical definition is actually his working model of the true, as when he says: "When Scripture speaks of truth, it means precisely what the man on the street means. Whether a person listens to a political speech or reads the Bible, he is called upon to judge the sufficiency of the evidences."[48] Carnell's test for truth is "systematic consistency," that is, a set of criteria that checks on internal self-coherence and an external fit with the facts of our experience.[49] The light of rationality common to all (John 1:9), provides the "univocal point of meeting between God and man"[50] and puts everyone on a level playing field of ability to engage in reason and provides a valid means of determining truth.

Being confronted with a revelation from God, man is therefore invited to submit it to the test of systematic consistency in order to verify its truth. Carnell advises to

> accept that revelation which, when examined, yields a system of thought which is horizontally self-consistent and which vertically fits the facts of history....Bring on your revelations! Let them make peace with the law of contradiction and the facts of history, and they will deserve a rational man's assent. A careful examination of the Bible reveals that it passes these stringent examinations *summa cum laude.*[51]

He triumphantly concludes: "In this entire system of salvation [in the Bible] there is nothing repulsive to the reason of man; there is nothing impossible, immoral, absurd, nothing inconsistent with the corpus of well-attested truth."[52] Carnell does not ask anyone to go against his rational instincts. He is confident that the Christian message will survive even the most meticulous scrutiny; the evidences for his message will withstand the most stringent investigation and will provide a secure resting place for faith. Carnell tries to defend the Bible as his governing authority; what he rejects is "the notion that authoritative decree per se, unaccompanied by rational evidences of its authority, can be a basis for faith."[53] That is, he wants more than biblical dogmatism; he wants an authority but not authority worthy of trust in itself.

Values

Carnell's second major contribution to apologetics appeared in *A Philosophy of the Christian Religion,*[54] in which he uses values as the point of contact between the gospel and society. Again his methodology assumes the truthfulness of the

---

[46]*An Introduction to Christian Apologetics*, p. 45.

[47]Ibid., p. 47.

[48]Edward John Carnell, *The Case For Orthodox Theology* (Philadelphia: Westminster, 1959), p. 82.

[49]*An Introduction to Christian Apologetics*, pp. 60-61.

[50]Ibid., p. 63.

[51]Ibid., p. 178.

[52]Ibid., p. 179.

[53]Ibid., p. 71.

[54]Grand Rapids: Eerdmans, 1952.

Christian message and assumes to verify it with the facts of our experience relative to values. Carnell begins by postulating Christianity as a value-option among other options and proceeds to show how it is the best option. He clears the ground of charges against the value of faith vis-a-vis knowledge by showing that we exercise faith every day of our lives in that of which we know little or nothing. On the other hand, Christianity *is* knowledge, that which is derived after carefully screening the evidences so that the heart may have an unambiguous place to rest.[55] He further answers the value-options of pleasure, economic security, pure rationalism, and humanism, among others.[56] Linking all truth with God and His revelation, the author advises that all pretenses to revelation be tested and scrutinized; that since we use coherence in all other realms, why should it be irrelevant in testing for revelation?[57] The criterion for testing revelation is values, and these values are administered by what Carnell calls the free (unprejudiced) self or the free man.[58]

Carnell appeals for the consistent and honest rational man to consider the values offered by the option of biblical Christianity. Just as he invited others to bring on their revelations, he now invites them in effect to bring on their would-be value-options, and he will show that the Christian message makes peace with our highest conceptions of values and theirs do not. Therefore it is in the highest traditions of reason to trust Christ as one's personal Savior and the essence of utter folly not to do so. This truth follows of the indisputable testimony of the evidences. "Spirit can be led to the God worthy of being worshiped only through the avenue of objectively veracious evidences."[59] "Jesus Christ is worthy of our faith and consequently ought to receive it because both his person and his doctrine are rationally continuous with the values which we have already accepted in ordinary experience."[60]

Morality

In *Christian Commitment*[61] Carnell articulates a third point of contact with culture, the common ground of "judicial sentiment," a moral oughtness growing out of "the moral and spiritual environment." The moral and spiritual environment encloses everyone, and it is formed by obligations of a moral and spiritual nature, sometimes called "the duties that already hold a person."[62] Man's environment is composed of the realities to which people are committed by existence itself. For example, the law of dignity is an essential part of this environment.[63] If one enters another's presence, the other person has a moral obligation to respond. Myriads of

---

[55]*A Philosophy of the Christian Religion*, p. 29.

[56]Ibid., pp. 53, 111, 223.

[57]Ibid., p. 491.

[58]Ibid., pp. 64, 155, 164, passim.

[59]Ibid., p. 450.

[60]Ibid., p. 495.

[61]New York: Macmillan, 1957.

[62]*Christian Commitment*, p. 32.

[63]Ibid., p. 56.

decisions of a moral and spiritual nature are made daily because of every man's participation in this enclosure. The moral faculties of every person are constantly at work in this moral and spiritual atmosphere as men fulfill their duties or claims legislated by the moral and spiritual environment. These duties are called the claims of the moral and spiritual environment. Morality consists of choices freely expressed through the necessities of the moral and spiritual environment.[64] "Rectitude forms the moral and spiritual environment of an upright heart."[65] This is but another way of saying that the person of God comprises this environment, for in Him we live and move and have our being.[66]

The judicial sentiment is the moral faculty that judges on the basis given it by the claims of the moral and spiritual environment.[67] If someone takes advantage of another, is rude, or even inadvertently violates the law of dignity, the judicial sentiment is aroused, and he is judged to be guilty. He has transgressed the claims of the moral and spiritual environment. He lacks rectitude at that point; justice has been miscarried to some degree. From this point Carnell transitions easily to God Himself. The judicial sentiment in all people implies and even demands an Administer of justice since the moral and spiritual environment is the basis upon which all judgments are made.[68] This Administrator must be God; He completes the moral cycle by fulfilling the judicial sentiment.[69] On this basis Carnell feels he has reasoned from human experience to the person of God, although he acknowledges the Bible as his authority for the fact that in God we live and move and exist.[70]

Extending the argument further, Carnell shows how the morality approach can help a person find God. Man knows it is morally wrong to be indifferent to those around him who show him favors, yet when it comes to *divine* favors, he not only fails to respond, he does not have the moral capability of changing himself. This is called the *moral predicament.*[71] What can such a person do in this case? The author suggests that he at least can be transparently honest before God; that while this will not solve the problem, it will provide "a clean moral platform on which to build."[72] Since the moral and spiritual environment is common to both God and man, God is obligated to reveal himself when the right moral conditions exist. "God is under the same necessity to extend life to the humble as he is to withhold it from the proud."[73] So if someone will but humble himself he will discover truth—truth as personal rectitude or uprightness: man as he corresponds

---

[64]Ibid., p. 66.

[65]Ibid., p. 39.

[66]Ibid., p. 41.

[67]Ibid., p. 92.

[68]Ibid., p. 103.

[69]Ibid., p. 108.

[70]Ibid., p. 101.

[71]Ibid., p. 129.

[72]Ibid.

[73]Ibid., p. 151.

to man in the way he ought.[74] He will discover truth by moral self-acceptance, by consistently submitting himself to the realities that already hold him in the moral and spiritual environment. In other words he will come to God.

Love

The last major contribution to apologetics by Carnell is *The Kingdom of Love and the Pride of Life*.[75] In this work he appeals to the law of love as the point of contact with modern society. He believes that the relationship between patient and analyst in modern psychotherapy is a basis for an apologetic. He confesses indebtedness to Freud for the apologetical significance of love.[76] Carnell develops the thesis that love is unconditional acceptance. Love is always kind, truthful, and humble without pretense.[77] What kind of an authority referees the kingdom of love? Carnell says it is the "convictions of the heart." This seems to be some intuitive sense of good that everyone, especially a happy child, possesses. "These convictions say that a person is good when he is kind and truthful, and that in the end a good person has nothing to fear....Since happy children are citizens of the kingdom of love, they enjoy an intuitive perception of virtue...[they] discover the meaning of virtue by listening to their own hearts."[78]

The happy child is used as the paradigm of the intuitions of the heart that form the basis of the book. Whatever a happy child feels in the raw stuff of his heart concerning love, evil, and fair play is the structure of the kingdom of love. The values a happy child takes for granted form the convictions of the heart in the kingdom of love. These convictions distinguish between a good man and an evil one. A good man is kind and truthful; he always does as he would be done to—an axiom in the kingdom of love.[79] These good people form the decent society which collectively acts as the good man. This society also follows the axiom. The convictions of the heart form the decent society that intuitively knows to condemn lying, cheating, murder, and theft. These persuasions of the society are the same as those which children draw upon to pronounce Cinderella good and her stepmother bad.[80] Anyone who would attack the best interests of a decent society would immediately be branded as a fraud. All moral improvements in society trace to the convictions of the heart.[81] These convictions of the heart are analogous to faith in God. It is the faith of a child in the outcome of a fairy tale elevated to a much higher proportion. Here the transition is again made to God. Only God can answer, or fulfill, the convictions of the heart.[82]

---

[74]Ibid., p. 16.

[75]Grand Rapids: Eerdmans, 1960.

[76]*The Kingdom of Love and the Pride of Life*, p. 6.

[77]Ibid., p. 7.

[78]Ibid., p. 17.

[79]Ibid., pp. 52, 95, 151.

[80]Ibid., p. 149.

[81]Ibid., p. 150.

[82]Ibid., p. 105.

Love, like the other common ground elements, is the common denominator between people and God and the common ground between people among themselves. Love flows out of the convictions of the heart. Little children can instinctively perceive virtue, but among adults it is the (consistent) good man and his kind in the decent society that can distinguish virtue from vice. The good man does the testing in the kingdom of love.[83] The good man thus stands with the upright man, the free man, and the rational man of Carnell's earlier works in verifying truth as man meets God.

Another familiar area of common ground is history, including archaeology. Pinnock argued: "If the Gospel cannot be sustained by historical data, it cannot be sustained at all. Myths and fables may be immune to historical investigation if only because they are in essence a-historical; but the incarnation of the Son of God belongs to the flesh and bone of history." Noting further: "The Gospel is about historical facts. Unless these can be examined and tested, preaching loses its integrity and conviction."[84] Gary Habermas employs the supposed independent testimony of history in *Ancient Evidence For the Life of Jesus*.[85]

Assumptions
Several assumptions mark the use of common ground. Without a valid, presupposed framework, the verification process could not work, and the use of common ground would be impotent. First, the neutral autonomy of the human mind is assumed in the verification/common ground procedure, taking for granted that man's mind is free, independent, and neutral with regard to God or any other "fact." Prejudice to any degree skews the verification process and makes common ground anything but common. A second assumption is the common rationality of all people. It is assumed that all have or can have common notions of logic, values, morality, love, or the meaning of history. That is, whatever is used as the common ground must have the common thinking of all in the verification process. It is this common rationality that creates an area of common ground that is equally accessible to all and can be a basis of appeal for all.

Third, it is assumed that there is a virtual one-for-one rational continuity between all people and God. Carnell says that John 1:9 (the "light" that lights everyone) is a "univocal point of contact between God and man."[86] In other words, man's rational nature, his ability to reason, is continuous with God Himself. It gives man the ability to think God's thoughts after Him. In practicality, this notion assumes logic is a common rational bond between God and human beings. Logic means the same thing to God as to man and, if used consistently, is common to all people with each other. Henry understands that "the Christian religion assigns

---

[83]In *The Case for Orthodox Theology*, Carnell follows the same thought in the chapter titled "Proof" (pp. 81-91).

[84]Clark Pinnock, "Toward A Rational Apologetic Based Upon History," *Bulletin of the Evangelical Theological Society* 11 (Summer 1968), pp. 147-48.

[85]Nashville: Thomas Nelson, 1984. See the report by Richard John Neuhaus of a debate between Habermas and British atheist, Anthony Flew, on the historicity of the resurrection of Christ ("History and Faith," *National Review* [Apr 15, 1988], p. 45). Neuhaus, a Roman Catholic, says Habermas won "hands down."

[86]*An Introduction to Christian Apologetics*, p. 63.

a critical and indispensable role to reason....Christian theology unreservedly champions reason as an instrument for organizing data and drawing inferences from it, *and as a logical discriminating faculty competent to test religious claims*" (italics added).[87]

The fountain head of this role for logic appears to be Gordon Clark, the mentor of many of the budding new evangelical thinkers while he was teaching philosophy at Wheaton College. Building on the Greek word *logos*, Clark boldly translates John 1:1: "In the beginning was logic, and logic was with God and logic was God." For him "the law of contradiction is not to be taken as an axiom prior to or independent of God. The law is God thinking."[88] Using this deified law, Carnell can exclaim with great triumph: "In this entire system of salvation there is nothing repulsive to the reason of man; there is nothing impossible, immoral, absurd, nothing inconsistent with the corpus of well-attested truth."[89] This rational continuity thus becomes the theoretical basis of new evangelicalism's "dialogues" with heretics and infidels and many other activities that bind Christians and non-Christians together in some kind of fellowship or common cause.

Fourth, the new evangelical methodology of verification and common ground presupposes the brute nature of fact or truth. A fact is brute when it just "is." In this approach it is assumed that a fact has no necessarily intelligible relationship to other facts (much less to God) and requires no universal for understanding. As such a fact is free-floating, self-explaining, self-fulfilling or self-satisfying, and independent. It is rootless; it stands on its own base and becomes something to which both God and man must conform, that both can appeal to, and can be used by man to prove the existence of God or at least to test and confirm the veraciousness of God's revelation-claims in Scripture. In the new evangelical proposal, truth is a body of independent brute facts that derives meaning from itself, is accessible to all, and can be used in proving, confirming, verifying, defending, and even presenting the Christian message.

Empiricism (i.e., sense experience) plays a large role in defining and verifying truth in this methodology. Carnell writes, "The true is a quality of that judgment or proposition which, *when followed out into the total witness of facts of our experience*, does not disappoint our expectations" (italics added).[90] Or, "while Scripture speaks of truth, it means precisely what the man on the street means. Whether a person listens to a political speech or reads the Bible, he is called upon to judge the sufficiency of the evidences, and if he is reasonably free of prejudice, he will bring the same criteria to the one task that he does to the other."[91] Bernard Ramm states that theological study has two foci—one in *experience* and the other in Scripture (italics added).[92]

---

[87]*God, Revelation and Authority*, 1:226.

[88]"The Wheaton Lectures," p. 67.

[89]*An Introduction to Christian Apologetics*, p. 179.

[90]Ibid., p. 45.

[91]*The Case For Orthodox Theology*, p. 82.

[92]Bernard Ramm, *The Christian View of Science and Scripture* (Grand Rapids: Eerdmans, 1955), p. 46.

THE DEFENSE OF THE FAITH

Carnell is probably the most articulate paradigm of the new evangelical apologetic methodology as regards removing the intellectual objections to, and the defense of, the gospel. His series "How Every Christian Can Defend His Faith," by its very title encompasses every believer and the method that each believer can use in presenting and defending his Christian faith. Two pertinent questions should be kept in mind as this method is analyzed: Is genuine New Testament Christianity being presented and defended? Is this something that *every Christian* can do?

Part I of his series deals with the existence of God. Reminding us that "apologetics is simply Christianity defensively stated," Carnell calls attention to its limitations.

> The sole purpose of any skilled refutation...is to prepare the ground so that the seed of the gospel can find good soil. This means that your aim should be twofold: first prayerfully seek to answer intellectual difficulties on the part of the unbeliever; then, when these have been met and the way is open, proceed swiftly with the sowing of the gospel seed, Preach Christ![93]

In answering a "genuinely sincere agnostic," for example, first "give him a glimpse of the variety and extent of proofs supporting Christianity, by pointing to as many as you can of the many evidences that God exists," evidences such as archaeological and scientific data, the unity and coherence of the Bible, the uniformity and design of nature, and the like. "If the person is impressed with this evidence, turn at once to the gospel....If, however, the objector appears unimpressed with the evidences you have listed, leave them and turn to logical reasoning." The purpose here is "to bring reason to bear on the preconceived convictions of the unbeliever....It is an attack on the skeptic's Maginot line so that the infantrymen—the evidences—may gain entrance."[94]

Part II handles the revelation of God and how to meet various objections to the need for and the idea of divine revelation. In a summary introductory statement, Carnell writes that "the Christian thus should be prepared to defend the fact of revelation, to present the Bible as the very Word of God, and finally to hold it up as a mirror which so clearly reflects the sinfulness of the unbeliever's heart that he cannot but see his need and cry out to God for saving mercy."[95] Part III is given over to attacks on the providence of God. Answering an attack on prayer, "the proper approach is to go back to the arguments establishing the existence of God and the reality of revelation. Then return to the question of prayer. When once God and revelation are shown to be reasonable, prayer will become reasonable, too."[96] The perennial problem of free will and God's sovereignty is answered by anecdotal parallels. "We can generally *predict* what a hungry child will do with a chocolate ice cream cone or how a woman with a new hat will act before a mirror. But

---

[93]*Moody Monthly* (Jan 1950), p. 312.

[94]Ibid.

[95]*Moody Monthly* (Feb 1950), p. 384.

[96]*Moody Monthly* (Mar 1950), p. 460.

this does not mean that the acts were not freely done" (italics his).[97] Since God's knowledge and ability transcend man's, the argument is that the tension between sovereignty and freedom thus virtually disappears or is at least made manageable.

The attack against miracles is a little more complicated to meet, but the author is optimistic: "The Christian may be courageous when men try to argue against the possibility of miracles, for the case against miracles is a tissue of fallacies."[98] Critics who deny miracles by appealing to a closed universe, which holds that natural law is binding on the entire universe, are answered by the Christian by appealing to an open universe—arguing for the *possibility* of miracles, noting that *history* will confirm their actuality. If the critic then argues that this makes the universe a little too open and thus unpredictable and science impossible, the advice is to assure him that "God has restricted [miracles] to a very small number."[99] That is to say, the universe is not *that* open; it is actually a closed system after all, but then again not so closed as to preclude miracles.

A similar tack used by others is to show that miracles are compatible with natural law. Arguing that if a needle will float in a bathtub, it is scientifically possible that the young prophet's axe head could float in a river (2 Kings 6:6);[100] or since "lizards and salamanders grow new tails, to make a new hand would not be impossible for God."[101] Furthermore, "nature furnishes many…examples [of virgin births—parthenogenesis] on the lower levels of life,"[102] presumably referring to certain self-pollinating plants and self-fertilizing insects. It is not difficult therefore "to believe in the virgin birth of Christ."[103] The scientific criterion for the explanation of a miracle is: "The first thing a scientist should say is that all our laws are 'probabilities.' Einstein demonstrated that point effectively. We know, for example, that although each electron behaves differently, the ensemble of electrons is predictable in behavior. *Yet if we have the slightest change in the organization of this activity we have a miracle*" (italics added).[104]

This apologetic methodology is in need of analysis and is open to several challenges which undermine its validity and trustworthiness of presenting and defending the truth claims of Christianity.

---

[97]Ibid., p. 461.

[98]Ibid., p. 460.

[99]Ibid., p. 461.

[100]"An Interview With Stanley W. Burriss, Gerhard Dirks and Lambert Dolphin Jr.," *Decision* (Nov 1966), p. 8.

[101]Ibid.

[102]Ibid., p. 9.

[103]Ibid.

[104]Ibid., p. 8.

17

AN ANALYSIS OF NEW EVANGELICAL APOLOGETICS

The foregoing apologetic methodology received official sanctioning in the 1960s as the new evangelical approach. With some variation, Carl Henry, Bernard Ramm, Clark Pinnock, Millard Erickson, Ronald Nash, and especially Edward John Carnell espoused the partial presuppositional apologetics. The leading ideas of this approach found roots primarily in Gordon H. Clark, the unofficial mentor of the new evangelical apologists. Clark and his followers called themselves presuppositionalists because they allegedly held to a starting point in philosophy and apologetics that was self-evident, axiomatic, and not deduced from a prior truth, a starting point they asserted was the Scripture itself. However, the new evangelicals' inconsistent adherence to a scriptural starting point displayed itself in their readiness to subject the Bible to verifying tests before the true accuracy could be asserted. Clark's position could more correctly be identified as presuppositional rationalism. The overall new evangelical position had many more elements of inductivism, empiricism, fideism, and evidentialism than true presuppositionalism.[1]

In the 1940s and 50s especially, the rival schools of apologetics were chiefly those of Clark and Cornelius Van Til, whose viewpoints differed significantly. Both were of the Reformed tradition theologically, but they differed sharply over the degree of depravity of the human intellect, the creator-creature distinction between God and man, and the ultimate incomprehensibility of God, especially as these doctrines intersected with philosophy and apologetics. I became convinced while in seminary in the later 1950s that the Van Til position is the biblical one, and it is from this perspective that the new evangelical apologetic will be criticized. Van Til was part of the original fundamentalist/evangelical coalition, at least in thinking and arguing, although for

---

[1]*Inductivism* is reasoning from particulars to general conclusions. It starts with independent "facts" as a given and from there constructs degrees of probabilities as proofs, verification, or evidences of Christianity. *Empiricism* appeals to the senses, usually in the form of "the scientific method," in determining truth in the process of proving, verifying, or evidencing Christianity. *Fideism* understands Christian philosophy and apologetics to be purely a matter of faith. Reason and argumentation are considered invalid and thus discounted altogether; one must simply believe. *Evidentialism* focuses mainly on objective, historical evidences supporting, proving, or verifying the truth-claims of Christianity.

him the name Reformed or Calvinist stood for the Bible and everything Christian. He did not consider himself a new evangelical; in fact, he was quite critical of early new evangelicalism.[2] Ronald Nash denies that Van Til was a new evangelical.[3]

The new evangelical apologetic methodology is ambivalent in at least three areas.

AMBIVALENCE ON DEPRAVITY

One of the ironies of theology is that self-confessed Calvinists could become functional Arminians in apologetics. All of the new evangelical apologists claimed to stand in the Reformed tradition on soteriology, but they all demonstrated a colossal inconsistency on the doctrine of total depravity. They denied completely any ability of the natural man to respond of his unaided free will to the call of God to salvation, much less man's ability to initiate some kind of overture to God. They had no patience with the Pelagian idea of the natural ability of the unsaved or with the Arminian concept of prevenient grace, i.e., enough redemptive grace is given to all the unsaved to offset the depravity of the will so that a truly uninhibited free choice could be made for or against Christ by means of this volitional equilibrium. They were far too Calvinistic for those notions; however, in philosophy and apologetics they denied or mitigated the effects of depravity on the human intellect (noetic sin).

Clark (rightly) criticized Abraham Kuyper for thinking that "the universal human consciousness is always able to overcome this sluggishness [i.e., noetic sin] and to correct mistakes in reasoning." Clark himself though, only weakly rejoins: "Perhaps the human consciousness is not always able to overcome sluggishness and correct mistakes in reasoning."[4] However his own rationalistic apologetic methodology seems to assume that the natural man can indeed override his cerebral "sluggishness," at least to the extent that he can test conflicting first principles and revelation-claims by the law of contradiction to see which gives the most coherent picture of the world.[5] Carnell disliked the "vague homilies on the 'noetic effects of sin'" and found depravity to reside primarily in the affections. Sin touches the mind only as it is made the servant of the affections.[6] "Although we cannot make ourselves righteous, we can be sorry for our want of rectitude. We *are* capable of humbling ourselves before God and our neighbor."[7] "God only asks humility, and humility is within the reach of one who feels even the faintest stirring of guilt in his heart."[8] "It can be argued with equal plausibility that not only are we obliged by the law of love, but that in a very meaningful sense we are natively capable of meeting it."[9] Carnell's concept of depravity here is extremely shallow.

[2]Cornelius Van Til, "The New Evangelicalism" (Philadelphia: Westminster Seminary, 1960, unpublished).

[3]*The New Evangelicalism* (Grand Rapids: Zondervan, 1963), p. 113.

[4]Gordon H. Clark, "The Bible As Truth," *Bibliotheca Sacra* 114 (Apr 1957), p. 161.

[5]*A Christian View of Men and Things* (Grand Rapids: 1952), pp. 32-34.

[6]*Christian Commitment: An Apologetic* (New York: Macmillan, 1957), p. 198.

[7]Ibid., p. 200.

[8]Ibid., p. 238.

[9]Ibid., p. 240.

Dewey Beegle, while not an apologist per se, attempted an apologetic response to inerrancy by reasoning that, "the human mind does not create the evidence which is determinative in the separation of truth from error. All human reason can do is *to function properly* with the data that are furnished it" (italics added).[10] The problem is that the human mind cannot "function properly" with the data because of the innate effects of noetic sin. Granted, Beegle is an Arminian, and one would expect his view of total inability to be anything but total, but his statement highlights the new evangelical methodology's problem of sounding exactly like Arminianism.

Millard Erickson's idea of depravity is also profoundly weak: "The Bible pictures man prior to conversion as being in some sense 'dead.'...He does not care about spiritual considerations, at least not very greatly."[11] The biblical picture, however, of the natural man, is one of hatred and active hostility against "spiritual considerations" and not a bland "I don't care very much about them."

The mind of the natural man is not neutrally autonomous, it is totally depraved. He does not accept or welcome[12] spiritual things from God. He is unable to do so because he regards them as foolishness (1 Cor 2:14). The mind of the unbelieving is defiled (Titus 1:15). The fleshly, unsaved mind is "hostile toward God; for it does not subject itself to the law of God, for it is not even able to do so" (Rom 8:7). Before conversion the person was "indulging the desires of the flesh and the mind" (Eph 2:3). Unbelieving Gentiles, and by legitimate extension all unbelievers, live in the "futility of their mind, being darkened in their understanding, excluded from the life of God" (Eph 4:17-18). The thoughts of the wicked are, "There is no God" (Ps 10:4; i.e., God is irrelevant). No one among the sons of men of his unaided mental energies "understands" God in the sense of seeking Him, doing good, and integrating Him into their world view (Ps 14:2-3; Rom 3:10-12). Sin has affected the whole of man's being; "from the sole of the foot even to the head there is no soundness in it" (Isa 1:6). The unsaved person is completely destitute of the unconditional love for God which He requires (Matt 22:37-38). He who is being asked to choose between conflicting first principles for the one with the most coherent world view has *already* formed a world view with himself at the very center. Of all the pictures or symbols depicting the natural man with reference to the absolute claims of God on him, the most poignant is the figure of death. He is "dead in trespasses and sins" (Eph 2:1), totally unresponsive to God, as completely unable to humble himself as he is to lift himself up to the streets of gold. If he is to have any relief epistemologically, intellectually, volitionally, or in any manner, there must be a unilateral work of divine grace that elicits a response of repentance and faith. The dead must be acted upon by being given life before any right response is possible.

---

[10]Dewey M. Beegle, *The Inspiration of Scripture* (Philadelphia: Westminster, 1963), pp. 63-64.

[11]*The New Evangelical Theology* (Westwood, NJ: Revell, 1968), p. 113.

[12]BDAG, s.v. *"dechomai,"* p. 221, lists "to be receptive of someone, receive, welcome" as a general meaning.

Man's rational continuity with God has been disrupted and distorted by the curse of original sin and its noetic effects. He can think, but he cannot think God's thoughts after Him without regenerating grace. He can only sin in varying degrees. He has not lost his mind; he has lost his holiness. He does not lack information; he lacks regeneration. The natural man has a totally contradictory rational/irrational standard by which he judges and evaluates everything.[13] Which aspect of the standard he uses is determined by his sinful nature and his compulsion to suppress the truth he already knows in his heart about God, sin, judgment, and the like (Rom 1:18−32). This congenital ambivalence systematically rejects offensive truth. The nearer the natural man comes to his need for God for whatever reason, the more energetically he will pursue this hypocritical inconsistency. Therefore, to try and meet the natural man on some kind of neutral, mutually agreeable common ground is impossible. It will only end in the believer frustratingly declaring that his opponent is hopelessly prejudiced against God. But the apologist who understands the noetic effects of sin already knows that the unbeliever is not only self-contradictory and prejudiced, but on his apostate principles is unable to account for any datum in the universe. This is to say nothing of the folly of asking such an one to judge or verify the cogency of the truth-claims of the Incarnation of Truth Himself. Even a Christian cannot conduct a totally unbiased verification process because he too has a sinful nature that vitiates the full implications of truth. Thus *no one* is able completely and honestly to verify the Christian revelation-claims. The only way out of the dilemma is to presuppose that the one living and true God, eternally existing in self-sufficient tri-unity, has revealed Himself inerrantly in the self-attesting Scriptures of the Protestant canon. This axiomatic first principle is a product only of sovereign divine grace.

AMBIVALENCE ON TRUTH AND THE ACQUISITION OF KNOWLEDGE

The Definition of Truth

Truth and fact are here considered as synonymous. Theologically, truth in God means that He is eternally self-consistent. His knowledge of Himself eternally conforms to His being. His knowledge and being are in perfect, absolute, and eternal correspondence. God exhaustively knows who He is and He is exactly who He knows Himself to be. This is more than divine self-consciousness but includes His decrees, purposes, motives, actions, and attitudes. Truth is not something arbitrary with God; it is not the product of His will. It is a matter of His being and knowledge in complete and everlasting self-coherence. Truth is constitutional with God. The Father is the "God of truth" (Ps 31:5), and He cannot lie (Heb 6:18). Christ is the truth (John 14:6), and the Holy Spirit is the truth (1 Jn 5:6). Truth, then, is that which corresponds with the mind of God. It is a propositional expression from God, that which God could state about any and all reality.

Truth is more than just that which corresponds to reality, since this notion implies that somehow truth is not a part of reality or that reality is some kind of an eternalized first principle that gives existence to truth—both of which omit the One

---

[13]Cornelius Van Til, *The Defense of the Faith* (Philadelphia: Presbyterian and Reformed, 1955), p. 237.

who is Truth Himself. The mind of God is the ultimate truth for every fact, proposition, person, event, circumstance, or exchange of energy in the universe since God alone has willed, created, sustains, and controls them either directly or indirectly. God knows exhaustively who He is and what He has willed; thus He alone determines truth for Himself and for all rational creatures external to Himself. Human beings can know truth as they think God's thoughts after Him. This means that truth for man must consist of or correspond with the truth-propositions of God's revelation in Scripture.

There are many properties of truth. For one, truth is intellectual; it is always the product of an intellect or mind. Otherwise it is a meaningless abstraction. By the same token, truth is propositional; it is subject and predicate material—concepts, ideas, and information. Propositions are the only material a rational mind can process and use. Non-propositional thought is an oxymoron that is totally self-destructive, to say nothing of its apostate presuppositions. Propositional discourse must be employed in any attempt to deny propositional discourse; it is axiomatic. Truth, then, is a character of propositions that correctly represents an actual state of affairs. Truth is one coherent system; it is a unity of interlocking propositions. It is infinite in scope because its source is God. Each truth is related to every other truth, and all is related to God. The truth is the whole; it is one and personal, and infinitely interlocking. Therefore, God is essential to *any* truth and thus to *all* truth. If He can be omitted from one truth, He can be dispensed with from every truth. A "moral" truth ("theft is sin") stands in the same objective sense as a "historical" truth ("Christ was born in the days of Augustus Caesar"). Without the self-contained tri-personal God, neither would have any meaning. There would be nothing but eternal chance, chaos, and impersonal flux.

What is more, truth as a systematic unity is only set forth in Scripture. Not all truth is found in the Bible or in what can be deduced from the Bible, but the Bible is the only sure foundation for a unified system of truth. Only the inerrant Scriptures testify authoritatively to the infinite God of truth and His exhaustively pervasive relations with the universe. There is no free-from-God or free-from-Scripture truth.

The Basis of Truth

In this setting, then, facts are what they are because of their relationship to God. They take on meaning by virtue of their interpretation by the triune God, i.e., their place in the eternal counsel of the sovereign God as well as their place in the temporal order which only He created, sustains, and controls. All facts are theistic facts; they find definition and "factuality" solely at the pleasure of the God of the Bible and His determination of whatsoever comes to pass. Christ's self-assertion, "I am the truth" (John 14:6), a claim found in one form or another in all of Scripture, declares that "all reality is created reality, that is, that the facts are what they are by virtue of the Word, who was 'in the beginning,' and that consequently they cannot be understood in terms of themselves, but must be seen in the light of the authoritative interpretation which the Word has given."[14] In other words, the

---

[14]Richard B. Gaffin, Jr., "Review of Dewey M. Beegle, *The Inspiration of Scripture*," *Westminster Theological Journal* 26 (May 1964), p. 236.

relation of one fact to another and to all facts, which gives meaning to any fact, can be known only on the basis that these relationships are exhaustively known by the omniscient God of Scripture. He knows them because He has willed these relations in His eternal counsel, and He has revealed these matters in the inerrant Scriptures. Facts and truth can be rightly comprehended only by those capable of understanding God and His revelation.

The unsaved may indeed make truth statements and retain factual propositions in their thinking, but they do so on principles inconsistent with their apostate free-from-God world view. They have unwittingly plagiarized truth/fact from Christian theism and mouthed it in a certain way, sometimes even using conventional God-talk. But they cannot knowingly affirm truth as genuine truth without the Scriptural world view that only comes through a regenerated mind. God must be included and is necessary for the correct interpretation— the truthfulness—of any so-called fact. He is the Ultimate Fact and Reality. Christ Himself indicated as much when He said, "If anyone is willing to do His will, he will know of the teaching, whether it is of God" (John 7:17), and, "you will know the truth and the truth will make you free" (John 8:32). This teaching brings us back again to John 14:6—the very enfleshment of truth is the self-identifying Christ of the infallible, self-authenticating Scripture of the Protestant canon. There is no free-from-Christ or free-from-Scripture truth.

The new evangelical thinking, on the other hand, posits Christ and His revelation as facts among other facts, a truth-option among other options, although perhaps the best option and the facts with the fewest difficulties. The Scriptures, however, present Him as *the* truth and the *only* option if man would ever know truth. In order to avoid the hated charge of circular reasoning, the new evangelical methodology speaks of a body of facts as if it were something independent, free-from-God, and objective to both God and man, and objective to all mankind with one another. This idea is unbiblical, as we have seen, as well as self-destructive. The new evangelical apologist knows that no fact or truth is free-from-God, he knows that God planned, made, upholds, and directs the movement of the entire universe; in other words, he knows from theology who God is and His all-pervasive relations with the universe. He should also know that in apologetics when he appeals to a stockpile of supposedly generic facts, he is actually appealing to God-created facts to prove or verify the existence of God and His revelation-claims. In other words, he too is reasoning in a circle! This methodology is confusing, self-defeating, and utterly futile.

One must reason from God to God-given and thus God-interpreted facts. If this method is denied, the only alternative is to reason from autonomous man to brute facts that derive meaning from themselves and are necessarily extracted by human interpretation.[15] This latter method creates a basket full of temporal rational

---

[15]This extraction of meaning from brute facts is technically impossible since the so-called facts have no self-included universals to make the particulars intelligible. In other words, there is no intelligible relationship between one particular fact to another in this free-from-God system. Everything arises out of an ocean of chance, contingency, and pure possibility—anything but the sovereign control of the God of Scripture. Any assignment of meaning to this blob of "facts" only betrays a prior commitment to an ultimate point of reference of some kind, which of course invites the rejoinder of circular reasoning. This again illustrates the necessity of the biblical presuppositionalist's first principle that the one living and true God, existing in self-sufficient tri-unity, has authoritatively revealed Himself in the self-authorizing Bible. Without this, nothing is intelligible; any reasoning to the contrary ends in nihilism.

probabilities from which one then must make an irrational, fideistic "leap" to the eternal God. But there is no direct line in theology, apologetics, or logic from any number of finite effects to an Infinite First Cause.[16] New evangelical apologists, of course, would be extremely loathe to admit anything so crass as an irrational leap to God. After all, in that system, apologetics is the handmaiden to faith and the arguments are designed to make faith intelligent. A closer look reveals that the system actually falls quite short of fostering the certainty of faith in the only God there is and in the eternal trustworthiness of his self-revelation in Scripture. Clark, for example, makes a very telling admission.

> If, nonetheless, it can be shown that the Bible, in spite of having been written by more than thirty-five authors over a period of fifteen hundred years, is logically consistent, then the unbeliever would have to regard it as a most remarkable accident. It seems *more likely* that a single superintending mind could produce this result than that it just happened accidentally. Logical consistency therefore is evidence of inspiration; but it is not demonstration. *Strange accidents do indeed occur, and no proof is forthcoming that the Bible is not such an accident. Unlikely perhaps, but still possible* (italics added).[17]

Elsewhere Clark appealed to an open universe where anything can happen. Concerning the virgin birth of Christ, he wrote: "Indeed, what with all sorts of biological surprises, a virgin birth seems even less impossible than the incarnation of Deity in human flesh."[18]

It appears that Clark has bet the apologetic farm at this point—and lost. He has asked the unbeliever to leap into an ocean of pure contingency, to stake his eternal destiny on what may prove to be a "strange accident," and to entertain the possibility that the very foundation of atonement may turn out to be no more than a "biological surprise." Clark has simply told the natural man what he has told himself repeatedly, i.e., that the Bible and the person of Jesus Christ may possibly be the products of chance historical anomalies, and that God Himself may actually be irrelevant after all. This is the problem with engaging in probabilities. The high probability that God exists and His Word is true has the correlate *possibility* that He might not exist and His Word might not be true. Is this making the content of saving faith more intelligible?

Carnell had his "penumbral zone," essentially a bin of agnosticism, mystery, and enigma where the shortcomings of evidences, probabilities, and accidents were thrown. He wrote:

> Revelation is fragmentary. "The secret things belong to the Lord our God; but the things that are revealed belong to us and to our children forever" (Deuteronomy 29:

---

[16]Carl Henry, for one, shows his ambivalence on this point. On the one hand he knows that "if one approached the cosmos on non-theistic premises, he was not driven by the evidence to a theistic conclusion" (*Remaking the Modern Mind*, p. 231). On the other hand, Henry wants to use empirical, essentially non-theistic, conclusions or "facts" to verify the Christian revelation-claims. But he simply cannot have it both ways without the charge of reasoning in a circle. If non-theistic thought cannot produce theistic conclusions, neither can non-theistic "facts" based on non-theistic premises *verify* theistic truth-claims.

[17]Gordon Clark, "Can I Trust My Bible?" p. 24

[18]Gordon H. Clark, "Incarnation: Fact or Theory?" *Christianity Today* (Dec 10, 1956), p. 5.

29). Whenever a systematic theologian becomes too systematic, he ends up falsifying
some aspect of revelation. It is extremely difficult, if not impossible, to coax all the data
of Scripture into neat harmony. One must preserve a penumbral zone in his theology;
new exegetical possibilities should be welcomed. "Now I know in part; then I shall
understand fully, even as I have been fully understood" (1 Corinthians 13:12).[19]

It is true that God and His relations with the universe are at bottom incomprehensible;
they cannot be fully known by a finite mind. But that is not what Carnell seems
to be referring to. He means that the high probability of evidences for truth in
apologetics carries its contrary, i.e., that it is also possible, though remote and
highly unlikely, for the whole evidentialist/verificationist scheme to collapse in
skepticism and worse. Using history as the common ground, Carnell maintains that
the raising of Lazarus is of the raw stuff of history theoretically open to the same
verification as anything historical. Yet he knows that the miracle of Lazarus is
impossible to verify by empirical means. This empirical lack is therefore deposited
in the penumbral bin.

Since Christian evidences do not form an airtight system that compels belief,
one is forced to choose between conflicting truth-claims. As such, the evidences
for the historicity, affirmations, and demands of Christianity all fall short of actual,
formal proof, attaining only degrees of probability, and one must still accept the
claims of Christ by faith as revealed in the testimony of a self-authenticating Bible.
This evidentialist/probability shortfall is put by Carnell into the penumbral zone.
But, like Clark, he also seems to make faith another irrational leap into uncertainty.

Clark and Carnell would both have been better advised to follow their
Reformed theological instincts and call for sovereign supernatural grace (i.e.,
divine illumination) to implant an intuitive certainty of Scripture's truthfulness
as a sure basis for divinely-endowed faith. In so doing they could have forgotten
altogether about "accidents," "surprises," and "penumbra," and had an apologetic
methodology informed by exegetical theology rather than logic and experience.
They would also have had a fully consistent, biblical presuppositionalism, and the
irrational "leap" would have been eliminated.

The Principle of Analogy

In the 1940s an open controversy erupted between Clark and Van Til over the
doctrine of the incomprehensibility of God.[20] The dispute focused on how one can
know God and His revelation (epistemology). Clark taught that there is a direct
identity between what God knows and what man knows if both know the same
thing. Van Til posited that nothing exists in man as it exists in God; therefore man's
knowledge is indirect, an "image" or a mirror of God's knowledge. Van Til charged
Clark with denying God's ultimate incomprehensibility, and Clark counter-charged
that Van Til's position made for skepticism about any knowledge of God.

---

[19]*Christian Commitment*, p. 285.

[20]Cornelius Van Til, *The Protestant Doctrine of Scripture* (Rippon, CA: den Dulk Christian Foundation,
1967), pp. 62-72; John Frame, *Cornelius Van Til: An Analysis of His Thought* (Philadelphia:
Presbyterian and Reformed, 1995), pp. 97-113); and Bradley J. Swygard, "The Basis For the Doctrine
of the Incomprehensibility of God in Gordon Clark and Cornelius Van Til" (Th.M. thesis, Dallas
Theological Seminary, 1991).

The options in the relation between God's knowledge and man's are three. One is the univocal (one identical meaning): knowledge is the same for God and man; there is an identity in content and understanding. Another is equivocal (two or more meanings): there is no point of contact between God's knowledge and man's. The third is analogical (similar but not identical meaning): man's knowledge replicates God's knowledge because nothing exists in man exactly as it exists in God. Clark's camp held to the first and the supporters of Van Till to the third. Neither would give place to the second option—equivocalism—which is the thread-bare neo-orthodox view that God is the "wholly other," thus ultimately totally unknown and unknowable.

Eqivocalism is an old Platonic, gnostic notion that the realm of deity is so transcendent that God (or the gods) and man never meet on any physical or metaphysical level. The two realms never truly intersect; at best they only "touch" as on a tangent. Theism becomes an open pantheon—"whatever gods may be," in Henley's awful words in "The Invictus." Equivocalism is simply a provincial brew of the Unknown God, the godless "ignorance" of the ancient Athenians (Acts 17:23). The realm of God or the gods is unknown and ultimately unknowable by human beings; it is an area that is totally enveloped in the fog of impenetrable mystery in the last analysis. It is completely apostate and thus stringently opposed by any Bible-believing thought.

The option of univocalism presupposes something outside of and above God to which He and man are both bound, some common point of reference. Carnell, for example, is thinking univocally when he says: "To be sure, we do not understand everything God has revealed in Scripture, but that is not to admit that the obscure parts are intrinsically irrational; rather it simply means that we have not studied them long enough. *Time and illumination alone stop us from understanding the entire revelation of God* (italics added)."[21] This statement elevates the human mind to deity because both God and man are bound to the same dictate or referent; both share the same continuum of Eternal Universal Reason (or "reason in general"). The difference is only a matter of degree. At this univocal point man can comprehend God's mind if only he had enough time, a view that seems to clearly deny God's ultimate incomprehensibility—a blurring of the line between the Creator and the creature. Man's elevation of himself is but another form of the human intellectual arrogance that is the sworn enemy of God and His truth-claims and of a truly biblical apologetic methodology. It is not too difficult to see that the new evangelical evidentialist and verificationist apologetics have laid the groundwork for what became a denial of the inerrancy of Scripture by those who wanted the inductive "phenomena" or "facts" to control the doctrine. This denial resulted in the bifurcation of the Bible into "revelational" and "non-revelational" verses, truth and error, and the search for the "canon within the canon" of Scripture—all governed and directed by human intellectual autonomy.

The option of analogy as developed by Van Til[22] contends that man is in some sense analogous to God because of man's creation in God's image. He is

---

[21] *An Introduction to Christian Apologetics*, p. 195.

[22] This principle has often been confused, unwittingly or otherwise, with the principle of analogy put forth by Thomas Aquinas in the 13th century. For the difference explained, see Gilbert B. Weaver, "Man: Analogue of God," in *Jerusalem and Athens: Critical Discussions on the Philosophy and Apologetics of Cornelius Van Til*, ed. E. R. Geehan (Phillipsburg, NJ: Presbyterian and Reformed, 1977), pp. 321-27.

an analogue of God in thinking, willing, being, and doing. He is a finite replica of God in certain areas, although he does not participate in the eternal divine essence or being of God. Man cannot cross the Creator-creature line of distinction, but he can and does mirror on a finite level the Creator's level. Nothing exists in man precisely as it does in God; no attribute of God is truly communicable. "Analogy" might better be termed "image relationship," "reflection," or "likeness." Man's thinking process reconstructs a finite replica, as it were, of God's knowledge.[23] Weaver suggests "image-like" for the relationship of analogy, likening it to seeing oneself in a mirror—a "mirroring."[24] "To say that God is incomprehensible is to say our knowledge is never equivalent to God's own knowledge, that we never know Him precisely as He knows Himself."[25] That is, there is no identity of *content.* Man must rethink/reinterpret God's knowledge of anything. However, *man* does the rethinking; the thoughts are still his, not God's. Man can have truth because he has been created as a self-conscious reinterpreter of God's knowledge of truth. To that extent there can be "an identity of meaning between God's words and man's, at least on those occasions when God uses human language,"[26] even though technically there cannot be an identity of content. "The Analogy does not mean that man cannot know the same truth that God knows. [It] means that the subjective comprehension man has of a given truth is not identical to that which God has of the same truth."[27] This knowledge by analogy is valid knowledge, just as a free act of man is valid even though it is at the same time the conscious object of God's all-encompassing decree of whatsoever comes to pass. Man's actions have genuine significance; they are not a charade. Repentance and faith, for another example, are both gifts from God, yet it is man, not God, that repents and believes. Man's repentance and faith are valid and are truly *his* even though they are grants from God; so with the two-level idea of truth and its knowledge.[28] "Human reason is not a simple linear extension of divine reasoning."[29]

The principle of analogy is the only thing that can save truth and knowledge from skepticism. God *can* be known; truth *can* be known. Man does not need to know everything in order to know something, because God *does* know everything, and man's limited knowledge is held with reference to God's exhaustive knowledge. Comprehensive knowledge must reside somewhere if there is to be true knowledge anywhere; a One must make the Many data intelligible; and knowledge must be unified or else men must yield to the despair of sheer diversity. Thankfully, no

---

[23]Jim Halsey, *For Such a Time As This: An Introduction to the Reformed Apologetic of Cornelius Van Til* (Phillipsburg, NJ: Presbyterian and Reformed, 1976), p. 50.

[24]Gilbert B. Weaver, "Gordon Clark: Christian Apologist," in *The Philosophy of Gordon Clark*, Ronald Nash, ed. (Phillipsburg, NJ: Presbyterian and Reformed, 1968), p. 304.

[25]John Frame, *The Doctrine of the Knowledge of God* (Phillipsburg, NJ: Presbyterian and Reformed, 1987), p. 21.

[26]John Frame, *Van Til the Theologian* (Phillipsburg, NJ: Pilgrim, 1976), p. 22.

[27]Weaver, "Gordon Clark: Christian Apologist," p. 304.

[28]Cornelius Van Til, *An Introduction to Systematic Theology* (Phillipsburg, NJ: Presbyterian and Reformed, 1978), pp. 27—28. See also Weaver, "Man: Analogue of God," p. 325.

[29]Van Til, *An Introduction to Systematic Theology*, p. 28.

one really yields to total despair. (The particulars of mathematics, for example, are given meaning by the universals of theorems, axioms, et al. The particulars of the alphabet are given validity by the universals of spelling and word formation. Words convey truth by means of grammar, and syntax.) For the Christian apologist the temporal one and many—universals and particulars—are intelligible and valid because they are created by, and interpreted by, the Eternal One and Many—the self-sufficient triune God of the inerrant Bible. He is eternally Three persons in One essence. On this basis, God's image-bearers can think God's thoughts after Him and have valid truth and knowledge.

The principle of analogy also reflects and preserves the biblical Creator-creature distinction. The preservation of this distinction upholds the very definition and essence of sin, which is to worship and serve the creature rather than the Creator (Rom 1:25). Sin intrinsically is self-made autonomy in an effort to destroy the Creator-creature relationship. In apologetics the big sin is intellectual autonomy. Man endemically refuses to rethink or reinterpret God's thoughts and interpretation of things as controlled by His written revelation. When the Christian apologist attempts to cross this line of distinction, as Clark and Carnell did in epistemology, he can rightly be charged with destroying the doctrine of the incomprehensibility of God. At the door of this assumption of intellectual independence, however minimal it may appear to be, all the deviations from Scripture that cursed new evangelical thought throughout the decades can be laid.

AMBIVALENCE ON AUTHORITY

Authority and Reason

Some new evangelicals admit that two authorities govern theology and apologetics—the Bible and human reason. Others, not being so bold, tacitly admit the same by using the empirical process of verifying the Bible's authenticity and truth-claims in order to be certain that provisional faith was not irrationally founded. Verification presupposes some sort of independent criteria by which to test divine authority—call this logic, systematic consistency, coherence, applicability, adequacy, or whatever. But without the governance of this outside, creaturely authority, the new evangelical apologists would face the dreaded charge of circular reasoning—of proving the Bible from the Bible.

What, then, is the ultimate religious authority for them? It appears clearly to be the authority of the independent criteria, rational and/or empirical, as administered by the thinking individual, to which the Bible is subjected to determine its consistency, coherence, and truthfulness. This testing/verifying process then dictates whether the Scriptures can be affirmed or rejected by thoughtful people. If the Bible is tested by certain criteria to determine and/or verify its truthfulness, then man is the ultimate authority. In this system, one reasons from man to God. This method assumes that reason, logic, and facts are prior to and apart from God and His revelation, or again one faces the charge of circular reasoning—proving God and revelation from God and revelation. In new evangelical apologetics, the Bible has authority only because it rests on the prior approval of whatever is used to verify it.

> While the new evangelicals do not use the terms, it might be appropriate to refer to the Bible as *legislative authority*, and to reason as *the judicial authority*....While the Bible not only states what is true, but also that its content is true, one cannot utilize it as his authority in the latter sense. He must decide on the basis of the evidence whether the claimed revelation is genuine. He is forced to do so on the basis of reason, whether he wishes to or not. In actual practice, all men do this, regardless of how naively or simply it may be done.[30]

Erickson, as an evangelical theologian, wishes not to hold to the *equal strength* of these two authorities and would probably make reason subordinate to Scripture. However, the distinction between legislative and judicial authority is not relevant because two *rival* authorities—Scripture and reason—still contend for supremacy. In Erickson's apologetic methodology, Scripture is actually subordinated to reason to verify its truthfulness and authority. The Bible is thereby denied the supreme and exclusive authority it claims for itself. Two or more authorities result in no ultimate authority.

Stephen Davis, a professing evangelical who believes errors are in Scripture, also purports the necessity of more than one authority. Facing the problems of an errant Bible possessing authority, or on what authority can one accept some portions of the Bible and reject others, he concludes: "It is true that no Christian who believes that the Bible errs can hold that the Bible *alone* is his authority for faith and practice. He must hold to some other authority or criterion as well. That authority, I am not embarrassed to say, is his own mind, his own ability to reason." "Reason has a critical function to play in *all* beliefs, religious as well as non-religious. Reason must help determine what the Bible says and, ultimately, whether or not what it says is acceptable." "It is quite true that the notion of 'good reason' is imprecise and flexible. It does not constitute an infallible criterion for what is and is not to be accepted in Scripture. This much I admit."[31] Although I personally would deny to Davis the label evangelical, and would dismiss his non-inerrantist views as intellectual sophistry, the truth is that he is recognized as an evangelical, and his view of human reason as an authority is a logical extension of his non-presuppositional approach to theology and apologetics.

Bernard Ramm forthrightly stated that "we define theology as the task of setting forth the claims of our knowledge of God, the verification of these claims, and the systematic and organic connections of our theological knowledge. Theological study has, however, two foci, one in experience and one in Scripture."[32] This has the sound of equivocation, if not more, as does the title of his treatise on biblical authority—*The Pattern of Religious Authority*.[33] Authority consists of a pattern, a mosaic, or a multi-faceted grid.

> The authority of God, of Jesus Christ, of Sacred Scripture, and of truth must be properly related, as well as proper regard given for human personality and

---

[30]Erickson, *The New Evangelical Theology*, pp. 201-02.

[31]Stephen T. Davis, *The Debate About the Bible* (Philadelphia: Westminster, 1977), pp. 71, 117, 126.

[32]*The Christian View of Science and Scripture*, p. 46.

[33]Grand Rapids: Eerdmans, 1957.

freedom. The result will be a mosaic of authority, with the central piece being the principle of authority....one could even speak of a chain of authority with the principle of authority being the first and most important link.[34]

> We must be most demanding in our process of differentiating the voice of God from the voice of man....That God may have spoken is also a genuine option, and *prejudice* of no species must blind the eye of the searcher to this possibility.[35]

Thus the Bible as a word from God is a "genuine option" and a "possibility" that may be worthy of the efforts of an unprejudiced searcher. This notion in turn sets up the need for an authority other than the Bible itself. The Bible cannot be a sole authority because Ramm rejects the idea of a "sheer appeal to authority" or the "exclusive claims to authority." "Principles of religious authority founded on a bare monistic principle soon founder." He wants "to steer a wise course between subjectivism and authoritarianism."[36] But in this mixture of the Bible and human experience, the exclusive truth-claims of Scripture can never be set over against the claims of non-Christian thought. The Bible is made to share in a mosaic or chain of authority, even though it may be the centerpiece of the mosaic and the main link in the chain. Apologetics, in effect, becomes a quibble over *how much* authority the Bible is allowed to have. And in this the evangelical apologist has nothing new to say to the natural man or to anyone operating on sub-Christian, non-Christian, or pagan principles. The absolute authority the Bible claims for itself has degenerated into an interminable hassle over degrees of authority, and true biblical authority ends up bearing little or no weight.

Authority and Logic

Clark elevated logic virtually to a place of deity by understanding John 1: 1 to mean "in the beginning was logic, and logic was with God, and logic was God." Logic is eternal and ultimate; "the law of contradiction is not to be taken as an axiom prior to or independent of God. The law is God thinking."[37] Carnell, following Clark, said: "The foundation of all meaning is the law of contradiction."[38] "The only demonstration of any absolute is this: Without the presupposition of its [the law of contradiction's] existence nothing else has meaning—not even the denial of that absolute."[39] Carnell, as noted earlier, clothed logic in the terms of systematic consistency and coherence. Nash, as noted earlier, added adequacy and applicability as further refinements. In other words, each of these terms is simply another name in the nomenclature for the law of contradiction. But is this law eternal? Is it ultimate? Does it belong to the realm of the Creator or the creature?

---

[34]*The Pattern of Religious Authority*, p. 18. For an extensive analysis of this book see Van Til, "The New Evangelicalism," pp. 13-22.

[35]Ibid., p. 16.

[36]Ibid., pp. 18-19.

[37]Clark, "The Wheaton Lectures," p. 67.

[38]*The Philosophy of the Christian Religion*, p. 184.

[39]Ibid., p. 186.

To say that logic as used by humans is simply God's thinking process is to break the Creator-creature distinction that is fundamental to the Scriptures, theology, philosophy, and apologetics. In truth, logic belongs to the realm of the created; it is creaturely in essence. It is an aspect of the image of God in man which, among other things, is rational. Creaturely rationality is patterned after God's all-encompassing rationality. Since nothing exists in man exactly as it does in God and no divine attribute is truly communicable, the law of contradiction rests on the inherent order that exists in the tri-personal God. God is exhaustively and eternally self-coherent, and He has endowed His image bearers with the ability to reason coherently on the temporal level. Since God is truth and cannot lie (Ps 31:5; Heb 6:8), "logical laws are elaborations upon the fact that God does not contradict Himself."[40] "Christianity holds that God existed alone before any time existence was brought forth. He existed as the self-conscious and self-consistent being. The law of contradiction, therefore, as we know it, is but the expression on a created level of the internal coherence of God's nature."[41]

Logic is valid and necessary for communication on the creaturely level. Human language itself is univocal; it is predicated on the law of contradiction. Proposition A cannot be non-A at the same time and in the same sense. Presuppositional apologetics does not deny the validity of this universal and unchangeable law that is constitutional with human beings. The validity of the law in not in question, but its *use* is the point of debate. The law of contradiction makes no sense outside of the Christian world view and the primacy of the counsel of the self-sufficient triune God. Logic is not God but presupposes the God and Father of the self-identifying Christ of Scripture, which is the most primitive and ultimate first principle of human predication in Christian apologetics and philosophy. The Clark-Carnell proposal is presuppositional in name only; all it presupposes is some kind of a self-referential first principle. In this case it presupposes logic as an absolute to which God Himself must conform. Rather than predicating logic on the person of God, it is used to test and verify God and His truth-claims, an obliteration of the Creator-creature distinction. Van Til asks: "Why did [Carnell] not tell us that the laws of logic must rest upon the order that God has created in the world and in the mind of man?"[42] Instead, logic is elevated as a standard above God by which creatures can pronounce upon the validity of His revelation-claims in the Bible via their estimation of how He conforms to this absolute law. On the contrary, the law of contradiction is to be used to receive and understand God's verbal self-disclosure in the self-authorizing Scripture. It cannot bear the weight put on it by the new evangelical apologetic methodology. It is a God-endowed tool to appropriate divine revelation, not to test it. It is a temporal principle not to be eternalized. Van Til is correct when he traces the laws of logic back to the world view of Aristotle.

---

[40]Greg Bahnsen, *Always Ready: New Directions For Defending the Faith*, Robert R. Booth, ed. (Texarkana, AR: Covenant Media, 1996), p. 149.

[41]Van Til, *An Introduction to Systematic Theology* (Phillipsburg, NJ: Presbyterian and Reformed, 1974), p. 11.

[42]"The New Evangelicalism," p. 8.

The laws of logic as they were worked out by Aristotle presupposed this notion of metaphysical participation [in deity]. And Carnell, following Clark, starts from the law of contradiction as based upon this pagan assumption of man's essential identity with God through the idea of participation in an absolute. The God of his own Christian conviction must be tested as to the truth of the revelation that he gives to men by this absolute which is superior to him.[43]

Authority and "Testing" the Bible

If the Bible is tested by created principles of human reasoning and logic as administered by the consistent rational man, then man is the ultimate authority. Somehow the absolute law of contradiction is prior to and apart from divine revelation. New evangelical apologists vigorously deny this conclusion of course, but their methodology leaves one with no other conclusion. This methodology is inverted; the Bible is not self-authorizing but instead rests on a foundation of logic in this system. In effect this system is telling God that He cannot speak His revelation until autonomous man with his absolute of logic allows Him. When God does speak, He must speak all His mind, withholding nothing; otherwise the human tester would not have all the necessary data to make a rational choice between conflicting truth-claims. It is fairly self-evident where the true locus of authority is in this methodology. Its first requirement is that Christianity, as a system of truth-claims, accords with "reason" and makes peace with the law of contradiction. After that it must pass muster with the facts of "experience." Authority that must jump through these hoops ceases to be absolute and final.

> It is needless to say that this procedure will appear suicidal to most men who study philosophy. Is it not by the help of man's own reason that we are to think out the nature of reality and knowledge? To accept an interpretation of life upon authority is permissible only if we have looked into the foundations of the authority we accept. *But if we must determine the foundations of the authority, we no longer accept authority as authority.* Authority could be authority to us only if we already knew that it had the right to claim authority (italics added).[44]

The new evangelical dislike of "sheer authoritarianism" eventually succeeded in destroying the absolute authority of God and His demands in Scripture and replacing it with autonomous human reason. Several reasons why this methodology became so popular among the early new evangelicals are evident. For one, rational apologetics had been in Protestantism to one degree or another since the eighteenth century when Bishop Joseph Butler put a Protestant facade on Roman Catholic, Thomistic philosophy and apologetics. Butler's thinking permeated evangelicalism, even in Reformed circles, culminating in the philosophy and apologetics of old Princeton Seminary especially in the evangelical/fundamentalist coalition of the early twentieth century. Also, this methodology coincided neatly with the intellectual and academic aspirations of the new evangelical break-off in the mid-twentieth century. The desire of the young intellectuals to make evangelical Christianity respectable in the market place of ideas and world views embraced the

---

[43]Ibid.

[44]Van Til, *The Defense of the Faith*, p. 49.

methodology; believing fundamentalism could not appeal to the modern mind.[45] The young intellectuals pursued doctorates in secular universities and liberal seminaries, and felt intellectually outclassed in those settings by their peers and embarrassed by their fundamentalist, revivalist backgrounds. The intellectual pride soon manifested itself when the intellectuals gained access to the levers of power within the new evangelical movement. As Carnell lamented to Henry, "we need prestige desperately."[46]

The struggle for prestige and acceptance by non-evangelical scholarship proved to be the undoing of the new evangelical movement over the last half of the twentieth century. Slowly the dikes of orthodox theology gave way to the increasingly virulent tides of unbelief. New evangelicals slowly ceded the absolute authority of an inerrant Bible to human intellectual autonomy. The decline proceeded unchecked by the new evangelical camp until the 1980s and early 1990s.[47] Whether the belated alarm will rescue evangelicalism from the fate of every other movement that has substituted man's authority for God's remains to be seen; probably it will not.

The vacuity of evangelical theology today can rightfully be traced to the loss of biblical inerrancy. This chapter has suggested that the doctrine of inerrancy was surrendered finally because the absolute authority of the Bible was vacated and its self-authorizing claims made subject to the inductive search for free-from-God "facts" to verify the Scripture's truthfulness to the satisfaction of creaturely rational autonomy.

The work of the Christian apologist is not to remove the intellectual objections to Christianity by rational argument from a plateau of supposedly common ground. His duty is to confront every part of the thinking of the natural man with *biblical* authority, allowing the Holy Spirit to accomplish His results in the heart and mind. A truly biblical apologetic method must remove all props of self-help and every vestige of intellectual autonomy of the natural man so that his only recourse is the sovereign grace of a loving God who has revealed Himself inerrantly in the self-accrediting Bible and the self-identifying Christ of the Protestant canon.

---

[45]For example, E. M. Blaiklock, "Conservatism, Liberalism, and Neo-Orthodoxy," *Eternity* (Aug 1960), p. 23; Ronald Nash, *The New Evangelicalism* (Grand Rapids: Zondervan, 1963), pp. 22, 26.

[46]Letter to Carl F. H. Henry, reported by Henry in his *Confessions of a Theologian: An Autobiography* (Waco, TX: Word, 1986), p. 137.

[47]Two examples will suffice: Francis A. Schaeffer, *The Great Evangelical Disaster* (Westchester, IL: Crossway, 1984) and David F. Wells, *No Place For Truth* (Grand Rapids: Eerdmans, 1993).

PART 7: SOCIAL INVOLVEMENT

In the 1940s and 50s, evangelicals charged fundamentalism with having little or no social concern, as noted in chapter one, and accused fundamentalism of being merely reactionary against the social gospel of liberalism. Fundamentalism allegedly was more concerned to win souls than to deal with society's structural sins or to contribute to charity and social welfare. "A more definite recognition of social responsibility" was one of the "changes" in evangelical theology noted in the coming-out article in *Christian Life*.[1]

---

[1]"Is Evangelical Theology Changing?" *Christian Life* (Mar 1956), p. 18.

18

NEW EVANGELICAL SOCIAL ACTIVISM

After the fundamentalist-modernist controversy of the 1920s, the fundamentalists, having lost control of the ecclesiastical furniture of the major denominations, began to rebuild their infrastructure around strong leaders in pastoral, educational, missionary, publicational, evangelistic, and similar ministries. A post World War II crop of young evangelical scholars and would-be leaders within the fundamentalist/evangelical coalition, who had not personally fought the modernists in the great conflict, had grown discontent with old-line fundamentalist militancy. Fundamentalism's lack of social involvement and activism distressed the younger evangelicals.

INITIAL ACTIVISM

Carl Henry fired the opening salvo against fundamentalism's alleged societal indifference in *The Uneasy Conscience of Modern Fundamentalism*.[2] He followed a decade later with another critique, *Evangelical Responsibility in Contemporary Theology*.[3] The bimonthly publication, *Christianity Today*, with Henry as the first editor, declared itself designed to "apply the biblical revelation to the contemporary social crisis."[4] Social concern proved a relevant factor in the formation of the National Association of Evangelicals in 1942. Evangelical social concern manifested itself also by the founding of the Committee for Postwar Relief in 1945 (renamed the World Relief Commission after the Korean War), the Committee on Social Action in 1951 to coordinate evangelical welfare efforts (later renamed the Evangelical Social Action Commission),[5] and World Vision International in 1950 to promote medical missions, child care, and other social ministries in Asia.

Another early attempt to outline some guiding principles for social involvement appeared in "The Christian and Social Reform" by Samuel Hugh

---

[2]Grand Rapids: Eerdmans, 1947.

[3]Grand Rapids: Eerdmans, 1957.

[4]Carl F. H. Henry, "Why 'Christianity Today'?" *Christianity Today* (Oct 15, 1956), p. 20.

[5]Bruce Shelley, *Evangelicalism in America* (Grand Rapids: Eerdmans, 1967), pp. 104-09. A brief history of the Committee on Social Action is given by Richard Pierard, "NAE's Social Awareness Grows," *Christianity Today* (Apr 9, 1982), p. 42.

Moffett.[6] He traced the social sensitivities of God's people beginning with the "social gospel in the Old Testament," citing the Mosaic Law on land tenure and the prophecies of Amos against the land barons. He also saw a "social gospel of Christ" based on the Lord's ministry of healing broken bodies and feeding the multitudes. From there he moved to the "charity of the early church" as seen in the commonality of the early church in Jerusalem. He then dealt with "justice in the growing church," predicated principally on Tertullian's dictum, "The only limit to Christian charity is the need of the people," which Moffett suggests was the basis of the Communist Manifesto's creed, "From each according to his ability, to each according to his need."[7] He carried his overview up to Emperor Constantine whose Christian social contributions he found ambivalent. The article concluded with some broad principles under the heading "toward the solution."

A common new evangelical response to previous fundamentalist social indifference included public confession of past disinterest and a new commitment to address the plight of fellow human beings. Public statements tended to raise the social consciousness of the evangelical movement and build momentum for some kind of an agenda for action. Even Billy Graham participated: "My belief in the social implications of the gospel has deepened and broadened," he said.[8] Elsewhere he noted concerning his early ministry: "I didn't relate my message sufficiently to social concerns and everyday life."[9] Daniel Fuller related an anecdote concerning his parents, Dr. and Mrs. Charles E. Fuller. Influenced by the fundamentalist movement, the Fullers "felt that the church should simply preach the Gospel and leave to other organizations the task of caring for people's physical needs." He reported that his mother later regretted this idea.[10] John R. W. Stott could report that "evangelical Christians are now repenting of the former pietism which tended to keep us insulated from the secular world, and are now accepting that we have a social as well as an evangelistic responsibility."[11]

These modest new evangelical beginnings accrued larger proportions in the 1960s, saw a flowering in the 1970s, and kept on growing in the 1980s, 90s, and early 2000s.

BUDDING ACTIVISM (1960s)

New evangelical social activism acquired fresh impetus in the mid 1960s, soliciting fears from fundamentalists that it was displaying some of the earmarks of the old social gospel of liberalism. David O. Moberg, a sociology professor at Bethel College, St. Paul, in 1965 wrote *Inasmuch*, a volume setting forth an agenda

---

[6]Samuel Hugh Moffett, "The Christian and Social Reform," *His* (December 1950), pp. 10-13, 15, 24-25. This was an address to a China Inland Mission personnel meeting in Shanghai. Moffett was trained at Wheaton College, Princeton Seminary, and Yale University. At the time he was teaching in a seminary in Nanking, China, under the Presbyterian Board of Foreign Missions (USA.).

[7]Ibid., p. 13.

[8]Billy Graham, "What Ten Years Have Taught Me," *The Christian Century* (Feb 17, 1960), p. 188.

[9]John Pollock, *Billy Graham—The Authorized Biography* (Grand Rapids: Zondervan, 1966), p. 21. See also p. 146.

[10]Daniel P. Fuller, *Give the Winds A Mighty Voice: The Story of Charles E. Fuller* (Waco, TX: Word, 1972), pp. 50-51.

[11]John R. W. Stott, *Christian Mission in the Modern World* (Downers Grove, IL: InterVarsity, 1975), p. 31.

for evangelical social involvement.[12] Moberg reiterated a rather common argument of the old fundamentalist/evangelical coalition regarding social involvement, namely that social improvement can be a tool of "pre-evangelism:"

> Social service is one form of evangelism. Welfare activities demonstrate love. They help prepare people to listen to the gospel by removing the barriers of problems that hinder them from hearing its proclamation.[13]

William Booth, founder of the Salvation Army in London in 1865, had originally employed the argument to give biblical legitimacy to the social activism of his new organization. His motto of "soup, soap, and salvation" became the rallying cry of the Army.[14] In time not only rescue mission work in large cities' slums but missions abroad in foreign fields adopted the policy of establishing clinics, hospitals, various forms of relief work, and other social benevolence in order to forge an opportunity for presenting the gospel.

The Association of Baptists for World Evangelism (ABWE) and many other fundamentalist or fringe fundamentalist missions organizations, adopted Booth's rationale of social ministry. The policy of ABWE is an example.

> Medical work has proved to be an effective means of gaining a hearing for the message of soul-salvation within an environment of love and concern. Accordingly, medico-evangelistic work is a valuable method in certain areas of the world. The policy of the ABWE is that spiritual healing is of definitely greater value than the physical healing and should receive the major emphasis. Hospital and clinic facilities shall be adequate for quality medical care, but compatible with the principle of evangelism and possible national administration.[15]

Donn Ketcham, a medical doctor with ABWE, coupled medical work with spiritual evangelism based on understanding Jesus' feeding of the 5000 "as an example of the use of a physical need as an opportunity to meet their spiritual, i.e., using the satisfaction of the physical needs as the modality by which He approached the spiritual need."[16] Summing up, he stated that "there is nothing wrong with the Christian and the church meeting the needs of society if the meeting of those needs clearly serves to facilitate the ability of the church to meet the spiritual needs of mankind," adding that "the church may include the first mandate [the cultural/ social mandate of Genesis 1:28] in its order of business if it is clearly a means to the end of preaching the gospel."[17]

Other prominent evangelicals passionately echoed the rising sentiments:

> An emphasis on the spiritual mission of the church should not blind us to the fact that social reforms must sometimes precede the preaching of the gospel....Jesus

---

[12]Grand Rapids: Eerdmans, 1965.

[13]Ibid., pp. 50-51.

[14]Quoted by Donald G. Bloesch, *The Evangelical Renaissance* (Grand Rapids: Eerdmans, 1973), p. 73.

[15]Harold Amstutz, in the forward to "The World Hurts: A Biblical Approach to Social Action," *ABWE Insight Series* 1 (1981), p. 5.

[16]Donn W. Ketcham, The World Hurts," p. 28.

[17]Ibid., p. 40.

fed the hungry so that people might perceive their spiritual hunger (John 6)....The great commission has theological priority over social service and political action but not always chronological priority.[18]

It can be said that social service is a fruit and evidence of our faith and also a preparation for the proclamation of the faith....The pre-evangelism of works of mercy is often just as important as evangelism proper in bringing men into the kingdom of God.[19]

Even though Christian social action is not oriented toward evangelism as its primary goal, yet it is part of the total task assigned by Christ. In performing that task, Christians will plant and water seeds that will yield a spiritual increase given by God (see I Cor. 3: 5-11). Social reform and social welfare are aspects of proclaiming the gospel.[20]

Social service thus becomes both the evidence of one's faith and a preparation for the proclamation of the gospel. The pre-evangelism works of mercy may be just as important as preaching itself in bringing people into the kingdom of God.[21]

Henry in 1965 set forth "four controlling convictions" to govern evangelical interaction with the social problems of the day.[22] He placed the new birth as the dynamic for social transformation, declared that the institutional church has no specific social mandate, that the church's impetus is through pulpit proclamation, and placed the responsibility for social justice and order on Christians as citizens of the civil government. He placed the mission of moral redemption on believers as members of Christ's church. Following Henry's counsel, later that same year evangelicals launched the periodical *The Other Side* as a mouthpiece for evangelical social concerns.

The *Christian Century* gave Billy Graham "two cheers" for his support of the social gospel. Quoting from a paper Graham distributed to members of the Central Committee of the World Council of Churches, the magazine reported: "There is no doubt that the social gospel has directed its energies toward the release of many of the problems of suffering humanity. I am for it! I believe it is biblical."[23] Henry devoted a chapter to the evangelicals and the social crisis in *Evangelicals At the Brink of Crisis*. He again stated that the institutional church's business is the proclamation of the word of God and not direct engagement in politics. He said, "It is not the task of the institutional Church to promote legislation, but it is the duty of Christians to advocate and support good laws and to lead the way in obeying them."[24]

---

[18]Donald G. Bloesch, *The Evangelical Renaissance*, p. 42.

[19]Ibid., p. 73.

[20]Ronald J. Sider, "Evangelism or Social Justice: Eliminating the Options," *Christianity Today* (Oct 8, 1976), p. 29.

[21]*Evangelical Dictionary of Theology*, s.v. "Evangelicalism" by R. V. Pierard, p. 380.

[22]Carl F. H. Henry, "Evangelicals In the Social Struggle," *Christianity Today* (Oct 8, 1965), p. 11.

[23]"Here and There," *The Christian Century* (Sept 27, 1967), p. 1213.

[24]Carl F. H. Henry, *Evangelicals At the Brink of Crisis: Significance of the World Congress on Evangelism* (Waco, TX: Word, 1967), p. 71.

In 1968 Sherwood Wirt, editor of the Billy Graham Evangelistic Association's *Decision* magazine, wrote *The Social Conscience of the Evangelical*.[25] That same year, Wheaton College professor, Millard Erickson, produced a sympathetic theological assessment of the new evangelicalism entitled *The New Evangelical Theology*.[26] He criticized fundamentalism for seeing sin only in its individualistic and not also its corporate dimension, for being an overreaction against liberalism, and for its futuristic, eschatological "kingdom then" doctrine to the neglect of a "kingdom now" with its social incumbencies.[27] He argued that some of Jesus' "benevolent miracles" were done primarily to relieve human suffering.[28]

Rufus Jones, general director of the Conservative Baptist Home Mission Society, tacitly approved of the 1967 burnings in Detroit and Watts by noting: "If we knew the poor better, we would understand that it [i.e., burning down their city] is the only way they can call attention to the hopelessness of their situation that worsens as the rest of society becomes more affluent."[29] He echoed a common refrain of the time that evangelicals should model Jesus Christ who was anointed to preach to the poor and liberate the bruised (Luke 4:18), and follow the example of the Old Testament prophets who announced judgment on those in Israel who oppressed the poor (Jer 22:13-16; Amos 5:11, 12; et al.).[30]

BLOOMING ACTIVISM (1970s)

The 1970s witnessed an outburst of new evangelical social activism, and the rhetoric and calls to action increased significantly. James Davison Hunter lists no fewer than twenty-eight books among the burgeoning evangelical literature on the subject during the decade.[31] Hunter also relayed a quotation from Billy Melvin, president of the NAE, that "social ministry in Evangelicalism and for the NAE came into its own in the early 1970s."[32] Robert Linder observed in 1975 that "a marked change of attitude on the part of millions of evangelical Christians in America toward social issues is under way."[33] Of interest is Hunter's evaluation that the 1970s enthusiasm for social justice was more on the "ideological level" than in actual practice[34] since it was "not entirely clear whether there was, in practice, any appreciable diminution of social ministry in conservative denominations after the Fundamentalist reaction."[35] Furthermore, he concluded:

---

[25]New York: Harper and Row, 1968.

[26]Westwood, NJ: Revell, 1968. Already in 1963 Ronald Nash, an evangelical philosopher by training and profession, had written *The New Evangelicalism* (Grand Rapids: Zondervan), a partisan apologetic for the movement. While useful in many respects, the work suffered from a complete lack of biblical and theological depth, and had nothing to say about the social motif of the movement.

[27]Erickson, *The New Evangelical Theology*, pp. 178-82.

[28]Ibid., p. 184.

[29]Rufus Jones, "Face Up to Poverty," *Eternity* (Jan 1969), p. 10.

[30]Ibid., p. 12.

[31]James Davison Hunter, *Evangelicalism: The Coming Generation* (Chicago: University of Chicago Press, 1987), pp. 256-57.

[32]Ibid., p. 42.

[33]Robert D. Linder, "The Resurgence of Evangelical Social Concern (1925-75)," in *The Evangelicals: What They Believe, Who They Are, Where They are Going,* David F. Wells and John D. Woodbridge, eds. (Nashville: Abingdon, 1975), p. 189.

[34]*Evangelicalism: The Coming Generation*, p. 42.

[35]Ibid., p. 41.

Social service initiatives such as rescue missions for drunkards and the disreputable urban poor, orphanages, homes for "fallen women," relief programs for immigrants and the needy (which included providing lodging and food as well as finding jobs for these people), and medical missions *were commonplace within nineteenth- and twentieth-century Evangelicalism* (italics added).[36]

As an evangelical sociologist, Hunter's analysis casts doubt on the somewhat oft-repeated charges of Fundamentalist social insensitivity.[37]

The magazine, *The Post American*, founded in 1971 by Jim Wallis attempted to raise the social consciousness of evangelicals and to address various cultural issues and problems. The periodical's name later changed to *Sojourners*. Wallis' magazine catered to Marxism, socialism, economic liberalism, and other radical 1960s enthusiasms.[38] In the 1972 USA presidential election, the Evangelicals for McGovern committee formed. McGovern campaigned on left-wing religious and political ideologies, notably those of the anti-Vietnam war protest. The committee aimed to "demolish the 'conservative-theology-equals-conservative-politics' stereotype."[39] Meanwhile Henry continued his call for evangelical participation in social initiatives with his more moderate approach of emphasizing the preaching of truth and righteousness. He, as before, regarded the liberal left and fundamentalist right as examples of social extremism. He was convinced that the next generation of young people would march for social justice and would do so under an "alien" banner if the evangelicals failed to attract them with biblical principles to combat "intractable social injustices."[40]

The Chicago Declaration

Evangelicals took a major step in social activism in 1973 when fifty evangelicals met in Chicago for a Thanksgiving Workshop. Out of that gathering emerged "A Declaration of Evangelical Social Concern," a nearly 500-word

---

[36]Ibid., p. 40.

[37]The charge of fundamentalist social indifference had long before been challenged by W. B. Riley, for forty-five years pastor of the First Baptist Church in downtown Minneapolis. In one of the last articles he wrote before his death, he bluntly refuted the charge by saying, "I grow weary when my brethren, who profess fundamentalism, concede that there is a social service on the part of modernists unknown to those of better faith. Such claims are chimerical....I have been in the ministry for sixty-four successive years. In that entire time I have never known the modernists of any of the cities in which I served, to accomplish any great social service....I have been in Minneapolis for fifty years. In that time I have fought the battles against crooked mayors, criminal conditions, illegal liquor, and for righteous elections. Again and again my brethren who believed the Word of God came with me to the battle; but in this entire time I have never known the combined endeavors of the modernist theologians to accomplish aught of social service....The social gospelers know little of social aid or social improvement" ("Critics in the Fundamentalist Family," *The Pilot* [Aug 1947], p. 344).

[38]Evangelicals Ronald Nash, Harold Lindsell, and Richard Quebedeaux tied *Sojourners* to Marxist ideology. A Wallis sympathizer, Boyd Reese, answered the charge by verbally finessing *Sojourners'* economic position, concluding that "the magazine integrates a sophisticated theological position with a carefully articulated non-Marxist political radicalism" ("Is *Sojourners* Marxist? An Analysis of Recent Charges," *TSF Bulletin* [Nov-Dec 1984], p. 16).

[39]Barrie Doyle, "Backing Their Man," *Christianity Today* (Oct 27, 1972), pp. 38-39. Prominent evangelicals on the committee were, among others, Tom Skinner, Ronald Sider, Lewis Smedes, David Moberg, Robert Webber, Richard Pierard, Stephen Monsma, and Anthony Campolo.

[40]Carl F. H. Henry, "The Tension Between Evangelism and the Christian Demand for Social Justice," *Fides et Historia* 2 (1972), pp. 8-9.

social-action statement commenting on the rights of the poor and oppressed, the injustice of international trade, world hunger, the need for both love and justice, and other such concerns. One of the more salient points read: "We must attack the materialism of our culture and the maldistribution of the nation's wealth and services." Prominent new evangelical signers were Henry, Samuel Escobar, Bernard Ramm, and Joe Bayly.[41]

The formation of the Evangelical Women's Caucus International in 1974 stemmed from the Chicago declaration's statement on women: "We acknowledge that we have encouraged men to prideful domination and women to irresponsible passivity. So we call both men and women to mutual submission and active discipleship."[42] The first national conference of the women's Caucus in 1975 seemed to turn the "mutual submission" language of the Declaration into the "full equality" of the sexes of the feminist nomenclature. Lucille Sider Dayton claimed Jonathan Blanchard (founder of Wheaton College), A. B. Simpson (founder of the Christian and Missionary Alliance), A. J. Gordon (founder of Gordon College), and evangelist Charles G. Finney as early evangelical leaders who advocated the full equality of the sexes.[43] Indeed, the leaders of the Caucus were not averse to the term "biblical feminism" to describe themselves. Virginia Mollenkott called for the "deabsolutizing of the biblical culture" which was simply the "sinful social order" of the first century into which the gospel came, that was divinely intended to be revolutionized by the gospel message.[44] She further contended that Paul was "a man of God in process," evolving out of his sexist rabbinical training on the subordination of women to his apparently mature Christian view of the equality of women reflected in Galatians 3:28.[45] The Caucus reaffirmed its support for the Equal Rights Amendment pending before the American people, and affirmed "solidarity with women attending the Catholic Women's Ordination Conference in Detroit the same weekend."[46] No less an evangelical leader than Rufus Jones, head of the Conservative Baptist Home Mission Society, testified at an "emotion-packed final worship service" that, after a struggle with a biblical passage presumably on the feminism question, "yesterday a Priscilla came and expounded to me the way of God more perfectly."[47]

Later, in 1986, a division arose within the Evangelical Women's Caucus International over several resolutions in favor of homosexual rights. These resolutions were pushed by Nancy Hardesty and Virginia Mollenkott, drawn up "in recognition of the presence of the lesbian minority in EWCI."[48]

[41]"Evangelicals on Justice Socially Speaking..." *Christianity Today* (Dec 21, 1973), pp. 38-39.

[42]Ibid., p. 38.

[43]Letha Scanzoni, "Evangelical Women and 'Biblical Feminism,'" *The Christian Century* (Dec 24, 1975), p. 1173.

[44]Ibid.

[45]Ibid.

[46]Ibid., p. 1174.

[47]Carol Prester McFadden, "'We're on Our Way, Lord!'" *Christianity Today* (Jan 19, 1975), p. 37.

[48]*Christianity Today* (Oct 3, 1986), p. 40.

The International Congress of World Evangelism

Probably the greatest impetus to social activism in the 1970s came at the 1974 International Congress on World Evangelism (ICOWE) at Lausanne, Switzerland. The Lausanne Covenant that came out of the International Congress strongly insisted on evangelical social involvement, reflecting principally the ideas and efforts of John R. W. Stott, rector of All Souls Church, London. Arthur Johnston wrote a significant volume documenting the rise of the social gospel in the missionary movement and its infiltration of evangelical missionary philosophy and activity culminating in Lausanne and in the subsequent influence of its Continuing Committee.[49] He considers Lausanne the turning point for evangelical missions and evangelism where the social gospel of the World Council of Churches (euphemistically called "the larger evangelism" or "holistic evangelism" by the social pushers) synchronized with traditional evangelical missionary philosophy to include sociopolitical action.[50]

The Student Volunteer Movement

Johnston demonstrates how liberalism's social gospel captured the missionary agendas of denominations and agencies beginning with the Edinburgh World Missionary Conference (1910), a gathering with a thin veneer of evangelicalism. The conference leadership consisted of members of the aggressive but theologically immature Student Volunteer Movement (SVM), an organization of evangelical students for foreign missions begun in 1886 under the direction of D. L. Moody and organized in 1888 with John R. Mott, president, and Robert Speer, traveling secretary. In less than three decades the Movement had fallen prey to the social gospel, mainly because of the theological ineptness of its student leadership and their ecumenical spirit that minimized Bible doctrine[51] and because of Arminian theology and the "synergistic principles of Methodism."[52] The SVM went downhill after 1920, becoming irrelevant as a missionary influence among churches by 1940. In 1959 it merged with the United Student Christian Council and in 1966 allied with the Roman Catholic National Newman Student Federation to form the University Christian Movement.[53]

David Howard gives ten factors that precipitated the decline and eventual collapse of the SVM, one of which was that "they shifted away from Bible study, evangelism, lifework decision, and foreign-mission obligation, on which the SVM had originally built. Instead they now emphasized new issues such as race relations, economic injustice, and imperialism."[54] Out of Edinburgh 1910 came the International Missionary Council that eventually merged with the World Council of Churches in 1961 at New Delhi, India. The union with the World Council finished the

---

[49]Arthur P. Johnston, *The Battle For World Evangelism* (Wheaton: Tyndale, 1978).

[50]Ibid., p. 40.

[51]Ibid., pp. 33, 36.

[52]Ibid., p. 37.

[53]David M. Howard, "The Rise and Fall of SVM," *Christianity Today* (Nov 6, 1970), pp. 15-17.

[54]Ibid., p. 16.

complete social gospel take-over of formerly-evangelical Protestant denominational and interdenominational missions originally spearheaded by the SVM.

The Berlin World Congress on Evangelism (1966)

Liberal social gospel mission work and evangelical missionary activity had been going their separate ways for several decades until a series of events led to a synthesis of the two philosophies at the International Congress on World Evangelism at Lausanne in 1974, chiefly through the labors of Anglican evangelical John R. W. Stott.

The stage-setting for Lausanne began with the 1966 Berlin World Congress on Evangelism, an evangelical alternative to the expanding influence of the liberal social gospel (noted as recently as 1961 when the International Missionary Council became part of the World Council of Churches).[55] Berlin 1966 held to the primacy of proclamation evangelism, but a *sub rosa* element wanted a much wider berth for social activism. Thus Berlin left some unfinished business because "the relationship of social action and social concern to evangelism required greater theological expression and application than it received....Berlin did not establish the theological basis for social action, even though it stood firm on proclamation evangelism as *the* mission of the Church."[56] As a result, a series of four regional evangelical congresses on evangelism, met, each of which incorporated measures to include social activism as part of the church's overall mission: Singapore (1968), Minneapolis (1969), Bogata (1969), and Amsterdam (1971). At Lausanne these measures were brought together to effectively bridge the gap or forge a synthesis between the social gospel of the World Council of Churches and the old evangelical idea of biblical missions. The Bogata congress was especially influential. At that conclave Canadian Samuel Escobar boldly declared that evangelical evangelism and social activism both were the responsibility of the church, although the official declaration of the Congress stopped short of specifically incorporating social work as part of the church's mission.[57]

The Lausanne Covenant

The International Congress on World Evangelism at Lausanne, Switzerland, funded heavily by the Billy Graham Evangelistic Association, was a ten-day conference that drew some 3,700 representatives together to consider the evangelization of the world by the year 2000. The representatives framed a Covenant to express the consensus of the assembly on a number of topics related to evangelism. Of special interest are the Covenant's pronouncements on social activism and even more relevant, the position of John Stott and his influence toward the incorporation of social justice as a "partner" of evangelism in the church's mandate or "mission."

The social gospel of liberal ecumenical missionary work changed the nomenclature of evangelism from "missions" to simply "mission." This verbal sleight of hand was introduced by the International Missionary Council of the

---

[55] Arthur Johnston, *The Battle For World Evangelism*, pp. 141-54.

[56] Ibid., p. 221.

[57] Ibid., pp. 255-57.

World Council of Churches to broaden the concept of the church's duty in the world, and to incorporate social activism into the traditional evangelical concept of evangelism and missions. To the churchmen of the World Council the new term carried an intended philosophical/theological change from the old thought of the church *in* the world to an identification of the church *with* the world community itself—humanity—as the redeemed body of Christ. The revolutionary emendation hinted at universalism, which evangelicals rejected, but to the liberal ecumenists it not only expressed their views on soteriology, it defined ecclesial labors solely in terms of recognizing and relieving society's perceived structural injustices instead of seeking individual conversions to Christ. "Service," i.e., social involvement in a world cosmically redeemed, became the "missional" imperative. The new evangelicals did not want service in that sense to be interchangeable with evangelism, but desired that social activity should "partner" evangelism. A tracing of "mission" in Johnston's index[58] reveals an interesting etiology of the term and its subsequent bearing on the "incarnational" vis-a-vis the "proclamational" distinction in philosophy of ministry in evangelical thought.

The Lausanne Covenant had several references to social activism but still maintained that "evangelism itself is the proclamation of the historical, biblical Christ as Saviour and Lord, with a view to persuading people to come to him personally and so be reconciled to God."[59] Nevertheless, the Covenant did "express penitence...for having sometimes regarded evangelism and social concern as mutually exclusive."[60] After having disclaimed social action as evangelism or political liberation as salvation, the covenant affirmed that evangelism and sociopolitical involvement are both part of Christian "duty" in the sense of Christian service or works that are evidence of faith.[61] The formal words of the Covenant do not convey the depth of the social gospel's penetration into the thinking of those who were at the congress, notably the thought of John R. W. Stott.

John R. W. Stott

Stott knew of the intent to expand the definition of "mission" by the social gospel ecumenists, but saw "no reason why we should resist this development,"[62] even though the new language grew out of the teaching that the church is the incarnational presence of God in Christ in a cosmically redeemed world. The "incarnational" idea must have caught Stott's eye because it became the centerpiece of his philosophy of evangelism that contained equal spiritual and social concerns. He synthesized the World Council's social gospel with old fundamentalism's biblicism to form a hybrid evangelical notion of mission. Stott appealed to Jesus' words in John 20: 21 ("as the Father has sent Me, I also send you") as setting forth both the command for the church's mission and the example of Christ Himself for doing it.

---

[58]Ibid., p. 414.

[59]"The Lausanne Covenant," as printed in *Christianity Today* (Aug 16, 1974), pp. 23-24.

[60]Ibid., p. 23.

[61]Ibid.

[62]"The Biblical Basis of Evangelism," in *Let the Earth Hear His Voice*, J. D. Douglas, ed. (Minneapolis: World Wide Publications, 1975), p. 66.

Stott acknowledged the evolution in his thinking on this subject. Previously he had believed that social responsibility was an outcome of new life in Christ, an errand taught to new converts from the repository of Jesus' teachings. Stott used to believe that the mission of the church was proclamation of the gospel. However, he changed his mind:

> The cumulative emphasis [of the biblical material] seems clear. It is placed on preaching, witnessing and making disciples, and many deduce from this that the mission of the church, according to the specification of the risen Lord, is exclusively a preaching, converting and teaching mission. Indeed, I confess that I myself argued this at the World Congress on Evangelism in Berlin in 1966, when attempting to expound the three major versions of the Great Commission. Today, however, I would express myself differently. It is not just that the commission includes a duty to teach converts everything Jesus had previously commanded (Matthew 28:20), and that social responsibility is among the things which Jesus commanded. I now see more clearly that not only the consequences of the commission but *the actual commission itself* must be understood to include social as well as evangelistic responsibility, unless we are to be guilty of distorting the words of Jesus (italics added).[63]

Elevating the social agenda to equal status with proclaiming the gospel meant, "that social action is a *partner of evangelism*. As partners the two belong to each other. Each stands on its own feet in its own right alongside the other. Neither is a means to the other, or even a manifestation of the other. For each is an end in itself. Both are expressions of unfeigned love (italics his)."[64]

Stott was searching for some kind of middle ground, a synthesis between evangelism that excluded social work and social activism as a substitute for evangelism. He concluded that three possible solutions existed. First, social action is a means to evangelism. Stott rejected social action in a complementary role with evangelism, viewing it as philanthropy with the "smell of hypocrisy," being simply "the sugar on the pill, the bait on the hook, while in its best form it gives to the gospel a credibility it would otherwise lack." The second possibility considers social action to be a manifestation of evangelism. Stott valued the second view, but it left him uneasy because it made "service a subdivision of evangelism, an aspect of proclamation." He also thought it compromised the integrity of Christian service born of unfeigned love because it still was only a means to an end. "If good works are visible preaching, then they are expecting a return; but if good works are visible loving, then they are 'expecting nothing in return' (Luke 6:35)." The third possibility viewed social action as a partner of evangelism, the position Stott affirmed.[65]

On the surface, it would appear that Stott's "partnering" and the "co-equality" of evangelism and social action are mutually exclusive. If each stands in its own right and neither is a means to the other nor a manifestation of the other, then what is the real relationship? If each is an end in itself, parity may be possible, but genuine partnering is not. Stott's definition of partnering is self-eliminating.

---

[63]John R. W. Stott, *Christian Mission in the Modern World*, p. 23.

[64]Ibid., p. 27.

[65]Ibid., pp. 26-27.

A radical social gospel minority at Lausanne saw sin "as provoked by sinful social structures, rather than by the response of man's sinful nature inherited from Adam."[66] The influence of Lausanne extended beyond 1974 through the efforts of the Continuing Committee to set up other conferences and meetings around the world to interpret and implement the 1974 Covenant. The later gatherings established formal contacts with the Roman Catholic Church and the World Council of Churches, expanding the role of social involvement in evangelical world evangelization and worsening biblical missions and outreach.

The Young Evangelicals

Lausanne 74 proved to be a watershed in social ideology for the new evangelicalism, but *The Young Evangelicals*,[67] a left-leaning work published the same year, engineered the most immediate short-term impact for the social ideologies. According to the cover, the book comprises "the story of the emergence of a new generation of Evangelicals" who feel destined to "one day assume leadership and eventually command the support of the majority [of evangelicals]" and whose "positive action...now will most likely decide the Evangelical posture as a whole in years to come."[68] The second generation evangelicals, emanated from the teachers and ideas of the first generation (or new evangelicals) on the scene since the 1940s. Fundamentalists had suspected and warned that the second generation of new evangelicals would deviate farther in doctrine and practice than the first generation. The ominous projections proved prophetic, yet the projections also fell short. The young evangelicals not only had compounded the errors of their forebears, they had come to hold them in contempt for their "conservative" notions. The accoutrements of the young evangelicals in the book are revolution, rebel, prophetic, young, free, dynamic, new, the people, and other notes consistent with the theological and political liberal-left.

In the matter of evangelism, the young evangelicals' motto, "Reaching the Whole Person," simply reiterated the social gospel of old liberalism baptized into more evangelical surroundings and nomenclature. By the evangelizing of the "whole person," the book meant reaching not only one's spiritual needs but "his life in corporate society, his relationship with other men and women and the social structures they create for themselves."[69] "Positive social concern and action are as much a part of the Gospel as personal salvation—they are reverse sides of the same coin."[70] This was the revolutionary portion of their social philosophy—maintaining the *equal* necessity of ministering to the body as well as the soul (reminiscent of John Stott's synthesis). Interestingly, the evangelism process does not necessarily begin with the soul before the body. Young evangelicals challenged the concept that a changed society needs changed individuals.[71] "New persons have *not*

---

[66]Johnston, *The Battle For World Evangelism*, p. 330.

[67]Richard Quebedeaux, *The Young Evangelicals* (New York: Harper and Row, 1974).

[68]Ibid., pp. 140-41.

[69]Ibid., p. 81.

[70]Ibid., p. 99.

[71]Ibid., pp. 14, 36, 81, 99.

inevitably produced a new society (italics his),"[72] so the traditional evangelical approach must be abandoned.

The implementation of the young evangelical social gospel, according to Quebedeaux, carried certain assumptions, one of which was that political liberalism with its mandate of social legislation financed by higher taxes articulated the only political stance compatible with the gospel.[73] Another assumption denigrated capitalism (the private ownership of the means and distribution of wealth), contending it was based on inherently selfish principles.[74]

To the young evangelicals depicted in the book, Leighton Ford, the evangelist to whom they looked for inspiration and accomplishment, embodied the dual form of evangelism. Billy Graham did not even meet their social-minded criteria. Among student groups, Inter-Varsity Christian Fellowship found favor and Campus Crusade for Christ met rejection from the young evangelicals. A new student organization, the Christian World Liberation Front, adopted the life style of the counterculture of the time, and exemplified the spirit of the young evangelical evangelism.[75]

The nature of the evangelical social gospel found expression in several areas. One popular issue proved to be sex. The young evangelicals relied on Bruce Larson to guide their search for "an authentic Christian sex ethic appropriate for the time,"[76] and studiously avoided the absolute Bible ethic applicable to all times. The ethic of these evangelicals declared that "masturbation can be the way God has given for easing what seems like intolerable tension;" that only an "implicit" case can be made for premarital chastity; that extramarital sex is more offensive to God than premarital sex; and that homosexuality is not to be condemned outright. They made a serious attempt "to find biblical justification for homosexual life and practice."[77]

Another area of social evangelism included the "politics of conscience," embracing the views of the political left as embodied in the thinking of Senator Mark Hatfield of Oregon;[78] racial justice as worked out by evangelist Tom Skinner;[79] egalitarian personal and social man-woman relationships;[80] and concern for poverty and the environment.[81] Another component dealt with personal conduct and enjoyment, which amounted to a crusade against the old fundamentalist/ evangelical taboos against drinking alcoholic beverages, smoking, card playing, social dancing, rock music, long hair, and movie attendance.[82]

---

[72]Ibid., p. 81.

[73]Ibid., pp. 81, 100, 115, 125.

[74]Ibid., p. 125.

[75]Ibid., pp. 86-98.

[76]Ibid., p. 104.

[77]Ibid., pp. 102-109.

[78]Ibid., 118-23.

[79]Ibid., pp.115-18.

[80]Ibid., pp. 109-14.

[81]Ibid., pp. 124-29.

[82]Ibid., pp. 129-34.

Quebedeaux's book represented a minority opinion within new evangelicalism and drew mixed reactions. Ramm, calling the group "Green Grass Evangelicals," took a positive stance toward them in general.[83] Henry, while offering some praise, took a fairly hard line against them, chastising them for failure to comprehend the real dynamics and blind optimism of their Marxist solutions. He admonished them for being unduly, if not ignorantly, harsh on "establishment evangelicals," by which he meant the original "new" evangelicals such as Henry himself, for their alleged failures.[84] Harold Lindsell, then editor of *Christianity Today*, wrote an irenic, fatherly response to the young evangelicals pointing out the unbiblical, Marxist flavor of their ideals, among other things.[85] *Newsweek* magazine reported the appearance of *The Young Evangelicals*, preceded by this note: "Moving Left: A shift to liberal—and even radical—politics has been building for several years among the 40 million theologically conservative evangelical Protestants in the United States," and cited the Evangelicals for McGovern Committee, the Chicago Declaration of Evangelical Social Concerns, and the activities of Billy Graham, Mark Hatfield, Leighton Ford, Jim Wallis, and others.[86]

Rich Christians

In 1977 Ronald S. Sider wrote *Rich Christians In an Age of Hunger* predicating social activism based on three epochs of revelation history. The first epoch occurred around the exodus of Israel from Egypt, a divinely planned event to free the Jewish slaves and end their physical suffering (Exodus 3:7-8).[87] The second epoch spanned the destruction and captivity of Old Testament Israel. When Israel oppressed, she went into destruction; when Israel was oppressed, it led to her freedom.[88] The third epoch covered the incarnation of Jesus of Nazareth, the God-man and His mission to free the oppressed and heal the blind (Luke 4:18-19).[89]

Sider supplies numerous Old Testament citations to show that God aids the poor and disadvantaged and casts down the wealthy and powerful because they gained their wealth by oppression and failed to feed the hungry.[90] He was curiously enamored with the Old Testament Sabbatical and Jubilee Years, and offered some suggestions as to how portions of the Law of Moses could be implemented today, at least principally, to alleviate poverty and hunger.[91] He implied strongly that

---

[83]Bernard Ramm, "Welcome 'Green Grass' Evangelicals," *Eternity* (Mar 1974), p. 13.

[84]Carl F. H. Henry, "Revolt on Evangelical Frontiers," *Christianity Today* (Apr 26, 1974), pp. 4-7. Jim Wallis, editor of *The Post-American*, gave a three-point reply to Henry (*Christianity Today*, June 21, 1974, pp. 20-21).

[85]Harold Lindsell, "Think On These Things: Advice to Young Evangelicals," *Moody Monthly* (Oct 1975), pp.117-21. This article was originally published by *The Other Side* (Apr 1975). See Ernest D. Pickering, *The Fruit of Compromise: The New and Young Evangelicals* (Schaumburg, IL: Regular Baptist Press, 1980) and my review article, "Second Generation New Evangelicals," *Central Bible Quarterly* (Winter 1974), for analyses of the Young Evangelicals from the fundamentalist perspective.

[86]"The New Evangelicals," *Newsweek* (May 6, 1974), p. 86.

[87]Downers Grove, IL: InterVarsity, 1977, p. 60.

[88]Ibid., p. 61.

[89]Ibid., p. 66.

[90]Ibid., p. 73.

[91]Ibid., pp. 88-94.

those who do not give to the poor are guilty of covetousness and should be church disciplined according to 1 Corinthians 5:21. Christians needing discipline are those "who demand an ever-higher standard of living while a billion hungry neighbors starve."[92] The author drew on eschatology by noting that the biblical picture of the coming kingdom age "suggests the kind of a social order God wills."[93]

Sider proffers ideas to deal with world hunger, such as the USA having a foreign policy that sides with the poor,[94] the correction of tariff barriers on international trade,[95] and the adoption of a new food policy based on the projection that by 1985 not enough grain would be available so 400 to 600 million people would be without it. Sider's scenario leads to a global conflict with North America having to decide who receives the scarce food.[96]

The Moral Majority

Another significant evangelical phenomenon began with the rise of the Moral Majority under Jerry Falwell (1979). Falwell, pastor of the Thomas Road Baptist Church and president of the Liberty Baptist College and Seminary, Lynchburg, VA, began the organization with the collaboration of influential pastors James Kennedy, Charles Stanley, Tim LaHaye, and Greg Dixon. Falwell's self-professed fundamentalist credentials looked suspect to mainline fundamentalists.[97] His profile fit new evangelicalism better, primarily because of his associations and activities with new evangelicals and others even more to the left theologically within the Moral Majority. Falwell spelled out the social platform of the Moral Majority clearly:

> Today Moral Majority, Inc., is made up of millions of Americans, including 72,000 ministers, priests, and rabbis who are deeply concerned about the moral decline of our nation, the traditional Mormons, Fundamentalists—blacks and whites—farmers, housewives, businessmen, and businesswomen. We are Americans from all walks of life united by one central concern: to serve as a special-interest group providing a voice for a return to moral sanity in these United States of America. Moral Majority is a political organization and is not based on theological considerations. We are Americans who share similar moral convictions. We are opposed to abortion, pornography, the drug epidemic, the breakdown of the traditional family, and other moral cancers that are causing our society to rot from within. Moral Majority strongly supports a pluralistic America. While we believe that this nation was founded upon the Judeo-Christian ethic by men and women who were strongly influenced by biblical moral principles, we are committed to the separation of Church and State.[98]

---

[92]Ibid., p. 124.

[93]Ibid., p. 206.

[94]Ibid., p. 207.

[95]Ibid., p. 210.

[96]Ibid., p. 214.

[97]Dave Sproul, *An Open Letter to Jerry Falwell* (Tempe, AZ: Fundamental Baptist Press, 1979); Bob Jones III, "The Moral Majority" (Greenville, SC: Bob Jones University, 1980, pamphlet); Bob Jones, "Letter to a BJU 'Preacher Boy,'" June 10, 1980 (Fundamentalism Archives, Bob Jones University, Greenville, SC); Bob Jones, "The Impossible Dream: A Book Review," *Faith For the Family* (Jan 1982), p. 13; and *The Moral Majority: An Assessment Of a Movement by Leading Fundamentalists*, compiled by James E. Singleton (no publishing data).

[98]Jerry Falwell, "An Agenda For the Eighties," in *The Fundamentalist Phenomenon*, Jerry Falwell, ed., with Ed Dobson and Ed Hindson (Garden City, NY: Doubleday and Co., 1981), pp. 188-89.

Falwell listed ten areas of common moral concerns the Moral Majority shares, such as separation of church and state, life begins at fertilization, traditional families, opposition to illegal drug traffic, opposition to pornography, support for the state of Israel and Jewish people everywhere, and equal rights for women, etc.

Progressive fundamentalists led the Moral Majority, and they propagated a social activism they had formerly opposed, now criticizing traditional fundamentalists for ignoring the social implications of Christianity. Falwell confessed: "Back in the sixties I was criticizing pastors who were taking time out of their pulpit to involve themselves in the Civil Rights Movement or any other political venture....Now I find myself doing the same thing and for the same reasons they did."[99] He also conceded: "In our reaction against the social gospel, we have ignored the social implications of the gospel in conservative Christianity. In the past five years we have become aware of that, and we acknowledge our wrong attitude. We must now make it a priority in the 1980s."[100] Kenneth Kantzer, on retiring as editor of *Christianity Today*, also noted the about-face in the professing fundamentalist camp.[101]

A primal point with the Moral Majority asserted that God had raised up the United States in the last days for world evangelization and for the protection of the Jews. It held that the United States is in a peculiar sense God's special nation in the last days and that the USA must remain free so she can perform her double duty (world evangelization and protection of the Jews). In order to remain free, America must be strong morally. Falwell concluded, "I don't think America has any other right or reason for existence other than these two purposes."[102]

Another factor undergirding the rationale of the Moral Majority lay in its grassroots of private citizens. While many fundamentalist pastors and leaders participated, as well as other clergymen and people from all sorts of religious backgrounds, they considered themselves to be involved only as citizens of the state and in no other capacity. Falwell said, "Moral Majority for me is definitely a movement in which I am involved as a private citizen—period!"[103] Religious and non-religious people populated the movement because no theological premise filtered membership or participation. Falwell explained: "The Moral Majority is a *political* organization. You're not going to hear doctrine there."[104] The Moral Majority dissolved in 1989, but attempted a revival in the 1990s.

CONTINUING ACTIVISM (1980– 2000s)

1980s

Hunter notes that in 1980, as in 1970, conservative denominations put 18% of their annual budgets into social needs (the same percentage as liberal

---

[99]"Where is Jerry Falwell Going?" an interview, *Eternity* (July-Aug 1980), p. 18.

[100]"An Interview With the Lone Ranger of Fundamentalism," *Christianity Today* (Sept 4,1981), p. 26.

[101]Kenneth Kantzer, "Reflections: Five Years of Change," *Christianity Today* (Nov 26, 1982), p. 14.

[102]"Interview With the Lone Ranger," p. 25.

[103]Ibid., p. 23.

[104]Ibid., p. 24.

denominations contributed). Though the appropriations had not changed, the *rhetoric* had. Social ministry as *an end in itself* came to be promoted. Hunter noted that 54% of the evangelical college and seminary students polled felt that the pursuit of social justice was "just as important" or "almost as important" as evangelism,[105] a position consistent with Stott's idea of the "partner" or collaboration of evangelism and social activity. Stott noted that "each stands on its own feet in its own right alongside the other. Neither is a means to the other, or even a manifestation of the other. For each is an end in itself."[106]

Frank Gaebelein (1982)

Frank Gaebelein, after duly noting that fundamentalism's social conscience "went into eclipse" during the heyday of the liberal social gospel,[107] assailed two assumptions which, in his opinion, restricted the exercise of the neighbor love which Christ commands. The first was: "Just preach the gospel so that people are born again and then changed people will bring about the needed social change." In his view this idea presented a "simplistic view of evangelism."[108] To him, the great commission *includes* social activism as a part of the "all things" that were to be taught to new disciples. Invoking the understanding of Albert Schweitzer on the parable of the lost sheep, he concurred that Christ saved the "whole sheep" and not just its soul.[109]

Gaebelein discredited a second assumption: "A conservative evangelical theology necessarily means a conservative social outlook." By a conservative social outlook he apparently construed a sociopolitical activism carried out by Christian as citizens in a private, not public or political, manner. He based his disagreement with the "old conservative social outlook" on the preaching of the Old Testament prophets, particularly Amos, who upbraided Israel for its societal sins and on the kingdom message preached by Jesus Christ that included evident social concern. He echoed the thoughts of Henry in *The Uneasy Conscience of Modern Fundamentalism*, lamenting the neglect of kingdom preaching in evangelical circles.[110] Gaebelein's conclusion implied that if evangelicals are going to have a conservative theology that takes seriously the whole of Scripture, they must adopt a liberal political philosophy.[111]

Douglas Frank (1986)

Douglas Frank criticized the failures of his fellow evangelicals to alleviate social problems.[112] While professing to be evangelical, his stance is decidedly

---

[105]James D. Hunter, *Evangelicalism: The Coming Generation*, pp. 41-42.

[106]John R. W. Stott, *Christian Mission in the Modern World*, p. 23.

[107]Frank E. Gaebelein, "Evangelicals and Social Concern," *Journal of the Evangelical Theological Society* 25 (1982), p. 17.

[108]Ibid., p. 19.

[109]Ibid.

[110]Ibid., pp. 20-21.

[111]Ibid., p. 21.

[112]Douglas W. Frank, *Less Than Conquerors: How Evangelicals Entered the Twentieth Century* (Grand Rapids: Eerdmans, 1986).

neo-orthodox in the tradition of Reinhold Niebuhr.[113] A review of a few of his assertions will reveal his thinking and agenda. Frank deprecates money and wealth, and understands "rich" to mean self-sufficient, not needing the grace of God, immune to disaster and the plight of the needy, and prone to build cities "as a human attempt to fashion a secure home on earth,...where God is not welcome because he is not needed." How this impacts Frank's example of Jesus who, after all, was "rich" before He became poor (2 Cor 8:9) is left unanalyzed.[114] Frank strongly dislikes the middle class,[115] and displays disdain for capitalism.[116] He quotes Karl Marx favorably a number of times.[117] He denigrates premillennialism in general and dispensationalism in particular as the psychological products of the social tumult of the post-Civil War unrest; they are eschatology schemes sanctifying an agenda for evangelicals to regain control of history.[118] For the same reason, he criticizes the victorious life movement that also began in the latter part of the nineteenth century, linking it with "charlatanism" and playing "mind games" with people's guilt over the social disasters of the day. He does not hesitate to associate Charles Trumbull, editor of the *Sunday School Times* and a vocal advocate of the victorious life, with Mary Baker Eddy, William James, Charles Filmore, and other "mind cure" proponents, faith healers, and such itinerants who preyed on the anxieties aroused in people by the industrial revolution.[119]

Carl Henry (1987)

During this period Carl Henry changed his philosophy of social involvement. Arguing that *The Uneasy Conscience of Modern Fundamentalism* (1947) "was not an angry diatribe against fundamentalism" nor an effort to "commend the modernist agenda," he reiterated that "fundamentalism as such sponsored no program of attack on acknowledged societal evils and ignored serious reflection on how evangelical ecumenism might impinge on the culture crisis."[120] He also conceded that what appeared to be a wholly negative fundamentalist ethic and an impingement on individual liberty ("don't smoke, drink, or gamble") "often has prudence on its side" in view of the virtually unrestrained ethical practices he observed of certain elements within the new evangelicalism.[121]

Henry confessed to "notable weakness" in his *Uneasy Conscience* proposals of forty years earlier. His original social philosophy viewed regeneration as the answer to social problems, believing that sanctified lives of individual believers would produce social changes that would roll back injustice and inequity.

> There was...a notable weakness in my concentration on regeneration as the guarantee of a better world. For *Uneasy Conscience* failed to focus sharply

---

[113]Ibid., pp. 77, 78, 79, 84, 85, 86, 89 91, 98, 102, 228, *passim.*

[114]Ibid., pp. 26, 29. See also pp. 6, 7, 13, et al.

[115]Ibid., pp. 127ff, 198, 201, 223, 261.

[116]Ibid., pp. 33, 34, 35, 39, 97, 98, 129, 221, 224, 227.

[117]Ibid., pp. 35, 41, 57, 98, 121.

[118]Ibid., pp. 68, 69, 73.

[119]Ibid., pp. 149-50.

[120]Carl F. H. Henry, "The Uneasy Conscience Revisited: Current Theological, Ethical and Social Concerns," *Theology News and Notes* (Dec 1987), p. 3.

[121]Ibid., p. 4.

on the indispensable role of government in preserving justice in a fallen society....Although redemptive vitalities in society continued to have priority in my thinking, seminars on social ethics during my 10 years at Fuller and later showed an enlarging emphasis on the state's mandate for preserving justice...many of us underestimated the indispensable importance of legislative coercion in a fallen society.[122]

Through the decade of the 1980s, Henry reiterated his criticism of evangelicals' political involvement because their endeavors lacked substance, were being done without a comprehensive social vision, and were void of political savvy. Instead, political efforts concentrated on a faith community's special-interest basis or what certain communities opposed at the moment. The activities of the Christian Reconstruction movement or the Moral Majority provided good ammunition for his criticisms.[123] He called for evangelical political action based on William Wilberforce's type of "divine compulsion to speak of public affairs in the context of transcendental justice and a universally binding social good" and not "solely an appeal to biblical considerations."[124] He spoke positively of an emerging social philosophy called "chartered pluralism," a project "not predicated on shared beliefs" but rather a co-belligerency based on the three tenets or universal notions of religious rights, responsibilities, and respect. On this platform "nothing precludes an interreligious or ecumenical cooperative public witness against injustice or for justice." Henry felt that cobelligerent cooperation would force the non-evangelicals into a corner, causing them to reflect on whether or not they could "afford" to get involved with evangelicals in social activism.[125]

John R. W. Stott

John Stott continued fleshing out his evangelical social philosophy during this period. From September 1979 to May 1980 Stott wrote a series of six articles explicating his social philosophy. The agenda he postulated revolved around two ideas: the "peacemaking" role of Christians in the world, and the need for universal opportunity for economic equality. In the first article, he calls for Christian peacemaking based on the beatitude of Matthew 5:9 and the incident in 1 Kings 12 where Rehoboam failed to pacify the economic unrest and adversarial atmosphere created by the regime of his father Solomon. From there he deduces management's necessity to abolish a "them—us" attitude in labor negotiations, to rectify the disparity between the high paid and the low paid, and with help from the parable of the laborers where "the laborer is worthy of his hire" (Luke 10:7), to institute a profit sharing plan so that all share in bonuses, pensions, stock, and other fruits of profits.[126] In the second article, Stott propounds a "whole [i.e., holistic] mission" on the whole church in which evangelism and social action are

---

[122]Ibid.

[123]Carl F. H. Henry, "Evangelicals Jump on the Political Bandwagon," *Christianity Today* (Oct 24, 1980), pp. 20-24; "Evangelicals: Out of the Closet But Going Nowhere?" *Christianity Today* (Jan 4, 1980), p. 19; "The New Coalitions," *Christianity Today* (Nov 17, 1989), pp. 26-27.

[124]Carl F. H. Henry, "The New Coalitions," p. 27.

[125]Ibid., p. 28.

[126]John R. W. Stott, "Peacemaking Is a Management Responsibility," *Christianity Today* (Sept 21, 1979), pp. 34-35.

joined, based on the biblical ideas of God being a God of social justice as well as personal redemption, the social dimension of Christ's kingdom preaching, and the example of Christ Himself of blending the spiritual and social, faith and works, and soul and body.[127]

Stott's third article emphasized the peacemaking role of the church in condemning the use of nuclear weapons of war, based again on the example of a pacifistic Christ. Stott explains Christ's seemingly contrary stances on violence and pacifism: "Yet his resort to violence in word and deed was occasional, alien, uncharacteristic; his characteristic was nonviolence; the symbol of his ministry is not a whip but the cross."[128] The fourth article continued in a similar vein, giving five initiatives whereby Christians can contribute to universal (though not unilateral) nuclear disarmament, ending on the note that national morality is more important than national security.[129] The fifth and sixth articles addressed the need for universal opportunity for economic equality, especially with the Third World as the chief beneficiaries. Stott appeals to the dominion mandate of Genesis 1:28, "the earth is the Lord's" dictum of Psalm 24:1, and the parable of the Good Samaritan to argue for "a fundamentally Christian quest to seek for all people equality of opportunity in education,...trade,...and in power sharing." The indictment of the rich man in Hades, in his opinion, did not come because he contributed to Lazarus' poverty but for acquiescing in the poor man's economic inequality.[130] Stott also calls for a careful examination of the goods and services which we appropriate routinely, and especially of the disparate wages and living conditions of those who make them and of the trade agreements by which they are made available to us. He also pleads for a simpler Christian lifestyle, lower than is actually affordable which, while not alleviating world poverty as such, would "be a sign and symbol of our Christian obedience, of our love for the needy, and of our resolve to imitate that grace of our Lord Jesus Christ who, though rich, became poor in order that through his poverty we might become rich."[131] Stott's proposals bring many interpretive and theological questions, some of which will be addressed later.[132]

Mankind's three-fold quest, consisting of aspirations that Christ incites by His Spirit that only He can fulfill, lay at the basis of Stott's proposals. The divinely instilled yearnings should then set the agenda for the church's mission. The first quest is for transcendence, an ultimate reality beyond the material universe. On his understanding of the Athenians and the Unknown God (Acts 17), Stott identifies this search for transcendence as a search for God.[133] The second quest is for human significance

---

[127]John R. W. Stott, "The Biblical Scope of the Christian Mission," *Christianity Today* (Jan 4, 1980), pp. 36-37.

[128]John R. W. Stott, "Calling for Peacemakers in a Nuclear Age, Part I, *Christianity Today* (Feb 8, 1980), p. 45.

[129]John R. W. Stott, "Calling for Peacemakers in a Nuclear Age, Part II, *Christianity Today* (March 7, 1980), pp. 44-45.

[130]John R. W. Stott, "Economic Equality Among Nations: A Christian Concern?" *Christianity Today* (May 2, 1980), pp. 36-37.

[131]John R. W. Stott, "The Just Demands of Economic Inequality," *Christianity Today* (May 23, 1980), p. 31.

[132]A comprehensive review and analysis of Stott's series is by Gary T. Meadors, "John R. W. Stott on Social Action," *Grace Theological Journal* 1 (1980).

[133]Ibid., pp. 125-29.

in terms of Viktor Frankl's idea of finding meaning to life which has been devalued through technology and other things.[134] The third quest is for community, the hunger of all humans for love and understanding as suggested by Mother Teresa.[135]

In 1987 Stott delivered the W. H. Griffith Thomas Lectures at Dallas Theological Seminary, reprinted in the *Bibliotheca Sacra*.[136] He began by saying:

> One of the greatest needs in today's church is for a greater sensitivity to the world. As true servants of Jesus Christ, believers should keep their eyes open, as He did, to human need and their ears cocked to the world's cries of pain. They should respond, as again He did, with compassion to the real issues of the day.[137]

Stott's second lecture began by speaking of the church's "mission" as being all that "Christ sends the church into the world to do," and he tries to steer a course between the liberal World Missionary Conference of Edinburgh (1910) and the "mislaid social conscience" of early 20th century evangelicalism.[138] He appealed to the Grand Rapids Consultation of 1982, an heir of the efforts of the Continuing Committee of Lausanne 1974, which said:

> (a) that social activity is a consequence of evangelism, since "faith works through love"; (b) that social activity is a bridge to evangelism, since "it can break down prejudice and suspicion, and gain a hearing for the gospel"; and (c) social activity often accompanies evangelism as its partner. "They are like the two blades of a pair of scissors, or like the two wings of a bird." This partnership is clearly seen in the public ministry of Jesus in which *kerugma* (proclamation) and *diakonia* (service) went hand in hand. "His words explained his works, and his works dramatized his words."[139]

Stott's idea of the church's mission to the world is summed up in "incarnational Christianity," the basis of which is the example of the ministry of Jesus and His words in John 17:18 and 20:21 ("As the father has sent me, I also send you"). Stott notes the "double identity" of the church—the church in the world but not of the world, the "holy worldliness of the church" in the words of Alexander Vidler.[140] "So believers are to enter other people's worlds (which is the implication of incarnation), as Christ entered theirs. That means entering their thought world and the world of their alienation and pain."[141]

1990s AND LATER

Michael Cromartie

The early 1990s began with evangelical assessments of their success and progress in social activism. Michael Cromartie gave a brief history of evangelical

---

[134]Ibid., pp. 129-31.

[135]Ibid., pp. 131-33.

[136]"Christian Ministry in the 21st Century," April 1988—January 1989.

[137]John R. W. Stott, "The World's Challenge to the Church," *Bibliotheca Sacra* 145 (1988), p. 124.

[138]John R. W. Stott, "The Church's Mission In the World," *Bibliotheca Sacra* 145 (1988), p. 244.

[139]Ibid., p. 244. Stott's quotes are from *The Grand Rapids Report, Evangelism and Social Responsibility* (Grand Rapids: Eerdmans, 1982), pp. 21-24.

[140]Ibid., pp. 246-47.

[141]Ibid., p. 247.

social action since the publications of Henry's *The Uneasy Conscience of Modern Fundamentalism* (1947), noting that the impetus for social involvement came with the rise of the Religious Right. Through the formation of the Moral Majority aided by the presidential campaign of evangelist Pat Robertson and his conservative connections. The Religious Right played a significant role in the election of Ronald Reagan and the ushering in of a politically conservative era. Comartie reported the disappointment of Henry and other "mainline" evangelicals with the "hijacking of the evangelical jumbo jet" that caught some evangelical leaders without an aggressive public agenda.[142] Ron Sider, president of Evangelicals For Social Action, complained: "We called for social and political action but instead we got eight years of Ronald Reagan."[143] New evangelical social activism had become dominated by leftists with their radical magazines and proposals. But their ideas were being ignored except for left-wing Catholics and liberal Protestants, causing evangelicalism to be "an opposition without teeth."[144] Cromartie's article concludes:

> The debates now revolve around prudential questions regarding which policies are in fact the most effective in meeting the normative standards of justice. Many times these are empirical questions that need honest exploration.[145]

The Calvin Center for Christian Scholarship

A conference sponsored by the Calvin Center for Christian Scholarship in Grand Rapids, MI, assembled to address the projected influence of evangelical activists. Journalist James Costelli saw a decreased influence by religious political activists that he attributed to a decline of confidence in organized religion.[146] Ralph Reed of the Christian Coalition saw it differently; he predicted an increased influence chiefly because the religious Right has a broader agenda "no longer focused exclusively on abortion, pornography, or prayer in school," but on issues such as the balanced-budget amendment being proposed in Congress.[147] Various suggestions and proposals were offered by others on both sides of the question of evangelicalism's anticipated social influence.

"Green" Evangelicals

The early 1990s also saw the rise of "green" evangelicals who were especially environmentally conscious, although ecological concerns were being urged

---

[142]Michael Cromartie, "Fixing the World—From Nonplayers to Radicals to New Right Conservatives: The Saga of Evangelicals and Social Action," *Christianity Today* (April 27 1992), p. 24. Thomas Atwood criticized the Evangelical Right "because it never built strong relationships with the mainstream evangelical establishment as represented by Billy Graham, *Christianity Today* magazine, and the National Association of Evangelicals" (Thomas C. Atwood, "Through A Glass Darkly: Is the Christian Right Overconfident It Knows God's Will?" *Policy Review* [Fall 1990], p. 46).

[143]Cromartie, "Fixing the World," p. 25.

[144]Ibid.

[145]Ibid.

[146]Thomas S. Giles, "Does 1992 Signal the Rising or Falling of Evangelical Activists?" *Christianity Today* (Nov 23, 1992), p. 52.

[147]Ibid.

already in the 1960s.[148] In August 1992 an "Evangelical Christianity and the Environment" conference convened in Michigan sponsored by the Au Sable Institute of Environmental Studies and the World Evangelical Fellowship. The conference met early two months after the Earth Summit held in Rio de Janeiro.[149] The Au Sable director, Calvin DeWitt, noted that "the forum was the first worldwide meeting of evangelical Christians to work seriously on the relationship between faith and caring for the creation."[150] Those gathered believed "the secular environmental movement reveals a deep spiritual hunger that evangelicals can respond to," apparently based on the idea that many of those in the Rio conference were attracted to the concept of a "force" holding the universe together. The main difference between the Michigan and the Rio conferences was that the evangelicals had a common faith in Jesus Christ that dispelled any pagan notions of a force or earth goddess.[151] The Au Sable forum also "linked earth keeping with a need for careful, thoughtful missions work."[152]

A new evangelical organization, the Christian Society of the Green Cross, began in 1993. This new formation, along with the Au Sable group and the continuing environmental/social ministries of World Vision International, led to the optimistic conclusion of Howard Snyder: "Here is something to celebrate: the goodness of God's creation, a growing public support for earthcare and evangelicals who are leading the way in the stewardship of the garden God has given us."[153]

In 1993 new evangelical spokesman and prolific writer Millard Erickson authored *The Evangelical Mind and Heart*, devoting two chapters to an evangelical theology and ethic of ecology.[154] He began with "the indictment of Christianity," principally echoing the complaints of Arnold Toynbee against some of the ecological attitudes of Christians as he perceived them.[155] Generally, Erickson's principles of ecology are well-taken, but some of his reasoning for them is theologically novel and stretched. For example, he understands that the servitude of creation in Romans 8: 18-25 can be justifiably interpreted to mean that

> humans, through their sinful activity, bring the creation into bondage. Nature is frequently the victim of human greed and selfishness, as they seek to obtain the maximum of material good at a minimum of cost. Their plundering and polluting of the environment enslave and bind it, affecting its ability to bear adequate witness to its Maker.[156]

---

[148]For example, Sherwood Wirt, *The Social Conscience of the Evangelical*, chapter 11, "The Defilement of the Earth," pp. 102-11.

[149]Joan Huyser-Honig, "A Green Gathering of Evangelicals," *Christianity Today* (Oct 5, 1992), p. 56.

[150]Ibid.

[151]Ibid.

[152]Ibid.

[153]Howard Snyder, "Why We Love the Earth," *Christianity Today* (May 15, 1995), p. 15.

[154]Millard J. Erickson, *The Evangelical Mind and Heart* (Grand Rapids: Baker, 1993), pp. 51-82: chapter 3, "An Evangelical Theology of Ecology," and chapter 4, "An Evangelical Ethic of Ecology."

[155]Ibid., pp. 51-53.

[156]Ibid., p. 55.

In contrast, the apostle Paul clearly traces creation's "slavery to corruption" to the Edenic fall of man into sin and its physical effects on the universe and not to human greed.

Another quirk to surface in Erickson's theology of ecology was his attributing of God's providential care and control over creation to His love. Using Christ's comparison of His benevolence toward sparrows with His care for human beings (Matt 10:29-31), Erickson concludes that both sparrows and humans are objects of God's love.[157] He does indicate one small caveat later, apparently in reference to plants, by saying "there are definite indications of divine pleasure (which may or may not be identifiable as love) with the creation below animals."[158]

Another questionable element of Erickson's theology of ecology is his idea that non-rational creation is an end in itself worthy of good stewardship regardless of any utilitarian value it may have for human beings.

> Human management of the creation does not mean that the creation exists solely for human benefit and use....This means that animals, plants, and minerals are not merely means to human ends. They are ends in themselves. They are not merely to be utilized and exploited, but cared for. Their welfare is the responsibility of the human, the caretaker of God's kingdom, who must see to it that they fulfil God's highest and best intention for them.[159]

Chicago Declaration II

In November 1993 a three-day meeting of evangelicals under the banner of an "evangelical renewal," transpired. The representatives believed that "the gospel… embraces the call to conversion and the summons to justice."[160] Sider, president of Evangelicals For Social Action, called for a declaration to give expression to an "incarnational kingdom Christianity" that is "holistic," combining evangelism and social transformation.[161] Out of the conclave emerged a brief document, signed by several hundred people, called Chicago Declaration II, the first Declaration having occurred in 1973. According to the report:

> The new declaration is divided into sections on thanksgiving, "weeping" over racism and other persistent social ills, "dreaming" of a renewed church and committed believers, a recommitment to evangelism as well as social engagement, and a final prayer for God to pour out his power.[162]

NAE

The National Association of Evangelicals took a sudden interest in race relations in the mid 1990s. In 1995 Don Argue became president, succeeding Billy Melvin who had served since 1967. Argue immediately called for a new agenda for the NAE that revolved around racial issues.[163] A new mission statement adopted by the executive committee called for more ethnic diversity and the grooming of African

---

[157]Ibid.

[158]Ibid., p. 58. Erickson had made the same point in his *Christian Theology,* 2nd ed. (Grand Rapids: Baker, 1983), p. 320.

[159]*The Evangelical Heart and Mind*, p. 61.

[160]Timothy C. Morgan, "Evangelicals Urge Social Renewal," *Christianity Today* (Jan 10, 1994), p. 47.

[161]Ibid.

[162]Ibid.

[163]Helen Lee, "Racial Reconciliation Tops NAE's Agenda," *Christianity Today* (Apr 3, 1995), p. 97.

American evangelical leaders. The NAE reorganized and initiated discussions with the National Black Evangelical Association that had broken with the NAE in 1963. In addition to Argue's concern over the prevalence of white membership in the NAE, he voiced concern that the Association too closely identified with the Republican party, an association that squelched dialogue with minorities. "I want to undrape the Republican flag that has draped evangelicals in recent times. There are some wonderful evangelical Democrats."[164] The new image of the NAE, according to one officer, was to be "less male, less gray, and less Anglo."[165] Argue resigned rather suddenly in 1998, and Kevin Mannoia succeeded him. While still quite interested in ethnic diversity (Mannoia pointed out that his new staff was multilingual), Mannoia sought to enlarge the constituency of the NAE by reaching out to non-evangelical organizations containing covert evangelicals.[166] The NAE's appeal, constituency, and effectiveness in the late 1990s had dwindled markedly (only 350 people showed up for the 1999 annual meeting), and the organization needed to reinvent itself.

At the 2000 annual meeting, the NAE continued its agenda of transforming culture and reaching out to other religious groups by electing its first black chairman and by changing its bylaws to include members of liberal groups, such as the National Council of Churches.[167]

John Stott

In the mid 1990s, at age 75, Stott still proclaimed social activism as much as ever. In an interview with *Christianity Today,* Stott attributed his growing social awareness to an enlarging vision of the person of God; that God is interested in the "whole of life—in justice as well as justification," that the idea of righteousness includes both personal holiness and cultural justice.[168] The theological basis of his social conscience also included the unique dignity and value of human beings in the image of God; therefore "anything that dehumanizes human beings should be an outrage to us, because God has made them in his image."[169] Stott reiterated his burden for the economic oppression of the poor, especially in Third World countries. Concurring with an African phrase, "an empty belly has no ears," he added, "When they're that poor, they *can't* respond to the gospel" (italics added),[170] rehearsing the old evangelical notion of social betterment as a pre-evangelism technique.

The King Legacy

The legacy of Martin Luther King, Jr. on the evangelical social and racial agenda was addressed in a lengthy article in the late 1990s, which can be summarized in a telling paragraph:

---

[164]"Argue to Assume NAE Helm," *Christianity Today* (Feb 6, 1995), p. 49.

[165]John W. Kennedy, "NAE Issues 'Evangelical Manifesto,'" *Christianity Today* (Apr 8, 1996), p. 101.

[166]Christina J. Gardner, "Power in Unity: Evangelical Leader Embraces New Strategy," *Christianity Today* (Apr 24, 2000), p. 25.

[167]Larry Witham, "Evangelicals Plan on 'Transforming' American Culture," *The Washington Times National Weekly Edition* (Mar 13-19, 2000).

[168]Roy McCoughry, "Basic Stott: Candid Comments on Justice, Gender, and Judgment," *Christianity Today* (Jan 8, 1996), p. 25.

[169]Ibid., p. 26.

[170]Ibid., p. 30.

For the church, King's legacy is as multifarious as the nation he sought to reconcile. While some revere him as a hero and a prophet of peace, others look on him with disdain, a fact that has been magnified by revelations of King's sexual improprieties and lapses in ethical judgment. Nonetheless, the enduring importance of King's life and achievements have led many evangelicals who once dismissed him as a rabble-rouser now to acknowledge the spiritual validity of his social mission.[171]

The article in the main was quite positive about King's vision and accomplishments, noting that only "a few Christian thinkers" remain unconvinced "of the religious purity of King's public message."[172]

Politics of Compassion

In the USA presidential campaign of 2000 the Republican party introduced the novel idea of the politics of compassion. "Compassionate conservatism" announced the theme of George W. Bush's campaign, and he won the presidency. The theme had its roots in the Project for American Renewal led by Senator Dan Coats from Indiana. Some new evangelicals salivated at the prospects for new meaningful social action. With the nation in a "one-way libertarian" mood, i.e., where government is thought to be obligated to the citizen but not vice versa, the editor of *Christianity Today* felt that "the new politics of compassion is just what we need to turn us away from individualism and toward right relations between people in community."[173] He added, "And there is no better place than a local church congregation to reconnect rich and poor."[174]

In 1999 an interesting and informative book on evangelicalism came out, and the chapter "Transforming Culture: Evangelicals and the Social Order" gave a fine documented overview of evangelical social thought and endeavors since the 19th century.[175] The chapter begins with evangelicalism's "rescue or reform" dilemma regarding a proper response to social problems. The "rescue" approach contended that individual sinners needed to be delivered from the wicked culture so that their regenerated lives could effect social change. The "reform" proposal believed that altering the social structures would be conducive to conversion and Christian nurture.[176] The rest of the chapter traces evangelicalism's activism in various social strata such as politics, women, homosexuality, civil rights, public schools, and support for Israel.

A new book promoting one of the newest offshoots of evangelicalism appeared in 2002, *The Younger Evangelicals: Facing the Challenges of the New World* by Robert E. Webber.[177] Webber describes postmodern evangelicals who wish to

---

[171]Edward Gilbreath, "Catching Up With a DREAM: Evangelicals and Race 30 Years After the Death of Martin Luther King, Jr.," *Christianity Today* (Mar 2, 1998), p. 22.

[172]Ibid., p. 25.

[173]"Reconnecting With the Poor: If People are Hurting, It's Our Business," *Christianity Today* (Jan 11, 1999), p. 40.

[174]Ibid.

[175]Robert H. Krapohl and Charles H. Lippy, *The Evangelicals: A Historical, Thematic, and Biographical Guide* (Westport, CT: Greenwood Press, 1999), pp. 131-42.

[176]Ibid., p. 130.

[177]Grand Rapids: Baker.

reach and minister to a postmodern culture. One of their main elements in ministry philosophy is social activism, especially in the areas of poverty and injustice.[178]

The new evangelical social agenda evolved over the decades as it addressed the tension between evangelism and social activism. In the beginning it was evangelism over social action. This was the original position of Henry in *The Uneasy Conscience* and of nearly all the new evangelicals for the next 25 years (1947-1970s). Evangelized and regenerated people should make a Christian impact on culture. In the 1970s, particularly through the influence of John R.W. Stott and the Lausanne World Congress on Evangelism, there arose the notion of parity wherein social activism became an equal "partner" of evangelism. In the 1980s social ministry began being promoted as an end in itself with its own inherent appeal apart from spiritual considerations. Finally, some left wing evangelicals elevated social activism over evangelism; it came to be understood as "exclusively legitimate" and the "essential Christian act."[179]

---

[178]Ibid., see especially chapter 16: "Activists: From Theory to Action."

[179]James D. Hunter, *Evangelicalism: The Coming Generation*, p. 45.

19

THE BIBLICAL IDEA OF SOCIAL ACTION

With every matter of faith and practice for Bible-believing Christians, the Bible must be the sole and final authority. The mere presence of a social or spiritual need does not legitimize non-biblical solutions or constitute a sacred obligation to address the needs. Biblical criteria form and inform the parameters for Christian social involvement.

BIBLICAL CRITERIA FOR SOCIAL ACTION

The Church Within Society

No social program is given in Scripture for the institutional church in relation to civil society in general despite the grave social problems in the New Testament world. In fact, the New Testament barely mentions the social climate of its world at all. Slavery, a pernicious social ill in the Roman world, is never addressed as a structural evil to be eliminated by social "partnering" with evangelism or in any other specific manner. Jesus, Paul, nor any other writer called for the abolition of slavery. Christian slaves heard commands to obey their masters and give a good account of their Christianity as well as their stewardship of the biblical work ethic (Eph 5:1-8). Christian masters learned of their own accountability to God and to avoid threatening (Eph 5:9). The lone example of an actual slave is Onesimus, a runaway who had stolen from his master Philemon and had in God's circuitous providence found Christ through Paul in prison. Paul's word on the subject is to Philemon, the slave holder, who is told simply to receive Onesimus back as a Christian brother and worker, with no comment on the structure of institutional slavery. If the new evangelicals and others are right in their theory of societal activism, Paul's actions and counsel were either in error or the Apostle was unforgivably apathetic. If Paul today would denounce entrenched structural evil in the United Nations sessions and in corporate board rooms across the world, as Carl Henry assumes he would,[1] it is surely not asking too much for the great Apostle to have written even a few such lines in private correspondence to a Christian friend.

---

[1]Carl F. H. Henry, *The Uneasy Conscience of Modern Fundamentalism* (Grand Rapids: Eerdmans, 1947), p. 34.

Liberal social gospel proponents have been baffled by this silence of Paul. Samuel Hugh Moffett, himself a professing evangelical, noted this fact.

> But you say, that [Old Testament social emphases] was the old dispensation. With the coming of Christ all things are become new. In the New Testament the atmosphere is changed. Jesus goes straight to the heart of things. He came to save sinners, not society. He dealt with problems of the heart, not with politics....This is all very true. Jesus Christ's unconcern, His indifference almost, with overwhelming injustices of Roman imperialism and Roman slave economy, is a source of great embarrassment to modern preachers of a purely social gospel. They can't quite forgive the Great Example for wasting time calming the storms on Galilee and in the human heart when He might have been lobbying at the Roman court, or getting out the vote in Galilee.[2]

Moffett's own answer to the dilemma is that the early church "saw statism, not slavery, as the basic social problem—a rather keen insight;" but even so "the Church balked at social revolution."[3] No biblical proof is given for this reasoning, and Moffett's proposed "statism" solution seems to sidestep the issue completely. Though Moffett points out that Jesus did have concern for the poor, hungry, diseased, and crippled—the physical and social ills "*of the world*" (italics added),[4] his overall explanation of the problem is unconvincing.

Slavery as generally practiced in pagan cultures is not biblically condoned or recommended; it is simply not addressed as a specific object of social reform by organized Christianity. What is clear, from both Testaments, is the dignity and worth of the human personality because of the image of God within each human being. The Bible objects to owning, trading, or selling another person as mere chattel property, but being indentured to another person, even for a lifetime of bond-service, is never prohibited and is simply ethically regulated (Lev 25:39-55; Deut 15:12-18; Eph 5:1-9).

While the organized church as such has no global social mandate, individual Christians are admonished to "do good to all people" (Gal 6:10), but this is in their capacity of citizens of earth. Believers are to be salt and light in civil society (Matt 5:13-16), preserving the culture from immediate social rot and bringing moral illumination into a darkened world. A Christian has his feet in two spheres: the church and the state. As a citizen of the state he has social obligations as a believer to fellow human beings, and he can participate in the amelioration of societal ills to whatever extent his resources, prudence, and the will of God indicate; however, this is not "Christian service" in the normal acceptance of the term. Whatever beneficial cultural impact an individual Christian may have is a by-product of his sanctification and implementation of Christian principles in his social milieu. Christians do not have biblical warrant to bring into the organized church programs and schemes of sociopolitical involvement in the name of "service."

---

[2]Samuel Hugh Moffett, "The Christian and Social Reform," *His* (Dec 1950), p. 11.

[3]Ibid., p. 13.

[4]Ibid., p. 12.

The pre-fall "dominion mandate" of Genesis 1:28 has been understood by some theologians as an obligation to the church, an interpretation usually due to the continuity of the one people of God in both testaments posited by covenant theologians. But this mandate is given to all men as human beings, not only to men as believers or covenant-keepers; i.e., *all* people are to "subdue" the earth for the benefit of mankind to the glory of God. The whole human race as a civil order, saved and unsaved, is under obligation to pursue true science, advance cultural betterment, and contribute to the furthering of a decent society.

The purpose here is not to explore the whole biblical idea of social ethics, but to encourage understanding of scripturally-informed creation ethics. Creation ethics are based on the one true and living God as Creator, man as a subordinate creature made in God's image, and the non-rational creation as subservient to man and his obligation to obey and glorify his Maker. This ethic is directed to man as man and is universally applicable in mixed society (i.e., saved and unsaved, or Jew and Gentile); it also transcends ages and dispensations. It is an ethic of general moral theism and basic morality, and is in part intuitive (Rom 1:18-2:16) and in part codified (Gen 9:5-7; aspects of the Mosaic Law, et al.). Included in this ethic are fundamental "human rights" such as the sanctity of life, marriage, the home, private property, and truth, among others. Creation ethics are binding on all people of all time and can be proclaimed by the people of God of all times individually or institutionally. All people can be reproved at any time for their violation of these ethics. Otherwise it would be impossible to find any basis of appeal to non-believers for right behavior.

The Church Toward Its Own

Christian social involvement embraces the social responsibilities the institutional church had towards its own people. The New Testament teaches the benevolence of the local church to its own members; it does not portray the church as the God-appointed watchdog over the social welfare of the world at large. The economic commonality of Acts 4:32-35 was of believers only and was not projected into civil society at large in fulfillment of some notion of a social mandate. In Acts 6:1-3 the local church developed a strategy to handle the social well-being of its own widows, not all the widows in the wider area. The Christians in Antioch contributed to the relief of the famine-stricken believers in Judea (Acts 11:27-30). Romans 12:9-21 gives direction to believers in practical affairs, but there is no social directive except "contributing to the needs of the saints" (v. 13). Paul gathered money from the churches of Macedonia and Achaia for the poor saints in Jerusalem (Rom 15:25, 27; 2 Cor 8-9). 1 Timothy 5:3-16 gives numerous instructions for the physical/financial support of the local church for its destitute widows, guidelines that demonstrate that the church's social program clearly was not intended for the greater civil community. James 2:15-16 involves a brother or a sister—a fellow believer—who is in need of food or clothing, and for whom mere platitudes are worthless gestures. James declares that the evidence of genuine, persevering faith is to "give them what is necessary for their body" (v. 16). In 1 John 3:17, the context is again limited to the saints and not the world at large; the material compassion is for a "brother" in need.

The Church and Israel

A third consideration in a Christian social philosophy acknowledges that the biblical understanding that the New Testament church and Old Testament Israel are not socially comparable institutions. Nationally, Israel was a religious-political entity—a theocracy, a God-ruled institution. Israel was basically a governmental entity that had a very wide social dimension much of which was peculiar to the nation. The Law of Moses expressed the divinely-given legal covenant that forged the Hebrew tribes into a kingdom of priests (Exod 19:6); it codified the constitution of the state of Israel in Old Testament history. It was an indivisible law code (James 2:10) that consisted of three aspects: moral, civil, and ceremonial. The Law of Moses uniquely belonged to Israel, not to the Gentile nations (Rom 2: 14), and it was incumbent only on the covenant community. Thus the questions are raised: Were the social demands of the Law to be imposed by Israel on the surrounding nations, and were those nations required to adopt the Mosaic Covenant as their own political infrastructures? The answers are plainly negative. The covenant obligations, including its social demands, were to be internalized by Israel alone and by those admitted to the covenant community through the required Levitical procedures. Israel did not have a mandate to establish Mosaic social justice world-wide.

In ancient Israel the civil and religious arenas were combined in the theocratic polity, in effect a *union* of church and state. The Law governed every aspect of the people's lives including the social sphere, and this in part sets the Old Testament people of God apart from the New Testament church. In order to head off the implications of this distinction, Moffett early in his article stated: "At the outset we must avoid the temptation to begin with the New Testament,"[5] implying that Israel's theocratic social demands are normative for the church of the present age.

Coming to the New Testament, we find that Israel's social arrangement does not exist for the church. A church saint lives in two separate spheres, the church and the state. But the New Testament teaches the *separation* of the organized church and the civil state (Matt 22:21) with the ideal being a free church in a free state. The church has been given no civil social agenda and the state has no religious or spiritual agenda. The church influences the state through the regenerated lives of the saints acting as individual Christian citizens in civil society and not as people ecclesially structured in a corporate body. A better social/civil order results from the operation of the gospel in personal lives. The only genuine alternative to this view is the modern theonomist, Christian Reconstruction, or Dominion Theology movement which is predicated on a rigid covenant theology and a postmillennial view of the final outcome of human history. In other words, in that view the present-day church is the "new Israel," and it has the mandate to "milllennialize," which is to reestablish the Law of Moses earth-wide by gradually Christianizing the existing social order. Postmillennial eschatology does not have a cataclysmic intrusion of Jesus Christ into human history that summarily ushers in a new international social order that will totally displace what preceded it.

---

[5] "The Christian and Social Reform," p. 11.

The NT Minister and OT Prophet

The fourth component to consider in Christian societal engagement is similar to the third: The New Testament minister and the Old Testament prophet are not on the same continuum of ecclesiastical labor because of the factors in the difference between Israel and the church. A religious figure in a theocratic state does not function in the same manner as one in a free church in a free state. The Old Testament prophets' message to their contemporary Hebrews often concerned the people's treatment of the orphan, the widow, the poor, and the stranger (alien) in the land. Underprivileged people were easily disenfranchised and taken advantage of. Consequently, the Law specifically provided for them, and anyone in ancient Israel who had a heart for God and the covenant was sensitive to these easily marginalized social groups. The prophets continuously called the people back to the social responsibilities of their divinely-revealed, God-given covenant. The impetus for the preaching of the Old Testament prophets is not comparable to the Great Commission of the New Testament preacher.

The Old Testament prophets, however, did not confine their preaching, and thus some of their ethical demands, only to the covenant community. Jeremiah, foreordained by God as a prophet "to the nations" (Jer 1:5; cf. 46:1), articulated six chapters of messages specifically to surrounding peoples (46-51).[6] Isaiah (13-23), Ezekiel (25-32), Amos (1:3-2:3), Obadiah, and Joel (3:3, 6) likewise denounced the sins of the nations, some of which were social evils. But the Old Testament prophets did not call the Gentile nations to the social ethics peculiar to Israel through the covenant. For example, the Gentile nations were not admonished to observe the sabbath, the food laws, the regulations regarding interest and loan collection, the reversion of property rights, etc.

One of the clearest truths of New Testament theology is that the Christian believer in the church age is not under the Law of Moses (Rom 6:14). No appeal to Jeremiah or Amos against social sins can be legitimately used as a paradigm for local church socio-political agitation. Since the Mosaic Law's social regulations applied to Israel alone, the nation had no commission to establish global justice or the equalization of wealth throughout the rest of the Old Testament world. The preaching of the Old Testament prophets must be understood in that light.

The Kingdom

A fifth consideration argues that the messianic Kingdom of God is not presently established nor is it incrementally penetrating society by the influence of the gospel.[7] If this is true, a "kingdom now" theology of social activism is without foundation. Covenant theology understands the Bible to teach a fundamental

---

[6]John Martin suggests that Jeremiah's prophecies were probably not for these nations themselves to read but were for the benefit of the chosen people that God will judge their enemies and keep His covenant promises ("Isaiah," *The Bible Knowledge Commentary* [Wheaton, IL: Victor, 1985], 1:1058).

[7]Donald W. Dayton saw this clearly as he discussed the rise of premillennialism as preached by D. L. Moody and its clash with the popular but fading postmillennialism as promoted by Charles G. Finney. "What is at stake here is not just the dating of the Second Coming of Christ, but a whole world view and differing conceptions of how God works in the world in relation to human activity" ("The Social and Political Conservatism of Modern American Evangelicalism: A Preliminary Search for the Reasons," *Union Seminary Quarterly Review* 23 [1977], p. 77).

continuity between Israel and the church, especially in the so-called covenant of grace. From the post-fall redemptive promise of Genesis 3:15, the covenant of grace, all subsequent covenants simply expand and further God's redemptive program and culminate in the new covenant of Christ's blood. As a result, anyone saved from sin participates in the covenant of grace and becomes part of the one continuing people of God, or the generic "church." Covenant theology consequently holds that Jesus' kingdom is the abstract sphere of salvation from sin, i.e., His dynamic spiritual rule in believers' hearts. In this view, Jesus in the first century offered and established His messianic reign in the hearts of all believers. He currently rules His "kingdom now" from the throne of David, typically identified with His present session at God's right hand. Since the historical kingdom of Old Testament Israel had a pronounced social dimension, and since the kingdom Jesus preached and established included social benevolence of all sorts, it is concluded that all church work is at the same time kingdom work. Since the work of the church, in this view, is to extend Christ's kingdom, it is irresistible logic to say that the institutional church is also to be socially engaged in the world. However, if the church is not the new Israel and Christ is not now sitting on David's throne, and the messianic kingdom is not in fact established today, then any social program built thereon evaporates.

Dispensationalism, a better approach to the Bible, understands the Bible to teach a fundamental theological distinction and discontinuity between Israel and the church in origin, purpose, and destiny. While redemptive unity is woven all through the Bible, God's dealings with mankind have a more comprehensive and primitive purpose than redemption in mind, namely His own self glory. Therefore His plan for the nation Israel differs from His plan for the church, and it is theological confusion not to see this distinction. Jesus performed His ministry in an Old Testament world and His kingdom officially extended only to the nation Israel (Matt 10:5-7). Since Jesus' kingdom was never defined or redefined and must have been clearly understood by the Jews, one is forced to conclude that Jesus offered the literal, earthly reign of Israel's Messiah foretold by the Old Testament prophets.[8]

To be sure, the kingdom Jesus, John the Baptist, and others announced to Israel carried clear-cut social and spiritual demands. Israel rejected the proffered kingdom (John 19:15), crucified the King, and the kingdom program was delayed until the end times (Matt 21:43) when it will be established at the second coming of Christ (Matt 25:34; Rev 12:10; 19:6). There is not presently a messianic kingdom of God in existence; there is no "kingdom now." The church is not the kingdom and cannot participate in any social proposals attributable to the kingdom, and for that reason there can be no tenable sociopolitical kingdom advancement by the church in the present age.

The recent dispensational revisionism known as "progressive dispensationalism" is a hybrid of traditional dispensationalism and covenant theology. It

---

[8]The whole idea of the Kingdom of God is masterfully presented by Alva J. McClain, *The Greatness of the Kingdom* (Grand Rapids: Zondervan, 1959).

too sees the eschatological kingdom as being inaugurated in the present age and thus implies a program of sociopolitical exercise for the church. Contributing factors in the formation of the revised dispensationalism include its sensitivity to the social rhetoric of the new evangelicalism and a disdain for historic dispensationalism's rejection of a "kingdom now" in any messianic sense. Historic dispensationalism has often been severely criticized for its lack of a social agenda for the institutional church of the present age, but progressive dispensationalism provides a medium between the social concerns of evangelicalism at large, and does so under the name of dispensationalism. The hermeneutical synthesis has given progressive dispensationalists respectability at the table of social agitation and activism.

The progressives' idea of the church as "a phase of the eschatological kingdom" forms the foundation for "a social ministry [for] the church."[9] This foundation is clearly explicated.

> From what base does the church speak to national justice and peace? From the progressive dispensational perspective, that base should be the future eschatological kingdom, which is known through direct prophecy, through the witness of past dispensations, and the manifestation of kingdom righteousness in the life of the church itself. The church must participate from a revelational base in which it seeks justice from within its own society and testifies from that base in its work for justice in the society at large.[10]

The progressive dispensational view and all views founded on "kingdom ethics" are internally self-destructive and ruinous in addition to being faulty exegetically and theologically. The reason is that kingdom ethics are for the in-group, they are for the citizens of the kingdom and not for the outsiders. By definition a mixed society or the "society at large," saved and unsaved, is not the in-group. While the kingdom ethics view may provide a word for social conduct within the kingdom community, it is too much of a stretch, and without biblical warrant, to impose those demands on the world at large. In terms of the kingdom idea, "no one can tell us with confidence what sort of [kingdom] social policy it requires in a mixed community;"[11] "nowhere in the New Testament is the Kingdom idea...made the 'way in' to social ethics in a mixed society. It appeals exclusively to those who are citizens of the Kingdom."[12] Therefore, any local or global social agitation imposed on the institutional church that is based on the ethics of Jesus' kingdom is self-defeating, impractical, and irrelevant.

There is quite obviously a definite correlation between one's eschatological scheme and any present social engagement in the name of Christ and His church.[13] McClain saw this with clear theological precision:

---

[9]Craig A. Blaising and Darrell L. Bock, *Progressive Dispensationalism* (Wheaton: Victor, 1993), pp. 285-86.

[10]Ibid., p. 289.

[11]Oliver R. Barclay, "The Theology of Social Ethics: A Survey of Current Positions," *Evangelical Quarterly* 62 (1990), p. 65.

[12]Ibid., p. 66.

[13]For further discussion on this point, see Wilber B. Wallis, "Eschatology and Social Concern," *Journal of the Evangelical Theological Society* 24 (1981), pp. 3-9; and Theo. J. W. Kunst, "The Kingdom of God and Social Justice," *Bibliotheca Sacra* 140 (1983), pp. 109-16.

> The identification of the Kingdom with the Church has led historically to ecclesiastical policies and programs which, even when not positively evil, have been far removed from the original simplicity of the New Testament *ekklesia*....But practically, once the Church becomes the Kingdom in any realistic theological sense, it is impossible to draw any clear line between principles and their implementation through political and social devices....Thus the Church loses its "pilgrim" character and the sharp edge of its divinely commissioned "witness" is blunted. It becomes an *ekklesia* which is not only in the world, but also *of* the world[14] (italics his).

The thoughts of John Sproule articulate the dispensationalists' conclusion:

> The social and political condition of the world will be radically improved only when Christ Himself returns to reign. Then, and only then, will true justice reign universally. It has never been God's plan in history to reconstruct a fallen world with fallen men. No *human* plan will relieve this problem.[15]

ENVIRONMENTALISM

Ecology as part of the new evangelical social agenda merits a closer look, especially its primal point that man is to serve the plant and animal world and his fellow human beings as part of his social stewardship. An evangelical attempt to make a theology of animal rights concluded: "This, then, is the biblical picture: Men and women *are* animals. They share creatureliness with the beasts. Saint Francis was right to address animals as 'brother' and 'sister'" (italics his).[16] Another noted that "within Christianity there is room for tremendous differences—room for the chicken farmer viewing his birds as meat-making machines, as well as for Saint Francis preaching sermons to them."[17] Andrew Linzey put it: "We are in the world to represent God and to serve the world."[18] Erickson sounded the same note when he counseled that "animals, plants, and minerals are not merely means to human ends. They are ends in themselves. Their welfare is the responsibility of the human,...who must see to it that they fulfill God's highest and best intention for them."[19]

Fundamental questions arise in this connection. Is man to serve creation? Or is man to be served by creation? Or is there some middle ground of mutual or complementary servitude? The biblical teaching strongly affirms that man in the image of God is to be served by the created order. The creation account itself makes this clear.

The creation account in Genesis 1 and 2 comprehends the universe or all that is not God. It is the only divinely revealed and hence the only infallibly authoritative record of the origin of all time-space-mass phenomena or exchanges of energy. More particularly the creation narrative is concerned with the earth—its

---

[14]Alva J. McClain, *The Greatness of the Kingdom*, pp. 438-39.

[15]John A. Sproule, "The Social Gospel Invades Evangelicalism," *Grace Seminary Spire* 10 (Summer 1981).

[16]Loren Wilkinson, "A Theology of the Beasts," *Christianity Today* (June 18, 1990), p. 21.

[17]Tim Stafford, "Animal Lib," *Christianity Today* (June 18, 1990), p. 23.

[18]David Neff, "Why Christians Should Care," an interview with Andrew Linzey, *Christianity Today* (June 18, 1990), p. 22.

[19]Millard Erickson, *The Evangelical Mind and Heart*, p. 61.

features and inhabitants; it has a general geocentric (earth-centered) perspective. However, the creation of man is the crowning glory of God's creative activity. The rest of creation is designed to serve man in providing food, clothing, shelter, and whatever is necessary to rule planet earth for God. The supplemental account of creation (Genesis 2) emphasizes day six, especially the creation and original activity of mankind. So the narrative is both earth-centered and man-centered. The creation of the heavens and the earth, then, was ultimately designed for the benefit of God's image-bearers, i.e., man and woman (Gen 1:27-28; 1 Cor 11:7).

The image of God in man finitely replicates the infinite Creator and enables man to enjoy the created order, fulfill God's mandate to rule the earth, have a loving relationship with his God, and glorify Him to the greatest extent possible. Therefore, to suggest that the non-rational ecological order possesses a kind of independent value necessitating man's servitude is specious. Nor do animals and the environment possess the inherent worth by which to command a moral parity with human beings to be worked out in some form of complementary flow chart. The rest of the created order is subservient to man even as man is subservient to God. The difference in servitude in both cases is based on factors that are *infinitely* qualitative. Animals no more deserve to be called "brother" and "sister" than man deserves to be called God. It is simply not the case that "if eyes were made for seeing, beauty is its own excuse for being."[20]

Of course mankind is to be a good steward of the environment as part of the husbandry of being God's vice-regent over creation through the dominion mandate of Genesis 1:28. Man's responsibility includes the humane treatment of animals (Prov 12:10: "a righteous man has regard for the life of his animal"), a mandate founded on the native inferiority of non-rational creation and the inherent worth of man as God's image-bearer who is the apex and crown of God's creative activity. However, man's stewardship obligation far from suggests that man and the animal/vegetable/mineral creation are on a level playing field in God's hierarchy of function. Precisely the opposite is true; man is king and all other created things are subjects (Psa 8:3-8, note the regal language).

THE MORAL MAJORITY

The Moral Majority, formed in 1979, gained public prominence during the 1980 presidential campaign. Jerry Falwell, the founder, articulated "An Agenda For the Eighties" in which he described the composition and purpose of the movement.

> Today Moral Majority, Inc., is made up of millions of Americans, including 72,000 ministers, priests, and rabbis who are deeply concerned about the moral decline of our nation, the traditional family, and the moral values on which our nation was built. We are Catholics, Jews, Protestants, Mormons, Fundamentalists—blacks and whites—farmers, housewives, businessmen, and businesswomen. We are Americans from all walks of life united by one central concern: to serve as a special-interest group providing a voice for a return to moral sanity in these United States of America.[21]

---

[20]Ralph Waldo Emerson, "The Rhodora."

[21]Jerry Falwell, *The Fundamentalist Phenomenon*, Jerry Falwell, ed., with Ed Hinson, and Ed Dobson (Garden City, NY: Doubleday and Co., 1981), pp. 188-89.

The Moral Majority is open to criticism form several angles. Its claim to be a purely political organization cannot be sustained. Clergymen especially cannot function merely as "private citizens" in the Moral Majority and men of the cloth on other occasions. They always carry the image of some kind of representatives for God, and their public appearances and pronouncements are interpreted in a religious sense or a sense in keeping with their status as Fundamentalist pastors, Roman Catholic priests, Jewish rabbis, etc. Furthermore, because of the impossibility of acting solely as private citizens in the political arena, the associations of the various religious groups within the Moral Majority are popularly understood and perceived as ecumenism.

Another criticism targets the Moral Majority's claim that America, more than any other nation (actually to the exclusion of any other nation), is ordained by God to evangelize the world, maintain freedom, and protect the Jews. The USA is not an "elect" nation; in fact there are no such nations in the world today, and none will exist until Israel looks to Him whom they pierced (Zech 12:10). The millennial kingdom will be established on earth in the *eschaton* with Israel again as the divinely favored nation. If America is destined to lead in the mass evangelism of the world, and if the USA is the protector of the Jews for their role in the end times, then it follows that the rapture of the church and the coming of Christ for His saints must occur in the foreseeable future or at least in the present generation.

The question still persists: Does God have a prophesied national agenda for any group except theocratic Israel? Is there a biblically revealed role for a specific nation, in this case the United States, in the present church age? Such is not the case. Governments in this age serve the interests of *individuals* so they can pursue the will of God in tranquility (Rom 13:1-7; 1 Tim 2:1-2). That God has a hidden agenda or a secret will for all nations, indeed for everything that comes to pass, is impossible to deny. But there is no biblical mandate for America, Japan, or Chile to serve the purposes of the modern state of Israel in view of the end times.

A third difficulty with the Moral Majority is the fact that there is no biblical or theological precedent for church saints merely to establish or restore non-sectarian morality in a nation, even though that morality may be theistic and in the "Judeo-Christian tradition." The implicit assumption is that to restore morality to America is to restore *God* to the nation. The theological implications of this idea are very uncomfortable; it sounds more like a throw-back to the secularistic, tired, and outdated concepts of the social gospel. In fact, George Marsden argues that the Moral Majority and fundamentalist thinking got the notion of a general moral consensus from Enlightenment thought with its basis in natural theology.[22]

If the Moral Majority type of response to the secular culture is inadequate, what would constitute a proper response? Several factors can be mentioned briefly.[23] (1) A Christian should be careful to maintain personal holiness and

---

[22]George M. Marsden, "Roots of the New Fundamentalism," *The Bulletin of Westminster Theological Seminary* (Winter 1983), p. 2.

[23]These basic proposals were put forth by Jeffrey R. Benson, "An Analysis of the Religious Right," (Unpublished notes, Spring Workshop, Central Baptist Theological Seminary of Minneapolis, 1983), with my own thoughts and biblical references added.

exhibit good works, normal ingredients of a viable Christian experience in any circumstance. (2) A believer must challenge the secular society with the redemptive claims of Christ and not merely with a call to old fashioned morality. Morality cannot stand on its own base; it is not self-defining. Morality without Jesus Christ and the truth-claims of the Christian witness is not enough. (3) The church can and should publicly proclaim biblical values and true biblical morality from a complete Christian agenda. A local church can be biblically oriented without being beholden to or intimidated by the distinctives of all the various denominations, sects, civic clubs, and fraternal orders. As such it can declare the total claims of the Christian world view and way of life to all. (4) A believer should not shun all political involvement. Full participation in the political process is a valid option for a Christian layman. The idea of the "salt of the earth" is primarily individual, not corporate or institutional; institutional churches should not become political power bases. (5) The church should adopt and maintain a non-antagonistic and non-belligerent profile and attitude toward civil authorities. The New Testament instructs believers to be in submission to the temporal powers for the Lord's sake (Rom 13:1-7; Titus 3:1; 1 Pet 2:13-14). Otherwise they will be subject to the judicial anger of the constabulary whose punitive authority is God-given (Rom 13: 2-5). Resistance is justifiable only when the government forces one to sin, because obedience to God trumps obedience to earthly rulers (Dan 3:18; Acts 4:19).

INCARNATIONAL MINISTRY

John R. W. Stott, and other evangelicals after him, promoted a philosophy of ministry based on Christ's words in John 17:18 ("As You sent Me into the world, I have sent them into the world") and 20:21 ("As the Father has sent Me, I also send you"). "Sent" is taken to mean service, and service by his definition includes not only redemptive service but social service as well.[24] Christ is our model for doing ministry, and He gave attention to the socially poor, needy, sick, and oppressed as well as the spiritually impoverished and destitute. Christians are sent by Christ into the world to incarnate or flesh out today His ministry while He was on earth, bringing redemption not only to personal depravity but to structural sin as well. An examination of the underlying assumptions and underpinnings of the view is in order.

At the outset, it must be noted that the "redemption" of society from its structural depravity is theologically vacuous if not totally erroneous. At best the idea is sensible only in terms of the final consummation of the salvation of the redeemed in the *eschaton* (Heb 9:28), but even this is individual. Exactly how sin can be predicated of society in its impersonal abstract corporate structures is not at all clear. Sin by definition is personal because it involves eternal liability before the perfect justice of the personal infinite God. There cannot be, in truth, "structural" sin that can hear a "social gospel" and be redeemed. Society can be reformed or ameliorated by truth and righteousness through the lives of individuals, but it cannot be redeemed in any valid sense of participating in the atoning benefits of Jesus Christ. The thought of redeeming American society or culture is, in the Bible and theology, virtual nonsense.

---

[24]John R. W. Stott, *Christian Mission in the Modern World* (Downers Grove, IL: InterVarsity, 1975), pp. 23, 24.

The weight of Stott's position rests on Christ's being "sent" by the Father into the world, a mission that becomes the paradigm for the church's service in behalf of Christ today. Did Christ's mission to earth have a definite social intent that was pre-evangelistic if not co-evangelistic? Did Christ's ministry in the area of physical disease, deformity, and death simply gain a hearing for the gospel He preached? Was His sensitivity to physical needs a true and independent "partner" of His gospel, neither contributing to nor borrowing from the gospel? Or was the physical/social side of His ministry for an altogether different purpose that bore secondary but beneficial effects on the recipients?

A true understanding of the "sent ministry" of Jesus Christ is gleaned from the context of John 17 and 20 and from examining the theme of Jesus' commission in the fourth gospel. Stott and others press their understanding of Jesus' commission through a preconceived philosophy of ministry. The commission accounts in the other gospels are virtually ignored. Why, in Stott's proposal, is the much clearer statement of the Great Commission in Matthew 28:18-20, for example, overridden by a dubious understanding of the more truncated "sending" idea of John? Parallel accounts seem to matter little. Stott asserts that "the crucial form in which the Great Commission has been handed down to us (though it is the most neglected because it is the most costly) is the Johannine."[25] What makes John's account the "crucial form" is never explained other than by emphasizing "sentness." Allegedly, Jesus culminates a string of individuals whom God sent into the world to minister His cause, such as Abraham, Moses, Joseph, and the prophets.[26]

John's theme of Jesus being sent does not bear the weight Stott places on it. John invests the term with thoughts of incarnation, obedience to the Father's will, dying as a sin-bearer, proclaiming the good news of release from guilt and moral bondage through faith, the promise of everlasting life, and more. Nor is the actual "sent" theme in John confined to the word "sent." Under normal rules of interpretation, the idea, sentence, or proposition, including synonyms, communicate thought, and such is seldom, if ever, restricted to one word and its use. In introducing the Logos, John said, "And the Word became flesh and dwelt among us" (John 1:14) and "Behold the Lamb of God who takes away the sin of the world!"(v. 29) Christ's "sentness" is immediately connected to His being the God-man and the world's atoning sacrifice. In John 3:17 Christ is sent so that "the world might be saved through Him." In John 4:38 the disciples are sent to "reap" the harvest, suggesting a proclamation that is associated also with "sowing" (vv. 36, 37). This proclamation is predicated on the Son's redemptive sentness in doing the will of the Father and accomplishing His work (v. 34) (cf. 5:19-20; 8:29). In John 6:38 Jesus is the living bread sent down from heaven to do the will of the Father for the certain salvation and bodily resurrection of the elect (vv. 37, 39-40), namely, those who "eat" this bread in saving faith (vv. 48-58). The sent ministry of the disciples involves testifying of Christ through the strength of the Holy Spirit sent by the Son from the Father to testify of Christ (John 15:26-27).

---

[25]Ibid., p. 23.

[26]Ibid., pp. 21-22.

In John 17 the sentness of Christ is defined as a mission of preaching and accomplishing redemption from sin. Whatever else one may note about His earthly ministry must be subservient to that. In Christ's prayer, His petition for the disciples is for them to disseminate his words (v. 8). Christ had accomplished the mission He was sent to do in manifesting the name of God (vv. 4, 6) and delivering the Father's word to His followers (v. 14), a word that had sanctifying power in the individual experience (v. 17). His sent mission becomes the rationale of the disciples' sent ministry (v. 18). The benefits Christ prayed for the disciples He also prayed for those who would become believers through the disciples' word (v. 20). A chain of communicating the revelation of God is extended from the Father, through the Son, through the Son's successors, to all who believe that word. Christ both heralded and accomplished His mission of redemption; His followers can only proclaim it, not accomplish it, in their sent mission from the Son. All of that inheres in this subject of sentness in John 17:18 and is gathered up as well in John 20:21 ("as the Father has sent Me, so send I you") with the addition of a special endowment of the Spirit's power (20:22) to sustain His sent ones in the proclamation of divine forgiveness (20:23) until the great outpouring at Pentecost a few weeks later.

The sent ministry of Christ, and thus of His followers, does not entertain any notions of social agitation except by the prejudiced interpretations of those committed to a social gospel. This truth is buttressed by noting how the Lord at times gave a very low priority to social and physical amelioration. In Mark 1 Christ had experienced great success in healing and in drawing the multitudes in Capernaum (vv. 32-34). But the next day, when everyone was looking for Him (v. 37), the Lord turned His back on them and declared that He had a more urgent ministry of preaching in nearby towns because, in His words, "that is what I came for" (v. 38). He continued a preaching ministry, accompanied by healing, throughout Galilee (v. 39). Whatever the purpose of His social concerns, it was not the primary thing in Christ's agenda, nor was it to draw a wider hearing for the gospel because He deliberately left the Capernaum multitudes, who were clamoring for physical relief, to go instead on a proclamation mission elsewhere in the region.

Similarly, in John 6 Christ fed the 5,000 hungry and needy people by a colossal miracle. But when they sought Him further He discerned that they were "loaves and fishes disciples" and not interested in being His true committed disciples (v. 26). The underlying point of feeding the 5,000 was that He was the Bread of Life (vv. 35, 48, 51) whose appropriation was by total commitment to Him for eternal life, a surrender that required a prior bestowal of divine omnipotence (v. 65). Committed discipleship proved costly and demanding, and fair-weather disciples proved their disinterest in anything beyond their physical relief by "not walking with Him anymore" (v. 66).

So what was the purpose of Jesus' social concern? Was it simply to relieve human suffering? Can the church today meaningfully incarnate the ministry of Christ in this area? Can Christians reduplicate the miracles of Christ in the social and physical realm?

Biblical miracles accredited a messenger and his message. For Christ, miracles were attestations that He was the Son of God, the Messiah of Israel with power to forgive sin and authority to sit on David's throne in the messianic kingdom He was announcing. In the power of His miracles the proffered but impending kingdom had "come upon" Israel of the first century (Matt 12:28).[27] Rejecting or misinterpreting His miracles equaled the rejection of the golden age of the Kingdom of God on earth and of eternal life itself. This rejection, of course, was what was done by Israel in the first century. The compassion of Christ for the physically needy and hurting served a purpose well beyond their present ills. Human relief from suffering and want was merely a by-product of the Lord's sent mission. Although a very welcome and beneficial by-product, it was one whose continuance is irrelevant to a philosophy of ministry for the church of the present age.

The miracles that confirmed the message of the apostles (Heb 2:4-5) were "powers of the age to come" (Heb 6:5), doubtless an oblique reference to the lingering offer of the kingdom that receded throughout the Book of Acts. Christ's successors on earth, the apostles, had appropriate attesting miracles (2 Cor 12:12). Miracles of exorcism and healing were foundational to the New Testament church, the period of its infancy and immaturity (1 Cor 13:8-13), but once the church matured, the need for miracles ceased.[28] A desire for miracles, or near-miracles, to mitigate human misery as a component of church outreach is an infantile reversion to a bygone day.

Arthur Johnston with near-prescience said Stott's new theology of the church's purpose "has dethroned evangelism as *the* only historical aim of mission."[29] But blame cannot begin with Stott, however; he did not start the downgrade toward the social gospel among the new evangelicals. The slide began in the 1940s with Henry's *The Uneasy Conscience of Modern Fundamentalism*. Stott simply but astutely blended evangelicalism with the social program of the World Council of Churches to form a not-too-liberal social gospel with a not-too-fundamentalist evangelism in a synthetic evangelical philosophy of mission. As with most social experiments that tilt toward the theological and political left, the result is often more a feel-good attitude on the part of the promoters than much of a dent in the myriads of social problems of the truly needy.

PRE-EVANGELISM SOCIAL ACTION

The church's mandate for its ministry is the Great Commission and its emphasis on making a whole disciple by means of evangelism followed by baptism and a continuing maturity in the context of a New Testament local assembly. The church does this through the proclamation of the gospel to the world and the instruction of believers in the "all things" which Christ commanded. These things are not just His spoken words recorded in the gospels, but also include the revelation of His apostles whose writings He pre-authenticated before His departure (John 14:26; 15:26-27; 16:12-15; 17:20). No overtones of social involvement infiltrate Christ's words or His apostles' writings. There is no indirect social stratum to the Great Commission even as there is none in any direct sense.

---

[27]Alva J. McClain, *The Greatness of the Kingdom*, p. 272.

[28]See the excellent treatment by John C. Whitcomb, *Does God Want Christians to Perform Miracles Today?* (Winona Lake, IN: BMH, 1979).

[29]*The Battle For World Evangelism*, p. 303.

One would expect that by now a biblical theology and philosophy of missions and evangelism would have been carefully worked out and accepted by the Bible-believing community, evangelical and fundamentalist. Such is not the case. Given the inherent new evangelical pragmatic tendency of promoting what is most productive, whether in evangelism, missions, intellectual dialogue, theology, biblical studies, apologetics, or ecclesiastical separation, it is not surprising to find it in social theory. Pre-evangelistic social activism is, unfortunately, not confined to groups that are far to the left of fundamentalism.

Social exercise as an opportunity to present the gospel is contrary both to the Great Commission with its divinely mandated heralding or preaching ministry of the church and to the complete sovereignty of God in personal salvation. Such a technique reflects an Arminian, woefully inadequate view of human depravity and inability. Biblical witnessing, preaching, or presenting the good news of saving grace is addressed to people in their *lostness* and their absolute inability to respond or make any kind of overture to God of their own unaided free will (Rom 3:11; 1 Cor 2:14). The gospel is not addressed to mankind in its physical, social, or emotional turmoil; these are but the symptoms of the problem, which is the innate hostility of the natural man to the living God (Rom 8:6-8). Society's injustices and inequities are due to the total depravity of individual human beings, and the gospel remedy is the unilateral divine intervention of saving grace that results in total surrender to Christ and complete abandonment to the truth-claims of Christianity. The gospel is the only solution to social ills, and this is the church's message to a mixed society (i.e., saved and unsaved) of hurting people. Repentance is a gift from God (Acts 5:31; 11:18; 2 Tim 2:24-25; Zech 12:10) and so is faith (Acts 14:27; 1 Cor 12:3; Phil 1:9; Heb 12:2; 2 Pet 1:3), and these both come by hearing the proclamation of the Word of God (Rom 10:8, 17) as it is accompanied by the transforming work of God's Spirit (John 6:65; 1 Cor 2:1-5). The belief that the natural man with an empty belly cannot respond to the call for repentance and faith is strange theology indeed. It is Arminian, if not Pelagian, in content; it assumes that one's stomach ultimately controls his response to the gospel, or else it presupposes some form of volitional equilibrium by which a person has no inclination for or against the gospel except through the glands. This is not only unscriptural, it is inherently unstable and self-destructive because it has no limiting notion. How much hunger must be satisfied before someone will respond to the gospel? Perhaps a chilly or cold person cannot exercise faith until he is given warm clothing or a heated house; if so, how warm must he be? This is to say nothing of his diminished self-esteem that must be shored up and his hierarchy of needs correctly aligned before the natural man is ready to surrender to Christ. But how psychologically adjusted must he be? In other words, the felt needs that must be satisfied before the gospel can be presented are endless, and evangelism based on meeting such needs is totally unproductive and thus of no use. Such an approach is an insult to God's sovereign grace and unlimited power to save whom He will by the means He has clearly established.

If social activism is not a legitimate evangelistic technique, fundamentalism itself is in need of rethinking its long practice of institutional missions. "Missions" (home and foreign) now covers activities far removed from preaching the gospel and establishing local churches. Doctors, nurses, lab technicians, crisis pregnancy centers, diesel engineers, radio technicians, pilots, mechanics, music teachers, English teachers, karate experts, magicians, and many others have for a long time been using the label "missionaries" or "Christian workers, " whose fundamental rationale seems purely social. Local church missionary budgets are bloated and clogged with those whose real New Testament ministry is non-existent, obscure, or at best "on the side." It is incongruous for fundamentalists to criticize new evangelical social agitation when their own missionary/evangelism philosophy is often bereft of a consistent proclamational, local church establishing motif.

PART 8: DOCTRINAL STORMS

The new evangelicalism has undergone some costly doctrinal upheavals with long-lasting effects. Despite the widespread opinion among new evangelicals that their movement is not a doctrinal one, theological issues continuously intrude themselves into their history and vie for attention. Indeed, the major differences between fundamentalism and the new evangelicalism arose essentially as doctrinal issues, such as separatism, social concerns, evangelism, apologetics, inspiration and inerrancy, among others. These internal controversies have not caused groups to break away from the evangelical movement because division, schism, and separation are the scarlet sins in new evangelical thought. What happens is that the *avant garde* ideas cause internal controversy and calls then go out for more prayer, more open-mindedness, more finessing, and more effort to find some kind of tolerable middle ground.[1] These summons may be accompanied by not-so-veiled charges of causing disorder in the body of Christ, but when the turmoil quiets down, the new element is simply absorbed into the general new evangelical movement, and life goes on in the name of Christian brotherhood. Meanwhile as the movement has become doctrinally diluted and less and less biblical there is internal debate about what an evangelical really is.[2] In the end, no one seems to be excluded from being considered an evangelical. There always seems to be "room at the evangelical table"[3] for all but the most extreme and bizarre views. This section will examine three doctrinal topics: the lostness of the heathen, the eternal fate of the wicked, and the "open theism" view of God.

---

[1] For example, in the eternal torment/annihilation dispute among evangelicals, the Evangelical Alliance Commission of Unity and Truth Among Evangelicals (in England) was established "to work for *consensus* of theological issues that test evangelical unity, and to provide, on behalf of evangelicals, a coordinated theological response to matters of wider public debate" (italics added). Robert A. Peterson, "Undying Worm, Unquenchable Fire," *Christianity Today* (Oct 23, 2000), p. 33.

[2] For example, Roger Olson, "The Future of Evangelical Theology," *Christianity Today* (Feb 9, 1998), pp. 32-50, with responses by Clark H. Pinnock, Thomas C. Oden, and Timothy George. David Neff, editor of *Christianity Today*, said that "evangelicals are still confused [as they were in 1955] about their role in society, divided as a body, *and even bewildered about what evangelical means*" (italics added) ("*Christianity Today* Predicts: More of the Same," *Christianity Today* [Dec 6, 1999], p. 36).

[3] Robert A. Peterson, "Undying Worm, Unquenchable Fire," p. 36.

20

THE STATUS OF THE
UNEVANGELIZED

NEW EVANGELICAL VARIATIONS

Evangelical thought went through, and is still enduring, a vigorous debate over the lostness of the unevangelized (heathen or pagans) and the fate of those who never heard the gospel of Jesus Christ. The subject in the religious world in general can be divided and subdivided into various categories, most of which would see some evangelicals in their number.[4] (1) Pluralism—all religions make it possible for a person to be rightly related to God. (2) Universalistic Inclusivism—all will be saved through Jesus Christ, but there are various ways that His saving benefits can be applied, such as (a) "Implicit faith"—people can come to Christ through general revelation and casting themselves on God's mercy; (b) "Anonymous Christians"—people who are Christians but do not consciously know it; (c) "Universal election in Christ"—all people are elect in Christ and thus all will be saved eventually. (3) Universalistic Exclusivism—all will come to God only through personal faith in Jesus Christ, usually in the afterlife. (4) Annihilationism—the finally impenitent will be reduced to non-being. (5) Eternal punishment—all the finally impenitent will suffer eternal punishment in hell either (a) both physically and spiritually, or (b) only spiritually. The traditional orthodox view has been that the wicked will endure eternal physical and spiritual suffering in hell. Unrest in the new evangelical ranks over this issue arose in the 1970s and continued to foment increasingly for nearly thirty years. For purposes of this section, two main issues and some of their implications will be noted and analyzed—the status of those who have never heard the gospel and the fate of the finally impenitent.

Exactly why or under what circumstances these matters arose within new evangelical thought and practice may be difficult to ascertain. From appearances,

---

[4]There are different ways of configuring the issue of the fate of the unevangelized. John Sanders has seven views (*No Other Name: An Investigation Into the Destiny of the Unevangelized* [Grand Rapids: Eerdmans, 1992]). *Four Views on Salvation in a Pluralistic World*, Dennis L. Okholm and Timothy R. Phillips, eds. (Grand Rapids: Zondervan, 1995), lists four. In an informative book, Millard Erickson examines six perspectives which resolve into five main issues. Generally he is inconclusive because of the "positive" and "negative" attributes he sees in all the positions (*How Shall They Be Saved? The Destiny of Those Who Do Not Hear of Jesus* [Grand Rapids: Baker, 1996]).

the "dialogue" technique once again seemed to cause a desire to meet modern culture and scholarship on their own terms; in other words, the need to be "relevant" and not appear to be obscurantist and too "fundamental."

Optimism about the nature and abilities of mankind represented the hallmark of liberalism and neoliberalism. It discarded the biblical doctrine of total depravity/inability in favor of the notion of the goodness and perfectibility of human beings. The concept of "sin" consequently degenerated into psychological maladjustment and social inequities, but an individual was never considered "lost" in the biblical sense. Liberalism was universalist, everyone was already "saved" and heaven-bound because no one was truly lost. Atonement for sin by penal satisfaction and eternal punishment for the wicked were abhorrent to liberals.

Neo-orthodoxy, in contrast to liberalism, exemplified extreme pessimism. It saw God as totally transcendent, the Wholly Other dwelling in *geschichte* (eternity), and man as an utterly finite sinner living in *historie* (time). Eternity and time, God and man, were in complete isolation except for the existential encounter with the "Christ event," a magical blip when eternity merely brushed against but never penetrated time. In this timeless moment man received a "revelation" of the Wholly Other or the Hidden God in Christ. Barthian neo-orthodoxy had a Christomonistic principle. This principle held that Christ is both the Elect One and the Reprobate One, subsuming the totality of God's Yes and No regarding all mankind. As such it could never shed the charge of universalism. Neo-orthodoxy, through its dialectical double-talk, tried to deny its implicit universalism by making hell and the eternal lostness of the wicked a philosophical "impossible possibility". Fundamental Bible-believers considered neo-orthodoxy as inscrutable nonsense.

The early fundamentalist/evangelical coalition adamantly opposed the universalism of liberalism, neo-orthodoxy, and many other cults and sects as well. As the American culture embraced relativism, it disdained any form of religious exclusivism, especially the evangelical doctrine of salvation through personal faith in Jesus Christ alone. Typically, certain new evangelicals lamented their negative status and tried to piece together some kind of a synthesis out of the open-endedness of cultural opinion and the exclusiveness of the biblical plan of salvation. They would not affirm that all human beings will go to heaven, but neither would they affirm that all those who had not put their personal trust in Jesus Christ would go to hell. Thus they hoped to recover some respectability in modern eyes by their eclectic, centrist approach to the issue.

As in several cases of evangelical avant-garde theological proposals, Clark Pinnock was the early pathfinder to the new thought. Not all new evangelicals, not even a majority of them, subscribe to the Pinnock model. In fact, some of his fiercest opposition is from within his own evangelical camp. But it was principally Pinnock who gathered up and systematized views that were novel to the traditional orthodox position.

In one of his works, Pinnock notes the contemporary polarity between the complete relativism of modern culture and the restrictivism of the evangelical gospel of eternal life through faith in Jesus of Nazareth. He accordingly feels the need for a middle way that widens God's mercy and extends His salvific purposes by acknowledging what is positive in other religions that contributes to human welfare. What is needed, in his solution, is a new "evangelical theology of religions" to catch up with modern thought, a "greater theological globalism" that opposes the old fundamentalist/evangelical "fewness doctrine" of traditional exclusivism.[5] For him, "the challenge of religious pluralism is not to abandon the finality of Christ, but to grow in the ability to enter into dialogue with those of other faiths, bearing a winsome and winning testimony to His saving power."[6]

In the forward to John Sanders' *No Other Name*, Pinnock asserted that evangelical theology has an "unresolved problem," the problem being the "credibility of God's plan to save humanity. Evangelicals say rhetorically that God desires all men and women to be saved, but their position logically denies all those outside the church any meaningful access to salvation." In his understanding, "many," including himself and other evangelicals, are finding it inconceivable that the vast majority of human beings will perish because they have not heard of Jesus Christ. He is sure that the book he is introducing will help close this "credibility" gap in evangelical theology. He notes that liberal scholars, such as John Hick, "have been making mincemeat out of us [evangelicals], arguing all too convincingly that evangelicals have nothing to contribute to the discussion of religious pluralism." He complains that both liberals and some evangelicals have noted for some time that evangelical theology on this point "is stuck in deep mud, having no new ideas to put forward and no defense to the serious criticisms made of it." Implying that ultimately the Bible is ambiguous and the prudent course to take on the subject is agnosticism, he concludes: "The judgments of God will contain surprises, of course, and we are in no position to give the final word on the final destiny of any group of people."[7]

The enginery behind this particular new evangelical creativity is once again the yearning for acceptance by the liberal and secular elites. Pinnock and many others felt compelled to be on the cutting edge of new thought; evangelicalism must provide fresh answers and demonstrate new relevance for every possible question and criticism. Eventually, evangelicalism's elasticity encloses these questionable, if not heretical, solutions within its fold. To be sure, opposition from within the new evangelical camp to some of these bold and aberrant proposals surfaces, but hardly anyone questions the evangelical credentials of these novelists. Rare is the new evangelical who suggests that the line between biblical orthodoxy and heresy is ever crossed and that those in the vanguard are outside the pale of biblicism and evangelical brotherhood.

In 1971 an article addressing the fate of those who never heard the truth-claims of Christianity appeared.[8] It may well have been a straw in the wind since

---

[5]Clark H. Pinnock, *A Wideness in God's Mercy: The Finality of Jesus Christ in a World of Religions* (Grand Rapids: Zondervan, 1992), pp. 12-13.

[6]Clark H. Pinnock, "Why is Jesus the Only Way?" *Eternity* (Dec 1976), pp. 14-15.

[7]Clark Pinnock, "Forword," in John Sanders, *No Other Name*, pp. xiii-xv.

[8]Joseph M. Ferrente, "The Final Destiny of Those Who Have Not Heard the Gospel," *Trinity Studies* 1(1971), pp. 55-62. *Trinity Studies* was published by the students and faculty of Trinity Evangelical Divinity School.

the question took on huge proportions within the new evangelicalism inside of just a few years. The author presented three possible answers to the question of the final destiny of the unevangelized. They are saved; they are lost; and, the author's preference, they are saved/lost. "The unevangelized can be either saved or lost, depending on their response to the revelation of God they have received."[9] Examples from the Book of Acts yielded instances of non-Christians who responded to some kind of inner promptings and were sent divine messengers who led them to faith in Christ, examples such as Cornelius (Acts 10), Saul of Tarsus (Acts 7:51-58; 9:1-18), and the Ethiopian eunuch (Acts 8:26-39).[10]

In 1975 Millard Erickson enlarged on the question. Finding a parallel with the convicting power of the law of Moses (Rom 3:19-20), he proposes that natural law can have a similar effect.[11] Just as one can be convicted of sin and brought into a reliance on God for salvation through the law, the convicting voice of natural revelation can also have such an effect. "This must then be the pattern (or a similar one) involved in the possible salvation of those who have only the natural law."[12] Since Christ is the only Savior, Erickson suggests that Romans 10:18 teaches that an implied knowledge of Christ goes out to all the earth through natural revelation. "Paul appears to say that men have heard through [nature]. If that be the case, then perhaps the essential nature of saving faith can be arrived at without the special revelation. Perhaps…it is possible to receive the benefit of Christ's death without conscious knowledge-belief in the name of Jesus."[13] He appeals to Old Testament believers as evidence that one can be saved apart from an explicit knowledge of Jesus Christ.[14]

In 1975 Harold Lindsell also propounded the view that God will send more light to a seeking heathen who has never heard of Christ. Many in the old fundamentalist/evangelical coalition agreed, and many contemporary fundamentalists still do today. Lindsell wrote:

> Let it be said that any one who really wants to know God even though he has no particular knowledge of the law or the Gospel will be given the opportunity to hear of Christ and to receive him as Savior. It is God's responsibility to make certain that whoever really wants the knowledge of God will receive it. *This has been demonstrated many times in the missionary situation*....One way or another God in his mercy will make known what the unsaved need to know if they really wish to know God (italics added).[15]

---

[9]Ibid., p. 59.

[10]Ibid., pp. 59-60. J. Ronald Blue said similarly: "Even when an unevangelized heathen appears to show an initial response in line with the revelation afforded him, as in the case of Cornelius in Acts 10, the Lord employs one of His servants to bring the fuller revelation of Jesus Christ necessary for salvation" ("Untold Billions: Are They Really Lost?" *Bibliotheca Sacra* 138 [1981], p. 349). John MacArthur likewise considers Cornelius to have had a seeking heart, to have lived up to the light he had, and one to whom God gave more light (*Romans 9-16*, The MacArthur New Testament Commentary [Chicago: Moody, 1994], p. 293).

[11]Millard J. Erickson, "Hope For Those Who Haven't Heard? Yes, But…," *Evangelical Missions Quarterly* 11 (1975), p. 124.

[12]Ibid.

[13]Ibid.

[14]Ibid., pp. 125-26.

[15]Harold Lindsell, "Universalism," in *Let the Earth Hear His Voice: International Congress on World Evangelization, Lausanne, Switzerland*, J. D. Douglas, ed. (Minneapolis: Worldwide Publications, 1975), p. 1212.

In 1976 Clark Pinnock, as usual, made waves by his bold new understanding on the status of those who never heard of Christ. Concerning the dilemma between the finality of Christ as the only way to salvation and the multitudes who have never heard of Him, Pinnock says, "One not very satisfactory traditional answer has been to insist that salvation can only be found in an explicit faith relationship with Christ." This is the "hardline view, which disagrees so badly with what we know about God's passion to save sinners."[16] To him, God notices who among the heathen really is in search of the Good. Pinnock is in agreement with some church fathers who "believed that those who lived by the *Logos* present in the world were in reality Christians *if their attitude was right*" (italics added).[17] Pinnock wanted to "focus on the desire for salvation which exists in many human hearts" as evidenced by the many world religions.[18] Drawing on 1 Peter 4:6 and 3:19 (the gospel preached to the dead), Pinnock posits a post-mortem opportunity in which for the heathen "the desire to believe which is accepted in lieu of explicit faith in Christ, is finally completed at death when we all encounter the true God." This is not a second chance; for them this will be their first chance. Of this Pinnock is certain: "God will not abandon in hell those who have not known and therefore have not declined His offer of grace."[19]

In the same *Eternity* article was a sidebar piece by the editor that notes the view of J. N. D. Anderson that ignorance does not disqualify one for grace because for grace "it is not so much knowledge as a right attitude towards God that matters."[20] Anderson goes on to quote another that "it is possible that an omniscient God will judge those who have never heard of Christ on the basis of what he knows would have been their response if they had heard."[21]

In 1978 Billy Graham caused great controversy in an interview in *McCall's* magazine, which reported:

> "I used to play God," [Graham] acknowledged, "but I can't do that any more. I used to believe that pagans in far-off countries were lost—were going to hell—if they did not have the Gospel of Jesus Christ preached to them. I no longer believe that," he said carefully. "I believe that there are other ways of recognizing the existence of God—through nature, for instance—and plenty of other opportunities, therefore, of saying 'yes' to God."[22]

As was his habit in such cases, Graham later claimed the interview gave an incorrect impression of his beliefs. In a prepared statement, he averred, "Contrary

---

[16]Clark H. Pinnock, "Why is Jesus the Only Way?" p. 15.

[17]Ibid.

[18]Ibid., p. 32.

[19]Ibid. Elsewhere he forthrightly stated of 1 Pet 3:19-20 and 4:6: "It seems plausible to suppose that Peter means that the gospel comes to the dead so that they 'might live in the spirit with God' if they respond to the proclamation they hear. In this way the universality of Christ's redemption is vindicated and made effective" ("The Finality of Jesus Christ In a World of Religions," in *Christian Faith and Practice in the Modern World* [Grand Rapids: Eerdmans, 1988], p. 163).

[20]Russell T. Hitt, "Have They Not Heard?" *Eternity* (Dec 1976), p. 15.

[21]Ibid.

[22]James Michael Beam, "I Can't Play God Any More," *McCall's* (Jan 1978), pp. 156, 158.

to what the article later suggests, I *do* believe that non-Christians are lost—whether they live in far-off countries or in America."[23] Explaining the "other ways of recognizing the existence of God," Graham noted that the Bible says:

> All men have some light given by God, both in the creation and in the human conscience. Whoever sees the footsteps of the Creator in nature can ask the God he does not fully know for help, and I believe God—in ways we may not fully understand—will give that person further light and bring him to a knowledge of the truth that is in Jesus Christ so he will be saved. He may use our preaching or he may use any other way he chooses, but ultimately it is God...who saves men.[24]

Stephen Davis, a professing evangelical, decried the "Christian triumphalism" of the fundamentalist "theory" that "Christianity has all the truth worth knowing;... that people who die as nonbelievers in Christ have no hope of avoiding eternal damnation."[25] His position: "I believe it quite possible that in the mercy of God non-Christians can be saved. But if they are, it is only through Jesus Christ, whom they do not affirm and of whom they may never have heard."[26]

Stanley Ellisen tried to address the lostness of the pagans in biblical fashion. He approached the subject with four main points. (1) Salvation is exclusively in God through Jesus Christ (Isa 43:11; Jn 14:6; et al.). (2) Christ is the world's only Savior (Isa 53:6; Gal 3:21; Rom 4:25). (3) Christ is a world-wide Savior (1 John 2: 2; 1 Tim 2:6; 2 Cor 5:19). (4) God gives further light to those who respond positively to His revelation in nature. "God has given all men the light of creation, providence, and conscience, each of which testifies to the existence, power, and glory of God. To those who acknowledge and seek Him, He sends the light of the gospel."[27]

John R. W. Stott declared his agnosticism regarding the eternal fate of those who have never heard the gospel. He is against universalism but sees an implication in the "surprise" of the sheep and goats (Matt 25) that one is accepted or rejected by God based on good works.[28] He is tolerant of the view that Christ in his foreknowledge could see what people would have done with the gospel and thus judge them accordingly, using the example of Korazin, Bethsaida, and Capernaum (Matt 11:21).[29] Stott does not believe everyone will have an opportunity for post-mortem repentance,[30] but is kindly disposed to the idea that some who have never heard of Christ can cry out to God for mercy in remorse for their sin and guilt, since Old Testament believers were saved without a personal knowledge of Christ.[31] But

---

[23]"Graham Explains Interview in McCall's," *Eternity* (Mar 1978), p. 11.

[24]"Graham's Beliefs: Still Intact," *Christianity Today* (Jan 13, 1978), p. 49.

[25]Stephen T. Davis, "Evangelicals and the Religions of the World," *TSF Bulletin* (Sept-Oct 1981), p. 9.

[26]Ibid., p. 10.

[27]Stanley E. Ellisen, "Are Pagans Really Lost?" *Conservative Baptist* (Spring 1983), pp. 6-9.

[28]John R. W. Stott and David L. Edwards, *Evangelical Essentials* (Downers Grove, IL: InterVarsity, 1988), p. 325.

[29]Ibid.

[30]Ibid., p. 326.

[31]Ibid., p. 327.

in the end he feels that "the most Christian stance is to remain agnostic on this question....The fact is that God...has not revealed how he will deal with those who have never heard [the gospel]."[32]

In 1988 Evert Osburn argued along four lines that hope for the unevangelized exists. First, "Just as the Israelites of the OT brought sacrifices to God...so may the unreached 'heathen' come to the one true God in repentance and faith and be forgiven."[33] Second, Romans 10:11-17 indicates that "apparently some of the gospel of Christ is known through general revelation apart from the written word."[34] Third, religious traditions are quite possibly based on an ancestral knowledge of the true God and have preserved enough of the gospel to lead to salvation.[35] Fourth, "since Christ and God the Father are equal...then sincere belief in the God of creation as the one and only true God is implicit belief in Christ (and the Holy Spirit, the other co-equal member of the Godhead)."[36]

Christopher Lamb poses the question: Is there truth in other religions? To him, "the answer... is quite straightforwardly: Yes. If this were not so there would be no possibility of communicating Christian truths to people of other faiths and religious traditions, since there would be no prior understanding, no vocabulary even, in which you could express the Christian faith itself."[37] Accordingly, "we should therefore treat other faiths as Judaism is treated in [the Book of Hebrews], not as enemies of the Christian faith but as—ever chronologically related to Christianity—forerunner of it."[38] Lamb does not feel that Jesus's words of exclusiveness in John 14:6 ("I am the way...no one comes to the Father, except by me") is a negative statement about other faiths but simply that the path to the Father is by way of the cross.[39]

Colin Chapman is pained at the thought that the unevangelized are hopelessly lost. His understanding of the exclusiveness of John 14:6 ("no one comes to the Father but through Me") is that people of other faiths may indeed have some kind of a relationship with the true God but that they can not relate to God "as father" except through Christ.[40] He knew of some devout Muslims who had a relationship

---

[32]Ibid. Leon Morris concurs with the agnostic approach: "We do not know what the fate of those who have not heard the gospel will be" ("The Dreadful Harvest," *Christianity Today* [May 27, 1991], p. 37). Amazingly, no less an evangelical leader and theologian than Kenneth Kantzer shares the same opinion. He concluded that "the fate of those who have never heard has been a troublesome issue throughout history. Yet Scripture has not given us enough information to resolve the problem" ("Preface," in *Through No Fault of Their Own?: The Fate of Those Who Have Never Heard*, eds. William V. Crockedtt and James G. Sigountos [Grand Rapids: Baker, 1991], p. 14).

[33]Evert D. Osburn, "Those Who Have Never Heard: Have They No Hope?" *Journal of the Evangelical Theological Society* 32 (1989), p. 368.

[34]Ibid., p. 369.

[35]Ibid., pp. 369-70.

[36]Ibid., p. 371.

[37]Christopher Lamb, "An Evangelical Theology of Pluralism: A Personal View," *Evangelical Review of Theology* 14 (1990), p. 81.

[38]Ibid., p. 82.

[39]Ibid., p. 84.

[40]Colin Chapman, "The Riddle of Religions," *Christianity Today* (May 14, 1990), p. 17.

with God because of the quality of their lives, but they would never think of calling God their *Father*.[41] Cornelius is exemplified as one who has "faith" in God, but who was not saved or justified. Such an one is in a different position from one who has no faith. He seems to side with those "respected evangelical teachers" who were questioning the lostness of all those in world religions who never knew of Christ.[42]

In a 1992 book-length treatise of the subject, Clark Pinnock in similar fashion amplified his views. He coined the term "pagan saints" to describe Old Testament believers who did not know of Jesus of Nazareth and never had explicit faith in Him, saints such as Enoch, Daniel, Noah, Abel, Melchizedec, Abimilech, Seth, Jethro, Rahab, Ruth, Naaman, the Queen of Sheba, and Job.[43] So today there is religious faith "neither Jewish nor Christian, which is nonetheless noble, uplifting, and sound."[44] Pinnock understands Paul at Athens (Acts 17:22-31) as "acknowledging the good intentions of the Greeks in worshiping the Unknown God....Evidently Paul thought of these people as believers in a certain sense, in a way that could be and should be fulfilled in Jesus Christ."[45] He believed that "many people in the other religions worship God, even if in ways that fall conceptually short of the revelation of God's nature which Christ brings."[46] "Religions do not present only the way of human self-justification. At times they also announce the grace and love of God. When they do, this Christian, at least, rejoices."[47]

In a fast-forward to 2001, noted Southern Baptist radio preacher, Charles Stanley, declared that God would not send to hell those who have not heard the gospel. "Would God send somebody to hell because they did not receive Jesus whom they never heard about, never had the privilege of knowing about? And my answer is: No, he would not."[48]

ANALYSIS

While it is neither practical nor necessary to investigate every tenet and assertion of the aforementioned new evangelical preachers and teachers, several load-bearing points call for analysis.

Heathen Ability

It has been assumed in the foregoing evangelical tenets that the heathen have the ability to make a positive response to natural or general revelation, an assumption based on both exegetical and theological error. Theologically, the doctrine of total depravity precludes any form of natural ability to make any kind of an overture or any form of a proper response to any revelation of God. The natural man is dead in

---

[41] Ibid., p. 18.

[42] Ibid., p. 19.

[43] Clark H. Pinnock, *A Wideness in God's Mercy*, pp. 22, 26,92, *passim*.

[44] Ibid., p. 92.

[45] Ibid., p. 32.

[46] Ibid., p. 46.

[47] Ibid., pp. 100-101.

[48] Charles Stanley, "Reconciling God's Love With His Justice," In Touch Ministries, July 31, 2001.

trespasses and sins (Rom 8:6; Eph 2:1), unwilling and unable to respond positively to the revelation of God and spiritual things in general (1 Cor 2:14). He is natively hostile toward God, being incapable of subjecting himself to the moral law of God (Rom 8:7). Sin has penetrated and affected the whole of his being: body (Rom 8:10), mind (Rom 8:5-6), heart (Jer 17:9), and will (Jer 13:23). The unsaved person is completely destitute of the love for God which His moral law requires (Matt 22:27-28). Only the sovereign intervening grace of God can change the natural man's disposition to sin and relieve his implacable enmity toward his Creator and Judge.

Simple and straight-forward exegesis of Scripture also reveals that the natural man cannot rightly follow the light of his conscience or the revelation of God in the material creation. He has no desire to know God because he uniformly chooses to worship and serve some aspect of the created order rather than the Creator (Rom 1:25). He is not capable of engaging in a "search" for the true and living God because *no one searches for God* (Rom 3:11[49]). Those who worship sticks and stones are renegades from God, not seekers of Him. Their heathenism is a form of their suppression of the truth by means of unrighteousness (Rom 1:18, 23). Idolatry among the unevangelized is no more a search for God than is homosexuality (Rom 1:26-27) and the other terrible items in the apostle's sin list (Rom 1:28-32). Granted, God's benevolence to all mankind *ought* to cause everyone to grope for and find Him because He is near at hand (Acts 17:25-28); the natural man is virtually drowning in an ocean of God's self-disclosing goodness. But there is a vast difference between what man ought to do and what he actually does. The reason for man's waywardness is his complete inability to do what he should do or, conversely, his inevitable *perversion* of God's revelation due to his total self-interest.

The case of the Gentile Cornelius is often brought up as one responding to God on his own, and the analogy is then made to the heathen responding to the sun or the lightning in his search for God. If Cornelius prayed and was heard (Acts 10:30-33), the unevangelized can also. The examples, however, are not comparable. For one, Cornelius was not an unenlightened aboriginal pagan seeking God by bowing down to fetishes and idols and responding to thunder claps. He was one who had a great deal of knowledge about God, a Gentile military officer attracted to the monotheism and ethics of Israel's divinely-revealed religion but who had not become a full proselyte because he was not circumcised (Acts 11:3). In truth, he was *not* living up to all the light he had or he would have become a believing convert to the revelation of God and had joined the covenant community by receiving circumcision, the sign of the Abraham Covenant (Gen 17:11). Furthermore, the narrative here is shot through with angelic activity, direct revelation, and miracle so that one is compelled to account for it as one of the significant transitions from Old Testament Mosaism to New Testament Christianity, from Israel's favored status to the full inclusion of Gentiles for the first time in God's plan. In other words, major dispensational factors are involved and,

---

[49]In all the research and sources consulted for this study, I found *no one* even remotely sympathetic to the idea that the heathen can seek for God who attempted in any way to come to terms with this verse.

as such, the experience of Cornelius is not normative, not truly repeatable, and not really germane to the discussion on the status of those who have never had special revelation.

God's Obligation

It is not correct to impose on God the responsibility to respond to heathen seekers, if it were even possible for them to seek Him. God is under no obligation to respond to any person because all have forfeited any claim to divine favor through Adamic guilt and personal rebellion. All are sinners by nature and by choice (Rom 3: 9-18, 23; 5:12, 16a, 17a). It is a fallacy of fallen thinking to understand God being obligated to His enemies in this fashion. It is unthinkable that God is under some kind of coercion to meet any human agenda, much less that of the natural man. God is not responsible to send more light, or a missionary, or a messenger of any kind to anyone.

"Natural" Gospel

It is a misunderstanding of Romans 10:17-18[50] to say that the gospel has gone out to all the earth through natural revelation. The text may sound as if Paul is saying that there is a gospel in natural or general revelation and that all the Jews, if not the world, have heard it but have not believed, but does the apostle imply that the "word of Christ" has gone to Jewry and the world through general revelation?

Since there are any number of texts that teach that conviction of sin and salvation from sin come only through God's special revelation in Scripture,[51] Paul cannot be referring to a "gospel in the stars" or a redemptive natural revelation, for there is none. The main purpose of natural/general revelation is condemnatory not salvific (Rom 1:20: "so that they are without excuse"). The unevangelized are eternally culpable for rejecting the light they do have from the true God, however minimal that may appear to be. In any case, the amount of natural revelation is not really the issue; any degree of divine light is perspicuous (Rom 1:19-20: what they know about God is "evident" and "clearly seen"). The culpability of the heathen stems from their suppression and perversion, by means of their endemic depravity (Rom 1:18), of the knowledge of God they already comprehend.

It is best to understand Paul in Romans 10:18 as using Psalm 19:4 and the universal witness of nature to God as an illustration or simile as to how the gospel has gone into the world, primarily the Jewish world in this chapter and this section of Romans (Rom 9-11). F. F. Bruce is correct: "It is unnecessary to suppose that Paul regarded Ps xix:4 as a *prediction* of the world-wide dissemination of the gospel; he means that the dissemination of the gospel is becoming as world-wide as the light of the heavenly bodies" (italics his).[52] Frederick Godet says similarly: "As the heavens and their hosts proclaim God's existence and perfections to the whole universe,...so, says Paul, with a sort of enthusiasm at the memory of his own ministry, the voice of the preachers of the gospel has sounded in all countries and in

---

[50]"So faith comes from hearing, and hearing by the word of Christ. But I say, surely they have never heard, have they? Indeed they have; 'Their voice has gone out into all the earth, and their words to the ends of the world.'"

[51]For example: 1 Cor 1:18; 1 Thess 1:5; 2 Thess 2:14.

[52]F. F. Bruce, *The Epistle of Paul To the Romans*, The Tyndale New Testament Commentaries, R. V. G. Tasker, ed. (Grand Rapids: Eerdmans, 1954), p. 209.

all the cities of the known world."[53] Robert Picirilli expresses it well: "What [Paul] means is that Israel has just as truly heard the gospel as has all mankind heard natural revelation."[54] Good explanations of the "parallelism" between general and special revelation in this passage are also given by John Murray[55] and E. F. Harrison.[56]

God's Foreknowledge

The appeal to God's foreknowledge as relief from the tension over the fate of the unevangelized is not well-founded. The idea is that God somehow will look ahead and see the decision a pagan would have made if he had heard the gospel of Jesus Christ and accordingly will allot to him his eternal fate. The theological and philosophical factors of this proposal are somewhat complicated and cannot be plumbed to any great depth here, but one basic point can be explored.

"Foreknowledge" as used in this case is simply God's omniscience as it affects the future. Biblically and theologically there are only two viable alternatives: God knows what *will certainly* come to pass, and He knows what *could possibly* have come to pass. Philosophers have proposed a half-way house, called "middle knowledge," by saying that God infallibly knows also what *would actually* have come to pass, but did not in every possible set of circumstances. The whole argument revolves around whether or not there is such a thing as a pure contingency (a genuine if, chance, accident, happenstance, or fortuity) in God's universe and whether or not it can be an object of God's knowledge of the future. Middle knowledge assumes that God can know a contingency as a certainty or actuality. He sees as a certainty and not merely as a possibility what would never happen in reality. In this case God foresees as an actuality the decision the unevangelized would certainly have made if they only would have had the opportunity.

In reply, it must be understood that God's omniscience, or His all-knowing, includes all things past, present, and future, immediately, simultaneously, and eternally, whether things actual or possible. This knowledge means that there are no unexplored possibilities anywhere; God's universe is not "open." God knows all possible exchanges of energy under all possible circumstances; He knows all that could happen, and He knows this by His reason and power. He knows all that He can or could do and therefore He knows possibilities only as possibilities and not as certainties or actualities. God also knows as actualities all that He will do because His will is exhaustive and He knows Himself exhaustively. God knows all future actualities because He has planned or decreed them. The Bible teaches that God has a single, all-inclusive and comprehensive plan, purpose, or will (Prov 16:4; Eph 1:11; 3:11). He foreordains whatsoever comes to pass and His plan is immutable (Isa 14:27; 43:13; Dan 4:35; Acts 13:29). There is no such thing as pure chance or a pure contingency with God; there are no undecreed events and no

---

[53]Frederick Godet, *Commentary on Romans* (Grand Rapids: Kregel, reprinted 1977), p. 388.

[54]Robert Picirilli, *The Book of Romans* (Nashville: Randall House, 1975), p. 212.

[55]John Murray, *The Epistle to the Romans*, New International Critical Commentary on the New Testament, 2 vols. in one (Grand Rapids: Eerdmans, 1977), 2:61.

[56]E. F. Harrison, "Romans," *The Expositor's Bible Commentary*, Frank E. Gaebelein, ed., 12 vols. (Grand Rapids: Zondervan, 1976), 10:114.

ultimately unfulfilled decrees. God can only know as a certainty what He has willed to happen, and since He has willed whatsoever comes to pass, He knows exhaustively all things external to Himself. He cannot therefore "foresee" what never will happen. What decision a heathen would have actually made if he had heard of Christ is simply not an object of divine knowledge. Middle knowledge ends up making a contribution to God's knowledge; that is, God "learns" the outcomes of supposedly pure contingencies. This is information *in addition* to His knowledge of what He foreordained as certainly to come to pass out of all the possibilities He contemplated. What is more, middle knowledge clutters God's mind with false and erroneous information. Of all the infinite vagaries of pure chance that God allegedly "knows" as certainties in His middle knowledge, only *one* is true, and that is the one that actually comes to pass. Middle knowledge is simply the heresy of a denial of God's omniscience and bears no weight in determining the status and eventual fate of the unevangelized.

Paul at the Areopagus

The Areopagus address of the Apostle Paul in Athens (Acts 17) does not attribute anything positive to those ancient idolaters. Paul is not suggesting that their altar to the Unknown God represents a search for the true God, or that somehow in the Unknown God they had inadvertently found the God of the Bible, and thus had found Christ, but simply did not know it. The apostle was not commending their paganism "as far as it went" and thus was going to supplement their theism and bring it up to speed.

An examination of the Mars Hill address reveals a direct confrontation between Paul and the Athenian philosophers, a virtual head-on collision that shows a complete antithesis of world views and starting points in understanding the God of New Testament Christianity. Paul had anything but a positive attitude toward the idea of an Unknown God. "Very religious in all respects" (Acts 17:22) and the "ignorance" to which he attributes their worship (v. 23) are actually quite negative in force. Verse 16 indicates that Paul's spirit was "provoked" (*paroxuno*, aroused, irritated and angry[57]), and verses 22 and 23 are an elaboration of Paul's emotional upheaval at their benighted worship in verse 16. Verses 22 and 23 are actually Paul's evaluation of the Athenians' religious situation. The "ignorance" (*agnountes*) he attributes to them seems to be an intentional allusion to the "unknown" (*agnosto*) god of the one particular altar. In other words, Paul practically reads back to them their profession of a lack of knowledge, or ignorance, as that which characterizes their whole religion.[58] What they worshiped as "unknown" or in "ignorance" is a comment on the *worshipers* themselves as being without knowledge rather than the object of the worship (the "god") being unknown. To these philosophers, in other words, the realm of God or the gods was not only unknown but in the last analysis *unknowable*. The Unknown God represented an open pantheon of the gods; there would always be an Unknown God in their pagan worship. The realm of deity would forever be enshrouded in total mystery and abysmal ignorance.

---

[57]BDAG, s.v., "*paroxuno*," p. 780.

[58]Ned B. Stonehouse, *Paul Before the Areopagus and Other New Testament Studies* (Grand Rapids: Eerdmans, 1957), p. 19.

By contrast, Paul was going to tell these philosophers about that which admittedly they did not actually know; he was going to tell them about the true God and inform them about that which they professed was unknowable. He was going to "inform them with regard to that concerning which they acknowledge ignorance."[59] His starting point was to assume the existence of and proclaim the absolute demands of "the God who made the world and all things in it" (Acts 17:24; cf., Gen 1-2). This was the God whom the Athenians already knew about deep down from natural revelation but which knowledge they perverted by relegating it to the realm of the unknown and unknowable and had publicly advertised the same by erecting their altar.

Paul's session at the Areopagus offers no support for the idea that the unevangelized are in a search for the true God and are rewarded with more light from a divinely-sent messenger. In the eyes of these godless philosophers Paul seemed as an "idle babbler" and a "proclaimer of strange deities" (v. 18), one who had a "new teaching" (v. 19) and who brought "strange things" (v. 20). He did not compliment them with the idea that their pagan unbelief was right "up to a point," nor seek some kind of common ground with their apostasy as a launching pad for biblical theism.

Pagan Saints

No substance can be established to the thought that Old Testament believers were "pagan saints" who then serve as a paradigm for those who embrace the supposedly Good in the world's religions. This idea is a serious blow to the unity of God's plan of salvation in the Old and New Testament eras to say nothing of the two millennia since. It is patently evident that God parceled out His self-disclosure in what is called progressive revelation; it was in "many portions" (Heb 1:1). This disclosure includes the information He gave in order to be in right relations with Him. No one puts it more cogently than Ryrie: "The *basis* of salvation in every age is the death of Christ; the *requirement* for salvation in every age is faith; the *object* of faith in every age is God; the *content* of faith changes in the various dispensations" (italics his).[60] The content of faith is the revelation of God; namely, *what* was actually believed.

The content of the faith of the Old Testament saints was obviously not the incarnate, crucified Lamb of God. The first hint of redeeming grace was the personified seed of the woman who would crush the serpent's (Satan's) head (Gen 3:15). This glimmer grew brighter throughout the Old Testament until the prophets were speaking of the name, character, mission, and even birthplace of the Coming One (Isa 7:14; 9:6; Mic 5:2). What the Old Testament believers saw as they "looked forward" to the final sacrifice for sin was not exactly what we today see when we "look back" to Calvary. The content of the saving faith of the Old Testament saint was essentially God's redemptive revelation up to that point accompanied by an animal sacrifice. God saved them "on credit" and ratified their salvation on the basis of the coming perfect final payment for sin to be made by the incarnate Son of

---

[59]Ibid.

[60]Charles C. Ryrie, *Dispensationalism* (Chicago: Moody, 1995), p. 115.

God. This gave their redemption, and that of all true believers, a genuinely ethical basis in divine atonement. The later cross work of Christ made final expiation for them; it was "the redemption of the transgressions that were committed under the first covenant" (Heb 9:15).

In no sense were Noah, Melchizedec, Job, and other Old Testament believers "pagan saints." The stream of special redemptive revelation, such as it was up to their day, reached them and they exercised God-given faith and were justified. While they were all approved by their God through the exercise of faith, they did not receive fully what was promised (Heb 11:39). With the finality of the once-for-all sacrifice of Christ, they are now "the spirits of the righteous made perfect" (Heb 12:23).

Post-mortem Salvation

The error of a post-mortem opportunity to believe on Christ is of no small proportion. Whether this encounter with Christ will be for all who die in unbelief, or for those who have not heard of Christ, or for those whom God foreknew would have accepted Christ had they heard of Him, is of little consequence. The whole idea of "another chance" or a probation after death is without any solid biblical, exegetical evidence, and seems manifestly to be a philosophical dogmatism to counter the biblical teaching on the lostness of those who have never been told of Christ. To say that John 14:6 means that no one can come to God "as Father," implying that one can come to Him in other capacities through the world's religions, is simply a theological quibble. Furthermore, to put weight on highly controversial passages as 1 Peter 3:10 and 4:6 is nothing short of exegetical desperation.

Our Lord's words in John 8:21, 24—that unless one believed Christ was who He claimed to be, that one would "die in his sins"—carry unmistakably the finality that one's lost condition at death is irreversible. In the account of the Rich Fool, Christ clearly indicated that when the fool's soul would be required of him (when he died), he would face the judgment of God for his spiritual bankruptcy in the midst of his selfish treasure-hoarding (Luke 12:20-21). There is no interval of time between his death and the imposition of the divine sentence. Pinnock makes no attempt to handle these texts in *A Wideness in God's Mercy*.

21

THE DESTINY OF THE FINALLY IMPENITENT

Apart of the controversy within new evangelicalism over the status of the unevangelized concerns the eternal destiny of the wicked. The theological debate emerged from re-examination of the final destiny of those who never heard the gospel of Jesus Christ. Eventually the question extended to all the unredeemed. In 1977 Fuller Theological Seminary altered its doctrinal statement in several areas, one of which had to do with a change concerning the status of the unredeemed dead. According to the report, the original statement consigned unbelievers to "eternal punishment"; that wording was changed to "the wicked shall be separated from God's presence,"[1] a noticeable reduction in the meaning and intent of the original article.

Universalism

At about the time of the Fuller Seminary revision, notes of universalism[2] began to appear from the left wing of the new evangelical movement. Richard Quebedeaux spoke of the "universalist impulse" among the new evangelicals.[3] He noted that both liberalism and neo-orthodoxy generally taught that all people were in fact reconciled to God and that God, being loving and merciful, would not let a human being languish in an eternal prison house of suffering and torment. He observed correctly that evangelicals resisted the Protestant tendency to universalism but went on to declare: "But certain discernible trends suggest that there has been a subtle shift in that direction among some leading evangelical intellectuals and activists at least."[4] His conclusion was both astute and chilling:

> The new willingness of many evangelical academics, pastors, and activists to have fellowship and engage in cooperative activities with Protestant liberals (who may deny some of the cardinal tenets of orthodoxy) and Jews, without trying to convert them, makes it difficult to believe that these same evangelicals regard

---

[1]"Doctrinal Changes at Fuller," *Christianity Today* (May 7, 1971), p. 40.

[2]Universalism teaches, for various reasons, that all humankind are and/or will eventually be saved.

[3]Richard Quebedeaux, *The Worldly Evangelicals* (New York: Harper & Row, 1978), p. 20.

[4]Ibid.

their not born-again colleagues as hell-bound sinners. Clearly, in the minds of such evangelicals, the boundaries between saved and lost have been obscured.[5]

Donald Bloesch, while disclaiming universalism, nevertheless seems to pine for it and comes close to embracing it. He does not wish "to build fences around God's grace," but in a hopeful spirit adds, "we do not preclude the possibility that some in hell might finally be translated into heaven."[6] This wishful note is surrounded by clauses such as "God's wrath,…[is] a demonstration of his love, which punishes for the sake of the sinner." Or, "even redemptive love is present in hell," that "hell is not a concentration camp presided over by the devil, but a sanatorium for sick souls who are ministered to by Jesus Christ." "Hell is included in the dominion of heaven." "The sufferings in hell are mitigated because Christ is present." "We affirm that the punishment in hell is both punitive and remedial." And, "hell is not outside the compass of God's mercy nor the sphere of his kingdom."[7]

Small pockets of universalism have existed since Origen, but the doctrine has never made much of an inroad in conservative Protestantism. Fortunately its following in new evangelicalism is likewise minuscule and appears to be making no discernible headway, despite a flurry of interest in the later 1980s.[8] The Bible so clearly states that the lost endure punishment everlastingly that only confirmed prejudice could see it otherwise.

Annihilationism

While universalism is practically discounted by most contemporary new evangelicals, annihilationism is a teaching that has not been ignored. Annihilationism holds that the finally impenitent will eventually be reduced to non-being or extinction. Whether that occurs at death, or after the final judgment at the end of the intermediate state,[9] or after a period of punishment in hell are questions for a more in-depth discussion than the present chapter provides.

In the 1990s Millard Erickson noted that the growing popularity of annihilationism had significantly increased among evangelicals.[10] Donald Carson spoke of the "rising number of self-confessed evangelicals who now publicly espouse some form of annihilationism."[11] Notices of annihilationism within the new evangelical community began to appear already in the 1970s. In 1974 John Wenham developed the rationale for later proponents.[12] In 1982 Edward Fudge

---

[5]Ibid., p. 21.

[6]Donald G. Bloesch, *Essentials of Evangelical Theology*, 2 vols. (New York: Harper and Row, 1978), 2:226.

[7]Ibid., 2:225-27.

[8]For example, "Universalism: Will Everyone Be Saved?" *Christianity Today* (Mar 20, 1987), p. 31.

[9]The intermediate state is that period of conscious existence between physical death and the end-time resurrection.

[10]Millard J. Erickson, "The State of the Question," in *Through No Fault of Their Own: The Fate of Those Who Have Never Heard*, William V. Crockett and James A. Sigountes, eds. (Grand Rapids: Baker, 1991), p. 31.

[11]D. A. Carson, *The Gagging of God: Christianity Confronts Pluralism* (Grand Rapids: Zondervan, 1996), p. 515.

[12]John Wenham, *The Goodness of God* (Downers Grove, IL: InterVarsity, 1974), pp. 27-41.

produced a lengthy volume on the subject of final punishment that espoused the extinction of the wicked.[13] That same year Steven Travis affirmed annihilationism as the better of the two main options: eternal conscious punishment or conditional immortality.[14] In 1984 Fudge produced an article designed to refute the traditional view of the eternal, conscious punishment of the wicked and to make a case for "the total, ultimate, everlasting extinction of the wicked."[15] In 1987 Clark Pinnock declared his preference for annihilationism. After lamenting that the evangelical doctrine of eternal punishment will make universalism nearly irresistible to "sensitive" Christians, he commended the extinction of the wicked as an appropriate alternative.[16] Pinnock's proposals did not seem to ignite much attention in the new evangelical ranks, quite palpably because his novel theological creations in his ever-leftward move away from biblicism earned him a certain amount of distrust and disinterest among many evangelical thinkers.

It took someone of the stature of John R. W. Stott to shake the new evangelicalism with his tentative openness to the idea of the extinction of the finally impenitent. In a 1988 dialogue with a liberal, David L. Edwards,[17] on subjects such as the gospel, Jesus Christ, the scriptures, and ethics, Edwards challenged Stott on the doctrine of eternal punishment. After reluctantly presenting some arguments in favor of annihilationism, Stott conceded that this was not the traditional view of evangelicals and that he was only tentatively, not dogmatically, espousing it.[18] The new turn of Stott and others drew scholarly but negative evangelical response.[19]

In 1989 respected evangelical scholar Philip Edgcumbe Hughes set forth the conditional immortality of the soul and its corollary, the extinction of the wicked.[20] In 1990 Pinnock wrote a definitive article on annihilationalism.[21]

Proponents of annihilationism put forward several arguments, such as (1) the conditional immortality of the human soul, (2) the unfairness or injustice of God in

---

[13]Edward Fudge, *The Fire That Consumes: A Biblical and Historical Study of the Doctrine of Final Punishment* (Houston, TX: Providential Press, 1982).

[14]Stephen Travis, *I Believe In the Second Coming of Jesus* (Grand Rapids: Eerdmans, 1982), p. 198. Conditional immortality holds that immortality is contingent on personal faith in Jesus Christ. Those who do not exercise faith are bereft of immortality and will suffer extinction as a consequence.

[15]Edward Fudge, "The Final End of the Wicked," *Journal of the Evangelical Theological Society* 27 (1984), p. 325.

[16]Clark Pinnock, "Fire, Then Nothing," *Christianity Today* (Mar 20, 1987), pp. 40-41.

[17]David L. Edwards and John R. W. Stott, *Evangelical Essentials: A Liberal-Evangelical Dialogue* (Downers Grove, IL: InterVarsity, 1988).

[18]Ibid., p. 320.

[19]For example, Robert L. Reymond, "Dr. John Stott on Hell," *Presbyterion* 16 (1990); Harold O. J. Brown, "Will the Lost Suffer Forever?" *Criswell Theological Review* 4 (1990); J. I. Packer, "The Problem of Eternal Punishment," *Crux* 26 (1990); and Packer, "Evangelicals and the Way of Salvation," in *Evangelical Affirmations*, Kenneth S. Kantzer and Carl F. H. Henry, eds. (Grand Rapids: Zondervan, 1990); and Robert A. Peterson, "A Traditionalist Response to John Stott's Arguments for Annihilationism," *Journal of the Evangelical Theological Society* 37 (1994).

[20]Philip Edgcumbe Hughes, *The True Image: The Origin and Destiny of Man in Christ* (Grand Rapids: Eerdmans, 1989), pp. 398-407.

[21]Clark Pinnock, "The Destruction of the Finally Impenitent," *Criswell Theological Review* 4 (1990).

eternal punishment and the contradiction this causes with His love and mercy, (3) the incompatibility of the nature of God's final victory over all evil with the actual existence eternally of sin and sinners (in hell), (4) the meaning of biblical terms such as eternal, fire, and destruction (destruction being interpreted as total obliteration), among others , and (5) the question of how the blessedness of the redeemed in heaven can be unaffected by the existence of those in hell. Two of the more crucial of these elements in the case for annihilationism will be discussed here.

Conditional Immortality

Annihilationists hold that human beings are not constitutionally immortal; for them it is not true that all people will have conscious, personal existence forever as a constituent element of their being. Immortality, in their view, is conditioned on faith in Jesus Christ and is not a native endowment of the human personality through the image of God. Only people of faith are endowed with immortality and for that reason will live forever in the eternal bliss of heaven. The finally impenitent are devoid of immortality and, as mere mortals, will be reduced by God to eternal extinction or non-being as a consequence of their unbelief. As Hughes says, "Immortality or deathlessness…is not inherent in the constitution of man as a corporeal-spiritual creature, though formed in the image of God, the potential was there."[22]

Part of the problem in the immortality dispute is apparently semantical. In the strictest sense only God possesses immortality (1 Tim 6:16), and He does so inherently and independently; His being is totally uncaused. In the more general sense of mere deathlessness, all humans are immortal by virtue of creation; they do not possess independent existence. Adam's body consisted of elements taken from the earth (Gen 2:7a) and his soul and spirit came directly from God (Gen 2: 7b). As the image of God (Gen 1:26, 27; 1 Cor 11:7), man as a person is a unity of the material and immaterial. At physical death, believers and unbelievers survive in a state of conscious existence (Ecc 12:7; Luke 16:22, 23). The soul and spirit of all mankind, saved and unsaved, cannot die or be killed (Matt 10:28), and their bodies will be resurrected so that they will face judgment and endless existence in either bliss or torment (Dan 12:2; John 5:28-29; 1 Cor 15:22: "all" shall be made alive). Man as the image of God is eternal because he was originally generated by the eternal God Himself. The unity of the human personality, that is, the union of body, soul, and spirit, is thus "naturally" immortal—constitutionally incapable of extinction. Furthermore, in Matthew 25:46, the existence or duration of both the righteous and the wicked are set in a parallel construction, and the existence of both is said to be eternal.

In a more technical theological sense, while the eternal felicity of the saved is termed "immortality" in the Bible (1 Cor 15:53), it means more than deathlessness or mere conscious survival beyond death. It has the positive idea of life—eternal life. The eternal perdition of the wicked is not known technically as immortality; it is called the second (or eternal) death.[23] But this death is not extinction or

---

[22]Philip Edgcumbe Hughes, *The True Image*, p. 405.

[23]Murray J. Harris seems to have captured this idea well: "All human beings survive beyond death, but not all will become immortal in the Pauline sense" ("The New Testament View of Life After Death," *Themilios* [Jan 1986], p. 47).

annihilation. Immortality is not specifically predicated of the final status of the unsaved; in fact, very little is said of the resurrection body of the unsaved at all. In eternity the unsaved will experience unending death. According to 1 Corinthians 15:53-54, immortality is not simply survival beyond physical death, it has the positive notion of eternal life in relation to the body.[24] The opposite is not non-existence but the second death as it affects the body—an eternal act of dying. Perhaps one could say that lost people are not subject to a *final* separation of soul and spirit from the body but are in a condition of continually dying in the eternal state, an unending execution in God's everlasting death house. The Scripture never teaches that the finally impenitent are reduced to non-existence.

God's Justice

John Stott believes that eternal punishment ruins the biblical idea of justice, and God's justice in particular. He queries that if God will judge everyone according to what he has done, "Would there not, then, be a serious disproportion between sins consciously committed in time and torment consciously experienced throughout eternity?"[25] Such divine punishment, Stott seems to be suggesting, would not only be unjust but unspeakably cruel.

Stott's view overlooks the fact that God's judgment is retributive. A sin against the infinite God takes on proportions of infinity; it requires infinite retribution. The response must be commensurate with the offense. Even human jurisprudence recognizes the link between the nature of a crime, the station of who or what it is against, and the appropriate sentence to be meted out. Is it unjust to incarcerate someone for forty or fifty years for a crime committed in a few minutes? Is shooting a horse any different from shooting the Governor? The questions are rhetorical.

Every sin, great or small by human standards, is against God (Ps 51:4), and therefore accrues infinite demerit. A finite being is required to pay this endless guilt in an unending amount of time. Only in this way are the perfect equity and retributive justice of God upheld. Anything other than eternal punishment slurs the character of God. Jesus, being the infinite God-man, could endure the infinite force of sin while on the cross and thus make an atonement for sin of unlimited value. Those who spurn His cross work have only one alternative, and God has only one recourse—eternal punishment. So instead of raising moral questions and arguments, eternal punishment *settles* all of them.[26] "If God is as good as the Bible says he is, if his character is as pure, if his life is as infinite, then sin is infinitely unpardonable and not momentarily mischievous."[27]

---

[24]Although a very common expression, there is really no biblical or theological substance to "the immortality of the soul." Biblical immortality for human beings affects the body. Soul immortality is more Platonic than Pauline. The conditional immortality of the soul is an oxymoron with no specific content and actually is counterproductive to theological understanding.

[25]John R. W. Stott, *Evangelical Essentials*, p. 318.

[26]David F. Wells, "Everlasting Punishment," p. 42.

[27]Ibid.

Advocates of annihilationism, based on a perceived miscarriage of justice in eternal punishment, betray a tragically deficient view of the character of God, especially His holiness, righteousness, and justice. Packer correctly noted, "The holy God of the Bible is praised no less for establishing righteousness by retributively punishing wrongdoers (Rev 19:1-5) than for the triumphs of his grace (Rev 19:6-10) [and] it cannot be said of God that expressing his holiness in deserved retribution mars his joy."[28] Wells's response to Pinnock's annihilationism, and by legitimate implication to all who hold to the ultimate extinction of the wicked, is severe: "[Pinnock's gospel] trades on a diminished view of sin, a modified notion of divine righteousness, and a restructured atonement." This, says Wells, is not more appealing, but less. "It is a gospel that has lost its nerve because it has lost its majesty."[29]

John Stott was honest and forthright enough to cite what seems to be the fundamental reason for rejecting eternal punishment, and that reason seems purely emotional and human-generated. "Emotionally, I find the concept [of eternal punishment] intolerable and do not understand how people can live with it without either cauterizing their feelings or cracking under the strain."[30] Although acknowledgments that emotions are not a reliable guide to truth, one is left with the lingering thought that annihilationism's exegesis is not very objective.

The duration of the punishment of the finally impenitent could hardly be more clearly presented in Scripture. Denial of eternal, conscious, penal suffering of the wicked necessarily must arise from cerebral or glandular, but certainly not exegetical, sources. Without going into a tedious word study of *aion* (age), *aionios* (eternal), *eis ton aiona* (forever), *eis ton aiona ton aionon* (forever and ever), it can be shown that God is eternal (Rom 16:26), as well as salvation itself (Heb 5:9), redemption (Heb 9:12), eternal life (John 3:16; 6:51; 10:28), the coming glory (1 Pet 5:10), Jesus Christ (John 12:34) and His Melchizedekian priesthood (Heb 5:6), the word of God (1 Pet 1:23), the throne of God (Heb 1:8), and the reign of the saved in the eternal kingdom (Rev 22:5). Those same words are used of the final abode of the wicked: eternal fire (Matt 18:8; 25:41), eternal punishment (Matt 25:41), eternal destruction (2 Thess 1:9), and eternal torment (Rev 14:11[31]). Only the most pedantic and prejudiced exegesis of Matthew 25:46, for example, could produce opposite, competing views of the duration of the eternal punishment of the goats and the eternal life of the sheep. The words of Moses Stuart on this subject, written well over one hundred years ago, have never been answered by annihilationists; indeed, his conclusion seems to have been purposely ignored and avoided.

---

[28]J. I. Packer, "Is Hell Out of Vogue?" *Action* (Sept-Oct 1989), p. 11, quoted by Robert L. Reymond, "Dr. Stott on Hell," p. 57.

[29]David F. Wells, "Everlasting Punishment," p. 42.

[30]John R. W. Stott, *Evangelical Essentials*, p. 314.

[31]Annihilationists insist that this "smoke" is an ongoing symbol of the previous extinction of the lost, but the text says it is the smoke of "their" torment, which is quite a different matter. That is, the torment itself is included in the designation of "eternal."

It does most plainly and indubitably follow, that, *if the Scriptures have not asserted the ENDLESS punishment of the wicked, neither have they asserted the ENDLESS happiness of the righteous, nor the ENDLESS glory and existence of the Godhead.* The one is equally certain with the other. Both are laid in the same balance. They must be tried by the same tests (italics his).[32]

The whole stand or fall together. There can, from the very nature of the antithesis, be no room for rational doubt here, in what manner we should interpret the declarations of the sacred writers. We must either admit the ENDLESS misery of hell, or give up the ENDLESS happiness of heaven.[33]

---

[32]Moses Stuart, *Exegetical Essays on Several Words Relating to Future Punishment* (Philadelphia: Presbyterian Board of Education, 1867), p. 82.

[33]Ibid., p. 89.

22

THE OPEN VIEW OF GOD

In the mid 1970s a resurgent Neo-Arminianism escalated rapidly within New Evangelicalism and is now challenging many traditional beliefs and historic doctrines, among which is the doctrine of God. One of the main contributors to this new rise is, as usual, Clark Pinnock. He acknowledges that the "open" view of God and the recent Arminian philosophical spin-offs originated in something less than biblical exegesis. He explained: "The trend began, I believe, because of a fresh and faithful reading of the Bible in dialogue with modern culture, which places emphasis on autonomy, temporality, and historical change."[1] His overriding burden is to make God credible to modern man. Elsewhere he spoke of his attraction to certain aspects of process theism.

> I am sympathetic with a number of motifs in process theism. I, too, see reality as open and not closed. And I think of God as relating to events as they happen, not timelessly....I hold to a dynamic theism which accepts the biblical portrayal of a God who works sequentially in a temporal process which is not an illusion.[2]

Earlier Pinnock traced the idea of undetermined, undecreed human freedom to some sort of intuitive feelings. He said, "Universal man almost without exception talks and feels as if he were free. He perceives himself to be a person capable of rising above his situation, of shaping his life and destiny, and of making a significant impact on history."[3] The new view of God, called "free will theism" or "open theism," is more fully delineated in *The Openness of God* by Pinnock and others.[4]

---

[1]Clark H. Pinnock, "From Augustine to Arminius: A Pilgrimage in Theology," in *The Grace of God, The Will of Man*, Clark Pinnock, ed. (Grand Rapids: Zondervan, 1989), p. 15. More recently John Sanders explained his change to open theism so that his theology would correspond with what he termed "biblically grounded piety" ("Does God Know Your Next Move?" *Christianity Today* [May 21, 2001], p. 40). This, of course, is quite subjective and harnesses Scripture to everyone's peculiar experience of "piety."

[2]Clark H. Pinnock, "God Limits His Knowledge," in *Predestination and Free Will: Four Views of Divine Sovereignty and Human Freedom*, David and Randall Basinger, eds. (Downers Grove, IL: InterVarsity, 1986), p. 147.

[3]Clark H. Pinnock, "Responsible Freedom and the Flow of Biblical History," in *Grace Unlimited*, Clark Pinnock, ed. (Minneapolis: Bethany Fellowship, 1975), p. 95.

[4]Downers Grove: IL: InterVarsity, 1994.

Gregory Boyd espoused a slightly modified form of the open theism view. He summarized his position by saying:

> Open theists...hold that the future consists partly of settled realities and partly of unsettled realities. Some things of the future are *possibly* this way and *possibly* that way....God knows the future as consisting of both unsettled possibilities and settled certainties (italics his).[5]

There are several crucial points in this new approach, such as the primacy of love in the attributes of God, the changeableness of God, the expanding nature of God's knowledge, and the limitedness of His power. What follows here is an analysis of what is perhaps the leading motif of this new view—*the ultimate contingency of God's will (or decree) in deference both to the absolute freedom of man's will and the ultimate randomness of the universe.*

CONTROLLING FACTORS OF OPEN THEISM

The Absolute Free Will of Man

The following are some quotations demonstrating the belief that man's volition is unfettered and totally free, sometimes called "significant freedom."

> To be sovereign does not mean that everything that occurs accords with the will of the sovereign or that the sovereign can bring about anything he or she wants. The ability of the sovereign to determine the outcome depends, in part, on the freedom granted to the governed. If those subject to the sovereign have freedom, then there are certain things that the sovereign cannot bring about.[6]

> God is a sovereign, not a novelist. He does not purpose or dispose everything that happens; his purposes are both general and specific, but they do not include every detail of human existence....This means, of course, that at times his plans and purposes are thwarted.[7]

> God limits himself in the creation of individuals who are free....If God has created us free to choose to love and serve him, then God cannot cause us to do so.[8]

> By inviting them to have dominion over the world (for example), God willingly surrenders power and makes possible a partnership with the creature."[9]

> [The impossibility for God to foreknow future actions] entails that future free decisions do not exist (except as possibilities) for God to know until free agents make them.[10]

The "Genuine Novelty" In the Universe

Pinnock and Boyd argue that pockets of pure chance exist in the universe, arguing essentially for an open universe where anything can happen.

---

[5]Gregory A. Boyd, *The God of the Possible* (Grand Rapids: Baker, 2000), p. 16.

[6]Bruce Reichenback, "God Limits His Power," in *Predestination and Free Will*, p. 105.

[7]Ibid., p. 117.

[8]Ibid., p. 108.

[9]Clark H. Pinnock, "Systematic Theology," in *The Openness of God*, p. 113.

[10]Gregory Boyd, *The God of the Possible*, p. 120.

[God's] sovereignty is not the all-determining kind, but an omnicompetent kind. God is certainly able to deal with any circumstances which might arise, and nothing can possibly defeat or destroy God. But he does not control everything that occurs.[11]

An important implication of this strong definition of freedom is that reality is to an extent open and not closed. It means that genuine novelty can appear in history which cannot be predicted even by God.[12]

The goals of [God's] plan are unchangeable (for example, to call people into fellowship with God). But the outworking of the plan is flexible and responsive to what happens. God is constantly making decisions which bear upon the realization of his will. God responds to events in time and works everything together for good. But it is not a controlled situation where nothing unexpected happens and everything turns out just as God wants.[13]

If God does not foreknow future free actions, it is not because his knowledge of the future is in any sense incomplete. It's because there is, in this view, *nothing definite there for God to know*!...one is not ascribing ignorance to God by insisting that he doesn't foreknow future free actions if indeed free actions do not exist to be known until free agents create them (italics his).[14]

The Ability of God to React to the Unexpected

Free will theism openly admits to an "ad hoc God," chilling as that may sound to orthodox ears. Rather than face the implications of this denial of God's omnipotence, open theists seem to think this enhances the abilities of God as He operates in an open universe which is suspended on pure contingency.

God has the power and ability to be...an 'ad hoc' God, one who responds and adapts to surprises and to the unexpected. God sets goals for creation and redemption and realizes them 'ad hoc' in history. If Plan A fails, God is ready with Plan B.[15]

Thus God at different times must adopt different plans and stratagems so that his ultimate purpose, the unification of the cosmos in Christ, can be achieved.[16]

Since Yahweh in his Son resolved to put himself in such a position [the risk of failure, being vulnerable, being affected by the world, etc.], we should see him as the defenseless superior power. As sovereign he is omnicompetent in his affairs with the world, but not omnicausal.[17]

---

[11]Clark Pinnock, "God Limits His Knowledge," p. 146.

[12]Ibid., p. 150.

[13]Ibid., p. 152.

[14]Gregory Boyd, *The God of the Possible*, pp. 16-17.

[15]Clark H. Pinnock, "Systematic Theology," p. 113. John Sanders reflects this same Plan A–Plan B scenario. "Moses' refusal to return to Egypt prompted God to resort to Plan B, allowing Aaron to do the public speaking instead of Moses" ("Does God Know Your Next Move?" p. 40).

[16]Bruce Reichenbach, "God Limits His Power," p. 118.

[17]John Sanders, "God As Personal," in *The Grace of God, The Will of Man*, p. 175.

In the open view there is little mystery involved in accepting that God can regret his own previous decisions. Once we understand that the future is partly open and that humans are genuinely free, the paradox of how God could experience genuine regret over a decision he made disappears. God made a wise decision because it had the greatest *possibility* of yielding the best results (italics his).[18]

[God is] the infinitely intelligent chess master.[19]

As the potter [in Jer 18] was willing to revise his vessel once the first plan was "spoiled," so God is willing to revise his initial plan when circumstances call for it. He is not a unilaterally controlling God; he is a graciously flexible God. The "clay" he works with is not lifeless but has a mind and will of its own, to which he responds appropriately.[20]

The Uncertainty of Bible Prophecy

Prophetic revelation in Scripture is perhaps the most easily recognized litmus test for the new view of God. If God is not omnipotent but omnicompetent, and if His plan and blueprint for the universe is not all-inclusive, then Bible prophecy can no longer stand. Unfortunately, predictive prophecy is completely eviscerated in evangelical open theism.

Prophecy is after all profoundly conditional and oriented to our response to God. We are not locked into a future course of events in which what we decide to do has no part to play in how things turn out.[21]

As it actually functions in the Bible, prophecy is primarily an expression, not of divine knowledge, but of divine agency. Its major purpose is not to provide information about the future, although it may indeed do that. Rather, its major purpose is to express God's intentions to act in certain ways and to assure people that God is directly involved in their lives.[22]

In a later work, Rice stated that prophecy "is a subtle and varied phenomenon," and God's prediction may (1) represent God's "intention to do something in the future irrespective of creaturely decision," (2) "express God's knowledge that something will happen because the necessary conditions for it have been fulfilled and nothing could conceivably prevent it," or (3) "communicate what God intends to do if certain conditions obtain."[23]

Even if we accept this way of interpreting Revelation [that its prophecies will take place at the end of history], it does not require that we believe that the future is exhaustively settled. The primary actors in this apocalyptic narrative are God and Satan, and it's not

---

[18]Gregory A. Boyd, *The God of the Possible*, p. 57.

[19]Ibid., p. 127.

[20]Ibid., pp. 76-77.

[21]Clark Pinnock, "Response to Bruce Reichenbach, 'God Limits His Power,'" in *Predestination and Free Will*, p. 139.

[22]Richard Rice, "Divine Foreknowledge and Free-Will Theism," in *The Grace of God, The Will of Man*, pp. 134-35.

[23]Richard Rice, "Biblical Support for a New Perspective," in *The Openness of God*, p. 51.

hard to understand how God could know very well the plans of both at the end of history without supposing that *all* of the future is settled in God's mind.[24]

A Corporate View of Divine Election

The traditional Arminian view of election to personal salvation is that in eternity past God foresaw who would manifest repentance, faith, and subsequent good works, and on that basis chose them to salvation. Historic Arminianism denied God a pretemporal choice since He based His decision on what was to transpire in time.

The new view of God does not grant Him a valid knowledge of the future, so the traditional Arminian view is discounted. Instead, a corporate view of election is substituted, arguing that God chose a group or corporate body but did not elect any individuals within that body. Those individuals will make up the body through the free exercise of their choice. Until that time their identity is unknown even to God.

> Three times in the verses just quoted [Eph 1:4-6] election/predestination is centered exclusively in Christ as a the key figure. This is the corporate solidarity or corporate personality concept so easy for patriarchal societies to understand and so alien to the western tradition of individualism.[25]

> The truth of eternal ecclesial election in Christ is the key to unlock the mystery being explained throughout Ephesians 1:19; 3:3, 4, 9; 5:32; 6:19.[26]

Regarding Acts 13:48 ("as many as had been appointed to eternal life believed"), William Klein says that "this does not necessarily imply a pretemporal election.... The Gentiles believed and entered the category of the appointed ones."[27]

> God pretemporally chose the church for salvation that is actualized by the work of the Spirit and the people's faith.[28]

> A major part of Christendom has never been able to accept the concept of the unconditional election of individuals as biblical....Many who oppose this concept assert instead that election is based on certain conditions which people may meet; and it is the election of a certain class or group, not the election of specific individuals.[29]

> In the same way that God predestined and foreknew the death of Jesus without predestining or foreknowing which individuals would condemn him, so God predestined and foreknew the church without predestining or foreknowing which specific individuals would belong to it.[30]

> In this context [Rom 11:2], Paul has Israel *as a corporate whole* in mind, not individual Jews, for one of his primary goals throughout Romans 9-11 is to show

---

[24]Gregory Boyd, *The God of the Possible*, p. 50.

[25]William G. MacDonald, "The Biblical Doctrine of Election," in *The Grace of God, The Will of Man*, p. 221.

[26]Ibid., p. 223.

[27]William W. Klein, *The New Chosen People: A Corporate View of Election* (Grand Rapids: Zondervan, 1990), p. 121.

[28]Ibid., p. 182.

[29]Jack W. Cottrell, "Conditional Election," in *Grace Unlimited*, p. 56.

[30]Gregory A. Boyd, *The God of the Possible*, p. 46.

that not all Jews are real Israelites....So too, in Romans 8:29 Paul is saying that the church as a corporate whole was in God's heart long before the church was birthed. But this doesn't imply that he knew who would and would not be in this church ahead of time. He predestined that all who choose to receive Christ would grow to be in the image of His Son. But whether particular individuals receive Christ and thus acquire this predestined image depends on their free will (italics his).[31]

AN ANALYSIS OF OPEN THEISM

The Correlativity of God and His Universe

God and His universe (including mankind) are in a reciprocal relationship in the new view, each needing the other to complement what is lacking. This view is an evangelical derivative of the pagan philosophy of process theism wherein God and the world are in some sort of a dipolar, mutual parity. This new view says that God needs man's freedom and an open universe to complement His sovereignty in order to give meaning and genuineness to the creation. Otherwise all would be a charade, mere puppetry on the strings of determinism. However, the universe also needs God to set goals and to give purpose to history; otherwise it would simply be a series of purely random events, a bracelet of beads without holes or string. In this view man also needs God to control the wilder side of his freedom or else life would become an impersonal, amoral chaos, a shoreless ocean of randomness and pure chance. In other words, God and the universe are tethered to each other and live off each other's wealth by taking in each other's washing.

As a matter of fact, the Neo-Arminian view of God embodies two incompatible, contradictory, and mutually destructive principles, because absolute human freedom destroys divine sovereignty, and true divine sovereignty does away with absolute human freedom. The one *eventually* eats up the other, but the modern Neo-Arminian wants it both ways. He wants an open universe (freedom and novelty) to authenticate his own autonomy so that he does not become a pre-programmed robot, but he also wants a closed universe (the sovereign will of God) to make it personal and meaningful so that he does not become a free-falling monster in the thin air of pure contingency. On the one hand, he ends with a universe full of particulars (absolute freedom and novelty) without any universal, and on the other, he has a worldwide universal bereft of particulars (a sovereign God with nothing to be sovereign over). The former (novelty and chance) is completely irrational and the latter (divine sovereignty and control) is totally rational, but both are held simultaneously in his mind.

The Bible condemns this correlativity. God is the eternal (Psa 90:12), independent/self-existent (Exod 3:14, the I AM), and infinite (1 Kgs 8:27) One. All else is temporal, dependent, and finite. God needs nothing outside Himself to define Himself nor anything against which to offset Himself for meaning. He is the self-contained and self-defining triune God.

The Breakdown of the Creator-creature Distinction

The Bible uniformly teaches the fundamental distinction between God and the universe (Gen 1:1; Acts 14:24). (The universe is defined as all that is not God.) The distinction between the Creator and all else is absolute; they are unmixed

---

[31]Ibid., p. 48.

categories. The gulf can never be bridged from man's side. To attempt do so is the very essence of sin (Rom 1:25); nothing exists in man as it exists in God. Any attempt to cross the breach from man's side is either to temporalize God or eternalize some aspect of creation. The divide can only be unilaterally crossed from God to man, and has been crossed in the incarnation, the giving of the Bible, and regeneration, to name some instances. However, these sovereign crossings still do not result in a confusion between the Creator and the creature or a fusion of the two distinct essences. For example, in the incarnation of the Son the divine and human natures are still absolutely distinct and indissoluble although inseparably united in the God-man.

The resurgent Neo-Arminian proposal of an open view of God and the ultimate free will of man confuses the Creator-creature distinction and results in a temporalized God and an eternalized creation. When God's will is made subservient to man's, the Creator is temporalized. When man's will is made equal, if not superior, to God's will, the creature is eternalized. When God willingly surrenders power and enters into partnership with man, He is temporalized. When man can frustrate the purposes of God so that He must go to Plan B (or C, D, E, or ?), man is eternalized. This is hopeless confusion and, like the correlativity principle, borders on blasphemy.

The Comprehensive Plan of God

God's ultimate plan or decree includes whatever comes to pass. Nothing is outside His all-inclusive purpose. No loose ends hang in God's universe; no pockets of novelty or randomness dot His creation. "He works all things after the counsel of His will" (Eph 1:11). "The Lord has made everything for its own purpose" (Prov 16:4). Some of the things in God's comprehensive plan are:

1. The stability of the material universe—Psalm 119:89-91.
2. The political influence and boundaries of nations—Acts 17:26.
3. The rise and fall of rulers—Romans 13:1.
4. The length of one's life—Job 14:5.
5. The circumstances of life—James 4:13, 15.
6. The free acts of men, good and bad—Ephesians 2:10; Acts 2:23.
7. The most trivial of circumstances—Job 36:32.
8. The certainty of prophetic events—Isaiah 14:24, 27.

The only alternative to an all-inclusive plan and purpose of God is caprice or sheer blind irrational chance, a conclusion inherent in the New Arminianism and contrary to the biblical view of God's plan. God's comprehensive purpose is voluntary (Psa 115:3—"But our God is in the heavens; he does whatever He pleases"), eternal (Isa 37:26—"Have you not heard? Long ago I did it, from ancient times I planned it. Now I have brought it to pass"), immutable (Isa 46:10—"My purpose will be established, and I will accomplish all my good pleasure"), and efficacious (Dan 4:35—"[God] does according to His will in the host of heaven, and among the inhabitants of the earth; and no one can ward off His hand, or say to Him, 'What have You done"). God's plan is certainly to be executed, and there are no unplanned entities in God's universe. He chose either to effect directly or indirectly whatsoever comes to pass.

Human Free Will

Human freedom can be defined simply as being rationally spontaneous, the ability to exercise volition according to the assessment that reason makes—the liberty of spontaneity.

> Wherever reason and the power of self-determination or spontaneity are combined in an agent, he is free and responsible for his outward acts and for his volitions.[32]

> Free agency is the power of self-determination in view of motives.[33]

The problem with free will theism is that it refuses to recognize the *bondage* of the human will due to the effects of total depravity, especially in the areas of sin, grace, and salvation. Human autonomy is assumed. However, the freedom of the will is not absolute. Man's rational spontaneity is circumscribed both by sin and its effects on one's dominant motives, and by finitude, especially the former. Therefore human beings are not in a state of moral and rational equilibrium, free from any persuasion or motivation.

Furthermore, this view fails to note that God can work in one's volition in a way that choices and actions are uncoerced. Dominant motives, resulting in actions, are controlled by God in a non-coercive manner (Psa 110:3; Prov 21: 1). God's all-inclusive plan entails *certainty* (Isa 46:10) but not *necessity*. Human freedom is fully compatible with the certainty of God's ultimate will, but not with necessity. Necessity involves coercion; certainty, in this regard, does not (note both the certainty and the rational/volitional spontaneity of the coming eschatological Assyrian [Isa 10:5,6; cf. vv. 7-19]).

Election to Salvation is Personal

To speak of a corporate entity bereft of any individual constituents is irrational and unbiblical. The Neo-Arminian plan originates from the logical necessities of the free will system rather than from sound exegesis and theology. On the surface, it appears that God could not even will a corporate body if the future is contingent, open, and undetermined. If He cannot will the future salvation of individuals, on what basis can He will a group of them? The open view of God proves too much here and renders any certainty of the future invalid. Free will theism has no limiting notion; it is open-ended with no logical or biblical stopping place short of total disorder and an abandonment of all teleology. If future personal actions and isolated events are impossible for God to plan and effect, then neither are corporate entities. Why limit God's future certainties to block entities? If one person or event can frustrate God's plan, on what basis can we deny that *every* person and *all* events may flout His ultimate will? Why is it not possible, in the free will view, for every person to opt out of the plan of salvation and thus frustrate the divine

---

[32]Charles Hodge, *Systematic Theology*, 3 vols. (Reprint ed., London: James Clark, 1960), 2:286.

[33]A. H. Strong, *Systematic Theology* (Valley Forge, PA: Judson, 1907), p. 360.

intention for even a corporate election? And if this frustration is possible, even theoretically, then any concept of election is a farce. It all amounts to nothing more than a bundle of special pleading.

The Bible unmistakably teaches a divine pretemporal choice of individuals to personal salvation, as these few clear texts demonstrate.

> 2 Thessalonians 2:13—"God has chosen you from the beginning for salvation through sanctification of the Spirit and faith in the truth."

> 1 Thessalonians 1:4—"Knowing, brethren beloved by God, His choice of you."

> John 6:37—"All that the Father gives Me will come to Me."

> Acts 18:10—[Concerning Paul's eventual ministry at Corinth] "I [God] have many people in this city."

> 2 Timothy 1:9—"[God] hath saved us, and called us with an holy calling, not according to our works, but according to His own purpose and grace, which was granted us in Christ Jesus before the world began."

While many would reject the Neo-Arminian view of corporate election, some would hold to the older Arminian view of election based on prescience or advance knowledge, i.e., election according to foreseen faith. The idea is that God in His omniscience foreknew who would believe and, on that basis, elected them to salvation.[34] This view is based on texts dealing with election and God's "foreknowledge" (Rom 8:29; 1 Pet 1:2).

While occurrences of the word foreknowledge sometimes refer to advance information (Acts 26:5; 2 Pet 3:17), these are not in contexts of salvation and, furthermore, the object of the foreknowledge is clear in each case. However, in contexts of election to salvation, "what" is foreknown is never stated. Rather the Bible says "whom" He foreknew (Rom 7:29); God foreknows *persons*. Arminians feel the force of this fact and admit that "although we are nowhere told what it is in the foreknowledge of God that determines His choice," their view of human freedom and responsibility "necessitates our *postulating* that it is man's reaction to the revelation God has made of Himself that is the basis of His election" (italics added).[35]

Proginosko (to foreknow) and its theological synonym *ginosko* (to know) have the idea of special regard for, personal interest or delight in, discriminating love and commitment toward. Something instrumental is involved in foreknowledge that the abstract foresight view fails to capture. In Acts 2:23 foreknowledge is in parallelism with the "predetermined plan" (lit. "the-having-been-fixed-will") of God ("this Man, delivered over by the predetermined plan and foreknowledge of God, you nailed to a cross"). The historical outworking of that foreknowledge is narrated in Acts 4:27-28 ("For truly in this city there were gathered together against Your holy servant Jesus, whom You anointed, both Herod and Pontius Pilate, along with the Gentiles and the peoples of Israel, *to do whatever Your hand and*

---

[34]For example, H. C. Thiessen, *Lectures in Systematic Theology* (Grand Rapids: Eerdmans, 1951), p. 344.

[35]Ibid.

Your purpose predestined to occur" [italics added]). To know/foreknow comes from the Old Testament idea of the verb *yadha* (to know). See the parallelism in Proverbs 27:23 ("Know well [*yadha*] the condition of your flocks, and pay attention [lit. set your heart] to your herds"). Note also Hosea 8:4; Amos 3:2; Genesis 18:19; and Exodus 33:17.

Foreknowledge in 1 Peter 1:2 can be understood correctly in either one of two ways. "According (*kata*) to the foreknowledge of God" can mean, in line with Romans 8:29, that God chose believers in accord with His special electing love, regard, and favor.[36] Or it can mean, on the order of the predetermined will of Acts 2:23 and the predestination of Ephesians 1:4, that God chose believers in accord with, or in keeping with, that overall foreordination which encompasses all things.[37] God's foreknowledge in election then is His eternal approving love and gracious affection. Election is God's pretemporal sovereign choice, according to His loving good pleasure, of all believers to salvation with all its accompanying means, obligations, and blessings.

Each ripple in the doctrinal storms delineated in the preceding three chapters, shows the deterioration of new evangelical theology and the new evangelical movement itself. In light of its relative cohesion in the 1940s, new evangelicalism is now fractured and fragmented over doctrines that were formerly attributed only to the cults and religion's lunatic fringe.

---

[36]Roger Raymer, "1 Peter," in *The Bible Knowledge Commentary*, New Testament, John F. Walvoord and Roy B. Zuck, eds. (Wheaton, IL: Victor), p. 840.

[37]Alan M. Stibbs, *The First Epistle General of Peter*, Tyndale New Testament Commentaries, R. V. G. Tasker, ed. (Grand Rapids: Eerdmans, 1959), p. 72. Edwin A. Blum, "1 Peter," in *The Expositor's Bible Commentary*, Frank E. Gaebelein, ed., 12 vols. (Grand Rapids: Zondervan, 1981) 12:219.

PART 9: CONCLUSION

23

EVALUATIONS AND PROSPECTS

The new evangelicalism has been slowly but decidedly moving toward neo-orthodoxy and beyond. This trend elicited warnings by early fundamentalists who sounded alarms over departures in the areas of revelation, inspiration, ecumenism, and other doctrines. Fundamentalists also feared that the strategy of "dialogue" would cause an acceptance of neo-orthodox and neo-liberal principles in the effort to find common ground and rapprochement with such scholars and leaders. The downward trajectory of new evangelicalism demonstrates the impossibility of maintaining a lofty rational objectivity and theological neutrality while exploring the so-called strengths of unbelieving scholarship for mutual enrichment, possible Christian fellowship, and organizational cooperation. The pacifistic and irenic spirit so necessary in dialogue circumvents a needed biblical confrontation and eventuates in toleration and, in some cases, an embracing of unscriptural ideas.

Millard Erickson noted in 1968 that the new evangelicalism "has been moving in the general direction of neo-orthodoxy. Some fundamental critics maintain that it already has moved to an essentially neo-orthodox position."[1] One need not look far for the names of those who at one time professed to be new evangelical but later embraced many non-evangelical tenets. One would be extremely reticent to apply to them any longer the name evangelical. Fuller Theological Seminary cannot be considered evangelical, largely due to the drift consciously engineered by David Allan Hubbard during his long tenure as president (1963-1993).[2] Billy Graham,

---

[1]Millard J. Erickson, *The New Evangelical Theology* (Westwood, NJ: Revell, 1968), p. 226.

[2]A very concise but informative account of Hubbard's success in changing Fuller Seminary's direction is given by Timothy Weber, "His Life and Ministry," in *Studies in Old Testament Theology*, eds. Robert L. Hubbard, Jr., Robert K. Johnston, and Robert P. Meye (Dallas: Word, 1992), pp. 21-27. The book was a tribute to David Allan Hubbard on his 65th birthday in honor of his 29 years as president of Fuller. Weber caught the genius of the Hubbard presidency in one sentence: "Under Hubbard's leadership, the course of Fuller Seminary was firmly set" (p. 24).

Clark Pinnock, Bernard Ramm, Donald Bloesch, Daniel P. Fuller, J. Ramsey Michaels, Robert Gundry, Stanley Grenz, Gregory Boyd, and others, have also forfeited the designation of evangelical, if their pronouncements, writings, and actions over the last few decades represent their true convictions.

Fundamentalists are not surprised at the decline because the greatest hedge against corruption by association (1 Cor 15:33) is the practice of ecclesiastical separation. Since the repudiation of this doctrine was the chief cornerstone of the new evangelicalism from its inception, the movement had a manifest destiny of deterioration in theology and ambivalence in practice from the beginning. Its anti-separatist obsession deprived it of the God-appointed means of preserving and propagating true Christianity. Carl F. H. Henry, Harold John Ockenga, Billy Graham, J. Elwin Wright, Edward John Carnell, L. Nelson Bell and Donald Grey Barnhouse, and others who labored unnoticed must bear the ultimate responsibility for the misfortunes of the new evangelicalism in the last sixty years. Their thinking set the sails of the movement back in the 1940s and 50s and, while they may lament the leftward plummet of their protégés, students, and ecclesiastical descendants, they contributed passively, indirectly and otherwise, to the movement's drift from its biblical moorings.

In 1969 Harold Lindsell made several predictions regarding his fellow new evangelicals. He foresaw theological deterioration, erosion of ethics and morality, substantial involvement in social and political activism to the detriment of the proclamation of the gospel, and defection to the ecumenical movement.[3] He seemed to be especially wary of social involvement, warning against the notion that "saved men will save society."[4] He observed almost caustically:

> Evangelicals must not accept the nonsense which says that if you feed men, house men, and clothe them, they will turn to the church. This is not true....The evangelical needs to be careful that he does not fall into the error created by those who insist that the church ought to be relevant....It is a fact that the Gospel is irrelevant to those whose eyes are blinded by sin....Ultimately the Gospel is relevant to the true needs of men and for us to try to debase the good coinage of the Gospel by vitiating it so that we can make it more attractive to men is to lose the Gospel and make it irrelevant.[5]

In a 1979 analysis, Harold O. J. Brown of Trinity Evangelical Divinity School concluded that "in the 1970s a challenge to evangelical identity arose within evangelicalism itself....Evangelicalism appears as a whole to have shifted leftward—theologically and politically—in the effort to defend liberalism's abandoned positions from militant secularism."[6] In his view, the new evangelical movement in 1979 had become "muzzled" after capturing "the highest peak of American political power—the election of Jimmy Carter as President late in 1976."[7]

---

[3]Harold Lindsell, *Evangelicalism and the Next Ten Years* (Wheaton, IL: National Association of Evangelicals, 1969), p. 7.

[4]Ibid., p. 8.

[5]Ibid., pp. 8-9.

[6]Harold O. J. Brown, "The Church of the 1970s: A Decade of Flux," *Christianity Today* (Dec 21, 1979), p. 23.

[7]Ibid., p. 21.

The next year Carl Henry expressed his regrets over the movement he had spearheaded.

> A decade ago I thought that late 20th century America might be on the move, however hesitatingly, toward a theological renaissance....Might not evangelicals who were beginning to wrestle with sociopolitical concerns also take theology more seriously? At present I see too little prospect for that.[8]

> During the 1960s I somewhat romanced the possibility that a vast evangelical alliance might arise in the United States to coordinate effectively a national impact in evangelism, education, publication, and sociopolitical action.[9]

Henry felt that the possibility of such a broad alliance, remote as it may have seemed, "was both shaped and lost...by evangelist Billy Graham" because "to call for an evangelical countermovement that might penetrate ecumenical ranks would have eroded ecumenical support for the crusades."[10] He lamented the fact that no evangelical leader or agency at the time had the dynamic to pull the movement together through the differences causing the new evangelical identity crisis.[11] He aired his complaints before the non-evangelical community through a liberal mouthpiece—*The Christian Century.*

Kenneth Kantzer gave a "mid-course self-appraisal" in 1983 in which he listed ten areas of weakness, such as weak institutions, reactionary tendencies and combative style, poor leadership, immature followers, and doctrinal and ethical ignorance."[12] He also gave several strengths offsetting the weaknesses, including evangelicalism's growing numbers (one third to one half of Protestants were allegedly evangelical), heritage, a coherent philosophy of life, and a self-correcting authority, the Bible.[13] Kantzer's appraisal seemed to err on the optimistic side.

Francis Schaeffer sounded the first undiluted critique and clear warning of Evangelicalm's looming demise. He pointedly named the biblical inerrancy/authority issue as the "watershed" issue dividing evangelicals.[14] Defections within the new evangelicalism on this doctrine led Schaeffer to warn: "*Compromising the full authority of Scripture eventually affects what it means to be a Christian theologically and how we live in the full spectrum of human life*" (italics his).[15] He saw looming on the new evangelical horizon a "new neo-orthodoxy" abetted by those who denied the propositional authority of the Bible in favor of forms of existential interpretation.[16] He castigated theologically trendy evangelicals who

---

[8]Carl F. H. Henry, "American Evangelicals In a Turning Time," *The Christian Century* (Nov 5, 1980), p. 1059.

[9]Ibid., p. 1060.

[10]Ibid.

[11]Ibid., p. 1061.

[12]Kenneth S. Kantzer, "Evangelicalism: Midcourse Self-Appraisal," *Christianity Today* (Jan 7, 1983), pp. 10-11.

[13]Ibid., p. 11.

[14]Francis A. Schaeffer, *The Great Evangelical Disaster* (Westchester, IL: Crossway, 1984), pp. 44, 51.

[15]Ibid., pp. 44-45.

[16]Ibid., p. 49.

seemed oblivious to the bleak results produced by neo-orthodoxy, particularly with the God-is-dead fascination.[17] Unfortunately, his warnings, having first sounded in the 1960s, were largely unheeded.

Lindsell's pessimistic view of the direction of the new evangelical movement saw that "evangelicalism today is in a sad state of disarray. In many quarters it has ceased to be what its founding fathers intended."[18] He saw the years 1940 to 1980 as the rising tide and influence of the new evangelicalism; however, since 1980 the foundations of the movement had been shaken and its constituency divided.[19] He felt the peak or "golden age" of new evangelicalism had been in the 1970s. Since then the movement had become diluted to where "it is difficult to define what and who an evangelical is."[20] He asks how one can be an evangelical if he does not accept the historical authenticity of Adam and Eve, the Mosaic authorship of the Pentateuch, the single authorship of Isaiah, the early dating of Daniel, the Pauline authorship of Ephesians or the Pastoral Epistles, the Petrine authorship of 2 Peter, or the omniscience of God. Lindsell affirmed that professing evangelicals had challenged these views[21] and, therefore the future for evangelicalism loomed frightful: "It is clear that evangelicalism is now broader and shallower, and is becoming more so. Evangelicalism's children are in the process of forsaking the faith of their fathers."[22] The foundation of the "Faith of their Fathers" had been biblical inerrancy, a doctrine Lindsell attempted valiantly to reaffirm.[23]

In 1986 Harold O. J. Brown expressed displeasure with the status of new evangelicalism and its future. To him, evangelicalism had become a kind of least common denominator of pietistic tendencies and "revivalistic fervor in Christianity, having much in common with more distinctive movements such as Pentecostalism and Fundamentalism, and also being subject to the criticism that it is fuzzy and not solidly biblical."[24]

Brown saw a multiplication of numbers in the future ranks of evangelicalism, but noted ominously that "following some of their intellectual leaders many evangelicals will tend to align themselves with mainline Protestantism and ecumenism and to play down the theological convictions and controversies that gave them their distinctives."[25]

In the mid 1980s Henry articulated disappointment with the movement he and others had fathered. In his autobiography's final chapter, titled "The Evangelical Prospects in America," he summed up his forecast:

---

[17]Ibid., p. 53.

[18]Harold Lindsell, "Evangelicalism's Golden Age," *Moody* (Dec 1985), p. 113.

[19]Ibid.

[20]Ibid., p. 114.

[21]Ibid.

[22]Ibid.

[23]Harold Lindsell, *The Battle For the Bible* (Grand Rapids: Zondervan, 1976) and *The Bible In the Balance* (Grand Rapids: Zondervan, 1979).

[24]Harold O. J. Brown, "Evangelicalism in America," *Dialog* 24 (Fall 1986), p. 191.

[25]Ibid.

I have two main convictions about the near-term future of American Christianity. One is that American evangelicals presently face their biggest opportunity since the Protestant Reformation, if not since the apostolic age. The other is that Americans are forfeiting that opportunity stage by stage, despite the fact that evangelical outcomes in the twentieth century depend upon decisions currently in the making.[26]

Elsewhere Henry expressed more disappointment and pessimism by observing that 1976, the "Year of the Evangelical," in which fifty million Americans professed to be born again, "marked the peak of a movement that had slowly emerged from its cultural ghetto through incentives like the Graham crusades, the founding of Fuller, and the launching of *Christianity Today* as a thought journal."[27] He placed further blame on his contemporary evangelicals:

The twentieth century in which evangelicals proposed to win the world for Christ in a single generation has in fact become the age in which religious atheism swept millions of persons into its ranks and in which political atheism now rules half the world's population and much of its land mass.[28]

The next year (1988) Henry again charged evangelicalism with gradually forfeiting its opportunities for global impact until its diversities now threatened to fragment the movement in the areas of evangelism, missions, education, literature, and the arts. The lack of a unified philosophy made various evangelical political efforts cancel each other out.[29]

Vernon Grounds, one of the early movers of the new evangelicalism among the Conservative Baptists, conveyed his own pessimism about the future of the movement. In the face of anticipated forthcoming problems and departures from truth in the coming generation, Grounds invoked the "GOK" (God only knows). Aside from what God knows, Grounds implied that his own knowledge provided little encouragement.[30] Ground's discouragement rose primarily from J.D. Hunter's evaluation of a cross-section of evangelical college and seminary students and the bleak outlook it posed for the next generation of evangelicals.[31]

Other negative evaluations appeared in the later 1980s and early 1990s, but it was David Wells, a theologian from the Gordon-Conwell Theological Seminary, who delivered the most penetrating and withering analysis of the movement's loss of sound doctrine.[32] Especially irksome to many was Well's willingness to expose and effectively kill many of new evangelicalism's sacred cows. His book chronicles and analyzes the breakdown of evangelical theology through Arminianism in the nineteenth century and modernism in the twentieth. Wells noted that the Second Great Awakening of the ninetheenth-century America, largely driven by

---

[26]Carl F. H. Henry, *Confessions Of a Theologian* (Waco, TX: Word, 1986), p. 381.

[27]Carl F. H. Henry, "The Uneasy Conscience Revisited: Current Theological, Ethical and Social Concerns," *Theology News and Notes* (Dec 1987), p. 3.

[28]Ibid., p. 8.

[29]McKendree Langley and Don McCrory, "A Conversation With Carl F. H. Henry," *Eternity* (Jan 1988), p. 20.

[30]Vernon Grounds, "American Evangelicalism: *Quo Vadis?*", *TSF Bulletin* (May-June 1987), pp. 7-10.

[31]James Davison Hunter, *Evangelicalism: The Coming Generation* (Chicago: University of Chicago Press, 1987).

[32]David C. Wells, *No Place For Truth: Whatever Happened to Evangelical Theology?* (Grand Rapids: Eerdmans, 1993).

Charles G. Finney and his "new measures" in evangelism, ushered in a new "Age of Protestantism,"[33] characterized by an overthrow of the Puritan-Calvinist beliefs of the First Great Awakening under Jonathan Edwards. In the new Age of Protestantism, the grandeur of God in His sovereignty succumbed to the majesty of man in his autonomy. God was almighty, almost. The Arminian trend coincided with the fundamental premise of the budding American democracy—the freedom of man.

Modernity, proved to be the legacy of the emancipated thought of the Enlightenment or the Age of Reason, a movement of ideas launched by the powerful, godless minds of philosophers in the seventeenth and eighteenth centuries. Modernity, called by Wells "Our Time,"[34] began between 1850-1875 at the instigation of technology and urbanization in an ocean of pluralism and multiculturalism. Modernity in principle rejected absolute truth or any unifying center to human thought and embraced the Unknown God of relativism. Relativism fostered a rootlessness in education, government, art, music, architecture, philosophy, morality, and, of course, religion. In theology, the Age of Reason first produced modernism, an optimistic web of religious thought in which nothing was off limits to the inquiring mind. This was followed by other forms of the same mental independence such as neo-orthodoxy and neo-liberalism.

In new evangelicalism the spirit of modernity mitigated stressing Bible doctrine in favor of an emphasis on cultural and personal "life," not unlike the path taken by the old modernism.[35] Evangelicalism soon became absorbed into the self movement where psychology instead of theology dominated. Happiness itself became an object of pursuit rather than a by-product of a right relationship with God and correct moral behavior. Being true to oneself (being all one is meant to be) took precedence over sacrifice for others. Wells showed that conformity, equality, the exaltation of the average, and the rise of a bland "Everyperson"[36] had become pervasive in new evangelicalism as well as in the general culture. In the forefront of this vacuous new thought stood the likes of Robert Schuller and his psychologized possibility thinking.[37] *Leadership Magazine* and *Christianity Today* also participated in the new relativism.[38] In the popular church growth movement, a community of "felt needs" set the church's agenda. Opinion polls and marketing manuals supplanted authoritative theology and preachers as guides of the new democratized faith. As a result seminary curricula emphasized relational, psychological, and CEO management type courses. Ministry tracks known for "breadth" rather than "depth" mushroomed at the expense of Bible truth. Enrollments and income increased, but theology disintegrated.

---

[33]Ibid., p. 31.

[34]Ibid., pp. 54-57, 61, passim.

[35]For this emphasis on "life" by liberals, see John Dillenberger and Claude Welch, *Protestant Christianity Interpreted Through Its Development* (New York: Scribners, 1954), p. 156.

[36]*No Place For Truth,* p. 189.

[37]Ibid., pp. 175, 178, 289.

[38]Ibid., pp. 113-14; 207-11.

Wells did not delineate a clear picture of the way out of the malaise in *No Place For Truth*, saving that for a later book. He did note, however, that "revival" (in the traditional sense of revivalism) was not really the answer. Instead, a thoroughgoing reformation with a genuine recovery of God and theology were needed.[39] The nineteenth-century revivalism of Charles Finney had been shaped by human techniques. Evangelicalism since then had "turned from dependence on God to management of God."[40] Wells argued that hope for a genuine and lasting extraction out of the present evangelical quagmire must return to the essential model of Jonathan Edwards and the First Great Awakening of eighteenth-century America.

The future of the new evangelical movement is bound up with its concept of ultimate religious authority. A struggle over this defining issue has been present from the movement's beginning. As was shown in the section on apologetics, the early new evangelical thinkers claimed the Bible as the final authority, but their verificationist/evidentialist methodology betrayed the claim by substituting an alien, free-from-God authority to test and verify God and His revelation-claims. The subtle shift led eventually to a surrender of biblical inerrancy and thus of a rightful claim to an absolute divine authority. Bit-by-bit, scholar-by-scholar, the new evangelicals brought themselves to their present impasse about authority. What is being advocated on the leading edge of evangelical thinking today is some sort of a religious jurisdiction that is non-authoritarian and non-absolute but also is not totally malleable and contemporary. Not wishing to choose between postliberal, culture-controlled relativism and old fundamentalist authoritarian absolutism, an attempt is being made to cut a middle channel by synthesizing the cultural-sensitive input of secular philosophy with the general tenets of the biblical story. The result has been a further drift from any genuine notion of absolute biblical authority to a vague, flat idea of an evangelical community consensus as a kind of court of appeal. This idea is expressed clearly and favorably by Robert E. Webber.[41] What this bodes for the future of the new evangelicalism is self-evident.

Movement away from absolute biblical authority has permeated the new evangelical ranks for some time. Some of this has been noted and analyzed in previous chapters. Some evangelicals have acknowledged the drift and voiced alarm. More recently a theological "megashift," a form of "new model" thinking has been going on that is "dividing evangelicals on a deep level."[42] Proponents of this latest new evangelical novelty, called postmodern, postclassic, or younger evangelicalism, are enthusiastic about the prospects it offers for dialogue with the current postmodern general culture. Clark Pinnock says that it is no exaggeration "to call it the most important religious development since World War II."[43]

---

[39]Ibid., pp. 283-301.

[40]Ibid., p. 296.

[41]*The Younger Evangelicals: Facing the Challenges of the New World* (Grand Rapids: Baker, 2002), Part Two, "The Younger Evangelical Thinkers."

[42]Robert Brow, "Evangelical Megashift," *Christianity Today* (Feb 19, 1990), p. 12.

[43]Clark H. Pinnock, *Tracking the Maze* (Eugene, OR: Wipf and Stock, 1998), p. 66.

A serious fracture within the new evangelical movement occurred in the 1970s when its leaders and avant garde thinkers reacted against Harold Lindsell and his exposure of those who were denying biblical inerrancy. Lindsell was the last of the "classic evangelicals."[44] Out of the authority vacuum, Robert Johnston proposed a consensus authority centered on a community of interpreters rather than that of an absolute, objective authority of the truth of Scripture. He termed his proposal "the collective wisdom of the best minds and spirits working together on the theological task of the church."[45] His approach has culminated in the "younger evangelical" movement that adheres to collective authority.[46]

Stanley Grenz advocated a "revisioning" of evangelical theology along the lines of postmodern thought, especially those of a "narrative" interpretation of Scripture that understands the Bible in terms of the general "story" of redemption rather than seeing Scripture as an inerrant text of propositions from God about redemption. Grenz complained that this latter approach focused on "epistemology or the cognitive dimension of faith, rather than toward our shared piety."[47] According to him,

> Central to evangelicalism is a common vision of the faith that arises out of a common religious experience couched within a common interpretive framework consisting in theological beliefs we gain from Scripture. As evangelicals we are persons who sense that we have encountered the living God through the gospel message of Jesus Christ. We describe this encounter by means of a set of theological categories derived from the Bible.[48]

For Grenz, doctrine describes a shared experience or a shared piety.

> More than the theological outlook itself, I believe, the way of experiencing the Christian life which as evangelicals we all share...lies at the center of the evangelical ethos. Our cherished theological commitments, in turn, are important insofar as they serve and facilitate this shared life-orientation.[49]

Grenz has it backward. Scriptural doctrine does not merely "describe" a shared experience, as though experience creates doctrine; biblical doctrine *defines* all valid religious experience. He wants evangelicalism to advance beyond a creed-based coalition to one originating from a common experience, a community of believers with shared convictions. Questions arise, however: precisely *what* do "believers" believe if Christianity is not defined by its propositions? And from *where* do the "convictions" originate that are shared? If convictions arise out of a pure vacuum, which is apparently the case, then the proposal is self-destructive and worthless.

---

[44]Douglas Jacobsen, "From Truth to Authority to Responsibility: The Shifting Focus of Evangelical Hermeneutics, 1915-1986 (Part II)," *TSF Bulletin* (May-June, 1987), p. 12.

[45]Robert K. Johnston, *Evangelicals At an Impasse* (Atlanta: John Knox, 1979), p. 147, quoted in Jacobsen, "From Truth to Authority to Responsibility," p. 12.

[46]Robert E. Webber, *The Younger Evangelicals*, pp. 87, 241.

[47]Stanley J. Grenz, *Revisioning Evangelical Theology: A Fresh Agenda For the 21st Century* (Downers Grove, IL: InterVarsity, 1993), p. 62.

[48]Ibid., p. 34.

[49]Ibid., p. 35.

Elsewhere Grenz contoured the infrastructure of a postmodern evangelical theology along three lines. First, it is post-individual. The "community" mediates to the individual in Christian matters.[50] Second, it is post-rational. Instead of theology fixated on and derived from rational propositions of the verbal revelation from God, theological propositions are merely the vehicles for the faith community to comment on and express its transforming religious experience of encountering God.[51] Third, it is centered on spirituality not doctrine. In other words, theology must be intensely "practical," or it is useless. In Grenz's words: "In the postmodern world we must reappropriate the older pietist discovery that a 'right heart' takes primacy over a 'right head.'"[52] Evangelical Roger Olson describes Grenz's theological method:

> Grenz emphasizes experience over supernaturally revealed propositional truth as the heart of Christian theology. He defines theology as reflection on the faith of the people of God—a second-order activity that provides useful models rather than the scientific deduction of intellectual truth from a mother lode of truth in Scripture.[53]

> Theology is second-order reflection on the faith....The essence of both Christianity and theology, then, is not propositional truths enshrined in doctrine, but a narrative-shaped experience.[54]

If theology is a second-order reflection on one's experience of the overarching narrative of redemption in the Bible, then where does ultimate authority lie? Obviously, the consensus of the faith community using all the resources of postmodern philosophy and biblical studies is doing the reflecting. Narrative-shaped experience as an authority consists of "employing a range of sources in a dialectical way."[55] Sadly, the emphasis on experience restricts theology as a correlation of propositional truths from God and also creates an authority that is purely relative. A secular/religious symposium of human thought is a perilously unstable authority. Postmodern evangelicals are aware that such a consensus authority may prove to be untrustworthy, and they labor vigorously to assert that it may not and has not yet happened. The defensive dogmatism is not convincing.[56]

One of the more oxymoronic quirks of the postclassic evangelicals is their quest for a non-foundational authority, a binary authority that tries to combine the text of Scripture with the context of culture in a non-absolutist and non-authoritarian way. Foundationalism holds that a philosophy or belief system must rest on a principle or principles that are transcendent, self-evidencing, or indubitable. Postconservative evangelicals are anti-foundationalists. Rodney

---

[50]Stanley J. Grenz, "Postmodernism and the Future of Evangelical Theology: *Star Trek* and the Next Generation," *Evangelical Review of Theology* 18 (1994), pp. 330-31.

[51]Ibid., p. 332.

[52]Ibid., p. 333.

[53]Roger E. Olson, "Postconservative Evangelicals Greet the Postmodern Age," *The Christian Century* (May 3, 1995), p. 483.

[54]Ibid., p. 481.

[55]Clark H. Pinnock, *Tracking the Maze,* p. 71.

[56]Ibid., p. 72.

Clapp, for instance, thinks "foundationalists need to admit that there is no such thing as safely and absolutely secured knowledge."[57] Having made that admission, Clapp argues, Christians as a faith community can engage non-believers in witness, pointing out to them the desirability of the change proposed for them in their lives and contextual interests. "By drawing others into Christian friendship, telling Christian stories and sharing Christian worship, we may alter the way others interpret their experience and introduce a new set of desires into their desires."[58] By "Christian stories" is apparently meant biblical narratives which serve as models with which one can identify.

Jonathan Wilson, an evangelical in quest of a non-foundationalist religious authority, finds a fertile source in the proposals and principles of postliberalism. Postliberalism has arisen out of the ashes of defunct and discredited liberal theology to form a religious rapprochement with rootless, non-absolutist, non-authoritarian, and secular postmodern philosophy. Wilson's eclectic evangelical authority construct is cobbled together with snatches from George Lindbeck with bits and pieces from the philosophy of Ludwig Wittgenstein. In an amazing note of triumph, Wilson exclaims: "By drawing on Lindbeck's proposal and extending it, I will develop a new evangelical paradigm of biblical authority rooted in practicing the gospel, living in community and interpreting the world."[59] It would probably be considered incredulous to ask where the actual contributions of the Bible itself are in this amalgam of authority.

The intellectual vanguard of the new evangelicalism in fewer than sixty years has found itself repudiating any absolute religious authority. Instead, it is advocating an appeal to an agreement among the Christian community. No longer does the individual Christian have an ultimately inerrant and infallible foundation in a series of revelation-claims and propositions in a divine-human book, the Bible. He must instead look to an elite cadre of intellectuals for some kind of direction divined from a smorgasbord of postliberal philosophy and biblical story.

J. D. Hunter, a sociologist, in his 1987 conclusions about evangelicalism, apparently could foresee what was on the horizon. Based on his analysis of a poll of evangelical college and seminary students, he noted concerning the evangelicals of the later twentieth century:

> There is less sharpness, less boldness, and, accordingly, a measure of opaqueness in their theological vision that did not exist in previous generations (at least to their present extent). A dynamic would appear to be operating that strikes at the very heart of the Evangelical self-identity. But what is one to make of it?....The evidence is suggestive of a common trend, one in which the theological tradition is conforming in its own unique way to the cognitive and normative assumptions of modern culture.[60]

---

[57]Rodney Clapp, "How Firm A Foundation: Can Evangelicals Be Nonfoundationalists?", in *The Nature of Confession*, eds. Timothy R. Phillips and Dennis L. Okholm (Downers Grove, IL: InterVarsity, 1996), p. 89.

[58]Ibid., p. 90.

[59]Jonathan R. Wilson, "Toward a New Evangelical Paradigm of Biblical Authority," in *The Nature of Confession*, p. 153.

[60]James Davison Hunter, *Evangelicalism: The Coming Generation*, p. 46.

The new evangelicals for many years have been rejoicing that they finally had come out of the fundamentalist social ghetto and into the mainstream of cultural life and thought,[61] and thereby have gained a certain measure of legitimacy and respectability in their new surroundings. Given that fact, Hunter raised a provoking question and gave an ominous answer:

> Certainly, in its move out of the ghetto, it [evangelicalism] has risked the unintentional contamination by the very reality it has tried to keep out. That this process has begun, there is little doubt. Where it will go from here is an open question. If historical precedent is instructive, *it becomes clear that these tendencies will probably escalate* (italics added).[62]

The intervening years have confirmed Hunter's probability assessment. The new evangelicalism as a movement has been incrementally winding its way toward evangelical extinction. If the postmodern proponents succeed in capturing the direction of the movement, then the movement is in the final stages of becoming totally irrelevant.

Having rejected the separatism of their fundamentalist heritage, the new evangelicals self-consciously pursued infiltration and dialogue as their new working principles. Their rationalistic type of apologetics and philosophy of religion, built by intellectual autonomy, made theology quite malleable for many. Denials of propositional revelation and verbal inerrancy led new evangelical theology to take a precipitous nose-dive in the later 1970s from which, as a general movement, it has never recovered. Some of its founders soon began to write the movement off as a prodigal son in a far county.

With its rejection of biblical inerrancy and consequent loss of ultimate religious authority, combined with an ever enthusiastic pursuit of the dialogue technique, new evangelicalism came to an impasse over what constitutes the gospel and what the New Testament church is all about. Worse, this blind alley caused a more monumental question—what is a Christian? The vanguard of new evangelicalism became increasingly mired in this vexing question as it sought cooperation and rapprochement with liberal Protestants and conservative Roman Catholics. *Biblically* the issue boils down to one's being either saved or lost, heaven-bound or hell-bound, one of God's people or Satan's. Scripture has no mediating position on the definition of a Christian.

When ultimate religious authority cannot be successfully identified, the gospel has no sure parameters. When the gospel cannot be precisely defined, what it means to be a Christian cannot be agreed upon. If the marks of a genuine Christian cannot be construed, then the question of what the Christian church is becomes moot. In liberal Protestantism the church became everyone and, in reality, was no one and thus nondescript. If everyone is a Christian, then no one is a Christian in this amorphous blob of religion. The new evangelicalism appears to be well on its way toward becoming such a conglomerate bereft of true biblical distinctives.

---

[61]Carl F. H. Henry, "The Uneasy Conscience Revisited," p. 3.

[62]Ibid., p. 49.

A movement that wants to be called evangelical and yet has to debate itself over what the genius of Christianity actually is, is putting the finishing touches on its own coffin. It seems certain that the new evangelicalism is incapable of self-correction.

24

ADDENDUM 1

The Younger Evangelicals: Facing the Challenges of the New World
by Robert E. Webber (Grand Rapids: Baker, 2002)

A REVIEW ARTICLE
ROLLAND D. MCCUNE

This book is an apologetic for and a chronicle of one of the latest editions in the ever-widening evangelical saga. Robert E. Webber is Myers Professor of Ministry at the Northern Baptist Theological Seminary and president of the Institute for Worship Studies. He taught at Wheaton College from 1968–2000. He has authored numerous books on the general subject of evangelicalism, the most recent being *Ancient-Future Evangelism* (Baker, 2003). The author's research and contact with his subject are aptly demonstrated in the book under review, although the ideas and practices of the new group he portrays are still largely from anecdotal accounts at this early point. In this book Webber "interprets the changing face of evangelicalism since about 1950 and projects where evangelicalism is going in the next decades" (p. 13).

Webber introduces the subject by placing the new movement, called the younger evangelicals, within the history of evangelicalism that spans roughly 1950–2000. From 1950–1975 a group flourished that he calls "traditional evangelicals" (what I would term "new evangelicals"). The group rose out of the old fundamentalist/evangelical coalition that itself had emerged from the fundamentalist-modernist controversy of the 1920s. The new or traditional evangelicals repudiated the essential motifs of the fundamentalists. From 1975–2000 a new stirring of "pragmatic evangelicals" appeared, baby boomers that turned against the traditionalists and created the mega-church, seeker-sensitive, market-driven, and generation-targeted philosophy of church ministry. From 2000 on into the 21st century, the latest wave has rebelled against the drastic innovations, self-esteem therapeutics, and crass commercialism of the boomer pragmatists. They are now returning to the past—pre-Constantine church practice, patristic theology, ecumenical creeds, and ancient liturgics, icons, and symbols—as a paradigm for doing church in a postmodern culture. They are known throughout the book as younger evangelicals (young in age or young in spirit), postmodern evangelicals, 21st century evangelicals, twenty-somethings, Gen X evangelicals, and millennial youth.

Webber lays out the flow of his thought well. Part one (chapters 1 and 2) is introductory, locating the recent vintage of evangelicals in the evangelical history of the twentieth century, mainly in the USA, and outlining the characteristics (24 of them!) of the new group. Part two (chapters 3–7) explains the impact of new forms of communication on the younger evangelical thinkers and how this has changed their approach to several critical issues. They have shifted from a disregard for history to a new appreciation of tradition, from didactic propositionalism to a story/narrative basis for theology, from rational apologetics to a verification of truth through its authentic embodiment in the communal church, and from a preoccupation with the invisible church to an emphasis on the visible church in ecclesiology. Part three (chapters 8-16) deals with the ways in which the 21st century evangelicals differ with their 20th century predecessors (the traditionalists and pragmatists) in ecclesial practice. To use the author's chapter titles: "Being Church: From Market to Mission; Pastors: From Power to Servanthood; Youth Ministers: From Parties to Prayer; Educators: From Information to Formation; Spiritual Formation: From Legalism to Freedom; Worship Leaders: From Program to Narrative; Artists: From Constraint to Expression; Evangelists: From Rallies to Relationships; and Activists: From Theory to [Social] Action." Part four (chapter 14) is the conclusion, diagraming Webber's vision of the new kind of evangelical leadership needed for the 21st century.

It would be impossible in this space to interact with each chapter of the book and its innovative proposals, although such a discipline would be worthy of the effort elsewhere. I will select what I consider to be four of the load-bearing points and respond to them. My stance, of course, is that of historic fundamentalism and, while there are varying eddies in the fundamentalist stream, some good and helpful and some otherwise, the main channel consists of a core of cardinal, non-negotiable theological teachings, the doctrine and practice of ecclesiastical separation, and an underlying *esprit* of militancy for the truth and against whatever would deny it or detract from it. Webber came out of a fundamental Baptist background and attended Bob Jones University, but subsequently shifted to what I would call a new evangelical position. Quite evidently he has become enamored with and a proponent of the latest expression of evangelical opinion. Accordingly, his interpretations and mine of the history, beliefs, and practices of the evangelical movement, as well as its present direction, rarely coincide.

History

Webber's feelings toward fundamentalism are patently negative, regarding it as sort of a pot hole in the ongoing evangelical movement. Evangelical history in the United States is marked off as (1) 1910-1925, the origins of the fundamentalist movement; (2) 1925-1945, fundamentalism; (3) 1945-1966, neo-evangelicalism;

and (4) 1966-2000, evangelical diversity consisting of the traditional evangelicals and the pragmatic evangelicals. In his thinking, the 1925 Scopes trial in Dayton, TN, marked the turning point when fundamentalism turned anti-intellectual, anti-ecumenical, and anti-social. It is probably too much ever to hope that fundamentalism will be seen by its opponents as anything but the villain of the so-called "monkey trial." The truth is that, while the fundamentalists took a hit in the court of public opinion thanks to a very prejudiced and unsympathetic media, the movement continued to flourish in the aftermath of Scopes and William Jennings Bryan.[1]

Fundamentalism has indeed been characterized as anti-ecumenical, if by that is meant that fundamentalists attempted to separate the liberals from their ecclesiastical environment and, that having failed, consequently had to separate themselves formally from the apostasy and its evangelical fellow-travelers. It was not until the rise of the new evangelicalism in the 1940s and 50s that ecumenism made its appearance within the original fundamentalist/evangelical coalition largely though the technique of ecumenical evangelism. This first took place openly at the 1957 Billy Graham New York Crusade with its inclusive policy of sponsorship and convert referrals, which fundamentalists resisted. Graham forced the issue and precipitated the final and irrevocable breach between the new evangelicalism and historic fundamentalism. In a pluralistic context of ministry where fundamentalists would be yoked with theological unbelief and apostasy, fundamentalism has always been and continues to be anti-ecumenical.

Concerning fundamentalism's anti-social action, the charge has been made that 20th century fundamentalism squandered a rich social sensitivity that it inherited from the Wesleyans and from the evangelicalism of the era from before the Civil War until the Scopes trial. On this subject I have two thoughts. One, the social activity of the Wesleyan movement and the social consciousness of antebellum evangelicalism as well as the pre-1925 evangelical/fundamentalist coalition has been hugely overdrawn. I do not discern a *distinct* social agenda for the institutional church in those times, the kind of programs being called for by the new evangelicals since the later 1940s. The Bible-believing churches did not consider themselves the divinely-appointed sentinels of the social conditions of their cultures. The care of Christians for the generally deprived and disenfranchised arose out of their individual lives in civil society as they fleshed out the implications of the Christian experience in good citizenry.

Two, pragmatically the social gospel and its theology have been a colossal failure, accomplishing little more than a feel-good attitude among liberal and evangelical churchmen, meanwhile totally devastating the philosophy and practice of the missionary enterprise in those circles.[2] Studies have shown that it is not clear that the rise of fundamentalism actually caused a loss of legitimate social ministry

---

[1]For a clear-headed and historically aware analysis of the Scopes trial and the subsequent fortunes of fundamentalism, see Gerald L. Priest, "William Jennings Bryan and the Scopes Trial: A Fundamentalist Perspective," *Detroit Baptist Seminary Journal* 4 (Fall 1999).

[2]This has been analyzed by Arthur P. Johnston, *The Battle for World Evangelism* (Wheaton: Tyndale, 1978).

among conservative Christian groups.[3] Furthermore, the evangelical lamentations over a lost fundamentalist social sensitivity and the calls for a revived sociopolitical activism, beginning with Carl F. H. Henry and Harold John Ockenga in 1947, were in reality more rhetoric than substance; little was actually accomplished. Even Webber notes that phenomenon (p. 31).[4]

As for fundamentalism being anti-intellectual, I have addressed that elsewhere,[5] but it too is part of the tired, old mantra against fundamentalism that continues on.

Authority

Any movement that wants to use the name Christian must justify its claims by an appeal to some kind of an ultimate authority. That authority may be autonomous human reason, the decrees of the church, or divine revelation. For historic evangelicalism the authority has always been an inerrant Bible. But for the younger evangelicals this has posed a dilemma: How can a postmodern culture, resting on a denial of virtually any kind of authority, be reached by those who ordinarily have been impelled by the absolute authority of an ancient book, the Scriptures? In sorting through this impasse, the new thinkers have abandoned the ultimate authority of the Bible in favor of a communal consensus of their intellectual elites as informed and shaped by patristic and medieval thought. The ultimate casualty of all this, of course, is exegesis of the biblical languages and its correlation into doctrinal propositions as the source of belief and practice. It is not surprising, then, that Webber's first appeal to any Scripture passage is on page 85, the second on page 86, and the third on page 95 in a book of only 230 pages of text!

As one analyzes the basis of authority for the way the younger evangelicals do theology, he soon realizes that their thought is governed by an underlying intuition or a sense of emotional satisfaction. The inner "still small voice" carries tremendous authority with them (pp. 193, 214). This stress on what is ultimately non-rational and non-cognitive as the basis of doing church is obviously fraught with all manner of difficulty, but it is their hope of reaching a postmodern, non-rational, non-judgmental, and authoritatively rootless culture for Christ. The question persists, however, is such theology and methodology truly Christian? Does this approach give a biblical and historically viable answer to the query, what is a Christian? In terms of its own proposals, it does not. In those terms the younger evangelicals are inherently unstable in theology and ecclesial practice and will not endure the challenges of the next fad of the contemporary culture even as, in their minds, their traditionalist and pragmatist evangelical predecessors did not. In fact, the newcomers may well have a shorter life span than either, and the underlying reason is the broad-based, pluralistic authority of younger evangelical group-think

---

[3]James Davison Hunter, *Evangelicalism: The Coming Generation* (Chicago: University of Chicago Press, 1987), p. 42.

[4]No less than George M. Marsden made this observation in *Reforming Fundamentalism: Fuller Seminary and the New Evangelicalism* (Grand Rapids: Eerdmans, 1987), p. 82.

[5]Rolland D. McCune, "The Formation of the New Evangelicalism (Part Two)," *Detroit Baptist Seminary Journal* 4 (Fall, 1999), pp. 121-30. Douglas Carl Abrams was perceptive: "As a group, fundamentalist leaders were well-educated" (*Selling the Old Time Religion: American Fundamentalism and Mass Culture, 1920-1940* [Athens, GA: University of Georgia Press, 2001], p. 9).

that will bring an even more accelerated deterioration of their cause than those against whom they are in revolt.

The Younger Evangelicals deprecates the cognitive, propositional (subject-predicate), and didactic thought-forms of ordinary human reason, especially of traditional evangelicalism, in constructing a theology of belief and practice from the written revelation of God. Here are a few examples. In Webber's dislike of the fundamentalist skepticism of unbiblical philosophical notions which he found in his college days at BJU, Webber adds, "This attitude still dominates fundamentalist Biblicism, a view that is based on the modern philosophy of rationalism [i.e., cognitive reasoning] and the scientific method of hermeneutics. *This method results in propositions of faith that deliver guaranteed truth, a hermeneutic not widely accepted by the younger evangelicals*" (italics added) (p. 28). He wishes to get away from a "truth-oriented" posture and "reasoned-based theology" to "a more experienced-based faith" (p. 45). He agrees with a current author that "the problem with a mere 'propositionalism' (a modern idea) is that you lose the power and force of the imagination…you lose the story and in so doing you lose the vibrant stuff." Thus the younger evangelicals know that "*they must minister in a new paradigm of thought* (italics his) (p. 48). "The freedom from rationalism, propositionalism, and logical analysis has revived the imagination, and we are beginning to see the fruits of empowered imagination in the new ministries formed by the younger evangelicals" (p. 51). "The importance of truth is not so much that it is understood but that it is loved and lived" (p. 52). For the younger evangelicals, "stating truths to which they are asked to commit is too modern. It's related to propositions and conclusions that have been developed by others outside their intimate community. Younger evangelicals enjoy the process of *shared experiences* from which they derive a sense of wisdom and direction" (italics added) (p. 53).[6]

For the younger evangelicals authority therefore becomes communal; it arises from within the church. This of course makes shambles of the doctrine of individual soul liberty, the freedom of conscience wherein every believer has the right and duty *personally* to come to Scripture directly and be taught and governed by the Holy Spirit. The corporate concept of authority rules out any such personal claim because that would, in their opinion, lead back to the old evangelical/ fundamentalist idea of individualistic faith, Great Commission ecclesiology, CEO pastors, personality cults, and empire building. In other words, individualism would destroy the idea of the church as a democratic community. Accordingly, the young evangelicals have decided, apparently through the feelings of the community, that certain ones who emerge with sufficient intellectual and personal abilities will be accepted as the authority. Webber not only affirms this but practices it as well as he quotes certain scholars and takes the testimony of successful anecdotal witnesses as authority for promoting the new paradigms of doing theology and ministry.

In an astounding overstatement, Webber claims that "classical Christianity

---

[6]More examples of this kind of assault on the propositional authority of the written Word of God can be found on pp. 69, 83, 94, 95, 96, 116, 123, 196, among others.

knew nothing of the concept of propositionalism as held by Christians after the Enlightenment" (p. 84), as if the Enlightenment invented the idea that meaning is in the subject-predicate sentence and not the individual word much less a feeling produced by the imagination or an intuition divined by the mystical still small voice. In inveighing against propositionalism, Webber has impaled himself on one of his own assumptions, which happens to be correct, that language is univocal. It is axiomatic as a result of the image of God in human beings that words cannot have two or more meanings in one and the same connection; A cannot be non-A at the same time and in the same sense, which is the genius of propositionalism. Yet the author uses propositional language to argue against the propositionalism of the Scriptures and true, historic Christianity. But he simply cannot have it both ways. By his own standard either his statements or the Bible's truth-claims, or both, are unintelligible.

When propositional formulations of truth from the written revelation of God are abandoned or deprecated, the only standard left is pure subjectivism in doing theology and doing church. In other words, if the mind is bypassed, the emotions and feelings remain as some sort of an ultimate criterion. This is to say that eventually one falls back on the glands for authority. And this is what Webber and the twenty-somethings duly propose as a final religious authority. For instance, in promoting the power of the imagination vis-a-vis propositional truth-statements, Webber quotes approvingly another: "Since imagination locates itself in time, it must also locate somewhere in space. Somewhere, in other words, it takes on a physical entity." The author then adds his own commentary: "If you can dream it, you can create it" (p. 50). But on what is the "dream" based? Since he has ruled out any cognitive content by circumventing one's intellect, what is left for the created "physical entity" that will emerge from the dream or imagination but glandular functions? Webber is optimistic about the "language of metaphor" that the younger evangelicals are embracing; it rides the tide of emotion and will revolutionize the senses. In the words of a recent author, it will make "our emotions and feelings— especially touch—cognitive extensions of our minds....*We will know through our feelings*" (italics added) (p. 68). This is surely confusion thrice confounded but aptly demonstrates the fact that if the mind is short-circuited, the glands are all that are left, accounting for the heavy mysticism and pietism that hangs over the younger evangelical agenda.

The subjective but normative power of the imagination in doing theology leads irresistibly to a subjective and fluid definition of truth. Truth must be rightly defined, in my judgment, as a character of propositions that represents a correct state of affairs. This "state of affairs" is the person of God and His all-encompassing decree of whatsoever comes to pass. Truth, in other words, is that which corresponds to the mind of God, and this gives truth a biblical, God-centered basis in theology and reality. If so, the younger evangelicals appear to have a most difficult task of affirming truth to say nothing of discerning truth from falsehood since truth cannot be absolute but must be flattened out to include everyone's feelings, especially those of the authoritative cadre of thinkers within the 21st century evangelicals. But if religious authority is relative to the culture's idea of authority, and if the younger evangelical's authority is relative to the magisterium of the movement's trusted think tank, then there is no solid basis of authority for anyone. Everyone is left floating in the shoreless ocean of relativity especially where spiritual and eternal truths are concerned. The younger evangelicals will protest that this is not the way it is, but in so doing they must employ authoritative propositional truth to deny or disprove the idea of the propositional nature of authoritative, divine, verbally revealed truth, and this, of course, is self-destructive.

Ultimate religious authority for these evangelicals is subjective (the communal consensus) and not objective in nature (biblical propositions). But it is impossible for authority to result from the unanimous feelings and consent of *every* believer within the believing community. Since authority is subjective, it can only be determined *arbitrarily* for the larger group, evidently by those most gifted and influential as leaders. And their choice for doctrine and practice is to return to the past and a formulated conflation of ancient patristic theology and pre-Constantine [prior to the 4th century AD] ecclesiology, medieval liturgy, and Reformation and Wesleyan ideas. This shift is a conscious deconstruction of traditional evangelicalism's thought-forms allegedly formulated with ingredients drawn from modernity, and a reconstruction of an ancient-future faith, a faith for the future built on the thought and ways of the past. "The younger evangelical is returning to basics, to broad strokes and an eclectic Christianity held together by traditions that have lasted for centuries" (p. 59). It must be stated again that this broad-based authority is theoretically a *consensus* of the believing community. "The younger evangelical is turning away from theology as ruled by reason and the scientific method toward theology as a reflection of the community on the narrative of Israel and Jesus" (p. 87). Theological reflection "is not an abstract objective discipline that is subject to reason, logic, or science. It is instead a communal reflection on God's mission that arises out of God's people as they seek to discern God's work in history and his present action in the life of the community" (p. 241).

With the negative attitude against propositional language formulations and a penchant for ambiguity, mystery, and the multi-dimensional in faith, theology, and worship (pp. 48, 49, 52, 185, 199), one is not prepared to learn that "*younger evangelicals are attracted to absolutes*" (italics his) (p. 52) and that "the younger evangelicals know that *they must stand for the absolutes of the Christian faith in a new way*" (italics his) (p. 48). The "new way" is to present the gospel as "story," which is "*not* a non-contradictory, rationally defended, logically consistent fact apprehended by cognitive acquiescence" (italics added) (p. 49). So it seems we are back to ambiguity after all in standing for the absolutes of the gospel and the Christian faith. I find this kind of dialectic utterly incomprehensible.

The question that remains to be dealt with is, are the church fathers a coherent and stable source of theology? If not, then the theological and ecclesial structure of the younger evangelicals is lost.

Historical theology teaches us that patristics is neither coherent nor stable. Just about any doctrinal variation (and aberration) can be found in the church fathers.

There is no consensus among them on the meaning, mode, recipients, and purpose of water baptism, or millennial issues; pre-, mid-, and posttribulationism have all been supported by selected fathers. Church polity, the person of Christ, and a host of other subjects including the nature of and the way to salvation and eternal life itself can be proven or disproved by an appeal to patristic thought. The fathers' knowledge of the biblical languages was quite deficient compared to today. Their theology in the main is immature and undeveloped at best; at worst it is heretical in many ways. It is hard to imagine a more unreliable source of authority.

In the middle ages ecclesiastical scholarship was deplorable. Since allegorism had generally prevailed for centuries, biblical exegesis had become sterile and the academia of the church was content largely to compile the theology of the fathers. Thus Roman Catholicism, Orthodoxy, and others developed an authoritative patristic theology that is with them to this day. Unfortunately, this is the mother lode out of which Webber and the younger evangelicals recommend that theology and ministry be drawn for a postmodern expression of evangelicalism and its ancient-future faith. Appeal to the fathers at the very best is an indirect and second-hand exposure to biblical exegesis and theology and accounts for the evident bob-tailed content and short-sighted outlook of the younger evangelicals' thinking and doing in a secular society, at least as depicted in the book. And I might add, I personally do not see a whole lot that is exegetically and theologically cogent in the church fathers that hasn't been said with more clarity and precision, and with far better exegetical foundation and theological correlation, by Bible-believing theologians and exegetes of the last century and a half. True, there were great theological controversies that yielded some outstanding confessions of faith in the days of the church fathers, but I would not consider these great expressions of doctrine as the kind of contributions that characterized patristic thought.

Apologetics and Evangelism

Apologetics and evangelism are intertwining and inseparable disciplines that concern the propagation and defense of a total witness to the truth-claims of biblical Christianity. The method and conclusion of both apologetics and evangelism are wrapped up and governed by a mutual presuppositional authority or starting point, whether it is that of autonomous human reason, the law of non-contradiction, a self-authenticating Bible that points to a self-identifying Christ, or whatever else. The younger evangelicals have cast their lot with some kind of a corporate religious conscience as the ultimate authority and most primitive starting point for their community's belief and practice. This carries the freight of arbitrary subjectivism for their interim, daily working basis for defining truth, formulating theology, constructing hermeneutics, conducting worship, and generally doing ministry, including how to defend and propagate the Christian faith. In other words, apologetics/evangelism is subject to the same notions of ambiguity, equivocation, imprecision, and lack of certainty that plague the other aspects of the younger movement.

The book's chapter on apologetics is subtitled, "From Rationalism to Embodiment." In brief this means that the younger evangelicals have moved the defense and propagation of the Christian faith out of the realm of argument and reasoned discourse based on the objective propositions and truth-claims of Scripture into the subjective and personal dimension—the "life" of the believing community.

There are four load-bearing points that I will address which are difficulties that prevent an understanding of how this new postmodern apologetic methodology can be either biblical or successful. The first is its non-propositional or non-foundational nature. I have addressed this in the previous section and will only mention it briefly. Foundationalism understands that a system of beliefs, to be coherent, must rest on presuppositions or first principles that are assumed at the outset because they are indubitable or self-evidencing—first principles that are authoritative because no greater authorization can be found for them. The younger evangelicals identify foundationalism with Enlightenment thought that was allegedly then adopted by evangelical thinkers. The younger evangelicals have rejected foundationalism in favor of a non-foundational construct for doing theology and ministry. In that sense they also wish to be considered postfoundational as compared to their evangelical predecessors.

It follows that if the Bible's authority does not reside in its propositional truth-statements, the process of conveying the message of the Bible will irresistibly be without a certain foundation. This is because, as I noted above, the method and conclusion in an apologetic methodology both begin with one's starting point or the presupposed foundational authority. If the younger evangelical begins with a subjective, in-house, corporate, and ambiguous authority, the method of presenting and defending the faith will proceed on that plane, and the conclusion of necessity will be an ambivalent, uncertain form of evangelicalism peculiar to the in-group. And this is exactly how the postmodern apologetic unfolds. Anti-foundationalism ends without fail in religious malaise and invites skepticism of the whole Christian enterprise. Biblical Christianity merely stands in line with the multitudinous other believing-without-knowing options in the world.

This methodology's result is at total cross purposes with the intended goal of the younger evangelicals, which is to make *committed* Christians in a rootless culture. That is to say, their postmodern apologetic/evangelistic technique betrays them in the end. It has nothing that makes New Testament Christianity unique, it has no way of showing the futility of false religions (Islam in particular is of concern to the younger evangelicals), and the truthfulness of Christianity and the exclusivity of Christ as the way to God (Acts 4:12) are muted. Apologetics, it seems, has been reduced to little more than unilateral, open-ended God-talk.

Webber begins his treatment of apologetics with an autobiographical introduction concerning his conversion experience that illustrates the younger evangelical methodology of doing apologetics and evangelism. One night, at his pastor father's behest, he consciously decided to

> acknowledge God and follow Jesus in baptism. I have always considered my baptism to be my first real conscious choice to affirm God's reality and to live in the pattern of Jesus' death and resurrection. This commitment was real, authentic, and actually radical, *even though it was not the result of knowledge* and certainly was not based on rational arguments or evidence that 'demanded a verdict' (italics added) (p. 94).

It is understandable that his coming to Christ was not based on rational arguments or empirical proofs since the biblical picture of saving faith is not such. But to say that saving faith does not involve intellectual content or result from knowledge is a problem. If by knowledge is simply meant demonstrable free-from-God proof derived by an independent, free-from-the-Bible apologetic methodology, well and good. But the rest of the chapter indicates that the author is simply affirming the non-foundational and thus non-rational structure of biblical authority. That the Bible is necessary to faith is indicated by his reference to Jesus' death and resurrection, but how His death and resurrection can be divorced from knowledge is to me unexplainable if indeed faith comes by hearing the Word of God (Rom 10:9). The implication here, and it is borne out in the chapter and various other parts of the book, is that faith is sacramentally structured in isolation from one's intellect. This is quite troubling to me but understandable in terms of the non-foundational construct the younger evangelicals have made for themselves.

A second point has to do with the subjective communal embodiment of apologetics which is the fulfillment of the non- or post-foundationalism chosen by the younger thinkers. If understanding and presenting the Christian faith are not to include commitments to propositional truth-statements in an inerrant Bible, what is to take its place? And whatever it is cannot be objectively authoritative. Once again we are back to the somewhat amorphous "community," the church which is the embodiment of the truth. As Webber says, "truth is not proven, it is embodied by individuals and by the community known as the church" (p. 101). Theological truth, in the post-foundational sense, is a "conversation" between the Bible, tradition, and the culture, "a mosaic in accordance with the ecumenical faith of the church throughout its history and on behalf of the church throughout the world" (p. 101; he is quoting another source). In other words, the Christian faith is true because it is old and has had innumerable adherents in its long history, and the living ones currently embody the truth in the believing community of the visible church. But what makes this community of adherents right and other ancient traditions (e.g., Islam) wrong? The proponents here admit that the new approach makes Christianity contestable and subject to debate just like Marxism, Hinduism, and others (p. 100). But this only makes biblical faith part of a smorgasbord of religious options, and who or what is to determine that the evangelical community has the absolute truth or that it even has superior insights about God and eternal life? Or is Christianity not the only viable way to God, and if not, why bother to do apologetics at all or even be evangelical? Post-foundationalism reduces all religions to God-talk and does nothing to make Christianity the embodiment of the truth and the others not.

A third factor is the corporate vis-a-vis the individual witness of Christians in the postmodern apologetic/evangelistic proposal. The younger evangelicals disapprove of the "Great Commission ecclesiology" (pp. 108, 122) that characterized the older evangelicals and indeed the church for centuries. Their model is that of a corporate witness to the truth-claims of the gospel. In that sense the church "does not have a mission, it is mission" (p. 109), and its missional function is not verbal so much as a communal dynamic that expresses somewhat metaphorically the Christian message. That is, the visible church demonstrates Christian spirituality holistically in authentic realness more than proclaims it to a listening world. Relationships rather than programs characterize ministry, and evangelism begins, not with a presentation of the plan of salvation, but with an invitation to begin a seeking journey into the things of God within the relationships of the believing community. The church is an "alternative community" (p. 118) of small groups that embody and exhibit Christian authenticity. "The goal of postmodern apologetics is to recover the role of the church as the interpreter and the embodiment of truth" (p. 104).

A fourth item concerns the lack of a proclamation motif of younger evangelical apologetics and evangelism. This is actually a subset of the previous point. As much as the postmoderns may dislike Great Commission ecclesiology, the New Testament could not be more clear and emphatic that preaching/ proclamation is the main business of doing church. This is seen not only in the Great Commission accounts (e.g., Matt 28:18-20) but in the life and ministry of the early church in Acts (e.g., 5:42) and the didactic exhortations of the epistles (e.g., Rom 10:15). Preaching is not confined to a homiletical sermon from the pulpit, nor is it limited to declaring the plan of salvation. But the evangelism methods of the New Testament are centered around the verbal proclamation of the message of divine grace whether in public or in private. To be sure, the younger evangelicals give a high place to preaching in the assembled community, but the content of the declaration is not very "evangelistic," instead it addresses the needs of the damaged and wounded spirit and encourages fellowship and meaningful interpersonal, communal relationships. One younger evangelical preacher put it clearly: "My preaching is not so much what I think they should hear but more a reflection on what they are going through and how God meets us in the midst of our troubles and joys" (p. 152). And as another explained: "Programs are important...[but] I'm a strong advocate of an embodied presence of Jesus," which means "that Jesus' presence is communicated in many other ways besides our words—such as compassion, encouragement, love, grace, kindness, service, etc....with no agenda to necessarily be telling them about Jesus. I believe He will be evident in the way we care for people" (p. 230). Preaching as a communication device in the postmodern setting is not "to transfer information" but "to stimulate the mind" (p. 68). As such, it is not reasoned discourse because postmodern man, including the younger evangelicals, are highly suspicious of propositionalism and they "reject the restrictions of print communication with its emphasis on knowing primarily through rational means" (p. 69). So there has been a shift to "embrace the more emotive, imaginative, and symbolic forms of communication" but, inconsistently it would seem, "without rejecting the significance of the spoken word" (p. 69). To accomplish this, the Bible is looked upon and communicated as a meta-narrative, an all-encompassing and universally applicable story of salvation that tells of God's work through the accounts of Israel and Jesus (p, 84). The truth reaches the hearer as he puts himself into the story and gains understanding by experiencing the narrative as a participant in the tradition (p. 91). A narrative interpretation of the biblical message is not dependent on any particular view of inspiration, especially not verbal inerrancy. As a result the younger evangelicals do not affirm inerrancy and show little interest in the subject since it is irrelevant to the overarching message of God in the story of Israel and Jesus.

This approach to communication is apparently the "soft sell" of the gospel that avoids propositionalism and authoritative pronouncements to be saved or to get right with God, and the like. Webber cites a successful young evangelical preacher who claims that for him communication "creates a beautiful atmosphere....They hear what they choose to hear. I cannot transfer meaning. I only give the setting in which people construct meaning....I hope people walk away with a certain need to fill in the spaces with their own experience of the one true God" (p. 68). This hazy, choreographic, you-connect-the-dots preaching is so self-evidently unlike the New Testament way of communicating the gospel that it would be redundant to criticize it further.

The post-foundational apologetics of the younger evangelicals is void of any idea of "defending" the faith. To the contrary, it is declared that the gospel needs no rational defense because it is capable of standing on its own; and, in one sense, that is certainly true. The gospel itself is, through the Spirit, "the power of God for salvation" (Rom 1:16). But believers are also called upon to make a defense, an *apologia*, an apology to those who ask a reason for their hope (1 Pet 3:15) because the unbeliever is "without a defense" (*anapologetos*, defenseless, without excuse) (Rom 2:1). But if the governance for apologetics is more of a feeling than authoritative biblical propositions and is a mosaic based on the ecumenical formulations of the church, it is unexplainable why this will not leave the millennial youth at everyone's mercy as they attempt to win to Christ a non-authoritarian, subjective culture on its own terms. There is neither a criterion nor a limiting concept as to whose feelings are correct, and if all emotions are eventually correct, none is truly right. And as well, verbal dialogue concerning faith and practice, if it is attempted at all, would soon degenerate into an endless haggle over which church father and whose interpretation of the ancient creeds is normative.

Ecclesiology

Ecclesiology means the study of the church, but it appears that for the younger evangelicals it is more about ecclesiasticism or the outward trappings of liturgy and formalism borrowed from ancient tradition. These objects and rites are designed to enhance postmodern worship and forward the spirituality of the community. This is clearly a violent reaction to the casual and highly informal flavor of the designer churches of their pragmatic evangelical predecessors. And in fact a deep-seated dissatisfaction with that form of doing church is justified and long overdue. Candidly, not a few professing fundamentalist churches are also in desperate need of a strong dose of reverence and order that would see an excision of the accelerated pace, breezy attitude, pockets of pandemonium, and the urge to be contemporary and "with it" that characterize much of their public services.

A couple of things stand out as characteristics of the younger ecclesiology that merit some note. One is its roots in the pre-Constantine church or the church prior to the fourth century. Younger evangelicals believe that with Constantine the church became a secularized civil religion that served as a "chaplain" and "caretaker" of the culture (p. 118), and this has continued to the present day. The Constantinian church over the centuries came to be operated and controlled by the professional clergy rather than a ministering people, sent out missionaries instead of itself being the incarnation of mission, and became in essence an extension or arm of the culture rather than an alternative community within the culture. The younger evangelical vision of a postmodern pre-Constantinian church is one that is intergenerational, intercultural, and postdenominational that operates within small groups characterized by diversity and an intimate relationship with Jesus Christ.

Another motif of the younger evangelical ecclesiology is its heavy liturgical formalism essentially borrowed from Romanism, Orthodoxy, Anglicanism, and other forms of ancient and medieval ceremonialism. This formalism incorporates a host of rites and symbols that include candles, prayers, crosses, icons, pictures, art, church architecture, sacraments (especially the Eucharist), initiation procedures, and other forms that promote "mystery, awe, wonder, [and] transcendence" in worship (p.199). What is more, all of the use of this religious paraphernalia can include the worship leader pronouncing absolution (p. 203)! The austere worship forms of the Celts, a fourth century group that became infested with Pelagianism, asceticism, and monasticism,[7] hold a particular fascination for the younger group.

One philosophical rationale for these observances is that "worship uses the material to proclaim that the invisible God who is wholly other is the very ground and meaning of material existence" (p. 198). But it seems to me that the Second Commandment forbids just that kind of practice. God is spirit and He is to be worshiped via the seat of one's personality, his spirit or the ability to think and reason, as this is informed and governed by revealed truth (John 4:24). The problem with these material objects is that, while intended to proclaim certain spiritual ideas, they soon become what they supposedly symbolize, i.e., they become sacramental. According to Webber, "'Sacrament,' refers to an action of God that is received, affirmed, treasured, and kept (Eph 3:3-6).[8] 'Sacrament' expresses the mystery of the union between God and man—effected by God, kept by man" (p. 181). The author goes on to state that the sacraments are to be observed "as a reception of *his work for us* and *our faith response to him*" (italics his) (181).

For example, faith understands that in the eschaton the created order will be freed from its slavery to corruption (Rom 8:21), but for the younger evangelicals the arts do not just symbolize this truth, they incarnate it. Webber says, "In worship

---

[7]Robert G. Clouse, "Celtic Church," *The New International Dictionary of the Christian Church*, ed. J. D. Douglas (Grand Rapids: Zondervan, 1974), p. 207.

[8]Webber traces the Latin word *sacramentum* back to the Greek word *musterion* (mystery) and uses Paul references to mystery in Eph 3:3-6 to prove his assertions about a modern day sacrament (pp. 180-81). But the biblical idea of mystery is anything but sacramental. It is revelation that God kept to Himself and revealed at an appointed time (Rom 16:25). Webber commits a hermeneutical fallacy that involves a completely illegitimate transfer and extrapolation of a Latin usage onto biblical Greek, leaving himself no basis for sacramentarianism.

the arts put wood, stone, and textile into a new and released form of praise. The arts are not mere decorations that enhance worship, nor are they illustrations of truth. Instead the arts *participate in their eschatological meaning*. They are creation put to praise" (italics added) (p. 200). That is, the physical materials of the arts become sacramental; they do not just portray eschatological truth, they *are* the eschaton in the midst of the assembly and have the mystical ability to bestow what they are on the worshipers.

This principle is applied in many other ways in the new millennial ecclesiology. Many younger evangelicals find in the Eucharist, for example, an especially poignant sense of the presence of God, an existential, momentary experience of the kingdom of God where the love of God in Christ's atonement "is on full and permanent display" (p. 182). The bread and cup constitute "a continuous rite of spiritual nourishment....On the divine side, the Eucharist is God's spiritual nourishment given to us" (p. 224). Some use a prayer that "asks the Holy Spirit to come upon the elements" (p. 204). The Benedictine *Lectio Divina* (Holy Reading), a very ritualistic reading of Scripture, is popular among the group. Icons are also highly recommended for worship, complete with eight rules for making an icon. The icon-making guide says that first "make the sign of the cross and pray in silence and pardon enemies," and at the end "have your icon blessed by putting it on the Holy Table...[and] be the first to pray before it" (p. 213).

All of the high church liturgy, formality, and sacramentalism of the younger evangelicals is very disconcerting to a biblicist. There is no attempt to locate these things in the Word of God, no effort whatever to interpret and correlate Scripture, nothing except a wholesale adoption of patristic and medieval forms that have been lifeless for centuries. This is so like the catenists of the Middle Ages, scholars that simply rearranged the thought of the church fathers and had no fresh exegesis of the Scriptures for themselves or the common people. Such rearranging and/or compiling of the fathers was done to enhance the sacramentalism of the dominant (Roman Catholic) church. The younger generation of evangelicals do not seem to appreciate how arid such religious thought had become in those days. Thus a question presents itself: How long will it be before dead formalism and theological and biblical sterility overtake the younger evangelicals? If medieval sacramentalism is popular among them today, can the beads and holy water be far behind?

Webber is probably correct to present this younger generation of evangelicals as a cultural reaction. It appears to be part of a general dissatisfaction of present day young adults with their boomer parents' ideas and ways. But while the newer evangelical thinkers want to be countercultural, i.e., against the forms of modernity with which they identify their predecessors, they are still very culturally conscious and wish to develop a postmodern evangelicalism that can interface with postmodern man on his own turf. And while these twenty-something evangelicals have leap-frogged well back of the twentieth century and appear to be in revolt against the current establishment, they are very much a part of its displacement, namely present-day postmodernity. They passionately wish to conform, convert, or change the face of their evangelical heritage to postmodernity's new thought and methods, that is, to contextualize the faith for a new day. How successful they will be remains to be seen, and if successful, will they be worthy of the name evangelical?

The younger evangelical movement and the promotion Webber gives it are reminiscent of the "young evangelicals" of the 1970s whose major prophet was Richard Quebedeaux[9] and minor prophet was Bernard Ramm.[10] They too were on a mission of change, from the new evangelicalism of Billy Graham and Carl Henry to a politically liberal post-American evangelicalism of the hippie movement and the countercultural anti-war protesters of the Viet Nam era. Their day came and went virtually without notice and made little impact. Then as probably now the promotion and hype were far greater than the substance; there was a lot less than met the eye. The young evangelicals of that time came across as a group of arrogant young turks who demanded to be seen and heard. The younger evangelicals of today are much more benign and seem not to be plagued by such visions of grandeur and greatness. But their emotionalism and lack of a stable authority for doing theology and church, their disdain for propositional written revelation, their failure and/or inability to rightly handle the sacred text, and their adaptation of medieval thought and practice all presage, in my judgment, a rather short evangelical life, if indeed they are even now genuinely evangelical.

---

[9]Richard Quebedeaux, *The Young Evangelicals* (New York: Harper and Row, 1974) and *The Worldly Evangelicals* (New York: Harper and Row, 1978).

[10]Bernard Ramm, "Welcome 'Green Grass' Evangelicals," *Eternity* (Mar 1974), p. 13.

25

ADDENDUM 2

Major Events In The New Evangelical Movement: 1942–2003

1942

- The formation of the National Association of Evangelicals in St. Louis, MO (April 7-8). Harold John Ockenga was the first president. Already in existence were the World's Christian Fundamentals Association (led by W. B. Riley) and the American Council of Christian Churches (led by Carl McIntire).

1947

- The publication of several articles in *Christian Life* magazine by Carl F. H. Henry, Harold John Ockenga, among others, calling for a new and broader expression of the fundamentalist/evangelical coalition.

- The publication of *The Uneasy Conscience of Modern Fundamentalism* by Carl F. H. Henry (Eerdmans) dealing mainly with social concerns.

- The founding of the Fuller Theological Seminary in Pasadena, CA.

1949

- Billy Graham's Los Angeles Crusade and the accelerated rise of his popularity.

1951

- Billy Graham's refusal of an invitation by fundamentalist ministers and leaders to hold a New York Crusade because he wanted a more inclusive representation on the crusade committee.

1953

- The renunciation of separatism by Donald Grey Barnhouse in his "New Years Resolution" article in *Eternity* magazine (January).

1954

- Billy Graham accepted the invitation of the National Council of Churches affiliated with the Protestant Council of the City of New York to hold a crusade, rejecting a second invitation from fundamentalists represented by Jack Wyrtzen.

- Edward John Carnell is named the first resident president of Fuller Theological Seminary.

- The publication of *The Christian View of Science and Scripture* by Bernard Ramm (Eerdmans), an attempt to harmonize the Bible and the theory of organic evolution by the proposal of "threshold creation" or "threshold evolution."

1955

- Donald Grey Barnhouse is featured in a series of TV programs put out by the Broadcasting and Film Commission of the National Council of Churches of Christ in the USA.

1956

- The publication of "Is Evangelical Theology Changing?" by *Christian Life* magazine (March), crystallizing new evangelical discontent with fundamentalism.

- The beginning of *Christianity Today*, the leading new evangelical thought magazine, Carl F. H. Henry, the first editor.

1957

- Billy Graham's public announcement of his inclusive policy of crusade evangelism (cooperation between evangelicals and liberal/neo-orthodox churchmen) at the annual meeting of the National Association of Evangelicals in Buffalo, NY (April 3).

- Billy Graham's New York Crusade (May 15–Sept 1) where his ecumenical, non-separatist policy of evangelism was put in place, became well known, and stirred much controversy.

- The departure of Charles J. Woodbridge from the faculty of the Fuller Theological Seminary because of its doctrinal drift.

- Donald Grey Barnhouse's discovery of fellowship with Seventh-day Adventists and Pentecostals.

- The news release by Harold Ockenga formally proclaiming the differences between the new evangelicalism and fundamentalism (Dec 8).

- A poll taken by *Christianity Today* in 1957 indicating that 48% of all evangelical ministers affirmed, while 52% were unsure or rejected, the verbal inerrancy of Scripture (reported Apr 26, 1963, p. 29).

1958

- The publication of *Cooperative Evangelism* by Robert O. Ferm (Zondervan), justifying inclusive, ecumenical evangelism.

1959

- The publication of *The Case For Orthodox Theology* by E. J. Carnell (Westminster), a bitterly caustic attack on fundamentalists and fundamentalism.

- The departure of E. J. Carnell from the presidency of the Fuller Theological Seminary.

1960

- The death of Donald Grey Barnhouse at age 65 (Nov).

- The publication of articles by Billy Graham and E. J. Carnell in the liberal *Christian Century* magazine (Feb, Mar) announcing to the liberal/neo-orthodox community their change of mind away from fundamentalism.

- The Billy Graham Evangelistic Association's launch of *Decision* magazine (Nov).

1962

- The Third Assembly of the World Council of Churches meeting in New Delhi, favorably received by new evangelicals, some of whose prominent leaders were in attendance.

1963

- The publication of *The Inspiration of Scripture* by Dewey Beegle (Westminster), an outright denial of the verbal inerrancy of the Bible by an evangelical.

- Billy Graham's Los Angeles Crusade with liberal Methodist bishop Gerald Kennedy as chairman of the general committee.

- The appointment of David Allan Hubbard as the president of Fuller Theological Seminary and the soon resignations of Harold Lindsell, Gleason Archer, and Wilbur Smith from the Fuller faculty.

- The publication of *The New Evangelicalism* by Ronald Nash (Zondervan), the first systematic attempt to justify and popularize the new movement by a recognized new evangelical scholar.

1964

- The occurrence of deviations on the doctrine of biblical inerrancy at the Bethel Theological Seminary, St. Paul, MN (Baptist General Conference).

- The enjoyment of a mutually warm fraternal meeting between Billy Graham and Cardinal Richard Cushing of Boston.

1966

- The convening of the World Congress on Evangelism sponsored by the Billy Graham Evangelistic Association in Berlin. Pentecostal minister Oral Roberts is welcomed, the first open new evangelical gesture to a Pentecostal healer.

- The meeting of the Wenham Seminar on the Authority of Scripture on the campus of Gordon College, Wenham, MA. Many evangelical scholars denied the doctrine of verbal inerrancy; most felt it is not to be a test of fellowship.

1967

- The dedication of the Oral Roberts University, Tulsa, OK (April 2), Billy Graham the featured speaker.

- The appointment of Harold Lindsell as the editor of *Christianity Today*, succeeding Carl F. H. Henry.

- The conferral on Billy Graham of an honorary doctorate by Belmont Abbey College, a Roman Catholic institution (Nov).

- The sudden death of E. J. Carnell at age 47.

1968

- The denial by Daniel P. Fuller, son of Charles E. Fuller, of biblical inerrancy, which caused great controversy.

- The move by evangelist/healer Oral Roberts to the liberal Methodist Church.

- The publication of *The New Evangelical Theology* by Millard J. Erickson of the Bethel Theological Seminary, St. Paul, MN (Revell), a favorable presentation and analysis of the movement. Erickson taught at Wheaton College at the time.

- The election of Billy Melvin as president of the National Association of Evangelicals.

1969

- The meeting of the ecumenical U. S. Congress on Evangelism in Minneapolis, MN, sponsored by the Billy Graham Evangelistic Association.

1971

- The publication of the revised doctrinal statement of the Fuller Theological Seminary which deleted belief in the verbal inerrancy of Scripture.

- The publication of *The Wittenburg Door* and *The Post-American* (later called *Sojourners*), both left wing, countercultural, new evangelical magazines asserting social activism.

1972

- The conferral of the Roman Catholic Franciscan Award on Billy Graham "in recognition of his contribution to true ecumenism" (April 21).

- The meeting of Explo '72, an ecumenical evangelical evangelistic campaign in Dallas, TX, aimed at reaching youth, sponsored by Campus Crusade for Christ.

- The rise in popularity of Robert Schuller and his "possibility thinking" doctrine and mega-church ecclesial practice.

1973

- An unqualified endorsement by the St. Louis Roman Catholic archdiocese of the Billy Graham St. Louis Crusade. Catholics served as counselors, and nuns sang in the crusade choir regularly.

- The launch of Key '73, a new evangelical, interdenominational, ecumenical evangelistic program to reach the North American continent for Christ.

- The formation of the Chicago Declaration, a statement of the need for social concern by fifty new evangelical leaders who met in Chicago's YMCA Hotel on Thanksgiving weekend.

1974

- The convening of the new evangelical, ecumenical Congress on World Evangelization in Lausanne, Switzerland.

- The campaign, Explo '74, an evangelical ecumenical thrust for evangelism in Korea.

- The publication of *The Young Evangelicals* by Richard Quebedeaux (Harper and Row), a favorable documentation of the rise and beliefs of a left wing element in the new evangelicalism.

- The formation of the Evangelical Women's Caucus International, a pro-feminist group advocating the full equality of the sexes.

1975

- The publication of *Man as Male and Female* by Paul King Jewett (Eerdmans) of the Fuller Theological Seminary, a pro-feminist book that discounts biblical statements on female subordination in the church and home, causing great controversy and headaches for Fuller.

1976

- The designation of 1976 as "The Year of the Evangelical" because of the supposed popularity of evangelical people and ideals. The Gallup Poll said that 94% of Americans believed in God; headlines said that Americans are "extraordinarily religious," and the like.

- The publication of *The Battle For the Bible* by Harold Lindsell (Zondervan), himself a new evangelical, exposing the hypocrisy of other new evangelicals on biblical inerrancy.

- The "Here's Life America" ("I Found It") campaign sponsored by Campus Crusade for Christ.

- The assertion of new evangelical Clark Pinnock that the heathen have an opportunity to be saved after death (*Eternity* magazine, Dec).

- The publication of "The Authority of Scripture at Fuller," a special alumni issue of the school's *Theology News and Notes* as a response to Harold Lindsell's charges in his *The Battle For the Bible*. It includes articles affirming less than full inerrancy by Clark Pinnock, Donald W. Dayton, and Paul S. Rees.

1977

- The formation of the International Council on Biblical Inerrancy in Chicago (Sept) with a ten year agenda of study, education, and publication; James Montgomery Boice, the first president.

- The publication of *Biblical Authority*, edited by Jack Rogers (Word) of the Fuller Theological Seminary, a reply to Harold Lindsell, *The Battle For the Bible*, and an attempt to defend an errant Bible by new evangelical scholars.

- The appointment of Kenneth Kantzer as the editor of *Christianity Today*. The periodical soon took on a more socio-political emphasis as well as a more evangelical populist flavor to boost sagging revenues.

- The expression of serious dissatisfaction with fundamentalist separatism by evangelist Jack Van Impe in a message at the Sword of the Lord convention in Detroit, MI (Aug).

- The announcement of serious dissatisfaction with fundamentalist separatism and other things by Jerry Falwell in an address to the Southwide Baptist Fellowship in Charlotte, NC (Oct).

1978

- The publication of *The Worldly Evangelicals* by Richard Quebedeaux (Harper and Row), further documenting favorably the radical and often heretical left wing of new evangelicalism.

- Doubts about the lostness of the heathen and Jews who die without Christ expressed by Billy Graham in *McCall's* magazine (Jan).

- The meeting of Summit I of the International Council on Biblical Inerrancy in Chicago (Oct 26-28) that drew up the Chicago Statement on Biblical Inerrancy.

1979

- The founding of the Moral Majority by Jerry Falwell and others, and its rise amid controversy and charges from fundamentalists of ecumenical compromise and capitulation to elements of the social gospel.

- The publication of *The Bible in the Balance* by Harold Lindsell (Zondervan), a sequel to his *The Battle For the Bible*, in which he answers his critics and provides additional evidence of new evangelical surrender on the doctrine of verbal inerrancy.

1980

- The discontinuance by former fundamentalist Jack Van Impe of city-wide evangelistic crusades because of alleged dissension and division caused by fundamentalist separatism.

1981

- The publication of *The Fundamentalist Phenomenon: The Resurgence of Conservative Christianity* by Jerry Falwell, ed., with Ed Dobson and Ed Hindson (Doubleday), a call for rapprochement between fundamentalists and new evangelicals.

1982

- The apology by evangelist Jack Van Impe, in his magazine *Perhaps Today,* to the Body of Christ for his separatism of past years (Nov).

- The retirement of Kenneth Kantzer as the editor of *Christianity Today,* being replaced by V. Gilbert Beers, a former professor at the Northern Baptist Theological Seminary in Chicago and a former editor with the David C. Cook Publishing Co.

- The death of George E. Ladd, a professor at the Fuller Theological Seminary, at age 71 (Oct 5).

- The meeting of Summit II of the International Council on Biblical Inerrancy in Chicago (Nov 10-13) that drew up the Chicago Statement on Biblical Hermeneutics.

1983

- The publication of *After Fundamentalism* by Bernard Ramm (Harper and Row) in which he affirmed the theological method (in effect the theology) of Karl Barth as the best evangelical answer to the philosophical framework of the Enlightenment.

- The departure of J. Ramsey Michaels from the faculty of the Gordon-Conwell Theological Seminary, Wenham, MA, over the denial of the doctrine of inerrancy as it pertained to the Gospel writers' use of sources and quotes, in his book *Servant and Son* (John Knox).

- The resignation under pressure of Robert Gundry of Westmont College from the Evangelical Theological Society over the use of redaction criticism in his commentary on Matthew.

- The production of an Open Letter by evangelicals at the World Council of Churches Sixth Assembly in Vancouver, BC, which condemned any who stood against participation in the WCC and pressed for more active involvement by evangelicals.

1985

- The conversion to Roman Catholicism of Thomas Howard, a Gordon College professor.

- The return of evangelist Jack Van Impe to city-wide crusades with the promise of preaching only a positive message of Christ's love.

- The death of Harold John Ockenga at age 79.

- The publication of *In Search of Unity* by Ed Dobson (Thomas Nelson), a not-so-veiled plea for fundamentalists and new evangelicals to have unity, on the order of *The Fundamentalist Phenomenon* (1981).

1986

- The convening of Amsterdam '86, an ecumenical evangelism congress sponsored by the Billy Graham Evangelistic Association that drew over 8,500 evangelists from all over the world.

- The publication of *Confessions Of a Theologian* (Word), an autobiography by one of the principals in the formation of the new evangelicalism—Carl F. H. Henry.

- The convening of Summit III of the International Council on Biblical Inerrancy in Chicago (Dec 10-13) that drew up the Chicago Statement on Biblical Application.

- A division within the Evangelical Women's Caucus International over resolutions favoring homosexual rights in deference to a lesbian minority in the Caucus.

1987

- The appointment of Joseph M. Stowell III, pastor of the Highland Park Baptist Church, Southfield, MI, as the seventh president of the Moody Bible Institute.

- The resumption of the course, "Signs, Wonders, and Church Growth," a charismatic-oriented class at the Fuller Theological Seminary. It had been taught from 1982–1986 but was dropped because of its divisiveness.

- The dismissal of Walter Bodine, Donald Sunukjian, and Jack Deere from the faculty of the Dallas Theological Seminary because of charismatic sympathies.

- The takeover by Jerry Falwell of the PTL ministries after the director, Jim Bakker, resigned because of sexual immorality.

- The formation of the Council on Biblical Manhood and Womanhood by conservative evangelicals, the result of an ongoing controversy within new evangelicalism over the gender roles of men and women.

- The publication of the article, "Universalism: Will Everyone Be Saved?" in *Christianity Today* (Mar 20), which focused on the growing new evangelical controversy over the lostness of the heathen and a pluralistic approach to finding salvation in the world's religions.

- The publication of "The Danvers Statement" by the Council on Biblical Manhood and Womanhood, a statement affirming the traditional evangelical understanding of the gender roles of men and women.

- The disbanding of the International Council on Biblical Inerrancy after completing its ten year goals of study, education, and publication, the most prodigious of which was the publication of six scholarly books, each a collection of essays on crucial issues in the area of inerrancy.

1988

- The publication of *Reforming Fundamentalism* by George M. Marsden (Eerdmans), an interesting and revealing history of the Fuller Theological Seminary.

1989

- The disbanding of the Moral Majority and the cessation of *The Fundamentalist Journal* by Jerry Falwell.

- The launch of AD 2000 Evangelism in Stuttgart, Germany, an ecumenical evangelical-liberal project, with the slogan, "All Christians should forget their differences and join forces to evangelize the world by the year 2000."

- The formation of Christians For Biblical Equality, a group of new evangelicals favoring man and woman egalitarianism.

- Evangelicals '89, a gathering of more than 350 Christian leaders at Trinity Evangelical Divinity School, Deerfield, IL, that gave concise definition to evangelical beliefs and practices, the results printed as *Evangelical Affirmations*, Carl F. H. Henry and Kenneth Kantzer, eds. (Zondervan).

1990

- The noticeable rise and popularity of the Church Growth movement and the "Designer Church" method of ecclesial extension.

- The founding of Promise Keepers by Bill McCartney.

1991

- The publication of *Recovering Biblical Manhood and Womanhood* (Crossway) by the Council on Biblical Manhood and Womanhood.

- The public debate among new evangelicals over the doctrine of eternal punishment. Some denied the eternality of hell and affirmed the annihilation of the wicked, bringing to a head the controversy simmering since 1982, if not earlier. The publication of *Four Views on Hell* (Zondervan) came in 1992.

1992

- The death of Bernard Ramm at age 76.

- The publication of *A Wideness in God's Mercy* by Clark Pinnock (Zondervan) in which he affirmed that the way to God and forgiveness can be found in other than formal Christianity.

1993

- The publication of *No Place for Truth* by David F. Wells (Eerdmans), a Gordon-Conwell Seminary professor who criticized the new evangelical movement for neglecting and then losing its theology and convictions to Arminianism, the self movement, the church growth movement, and other deteriorating sidetracks.

- The publication of *The Evangelical Heart and Mind* by Millard J. Erickson (Baker) offering some "perspectives on theological and practical issues" and a somewhat pessimistic outlook on the future of evangelicalism.

1994

- The release of ECT, "Evangelicals and Catholics Together: The Christian Mission in the Third Millennium," a twenty-five page statement drawn up by some thirty new evangelical and Roman Catholic representatives convened by evangelical Charles Colson and Roman Catholic Richard John Neuhaus.

- The publication of *God In the Wasteland* by David F. Wells (Eerdmans), a sequel to his *No Place For Truth*, in which he surveys the theological vacuum in the younger generation of evangelicals and offers remedial proposals.

- The publication of *Where is Evangelical Theology Going* by Millard J. Erickson (Baker), an assessment of the direction of evangelicalism.

1995

- The publication of *Four Views on Salvation in a Pluralistic World*, Dennis L. Okholm and Timothy R. Phillips, eds. (Zondervan), a series of essays by new evangelicals (except for liberal John Hick) on the pluralist, inclusionist, and exclusionist positions.

- The naming of William Franklin Graham by the Billy Graham Evangelistic Association to First Vice Chair with direct succession to the Chair and CEO "should his father become incapacitated."

- A meeting of a group of evangelical scholars (James M. Boice, Roger Nicole, Alister Begg, Tom Nettles, Albert Mohler, Jr., John Hannah, and David Wells) with J. I. Packer, Bill Bright, and Charles Colson on the ECT controversy. This resulted in ECT II, a five-point statement of clarification, the second phase of ECT.

- The election of Don Argue succeeding Billy Melvin as president of the National Association of Evangelicals, who immediately called for a new NAE agenda revolving around racial issues.

1996

- The publication of *How Shall They Be Saved?* by Millard J. Erickson (Baker) addressing the lostness of the heathen/fate of the unevangelized controversy in new evangelical circles.

- The first major meeting of The Alliance of Confessing Evangelicals, a group of Reformed theology oriented scholars and churchmen, in Cambridge, MA (Apr). It drew up the Cambridge Declaration, stressing the five "solae" (Scripture, grace, faith, Christ, and the glory of God), and criticized several things in evangelicalism, including the ECT efforts.

1997

- The publication of *Just As I Am* by Billy Graham (Harper and Row), the autobiography of Billy Graham.
- The publication of *The Evangelical Left* by Millard Erickson (Baker)
- The production of "The Gift of Salvation," an ECT document that stated what evangelicals and Catholics mean by the gospel (Dec), the third phase of ECT.

1998

- The response of The Alliance of Confessing Evangelicals to "The Gift of Salvation," with "An Appeal to Fellow Evangelicals" saying that "The Gift" added nothing new to the Roman Catholic problem of imparted vis-a-vis imputed righteousness in justification.
- The publication of "The Future of Evangelical Theology," by new evangelical scholar, Roger Olson, noting that "evangelicals are confused about what evangelical means," tacitly showing how doctrinally diluted the new evangelicalism has become (*Christianity Today*, Feb 9).

1999

- The fourth phase of ECT, "The Gospel of Jesus Christ: An Evangelical Celebration," a 3,400 word document endorsed by 125 Christian leaders that seemed to satisfy The Alliance of Confessing Evangelicals.
- The election of Kevin Mannoia succeeding Don Argue as president of the National Association of Evangelicals, whose main project was enlarging the NAE membership by reaching out to non-evangelical organizations such as the National Council of Churches that contained evangelicals.

2000

- Publication of *The God of the Possible* by Gregory Boyd (Baker), an explication of open or free will theism by a faculty member of the Bethel College, St. Paul, MN, and a minister with the Baptist General Conference.

2001

- The publication of *The Smell of Sawdust: What Evangelicals Can Learn From Their Fundamentalist Heritage*, by Richard Mouw (Zondervan), the president of the Fuller Theological Seminary, a somewhat nostalgic, mildly olive-branch-extending look on some of the days of the old fundamentalist-evangelical coalition.

2002

- The publication of *Renewing the Center: Evangelical Theology In a Post-theological Era by* Stanley Grenz (Baker), one of the latest left wing expressions of anti-foundationalist, post-absolutist evangelicalism that attempts to meet and win a rootless, post-modern culture on its own terms.

2003

- The death of Carl F. H. Henry at age 90 (Dec 7).

- The publication of *The Younger Evangelicals: Facing the Challenges of the New World* by Robert E. Webber (Baker), a sympathetic commendation of the latest, post-modern form of evangelicalism that advocates a return to the authority of patristic theology and a resumption of ancient liturgy and ecclesiasticism. See my review in Addendum 1.

- An attempt made to expel open or free will theists Clark Pinnock of McMaster University and John Sanders of Huntington College from the Evangelical Theological Society (Nov). Theologian Roger Nicole brought formal charges against the two saying their idea of openness precluded the freedom of God. He charged that the future is therefore indeterminate and thus impinged on God's knowledge and the accuracy of biblical prophecy. This in turn meant that God cannot know the future precisely but only with varying degrees of probability. The charge failed to garner the necessary votes of the ETS members present, raising the prospect of the formation of a new society of evangelical scholars.

SELECTED ANNOTATED BIBLIOGRAPHY

Ashbrook, John E. *New Neutralism II: Exposing the Gray of Compromise.* **Mentor, OH: Here I Stand Books, 1992.**
 A sequel to the book by his father, William E. Ashbrook, *Evangelicalism: The New Neutralism.* Updated material is given on areas of new evangelical neutralism such as music, Roman Catholicism, ecumenical evangelism, Fuller Seminary, National Association of Evangelicals, and Campus Crusade for Christ. Leaders such as Bill Bright, Billy Graham, Jerry Falwell, and others are biblically assessed.

Ashbrook, William E. *Evangelicalism: The New Neutralism.* **8th Printing. John Ashbrook, 8686 Hilltop Drive, Mentor, OH 44060, n.d.**
 One of the very early (first published in 1958) if not the first definitive analysis and warning concerning the new evangelical movement by a knowledgeable fundamentalist pastor. The author covers a wide range of crucial ecclesiastical issues and areas of Bible truth that are being compromised by the new coalition of evangelicals due to their non-militant, neutral stance. New evangelical leaders and institutions are examined in light of the Scriptures and historic fundamentalism.

Balmer, Randall. *Encyclopedia of Evangelicalism.* **Louisville, KY: Westminster John Knox, 2002.**
 A wealth of information on the old fundamentalist-evangelical movement and the later new evangelical coalition including hundreds of articles on persons, institutions, events, and issues.

Beale, David O. *In Pursuit of Purity: American Fundamentalism Since 1850.* **Greenville, SC: Unusual Publications, 1986.**
 The definitive historical account of the fundamentalist movement, including an extensive and excellent bibliography, written by undoubtedly the most knowledgeable fundamentalist scholar of the history of fundamentalism.

Bebbington, David. *Evangelicalism in Modern Britain: A History from the 1730s to the 1980s.* **Grand Rapids: Baker, 1992.**

A history of evangelicalism in Britain going back to the 18th century Wesleys, Whitefield, Independents, Particular Baptists, and others, and ending with the 20th century influences of John R. W. Stott, J. I. Packer, and others. While the author does not so state, the movement obviously deteriorated to something considerably less than a robust biblical, evangelical state of health. The author develops the changes and fortunes of UK evangelicalism in terms of the impacts of culture, Enlightenment thought, and philosophical Romanticism. Biblical criteria seem not to be given much of a berth. The book is informative, well-researched, and well-written.

Beegle, Dewey. *The Inspiration of Scripture.* **Philadelphia: Westminster, 1963.**

The first book-length, systematic denial of verbal inerrancy by a new evangelical. The author forthrightly declares that it is useless to argue for inerrant autographs when they no longer exist, that there is no theological difference between autographs and copies as far as inspiration is concerned, and that all we can press for are certain correct "key words" in the doctrine of verbal inspiration/inerrancy.

Butler, Farley P. **"Billy Graham and the End of Evangelical Unity."** **Ph.D. dissertation, University of Florida, 1976.**

A scholarly, well-written, and copiously documented account of how the policies intrepidly pursued by evangelist Billy Graham made a needless and irrevocable breach in the old fundamentalist-evangelical coalition of the early 20th century. The author demonstrates how the inclusive evangelism of the mid 1950s made reconciliation impossible between the separatist fundamentalists and the less restrictive and broadminded evangelicals, and how the two camps took increasingly divergent paths.

Carnell, Edward John. *The Case For Orthodox Theology.* **Philadelphia: Westminster Press, 1959.**

An early quasi-apologetic for the new evangelicalism as part of a trilogy along with volumes on neo-orthodoxy and liberalism published by Westminster Press. This work is a bitterly caustic attack on fundamentalists and fundamentalism by one who grew up in a fundamentalist milieu. Carnell backed away from affirming the full verbal inerrancy of Scripture by leaving the question open as to whether the Holy Spirit providentially kept the Chronicler from copying any errors that may have been in the public documents and genealogical lists which he used in recording the history of Israel. The author also reflected the idea of "degrees" of inspiration/authority by elevating Galatians and Romans above the other books of the Bible in authority, with Romans being the more fruitful of the two. Carnell was on the early faculty and also served as president of Fuller Theological Seminary.

Carpenter, Joel. *Revive Us Again: The Reawakening of American Fundamentalism.* **New York: Oxford University Press, 1997.**

Probably the best, most balanced, fair, and well-written history of the fundamentalist movement from the 1920s to the 1950s by a non-fundamentalist.

Cohen, Gary G. *Biblical Separation Defended: A Critique of Ten New Evangelical Arguments.* **Philadelphia: Presbyterian and Reformed, 1966.**

Mainly an analysis of Robert O. Ferm's book, *Cooperative Evangelism*, showing the biblical, exegetical, and theological weaknesses of the arguments for inclusive evangelism.

Dalhouse, Mark Taylor. *An Island In the Lake of Fire: Bob Jones University, Fundamentalism, and the Separatist Movement.* **Athens, GA: University of Georgia Press, 1996.**

A generally fair appraisal by a non-sympathizer toward fundamentalism demonstrating the militant conservatism and separatism of BJU (a trail blazed by Bob Jones, Jr.), the evangelistic successes of Bob Jones, Sr., the issues with Billy Graham and inclusive evangelism, and events that helped mold the BJU separatist position.

Dollar, George W. *A History of Fundamentalism in America.* **Greenville, SC: Bob Jones University Press, 1973.**

The first book-length history of fundamentalism written by a self-confessed fundamentalist. The work is enhanced by an excellent biographical index of fundamentalism's leaders and contributors as well as some of its enemies and antagonists.

Dorrien, Gary. *The Remaking of Evangelical Theology.* **Louisville, KY: Westminster John Knox, 1998.**

A non-evangelical author that is fairly perceptive of the slow leftward change by the new evangelical theology through some of its theologians such as Clark Pinnock, Bernard Ramm, and Stanley Grenz among others.

Elwell, Walter, ed. *Handbook of Evangelical Theologians.* **Grand Rapids: Baker, 1993.**

A series of short, factual biographies of older evangelicals and more recent new evangelicals that is helpful in evaluating some of the principal new evangelicals and their backgrounds.

Evangelical Action! *A Report of the Organization of the National Association of Evangelicals For United Action.* **Compiled and edited by the Executive Committee. Boston, MS: United Action Press, 1942.**

A publication of historic importance because it gives the background of the formation meeting of the National Association of Evangelicals in April 1942 in St. Louis, MO. Included are the major addresses, signers of the original call for the meeting, and a roster of the delegates present at the meeting. The assembly was composed of a who's who in the fundamentalist-evangelical coalition of the time.

Erickson, Millard J. *The Evangelical Heart and Mind.* **Grand Rapids: Baker, 1993.**

A development of "perspectives on theological and practical issues" and a somewhat pessimistic outlook on the future of evangelicalism by a well-known new evangelical scholar. Other works of a similar general nature by the same author are *Where is Evangelical Theology Going?* (Grand Rapids: Baker, 1994) and *The Evangelical Left* (Grand Rapids: Baker, 1997).

Erickson, Millard J. *The New Evangelical Theology.* **Westwood, NJ: Revell, 1968.**
A favorable analysis of the new evangelical movement by a professor at the time at Wheaton College. Subjects treated are historical development, the Bible and authority, various doctrines, apologetics, ethics, and general trends of and reactions against the new evangelical movement. The book has a tone of officially setting forth the main beliefs and practices of the early new evangelicalism.

Falwell, Jerry, ed., with Ed Dobson and Ed Hindson. *The Fundamentalist Phenomenon: The Resurgence of Conservative Christianity.* **Garden City, NY: Doubleday, 1981.**
An attempt by professing fundamentalists to forge a rapprochement between fundamentalism and the new evangelicalism. A smaller publication with a similar call is by Ed Dobson, *In Search of Unity* (Nashville: Thomas Nelson, 1985).

Ferm, Robert O. *Cooperative Evangelism: Is Billy Graham Right or Wrong?* **Grand Rapids: Zondervan, 1958.**
The first and only major apologetic for the inclusive, ecumenical evangelism of Billy Graham and all new evangelical evangelists thereafter. This book was sent free of charge to pastors, missionaries, professors, and college and seminary students. Arguments are given for inclusive evangelism; fundamentalist/separatist objections are answered. The book came out just as non-evangelical sponsorship and open-ended convert referrals to churches of choice were adopted as official policy among new evangelicals, causing great controversy and rebuttal from fundamentalists.

Graham, Billy. *Just As I Am: The Autobiography of Billy Graham.* **San Francisco: Harper SanFrancisco Zondervan, 1997.**
A massive tome of over 700 pages covering the Graham saga from his ancestry to the year of publication and a revealing window into the new evangelical movement. Aside from the innumerable events recounted, there are the many liberal, neo-orthodox, and Roman Catholic contacts that are portrayed. The impression is given that these kinds of friendships were made and used from the beginning of his major crusades. This impression is disingenuous at best and certainly inconsistent with the persona advanced by the public relations of the early years. Of help and interest is the chronological list of the Graham crusades from 1947 to 1996.

Grenz, Stanley. *Revisioning Evangelical Theology.* **Downers Grove, IL: InterVarsity, 1993.**
A book representing the *avant garde* left wing of the new evangelicalism as it tries to make evangelicalism compatible with a post-modern culture. Post-modernity rejects absolutes in favor of an open-ended universe of contingency, including the area of "truth." The author and others of his ilk are self-confessed post-modern, post-conservative, and reconstructed evangelicals who want to frame Christianity in terms of the non-absolutist authority of a communal consensus of the younger evangelical "church" in order to reach a rootless and non-authoritarian culture. Other works in this vein by the same author are *Theology For the Community of God* (Grand Rapids: Eerdmans, 1994) and *Renewing the Center: Evangelical Theology in a Post-theological Era* (Grand Rapids: Baker, 2002).

Gsell, Brad K. *The Legacy of Billy Graham: The Accommodation of Truth to Error in the Evangelical Church.* **Charlotte, NC: Fundamental Presbyterian Publications, 1996.**

A fundamentalist's evaluation of the negative effects of the Billy Graham inclusive policy in uniting evangelicals and non-evangelicals for purposes of mass evangelism.

Harris, Harriet A. *Fundamentalism and Evangelicals.* **Oxford: Clarendon Press, 1998.**

A non-evangelical examines the two named groups mainly in terms of philosophy and issues in biblical apologetics. The book is scholarly, analytical, and worth reading. The author gives a helpful glossary of fundamental and evangelical institutions and an exhaustive bibliography.

Henry, Carl F. H. *Confessions of a Theologian: An Autobiography.* **Waco, TX: Word, 1986.**

An inside look at the formation of the new evangelicalism from the viewpoint of one of its most energetic and capable founders, as well as accounts of some of the key events in the movement's history. The book is interesting, informative, surprising at times, and well-written.

Henry, Carl F. H. *Evangelicals At the Brink of Crisis: Significance of the World Congress on Evangelism.* **Waco, TX: Word, 1967.**

An assessment of the new evangelicalism in light of the 1966 Berlin World Congress on Evangelism. Four proposed crises face the movement: theology, evangelism, social activism, and ecumenism. Of special interest is the author's concern over the large presence of Pentecostal, charismatic, and other out-of-the-mainstream elements in the National Association of Evangelicals. Henry's startling query is whether or not it is time to revamp the NAE or begin a whole new organization.

Henry, Carl F. H. *Remaking the Modern Mind.* **Grand Rapids: Eerdmans, 1946.**

An evaluation of the state of modern philosophy in the post World War II era accompanied by a subliminal criticism of fundamentalism's cerebral inability and lack of involvement in the life of the mind.

Henry, Carl F. H. *The Uneasy Conscience of Modern Fundamentalism.* **Grand Rapids: Eerdmans, 1947.**

The opening salvo against fundamentalism's alleged lack of social sensitivity by a young, progressive scholar and leader in the development of new evangelicalism. It was the first book-length proposal of new evangelical activism in the socio-political arena.

Henry, Carl F. H., and Kenneth Kantzer, eds. *Evangelical Affirmations.* **Grand Rapids: Zondervan, 1989.**

"Evangelical Affirmations '89" was a gathering of more than 350 Christian leaders at the Trinity Evangelical Divinity School that gave concise definition to evangelical beliefs and practices. The results and conclusions are printed in book form.

Hunter, James Davison. *Evangelicalism: The Coming Generation.* **Chicago: University of Chicago Press, 1987.**

An analysis of the thinking of younger evangelical students by a sociologist. Students from sixteen evangelical institutions of higher learning across the USA were given a questionnaire. The survey found that evangelical students and their institutions are more amenable to social drinking and fewer restrictions on student conduct, and are favorably disposed to neo-orthodoxy, organic evolution, and the psychology of self-esteem. Fewer and fewer hold to eternal punishment. Hunter acknowledges the problem of answering, "What is an evangelical?" The author muses over whether conservative Protestantism is heading into a split between the "separatists" and the "moderates."

"Is Evangelical Theology Changing?" *Christian Life.* **March 1956.**

A ground-breaking article in which a symposium of evangelical scholars discusses ten areas where evangelical theology is undergoing rethinking, reevaluation, restatement, and change. The areas concerned the Bible and science, the work of the Holy Spirit, the doctrine of biblical inspiration, varying views of eschatology, social responsibility, and dialogue with non-evangelicals.

Johnston, Arthur. *The Battle For World Evangelism.* **Wheaton: Tyndale House, 1978.**

An historical tracing of the inroads made by the liberal social gospel into evangelical missions and evangelism. The penetration began with the early evangelical Edinburgh Conference of the Student Volunteer Movement (1910) and was climaxed by the influence of John R.W. Stott at the International Congress of World Evangelization in Lausanne, Switzerland (1974) sponsored by the Billy Graham Evangelistic Association.

Lightner, Robert P. *Neo-Evangelicalism.* **Findlay, OH: Dunham, 1962.**

The first analysis of the new evangelical proposal by a fundamentalist theologian along four lines: developments (history), doctrines, difficulties, and dangers. A later revision over a slightly different title added a section on further developments (*Neoevangelicalism Today.* Schaumburg, IL: Regular Baptist Press, 1978).

Lindsell, Harold. *The Battle For the Bible.* **Grand Rapids: Zondervan, 1976.**

A leading new evangelical scholar unmasks the hypocrisy of many of his peers who publicly affirm the verbal inerrancy of the Bible but inwardly do not believe it. The book sets forth the orthodox doctrine of Scripture and shows that it is the historic position of the Christian church. He also exposes the duplicity of various evangelical groups such as the Lutheran Church–Missouri Synod, the Southern Baptist Convention, Fuller Theological Seminary, and others. Unfortunately the author is inconsistent by not considering inerrancy a test of organizational fellowship while at the same time holding it to be a test of evangelical orthodoxy.

Lindsell, Harold. *The Bible in the Balance.* **Grand Rapids: Zondervan, 1979.**

A sequel to *The Battle For the Bible* and an interaction with the negative criticism of the former book. The author proved that his original assertions were correct and added further evidence of the same.

Marsden, George M. *Fundamentalism and American Culture: The Shaping of Twentieth Century Evangelicalism: 1870–1925.* **New York: Oxford, 1980.**

An account of the rise of fundamentalism from its roots in the revivalism of D. L. Moody in 1870 to what he terms the "debacle" of William Jennings Bryan and the Scopes evolution trial in Dayton, TN, in 1925. While not holding, as many other do, that fundamentalism is a purely social reaction to the effects of industrialization and Enlightenment thought in the USA, he also does not see its essence in its doctrines and organizations. However, he does retain the notion that the American culture made a sïgnificant contribution to the formation and fortunes of the fundamentalist movement.

Marsden, George M. *Reforming Fundamentalism: Fuller Seminary and the New Evangelicals.* **Grand Rapids: Eerdmans, 1987.**

One of the best windows into the development of the new evangelical coalition that broke away from fundamentalism in the 1940s as seen through the founding and ongoing of Fuller Theological Seminary in Pasadena, CA. The history of Fuller, the flagship new evangelical think tank, is a moving picture of the new evangelical movement as a whole.

Marsden, George M. *Understanding Fundamentalism and Evangelicalism.* **Grand Rapids: Eerdmans, 1991.**

In the words of the Preface, "This book provides an overview of the history of American fundamentalism and evangelicalism plus interpretations of some important themes." Marsden is a careful and generally fair scholar who is sympathetic to the new evangelicalism. The history consists of the rise of fundamentalism from 1870–1930, and the fortunes of evangelicalism since 1930. The interpretations concern politics, Enlightenment and creationist science, and the contribution of J. Gresham Machen of old Princeton Seminary.

Matthews, Victor. *New Evangelicalism: An Evaluation Through Its Literature.* **Schaumburg, IL: Regular Baptist Press, 1971.**

A small booklet by a fundamentalist reviewing some of the new evangelical publications.

McGrath, Alister. *Evangelicalism: The Future of Christianity.* **Downers Grove, IL: InterVarsity, 1995.**

An overly optimistic outlook on the fortunes of evangelicalism given by a new evangelical from the UK.

McLachlan, Douglas R. *Reclaiming Authentic Fundamentalism.* **Independence, MO: American Association of Christian Schools, 1993.**

A fundamentalist author's thesis that fundamentalism has been captured by elements alien to its genius, mission, and the Scriptures and therefore is in need of having its authenticity reclaimed. The book advocates a recovery of a biblical balance in crucial areas such as Calvinism/Arminianism issues, preaching and proclamation, leadership, and organizational separation.

Moritz, Fred. *"Be Ye Holy": The Call to Christian Separation.* **Greenville, SC: Bob Jones University Press, 1994.**

Essentially the dissertation for the D.Min. degree at Bob Jones University by a fundamentalist and general director of a fundamentalist mission agency. Personal and ecclesiastical separation are grounded in the transcendent holiness of God, and biblical separatism is shown to complement biblical evangelism.

Murray, Iain H. *Evangelicalism Divided: A Record of Crucial Change in the Years 1950–2000.* **Carlisle, PA: Banner of Truth Trust, 2000.**

The problems and misfortunes of evangelicalism principally in Great Britain as depicted by a biblically conservative Englishman. The book opens with a brief history of the formation of liberal theology and the controversy it generated in America. It goes on to show the influence of Billy Graham and his inclusive evangelism policies in England and the opposition they received from Bible believers led mainly by D. Martyn Lloyd Jones. Leading evangelical churchmen such as J. I. Packer, John R. W. Stott, and others eventually acceded to and joined in with the changes brought by the new evangelicalism and thus weakened considerably the Bible-believing separatist cause in the UK.

Nash, Ronald H. *The New Evangelicalism.* **Grand Rapids: Zondervan, 1963.**

The first systematic attempt to justify and popularize the new evangelical movement. The book began with a brief foray into the historical setting for the new evangelicalism, followed by chapters on the Scriptures, the church, apologetics, and an attempt to answer the new movement's critics. The author, a philosopher, was unable to grapple with the theological and ecclesiastical issues generated by the new evangelical coalition. Consequently his work was marred by a lack of theological precision and meaningful biblical correlation. Some chapters had no Scriptural input whatever making the book of limited value in commending the new evangelicalism.

Noll, Mark A. *The Scandal of the Evangelical Mind.* **Grand Rapids: Eerdmans, 1994.**

The argument by an evangelical historian at Wheaton College that evangelicalism has lost or abandoned the life of the mind at the hands of anti-intellectual fundamentalism as expressed in dispensationalism and elements of the holiness movement such as charismaticism and Pentecostalism.

Noll, Mark A. *Between Faith and Criticism.* **San Francisco: Harper and Row, 1986.**

A new evangelical scholar speaks of the achievements of evangelical scholarship but warns of the perils of getting into the mainstream of philosophical, theological, and critical thought.

Pickering, Ernest D. *Biblical Separation: The Struggle For a Pure Church.* **Schaumburg, IL: Regular Baptist Press, 1979.**

A leading fundamentalist pastor, scholar, author, professor, theologian, and missionary recruiter analyzes the main issue that divided the fundamentalists from the new evangelicals—ecclesiastical separation. A short history of the separatist conflict going back to the second century AD is given, the Scriptural basis of ecclesiastical separation is laid out, and anti-separatist arguments are scrutinized and answered.

Pickering, Ernest D. *The Tragedy of Compromise: The Origin and Impact of New Evangelicalism.* **Greenville, SC: Bob Jones University Press, 1994.**

A brief history of the fundamentalist-modernist controversy and the rise of the new evangelicalism followed by an analysis of ecumenical evangelism of the Billy Graham variety, the proposals of the "young evangelicals" of the 1970s, the church marketing philosophy of local church ministry, and the marks of the "new" new evangelicalism including the subtle drift of the time toward it.

Pickering, Ernest D. *The Fruit of Compromise...the New and Young Evangelicals.* **Schaumburg, IL: Regular Baptist Press, n.d.**

An account of the rise of the second generation of new evangelicals in the 1970s who were discontented with the views and direction of the founders of the original new evangelical coalition. The author gives a short historical background and goes on to examine the leading characteristics of the break-away group.

Pinnock, Clark. *The Scripture Principle.* **San Francisco: Harper and Row, 1985.**

A denial of the verbal inspiration/inerrancy of Scripture by an ever-changing new evangelical scholar. The book advocates degrees of inspiration, sees no theological distinction between autographs and copies of Scripture, and attributes certain historical accounts in the Bible to legend or the like (e.g., Jonah is considered "didactic fiction").

Pinnock, Clark. *A Wideness in God's Mercy: The Finality of Jesus Christ in a World of Religions.* **Grand Rapids: Zondervan, 1992.**

A one-time evangelical ever on a leftward pilgrimage denies the absolute uniqueness of Christianity as the only way to God and heaven, denies that a conscious knowledge of Jesus Christ as necessary to salvation, and affirms a post-mortem opportunity for the unevangelized.

Quebedeaux, Richard. *The Young Evangelicals: Revolution in Orthodoxy—The Story of the Emergence of a New Generation of Evangelicals.* **San Francisco: Harper and Row, 1974.**

A brief history of a second generation of 1960s and 70s new evangelicals and their rebellion against their first generation founders and forbears in the new evangelical coalition. The new group consists of the era's hippies, flower children, counter-cultural Christians, and vehement opposers to the Vietnam War. They are liberal in political philosophy, friendly to neo-orthodoxy and the liberal social gospel, and are in favor of a "post-American" national culture configured along the lines of political and economic socialism or welfare statism. A further favorable documentation of the radical, left-wing, young evangelical proposals was given by the same author in *The Worldly Evangelicals* (San Francisco: Harper and Row, 1978).

Ramm, Bernard. *After Fundamentalism: The Future of Evangelical Theology.* **San Francisco: Harper and Row, 1983.**

A former member of the original evangelical-fundamentalist coalition who studied under neo-orthodox theologian Karl Barth apparently completes his journey from evangelicalism to new evangelicalism to neo-orthodoxy, especially concerning the doctrine of the Scriptures and their authority.

Ramm, Bernard. *The Christian View of Science and Scripture.* **Grand Rapids: Eerdmans, 1954.**

A new evangelical decries fundamentalist scholarship and its narrow approach to the Bible and science. The book is an attempt to harmonize Scripture with the modern scientific theory of organic evolution by means of "threshold evolution" or "threshold creationism" wherein God fiatley created new life forms at strategic levels and governed their evolution according to the uniformitarian assumption of infinitesimally slow change over unlimited amounts of time.

Rogers, Jack, ed. *Biblical Authority.* **Waco, TX: Word, 1977.**

A series of essays by new evangelical scholars edited by a professor at the Fuller Theological Seminary as a response to Harold Lindsell's *Battle For the Bible*. Among other assertions, the book attempts to show that verbal inerrancy was not the historic doctrine of the church and, further, that a denial of an inerrant Bible does not have a "domino effect" of deviation from other crucial doctrines.

Rogers, Jack, and Donald McKim. *The Authority and Interpretation of the Bible.* **San Francisco: Harper and Row, 1979.**

Two new evangelical scholars give a lengthy tracing of the doctrine of verbal inerrancy through historical theology, concluding that the doctrine of inerrant autographs is a product of the old Princeton Seminary mentality and not the belief of the historical church. A withering rebuttal of the Rogers–McKim proposal was written by John D. Woodbridge, himself a new evangelical, in which he demonstrates with massive documentation the false premises, poor research, sloppy scholarship, prejudicial use of evidence, and unwarranted conclusions of Rogers and McKim (*Biblical Authority.* Grand Rapids: Zondervan, 1982).

Russell, C. Allyn. *Voices of American Fundamentalism.* **Philadelphia: Westminster, 1976.**

A series of informative biographies of some of the leaders in fundamentalism by a historian who is not himself a confessing fundamentalist.

Schaeffer, Francis A. *The Great Evangelical Disaster.* Westchester, IL: Crossway Books, 1984.

A new evangelical scholar, author, and lecturer sounds one of the first definitive warnings to fellow new evangelicals of the impending disastrous collapse of evangelical theology due to departures on the doctrine of the verbal inerrancy of the Scriptures. The author sees biblical inerrancy as the great watershed teaching of the Bible and theology. Deviations from this doctrine are the beginning of a downhill slide of compromise and loss of orthodox doctrine.

Sidwell, Mark. *The Dividing Line: Understanding and Applying Biblical Separation.* Greenville, SC: Bob Jones University Press, 1998.

A member of the faculty of Bob Jones University develops separatism in terms of its theological context and applies it to the areas of the world, false teachers, and disobedient Christians. Chapters are devoted to the new evangelicalism, neo-orthodoxy, liberalism, the charismatic movement, and Roman Catholicism. A brief but excellent glossary of terms is included.

Singleton, James. *Fundamentalism: Past, Present, Future.* Tempe, AZ: Fundamental Baptist Press, 1884.

A small booklet by a long time fundamentalist who has some proposals for constructive change within the movement.

Stevick, Daniel. *Beyond Fundamentalism.* Richmond, VA: John Knox, 1964.

A C. S. Lewis-like fictitious correspondence between "Spermologist," an allegedly thinking evangelical, and "Theophilus," an older and presumably wiser non-fundamentalist. The two discuss the supposed problems and inconsistencies within the fundamentalist-evangelical position on the Bible and doing church. It is actually an autobiographical call for the discontented, progressive types within the broad fundamental-evangelical spectrum to move beyond their confines either by agitating for change within or by outright departure for a more free and open ecclesiastical environment.

The Fundamentals: A Testimony to the Truth, R. A. Torrey, A. C. Dixon, et al., eds., 4 vols. Grand Rapids: Baker, 1980 reprint.

A series of booklets originally published in 1910–1915 by evangelical/fundamental scholars under the benefaction of Milton and Lyman Stewart and distributed free of charge. The essays in the series exposed and refuted the unbelief of liberal thinking on crucial areas of Bible-believing Christianity, and expounded and explained the truth of biblical teaching. The series was in part the basis of the term "fundamentalism."

Van Til, Cornelius. "The New Evangelicalism." Unpublished syllabus, Westminster Theological Seminary, n.d. (ca. 1960).

An early but negative appraisal of some of the original thinkers of the new evangelicalism from the standpoint of Christian apologetics, theology, and philosophy.

Webber, Robert E. *The Younger Evangelicals: Facing the Challenges of the New World.* **Grand Rapids: Baker, 2002.**

An apologetic for and a sympathetic portrayal of the most recent vintage of the evangelical movement by one who grew up in fundamentalism and was a former professor at Wheaton College. See my review article in the Addendum.

Wells, David F. *No Place For Truth: Or Whatever Happened to Evangelical Theology?* **Grand Rapids: Eerdmans, 1993.**

A stinging expose of the loss of biblical doctrine in the new evangelical movement written by a fellow new evangelical theologian from the Gordon-Conwell Theological Seminary. The book shows how post-modern philosophy, the psychology of the self movement, and the new marketing forms of ministry adapted from the business world have left sound theology in shambles. It also shows how the Calvinistic emphasis of Jonathan Edwards and the First Great Awakening of the 1700s deteriorated into an Arminianized manipulation of human emotions led by Charles G. Finney and his "new measures" in the evangelism of the Second Great Awakening of the 1800s. The grandeur of God in His sovereignty was displaced by the majesty of man in his autonomy. The author wrote a sequel in which he surveys the theological vacuum in younger evangelicals and offers some antidote (*God in the Wasteland*. Grand Rapids: Eerdmans, 1994).

Woodbridge, Charles. *The New Evangelicalism.* **Greenville, SC: Bob Jones University Press, 1969.**

A brief evaluation of the new evangelical movement that was gathering incredible speed by a fundamentalist scholar, author, and lecturer who was one of the early faculty members of the Fuller Theological Seminary that resigned because of the compromise and leftward drift of the school.

SCRIPTURAL INDEX

Revelation

TOPICAL INDEX

Y